The Multimedia Handbook

The Multimedia Handbook provides a comprehensive guide to the wide range of uses of multimedia. Multimedia has moved from a technology looking for an application to widespread implementation in many fields such as sales presentations, education, training, business, museums and art galleries, medical systems and scientific applications, with numerous uses in the fields of entertainment and leisure. Tony Cawkell details the huge array of authoring software which is now available, as well as the distribution of multimedia data by telephone, cable, satellite or radio communications.

Part one of the *Handbook* introduces the technology for the non-specialist. Part two covers multimedia applications and markets. There is an extensive bibliography, a glossary of technical terms and acronyms with a full index.

This book is suitable for professionals wanting to find out more about multimedia, as well as for media students.

Tony Cawkell founded Cawkell Research & Electronics Ltd, a company which designed and manufactured precision electronic measuring equipment. He moved to ISI and set up a European sale organization for that company, subsequently becoming Vice President of Research and Development. In 1980 he left to form Citech Ltd, information and technology consultants.

The Multimedia Handbook

Tony Cawkell

A BLUEPRINT BOOK
published by Routledge
London and New York

First published 1996
by Routledge
2 Park Square, Milton Park, Abingdon, Oxon, OX14 4RN

Simultaneously published in the USA and Canada
by Routledge
270 Madison Ave, New York NY 10016

Reprinted 1998

Transferred to Digital Printing 2005

Typeset in Times Ten by Keystroke, Jacaranda Lodge, Wolverhampton

British Library Cataloguing in Publication Data
A catalogue record for this book is available from the British Library

Library of Congress Cataloging in Publication Data
Cawkell, A. E.
    The multimedia handbook / Tony Cawkell.
      p.   cm.
    Includes bibliographical references and index.
    (alk. paper)
    1. Multimedia systems. I. Title.
    QA76.575.C33   1996
    006.6—dc20
    96–6079

ISBN 0–415–13666–0

Back cover photograph A data translation board being plugged into a computer
Source: Data Translation

Printed and bound by Antony Rowe Ltd, Eastbourne

Contents

Figures

Tables

Preface

Multimedia has become a very large and diverse field of activity. Its fuzzy boundaries merge into Information Technology. Disk storage, creative aspects like authoring, transmission protocols, standards, politics, and networks called superhighways are examples of activities where technical matters, creative work, applications, politics, and marketing hype are intermingled.

Two particular problems have been encountered in trying to arrange this book.

First, technical explanations may be unwanted. For example, a reader interested in the effectiveness of multimedia systems for teaching may not want to wade through technical data. Accordingly, technology is mainly confined to separate chapters. However, it is not possible to explain, for instance, certain CD-I applications without constant reference to the technology.

Second, not all of the information about a particular subject can be covered in one place – some aspects of it may be more appropriately covered in another chapter. On the other hand, a subject becomes fragmented if separate aspects of it are made to fit the 'right' chapter. In this book an attempt has been made to put major aspects of a subject in the chapter where a reader would expect to find it. The ambiguity of its different aspects sometimes makes this a difficult choice, but the book has a comprehensive index.

In those parts of the book where technical explanations are required I have tried to keep them simple. If jargon or acronyms are used, their meaning will be found in the glossary. I hope that the large collection of references will be useful.

A.E. Cawkell

Acknowledgements

I acknowledge the help provided during the writing of this book from the organizations listed below who have permitted certain illustrations to be published here.

Access Software
Adaptive Solutions
Adept
Adobe Systems
Asymmetrix
British Library
BT
Data Translation
IBM
Iterated Systems
Kodak
Lannet
LiveWorks
Loughborough Sound Images
Macromind
Microsoft
National Gallery
NEC
Panasonic
Picture Cardbox
Queen's University, Belfast
Scientific Microsystems
Silicon Graphics
Tektronix Ltd
Uppsala University
University of Southampton
Valentine Riverside Museum
Videologic

Part I

Background and technology

Chapter 1

Introduction

'When *I* use a word,' Humpty-Dumpty said in rather a scornful tone, 'it means just what I choose it to mean – neither more nor less.'

'The question is,' said Alice, 'whether you *can* make multimedia mean so many different things.'

'The question is,' said Humpty-Dumpty, 'which is to be master – that's all.'

(With apologies to Lewis Carroll)

WHAT IS MULTIMEDIA?

'Multimedia' supposedly means 'The processing and presentation of information in two or more media', so computers which are capable of handling text and simple graphics, available for many years, could be called 'multimedia computers'. However, so many extra attributes have been developed that the word now usually means the processing and presentation of at least text, graphics, and pictures, if not animation and motion video, usually in colour with sound. There are many systems and activities within multimedia's fuzzy-edged border including hypertext, image processing, compression systems, colour electronics, input technologies like scanners, cameras, and picture frame grabbers, output technologies such as displays and reprography, transmission systems, Virtual Reality, and visualization. Compact Disk media and techniques, electronic books and journals, and videoconferencing are multimedia, as are computer games and home shopping.

References are sometimes regarded as indexing terms – a well-devised collection of cited items about different aspects of the subject of the citing publication should reflect the subject content of that publication. At a late stage of writing this book I noted that there were 421 references to multimedia (subsequently to become nearly 500) distributed as shown in Tables 1.1 and 1.2. In Table 1.1, the date of 421 references in the *Multimedia*

Table 1.1 References

Date	Number of refs
1920–1939	1
1940–1969	11
1970s	13
1980s	48
1990s	348

Table 1.2 Early cited authors

Date	Author
1924	H. Nyquist
1945	V. Bush
1948	C.E. Shannon
1952	D.A. Huffman
1960	C. Cherry
1960	C. Mooers
1962	M. McLuhan
1963	A.H. Reeves
1965	I. Sutherland
1966	C. Cleverdon and M.E. Lesk
1969	J.-J. Servan-Schreiber

Manual to the literature of earlier decades are shown. This was the situation when the book was nearly completed in June 1995. The twelve authors of the earliest papers cited up to the end of the 1960s are shown in Table 1.2. These authors are notable pioneers who contributed to the foundations of the subject. Their papers contain not a whiff of multimedia *per se*. They were writing about coding, transmission, information systems, and politics. Thus Harry Nyquist and Claude Shannon wrote seminal papers about data rates – an important consideration when the electrical transmission of multimedia information is being discussed. Vannevar Bush did much more than write a famous article entitled 'As we may think'. He was the prime mover in attempting to devise code-breaking machines during the First World War and could be called 'the world's first information scientist'.

Incidentally, we may note that Newton's remark 'If I have seen further, it is by standing on the shoulders of giants' does not seem to be applicable to the pioneers of technology and engineering. With a few notable exceptions such as the authors listed above, and unlike authors who have published in *Science*, heavily cited technologists and engineers who could be nominated as 'giants' are relatively rare.

The references indicate the rate of expansion of multimedia publications. As at June 1995, 40 of the 348 references to the publications of the 1990s

Table 1.3 Top ten cited journals

Journal	No. of citations
Byte	18
Computer	13
Information Services and Use	12
Archives and Museum Informatics	11
IEEE Multimedia	7
Advanced Imaging	7
Journal of Information Science	6
Journal of the American Society for Information Science	6
Proceedings of the IEEE	6
IEEE Spectrum	5

are to 1995. Looking back from 1996 we may expect at least half of them to be to 1995. Of the citations in this book, 135 are to non-journal items, but journals predominate and the top ten by citations received are shown in Table 1.3. To some degree, Table 1.3 reflects personal information-collecting habits. For example, as the editor of *Information Services & Use* I have been moving it in the multimedia direction. *Archives and Museum Informatics* reflects the movements of Museums and Art Galleries into multimedia systems.

These journals show that the range of activities covered by the term 'multimedia' is wide. Lower down a list of diverse publications you will find journals like *Library Trends*, *Human Factors*, *Pattern Recognition*, *Radiology*, and *Telecommunications Policy*. In consulting earlier publications I found relevant articles about 'A computerization project for the Archivo General de Indias', 'McLuhan and Mumford: the roots of modern media analysis', 'Why books will survive', and 'A prototype electronic encyclopaedia'.

Sometimes esoteric developments are introduced. In 'A computerization project for the Archivo General de Indias', there is an illustration of a letter from Columbus about Amerigo Vespucci, who gave his name to the continent. It is so badly stained that it is difficult to read. In a second illustration we see it after it has been subjected to image processing. It appears to be written on clean white paper.

In *The Gutenberg Galaxy*, written in 1962, Marshall McLuhan suggested that communications media determine the nature of social organization. 'New media provides humans with new psychological-structural equipment,' he said.

Lewis Mumford (1963) thought that 'by centring attention on the printed word, people lost that balance between the sensuous and intellectual, between the concrete and the abstract . . . to exist was to exist in print: the rest of the world became more shadowy'. Mumford also thought that McLuhan was pressing forward in the interests of the military and commerce.

Carey (1981) imagines a scenario where the 'sole vestige of the world of concrete forms and ordered experience will be the sounds and images on the constantly present television screen or such abstract derivative information as can be transferred to the computer'. In the event, these words, written before multimedia existed, could turn out to be a description of a rather unpleasant future. If such a scenario arrives, it will depend on the wide-spread distribution of multimedia programmes, particularly entertainment programmes, which will in turn depend upon the success and time of arrival of the 'Information Superhighway' discussed in chapter 8. It has been suggested that this phenomenon should be called the 'Information Super-hypeway'; however, it probably will arrive – eventually.

The bones of the multimedia idea can be seen in the schemes incorporated in the Star machine devised in the late 1970s by the people at Xerox's Palo Alto research laboratories, where systems were designed for creating drawn designs (graphics) and combining them with text. Shape fitting and scaling operations could be carried out. Digitized sound was also discussed at Xerox (Smura 1986).

The idea of *interactivity* was introduced in the early days of computing. An interactive multimedia system prompts a user to make a response – for example, by providing alternative choices for pursuing a chosen course of action. A menu containing a list of possible actions may be displayed and the user is asked to choose one. More elaborate procedures were introduced such as hypertext's 'button' options, and later a range of control operations was offered to users in computer games with the aid of joystick, trackball, or mouse. In most other information/entertainment systems such as television and film, the user is a passive observer.

MULTIMEDIA PHILOSOPHY

Multimedia has got beyond the flash-in-the-pan stage when it was hyped up by manufacturers to join VCRs, camcorders, desktop publishing, DAT, and other gadgets which we can apparently no longer do without, but which are running out of steam. The boundaries between information, entertainment, education, and commerce are becoming even fuzzier. Will multimedia online databases, greatly enhanced by graphics and sound, appear with 'a controlled pictorial index language whose terms are the descriptors of the significant structure in digital images', as confidently claimed by Bordogna *et al.* (1990)? It is already being claimed that 'Multimedia databases will radically change the way you look and work with information' (Shetler 1990).

Shetler's Binary Large Objects (BLOB) database 'presents you with any combination of data fields, images, and text objects' and may contain 'spreadsheets, graphs, fax, object-code modules, satellite data, voice patterns, or any digitized data . . . it could be very large – up to 2 gigabytes' ('satellite data' are the same as any other data but it sounds impressive). For online access you will have to await the arrival of SONET (optical) telecoms otherwise it will take a week for the stuff to arrive. It should be added that BLOBS is already almost obsolete, having been overtaken by improved techniques.

Why shouldn't the presentation of information about, say, houses for sale be accompanied by the sights and smells of the neighbourhood? The enterprising estate agent who sends you an entertaining disk could steal a competitive advantage. Why shouldn't shareholders receive clips on a CD showing the products of their company in use, together with the report (which would be much more interesting if you could jump to any section via a hypertext link) which they receive annually from the chairman? Indeed, why in the home of the late 1990s shouldn't 'the multimedia machine be a computerised entertainment centre combining the functions of today's audio and video systems, television set, games machine, and home computer?' (Cookson 1990).

All these things may happen, although in a review of Macromind Director software in the October 1990 issue of *Byte* the writer says, 'The Overview Module allows business people to create excellent presentations easily.' For others, 'easily' is not the right word at all. In the very next issue of that journal, the potential user of a multimedia board (an experienced computer person) – advertised as being for 'reasonably knowledgeable people who aren't computer experts' – complained about it. She found that 'there was not one single sentence in the instruction manual that she understood!'

A related subject was discussed in a UK national newspaper (Virgo 1990): 'Organisations buying computer systems generally ignore the largest costs . . . the cost of disruption and training is commonly up to double the cost of developing and testing the software which is itself double the cost of the hardware.' To cover the cost of the technical effort and expertise needed to acquire and use appropriate multimedia hardware and software, together with the time and the artistic and creative effort required for providing a presentation, you should probably double the number again.

On the other hand, liberation is available to offset some of these constraints. Multimedia processing, particularly motion video processing, is much less constrained than it was. Real time graphics processing requires about 20 Mips, and fast rendering to produce photographic realism requires 300 Mips. Power, storage, and run-time are much improved and this kind of power is becoming available.

Graphics processing, which incorporates a dedicated computer within a computer, is advancing rapidly. IBM rhapsodizes about its PS/2 90 and 95 machines which 'thanks to dazzling XGA (Extended Graphics Array) . . .

(provide) a new standard in high resolution quality, conjured up in the blink of any eye'.

The other liberating factor is compression. Compression joined the ranks of over-hyped multimedia-related topics comparatively recently. CCITT Standard H.261 has been agreed and a Codec enabling videoconferencing to be carried on at bit rates of from 64 Kbps to 2 Mbps is already used by British Telecom. This is a proven application, not a pious hope.

Digital television speeds for high-quality colour picture reproduction are normally over 200 Mbps, but British Telecom claims that, at the 2 Mbps rate used for teleconferencing with the codec, 'it requires a keen eye to spot the difference between a compressed and a broadcast picture'. Much higher compression ratios are being developed for multimedia and television transmission purposes and the effect in terms of transmission, storage, and other economies will be considerable.

Plain vanilla business or information product providers have not yet acquired the gizmos needed to add the necessary multimedia pizzaz (to use some foreign but explicit words), nor have consumers yet acquired the gadgets to use them. But these difficulties are temporary. As one impetuous commentator suggested: 'Dismiss the problems and don't attempt to justify the cost of intangibles like your new multimedia fun-image – it's an act of faith.'

GROWTH AND FUTURE

Some chapters include a discussion about the future prospects for the subject covered in that chapter, but 'Prospects and growth' for multimedia in general are described in chapter 18.

Chapter 2

General functions and technology

INTRODUCTION

Authoring for CD-ROMs, CD-Is, etc. cannot be done unless an author considers the possibilities and constraints of the technology and content design together. Similarly, music and voice technology and application are so closely related that they merge into each other. In these cases it is unhelpful to attempt to relieve the user of the need to understand the technology by confining it to this chapter. Technical aspects and general functions that may be considered in isolation from applications are discussed here.

HUMAN ASPECTS

The acuity or resolving power of the eye is its ability to distinguish between two closely spaced objects. It varies according to the luminance, colour, and type of the object, and also according to a number of physiological characteristics such as fatigue and the aperture of the pupil. For these reasons it is hard to provide 'typical' information.

Lord Rayleigh – most of whose pioneering work on light and sound, carried out in the nineteenth century, needs no updating – estimated the eye's resolution to be about 40 seconds of arc. If an average could be quoted it would probably be larger – 1.5 to 2 minutes of arc. Other important properties of the eye include its frequency response, sensitivity to colour and white light, and its reaction to discontinuous images such as a flickering image or sudden bright flashes. The eye can detect very small changes in colour – as small as 0.0003 in chromaticity between two sample colours. Chromaticity is a measure of the ratio of the primary colours needed to produce a particular colour. A fully dark-adapted eye can detect white light at a level of about 0.000001 candela per square metre. (The candela is the SI unit roughly corresponding to the illumination provided by a standard candle.)

For a light source to be free from flicker (as in recurring CRT frames), the flicker frequency must be higher than 10, and these days is often made higher for CRTs than is dictated by the 50 or 60 Hz a.c. mains frequency. The term 'frequency response' is used with respect to the eye because light is a form of electromagnetic radiation characterized by frequency, velocity, and wavelength. The eye responds to light of 4000 (extreme violet) to 7700 (extreme red) Angstrom units (Au) (1 Au = 10^{-10} metres). To express the frequency of light we need to use Terahertz (THz) units (1 THz = 10^{12} Hz). The bandwidth of the eye's colour range is 390 to 750 THz. The potential for information transmission within this range is enormous. If it could be used for the purpose, about 3.7 million 100 Mbps digital television channels could be accommodated. These figures do not imply that the eye can process visual information at this rate, although they do indicate the huge bandwidth availability in optical transmission (fibreoptic) systems.

Information in the form of print on paper, displayed on film, on a micro-film viewer, or on a screen, must be resolvable by the eye, adequately illuminated or of adequate brightness, and aesthetically pleasing. The chemical grain structure on photographic film is equivalent to about 400 lines/mm and may become intrusive when 35 mm film is blown up for a large print. The image of these randomly distributed grains will be projected in different positions on the successive frames of electronic displays; wanted data are repeatedly overlaid. The 'signals' integrate, the 'noise' does not, so noise is not usually intrusive.

Choices involving the range of fonts, size of typeface, layout of text and the use of white space and colour have been available for some years. Printed information has been developed to suit human requirements by a process of evolution. These factors have been well reviewed by Reynolds (1979), who also provides a background of knowledge for newer electronically based applications. Formats, margins, headings, layouts, human scanning and reading activities have been discussed by Keen and Armstrong (1980).

Because we are now required to assimilate so much information, particular attention has been given to condensations in the form of titles, abstracts, summaries, indexes, etc. Unfortunately indexing, which is just as important for pictorial as it is for textual information, has not been given sufficient attention in new applications – for example in picture collections. The glamour and novelty of new technology obscure the ever-present indexing requirement. Its difficulties and supposedly boring aspects are rarely mentioned. They are considered to be unsuitable for inclusion in an ebullient literature or talked-up sales propaganda.

Another aspect which is receiving increasing attention is the effect upon human vision and posture of prolonged viewing of a screen. For a time some extreme for-or-against reports were published (Cawkell 1991a). More recently the matter has received serious attention, followed by official recommendations and litigation. Davies and Bianchessi (1994) provide some common-sense examples of the precautionary measures that should be taken.

ANALOGUE AND DIGITAL DATA

In a digital computer an accurate oscillator, known as a clock, generates a continuous sequence of pulses at a precise repetition rate. Each step in step-by-step computer operations is triggered by a clock pulse. All the steps in thousands of circuits triggered by clock pulses are accurately timed and occur synchronously. In addition to being controlled by timing or triggering pulses, the circuits collectively perform operations on pulses which represent data.

Humans process analogue information, so for within-computer operations analogue/digital and digital/analogue converter circuits are required for conversion purposes. Coded groups of pulses may represent the original analogue values of some physical change such as sound level, light level, etc., in digital form. Computer circuits may add, subtract, or store 0 or 1 impulses, usually called bits, to accomplish some task under the control of a program.

Levels of sound and light are perceived as a continuous range of smoothly changing analogue values by the ear and the eyes. To be processed by multimedia digital computers, the values must be changed into small, closely spaced electrical steps where the change in the numerical value of each step follows the original waveform with sufficient accuracy for its purpose and may be processed by a digital computer. Suppose that grey levels between black and white are digitized as 256 different numbers, each representing a 15.6 millivolt increment up to 4 volts maximum. A given level would be digitized as a coded 8-bit value (2^8 = 256) for processing, an operation known as Pulse Code Modulation (PCM). After being stored in the machine and just before being applied to the display, it will be converted back to its original voltage by a D/A converter so that a luminous point on the CRT screen (pixel) is displayed to produce the original grey level.

Colour systems require three D/A converters in order to convert digital levels representing values of red, green, and blue, to the analogue values needed to produce the sensation of a particular colour when the CRT's RGB beams strike a triad element on the screen. Colour electronics is described later.

OPERATING SYSTEMS, DATA, AND FILES

An operating system is a suite of programs which perform computer management functions and organize and allocate the resources needed to do a job. The major operating systems are DOS, OS/2, Unix and related systems, and System 7 used by Apple. These well-established systems will soon be joined by improved systems such as Chicago (Windows 95) and Daytona.

The operating system's functions are usually invisible to the user, as operations are often controlled by pointing to a symbol displayed on the screen and executing a function by depressing a button on a mouse. Formerly it was necessary to type a string of characters accurately.

There are usually two main kinds of file processable by a digital computer – program data files, used for housekeeping and control purposes, and user's data files. User's files may be created, stored, retrieved, edited, etc., by their names. They may be very long – the length may be limited only by practical considerations, for instance, a requirement to store a large file in one piece on a backup disk. Text files are usually relatively small. A page of text containing 500 words occupies about 5000 bytes of storage. A picture file may be relatively large, requiring megabytes of storage.

One important function, often encountered by users, is that of transferring files between different machines. For example, the publicity blurb says that 'Macintosh PC Exchange enables you to move files from PC to Mac as easily as you can between two Macs.' It would be reasonable to assume that it must be easy because many of the millions of DOS users will surely have checked with Apple dealers before buying a Mac, so that by now DOS–Mac file transfers are routine. A Mac may be able to read files from, say, a 3.5" PC/DOS diskette plugged into it, but can the files then be used in the Mac in the same way as they were used in the PC? Until recently a visit to Mac dealers with a PC disk containing a DOS/Word Perfect WP file would reveal that a page reproduced on the Mac via PC Exchange and Mac Word Perfect software looks very different from the original and needs to be completely re-edited.

An 'Apple DOS Board' was introduced in the States in February 1964. It was targeted at 'the home office, where multiple users have different platform needs e.g. kids using Macs at school and the small office where folks don't have an expert and don't care to wrestle with technology'. But the product would not be needed at all if it could be done already, as had been claimed previously. By 1995 most Apple machines contained built-in conversion arrangements.

TEXT

Text used in multimedia is likely to have been composed on a word-processing machine. When using a WP machine, an author specifies the layout and appearance of a document with a set of codes which determine margins, font, line and character spacing, and so on. The author may also have stored a standard set of formatting codes in a file which is retrieved on to every document so that all pages and documents have the same appearance. Several such code sets, specifying different-looking documents, may be stored and retrieved as needed. Layout and text codes may be peculiar to the WP machine, so if the text is sent on disk (instead of as print on paper, or as 'camera ready' print on paper) it cannot be used by a publisher unless he has a machine which can read the codes.

Demonstrations on the dealer's premises are likely to be inadequate for buying a WP system. A good dealer should allow a buyer to use a system for 14 days on a sale-or-return basis. The microcomputer world is a highly competitive one and it is easy to be swayed by marketing hype emphasizing speed (above all), new features, etc., most of which may be of little use for many applications.

CAMERAS

'Pictures' for multimedia may be images scanned from print on paper, 'photographs' of still objects taken with a camera which produces electrical signals from incoming light, motion pictures taken with a camcorder, or moving or still pictures captured as a television picture frame, or succession of frames, with a special board plugged in to a computer.

Cameras for capturing pictures for multimedia applications usually embody a matrix of Charge Coupled Device (CCD) sensors upon which the image is focused. Each sensor is capable of producing an electrical signal proportional to the incident light. Resolution depends on the size and spacing of the CCD elements. CCD response time depends on the maximum rate at which a charge can be built up in response to incident light, on the rate at which the charges can be read out, and on the illumination intensity. Colour is recognized as described in the section on colour scanning which follows. CCD signals varying according to the light value may be digitized to two levels corresponding to black or white, or digitized in steps corresponding to levels from 'black', through grey values to 'white'. Shutters are not usually necessary because software controls the period of time during which light falling on the CCD is accepted. Currently available CCDs can be read out at a frequency of 20 MHz or more so that with sensors arranged in a strip for, say, 300 pixels per inch resolution, the 8.7 million black/white pixels generated from a scanned A4 page can be handled in much less than a second. Sensor response time is not a speed constraint.

In 1994 several new digital cameras appeared. The Apple Quicktake 100, selling for about $650 with software, will take daylight or flash colour photographs which are stored in memory as compressed 640×480 pixel images. The camera is battery powered and the images are downloaded into Macs or PCs via an interconnecting cable.

The Kodak Professional DCS 200 digital camera is advertised at 'under $10,000', and sells at about £7000 in the UK. It will store up to 50 colour pictures on an internal hard drive. Downloading into Macs or PCs is via an SCSI interface. A CCD matrix of about 1500×1000 elements is fitted producing 8-bit per colour 24-bit 4.5 Mbyte (36 Mbit) images.

The AP/Kodak 'AP News Camera 2000' version of the DCS 200,

software is available for a Mac (the Apple Macintosh nearly always seems to be the starting point), enabling transparencies or discs to be created in-house and sent to a bureau for plate-making which is entirely satisfactory. A bureau in Oxford, UK, called Typo Graphics will provide film for printing, created from customer's material, at about £115 per page according to content. They do it with a Mac II, Truvel colour scanner, and a Linotronic 300. Software called PhotoMac is used to produce colour separation files. Typo Graphics claim that this is a 'stepping stone to high quality colour'. The interesting question is what standard is demanded by people who want to get their leaflets, house journals, magazines, etc. produced in colour.

The methods described above seem to be good enough for some but not for others. Evidently good colour printing still needs up-market equipment and expertise. If you want to produce good-looking material in colour you can always paste colour items on to DTP-produced pages and send them away for printing. The best-value route to quality printing is probably to adopt the 'Apple Mac–Quark XPress–Scitex Visionary' process. The minimum equipment needed is a Mac II machine with Visionary software – price around £16,000. Visionary is a modified version of the Quark XPress DTP software which produces files of Scitex formatted data. Alternatively, it will convert any Postscript file into Scitex. This outfit may not be justifiable for colour image output from computer-created graphics. It could be justified for pictorial illustrations scanned in colour by a colour scanner; the scanner will cost a few thousand pounds. Visionary software generates special files for use by a bureau with Scitex equipment, in particular a 'Page Geometry file' which specifies the CMYK value of each pixel in an image. The Scitex equipment (a Scitex workstation costs £200,000) then takes over to produce the transparencies for printing. The results are likely to be superb.

By now out of date, a table of 'Desktop Options' has been published by Neville (1989). It lists the approximate costs for printing systems starting with simple WP and DTP and progressing to a self-contained comprehensive colour system costing £80,000, plus desirable extras of £70,000 with running costs of £800 per week. The cost given for this last system includes the production of film separations.

BROADCAST ANALOGUE TELEVISION

The commercial broadcast television industry strongly influences trends in multimedia systems. Most equipment displays are based on television systems. They provide a convenient source of image frames which are 'grabbed' from a TV source and then usually digitized for multimedia purposes. The revolutionary changes in television such as digital HDTV and digital regular television will profoundly affect multimedia practice and so are discussed here in some detail. A good understanding of television is almost essential to anyone interested in multimedia.

Table 2.1 Representative scanners

Model	Manufacturer	Order of price (£s)	Interface	Micro-computer	Resolution	Speed docs/min.	Paper size	Colour	Notes
810C	Focus	735	SCCI	PC	400 × 800	6	A4	Yes	3-pass
LEOscan610	Focus	795	DMA	PC	300 × 300	10	A4	No	
11 SP	Microtek	895	SCSI	PC/MAC	30 0× 300	12	A4	No	
Scanjet 11CX	Hewlett-Packard	930	RS232	PC/MAC	400 × 400	3	A4	Yes	
Colour 1	Apple	1145	SCSI	MAC	300 × 300	3	A4	Yes	
LEOscan1210	Focus	1995	DMA	PC	300 × 300	12	A4	No	
IS 410	Ricoh	2500	SCSI	PC/MAC	300 × 300	10	A4	No	
M3096	Fujitsu	4400	RS232/SCSI	PC/MAC	400 × 400	27	A3-A5	No	
TZ-3	Microcad	8500	SCSI	MAC	600 × 600	2"/sec	A3	Yes	V. large objects

Abbreviations and acronyms
DMA   Direct Memory Access
SCSI   Small Computer System Interface
RS232   Standard computer interface for serial data

Modern scanners usually consist of a scanning head containing a single row of sensors, instead of the rectangular matrix used in cameras. An illuminated page is moved in very small steps relative to the head. The head remains over a strip of the page long enough for each sensor to generate a charge proportional to the incident light and for the electrical data from the row of sensors to be streamed out. The head then moves on to the next strip, and the process is repeated until the whole page is scanned.

The mechanical arrangements are either 'flatbed' or roller feed. A flatbed scanner consists of a glass plate beneath which the sheet of paper to be scanned is placed, face down. The head then moves along beneath the glass, scanning data from the illuminated page. The glass plate is usually large enough to accept a page of an opened book placed upon it, or the two pages of an opened book which face each other. A roller-fed scanner accepts sheets to be scanned. A sheet is moved across a stationary scanning head. Roller-fed scanners are unsuitable for book scanning. A typical head is 8.5" long with sensors spaced at 300 per inch along it. A whole A4 size page is scanned in a few seconds. The electrical data are digitized at two levels for 'bilevel' images and usually at 256 levels for halftone images.

By 1994 there were over 100 different models to chose from on the UK market. UK scanner prices range from about £700 upwards. The market in Western Europe was believed to be about $470M in 1992, growing at over 20 per cent per year.

Bilevel scanning

In two-level (bilevel) scanning, arrangements are made for each sensor to generate an impulse when the incident reflected light exceeds a fixed value, representing a 'white' pixel, or no impulse when the light is below that value, representing a 'black' pixel. This method is used for pages containing text (in circumstances requiring that the text be scanned to provide an image of a page rather than a coded version) and/or for 'line art' such as diagrams or sketches.

The simple method, where the output from each sensor is quantized at a fixed level for digital coding, is called 'fixed level thresholding'. It has its limitations because when an edge representing a change from black to white, or vice versa, occurs across a scanned element, the software must decide to represent it as either 'black' or 'white'; the larger the sensor element the more pronounced is the generation of a ragged edge by a row of sensors to represent a smooth edge in the original. Various techniques have been used to avoid this effect including 'average thresholding', which offers some improvement.

Halftone scanning

Black and white reproduction is adequate for text or line drawings, but halftones are needed for illustrations. The eye can perceive quite small changes in the 'grey scale' or in 'grey levels' – that is, in tonal levels in the range white through to black. For halftone digitization, the voltage level generated by a sensor in proportion to the intensity of the incident light is quantized into a series of fixed values representing a 'grey scale'. Two hundred and fifty-six levels are considered satisfactory for most purposes – the grey level of each pixel is the degree of brightness corresponding to a digitized value. Thus on a scale 1 to 255, grey level 201 would be represented as the 8-bit number 11001001. An 8-bit 256-level system increases the number of bits required to represent a 300 pixels/inch black and white picture on a 19" screen from 16.4 Mbits for bilevel to 131 Mbits for a 256-bit grey scale. Storage requirements are 2.05 and 16.4 Mbytes respectively.

Colour scanning

For scanning pages in colour, the CCD array makes three passes, letting in light through three different colour filters during each pass. Alternatively, the scan is carried out in a single pass using three light sources – red, green, and blue – which illuminate each line of the image to be scanned in sequence. Single-pass colour scanning may also be done by illuminating the image with a white light source and directing the reflected light through three dichroic filters on to three CCD strips. Each dichroic filter allows only one of the primary colours to pass through it. If each CCD specifies its colour in 8 bits, a 24-bit colour signal is sent to the computer. This is the method uses in the HP ScanJet IIc.

Typically a colour scanner is flatbed, generates not less than 300 dots per inch, provides 24-bit colour or 8-bit grey scale scanning, and includes software for OCR. A colour scanner may take from 100 to 400 seconds to scan a 'standard' image requiring 14 Mbytes of storage.

The human perception of a colour, described in a later part of this chapter, is defined by the CIE colour co-ordinate system in terms of the proportions of primary colours present. To produce good colour in scanning and reproducing equipment, account must be taken of the colour passed by each filter, and of the characteristics of the reproducing device, usually a Cathode Ray Tube (CRT). Faithful colour reproduction requires that special design and calibration be carried out for the performance of scanner colour filters and the CRT monitor to be used with them. Commercially available scanners and monitors will produce results which are good enough for most purposes, but are inadequate for fine art reproduction. A procedure for design and colour calibration has been described by Delp *et al.* (1991).

Scanner types and applications

When scanners were developed for the DTP market in 1985/1986 the software provided with them performed certain basic functions considered at the time to be impressive. For example, the software provided to run the Microtek MS-300A scanner on an Apple Macintosh controlled the scanning action and compression and decompression, enabled the user to select 'line art' or 'halftone' modes, set brightness and contrast levels, and saved the scanned image file in several alternative formats compatible with different DTP software. The simplest scanners are the small hand-held devices which can be manually swept across a part of a page of up to about 4 inches in width. The scanner is held over a strip of the page and swept slowly along it. An on-paper copy of the strip emerges as the sweep progresses. More expensive high-speed machines are available for dealing with high-volume document scanning, but page mechanical handling continues to be a speed constraint, particularly for bound volumes, single paper in assorted sizes, or pages with crinkled or bent edges.

To assist in the problem of scanning easily damaged rare books, the British Library and Optronics (Cambridge, UK) collaborated to produce a commercially available CCD scanner. The scanning CCD strip and a light source free of ultra-violet radiation are mounted behind a glass plate on the side of a V-shaped book-size box. The box is lowered just to touch the page of a book which is supported on a cradle, enabling it to be opened at 80 degrees to match the V of the box. The cradle is rotatable so that the opposite page may be scanned.

The Library of Congress (LC) put in hand one of the earliest large-scale scanning operations in 1978. It awarded a contract to Integrated Automation to provide scanners, Winchester disk temporary storage, Thomson jukebox 100 Gbyte optical disk WORM storage, laser printers, workstations, and monitors. System control is provided by a minicomputer connected to an IBM mainframe. The pages from a 3-year run of 74 prime scientific journals and other document collections were digitized and indexed to provide a test database. Within-LC users searched the database from their terminals and pages retrieved from the optical discs were passed to the terminals for viewing. Monitor resolution was 300×150 pixels/inch, printers 300×300. A mainframe computer received commands from terminals, searched LC databases, and passed retrieval commands to the minicomputer, which sent page images to requesting terminals. The objectives of the experiment were to preserve digitized copies of important documents, test alternative technologies, and assess user reactions.

In ongoing work at the National Library of Medicine, the objectives and equipment are broadly similar but particular attention has been paid to the throughput rates of material of variable quality. A special scanning jig has been constructed for turning over book pages easily and scanning them. The material to be scanned may consist of reasonably good quality bilevel pages, poor contrast faded bilevel pages on yellowing paper, variable contrast pages with stains and bleed-through, pages containing halftone (grey scale) material, or compound pages with mixed text and halftones. At input stations image enhancement is applied; compound pages are split up into, different sections according to enhancement requirements and then recombined into a single page. Indexing is unnecessary because the pages will have already been indexed under the NLM Medline system and records are available from within that database. Page storage is on local 20 Mbyte (160 Mbit) Bernouilli discs. The average compression ratio per page achieved for a particular collection is 14, enabling about 600 pages scanned at 200 dots/inch, each containing about 3.7 Mbits of uncompressed data to be stored per disk. The stored pages are periodically transferred to the main, optical disk, storage. The average throughput time per page input from bound volumes with this system is 50 seconds, inclusive of preparation, capture, quality control, and archiving to optical disk.

In a project at the Centre de Documentation Scientifique et Technologique (CDST), Paris, a division of CNRS, all aspects of an 'electronic document delivery service' were tested by delivering pages taken from current issues of 100 prime biomedical journals to users requesting them. Integrated Automation scanners digitizing at 200 pixels/inch, CIT/Alcatel laser printers, and a Thomson optical disk were used. The objectives were not particularly to test throughput times and problems with indifferent documents, but to study the behaviour of scientists in a real fee-paying situation which involved details like copyright payments to journal publishers, effective telecommunication links, etc.

During scanning operations at the Railway Museum, York, some photographic adjustments were required at the time of scanning which slowed up operations. While a scanning rate of 20 negatives per hour was sometimes achieved, Christine Heap, who is in charge of the work, says that the average rate was 5 to 6 negatives per hour (private communication, 1993). The scanning equipment supplied by Primagraphics incorporates a special camera, stand, and light box costing about £10,000. Primagraphics can also supply equipment which makes adjustments during scanning automatically – for example, contrast enhancement may be done by histogram processing.

In all scanning systems, page conversion cost is very sensitive to conversion time. It can vary from 3 pages per minute for desktop scanners designed for PC-based systems to 30 ppm for high-speed scanners such as TDC's Docuscan DS-2400, in which both sides of the documents are captured at one pass. Page sizes and paper thickness/quality will be different with non-uniform content and contrast. Page edges may not be flat. Other kinds of incoming paperwork such as delivery notes, invoices, orders, etc. may be worse. At the other extreme, pages to be scanned could come straight from a printing house as a pristine ream of A4 100 gramme paper carrying contrasty text, already containing terms required for indexing printed in a fixed position on each sheet. Such sheets could be fed into a scanning machine at high speed by the kind of paper-handling system used on fast copying machines.

Modern scanners include the Microtek Scanmaker machine, which can scan black and white, negative or colour 35 mm slides at 1850 dots per inch with an 8-bit grey scale or 24-bit colour. Special scanners are available for scanning slides to provide images of from 1025×1500 up to 4096×6144 pixels. The Kodak RFS 2035 35 mm Plus film scanner, for example, will scan a frame to generate 2048×3072 pixels in 40 seconds. 3D scanning may be carried out using a technique called 'laser stripe triangulation'. A laser beam scans over the surface, capturing several hundred points. Multiple images from different viewpoints are needed and images may be captured either by using several sensors or by moving the sensor around the object.

Some attempts have been made to standardize the formats of image files, particularly in regard to introducing scanned images into a desktop publishing system. The TIFF (Tag Image File Format) Standard seems to have gained some support from manufacturers. The most important part of TIFF is the set of tags describing the image and which are read by the computer in order to produce the image in the required form, whatever type of scanner or computer is being used. Tag information covers matters like number of bits per pixel, horizontal and vertical resolution, grey scale or colour details, compression system used, page number, etc.

DISPLAYS

Various display devices are starting to make the Cathode Ray Tube (CRT) less ubiquitous than it was, but the CRT exhibits 'the sailing ship effect' – sailing ships competed for much longer against steam than was expected because of various improvements. The performance of CRTs has improved remarkably and is still improving. For picture reproduction it still reigns supreme.

Photometric considerations

Having evolved in order to perceive reflected sunlight, the eye is sensitive to light from ultraviolet to infrared within the electromagnetic radiation spectrum of wavelengths between 400 to 700 nanometres (1 nm = 10^{-9} metres) centred around the wavelength of the sun's emission. This band of extremely short wavelengths corresponds to the wide frequency band embracing the wavelengths of the colour spectrum. In these days of fast data transmission, the attraction of the inherent bandwidth for light confined within a fibreoptic cable for data transmission media becomes very obvious.

Light produced by an electronic display has to be of adequate intensity, often vaguely described as its 'brightness'. A more scientific term is luminance in candelas per square metre (cd/m^2). Visual perception of a pattern depends crucially on contrast. This becomes very noticeable when the controls are adjusted on a CRT display. Characters may become hard to distinguish and may be lost in the background luminance when the controls are wrongly set.

Another aspect of importance, particularly with CRT displays, is the need for an absence of flicker. An image persists in the brain for a short period after light received from it by the eye has been extinguished, but for a light source to be free of flicker under any conditions the repetition frequency needs to be 50 Hz or more.

CRT display methods and techniques

The CRT has endured because the mass market for monochrome, and later colour television, has provided the incentive for the R&D effort needed to increase the performance and size of an evacuated glass tube with some precision metalwork inside it. The CRT is a cheap, mass-producible, if non-ideal, display device. The monochrome CRTs in use today are no different in principle from those developed by Von Ardenne in the early 1920s. A narrow beam of electrons hits a screen coated with a fluorescing material within an evacuated glass tube. A bright spot appears at the point of impact. In most CRT displays the spot traces out a raster produced by deflecting the electron beam with an external magnetic field applied horizontally to form a line, and with a second stepwise magnetic field applied vertically so that a succession of closely spaced lines is produced. During its rastering progress the spot may be switched on or off or varied in brightness by a voltage applied to a beam-control electrode. The completed raster frame filling the screen is rapidly repeated fifty or more times per second. If beam switch-ons occur at the same moments in each frame, apparently stationary patterns or pictures may be produced by a succession of frames. Alternatively, in vector displays, the spot is deflected by applied magnetic fields to form lines, circles, shapes, etc., which appear to be stationary because of frame repetition as with a raster display.

Resolution and bit rates

For electronic processing purposes, text and images are handled as dot structures. For good quality graphics, 300 dots per inch is considered to be desirable and there is a trend towards even higher resolutions. Consequently, a very large number of dots or pixels are contained on an A4 size page or '19 inch' screen, as shown in Table 2.2. Thus, when a pixel must represent any one of 256 different colours and there are 300 of them per square inch on a 19" screen, 131 Mbits (about 16 Mbytes) will be displayed in total.

The number of bits becomes larger as the resolution is increased and larger still as the amount of data per bit is increased for halftones or colour. The *bit rate* required when all the screen pixels are 'refreshed' in order to

Table 2.2 Displayed bit rates

Pixels/in	Pixels/mm	Pix./ Char.*	Pix./19"CRT# Hor. × Ver.	Total Mbits for 19"CRT# 1-bit	8-bit	24-bit
400 × 400	15.75 × 15.75	22	6240 × 4680	29	232	696
300 × 300	11.8 × 11.8	17	4680 × 3510	14.4	131	394
200 × 200	7.87 × 7.87	11	3120 × 2340	7.3	58	175
100 × 100	3.94 × 3.94		1560 × 1170	1.8	14.4	43.2
		Screen fill bit rate		1740	13920	41740
		at 60Hz (Mbits/sec.)		984	7872	23616
		corresponding to last		438	3504	10500
		three columns above		108	864	2592
		Storage required (Gbytes)		5.437	43.5	130.5
		for 1 minute motion-video		3.075	24.6	73.9
		corresponding to same		1.37	10.9	32.8
		three columns		.337	2.7	8.1

* Number of pixels in 1.4mm high (4 point) character.
# 19" CRT display area is assumed to be 15.6" horiz. & 11.7" vert.

display a steady image then becomes very high. Bit rates are a major constraint limiting the rapid reproduction of successive highly detailed frames on cathode ray tubes.

A sense of scale can be visualized in terms of a 4-point character which is about 1.4 mm high. If the pixel density is 200 per square inch, the vertical part of a 4-point character (about the smallest normally reproduced on a printed page) would contain about 11 pixels and would appear to be solid. It is often argued that a resolution of 300 × 300 pixels/inch is necessary to define fine structures in images if they are to look smooth rather than slightly jagged. Opinions about better requirements tend to be more forcibly expressed as the availability of suitable equipment increases and prices fall.

In CRT displays, for easily readable characters constructed from bright dots, a dot structure of not less than 7 (horizontal) × 9 (vertical) dots, with at least one dot between characters, is needed, with one dot between character ascenders and descenders in successive rows.

The size of the fluorescing spot is an important factor in determining CRT resolution. Reduction of spot size continues to receive the attention of CRT manufacturers who have turned to special electronics and deflection coil design to reduce spot size. Dynamic focusing provides more uniform sharpness over the screen area and an elaborate scheme called Digital Dynamic Convergence (DDC) is sometimes used to correct non-uniform resolution caused by production variations. The characteristics of discrete areas of the screen are corrected by data stored in read only memories controlling each area.

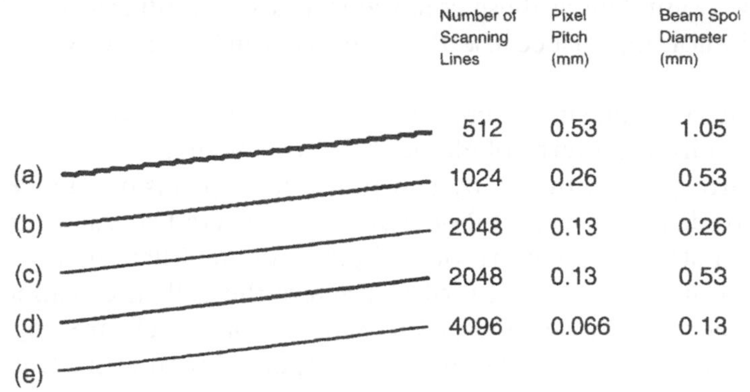

	Number of Scanning Lines	Pixel Pitch (mm)	Beam Spot Diameter (mm)
	512	0.53	1.05
(a)	1024	0.26	0.53
(b)	2048	0.13	0.26
(c)	2048	0.13	0.53
(d)	4096	0.066	0.13
(e)			

Figure 2.1 Resolution effects
Source: AEC

The relative effect on the smoothness of a diagonal line at different resolutions when displayed on a cathode ray tube is shown in Figure 2.1. The effect is most noticeable at certain angles and may be particularly noticeable at the edges of circular objects in pictures. Line (b) is typical of the effect on a good monitor and is barely noticeable at normal viewing distances.

In shadow mask colour tubes the resolution is mainly determined by the pitch of the shadow mask holes. In high-quality tubes the inter-triad resolution is about 0.5 mm. However, Hitachi offer a colour monitor (at a high price) with a triad pitch of 0.21 mm and 2730×2048 dots on the screen.

Maximizing cathode ray tube performance appears to be a black art. If high-quality reproduction is required, a user should conduct tests using an image carefully selected for the purpose before selecting a monitor, and use the same image for all tests.

For graphics and video a slightly different aspect of bit rates needs consideration. A user may want a change of graphic display or a succession of motion video pictures to be displayed as an immediate response to a command. Delays longer than a few seconds may be unacceptable. 'Fill screen' bit-rate times have improved greatly but so have processing demands. This aspect needs pre-purchase attention for demanding applications.

Reproducing a pattern on the screen

The speed of the spot is accurately controlled in CRT displays. During a scan, the time interval between the moment when the spot crosses a point on the screen's surface and then crosses the same point again during the next frame is accurately known. Consequently, a bright blob can be made to appear at the same position on the screen during each frame if the CRT beam is momentarily switched on at fixed time intervals. Because the frame is rapidly repeated or 'refreshed', the eye perceives an apparently stationary dot at that point. Under these conditions a raster is still traced out, but lines or dots do not appear because the beam is switched on only at one instant per frame.

One way of displaying a screenful of characters is to organize a series of character cells as patterns of elements in rows with, say, 1000 elements in a row, to correspond with row-by-row positions of pixels on the CRT screen's surface. To display a screenful of characters, selected character patterns are read into a store as a pattern of 'on' pixels defined within, say, a 7×9 dot matrix. To display a screenful of characters the cells are scanned, row by row, in synchronism with the beam, and the 'on' pixels are applied to the CRT's control electrode. The process is repeated with every frame.

Half-tones, colour, and bit-rate reduction

On a high-quality screen there may be over 1000 lines, each capable of sustaining 1000 pixels, being repeated 50 times per second. The time available for switching the beam on and off may be as little as 10 nanoseconds (1 ns = 10^{-9}) or one hundredth of a millionth of a second. When switching continuously at 10 ns intervals to produce a succession of dots, the speed is 100 million times per second, or 100 Mbits/sec.

To reproduce halftones or colour, extra data must be provided with each pixel. Thus for 16 halftones, 4 bits must be read out of a store increasing the on–off rate, in this case, from 100 Mbits/sec to 400 Mbits/sec – a speed which has become achievable only recently.

The high bit rates and large memories required for raster scanned displays have prompted various bit-reduction techniques. Compression or data reduction schemes have been in use for some years and they have become essential in intermediate stages such as data transmission and storage (see chapter 3). However, if, say, half the screen of a CRT display is occupied by a uniformly grey sky, every pixel must be wastefully controlled by successions of bits to hold it at that particular grey level. It would seem that bit rates at the CRT itself cannot be reduced.

But instead of struggling with circuit designs of the requisite bandwidth for conveying bits at very high speeds, memories can be organized to store data and deliver them simultaneously – the so-called 'bit plane' technique discussed later in this chapter.

Vector drawing

Vector drawing, which has come into its own for Computer Aided Design (CAD) applications, brings with it bit-reduced images as a bonus. In recent years vector drawing has been introduced into microcomputer software. Graphics created in the Apple Lisa machine were stored as the co-ordinates of points along outlines generated automatically when the user created drawings. 'Tools' were provided for assembling and manipulating outlines. Circles, lines, rectangles, polygons, etc. could be modified to form drawings. In the Macintosh, similar facilities are provided for graphics. This type of software enables special graphic effects to be achieved economically and easily. With the software package called Adobe Illustrator (see chapter 6), capitalizing on a language called Postscript, extraordinary computer-aided artistic effects can be produced.

Monitors

In TV receivers or TV-type monitors used as computer displays, data which are input to an 'RF' (Radio Frequency) socket pass through the TV's limited bandwidth amplifier, which causes picture element spreading. Text quality suffers if more than about 25 rows of text are used with 40 characters per row. In higher-quality monitors, data from the computer go direct to the monitor's video amplifier – the last electronics unit before the CRT.

The arrival of the inexpensive laser printer, capable of 300 pixels/inch, raised demands for improved resolution. There is nothing like an up-market push for creating a demand which did not previously exist. The resolution of CRT monitors still lags a long way behind such printers. Some manufacturers offer up to 200 pixels/inch in special-purpose monitors, and 300 dots per inch resolution is available at a high price. Larger, higher resolution monitors are desirable for the better assessment of pages that are to be printed, particularly for graphics with fine detail. Some people are prepared to pay for a high-quality monitor with, say, an A4 size screen in addition to the screen provided with a microcomputer, in order to get as near to WYSIWYG – What You See Is What You Get (on the printer) – as possible. There is also a demand for high-quality colour monitors.

The separate 19" monochrome monitors now being supplied with desktop publishing and multimedia equipment come with the necessary software and/or a plug-in board for the associated microcomputer. A board may include its own processor and storage needed to handle the larger number of picture elements. These monitors typically display a total of about 1 million pixels, equivalent to about 90 pixels/inch.

Microcomputers offering colour usually provide for fairly high resolution with a limited colour range. A larger range of colours, available on the screen at one time, themselves selectable from a much larger 'palette' are usually displayable only at lower resolution for reasons of economy in the CRT drive circuits.

Most CRTs have semi-rectangular screens with curved edges and both CRT manufacturers and monitor suppliers quote the size as a screen diagonal measurement. The usable display area is considerably smaller. The monitors normally supplied with microcomputers are much better than they used to be and are quite adequate for working with text. For looking at a clearly legible complete page or at good quality illustrations in colour, something better may be needed.

The display requirements for text or diagrams in colour, and for illustrations in colour – or for that matter, for text or diagrams in black and white and halftone illustrations – are rather different. In text and diagrams, resolution may be of prime importance. In illustrations, particularly 'pictures' – that is, artistic works – it is the colours or halftones, and their gradations and range which are usually of greatest importance.

In high-quality CAD/CAM workstations high-quality high-resolution colour CRTs are fitted with complex electronics capable of facilities for image processing and manipulation needed for engineering design work. Table 2.3 shows PAL and NTSC digitized frame bit capacities and the range of bit capacities for selected monitors under given conditions. The last three columns show the time it would take, at given rates in bits per second, to transmit one screenful of data over a telecoms link. For example (first line), 1.41 Mbits would take 0.37 minutes at 64 Kbps (8 Kbytes per second), and 0.056 seconds at 25 Mbps. Note that it takes over 8 minutes at 64 Kbps to send a single high-quality picture, such as might be represented by the 24-bit 31.4 Mbit data from the Chugai monitor.

The last monitor, the Nokia Multigraph, represents the state of the art in colour monitors – the first 1600×1200 21" colour monitor available as at January 1995. It is priced at $3225. Its maximum refresh rate of 80 frames/sec requires a very wide bandwidth in the driving electronics.

The details given in Table 2.3 include one high-quality monochrome example for comparison. A major reason for the superiority of the Flanders Exact 8000 is the small size of the single-beam spot compared with the size necessary to provide a tri-beam triad spot in colour tubes. The resolution of the Exact approaches 300 pixels/inch.

If what is being viewed is going to be printed then a good representation on the screen of what will ultimately be seen on paper is desirable. In multimedia a full-size representation of a whole page under preparation is a considerable advantage. Resolution and colour will still fall well short of what can be achieved with print on paper unless a very costly monitor is used. Know-how, experience, and additional facilities are needed to relate CRT colour to printed colour.

Principal (Haslingden, Lancs., UK) supplies the Spectrum/24 card for an Apple Macintosh II machine using Apple's 32-bit Quickdraw software. Principal can also supply the Supermac 19" monitor, which uses a Trinitron tube displaying 1024×768 pixels – about 72 pixels/inch on this screen. No doubt the result is a good quality image in colour but it's not clear how the monitor 'can add dramatic impact to publishing' as claimed, because the documents will be printed, not viewed on the monitor.

Cote and Diehl (1992) provide a list of 24 monitors, each with their various features described, in the price range $649–$2699. They recommend the

Table 2.3 Bit/byte capacities of selected monitors

Screen/frame example	Resolution Vert.	Resolution Horiz.	Bits per pix.	Total Mbits	Total K or M bytes	Duration at 64 Kbps (mins)	Duration at 1 Mbps (secs)	Duration at 25 Mbps (secs)
Original	512	342	8	1.41	176K	.37	1.41	.056
Apple	512	342	16	2.82	352K	.73	2.82	.112
	512	342	24	4.2	525K	1.1	4.2	.17
NTSC Frame	640	480	8	2.46	307K	.64	2.46	.1
(typical)	640	480	16	4.92	615K	1.28	4.92	.2
	640	480	24	7.37	921K	1.92	7.37	.295
PAL Frame	768	512	8	3.15	394K	.82	3.15	.126
(typical)	768	512	16	6.29	786K	1.64	6.29	.25
	768	512	24	9.44	1.18M	2.46	9.44	.38
NEC current	1024	768	8	6.29	786K	1.64	6.29	.25
Monitor	1024	768	16	12.58	1.57M	3.28	12.58	.5
	1024	768	24	18.87	2.35M	4.91	18.87	.755
Chugai current	1280	1024	8	10.48	1.31M	2.73	10.48	.42
Monitor	1280	1024	16	20.97	2.62M	5.47	20.97	.84
	1280	1024	24	31.46	3.93M	8.2	31.46	1.26
Flanders Exact	2560	3300	8	67.6	8.45M	17.6	67.6	2.7
Mono Monitor	2560	3300	16	135.2	16.9M	35.2	135	5.4
	2560	3300	24	202.75	25.34M	52.8	203	8.1
Nokia Multigraph	1600	1200	8	15.36	1.92M	4.0	15.36	.61
445X Monitor	1600	1200	16	30.72	3.84M	8.0	30.72	1.23
	1600	1200	24	48.08	6.01M	12.5	48.08	1.92

multiscan Viewsonic Seven 17" monitor at $1399, with a dot pitch of 0.28 mm and a maximum resolution of 1280×1024 pixels, but that list is already out of date. Information provided here as at April 1995 about monitors will almost certainly already be out of date, such is the rate of change.

At the time of writing, SuperMac were offering the 21-TXL 21" monitor providing multiple resolutions up to 1600×1200 pixels at about £2500 in the UK. However, the associated cards to drive it may cost up to about £4000. The boards include conversion from RGB to CMYK for publishing and twin 80 MHz DSPs for driving Adobe Photoshop applications.

Good quality colour is now available on a variety of other display devices which are gradually being introduced in competition with CRTs. So far the most successful competitor is the semiconductor screen formed from an array of active matrix supertwisted nematic Liquid Crystal Diodes (O'Mara 1992) – known as AMLCDs. At present colour AMLCDs, with advantages in size and power consumption, compete with CRTs only on portable computers.

A good example (Smarte 1992) is the Toshiba T4400SXC notebook computer which uses a screen containing nearly 1 million LCDs, each with its on-screen controlling transistor. It provides 256 colours at one time out of a 185,000 palette. As costs come down, especially for larger sizes, LCDs will become more widely used, particularly in HDTV receivers where the size limit for large, heavy CRTs is about 40" (diagonal). A 110" LCD screen has already been made. For the moment, CRTs remain supreme for the presentation of good colour at reasonable prices.

COLOUR

Introduction

Colour CRTs represent a substantial alteration in the basic CRT design. The colour tubes in use today are similar to the shadow-mask tube, introduced for colour television in the 1950s. Later a successful variation – the Trinitron tube – was developed. The result of this competition was a range of substantially improved shadow-mask tubes.

The rate of advances in technology being what they are, we are justified in asking, 'Since we see the world in colour, and artists usually represent it in colour, why can't we also always see it reproduced on an electronic display or as print on paper in colour?' The answer at the moment seems to be that we are prepared to pay more to see certain images in high-quality colour closely resembling the colour of the original – for example, the reproduction of a Turner in a fine art book. However, processing and printing good quality colour are still relatively expensive and are becoming more expensive. Some companies will pay extra to ensure that their products are presented to the public reproduced in the best possible colour. Advertisers who want to present a food product at its most succulent have to decide, on the basis of colour realism and cost per consumer reached, whether to advertise on paper or on colour TV. A whole-page advertisement in colour on coated paper in a high-circulation newspaper may cost up to £42,000 in the UK.

Advertisements excepted, newspapers consist mainly of text and so the effect of enhancement of the whole publication by colour is somewhat limited. Colour supplements (for which a better name would be 'advertising supplements') printed on higher quality paper to provide better colour are commonplace.

Desktop publishing costs are falling rapidly but are still too high for colour to be much used, although the magazines covering the field would have us believe otherwise. Costs will continue to drop and the know-how of colour printing will gradually become less essential as the software becomes more sophisticated. Colour printing will gradually spread downwards through the market.

For multimedia presentations, computers with displays in colour, plug-in boards for handling images in colour with special effects, and DSP and accelerator boards are virtually essential. Improvements at lower prices are an almost monthly occurrence and, as the demand for multimedia systems increases, better, faster displayed colour may be expected.

Defining colour

Colour is specified in terms of *hue*, determined by the frequency of the radiated energy, *saturation* (purity) – the amount of white light present, and *luminosity* (brightness). The sensation of a particular hue may be invoked either by the radiation of a particular wavelength (specified in nanometres (nm), $1nm = 10^{-9}$ metres) or by the wavelength generated by a mixture of colours.

For measurement purposes a given colour may be specified by matching against a colour composed of measured proportions of the primary colours red, green, and blue. Special instruments called colorimeters are available for the purpose. Equal proportions: 0.33 of red + 0.33 of green + 0.33 of blue = 1 = white. Any other colour may be reproduced by variations of these proportions. The coefficients (proportions) are called *trichromatic units*. The tri-stimulus theory of colour was advanced by Clerk-Maxwell in 1856 and has stood the test of time; it is supposed that the retina of the eye is composed of three types of receptors sensitive to the proportions of primary colours present.

These ideas were noted by the Commission Internationale de l'Eclairage back in the 1920s who put forward the CIE Chromaticity Diagram shown in Figure 2.2.

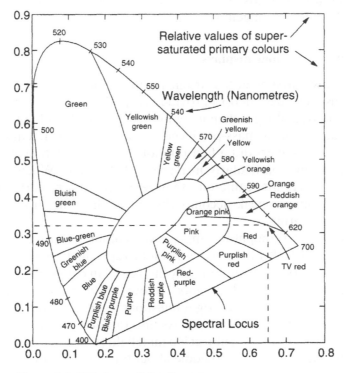

Figure 2.2 CIE chromaticity diagram
Source: CIE

This diagram has assumed particular importance for measuring and specifying colour as produced by Cathode Ray Tubes (CRTs) for colour television. The y and x axes represent the proportions of green and red (and in consequence blue since pR + pG + pB = 1) to produce the range of colours shown.

The wavelength of hues is shown round the edge of the diagram. The typical range of colours provided by a colour CRT – its 'colour space' – could be shown on this diagram as a triangle with its apices some way inside the corners of the diagram (e.g. one apex at 'TV red' as shown), not providing a complete colour range, but considered to be good enough for most purposes.

The above remarks apply to colour produced by radiated light. The sensation of colour generated from coloured painted or printed surfaces is produced by selective absorption of the component colours of white (ideally) light. What we see are the components which are reflected. If the surface is viewed by reflection from a source which is not pure white, the reflected components will of course be different.

Printed colour is produced by laying down the 'subtractive' colours cyan (turquoise), magenta (bright pink), yellow, and black (as opposed to RGB radiation, which is additive). Some colour printers use 'process' ribbons having lengthwise bands in these colours. Combinations produce other colours, e.g yellow + magenta = red; cyan + magenta = blue.

Reproduction in colour displays

Most people will first meet 'electronic colour' in their TV set. Colour television systems were designed to provide acceptable colour from a television signal transmitted along a channel of limited bandwidth, able to be decoded and reproduced on a mass-produced domestic receiver. Unquestionably the ingenious designers did a first-rate job, subjected as they were to these severe constraints, particularly in respect of the tube. When TV shadow-mask colour CRTs first came out, they represented a remarkable achievement – probably *the* peak accomplishment at the time in mass-produced precision engineering.

If a person buys a computer complete with colour monitor and appropriate software, the part of it dealing with colour reproduction should not introduce difficulties. But anyone seriously interested in colour who also wants to capture, create, or reproduce good colour graphics with special effects needs to know how to ask the right questions in order to be able to buy the right equipment. For assembling a system, rather than buying a complete integrated tested outfit, the subject is a minefield (unless he/she is a computer buff who has unlimited time to fiddle about for the love of it).

Colour electronics

A great deal of data has to be managed for storing, processing, or communicating images in colour. An 'image' in this context means a 'bit-mapped image' – that is the representation of an image by an array of very small picture elements sometimes called pels, but usually pixels. Good quality requires that there be a sufficient number of pixels to define the fine structure of an image ('high resolution'), that tonal qualities are realistically presented, and that a good range of colours is displayed.

Shadow-mask colour tubes have three electron guns. Their focused electron beams pass through holes in a mask (grid) allowing each beam to strike the phosphor screen only at specific locations. The screen is made up of triads of three dots which glow red, blue, and green respectively. The alignment of the mask holes with a dot of a particular colour in each triad is such that the beam from the 'red' gun can only strike a red dot, the 'blue' gun only a blue, and the 'green' gun only a green.

Trinitron tubes embody a grid called an 'aperture grille' mask which is slotted vertically, causing electrons to provide almost continuous vertical excitation, eliminating the small 'dead border' area present in shadow-mask tubes. In spite of improvements in the design of shadow-masks, Trinitrons are still claimed to provide slightly better quality.

The eye perceives a colour produced by the combined effect of the dots or vertical strips in each triad. Colour signals applied to each gun control the contribution of each dot to the overall colour of the triad. The triad pitch is about 0.5 mm in shadow-mask colour tubes. With some overlapping of displayed elements this represents a density of up to about 100 triads or pixels per inch.

The current in a gun is infinitely variable so if each gun is controlled by an *analogue* signal which varies according to the proportions of red, green, and blue in each pixel, colour reproduction should be good. This is the way it is done in television systems; the colour is as good as the whole system allows – from the TV camera, through the transmission channel and the circuits in the TV receiver to the tube. The eye perceives the particular colour produced by the combined effect of the dots in a triad, each glowing with a particular intensity. In the case of television and in some computer systems, three sets of analogue colour data are directly applied to the electron guns. In digital systems, three separate bit groups are converted into three voltages (analogue data) and are then applied to the three guns to produce the required beam intensities.

Digital computers work in bits – signals are either on or off. If the beam in a single-gun CRT is switched on by one impulse or data bit for a few microseconds during its traverse across the screen it will produce one dot or pixel. A pattern of such 'on' or 'off' pixels, rapidly repeated, can be made to represent a 'bilevel' ('black and white') image.

Colour electronics in digital systems is handled in two ways. The earliest and the simplest is quite adequate for the reproduction of text in a number of different colours. An on–off arrangement as just described is used, but with three guns instead of one. A 4-bit control signal provides 16 colours from 16 possible on or off combinations of R, G, B, and intensity. This arrangement has been extended to a 6-bit system providing 64 colours with R,r, G,g, and B,b, where RGB represents full intensity, and rgb represents, say, half intensity.

The controlling electronics called 'TTL' (Transistor–Transistor–Logic) involves straightforward switching and is quite simple. However, the principle becomes less attractive for a larger number of colours requiring more wires in a cable and wider bandwidth to deal with faster data.

In the second (digital) system, devised to provide a much wider range of colour more conveniently, data are transmitted, stored, and processed in *digital* form and three sets of digital signals, specifying multiple levels of red, green, and blue intensity in bits, are fed to three digital-to-analogue converters (DACs) which translate the signals into voltage levels. The DACs connect to the three guns in the tube to control the current intensities.

Each triad in the CRT's 'picture frame', typically totalling $640 \times 480 = 307,200$ elements, must be repeated 50 times a second or more to provide a flicker-free image, so the total *bit rate* becomes $307,200 \times 50 = 15.4$ Megabits per second (Mbps). The amount of additional data required to provide multi-level colour control as well raises the total to a much larger number than in the simpler methods already described (see Table 2.2).

The 'bit plane technique' (see Figure 2.3) is one way of reducing bit rates in grey scale and colour systems. A plane is a store holding as many elements as there are pixels on the screen. The box diagram shows a 4-plane 4-bit per pixel system with 4-bits being read out to represent pixel number 187 in a row near the top of the screen. For example, a 1280×1024 display with 12 bits per pixel would have 12 planes, each containing 1280×1024 storage elements. When a particular pixel is required to be displayed, the contents of the 12 storage elements in the same position on each plane representing the data for that pixel are addressed. The data are read out in parallel to the screen. The rate per plane is one-twelfth of the rate of the single store which could otherwise be needed.

In a microcomputer with good colour there is likely to be a 24-bit system with 8 bits for each gun providing up to 2^8 or 256 different colours at one time on the screen. A *'palette'* is also provided, from which these colours are selected from any combination of the 256 levels of each gun. The palette changes the combinations so that different sets of 256 colours are displayed, providing for $256 \times 256 \times 256 = 2^{24} = 16.78$ million different combinations of colours available for display.

A change in the colour combination for any gun is performed by a memory called a 'Colour Lookup Table' (CLUT) situated just before the

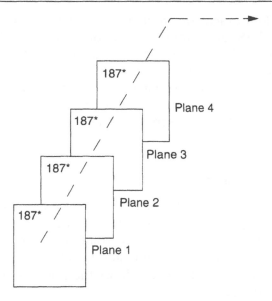

Figure 2.3 Bit plane operation
Source: AEC

DACs. To change the colour of a pixel, the CLUT memory location for that pixel is addressed. At that address resides a new word which has been programmed into the CLUT to represent a particular colour. The colours represented in the CLUT, usually 256, are chosen from the much larger 16.78M palette and may be changed rapidly. This word is output to the DACs to represent the new colour. All screen pixels are processed in this manner in order to change the colours in the whole display. Thus, while only these 256 colours may be present on the screen at one time, a different 256 may be presented shortly afterwards.

Colour matching

Once the handling of a large number of colours on relatively inexpensive equipment was solved, attention was focused on exact colour selection and matching, and on the relationship between colour as perceived on a CRT and as printed on paper. In 1989 Tektronix introduced a software package costing $50 called TekColor. It provides adjustments for colour while the user observes both CRT RGB colours and equivalent CMYK values from the printer on the screen. Adjustments may be made in order to achieve a match between the two. Colour selection and numerical readings given during the adjustment process conform to the CIE model mentioned earlier. The system runs on a Mac and supports a number of different monitors and printers.

In addition, a small table appears on the screen showing values for the Hue, Intensity, and Saturation (HIS) of a particular selected colour. To produce that colour exactly on another occasion, the same values are set up in the table. The HIS values are transformations of RGB values represented on the CIE diagram. Kodak have introduced a Colour Management System which reads the colour spaces used by colour reproduction devices and converts them into a descriptive language (Blair 1992). When a computer is connected to a particular printer and an image is displayed on the CRT, the CRT is controlled to represent the image in the colours which will be reproduced by the printer.

Systems for colour and graphics

Improvements have evolved through *de facto* Standards set by Apple and IBM. When the Apple Lisa machine was introduced, its 720×364 pixel monochrome display was considered revolutionary. IBM started with its CGA arrangement for colour, progressing to VGA. Other suppliers have introduced enhancements. Table 2.4 shows the titles and characteristics of some available arrangements.

At the present state of the art for reasonably priced microcomputers with small monitors, resolutions up to about 640×480 with 256 colours are available – about 80 pixels/inch on a small 8" × 6" screen. For resolutions of 100 pixels/inch or more, requiring more bits, the number of colours is often reduced in order to reduce the bit rate. For good colour with high resolution, higher prices must be paid for special processing cards and special monitors. Large high-resolution monitors driven by their own special plug-in cards are available at higher prices (see Table 2.3).

Table 2.4 De facto screen Standards

Title	Screen resolution	Max no. of screen cols
CGA	320×200	4
CGA	640×200	mono
MAC	512×342	mono
EGA	640×350	16
Enhan. EGA	640×480	16
HGC	720×348	16
Amiga	640×400	32
VGA	320×200	256
VGA	640×480	16
VGA	720×480	16
Super VGA	800×600	16
MAC II	640×480	256
MCGA	620×480	256
8514/A	1024×768	256
Amiga spec'l	1280×400	32
Apple spec'l	1024×896	256

PRINTING AND PRINTERS

Halftone reproduction

Dye-sublimation printers can print variable-sized dots for reproducing halftones. Most of the printers to be described – dot-matrix, inkjet, the thermal printer family, and laser printers – cannot. Instead, halftones are displayed or printed with the aid of software to provide simulated tonal effects by variable dot clustering, enabling bilevel printers to print acceptable halftones. Very small areas are filled with a variable number of dots by 'dithering' (filling with a dot pattern) in order to produce from white through grey shades, to black when the area is full. The illustration *Boats at San Francisco* in Figure 2.4 shows a dithered picture printed on a 300 dpi laser printer.

Larger dot-filled areas produce better halftones at the expense of a loss of detail, since the small dots which would otherwise resolve fine detail are replaced by these areas which now become the smallest displayed visible elements. But 600 dots per inch laser printers enable the areas of clustered dots to be made smaller without reducing the number of dots enclosed in them, to restore detail otherwise lost. Moreover, the smaller dots enabled an improved method called 'ordered dither' to be introduced.

A photograph ('bromide') of a continuous tone illustration, used by printers to make a printing plate, is taken through a piece of glass with closely spaced lines ruled on it. This 'screen' produces lines of variable width corresponding to grey levels on the photograph which take up ink on the

PRINTING: HALFTONE REPRESENTATION BY DITHERING

Figure 2.4 300 dpi 'dithered' picture
Source: AEC

plate and produce a halftone reproduction. The screen is usually rotated through an angle – often 45 degrees – to avoid interference effects associated with vertical or horizontal lines in the original. A screen of 150 lines or dots per inch is adequate for very good quality reproduction of printer illustrations. Detail scanned in at a higher resolution will not then appear. Since the quality of reproduction of the tones in an illustration is usually of greater importance than the fine detail, attention is shifted to good reproduction of a wide range of tones, ideally at least 256, sensed during scanning.

The number of halftones that can be printed depends on the number of printed dots per inch (since the size of the smallest dot effectively dictates the tonal range) and the screen pitch, as calculated from the expression:

$$\text{Number of halftones} = \text{printed dots/inch}^2/\text{screen pitch}^2 + 1$$

If the printer can provide 300 dots/inch and the screen pitch is 150, the number of halftones (nH) can be:

$$nH = (300^2/150^2) + 1 = 5$$

The '+1' is for the non-printed halftone 'white'. If a 'high-resolution' printer – such as a Linotron 300 running at its maximum 2540 dots/inch is used, and the screen is 150:

$$nH = 2540^2/150^2 + 1 = 287 \text{ (approx.)}$$

assuming, of course, that this amount of halftone data was input.

Dot matrix printers

Dot matrix printers are the least expensive. In the better quality versions 24 pattern-forming needles shoot out against an inked ribbon to impress a pattern on to paper. They can provide acceptable characters at 300 dots per inch. The inexpensive DEC LA95 colour dot-matrix printer, introduced in 1993, provides 24-pin 300 dots per inch in colour and is claimed to print 240 characters per second with good quality.

Inkjet printers

Modern inkjet printers use a powered ink chamber/nozzle arrangement. A piezo-electric crystal, which will bend or deflect when a voltage is applied to it, is used to apply sudden pressure to a flexible ink chamber and blobs of ink squirt out as the printing head scans across the paper. Resolution is up to 300 pixels/inch. The inkjet technique lends itself to one-pass colour printing. The head contains several squirters, each containing inks of different colours which are controlled to squirt as necessary to produce appropriate combinations. The speed of inkjet colour printers depends on what they are printing. Simple Postscript (see below) graphics in colour take about twice as long as the same without Postscript, while a complex coloured illustration may take twice as long again – perhaps several minutes.

Thermal printers

Thermal printers work at up to about 200 characters per second (about 3 pages a minute) and can be programmed to print graphics. A fast thermal printer might by now have been expected to appear as a cheap image printer in quantity production, resembling a fax Group 3 printer with a resolution of 200×200 pixels/inch. However, fax print can deteriorate by chemical action if left in contact with certain types of surfaces.

Simple thermal printers have been overtaken by special types of thermal printer for providing high-quality colour printing as described in the next sections.

Thermal wax colour printers

Pages in colour of reasonable quality, printed directly by thermal colour printers, can be produced for small print runs, or for the 'proofing' of pages to be further processed. Today's thermal wax colour printers transfer colour from a ribbon composed of sequences of four page-size panels coated with pigmented wax in CMYK colours. The same panel sequence repeats along the ribbon. The print head contains small dot-size printing elements which are heated to melt the wax and transfer it to the paper. The printer makes a separate pass to transfer each colour. Accurate registration is necessary. Such machines will print on plain paper, usually at 300 dpi. The speed depends on what is being printed.

Dye sublimation colour printers

These printers belong to the family of thermal printers but contain further refinements. Dye sublimation thermal printers are used for colour printing where the best available quality is required. Since dithering is not needed, they produce higher resolution printing although small text sometimes appears with a slightly fuzzy appearance. They use dyes, not inks and special paper. The dye turns into a gas before deposition on the paper. Different colours are produced by the superimposition of primary colour dots, not by 'area fill' as in dithering. Smooth continuous tone images are printed because dots tend to diffuse slightly into each other – hence the excellence for colour or halftones. Again, speed depends on what is being printed.

The Fargo Electronics company has produced a printer which prints with a choice of thermal wax or dye sublimation in the same machine. The price is far less than that of other printers and it is smaller and lighter. Although the machine is reviewed as having some disadvantages, its print quality is said to be only slightly lower than that of printers of a much higher price. Figure 2.5 is printed from a Tektronix Phaser 440 dye sublimation colour printer. It shows the kind of quality to be expected from such a printer. Note that in this case there is no sign of blurring on 4-point text.

Figure 2.5 Printed by a Tektronix Phaser dye sublimation printer
Source: Tektronix

Laser printers

Laser printers usually consist of a photosensitive drum on to which the modulated beam from a laser is projected. Beam raster-scanning is produced by rotating mirrors – the way scanning was done on the earliest projection television systems. Paper is rolled against the drum surface and the charge pattern transferred from the drum is made visible on paper by heat-fused toner.

The introduction of the Hewlett Packard (HP) 300 dots per inch (dpi) Laserjet printer in 1983 revolutionized lower-cost DTP reprographics. It would be more correct to say that HP and Apple between them made DTP possible. The Laserwriter, HP Laserjet, and Cannon's laser printer will print an A4 page at a resolution of 300×300 pixels per inch at 8 pages per minute under favourable conditions – that is, when they are repeatedly printing copies of the same page containing an 'average image'.

It may take many minutes to print each page of a succession of different highly detailed pages. Consumables associated with a laser printer such as toner, drum assembly, etc. typically average a cost of about 4 cents per page. Speeds depend on the printer manufacturer's hardware, the driver software which converts DTP page formats from Pagemaker, Ventura, etc. into Postscript, and the interpreter program which changes Postscript into laser printer bit-map format. For the highest quality of illustrations a machine such as the Lasermaster Unity 1200XL will print at 1200 dots per inch providing excellent quality. It uses a 33 MHz Risc processor, so it is also fast.

Colour laser printers are expensive but QMS have recently produced such a printer selling for around $12,000. It produces 300 dpi colour images by making four passes, using a belt with the adherence of a toner of a different colour at each pass produced by a laser sweeping out a pattern for each of the four colours. The printer can also be used to produce black and white copies. Its main advantage is the low cost per copy – much lower than wax or dye sublimation printers.

Postscript

Because Postscript is a programming language, instructions can be written to make a laser printer beam move anywhere in almost any manner to print almost anything. For most purposes, the ready-programmed printing control facilities available when Postscript software is supplied with a laser printer are sufficient, and no programming is needed. More information is provided in chapter 6.

Colour printing techniques

There is a quality gap between printing colour directly on to paper from a DTP or multimedia system using one of the several kinds of relatively inexpensive colour printer now available, and printing by overlaying from colour separation transparencies. With a direct colour printer, all that the user sees is the print in full colour emerging from the printer, the process of constructing the image from its component colours being managed by the machine. The results are moderate to good, and getting cheaper and better. The machine may take some minutes to produce the first print and then produces each subsequent copy rather more quickly. The method is suitable for short printing runs.

Colour separation printing involves the preparation of four transparencies – the contents of black and white films carrying data about those parts of an image containing the colours cyan, magenta, yellow, and key (black) (CMYK) respectively. A colour print is produced by first making four printing plates from the transparencies, and second, performing four printing passes using inks of different colours from each accurately aligned plate. After that copies are produced at high speed.

Direct colour versus colour separation printing

The perceived colour of inkjet and thermal printers which directly produce colour prints depends on the relative proportions of inks or dyes used in each pass. Postscript, the printer control language widely used with laser printers, changes bit-mapped images into plotted descriptions which are independent of printer resolution; high-resolution printers produce high-resolution images. The special thermal printers previously described enable very good quality to be produced from a microcomputer – in some cases good enough for 'colour proofing' – that is, checking what an image will ultimately look like when printed from separations.

'Gamma correction' facilities may be included when high quality is required – 'gamma' being the linearity relationship between input and output data. As with cathode ray tubes, gamma correction is necessary in printers for the best results in order to correct for non-linearity between input and output.

Professional human printers would disagree with the idea that a thermal printer colour proof is good enough for approving material to be reproduced later along the chain. The present method of proofing is to have a 'cromalin' (patented by Du Pont) proof sent back from the printing house, with colours closely resembling those to be finally printed. It seems doubtful whether human printers can still justifiably criticize quality, given the remarkable quality of dye sublimation printing. However, there still appears to be a gap between 'low end' colour printing and professional colour printing. Low end means direct colour printing, or for longer print runs, printing from software claimed to be able to produce separate files containing colour data or colour separation transparencies destined for plate-making.

Some hardware/software suppliers and information technology magazine article writers would disagree with the above comments. They would say that software is available for a Mac (the Apple Macintosh nearly always seems to be the starting point), enabling transparencies or discs to be created in-house and sent to a bureau for plate-making which is entirely satisfactory. A bureau in Oxford, UK, called Typo Graphics will provide film for printing, created from customer's material, at about £115 per page according to content. They do it with a Mac II, Truvel colour scanner, and a Linotronic 300. Software called PhotoMac is used to produce colour separation files. Typo Graphics claim that this is a 'stepping stone to high quality colour'. The interesting question is what standard is demanded by people who want to get their leaflets, house journals, magazines, etc. produced in colour.

The methods described above seem to be good enough for some but not for others. Evidently good colour printing still needs up-market equipment and expertise. If you want to produce good-looking material in colour you can always paste colour items on to DTP-produced pages and send them away for printing. The best-value route to quality printing is probably to adopt the 'Apple Mac–Quark XPress–Scitex Visionary' process. The minimum equipment needed is a Mac II machine with Visionary software – price around £16,000. Visionary is a modified version of the Quark XPress DTP software which produces files of Scitex formatted data. Alternatively, it will convert any Postscript file into Scitex. This outfit may not be justifiable for colour image output from computer-created graphics. It could be justified for pictorial illustrations scanned in colour by a colour scanner; the scanner will cost a few thousand pounds. Visionary software generates special files for use by a bureau with Scitex equipment, in particular a 'Page Geometry file' which specifies the CMYK value of each pixel in an image. The Scitex equipment (a Scitex workstation costs £200,000) then takes over to produce the transparencies for printing. The results are likely to be superb.

By now out of date, a table of 'Desktop Options' has been published by Neville (1989). It lists the approximate costs for printing systems starting with simple WP and DTP and progressing to a self-contained comprehensive colour system costing £80,000, plus desirable extras of £70,000 with running costs of £800 per week. The cost given for this last system includes the production of film separations.

BROADCAST ANALOGUE TELEVISION

The commercial broadcast television industry strongly influences trends in multimedia systems. Most equipment displays are based on television systems. They provide a convenient source of image frames which are 'grabbed' from a TV source and then usually digitized for multimedia purposes. The revolutionary changes in television such as digital HDTV and digital regular television will profoundly affect multimedia practice and so are discussed here in some detail. A good understanding of television is almost essential to anyone interested in multimedia.

For the first hundred years or so of electrical communication systems, speech was conveyed along wires as an *analogue* signal – a voltage from a microphone varying in proportion to the applied sound pressure level. The signals transmitted when the first electronic television systems arrived were also analogue.

For the purposes of this chapter, a television camera may be considered as a tube containing a plate upon which are mounted rows of very small photo-electric elements capable of generating a voltage proportional to the incident light. Light from the image is focused on to the plate which is scanned, row by row, by an electron beam. The element voltages are read off in a continuous stream and the scanning action creates a series of closely spaced lines of voltages forming a complete 'field' representing a snapshot of the image in electrical form. The process keeps repeating so that the camera tube outputs an analogue (continuously varying) voltage, field after field. A video frame is formed from two interlaced fields, lines from the second field falling between lines from the first – a way of reducing both flicker and transmission channel bandwidth. Synchronizing pulses are added. At the receiver, the scanning electron beam of a Cathode Ray Tube (CRT), running at approximately the same rate as the beam in a camera, is pulled into exact line, field, and frame synchronism by received synchronizing impulses. The video data on each line are applied to the CRT beam to vary the brightness.

These 'all analogue' principles were used in the EMI system adopted when the BBC inaugurated the first electronic public TV service in the 1930s, having rejected Baird's alternative. In the United States NTSC colour television was developed later using the analogue TV Standard RS170 – a modified version of the basic arrangement just described.

In colour television, a colour TV camera amounts to three cameras viewing the image through red, green, and blue (RGB) filters and outputting three signals and a luminance (average brightness) signal called the 'Y' signal. The RGB signals are combined in a special way as 'chrominance' signals to represent the hue and saturation values (as defined in the earlier section 'Defining colour') for each minute area of the image as these areas are successively scanned. These data, with a colour-burst reference signal added for decoding at the receiver, together with Y signals, comprise a spectrum of broadcast television signals occupying, in the NTSC case, a band 4.25 MHz wide. Special arrangements were implemented so that existing black and white TV sets could reproduce black and white pictures simply by ignoring the chrominance and colour-burst signals. A colour receiver decodes the composite chrominance/luminance data into the RGB components which are applied to the three electron beams of a colour CRT. The beams produce a pixel by illuminating a three-element dot on the screen. The dot is formed from three chemicals which glow red, green, or blue with an intensity in proportion to beam currents when struck by the scanning

RGB beams. The combined glow produces a pixel perceived as being of a particular colour.

There are three major TV systems in the world – NTSC in North America, some parts of South America, and in Japan and the Philippines, SECAM in France, Eastern Europe, and the USSR, and PAL in other countries. The differences stem mainly from political confrontations which arose when the systems were being introduced. There are certain technical differences as well as differences in A.C. mains supply frequencies and numbers of scanning lines; TV receivers are not readily interchangeable between the different systems.

DIGITAL HIGH DEFINITION TELEVISION (HDTV)

Space in the frequency spectrum available for television broadcasting is at a premium and much ingenuity has been applied to cramming sufficient analogue information into as narrow a bandwidth as possible – yet still providing a decent picture on the television. High Definition Television (HDTV) requires still more bandwidth.

The idea of replacing a world-wide investment in television broadcasting and receiving equipment worth billions of pounds/dollars/marks/yen, etc. by something different is an exercise in the art of the possible which has been accompanied by much political agonizing, briefly summarized below. Netravelli and Lippman (1995) estimate that there are nearly one billion TV receivers in the world today – representing a vested interest of enormous value and an equally valuable market for an improved system to replace it.

A Japanese proposal to launch High Definition Television (HDTV) with 1125 lines was made at a 1985 international meeting in Geneva – the scheme would wipe out POAT – Plain Old Analogue Television. The world closed ranks and came up with various alternatives. Subsequently technological progress encouraged ideas about the possibilities of digital television – so much so that if HDTV is to be introduced, the shift from conventional analogue TV directly into digital HDTV is the way to go. In view of the inevitability of the all-digital approach, changing from analogue TV to analogue HDTV would be an immensely expensive intermediate digression. Most HDTV ideas include a displayed picture resolution of 1100 lines or more, a wide screen more like a cinema screen, and a generally higher quality of sound and vision without the intrusion of various artefacts which affect conventional television systems.

Schreiber (1995) provides an outstanding review of the prospects for HDTV at both the technical and political levels.

It was thought that all-digital systems were very far into the future. Digital proposals had often been viewed as roundabout efforts to delay

HDTV. Likewise it had been the generally held (but incorrect) view that *any* amount of compression would be unacceptable because of loss of quality.

Schreiber believes there should be a market for HDTV at about $3000 for a receiver, comparable with the price when earlier systems were introduced, but points out that it took ten years for a 1 per cent penetration of the market by those systems. He continues with a comprehensive review of a range of technical factors, emphasizing the immensity of the problems that must be overcome during such a revolutionary change.

The world thought again about HDTV systems when the General Instrument company demonstrated a feasible *digital* television system at Chicago in 1990 – an event which disturbed mainline thinking, which had not expected such systems to appear so soon. In the United States it is now proposed to jump straight to an all-digital HDTV system whilst taking account of the existing needs of a very large customer base continuing to use NTSC receivers. For more information see Toth *et al.* (1993).

Some kind of HDTV service is expected to start in the United States during 1996. This rate of change has been made possible through an alliance ('The Grand Alliance') called the Advanced Television Research Consortium (ATRC) of erstwhile competitors – Thomson, AT&T, General Instrument, Philips, Zenith, and Sarnoff.

The major factors in a proposed US HDTV Standard being considered by the US Federal Communications Commission (FCC) at the time of writing will include a resolution specification providing for about six times the resolution of NTSC, progressive scanning – that is the scanning of each line in sequence to form one frame instead of interlaced scanning in which two scanned fields form one frame – at 60 frames per second, MPEG-2 compression, a picture aspect ratio of 16:9 instead of the current 4:3, the absence of artefacts, Dolby surround sound, and packet data transmission (Anon. 1995g). A major difference in design principles will probably form part of the system. It will use an elaborate method of coding and decoding at transmitter and receiver to allow for different levels of performance, and therefore differences in the price of receivers used for different purposes, e.g. 'expensive' main receiver, 'cheap' second receiver, etc. Schreiber suggests three levels of performance which would require expensive processing 'far in excess of today's most powerful personal computers . . . the chips required are exceedingly complicated'.

Political action has affected the HDTV versus NTSC campaign. In September 1988 the FCC stipulated that NTSC receivers must not be replaced; HDTV signals should be transmitted in such a way that NTSC sets could receive the programmes or they should be transmitted on a separate channel. In both cases the programmes would be seen on NTSC sets, but special sets would be needed to display them in HDTV form. Current thinking now visualizes a 'simulcasting' system, similar to the arrangement used when 405-line TV in the UK was replaced by a 625-line system. In other words, broadcasts to the NTSC Standard will continue in parallel with HDTV. The old system will be phased out after a very long period of time.

Early in 1989 the Defence Advanced Research Projects Agency (DARPA) invited proposals for HDTV receiver displays and processors. It received 87 and selected 5 for funding out of its $30 million allocated for the purpose. An HDTV Bill was introduced in the House of Representatives in March 1989 to provide funding for an industry consortium. The HDTV Standard includes the compressing of data into the currently available 6 MHz channels requiring data compression of about 5 times, since the uncompressed data need a bandwidth of at least 30 MHz. To be accomplished digitally, a set of motion vectors to be used for frame-to-frame prediction will be used. Still portions of scenes can be encoded in a much simpler manner. HDTV will provide the opportunity for a complete change to true all-digital television, but whether it will be seized on, or missed by implementing a hotch-potch of compromises for political reasons, remains to be seen.

In Europe the EC provided funds under the Eureka programme for a different approach tied up with satellite operations called MAC; the work has been beset by political and technical problems. The EC had agreed to provide an HDTV subsidy of $276 million towards development costs but in September 1993 said it would provide $7200 per hour of actual transmission, reducing to $3000 per hour after the first 50 hours.

However, in a communication dated 17 November 1993, the Commission announced that the MAC policy will be replaced by something which is 'neutral on analogue or digital technology' (EC, *I&T Magazine*, Winter 1993). In other words it will sit on the fence. This was believed to mean that the EC had abandoned MAC in spite of the efforts made by Thomson and Philips to continue with it – efforts which the commissioner chose to ignore. It is not clear whether these two companies had by then already decided that it was better to join the US alliance. In December 1993 it was confirmed that the EC had written off the MAC investment of about £1 billion following general agreement on the MPEG2 compression Standard, eventually published in 1994. The Standard recommends a means, already well tested, of compressing recurring data by 100 times or more without much loss in quality, further easing the arrival of bandwidth-hungry HDTV. A digital HDTV Standard is expected in 1995. The new commissioner, Martin Bangemann, said, 'It appears that systems of the future will be digital.'

The Japanese have been running a service called HIVISION Muse – a 1125-line wide screen system – since 1989. Various other alternatives have been considered and experimented with, including digital HDTV transmission. However, the Japanese seem to have assumed that digital HDTV is the way to go but their effort now appears to be in a less controversial field at which they excel – Video Tape Recorders (VCRs). They are developing a VCR which will work on any system which may appear, digital or otherwise.

The possible social effects of HDTV have received some attention in a 1992 report from US Worcester Polytechnic Institute, following interviews with major figures in the TV field. 'The sheer size of HDTV will make TV an even more important and potent medium.' The effects may include 'making TV the main contact with the world . . . and an increase in the side effects of television culture'.

DIGITAL TELEVISION

Analogue TV broadcast schemes provide inadequate performance in a number of respects because of the design economies made to cater for the need to transmit a lot of data through systems in which inexpensive mass-produced receivers are the most important component. Quality suffers because of the passage of TV signals through a chain of mainly analogue paths.

Netravelli and Lippman (1995) believe that 'we are on the threshold of a major technological, market, and business disruption caused by digital television'. They identify certain key factors:

- Proven algorithms for high-quality compression
- Inexpensive powerful circuits for processing, storage, and reconstruction of video data
- Direct consumer access to information providers
- Convergence with other information sources
- Personal computer market for consumers growing faster than the business market
- Extension of networks in commerce.

Moreover, unnatural effects are produced in existing TV from colour artefacts such as 'dot-crawl', from patterning of various kinds, from scanning artefacts such as flicker and low-frequency patterns, and from bandwidth constraints which limit picture detail and produce a break-up of motion. The provision of a digital TV service, whether HDTV or not, should considerably improve general performance. The benefits of digitization in overcoming problems associated with noise and amplification, and the comparative ease with which processing may be carried out on digital systems, are well known. The present digital state of the art is demonstrated every day on public television in special effects in which digital processing is extensively used before conversion to analogue format. Extraordinary effects are now often used in advertisements, often produced on equipment supplied by Quantel of Newbury, UK – masters of the art of TV effects creation. Digital television, operated within the confines of what is politically and economically feasible, is a complex business and it is not easy to relate what is done for TV purposes to what is done in computer systems. Eventually all television will be totally digital, including the receivers.

Sandbank (1990) suggests that the development of semiconductor memories provided a significant impetus. Early special digital effects – such as showing successive positions of billiards ball after a cue stroke – were introduced some years ago.

While the vested interests in prolonging the life of POAT are enormous, recent events have increased the probability of the arrival of digital television sooner than was expected. What does the future hold for POAT? If digital HDTV arrives quickly it seems likely that POAT will be left to soldier on for the time being – rather like UK 405-line TV when 625-line colour was introduced. Of course, digital HDTV won't arrive that soon. The air of immediacy attached to changes of this kind arises because the news ballyhoo is rarely accompanied by a time of arrival forecast which will prove to be accurate. If a service really is launched in the US in 1996 it might first appear in Europe in the year 2000 and catch on during the following five years.

PICTURE QUALITY ASSESSMENT

Scherr (1979) devotes a chapter in his classic work to 'performance evaluation', describing methods of measuring a number of characteristics of displays, but he does not discuss that elusive subjective assessment called 'quality'.

Barten (1989) provides an equation for the Square Root Integral (SQRI) which he claims expresses the resolution quality of a display in units of 'Just Noticeable Difference' (JND), where 1 JND gives a 75 per cent correct response in a two-alternative forced-choice experiment. The equation takes account of the optimum viewing distance for a given display size.

Jacobson (1993) provides a good review of the subject, claiming that

> The quality of images, as perceived by observers has no rigorous definition. Individual observers viewing a reproduction have their own criteria for judging its technical quality and a consensus view can be found for what may be described as good or bad quality, but to quantify how good or bad image quality is, is even more difficult.

Jacobson believes that a satisfactory combination of several measures already proposed, including SQRI, to provide a single figure of merit for 'total quality assessment . . . is not likely to be achieved for many years'.

The fact is that the subjective assessment of the quality of a television or multimedia image has received insufficient attention. Parts of a system may cause a degradation of quality, or some degree of quality loss may be deemed acceptable as a trade-off against some other kind of improvement – for instance, some degree of compression. The absence of any yardstick makes valid comparisons difficult. If one system compresses data by five times for some loss in quality and a second compresses it by fifty times for some loss in quality, it cannot be said that the first is 'better' than the second, or vice versa, in the absence of some measure of acceptable quality loss.

The circumstances of a viewer obviously make a difference. A critical viewer in a studio, the viewer of an expensive domestic receiver, and the viewer of a small portable have different criteria for assessing quality. The effects of picture quality judged subjectively by the viewing public are discussed by Schreiber (1995). He reports tests at MIT in which audience preference for studio-quality HDTV pictures over studio-quality NTSC pictures was small. However, 'it is not possible to receive digital TV pictures that are seriously degraded by channel impairments while badly degraded NTSC pictures in homes are the norm'. There was no evidence that a wide screen was a very important feature but 'the single parameter of the display that overshadowed all others, including sharpness, was image size'. Apparently a viewing public conditioned by viewing high-quality pictures in the cinema seem happy to accept relatively low picture quality on their TV sets at home. If quality is not that important, presumably we must look for factors other than the high quality promised for HDTV as a reason for paying a substantially higher price for a receiver.

USING TELEVISION DATA IN A MULTIMEDIA COMPUTER

The size of the analogue television broadcast industry has encouraged the mass production of equipment which provides a source of pictures and images in analogue television format. It includes television receivers, television cameras, recorded television programmes on tape or disk and so on.

It is not essential to digitize TV analogue video data for all multimedia applications. For Laserdisc optical disk players, for example, the TV analogue signals are recorded on the disk and the data are played back as if they were a conventional TV signal. Digitization incurs a penalty because a digitized signal occupies a much wider bandwidth. For most applications the bandwidth disadvantage incurred by using already digitized or digitized analogue data is overridden by the great advantage of being able to process it on a digital computer. At the output of a multimedia system the data are normally converted back to analogue before being applied to the CRT display.

Television sets and computers both use CRTs and raster (line-by-line scanning) displays and produce similar-looking pictures. However, they are technically very different. Any device for TV/computer image handling must reconcile these differences which are mainly to do with frame formats, digitization, and field, frame, and line timing (synchronization).

NTSC analogue interlaced fields form a 525-line frame. When digitized, say, in the circuits of a frame-grabber board, the format typically becomes

640×480 pixels. PAL interlaced fields forming 625 lines per frame typically digitize at 768×512 pixels. Consequently, the line frequencies of the two systems are different.

The non-interlaced displays of digital computers have tended to be 'standardized' as 'EGA', 'VGA', etc., containing different numbers of pixels, running at different line frequencies so an even greater range and a larger number of variables must be considered when an external monitor is being added.

Frame grabbers

It was realized, probably around 1985, that several technologies had reached a point where they could be combined to provide advances in imaging. Facilities for managing the volume and speed of data representing a high-quality colour image started to become available on microcomputers. 'Frame grabbers' have received special attention. They are often supplied in the form of a plug-in board to receive and store monochrome or colour picture frames from television receivers or cameras, often with provision for digitizing and processing the stored image in various ways before using it.

A substantial new industry for the supply of plug-in cards for microcomputers has appeared. The cards capture TV frames from a conventional TV tuner and decode and convert the analogue data into a form suitable for editing into, for example, pictures overlaid with captions for incorporation into multimedia presentations. State-of-the-art developments in microcomputers enable the bits from such sources to be processed and stored, but speed constraints in the input boards, and more especially at the display end of the micro, restricted the essential requirement of transporting a sufficient number of bits to reproduce an image with the required quality at full-screen size in a reasonable period of time until quite recently.

In a microcomputer fitted with a frame-grabber board, the user observes a television programme from one of the sources listed above and selects a single frame by pressing a key. The frame is then stored and displayed for processing. As the frame could come from any one of a number of different sources with different characteristics, the frame grabber must ideally be able to cope with whatever range of sources the user has in mind. The associated multimedia machine should be able to display a frame satisfactorily, and be able to output it to suitable media for presentation or other use. The important matters which the board must cope with are to modify the characteristics of the grabbed frame so that it may be viewed as a stable image on the screen and on an external monitor if one is used, and to provide facilities for editing it. The most generally required edit function is to overlay captions created on the computer for viewing by the user as a composite picture recorded on tape, or possibly for viewing as print on paper.

For example, a board such as Raster Op's 364 (Santa Clara, California), used in a Mac II computer, enables 30 frames/second in 24-bit colour video to run in a window on the screen. As the live video continues, single frames may be captured provided adequate storage is available. Any frame can be captured with a single keystroke, saved either in RAM storage on the board or on disk, and displayed full-screen size.

Frame grabbers and picture processing are discussed in more detail in chapter 4.

VIDEO, BIT RATES, AND DISPLAYS

Video terminology

To manage multimedia video it's as well to be aware of the major technical terms which slip off the tongues of the *cognoscenti* to convince you that they are the experts. It's not easy to look up the meaning of some of these terms so they are included here in alphabetical order. Short definitions are also included in the Glossary.

Composite video

A video signal consisting of a single stream of luminance and chrominance signals conveyed in a two-conductor screened cable usually fitted with inexpensive RCA plugs and sockets. Reproduction is of lower quality than S-Video.

Genlock

A means of synchronizing different video signals. A common example is the synchronizing of a computer image containing text, with a video image on which it is overlaid, in order to obtain a steady picture.

Hi-8

High band 8 mm wide (0.315") tape format. A tape format housed in a smaller cassette than VHS as used in domestic camcorders. 'Hi' indicates the same advantages versus ordinary tape as S-VHS versus VHS.

S-VHS

Super VHS. A tape having the same dimensions and format as VHS tape but carrying analogue video of higher resolution and good quality stereo sound. To appreciate the benefits the tape must be played on an S-VHS deck.

S-Video

Separated Video. Video conveyed as separate luminance and chrominance signals within screened cable containing four conductors usually fitted with relatively expensive BNC plugs and sockets. Provides results of higher quality compared with composite video.

Sync

Synchronizing. Arranging that separate, often recurring, events which require to be reproduced at the same instant always start at the same instant and remain in step with each other. Video synchronism between the frames and lines of separate video devices in a system is essential to provide a stationary presentation of special effects.

Timebase corrector

A device which inhibits the transmission of a video frame until it receives a synchronizing signal. For example, each frame is stored until the arrival of a sync signal.

Time codes

An essential requirement for video and audio editing, whereby each video frame is made uniquely identifiable by recording an hours-minutes-seconds-frames SMPTE time code on the space between frames. Audio time codes may be recorded on one of the tracks on an audio track. Some tape decks display the time code value – an accurate aid for synchronizing audio to video or to rewind the tape to a specific frame.

VHS

Video Home System. The standard format used for the ½" (12.7 mm) wide magnetic tape in analogue VCR (Video Cassette Recorder) cassettes.

TV digitization and bit rates

Public broadcast digital television is coming for several reasons: there will be a greater choice of programmes, the picture will be better and so will the stereo sound. When high definition television (HDTV) arrives, it will be digital. Later, the arrival of digital interactive TV and converging digital sources on the information superhighway will demand it.

Digital signals may be compressed at the transmitter and decompressed at the receiver by inexpensive chips. They then occupy much less space in the transmission channel – and channels are in short supply. Advances in 'multiplexing' enable a number of channels to be transmitted independently within a single channel which occupies the same space as it did originally. About twenty new channels will become available in the UK. Today's TV services will linger on for some years. Until the industry changes over to digital television, the digitization technique defined by the International Telecommunications Union and specified in CCIR 601 (1986) will continue to be used.

System technical details are still being debated. A set-top box probably costing a bit more than a satellite box will be needed. A buyer will have to decide between the price of the new box with increased programme choice, and what he or she already has. Some manufacturers may make complete digital receivers providing other improvements.

In analogue TV luminance (brightness), and red (R), green (G), and blue (B) signals, added in appropriate proportions to provide any colour, are combined as Y (luminance value) and the colour difference (chrominance) signals:

$$C_r = R - Y, \text{ and } C_b = B - Y. \quad Y = 0.299R + 0.587G + 0.114B \ (= 1)$$

Y, C_r and C_b are sampled at 13.5, 6.75, 6.75 MHz respectively ('4:2:2 sampling'), each sample being represented by an 8-bit number. It may be changed for lower bit-rate, lower-quality pictures, for example to 2:1:1 (Sandbank 1990: 9). In practice, a PAL frame digitizes to 576 lines at 720 pixels per line, each pixel comprising 720 Y (Luminance) samples per line and 2 x 360 C_r and C_b (Chrominance) samples per line at 8 bits per sample with a 25 frames per second repetition rate, so the bit rate is:

$$576 \times 1440 \times 8 \times 25 = 165.89 \text{ Mbps}$$

whereas for NTSC a frame digitizes to 480 lines at 640 8-bit pixels per line with 1280 C_r and C_b, 8 bits and 30 frames per second which is:

$$480 \times 1280 \times 8 \times 30 = 147.5 \text{ Mbps}$$

Ideally it should be possible to move a still or moving picture from any source in colour and in any desired resolution on to a CRT screen at a speed which is as fast as the viewer's ability to perceive it. In the case of motion video, pictures must be repeated fast enough for inter-frame motion to appear to be natural.

In multimedia operations such as changing graphics, stored pictures, etc., a new image should be presented almost immediately following the action or request made to obtain it. The new picture must be at its designed size – either 'thumbnail', specified window size, or full screen. A stream of data must flow very rapidly on to the screen. If the bandwidth is f Hz, the maximum possible signalling (baud) rate in a noiseless channel is 2f bauds per second with n bits per baud. For example, the bit rate at 3 bits per baud could be up to 6 Mbps in a 1 Mbps channel. In practice the rate would be slower because of noise (see chapter 8).

Until very recently, the technology was not developed to the point at which bits could be shifted at a rate adjudged to be 'acceptable' by a user for the reproduction of still or motion video pictures. What is and what is not acceptable depends on numerous factors. Unless the user has noted the processing delays and picture quality during a demonstration of a system with a relevant application, at a quoted price, he or she will not know whether the delays and quality will be acceptable for their particular application because they are not specified. There are so many different circumstances and possible applications that 'waiting time' and quality are difficult to specify.

For instance, a user interested in a machine's ability to perform ray-tracing, rendering, etc., for 3D photorealistic graphics, may or may not appreciate that a waiting time to do this kind of job is normal for equipment of reasonable cost and average power. Upon the delivery of a system, the user may be disappointed, neither having known the right questions to ask nor having seen the right demonstration to be able to decide on the adequacy of the system for the required purpose.

The development of motion video

Although the Mac II has been superseded by improved machines, it is still in wide use. The main video and motion video functions which can be handled using a Mac II or more recent machines having 4–8 Mbytes of RAM, at least 80 Mbytes of disk, a colour monitor, and a variety of third-party plug-in boards and software are to:

- Capture and digitize video frame-by-frame with a 'frame grabber', and output frames with added animation frame-by-frame under Hypercard control;
- Replace video data in a given colour (the 'key' colour) with a different set of video data if you want to add special effects;
- Import TV-standard NTSC or PAL motion video from a Hypercard-controlled videodisk player or a camera, and display it in real time in a window on the Mac's screen or on a separate monitor. A Mac II system is not fast enough to allow full-screen colour at TV resolution, although later Apple machines are able to do so;
- Overcome speed constraints by connecting the monitor directly to the video source, such as a videodisk player, for the direct full-screen colour TV resolution display of motion video, and control the videodisk from Hypercards to display a wanted picture. Present other material, for instance text, synchronized with a picture on the Mac's screen;
- Overlay and synchronize ('Genlock') Mac text and graphics non-interlaced picture data, with the imported interlaced composite TV signals (which contains all the synchronizing and picture data within the

signal). Record the composited pictures in NTSC or PAL format on VHS, or better S-VHS videotape for presentations elsewhere;

• Use the tape for mastering videodisks for interactive presentations. The random access seek time for Level 3 Laservision-type Constant Angular Velocity (CAV) videodisk players with Hypercard control via an RS232 connector, ranges from 3 seconds to 0.5 seconds for more expensive models.

A separate good quality monitor is desirable for these operations and essential for some of them. Monitors, or more particularly the CRTs inside them, continue to improve. The currently most popular ones are probably the 14" and 17" (screen diagonal) 640×480 pixel (IBM VGA resolution) monitors. The colour tube alone costs about \$300.

By the time LCD or other types of display panels become comparable to CRTs in performance, CRTs will probably have been improved to provide 1500×1500 pixels and will cost \$100, so the CRT will be around for some years yet.

The line scanning speed of Mac II's normal 640×480 display is fixed but third-party video adaptors offer alternatives, such as rates between 800×560 for the 37" Mitsubishi monitor (at £6000), up to 1365×1024 pixels. Scanning speeds and frame rates are likely to be different in the various adaptors available.

An auto-tracking monitor where the scanning rate automatically synchronizes, is the best choice. Typical ranges are 30–57 KHz horizontal and 40–75 Hz vertical. Another desirable feature in monitors is their capability of running from NTSC or PAL composite video signals, RGB analog, or RGB TTL. With these alternatives the monitor should cope with almost any requirement.

Motion video, usually in either NTSC or European PAL analogue form, may be imported from TV receivers, cameras, videotape, or videodisks. Data are displayed on a TV CRT by smooth pixel-to-pixel changes of brightness and colour in direct proportion to the light reflected from the original objects. As previously mentioned, the NTSC system uses 525 scanning lines per frame repeating 30 times per second. PAL uses 625 lines repeating 25 times per second. Both systems use interlaced scanning in which the frame is divided into a field of odd-numbered lines followed by a field of even-numbered lines, providing 60 and 50 fields per second respectively, reducing the flicker which would otherwise be noticeable.

Computers, or boards plugged into them, able to accept interlaced TV signals, include circuits for producing synchronized non-interlaced frames from frames containing interlaced fields.

In January 1993 Intel claimed that digitized compressed/decompressed motion video could be viewed full-screen at 30 frames per second with Microsoft's 'Video for Windows' software, a 386 DX-33 micro, and an i750 accelerator board. As at November 1993 there was some controversy about this claim, with Microsoft arguing that it was premature. In February 1994, Intel claimed that MPEG was an unsuitable method of compression for mass usage.

Videologic demonstrated a CD full-screen motion-video system at a 1993 exhibition. It consisted of two cards plugged into a 486 PC – a DVA-4000 card which will accept RGB computer input and PAL or NTSC colour television signals from a video cassette recorder; Laserdisc player or TV tuner; MediaSpace card for compression/decompression which incorporates a C-Cube CL-550 chip and an Inmos T400 transputer.

The 640×480 8-bit colour display screen must be filled 25 times per second to provide TV pictures of reasonably good quality – a screen-fill rate of about 61 Mbps. The procedure is to record compressed TV on to the machine's hard disk, and then shift the data on to a Philips Writer to record it on a CD. Subsequently, the CD is placed in a Pioneer DRM604X variable-speed CD player and played back into the micro in order to be decompressed and displayed.

The Pioneer can deliver data at up to four times the normal CD player rate – up to 612 KBytes per second or about 5 Mbps. But the TV data delivered for decompression need be at a rate of only 1.2 Mbps or about 150 Kbps, representing the original data rate of 61 Mbps after 50:1 compression. The 640 Mbyte disk will provide 640/0.15 seconds or about 71 minutes of TV of adequate quality.

This exercise is of interest because it shows how an intermediate stage of reproducing full-screen video on a micro was achieved. Such is the rate of progress that by early 1994 Radius (San José) had developed their VideoVision system comprising a video interface card, a JPEG compression/ decompression card, and a 16-socket connector panel. This system, plugged into a fast Mac such as the 80 MHz 8100/80, provides full-screen motion video at either 768×576 PAL or 640×480 NTSC, with 24-bit colour, at 25 or 30 frames per second (see also chapter 6, p. 165). The system is compatible with Apple's Quicktime software, which means that it will work with a large number of applications. Quicktime itself provides compression of 8:1. VideoVision provides 50:1.

The connector panel provides for 8-bit stereo or mono sound input, digitized at 11 or 22 KHz – a surprisingly low rate in view of the performance of the rest of the system. Sockets are also provided for S-Video and two composite video inputs, and for SMPTE time codes provided by special software. Output sockets include S-Video, composite video, and stereo sound. The total cost of all the items described in the last two paragraphs is about £12,000.

GRAPHICS

The term 'graphics' now seems to be used for certain operations not covered as 'picture processing' or 'image processing', but describing particular images or user-controlled operations thereon, often requiring special plug-in graphics processing boards.

Graphics Standards for 'mainline computer purposes' are the outcome of work which started around 1974, as described in chapter 9.

The esoteric world of computer graphics design and display on high-quality CRT colour workstations is moving on from flat polygonal areas filled with one colour and 'wire frame structures', as used for the 3D graphics in Computer Aided Design (CAD), to special effects for greater realism. Techniques called Gouraud Shading and the more sophisticated Phong Shading for altering individual pixels were introduced in the 1980s to produce smooth changes in shading. Further developments enable surfaces with a 'textured' effect to be produced.

In late 1988, lifelike effects were introduced to provide results comparable to those produced in special photographic work, particularly in the field of business presentation graphics. A company called Pixer gained some acceptance for its '3D modelling to visual attributes' interface as a Standard to make the connection between computer graphics software and visual attributes software. Pixer's photo-realistic 'Renderman' software is compatible with PHIGS.

The problem of the rapid transfer of text and graphics in colour has been eased by the arrival of Graphics System Processor (GSP) co-processor chips, a specialized version of a Digital System Processor (DSP). A GSP consists of two separate processors – the graphics processor, which receives CPU commands from a special instruction set, and the display processor.

An extraordinary effort has been put in by the chip manufacturers to develop fast, high-resolution colour graphic controllers to be installed as plug-in cards to be used in conjunction with special monitors. The objective seems to be to provide advanced facilities for engineering design work, desktop publishing, and multimedia with sufficient power to manipulate high-resolution multi-colour images. Facilities enable a user to create designs with special shading, surfaces, and textures, or, in less exotic applications, to create multiple windows and shift data about within them at high speed.

Graphics co-processor boards, many based on the Texas 34010 chip or its successors, are likely to possess more power than the micro into which they are plugged and may add several thousand dollars to its price. For example, one of the earliest, the Artist T112 from Control Systems, provides a resolution of 1280×1024 with 256 colours from a palette of 16M. An on-board 50 MHz processor is required to provide sufficient speed for special applications.

The Hitachi HD63484 graphics co-processor chip was announced in 1984 but the main contenders still seem to be the Texas 34010 and the Intel 82786. GSPs are associated with an important new component – a special form of buffer memory called a Video Random Access Memory (VRAM). The results of GSP manipulation are viewed on high-resolution colour CRTs from Hitachi, Cointran, and others. A GSP, given the appropriate command, can execute complex operations on large blocks of pixels and can address (typically) 128 Mbits of memory, adequate to hold a high-resolution representation of a page to be displayed or printed in colour, together with other data.

The Texas 34010 32-bit GSP contains over 30 32-bit registers and can be programmed in high-level languages – for instance, to control animation in real time. Pixel colour control is handled by an associated chip – the 34070 Colour Palette – capable of displaying any 16 colours in one displayed frame selected from 4096 different colours.

The manufacturers have coined appropriately dynamic words to convey the explosive urgency of these chips. A 'barrel-shifter' – for use in specialized graphics applications – enables a pixel field to be rotated. Bit Block Transfer (BitBlt) describes the important function of moving pixel arrays (whose size is programmable) *en bloc*. 'Pixblitting' (PixBlt) means the moving of multiple-bit pixels, the extra bits specifying halftones or colour. PixBlt enables the user to move one large or a number of small pixel arrays rapidly from a source area and fit them into a destination area of a different size – as, for instance, when transferring pixels between windows. The software, anticipating that 'window clipping' may be required, inhibits operations on pixels which would lie outside the new window. Pixels from a source and destination array may be combined, thereby producing a different colour, or a pattern of designated pixels in the destination array may be made 'transparent' so that, when the source pixels are moved, some appear through 'holes', producing various special effects. Small pixel arrays representing characters in special fonts can be fitted into new positions.

More recent applications of BitBlt techniques include an instruction which uses run-length compressed descriptions of complex objects. Butterfield (1994) provides an example of moving a line 8.5 inches long at 300 dots/inch from one location to another. The bit map representation of such a line occupies 300 bytes of memory, but a BitBlt instruction to create it requires only 10 bytes.

Processing of this kind requires logical mathematical operations to be carried out at high speed. With a GSP, delays in the execution of these effects are hardly noticeable. Without a GSP, delays would probably be intolerable, even with elaborate programs and additional chips. GSPs could not work at these very high speeds with a conventional display RAM where the update of a stored representation of the screen image, and continual CRT refreshing operations, operate in turn through a single port. In 'two-port' VRAMs, updating and refresh proceed in parallel. The VRAM contains a 'shift register', which is filled with a row of bits during the brief interval between CRT scanning lines. When the line commences, the bits are clocked out to form a line of displayed pixels for refresh purposes. The effect on performance is sensational – there may be a 40 times reduction in 'overhead' refresh time-wasting.

Graphics signal processing was used to produce the extraordinary special effects and animation used in the film *Jurassic Park*. A specialist in this area is the British company Parallax Graphics Systems formed in 1990 which produced their Advance software for workstations made by Silicon Graphics such as the Indy described in chapter 5. Advance software is a *tour de force* well worth its price of over £4000.

Parallax also produce a yet more advanced system for cartoons which costs up to £40,000. Systems of this kind are a challenge for Quantel, leaders for several years.

New kinds of special effects for television continue to be introduced and are reviewed by White (1994). Morphing effects (smoothly changing one image into a different one) were all the rage in 1993, says White. A morphing program for a Mac can now be purchased for just £130.

The recently developed Texas Instruments' MVP, which can handle a range of functions processed in parallel on one chip formerly requiring several chips, should provide improved multimedia performance particularly in the real-world real-time data processing of voice and video. Such chips are now called Advanced Digital Signal Processors (ASDPs) because the generalized design will support any new algorithm within a range of different types providing for advanced programmes and greater power. The MVP embodies five parallel processors on one chip running at 40/50 MHz which makes it capable of a performance equivalent to at least 10 normal DSP chips. It can shift bytes at an extraordinary rate – 2.4 Gbytes of data, 1.8 Gbytes of instructions, and 400 Mbytes of data into off-chip memory – *per second*. It achieves this by processing 64-bit words in parallel. 2.4 Gbytes per second is, of course, almost 20 Gbits per second – a rate which appeared to be quite impossible a few years ago. When the potential of the chip is realized in multimedia machines, processing constraints in applications like videoconferencing, high-resolution full-screen full-frame rate motion video, virtual reality, etc. will be greatly reduced. The problem of shifting such data through transmission lines of inadequate bandwidth will then become even more acute.

ACCELERATORS

The software which became available for providing full-screen high-resolution images in 24-bit colour in 1992 exceeded the rate at which images could be reproduced within a reasonable response time. At their maximum bit rates, machines were still too slow. Block transfers (BitBlts), sometimes involving the movement of huge blocks of pixels, perform a frequently used function which must be done quickly.

An accelerator may be described as a type of GSP specifically designed to reduce the time taken by an unaided microcomputer to reproduce a screen of data. With Windows, the solution is to add an accelerator card, usually based on a chip called the S3 with a Windows video driver. In 1992 the Orchid and Diamond cards appeared. They speeded up operations considerably.

In 1994 several new methods of acceleration were announced, enabling full-screen motion video to run at 30 frames per second. Alternatively, the response time to a command requiring a new full-colour high-resolution single-frame picture to be reproduced on a CRT is much reduced. The Matrox Ultima-VAFC (VESA Advanced Feature Connector) board, for example, uses the VAFC 32-bit standard to run 1280×1024 pixel motion video at 30 frames/second (Lockwood 1994). The board costs \$649.

The Thunder/24 24-bit accelerator card from Supermac, a part of Apple, was listed at £1995 in the UK during May 1994. Supermac claims that with this card 'you get an unrivalled 4000 per cent increase in Quickdraw performance' compared with the normal speed of Quickdraw on a Quadra 950. 'No more waiting for the screen to scroll, zoom, pan or redraw,' says the advert – 'it will execute in seconds rather then minutes.'

The Videologic 928 accelerator board for Windows also includes the VESA media channel – a fast bus which transports uncompressed video between digitizer and compressor, and between decompressor and output. The part of a microcomputer with a bus and output circuits unable to run at the speeds called for by current displays is relieved of the task. The board – a self-contained computer with its own VESA bus controlled by a 32-bit graphics processor – takes it over.

VESA stands for the Video Electronic Standards Association, which is supported by a number of major manufacturers. The VESA or VL bus is independent of the bus of the host microcomputer and can convey data at the speed required by high-resolution 24-bit colour displays. A 1280×1024 pixel 24-bit colour display repeated 30 times per second requires a fill rate of 943 Mbps or about 118 Mbytes/sec. If a 76 Hz refresh rate – that is, the screen if filled 76 times per second – is used, the data rate must be about 2 Gbps.

Boards like the Videologic 928 should increase fill rates by at least ten times compared with a VGA adapter with an ISA bus.

New developments in RAMs with 2-port access called VRAMs are expected to provide data transfer rates previously unheard of – probably over 600 Mbytes or 4800 Megabits (4.8 Gbits) per second. This rate is already being approached by the 2 Gbps fill-rate just mentioned – a rate calculated by simple multiplication. A 1280×1024 pixel 24-bit colour display frame contains about 31 Mbits of data. With the 76 Hz refresh rate as now used in a number of monitors, the bit rate becomes 2.3 Gbits/second.

These remarks confirm the earlier comment that 'waiting time' is a factor to be considered in multimedia equipment. A user operating a multimedia system expects to get an immediate response to a command.

If the response to a command needs to be measured in minutes, the software is calling for unrealistic hardware performance. Perhaps the user will get what he wants one day when hardware bit-rates catch up. An extra payment of up to about £2000 used to be required for the accelerator boards described in the previous section, but prices have dropped rapidly. A Videologic 928 board with 1 Mbyte RAM and sound costs about £400 in the UK.

In 1995, accelerators with data paths 64 or even 128 bits wide have become available for 24-bit graphics. These wide data paths interconnect a graphics chip with video memory and sometimes out to the digital/analogue convertors at the CRT's data input point as well. Special accelerators enabling PCs to handle 3D graphics are another 1995 development.

There is no upper limit to the processing speed needed for more realistic 3D graphics for Virtual Reality (VR) applications and the power required is likely to be supplied by accelerator boards. The 'Winmark' is a benchmark recently introduced to provide a speed comparison figure implying certain tests to cover typical modes of operation.

Accelerators usually rate in the region of 5 to 25 Winmarks, but 100 Winmark devices such as the Glint 3D which will run at 2.5 billion operations per second, are now available. VR scenes are constructed out of computer-drawn polygons – that is, multi-sided figures. The Glint, a complete system on a chip, will generate 300,000 shaded anti-aliased transparent polygons per second. Speeds of millions of polygons per second are needed to make VR really convincing.

VIDEO ON DEMAND AND INTERACTIVE TELEVISION

VOD and interactive television are services likely to run on an information superhighway (see chapter 8). They appear to have generated great interest and wild speculation. There are several non-technical aspects, but the subject is best discussed as a whole here, instead of being split between chapters 2 and 8.

Technology is a major hunting ground for a media which relies for its appeal on new stories. The information superhighway was seized upon as a field of limitless opportunity – the kind of concept enabling the press to fantasize to its heart's content; everybody loves a fantasy. Video on Demand sounds like technology and therefore has a lower appeal than the IS; even so, it has been trotted out quite often in recent months.

Just as the Internet seems to lend feasibility to the superhighway idea, so do networks like cable-TV lend feasibility to VOD. An intermediate stage in the development of VOD and interactive television has been devised by the Videotron cable television company. By using a simple set-top box which switches between four cable-TV channels running inter-related programmes, an illusion of interactivity is conveyed. For example, in a comedy show a new comedian may be chosen by a viewer if the provider runs comedy shows with a different comedian on four different channels. The viewer can choose the comic he likes best.

Ovum provides information about interactive television activities in Lee *et al.* (1995). They claim that over 50 trials are in progress, planned, or have been completed. Ovum states that 20,000 homes will participate in trials during 1996. Telecommunication companies have been encouraged by deregulation programmes in the US and Europe and see an opportunity to compete with the cable companies. In Europe, point-to-point interactive services are not restricted by regulation. Ovum states that BT has been encouraged by the range of its version of ADSL over subscriber loops at 2 Mbps with a 9.6 Kbps control channel. At about 6 Km, 92 per cent of the network should be usable. The technology so far adopted in Europe, North America, and the Far East is fairly evenly balanced between ADSL and ATM, as dictated by network availability. The telephone companies own the local loops so they are more likely to opt for ADSL, cable owners for ATM.

Major trials planned and in progress are shown in Table 2.5 ranked by number of households participating.

Hong Kong Telecom, with 57.5 per cent of its shares held by Cable & Wireless, London, is not shown; it is a late starter but has ambitious plans. A service will start in mid-1996 and expects to connect to 60,000 homes in 1997, rising to 340,000 by 1999. It will use both ADSL and fibre with ATM switching.

Some trials offer a number of different services, but VOD, with the possibility of offering a selection from a huge range of films and interactive multimedia programmes, is probably considered to be the most important. Home shopping and games come next, says the Ovum report. Ovum says that customer charges are made in some trials but does not stress a crucial

Table 2.5 Major VOD trials

Operator	Place	Number of households
Bell South	Atlanta	12,000
Deutsche T'kom	Stuttgart	4 000
Time Warner	Orlando	4 000
BT	Colchester/Ipswich	2 500
Nynex *et al.*	Manhattan	2 500
Bell Atlantic	Virginia	2000
Westminster Cable	London	1 000

point. Trials will enable the technology to be tested and some information about customer preferences may become evident, but what they will not reveal is demand at a given price when a choice from programmes exceeding a critical mass is also provided. Pessimistic estimates have been made about the time required to recover system investment. The price that an audience of unknown size is prepared to pay to be able to select from, say, 5000 different programmes of entertainment is unknown.

According to Ovum, the major equipment supplier is the US company BroadBand Technologies, with their FLX system for switched digital interactive services. It uses fibre links transporting multiplexed data to a node which serves up to 32 homes, distributing the video from the node over copper cable to customers. Bell Atlantic has chosen an FLX system.

Several VOD trials are currently in progress. A Canadian company called UBI appears to be already operational, claiming a large number of customers in Canada and the UK. It says that this year it will start installing its system in 34,000 homes, to be completed during 1996/7. It also claims that it has already arranged for 40 different services including e-mail, catalogues and home shopping, home banking, games, and home energy management.

The Videotron company has installed a fibreoptic cable linking the Saguenay area, where the UBI service is running, to Quebec. The network will have a bandwidth of 625 MHz capable of transporting 77 analogue or 200 digital channels.

There is frequent news about companies prepared to chance their arm and make a substantial effort to start up in this new field. BSkyB announced a new service in June 1995. The service responds with a 'personal teletext page' after receiving a request for information by telephone. One benefit of using a satellite channel for the purpose is that the bandwidth constraints of conventional teletext 'spare TV channels' are removed, enabling a much faster response to be provided.

The realization of genuine VOD may come sooner than was expected according to Fuhrt *et al.* (1995). The authors provide a list of the kind of interactive television services that they expect to see provided in distributed multimedia systems. A diagram shows how a network for 80 million subscribers might be organized. The system consists of an ATM Wide Area Network (WAN) with a number of large servers connected to it, each server storing data produced by an information provider. One hundred Metropolitan Area Networks (MANs) are connected to the WAN, each with 800 'head ends' (local distribution centres). Each head end services 1000 households. Thus the 80 million households are made up of 100 MANs × 800 head ends × 1000.

Having proposed a general arrangement, the authors continue with a description of alternative media and technologies, but suggest that in the future there will be a 'unified technology' embodying several media, topologies, and protocols – perhaps using the information superhighway – with 'the ultimate all-purpose set-top box' to deal with it. Alas, the proposed architecture of the ultimate set-top box shown in the same article falls well short of this ideal. The box is fed from something depicted as a cloud labelled 'network infrastructure'. Under 'Interoperability' ten different Standards groups are mentioned, but we are not informed how multiple connections to multiple media with an easily understood user interface control from one box will be arranged. This is, of course, a major question, which will be answered later rather than sooner – will there be a period of competing media and several boxes to receive them, leading to a single successful user's control box?

'Video on Demand' (VOD) usually implies digital motion video with some interactivity – a home user should be able to select information which includes motion video in colour with sound – for example, a 'television entertainment programme', which requires very little user interaction. Much of these kinds of data will probably be delivered one-way for domestic consumption, but the demand for services with greater interactivity – for example, for home shopping, education, videoconferencing, or games – is expected to grow. VOD constraints include time availability, acceptable delivery rate, bandwidth, and storage, the same constraints that exist for other branches of multimedia – all talked-up well ahead of their possible arrival date.

Elapsed time, acceptable delivery rate, and channel bandwidth are intertwined. 'Acceptable delivery rate' means that the rate of delivery for whatever is demanded must be in line with the client's expectations in terms of price and quality of service (QOS). Clients are conditioned by TV, so for entertainment a comparable continuous flow of data should be received. Adequate frame rates, picture resolution, and sound quality are the major requirements. The bandwidth of the channel has to be sufficient to convey the data quickly enough to provide an acceptable service.

Appropriate storage arrangements are just as intractable. At the present state of the art there is no way by which a client from a global audience could receive video data of whatever kind with an acceptable QOS from any provider within a few seconds of asking for it. Information providers must, of course, expect to have to supply the more popular material to a large number of clients simultaneously – a function performed by broadcast television without difficulty.

One potential way of meeting this requirement is to maintain a number of sites for local storage, each designed to serve a given community of clients. This is a tall order bearing in mind the number of information choices which are likely to become available and the volume of data which must be shifted to execute requests.

'Degrees of interactivity' also affect the issue. At one end of the scale a client needs to send an instruction which could consist simply of data informing a supplier of the position of a cursor on a menu showing choices. At the other extreme, say, for videoconferencing, a two-way flow of data conveying audio and visual information must be transported.

A number of authors have ventured proposals which are considerably less ambitious than those made by Fuhrt *et al.* just discussed. Little and Venkatesh (1994) list several VOD-like features which could be added to television programmes:

- Choosing a programming source
- Skipping or selecting commercials
- Providing the user-control facilities available on a video recorder for received programmes
- Providing access to information available via hyperlinks
- The incorporation of a personal profile for seeking wanted items
- An interface for viewing parallel data streams (as provided by some cable-TV providers who display current programmes from a number of channels in small windows)
- Secure mechanisms for private data such as money transfer.

They also classify interactive services according to the degree of interactivity:

- Broadcast service; no interactivity
- Pay per view; minor interactivity
- Quasi-VOD with programmes allocated to interest groups. Selection by switching to another group
- Near-VOD by connection to several channels running the same pro-gramme skewed in time by, say, 5 minutes enabling 'forward' and 'reverse' operation by switching channels
- True-VOD with control signalling from user to provider for interactivity.

But Little and Venkatesh are also extraordinarily optimistic:

> The availability of enormous communication bandwidth and computing power has made it possible to process and deliver information on a per-session per-user basis in real time. The ability to process information at the source enables the information provider to extract relevant data and modify their characteristics to specific tastes.

The authors continue with a masterly understatement: 'Developing this new information delivery infrastructure requires considerable planning and effort.' Paradoxically, the remainder of the article is a very good summary of the immensity of the problems that must be faced.

VOD is best considered in terms of realistic transmission rates, methods of storage, transmission techniques, and compression ratios. A one-hour programme at the 5 Mbps rate would generate 18,000 Mbits or 2250 Mbytes (2.25 Gbytes) of data. The programme could be compressed from uncom-pressed data running at 200 Mbps – a 40 times compression which should be achievable for motion video of acceptable quality.

The consequences of dealing with the thousands, or hundreds of thousands or more, of hours of programmes required to provide anything like a choice of, say, movies, to a large population are under consideration. The main lines of thought seem to be about filling storage units distributed round the country at the lowest possible transmission costs in order to provide for local communities. For example, Papadimitriou *et al.* (1994) suggest a 'personalized' multimedia service in which a 'personal service agency (PSA)' decides what programmes each user is likely to request. The PSA unit works rather like the 'Selective Dissemination of Information (SDI)' systems used for picking out printed articles of interest. The PSA maintains an interest profile for each user, from whom it receives 'relevance' feedback in order to improve the profile. By this procedure the data supply to each user is reduced to a relatively small part of the total information available.

Even assuming that storage costs continue to drop, the cost of an adequate storage cache for each user is considered to be unrealistically high so 'neighbourhood temporary caches' are organized for a user group. The authors consider how to reduce both the size of a cache and the transmission time needed to fill it. They provide an example for three users who want to see the same programme on the same day at different times, for which the total service costs are claimed to be $51 – i.e. $17 per user. This is a small step towards a situation where thousands of users simultaneously request the same programme at slightly different times, together with a provision for people to switch to another programme at any instant.

Doganata and Tantawi (1994) consider the design of a 'super video storage' server capable of supplying thousands of video streams. As they point out, customers would like a choice of thousands of movies in a situation where Oscar nominations might cause a surge in demand for a particular movie. They state the obvious: 'Video server designers would prefer to include in their menu only those movies just popular enough to justify their storage and communication costs.'

Aspects of the design of a server controlling tape, disk, and semiconductor storage are shown here:

- The design is based on the estimated *demand* and *duration* of files;
- Storage is based on a tape library (up to 15 terabytes), disks (2 Gbytes per disc) and RAM for movies with a very high demand;
- The system ensures that video files are in the right place at the right time;
- If the cost of the server described is $8M, this cost would be amortized in 2 years if 4000 homes viewed an average of 3 movies per week at a price of $5 per movie;
- The design caters, for 10,000 movies each of 1.5 hours' duration delivered at 1.5 Mbps;
- Demand is based on both video-on-demand and video-on-schedule, the former requiring that more movies are stored in RAM;

- Files are moved into appropriate storage according to demand probabilities.

This design is interesting because it indicates that a VOD system of feasible size which at first appears impossible to achieve might, in fact, be feasible. Some 10,000 movies, each playing for 1.5 hours recorded for delivery at a compressed speed of 1.5 Mps, require 8 terabytes of tape storage. The design allows for demand skew – meaning that movies may be ranked by probability of demand, enabling the requested demand rate to be calculated to give the number of times a given movie is likely to be required in a given time interval. Other design aspects are shown.

Gemmell *et al.* (1995) discuss the basic requirements for a server required to offer multimedia files on demand – a similar requirement to the one just discussed. The server is required to supply stream buffers (units for temporary storage) at the data rate needed to ensure continuity of playback – a somewhat different requirement from a VOD movie system. The authors discuss the problem of disk scheduling in multiple data stream retrieval – including the case when different streams are delivering data from different parts of the same file. The scheduling is arranged so that one reading head is able to deal with several streams, a situation made possible because disk data delivery is faster than stream delivery. Some of Gemmell's data for storage options is show in Table 2.6.

Home banking still seems to be one of the 'standard service attempts' for electronic information services. It appeared to be just the kind of service that would appeal to domestic viewers. This has not proved to be the case. Several banks in different countries have attempted it but it has failed to take off. If the situation changes and home banking becomes one more service among a collection used by a very large number of homes which have become accustomed to using interactive services, its prospects might improve.

Nahrstedt and Steimetz (1995) think through the difficult problem of resource management in multimedia networks. Pending specifications or Standards covering resources and QOS, they provide examples of QOS parameters such as picture frame resolution: 'At least 720×576 pixels' and 'Packet loss for compressed video less than 10^{-11}'.

Table 2.6 Storage details

Feature	Magnetic disk	Optical disk	Small tape	Large tape
Capacity	9 Gbytes	200 Gbytes	500 Gbytes	10 Tbytes
Transfer rate per second	2 Mbytes	300 Kbytes	100 Kbytes	1 Mbyte
Cost ($)	5000	50,000	50,000	500K–1M
Cost per Gbyte ($)	555	125	100	50

Systems being planned or tested

A number of interactive systems are being tried out as listed in Table 2.7.

The imagination of Fuhrt and his colleagues is well exceeded by a company called the Teledesic Corporation, who revealed their ideas at the Compcon 95 meeting (Myers 1995). The major owners of Teledesic are Craig McCaw and Bill Gates. They are considering a network based on 840 satellites in low earth orbit – a number which will take more than two years to launch because of the strain on launching facilities. The cost will be about $9 billion and the satellites will cover virtually the entire population of the world.

More localized is the plan being considered by the Lawrence Livermore National Laboratory to install a fibreoptic ring round San Francisco bay. It will run at 10 Gbps and connect the Livermore Laboratory with Pacific Telephone, University of California at Berkeley, and Sprint. The last service listed (at Ipswich UK) announced its intention to start up an 'inter-active multimedia services' trial, expected to last for up to two years, in June 1995. Three service franchises covering home shopping, home banking, local government, and educational services will be selected for the benefit of the 2000 customers for the trial service. The three phases of the trial will cover technical testing; field trials of networks, services, and billing arrangements; market trial for testing the appeal of the services to fee-paying customers.

Some information was published by Christine Blank in May 1995 (Blank 1995) about a VOD interactive system which is being tested on 45 homes in Orlando, Florida, scheduled to be available in 4000 homes before the end of the year. It is one of the first to use new technology which will soon be widely adopted – ATM switching (see chapter 8). A diagram of the network is shown in Figure 2.6. When a request is received from a terminal via the reverse control channel, the requested movie starts within a second. The movie is packetized by the server and sent to the ATM switch via the 155 Mbps channel. It then goes via the Quadrature Amplitude Modulator

Table 2.7 Interactive TV service trials

Place	Company	Service
Carritos, CA	GTE	Simple VOD
Montreal, Canada	Videoway	Quasi-VOD over cable
N. Virginia	Bell Atlantic	VOD over ADSL
New York	Nynex	VOD trials
New Hamps/Cambridge	Continental Cable	Compuserve over cable
California	Sega	Interactive games
Boston, Mass.	GTE	Various
Cambridge, UK	Acorn/Anglia TV/Camb. Cab.	Services (ATM)
Ipswich, UK	BT	Services (ADSL)
UK	Bell/Nynex/Telewest	VOD trials

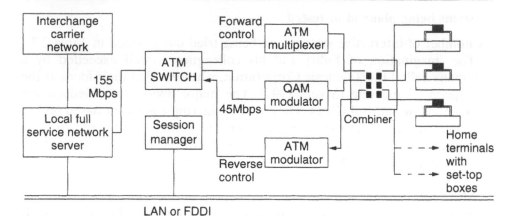

Figure 2.6 The Orlando full service network
Source: AEC

(QAM) where it is converted to RF signals within a 6 MHz band, and the combiner, to the terminal's set-top box. Digital control data pass via the ATM multiplexer and combiner to the set-top box. The combiner-to-terminal channels are fibreoptic. The set-top box separates the digital control and analogue data, and decompresses the latter. A connection cable between the system and a block of users carries 13 6 MHz signal channels, control signals in their own channels, and 13 return channels. The system embodies new techniques including SONET protocols to carry ATM data (see chapter 8), MPEG 1 compression, and set-top boxes with which there have been a series of problems, as might be expected. A hundred movies will be made available by the year's end, together with home shopping, news, music on demand, and educational services. The crunch comes when the system is priced at a profit-making level and the number of customers prepared to pay is discovered.

BT owns most of the telephone network in the UK. In 1990 it carried out trials with fibreoptic lines to households at Bishops Stortford with GEC Plessey (GPT), BICC, and Fulcrum, for multi-channel TV, access to a videodisk library, and teleworking. The trials ended in 1992. In November 1994, BT dropped its plan for a £15 billion fibre information superhighway after the government refused to lift the ban on BT's entry into TV broadcasting.

BT will make the most of the enormous investment in the 'copper loop' which provides it with an entry to businesses and homes. Regulatory legislation does not appear to prevent it from offering services such as VOD. It started trials in the spring of 1994 although Oftel warned it in November 1994 that a full system must be consistent with UK policy. The trials are mainly based on DMT ADSL (Discrete Multitone Asymmetric Digital Subscriber Loop) in which the maximum bit rate of the PSTN, nominally about 140

Kbps, is extended by equalization and the selective use of frequency bands within the channel, to up to about 2 Mbps. 'Asymmetric' means that the return path from a subscriber works at a lower rate. Delivered acceptable television pictures from, say, an 80 Mbps service, compressed by 40:1, could be viewed over such a system.

BT announced technical trials in 1993 for about 2000 households in Colchester, Essex. It would be using material from the Sears group and W.H. Smith for home shopping, Thomas Cook for holidays and travel, the BBC, Carlton, Kingfisher, Granada, and Pearson for TV programmes, sport from BSkyB, and music from BMG Video, EMI, Polygram, Sony, and Warner. BT's starting choice menu for the market-trial, starting in 1995, is shown in Figure 2.7. A massively parallel computer with an Oracle media server and nCube software is used at the head end. Set-top boxes supplied by Apple consist of LC475 machines with MPEG decompression and Quicktime, receiving data at 2 Mbps. Viewers' requests, sent at the 64 Kbps rate, are received at a central point via an ATM switch. No further announcement about technical progress was made but in June 1995 BT made a further announcement about marketing so presumably technical

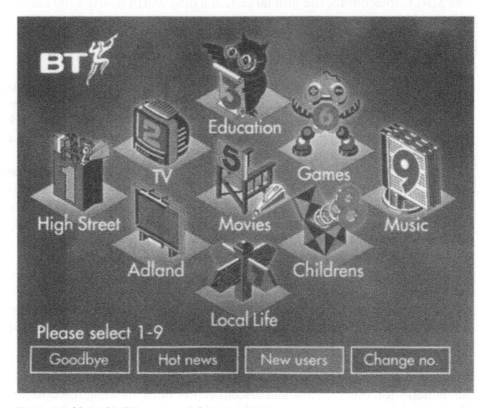

Figure 2.7 Menu for BT market-trial programmes
Source: British Telecom

tests had been satisfactory. With regard to interactive television for its trial users, now increased to 2500, there would be a monthly charge of about £5 and for movies a 'pay and play' charge of £1.50 to £3.99 with a choice of 'several hundred hours'.

The ATM network associated with the superbox for the Acorn/Cambridge consortium has been described by Wray *et al.* (1994). Each component such as a camera, audio system, display, etc. is treated as an 'ATM direct' module controlled by an ARM Risc processor, each module being directly connected to the network. The network will convey 'Many streams of multimedia data, perhaps thousands, which are active simultaneously.'

In March 1995 the trials were stepped up with the installation of ICL PIM (Parallel Interactive Media) Servers. A PIM Server embodies an ATM 155 Mbps interface and 240 Gbytes of storage. One PIM Server will support up to 7000 users watching, among other programmes, any of 1000 compressed feature films.

Further VOD trials on cable are expected in the UK on a similar scale to BT's, run by Bell Cablemedia, Nynex, and Telewest. These three companies serve about half of UK subscribers. Telewest, the largest operator, took over SBC Cablecomms, the fifth largest, in a deal worth nearly £700 million in June 1995.

Regulatory and technical problems

In the United States optimism about future broadband networks was followed by a rash of new companies and large contract awards. A company called Raynet did a substantial amount of work on fibreoptic network systems, but in 1994 its parent company, Raychem, withdrew support after losses of $500 million had accumulated.

In the United States the FCC's 1992 decision to allow telephone companies to offer video services was followed by a number of requests for permits. Companies must specify and keep separate the costs of a video service from telephones services. Permits have been slow in forthcoming and Perry (1995) reports attempts to load telephone services with most of the fibre installation costs intended for video.

Cable companies do not have this problem, but also according to Perry, the Orlando scheme – a joint effort between Time Warner, Scientific Atlanta, Silicon Graphics, and Anderson Consulting – scheduled to start in April 1994, has still failed to work properly. Software and engineering problems have been harder to solve than was expected.

Of course the UK press has seized upon pessimistic reports about organizations which have not yet succeeded in the cable business. It is said that penetration rates are low and disconnection rates are high; it is doubted whether cable will ever be as popular in Britain as in North America. It is too early to make such assumptions. There will certainly be some more failures. It is an expensive and risky business to find out more about people's information and service requirements, and their propensity to pay when they are going to have to change their behaviour in the expectation of receiving unknown benefits. Success will come if a sufficiently large proportion of up-market people spread the word to the remainder and both the keeping up with the Joneses and the new toy syndromes exercise their persuasive powers.

Chapter 3

Compression

INTRODUCTION

Compression systems have become of major importance because multimedia has introduced data speeds and volumes well in advance of the handling capabilities of transmission and storage systems. The incentives to develop compression systems will be obvious from Figure 3.1 (after Fuhrt 1994). General compression principles are applicable to CDs but CD-specific compression is discussed in chapter 11.

Simple methods of compressing large databases have been used for some years (Alsberg 1975). For example, in a personnel record a fixed-length one-bit code in a 'gender' field to replace the 8-bit characters M or F for male or female immediately provides an 8:1 compression for every occurrence of those words. In Huffman codes (Huffman 1952), the letters of the alphabet are arranged in order of probability of occurrence and are allocated variable length codewords. Thus E is 101 and Q 0111001101. Like the Morse code, the net effect is that the total number of bits used to represent a passage of text will be much less than would be the case if a fixed length code was used.

Systems transmitting information in a succession of frames, as in a television system, present compression opportunities because 'information' need only be transmitted when there are changes – an unchanging scene generates no new information.

Television system bandwidth, an expensive resource, is wide enough to cope with fast rates of change when they occur – the motion of a racehorse, motion in athletic events, etc. But for most of the time all that is needed is the narrow bandwidth required to transmit relatively slow changes of scene. When an area of uniformly blue sky is transmitted for, say, five seconds of viewing time, that area could be transmitted in a single frame, stored at the receiver, and continuously displayed until the scene changes. Such an ideal scheme is easier to talk about than do but it illustrates the general principle – when there is no change, generate a code to tell the system to send no new data until a change occurs.

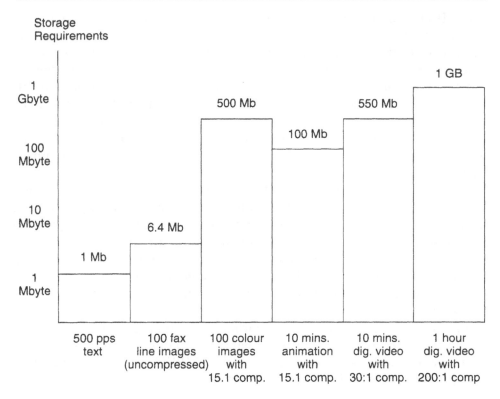

Figure 3.1 Storage requirements for data types

Source: After Fuhrt (1994)

Another method called 'progressive coding' has been described by Yeh (1989). It has been used for 'image browsing' in order to allow just sufficient information about the content of an image to be sent down a line of limited bandwidth, e.g. a telephone line. The method was standardized in 1993 as ISO/IEC IS 11544 under the aegis of the CCITT and ISO JBIG (Joint Bilevel Image Group) committee. The general principle of implementing JBIG progressive coding is to digitize a picture into a small number of bits. They are sent down a line in a relatively short period of time, as dictated by the line's bandwidth. The transmission is then repeated with improved digitization requiring more bits, taking a longer period of time, and so on. The user stops the transmission either when he or she has seen enough to decide that the image is of no interest, but if necessary allowing the process to continue to a reproduction with the best available quality.

Much work has been done on compressing facsimile data to enable detailed images to be transmitted quickly. Stand-alone scanning machines, as used for multimedia work, have inherited the methods used – they have been found to be good working compromises providing effective compression with reasonable compressing and decompressing processing times (Mussman

1977; Bodson and Schaphorst 1983). In facsimile systems, run length coding is used in which a row of data is stored and runs of black or white bits are identified. Codewords for numbers of bits have been previously stored in lookup tables for black and white bits. The machine looks up the codeword for less than but nearest to the number of bits in the run and then inserts the difference in binary code. For instance, if the number of black bits to be compressed is 865, and short codes are given in the black lookup table for 850 and 900 bits, the machine selects the code for 850 and follows it with the number 15 in binary. A similar, but inverse, process takes place before image reproduction.

The time taken to compress and decompress, and the compression ratio achieved – that is, the ratio of the amounts of data in the uncompressed and compressed image – vary according to page contents, the compression algorithms (rules) used, the power of the processor, and whether or not special chips are used for the purpose. For a short business letter consisting of lines of text with much white space the compression ratio could be 20 to 40, while for a page consisting of halftone illustrations there may be no compression at all.

For a good general review of earlier data compression methods see Lelewer and Hirschberg (1987). Aravind *et al.* (1993) have described the JBIG system described above and the JPEG, MPEG, and H261 methods of compression are described later in the chapter.

COMPRESSION SOFTWARE FOR MICROCOMPUTERS

In 1990 a number of compression packages for PCs were reviewed in *PC User* magazine (Price 1990). They were said to achieve compression partly by compacting DOS files which are allocated more space in the DOS file-cluster arrangement than they really need, and partly by using algorithms for variable length coding, Huffman encoding, or the Lempel-Ziv algorithm (as used in the latest modems), in which short codes are allocated to high-frequency strings and stored. Each time a stored string recurs the code is sent in lieu.

The main microcomputer application seems to be to compress files during disk backups. The compression ratios obtained are not large but worth having. They provide from 25 per cent to about 50 per cent file compression, nearly always performing better on text files than on programme files.

Software prices range from £8 to £150. Higher priced software includes compression among several other 'utilities'.

SPEECH DIGITIZATION AND COMPRESSION

Speech was one of the earliest data types to be studied; not so long ago all telecommunication *was* speech telecommunication. Speech continues to receive attention, particularly in the context of cellular radio and synthetic speech. For multimedia digitized speech, compression is almost essential otherwise storage requirements become excessively large (see also chapter 6).

Some remarkable results were obtained in the early work on vocoders. In a vocoder, speech is analysed in terms of the vocal tract parameters which created it. The speech is reproduced by using a pulsed sound source modified by vocal tract parameter data. The information needed to provide very artificial but understandable speech created in this manner has been achieved with a transmission rate as low as 0.1 to 0.4 bits per sample.

Considerable compression development work (Jain 1981; Haskell and Steele 1981) followed the adoption of digitization – implemented because the handling of data in digital form provides substantial advantages over analogue. The principles, advantages, and bandwidth disadvantage are described in chapter 2.

Speech compression is the art of ingenious methods of bit reduction. A crude way of doing it, which results in a steady reduction in quality and the introduction of quantization noise, is to simply reduce the number of samples taken. The variations and improvements on PCM include Adaptive Differential PCM (ADPCM) using 4 bits per sample. Continuously Variable Slope Delta Modulation (CVSDM) with only 1 bit per sample 32,000 times per second, and a relatively new method dependent on chip processing power called Codebook Excited Linear Predictive coding (CELP) are also used. CELP analyses the speech pattern during a short interval of time and consults a 'speech pattern reference table', compiled from speech pattern statistics, which shows what kind of pattern is most likely to follow a given pattern. It then applies the difference data between two adjacent patterns and sends them as the second pattern. The result is a very low bit rate of under 5 Kbps.

H.261 CODEC

The H.261 Codec was developed under the aegis of CCITT study group XV formed in 1984. It was the first compression system to be able to benefit from chip implementation. Its intention was to provide for video transmission over the ISDN. It was needed to provide a standard method of compression for videoconferencing schemes. It compresses pictures to a 352 × 288 line image in what is known as the Common Intermediate Format (CIF) providing 30 frames/sec at a bit rate of 64 Kbps.

The final recommendation proposed bit rates at p × 64 Kbits/second where p is between 1 and 30, for use on lines with bandwidths up to 2 Mbps. H.261 embodies DCT encoding as in the JPEG system described in the next section, but it also uses inter-frame coding to compute frame-to-frame differences resulting from motion – a method which is also embodied in MPEG, described in the next section.

TRANSFORM CODING AND JPEG

The number of possible patterns in even a very small image, of which only a small fraction, virtually impossible to compute, will form meaningful images, can be 10^{614}. The enormity of this number is evident when compared with the 1.3×10^{26} molecules in a gallon of water (Jain 1981).

The mathematical process known as the Discrete Cosine Transform (DCT) is a classic example of the elegant use of the compact processing power currently available to perform the elaborate operations in real time needed to substantially compress data 'on the fly'.

In the version of DCT incorporated in the Joint Photographic Experts Group (JPEG) standard for still images – worked out by ISO and CCITT groups – a digitized image is coded by processing blocks of 8×8 pixels in sequence from left to right and from top to the bottom of the picture. Each block is scanned in order to generate information about the rate of change between the pixels present. A checker-board pattern in a block would produce a stream of high-frequency data elements, an all-white or all-black block would represent a low-frequency change. Most of the 'information' in the block is confined to the high-frequency elements which are Huffman-encoded – a highly economic code. Decompression goes through the same processes in reverse.

The actual implementation of compression chips (Apiki 1991) started when the impending Standardization of JPEG algorithms, to be specified by ANSI and ISO, became known. The Inmos A121 chip was developed during 1989 to handle this type of operation. It runs at 320M operations/second, taking 3.2 microseconds to carry out an 8×8 DCT process and 15 ms to handle a 625×625 pixel image.

In April 1990 the 27 MHz C-Cube Micro-system type CL550 chip, designed to perform according to the JPEG standard, was announced. The price was $155 in quantity. It will compress an 8-Mbit video frame by 10 times in 0.033 seconds. Alternatively, it will compress a 200 Mbit high-resolution full-colour still picture to 8 Mbits in 1 second.

A 1992 advertisement of the Leadview board and software says that the Leadview system will provide compression ratios between 2 and 225 times, with compression times of 8 to 10 seconds. 'We are so sure you'll be impressed,' says the advert, 'that we include a 30-day money back guarantee.'

SGS-Thomson have also developed a JPEG processor – the STI140 – which will compress/decompress colour still pictures at a rate of 30 frames per second, providing compression ratios of up to 30:1. It sells at $200 in lots of 1000.

In June 1991, Philips announced that a C-cube chip would be used in up-rated CD-I players. It will enable about one hour of video plus audio to be accommodated on a 650 Mbyte CD-I. Compression will enable the data rate to be slowed down to less than 1.5 Mbits/second.

In June 1994 Iterated Systems offered Colorbox Pro containing the FTC III compression acceleration board dealing with resolutions of up to 1280 × 1024 24-bit colour, or 8-bit grey scale data, claimed to be capable of compressing a 3.9 Mbyte file into 32 Kbytes 'without appreciable loss of image quality'. The price, including decompression which is carried out by software only, is £2495.

Current discussion centres on whether it is better to use one chip – a 'fixed performance general solution' – or to implement the Standard with several chips and software. The Standard provides for several variations, so the second approach enables a 'custom-built for the application' system to be provided (Cavagioli 1991). Cavagioli also describes the way the JPEG effort developed and gives a description of its features.

Numerous devices now incorporate chip-implemented compression schemes to the Standard which provides for 'lossless' and 'lossy' compressed images. For lossless compression a 2:1 compression ratio is achieved – output and input pixels are identical and there is no visible difference between compressed and uncompressed pictures. For lossy compression at a ratio of about 30:1 the degradation becomes noticeable. Leonard (1991) provides a set of pictures including one showing just acceptable 32:1 compression; at 300:1 the picture is still just recognizable but fine detail is lost and edges are very ragged.

JPEG compression works by compressing the halftone or colour bits which are applied to the beam or beams as voltages to change the intensity level of a displayed pixel. Because of the importance of the maximum bit rates that can be delivered by different media – for example, CD-ROMs, video recorders, etc., an important objective is to compress pictures to the bit rate which a particular medium can deliver. The delivered data are later converted into real time data by the decompression software running on the associated machine.

Instead of ratios, compressions are often expressed as 'bits per pixel'. Cavagioli (1991) provides a subjective assessment of JPEG compression ratios from original 16-bit per pixel pictures as follows:

bits/pixel	compression	assessment
8	(2:1)	'Lossless'
1.5	(11:1)	'Indistinguishable from original'
0.75	(22:1)	'Excellent quality'
0.25	(64:1)	'Useful image'
0.10	(160:1)	'Recognizable image'

Whether others would agree with these subjective assessments is another matter (see Picture Quality Assessment in chapter 2).

VIDEO: STILL, MOTION, AND COLOUR COMPRESSION

In television, and for computers using similar types of display, a CRT screen is filled with a frame of pixel data representing an image to be immediately followed by another, usually very similar, frame. A succession of frames is displayed at a rate of at least 25 per second to provide a flicker-free, apparently continuous picture. Motion is conveyed by usually small frame-to-frame changes – motion may appear to be jerky if it is fast enough for the part of the image in motion to move an appreciable distance from frame to frame.

The development of fast cheap processing devices enables a frame-to-frame examination to be carried out to detect areas within which motion or a change of scene is occurring, and to supply a stream of data about those areas. This field has been the subject of intense activity for many years, one of the pioneers being Professor Cherry working at Imperial College (Cherry and Gouriet 1953). A company called Cawkell Research & Electronics, adopting some of Cherry's ideas, conducted some work (prematurely) to send TV pictures along a telephone line (Cawkell 1964).

For digitized motion video, the delivered bits, after decompression, must run at the designed rate for the application. For example, for 30 US television frames per second to be delivered to a US television receiver or computer screen and to provide good quality pictures, the data rate must be about 28 Mbytes/second or 224 Mbits per second for high quality.

A variation of JPEG called Motion-JPEG is JPEG speeded up to enable motion video to be compressed and decompressed in real time. However, the Moving Picture Experts Group (MPEG) Standard, described by Le Gall (1991), and Syed and Williamson (1993) will become the preferred method. The objective is to compress TV bit rates down to 1 to 1.5 Mbps or lower. Good quality pictures, having been compressed/decompressed with compression ratios of over 100:1, are required.

Agreement on the requirements for the Moving Picture Experts Group Standard was reached at a meeting in Sydney, in April 1993. MPEG-1 is required to deliver video from a CD at 1.416 Mbps. This provides a resolution of typically one quarter of digitized NTSC or PAL television signals – 352 × 240, or 352 × 288 pixels respectively.

The MPEG-2 Standard is intended to provide standard NTSC or PAL resolution – 704 × 480, or 704 × 576 pixels at data rates of 4 or 8 Mbps. MPEG-2 will be able to handle HDTV video and since MPEG-1 is a subset of it, any MPEG-2 decoder will decode MPEG-1 video syntax. Compression is provided by using transform coding in which an image, or sections of it, are processed in mosaic-like samples. With MPEG-2, the source sends pictures with redundant spatial and temporal information removed, but incorporates coded inter-frame data enabling a receiver to decode and reconstruct the pictures. High compression ratios of up to about 200:1 may be achieved because successive TV frames often contain similar information. In normal

TV transmissions, data about every pixel must be sent. In MPEG-2, most of the data relating to individual pixels forming similar scenes in a Group of Pictures (GOP) are not transmitted.

MPEG-2 encoding takes place in two stages – intra-frame JPEG encoding, and inter-frame difference encoding. Inter-frame encoding for a pixel block in a particular frame is carried out with reference to the position of the same data in past and future frames. The general principle of inter-frame coding may be visualized as follows. If three successive frames are stored before transmission, a pixel block depicting part of an object in motion could be in three different positions in each frame. The positions of the same or a very similar block in the frames are found by a frame-to-frame 'best matching' technique. When the frames are transmitted in the order 1, 2, 3, frame 2 block is transmitted not as a block of pixels ready to be displayed, but as 'interpolating' positional data. When decoded at the receiver, the interpolating data causes the pixel data from frame 1 to be installed in its correct new position in frame 2. This 'double' complex encoding procedure enables a good deal of redundant data to be removed before transmission so that far fewer bits need be transmitted to describe each frame.

Several companies have announced motion video compression products – UVC Corporation supply a card providing up to 500:1 compression for multimedia applications, Intel offer their JPEG i750 DVI motion video processor, and NEXT computer includes compression for special effects with their newer machines. However, so far as is known, the techniques used are not to the newer MPEG standard.

Early progress was reviewed by Tonge (1989), who starts by pointing out that the bandwidth required for HDTV is at least five times that of current TV. Compression research has been further stepped up in view of the expected advent of High Definition Television with the objective of reducing the required channel bandwidth.

Until the revolutionary proposals for all-digital TV systems were announced in 1993, 'sub-sampling' compression methods seemed to be popular for the compression of HDTV signals. This method is used in the Japanese MUSE and in the European HD-MAC systems. The TV signal is sampled for coding purposes at a rate lower than the rate required (Nyquist criterion) to reconstruct the waveform completely. A 40 per cent reduction in the required bandwidth may be obtained. Very little deterioration in picture quality can be observed when a new type of digital comb filter is used. The filter is designed to deal with distortion in the frequency spectrum which would otherwise occur.

In 1992/93 MPEG Standards were extended into MPEG versions 1 to 4. MPEG-1 for CD-ROM bit rates up to 1.5 MHz was published in 1992. MPEG-2, designed to cover bit rates in cable, optical fibre, or satellite systems, was published in 1994. MPEG-3 has been incorporated into MPEG-2, and a yet more ambitious MPEG-4 is now under discussion. It will operate within a number of TV frame and line formats and rates up to resolutions of 1080 lines.

VIDEO COLOUR COMPRESSION

Compression schemes based on reducing the amount of colour data have been developed, especially for CD-I systems (Anon. 1992a). Colour electronics and reproduction are discussed in chapter 2.

PAL digitized television signals providing a high-quality picture are usually $720 \times 576 \times 24$-bit colour = 10 Mbits (approx.) per frame. Colour data are RGB 8:8:8 – each colour is reproduced in $2^8 = 256$ levels, providing for a possible $256 \times 256 \times 256 = 16.8$ million (approx.) colours. As an example, CD-I uses $384 \times 280 \times$ RGB 5:5:5 – 15-bit colour = 1.6 Mbits (approx.) – already a compression of about 6 times. While comparing unfavourably with 10 Mbit PAL, this seems to be acceptable to most people used to the quality provided by the average TV receiver.

Colour Lookup Tables (CLUT) are also employed as described in chapter 2, and may be used to provide more compression than a 256-colour 8-bit arrangement by reducing the size of the table down to 16 (4 bits).

Further compression in CD-I is obtained with a coding technique called Data Luminance Colour Difference, usually known as DYUV, which records colour when successive pixels differ. As used in CD-I, the average extra compression provided is about 2.5 times, reducing a frame to about 700 Kbits (87 Kbytes). Run-length coding, discussed earlier in this chapter, is also available in CD-I for animation – the larger the areas of unchanging colour, the more the data can be compressed. Finally, yet another technique called Quantized High-resolution Y (QHY) may be used as well. It works by interpolating luminance (Y) signal values.

EDGE ENCODING AND COMPRESSION

Quite a different approach has been researched for some years, again based on omitting redundant information. An edge or boundary following a sequence of identical pixels is a change of information requiring the handling of high-frequency data. If edges can be satisfactorily detected, the potential for compression exists, provided that fewer bits are used in the implementation of the scheme than are used in conventional reproduction.

Current work on this approach has been described by Lee and Liu (1989). Low-frequency parts of the image are filtered out and coded by transform coding. Changes are detected by taking every pixel and checking its edges by examining the pixels above, below, and on both sides of it. A scheme for encoding the changes is described. The coded data from which the image may be reconstructed consist of a combination of the low-frequency and the edge data. Compression ratios of 23:1 are claimed.

FRACTALS

The 1989 *OED* defines 'fractal' as 'a mathematically conceived curve such that any small part of it, enlarged, has the same statistical character as the original'. Shapes described mathematically, later to be called *fractals* by Mandelbrot, were discovered in France by Poincaré and Julia but it was Mandelbrot who realized their significance in the 1970s. Fractal geometry is about 'scale invariance', a property of natural objects first fully appreciated by Benoit Mandelbrot. It is based on the fact that small portions of an object often resemble larger parts. Mandelbrot noticed that the coastline of Britain looked much the same when viewed from different distances. The collection of inlets and peninsulas visible at 5 m looks similar to the larger collection visible at 30 m of which the smaller collection has become a part.

Michael Barnsley, working at the Georgia Institute of Technology, Atlanta, devised computer algorithms which take portions of complex images and perform transformation operations on them called Iterated Function Systems (IFS) from which a set of points may be plotted providing a coarse image of salient features called Fractal Transform (FT) codes; information about the spatial relationship between points is preserved in the codes, enabling the original image to be reconstructed by an iterative scaling-up process.

The reduction process amounts to the elimination of redundant geometric information. The compression ratio between the original and the reduced image and the time taken to compress depend on the complexity of the shapes present in the original. Some parts may exhibit great redundancy; in others there may be very little. Normally over 700,000 bytes (5.6 Mbits) per frame are necessary for motion video, but about 1037 bytes per frame – a compression ratio of about 670:1 – was shown in an early Barnsley demonstration. A high-quality compression board for plugging in to a 386 PC microcomputer with 640K memory and hard disk, is sold by the company for £6000 with software for around £2000. It will accept 24-bit colour input files in various formats. A system user could compress a file to, say, 10 Kbytes and send it on disk or transmit it very cheaply to another location and load it into any suitable micro which contains the decompression software – for instance, a 286 or higher machine with 640K and a VGA display. The resident decompression software is licensed at £95 per user for up to 100 users, with reductions for larger numbers. No special hardware is necessary for decompression. The results obtained by these new compression systems are open to different interpretations and it seems necessary to proceed with caution.

Beaumont (1991) has described the principles of fractal compression in some detail, using a number of illustrations to show effects in working systems. He describes a scheme which compresses an 8-bit per pixel halftone picture into a picture requiring only 0.8 bits per pixel – that is a 10:1

compression – 'without introducing artefacts obvious to the untrained eye. Compression down to 0.5 (16:1) produces visible artefacts but the picture quality is still reasonable.'

Raittinen and Kaski (1995) assessed several methods of compression, including Barnsley's fractal compression method and JPEG. They used the well-known 'Lena' image for quality comparisons. The authors conclude that 'none of the tested fractal compression methods yield significantly better results than JPEG when a reasonably low compression ratio is used. Fractal compression methods may, however, be notably better when an extremely high compression ratio is required.'

Beaumont's modest results may be compared with Figures 3.2(a) + (b) (by permission of Iterated Systems), although the pictures probably suffer a little from being re-reproduced. They demonstrate resolution independence and mathematical zoom-in. In conventional zoom-in both the size of the image and the size of the pixels change. The upper image shows a zoom-in, still at a resolution of 1280×600 pixels, although it is only one-quarter of a 1280×600 image scanned into the system. It was printed after decompression from a 10 Kbyte compressed file. The lower picture, also printed from a 10 Kbyte compressed file, is zoomed in to provide a picture of 5120×3200. The printer used is a Mitsubishi 600 dots/inch printer. An effective compression ratio of nearly 5000:1 is claimed. The picture quality does not seem to have suffered much from this enormous ratio.

The time taken to compress and decompress presumably depends to some extent on the power of the machines being used. It could be 10 minutes for compression but only a few seconds for decompression. Using this system a very large database containing high-quality pre-compressed pictures could be easily stored in megabyte instead of gigabyte capacity. A few seconds for the decompression of a retrieved picture would be acceptable.

This dramatic performance is what is claimed by the supplier. Different users express different opinions about performance and picture quality. One user at a large research organization says that the obtainable compression ratios and quality are no better than those obtained with alternative proprietary systems and they will not be using this one; the appearance of compressed pictures depends very much on their content, and acceptability is different for different users. However, some commercial users find the system acceptable for use at very high compression ratios.

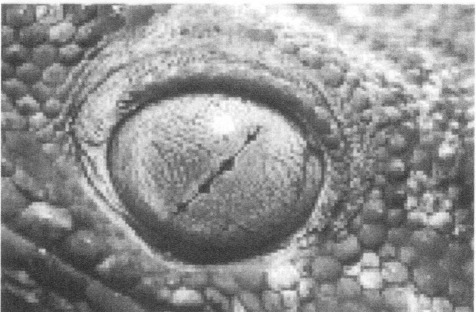

Figure 3.2 (a) and (b) Fractal compression

Source: Iterated Systems

Chapter 4

Image processing

INTRODUCTION

Image processing as used here means improving images or pictures and generating special pictorial effects. These operations rely heavily upon matrix algebra, Fourier transformations, etc., the mathematical language used to describe them. It is not easy to translate this language into English narrative. However, an attempt will be made to describe some of the basic operations upon which image-processing systems depend with the minimum of mathematics.

Much of the maths and many of the algorithms were developed some years ago and are described in textbooks such as Gonzalez and Wintz (1987), Pearson (1991), Pratt (1991), Low (1991), and Russ (1995), which brings the subject up to date. In the early 1980s image processing with relatively inexpensive hardware was in its infancy. In the 1990s, technology, computer power, and algorithms have become available for pixel-by-pixel processing on computers priced at $3000 or less. The rate of improvement and falling costs of hardware, particularly in respect of low-cost high-speed processing, are encouraging more experimenters into this area of research. Progress towards non-word content recognition (chapter 10) has advanced to the point where it is being used in practical applications.

The operations to be described cover the processing of the horizontal, vertical, and temporal dimensions of an array of pixels representing an image. The speed at which these operations can be performed is increasing all the time as a result of the introduction of parallel processing and faster chips.

A masking operation, commonly used in image processing, gives a good idea of the processing possibilities with the power now available in an inexpensive machine.

Gonzalez and Wintz, quoting the kind of performance that was available in 1986, say that the application of a 3×3 pixel mask (described below) to a 512×512 image requires 9 multiplications and 8 additions for each pixel location – that is, a total of 2.35 million multiplications and 2.097 million additions. When this was done with the Arithmetic Logic Unit (ALU) and frame buffers which were available at that time, the operations took about 0.3 seconds. Processing duration increases in proportion to the mask size. For example, processing a 4×4 mask would take about 0.53 seconds.

Pearson says that it would take about 3 seconds to process a 3×3 mask on a 512×512 8-bit image. Assuming that Gonzalez and Wintz were referring to a 1-bit image, this duration is of the same order. Pearson mentions that the speed may be increased according to the number of processors involved in the operation. Thus three processors would decrease the period to 1.1 second.

In the year when Gonzalez and Wintz's book was published and four years before Pearson, the LSI Logic Corporation was selling a chip-set capable of performing 60 billion binary operations plus one billion (10^9) 8-bit $\times$ 8-bit multiplications per second.

In 1993 a company called Adaptive Solutions (Beaverton, Oregon, USA) introduced its Connected Network of Adaptive Processors (CNAPS) chip. A CNAPS chip consists of 64 processors, called Processing Nodes (PN) in parallel. Up to 8 of these chips may themselves be connected in parallel, producing a total of 512 processor nodes. The device may be used for several of the operations described elsewhere in this chapter.

A method of thresholding (setting an image to two levels) an 8×8 array of image pixels is shown in Figure 4.1. It is imagined that an 8×8 pixel area of an image is to be thresholded with each of 8 processors being responsible for one column. When loaded, the arrangement will be as shown in the square at the bottom of the figure. The values of the pixels are then changed by an instruction passed to the processors via the common input bus. If the arrangement is extended to a full array of 512 processors, then the change of values in a 512×512 pixel array would be accomplished in 308 microseconds.

The system could be used for a convolution operation where it is required to move a kernel or matrix of $m \times n$ pixel values over all the pixels in an image. For example, to convolve a 7×7 kernel with a 512×512 image would take 9.55 milliseconds.

The system is also claimed to be suitable for performing JPEG compression (chapter 3). In this case it would carry out the operation in 4 stages – DCT transformation followed by quantization to filter out high-frequency components, run length coding to compress the result, and Huffman encoding for providing a second stage of compression. It is claimed that this operation can be carried out on a 512×512 pixel grey scale image in 33 milliseconds.

Note that in 1987 the time periods for carrying out processing operations were being expressed in seconds. In 1993 the times to carry out broadly similar operations are being expressed in milliseconds or microseconds. This rate of progress enables routine processing operations to be carried out today which had not been imagined six years ago.

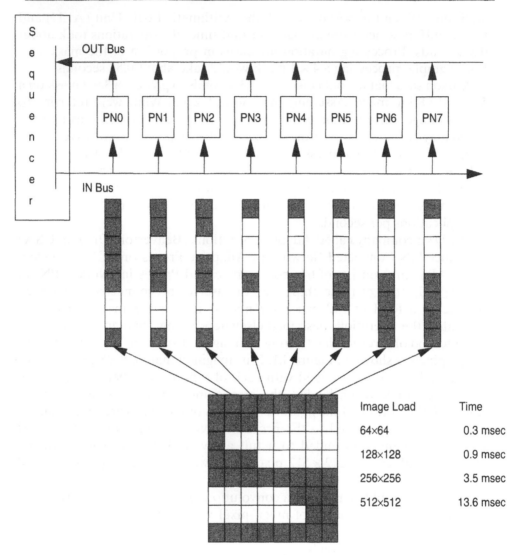

Figure 4.1 Thresholding array

Source: By courtesy of Adaptive Solutions Inc.

EXAMPLES OF PROCESSING TECHNIQUES

Many different types of processing procedures are needed for improving or enhancing pictures, for certain picture matching and retrieval techniques, for special effects such as morphing, and for artistic and special effects with colours. A number of them are described below.

Aliasing

A term used in various contexts to indicate the presence of imperfections in a picture introduced by processing operations – for example, the effect of using an insufficient number of data points when attempting to represent a continuous function by a dot structure.

Colour processing and special effects

Colour variations may be substituted for brightness levels in situations when it is necessary to provide a wider range of easily detectable gradations than can be detected in halftone or grey scale picture. A human eye can readily detect about 30 shades of grey, but can easily discern differences between hundreds of different colours. The 'pseudo-colours' created by grey level to colours conversion may obscure the real detail in some types of picture, but will be very helpful in others. Russ (1995: 33) shows a striking illustration of the effectiveness of changing the small features in a microscope grey scale image into different colours according to feature size.

The arrival of colour for microcomputers prompted the introduction of a huge range of colour-processing software for colour correction processing, filling and painting objects, and producing special effects. The potential is best described by discussing Adobe Photoshop software, which became established as the standard colour image-processing software for Macintosh machines. Later it became available for Unix and Windows. Photoshop 3.0 is a Power PC version introduced in 1994.

In addition to the painting, retouching, colour correction, and special effects which were possible on the previous version, Yager (1993) summarizes the new features in Photoshop 2.5 for Windows as 'quick mask mode, dodge and burn, brushes and channels palettes, pen tool, duotones, variations interface, and new special effects filters'. In Photoshop 3.0, the native Power PC version, more new features are included such as lighting effects, image layering, and a 'dust and scratches' remover.

The most remarkable manifestations of multimedia special effects are visible on our TV screens every day. The attraction of the special effects new toy and its entertainment and advertising value is reflected in the numerous special effects packages available from third-party suppliers (McClelland 1994). For example, Paint Alchemy (from Xaos Tools) provides a choice of 75 different brush shapes with control of layering, angle, size, and transparency of brush strokes which enable various styles of 'hand-painted' pictures to be produced. Andromeda Series 2 (from Andromeda Software) will produce the extraordinary effects beloved by TV advertisers such as spinning a three-dimensional object with a picture wrapped round it.

Convolution with a mask or template

A multiplying and summing operation – for example, between the pixel values in a mask/template and the value of each image pixel beneath the mask. The value of each pixel in the mask is multiplied by the value of each underlying picture pixel, and the sum of these results becomes the new value, e_x, of pixel e (Figure 4.2 (a)) in the new image. If it was required to modify the value of the centre pixel e to a new value, e_x which is the average value of the 8 pixels immediately surrounding it, the mask, as in (b), is laid over a part of a picture (a) so that e1 overlays e. A multiplying and adding operation is then executed to produce:

$$e_x = 1/9 \ (a1 \times a + b1 \times b \ldots\ldots\ldots\ldots i1 \times i) \tag{1}$$

In general, the values of the coefficients a1, b1, etc. may be set to the values required to produce a new picture having the required characteristics. This type of operation is widely used in image processing.

a	b	c
d	e	f
g	h	i

a1	b1	c1
d1	e1	f1
g1	h1	i1

(a) Pixel values in a
small area of the picture
centred at pixel e

(b) Coefficients in a
mask overlaying the area
in (a)

Figure 4.2 Convolution with a mask

Source: A.E. Cawkell

The operation is carried out for every pixel in a picture – equivalent to laying the mask successively over every pixel, each of which assumes a new value to form an entirely new image which is the result of the convolution. Mathematically, the convolution (as in (1) above) of the Mask/Template, T $(n \times m)$ and the picture P $(N \times M)$ is expressed as:

$$T \times P(N,M) = \sum_{i=0}^{n-1} \ \sum_{j=0}^{m-1} \ T(i,j) \times P(N+1, M-j)$$

Edge detection

Edge detection is applied after sharpening has been used for edge highlighting – for example, by gradient edge-generation pixels. This operation may be performed by comparing the levels of adjacent pixels and, where the gradient is below some arbitrary level, reducing them to black. Pixels with a gradient above that level are made white. Accordingly, a white line will be generated signifying a continuity of change corresponding to an edge on the image. However, edge detection is more difficult than this for edges in textured regions and for colour pictures. See Pratt (1991, chapter 16), for more information.

Filter

'Filtering processes' and 'filters' are general terms used to describe various kinds of filtering operations, for example, to exclude unwanted frequencies in order to reduce aliasing after Fourier analysis.

A filtering action can also be effected by changing the value of pixels in a picture. For example, the 3×3 low-pass mask, as in Figure 4.3 (a), when 'moved over' all parts of the picture pixel area (b) produces the new picture (c) (after Low 1991). The 'noise' pixel (6 in 4.3 (b)) will disappear in the new picture.

(a) (b) (c)

Figure 4.3 Filtering

Fourier analysis

Fourier analysis is used to convert a picture into a form which can be more easily processed, filtered, etc., using suitable algorithms for manipulating its contents, particularly when including filters. A rectangular single impulse of length t seconds will become rounded off when passed through a channel of finite bandwidth. The reason is that the pulse is composed of sinusoidal waveforms of different frequencies and the faithful transmission of its edges require that the channel will pass the very high-frequency components of which the edges are composed. The component frequencies occur regularly at f, 2f, 3f, 4f, etc., where f = 1/t. Thus if the pulse length is 100 milliseconds = 0.1 seconds, f = 1/0.1 = 10 Hz, 2f = 20 Hz, etc. The amplitude of these harmonically related frequencies steadily decreases, making them easier to filter with a low-pass filter. The determination of these components is known as Fourier analysis.

A similar principle holds for recurring data, although there are some different consequential effects. The process of sampling the amplitude of a continuous waveform at appropriate intervals so that it may be represented in a 'discrete' form is known as the Discrete Fourier Transform. If a waveform band-limited to a frequency f is sampled to determine the amplitude at intervals spaced 1/2f seconds apart, the waveform will be completely defined by these samples.

An associated operation known as Fast Fourier Transform is based on the speed advantage obtained by a method for reducing the number of multiplications and additions required when 'discretizing' a continuous series.

Gradients

A gradient is formed by the value difference between adjacent pixels. The gradient will be large when there is a large difference between adjacent pixels – as at edges in pictures. A gradient image of an edge can be computer-generated based on a continuity of large gradients.

Histogram

A diagram in which the height of a column or the length of a row represents the number of occurrences of a value such as intensity. The examination of a histogram of the intensity or grey levels in an image may be indicative of the value at which to set the threshold or transition level from black to white.

Mask

A 'mask' or template is an array of pixel values arranged in a grid-like box of 2×2, 3×3, or $m \times n$ size. It is stepped across the grid formed by a corresponding number of pixels in an image. At each step the values of the image pixels are changed – a process known as convolution – in order to modify, enhance, or otherwise process the picture. See also 'Convolution'.

Perspective transformation

The modification of an image so as to simulate a different viewpoint. It requires operations based on a camera model.

Quadtree processing

A method of splitting regions of an image to isolate individual within-scene objects. An image is split into smaller and smaller quadrant-shaped regions and then different regions are merged according to certain rules. Object areas and perimeters may be expressed in terms of bit quad counts.

To produce a quadtree a black and white image is split into four quadrants. Each quadrant is in turn split into four and so on. The entire image can then be represented by a quadcode representing the position of any sub-quadrant in the hierarchy. A number of sub-quadrants will contain all white, or all black pixels. Information need be saved only about the smaller of these two classes, the existence of the majority type being implied. By omitting the implied class, a substantial degree of compression may be obtained.

The idea is most effective when a picture contains large areas containing all black or all white pixels. Dash (1993) shows that it is equally effective for coloured pictures and for those with a rectangular format. He suggests that quadtrees may be useful for other applications such as 'spatial analysis in desktop mapping, geographic information systems, pattern recognition, and CAD applications'.

Boundary matching, bug following, curve fitting and segment labelling

Methods of identifying and specifying the closed contour of image segments. For example, a bug follower describes the motion of a spot which crosses and recrosses boundaries, turning left or right according to certain rules, therefore producing a somewhat ragged outline of an enclosed area.

Scaling, rotation, and warping

These effects are produced by mathematical operations using a set of moments which are invariant to rotation and scale changes. Warping is a method of changing the shape of an image using mathematical operations to produce effects as if the image was printed on a flexible rubber sheet.

Shrink-wrapping

A term used to describe the close-contouring of an object with an edge-following outline using a special algorithm after it has been roughly outlined by a user.

Sobel operator

A mask or template containing values which accentuate edges.

Template

See Mask.

Template matching

A method of comparing a query object of interest with all the objects in a database. The query object of interest is sequentially scanned and compared for similarity with all the objects in the database which have been similarly scanned. The usual procedure is to generate a difference measure between the query object and the unknown objects. The database objects showing the smallest difference are considered to be the best matches. The method is computer-intensive since an enormous number of unknown objects may need to be compared against the query object.

Thresholding

A method of changing a grey-level picture into a bilevel picture. All the grey levels below a certain value are set to zero brightness or all the levels above a certain level are set to maximum brightness. An example of executing this operation is shown in Figure 4.1.

Outlining

Work continues on improving on processing methods, or a combination of methods, which are required for object identification. Daneels *et al.* (1993), who use a two-stage method based on Kass *et al.*'s (1988) 'snakes' algorithm, devote a paper solely to the subject of interactive outlining. Object outlining is provided as a part of many software processing packages. The user outlines an object with a few points, perhaps three or four, or whatever minimum number is needed to make it clear which object is of interest. The machine then accurately traces the border of the object which was crudely indicated by the user. Samadani and Han (1993) review several procedures which are available for finding boundaries. In Haddon and Boyce's (1989) method for edge-based segmentation, each pixel is paired with its nearest neighbours and examined to discover whether it forms part of a boundary.

PROCESSING HARDWARE AND SOFTWARE AND SOFTWARE PACKAGES

Processing boards are likely to contain more power than their host micro-computer. Major operations possible for frame grabber and processing cards for PC AT-compatible microcomputers from Data Translation are listed here:

- Geometric processing
  e.g. Rotate an image with or without bilinear interpolation
- Statistical analysis
  e.g. Compute a histogram
- Image enhancement
  e.g. Perform general $n \times m$ floating point filtering on a frame buffer
- Morphological filtering
  e.g. Perform grey-level dilation, erosion, opening or closing of an image

- Frequency analysis
  e.g. Fast Fourier Transform of frame buffer
- Arithmetic processing
  e.g. Add or subtract a constant in a frame buffer
- Chain support
  Declare and end a function chain
- Memory management
  Allocate or free a buffer on DT2878
- Data transfer
  Write a buffer of data to a disk file
- Buffer manipulation
  Threshold an image

A diagram of the DT2871 frame grabber is shown in Figure 4.4 and the associated DT2878 Advanced Processor in Figure 4.5. The DT2878 card itself is shown in Figure 4.6. A software package called the Advanced Image Processing Library provides the range of image-processing operations, some of which are shown in the list above. Input to the frame grabber is an interlaced NTSC 60 Hz or PAL 50 Hz image.

Having been digitized by the Analogue/Digital converters, the colour components are changed from RGB to HSI and stored in three 512×512 8-bit buffer memories. A fourth buffer of the same size is used for different overlay patterns.

Processing facilities provided with the associated software include operations on single or groups of pixels, convolutions (operations for noise removal, edge enhancement, etc.), producing and controlling overlaid graphics or text, and many others. To make processing easier, RGB may be converted to HSI (Hue–Saturation–Intensity) data. Processing then usually requires the examination of only one component instead of three. See Sezan and Tekalp (1990) for more about the restoration of image defects.

Applications of the Data Translation DT3852 frame grabber have been described by Jagadeesh and Ali (1993). The board was tested when plugged into a 486DX2 66MHz computer. Jagadeesh says that Data Translation have 'every reason to be proud of their board'. It can accept four interlaced or non-interinterlaced monochrome or colour inputs. The board has been used to analyse heart movements in a micro-organism. 'Many details of image acquisition, video set-up, and memory allocation are organized into well thought out, albeit complex, data structures,' say Jagadeesh and Ali. The board comes with data communication facilities running at 4.5 Mbytes per second. Figure 4.7 shows a Data Translation card being plugged in to a computer.

Loughborough Sound Images, Loughborough, Leics., UK, specialize in Digital Signal Processors for mathematically intensive tasks such as real time image processing. Between 1982 and 1992 their DSP boards, embodying the

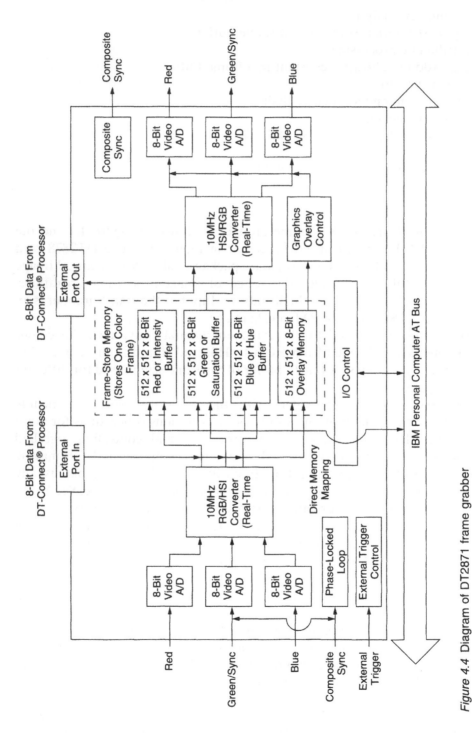

Figure 4.4 Diagram of DT2871 frame grabber
Source: Data Translation

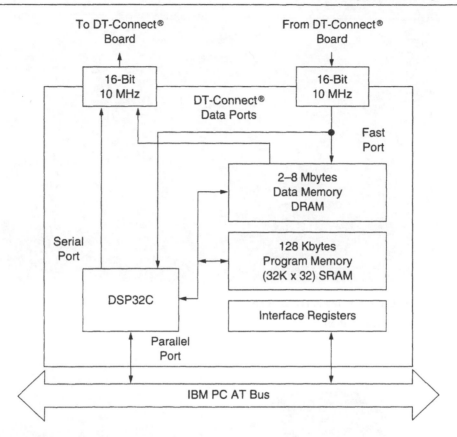

Figure 4.5 Diagram of DT2878

Source: Data Translation

Texas TMS320 series of processors, have incorporated the TMS32010 with 50K transistors and a power of 5 mips working at 20 MHz to the TMS320C90 with 500K transistors and a power of 40 mips working at 80 MHz. The card shown in Figure 4.8 embodies eight of these units providing a processing power of 400 mips.

APPLICATIONS

This advanced technology may be very impressive but what is its usefulness in multimedia applications? Data Translation's Global Lab image (GLI) software is devoted to enabling advanced specialized image processing and analysis, mainly in the medical area, to be carried out with its range of frame grabber hardware. In addition to the usual histogram, filter, and FFT operations it provides for low light, false colour, and image component separation and counting operations. Figure 4.9 shows the GLI software being used to collect shape, size, orientation, location, and average density data.

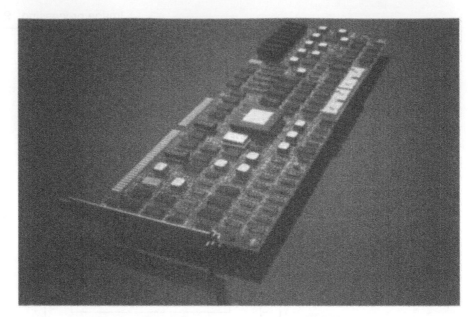

Figure 4.6 Data translation DT2878 card
Source: Data Translation

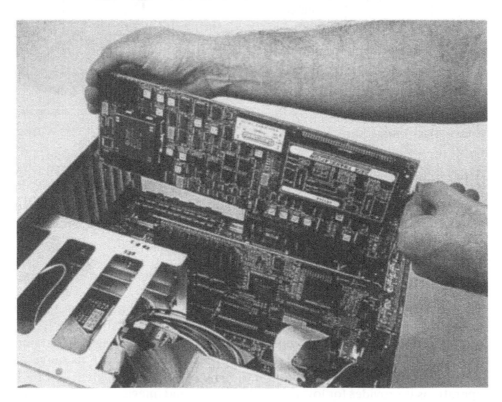

Figure 4.7 A data translation board being plugged into a computer
Source: Data Translation

Figure 4.8 The Loughborough Sound Images 8-unit TMS320C52 400 Mips DSP

Source: Loughborough Sound Images

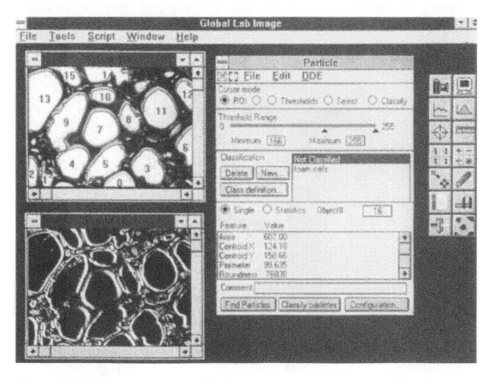

Figure 4.9 Data Translation's Global Lab

Source: Data Translation

Image processing may be used to enhance, clarify, de-blurr, or otherwise improve images. Good resolution and enhancement of thresholds can be useful for emphasizing image features.

Processing is being used to good effect on the IBM, Spanish Ministry of Culture, and Ramon Areces Foundation project to index and preserve the Archivo General de Indias collection (Anon. 1992c). The collection is stored in the Casa Lonja, Seville. The image archive consists of about nine million images.

Thresholding and filtering operations are particularly helpful. Neighbour-hood averaging and median filtering are described by Russ (1995) in chapter 3 of his book. In neighbourhood averaging, pixel brightness values in a large number of small regions of an image are added together and the average value is used in the construction of a new image. The size of the regions may be from 3×3 pixels up to 7×7. Another method based on colour thresholding is described in Russ's chapter 6. A colour in a particular region or regions is determined and the region is isolated by excluding all other colours.

Figure 4.10 shows how thresholding at level 5 throws up a character displayed with a range of only 13 halftones.

Figure 4.11 shows a scanned document before and after the removal of staining. The document is a letter from Columbus, dated 5 February 1505,

Figure 4.10 Character thresholding
Source: IBM

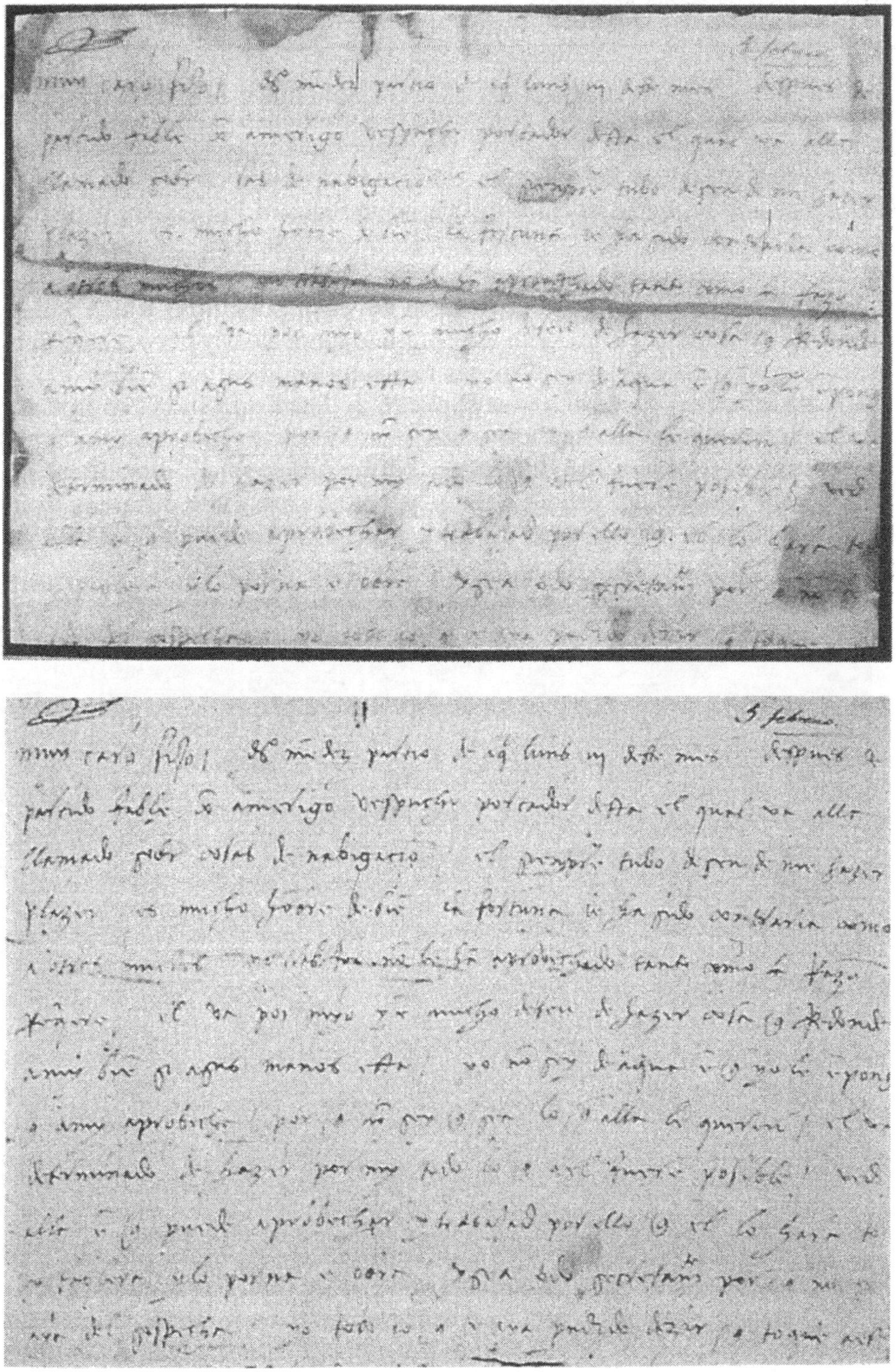

Figure 4.11 (a) and (b) Picture cleaning

Source: IBM

to his son Diego, concerning discussions with Amerigo Vespucci. Vespucci was a contractor who supplied provisions to Columbus's expeditions; he also sailed in an expedition to explore the Venezuelan coast. The continent was named after him following an exaggerated description of his travels. The stains and background markings shown in Figure 4.11 (a) were probably removed to produce 4.11 (b) by simple thresholding or by using more sophisticated methods as described by Russ, cited above.

The use of 'false colours' to distinguish between gradations which would otherwise be difficult to see, or to differentiate more clearly between objects in an image for classification purposes was mentioned earlier. Figure 4.12 is a striking example of a false colour application. The figure shows an agricultural area photographed from a satellite. Four identical versions of the same photograph are shown. The differences between them were introduced by false-colour processing; although the new colours are quite different from the actual colours, perception of the photos is changed and detail is revealed.

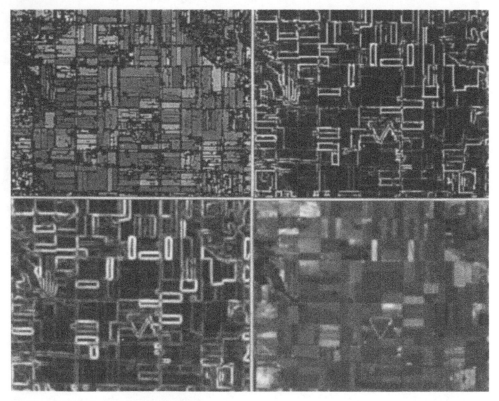

Figure 4.12 False-colour processing

Chapter 5

Multimedia computers and systems

MICROCOMPUTERS

The major parts of a microcomputer are the microprocessor Central Processing Unit (CPU), Main Memory (and associated Cache Memory), input/output controllers interconnected by multiple-line buses, and peripheral devices such as keyboard, disks, display, and printer.

To relieve the CPU processor of certain sub-tasks which are becoming increasingly complex, subsidiary semi-autonomous processors controlled by the CPU have been developed. Many current machines include at least one of them.

Microcomputer operations typically progress in a series of 'fetch–execute' cycles in a step-by-step manner, initiated by, say, a typed command from the operator to start a program. The operation continues until the required program sequence is completed. Appropriate buses, that is, interconnecting links, are switched to interconnect the appropriate units during data transfer and a program counter keeps track of each step. Bytes of data are moved into and out of memory to various part of the machine – say, to a port to which a peripheral device is connected. A port is the point of exit/entry for a peripheral unit. A peripheral will generate an interrupt signal to indicate readiness to communicate. In accordance with prearranged rules about handling priorities, the CPU will then transfer the data to the programmed address. Alternatively, a byte might have to be moved into the CPU to be added to another number stored in the arithmetic circuits as a result of an earlier instruction.

Since a series of CPU-controlled byte-by-byte transfers is relatively time-consuming, most microcomputers include a Direct Memory Access (DMA) routine – a fast method of exchanging data. The CPU temporarily surrenders control to the input/output controller.

The clock is a pulse-generator with its pulse repetition frequency accurately controlled by a crystal, so each pulse in a continuous train of pulses is spaced accurately from the next. Hundreds or thousands of circuits execute parts of an instruction, usually by switching to a different state when triggered together by a clock pulse. The next clock pulse triggers the circuits again, and so on, until the complete instruction is executed.

The major functions of a CPU are to receive, process, and deliver data under program control to and from addressed locations. It contains small stores called registers. The Instruction Register permanently stores the Instruction Set of codes for controlling a complete process such as adding, subtracting, or dividing data items and moving data from one addressed location to another. Other registers store memory addresses for data, sub-routines retrieved from memory, and temporary data in the course of being processed.

Processing takes place in the Arithmetic Logic Unit (ALU), which contains programmable circuits for arithmetical operations, registers for storing temporary results, and frequently used addresses. The clock, part of the CPU, triggers the succession of events in the ALU and its registers.

Advances and growth

Advances in CPUs have been mainly responsible for microcomputer performance improvements. Matching improvements in other parts have followed and the performance of complete microcomputers has steadily improved. Sometimes expected or actual advances in the technology of these other parts have been advances in their own right – for example, advances in display technology and Graphics Signal Processor (GSP) chips. Further advances are of course on the way.

IBM points out that 'Customers in 1981 were impressed by the original PC's 4.77 MHz 8088 processor, its 16 Kbytes of memory and 160 Kbytes of floppy diskette storage.' Referring to their PS/2s, the IBM note continues: 'Systems configured with the new 50 MHz card benchmark at over 57 times the performance of the original PC; they offer over 1000 times the memory capacity (64 Mbytes) and 10 thousand times the storage (1.6 Gbytes).'

According to International Data Corporation (1993) there were about 86 million business microcomputers installed worldwide in 1990, predicted to rise to 118 million in 1993. Of the 1993 total, it is estimated that 37 per cent would be connected to LANs. A higher percentage would be connected to LANs in the United States than in Europe; of the 1993 total, 43 million business machines were installed in the United States, of which 59 per cent were connected to LANs. Of the 26 million machines in Europe 48 per cent were LAN-connected.

SEMICONDUCTORS

Introduction

A transistor is a semi-conducting device invented by Bardeen, Brattain, and Shockley in 1947. They experimented with semi-conductive rectifiers similar to those used on the earliest 'crystal radio' receivers. The inventors duly received a Nobel Prize. Semiconductor versions of the valve wartime circuits developed by Alan Blumlein, F.C. Williams, and others soon appeared, but the transistor versions worked much faster, occupied far less space, and dissipated very little heat.

In 1968, Noyce and Moore, backed by Seymour Fairchild, a camera inventor, who provided them with $1.3 million of venture capital, were mainly responsible for founding the 'Silicon Valley' semiconductor industry around San José, California. Two microprocessor leaders emerged – Intel and Motorola. In the late 1970s Intel received a contract for the IBM PC which was launched in 1981. This established the 8088 16-bit processor as the *de facto* standard. In 1949 the EDSAC computer contained 3000 valves, consumed 15 Kilowatts of power, and occupied a special room. In 1989 a chip containing over 1 million transistors appeared (the 80860). It was infinitely more powerful than EDSAC and occupied a few square centimetres.

A transistor functions in many respects like a radio valve (US 'tube'). It amplifies a signal applied to a control electrode, or if a larger control signal is applied, the current through it may be cut off, so the transistor acts like a switch. But a transistor generates very little heat, is very reliable, and is very small. Improvements in technology have enabled its size to be further reduced and its other properties to be improved, particularly when it is used as a fast switch. Increases in switching speed have resulted in major advances in logic gates, the basic circuit elements in a microprocessor.

We usually assume that light or an electric current travel between two points almost instantaneously. An electric current takes about 1 nanosecond (1 ns = 1 thousand millionth of a second) to travel along a wire 30 cms long. During March 1990 IBM succeeded in running an experimental transistor at 75,000 MHz; each cycle then lasts for about 13 picoseconds (1 ps = 1 million millionth of a second). The semi-conducting layers in this transistor are 2 millionths of an inch thick. Clearly the effect of circuit connecting links is becoming increasingly important.

A transistor is formed from two types of semi-conducting materials – 'p-type' and 'n-type'. The atomic structure is such that the p-type material will accept electrons from n-type material. When such materials are deposited in layers, and the appropriate potentials are applied between them, the transistor, in conjunction with suitable circuits, may be used as an amplifier, or as a switch.

Until comparatively recently there were two major planar (layer-by-layer fabrication) technology products – bipolar and MOS (Metal Oxide Silicon). Bipolar transistors are made in p-n-p and n-p-n forms. In the MOS, sometimes called a Field Effect Transistor (FET), the field near the 'gate' electrode controls the conductivity of the silicon between two p-type regions.

The fastest working devices at present are bipolar Emitter Coupled Logic (ECL) circuits, which reduce switching delays to the absolute minimum. In spite of that, integrated circuits as used in computers are now predominantly MOS devices because they are easier to manufacture and consume less power.

The pioneering Intel 8080 processor, still in widespread use, uses N-MOS. N-MOS is also used in later microprocessors such as the Intel 8086 and 80286. In 1974, RCA manufactured the Complementary Metal Oxide Silicon (C-MOS) 1802 microprocessor and this technology was adopted by others as improved manufacturing techniques made production feasible. One compelling requirement – offered by C-MOS – was the need for low power consumption in small portable applications like digital watches. Also in C-MOS memories, data remain stored as long as power is applied, unlike memories using earlier transistors which require 'refreshing' every few milliseconds by a charging current.

The microscopic size of a transistor enables thousands, or hundreds of thousands, of them to be formed by chemical deposition methods in an extremely small space. The transistors may be interconnected to provide electronic circuits of extraordinary complexity and performance, the arrangement being manufactured as an Integrated Circuit (IC) or 'chip' – a very small container, with numerous metallic connections to the circuits contained within it.

From the 1950s onward, methods have been introduced for the mass production of interconnected transistors with other circuit elements on a small slice or wafer of silicon in order to provide more uniform and more reliable performance, with more components packed into a smaller space and faster switching speeds with less power and less heat dissipation. Each complete circuit element with its thousands of transistors is cut from the wafer and sealed into a small plastic container. Fine wire connections are made between the IC and pins protruding from it. The pins match mating sockets mounted on a printed circuit board.

Integrated circuits have enabled more and more information to be processed faster at lower cost. The name Very Large Scale Integration (VLSI) was the phrase used to describe the process of depositing large numbers of circuit elements on one chip – say 25,000 or more gates with dimensional control down to 0.5 micrometres. The ways to make faster processors are to increase the clock speed, which will increase power demands and heat dissipation, or to change the architecture, which is likely to result in a size increase, or to increase the number of transistors, which will increase size and heat dissipation.

Processor progress

The Intel 80286 commercially available microprocessor embodies 130,000 semiconductor elements on a square chip with sides of little more than 0.25 inches. The microprocessor used by Hewlett Packard as a CPU in their

32-bit microcomputer uses nearly half a million elements on an even smaller chip. An electron beam is used to make the masks required for its manufacture to enable conductors to be spaced 1 micrometre apart with 1/4 micrometre tolerance (1 micrometre = 10^{-6} metres = 0.000001 metres = 0.00004 inches (approx.)).

In 1986 it was suggested that later in the 1980s the target would probably be raised to 1 million transistors per chip. In 1987 the 32-bit Intel 80386 and Motorola's 68020 microprocessor were announced. There was a good deal of controversy about the speeds of these chips when used in micro-computers. The 386 was believed to be faster on average although the different characteristics of the machines in which they became available made chip comparisons difficult.

In April 1989 Motorola announced 1.2 million transistors on a single chip – the 32-bit 68040 (sometimes called Complex Instruction Set computer or CISC, competing with RISC described below), beating Intel's announcement of the 80486 by a few weeks. A chip containing over 1 million transistors had arrived on time as predicted. It offers four times the performance of the 68030, and is compatible with it and with earlier chips in the series.

The Intel 80486 – compatible with the earlier 286 and 386, and able to work with software designed for those processors – includes a maths co-processor, cache memory, and memory management on the same chip. It is designed to be clocked at 25 MHz (minimum), and to process 20 million instructions per second (Mips).

In 1990 TRW/Motorola announced that they could provide a chip – the CPUAX – containing 4 million transistors, capable of operating at 200 Million Floating Point Operations per Second (MFLOPS). There are a number of redundant cells in the chip's cellular design. If any cell fails, the chip repairs itself by connecting a replacement cell. In September 1989 Intel announced the 80960 specifically to handle input/output-intensive operations such as Local Area Network (LAN) control.

Since the arrival of the 80486, processor competition has further intensified. The arrival rate of new chips has reduced to months rather than years so the information provided in this chapter will soon be out of date. However, the date at which machines embodying new chips can be purchased is what matters to most users and that takes longer, so by the time you read this chapter, machines embodying chips mentioned below should soon become available.

The resources of the big manufacturers enable them to offer processors at prices which may or may not indicate the long-term winners – in so far as success is determined by competitive prices. For instance, Intel reduced the price of its slowest Pentium from $675 in April 1994 to $418 in July 1994. That price reflects company decisions about the amortization rate on the investment in the chip, the current cost of production, the policy of the company in regard to cutting the price when considering profits, and the competition between other products in its own range and between its own and other companies' products.

The newest processors include the 100 MHz Intel P5 or Pentium chip containing 3.1 million transistors. Its successors, the P6 and P7, will soon follow it. The DEC Alpha 21164 RISC processor contains 9.3 million transistors, will operate at up to 300 MHz and provides about 500 pins for connection to external circuits. It will execute 1.2 billion instructions per second.

RISC chips include caches, pipelining, and wider channel bandwidth, with a view to completing an instruction in one machine cycle instead of the many cycles usually required. RISC chips first appeared in a series of chips or chip sets, all using CMOS technology led by Inmos with the T800 and Novix with a specialized chip for image processing. The idea was taken up by IBM, using its own or Intel chips, and gathered pace when the Sun company, leading workstation supplier, introduced its Fujitsu-manufactured SPARC chip in 1987. RISC chips, like the 80860, are not compatible with the 286/386/486 series because they are primarily designed for use in workstations with the UNIX operating system.

Speed and its measurement: benchmarks

In general, semiconductor speed is inversely proportional to element size. It has been said that minimum size is somewhere between 0.5 and 0.1 micron spacing between circuit elements, at which point further developments in optical lithography (the basis for design layouts) would not be possible.

The number of transistors produced doubles every year. In each year more transistors are made than were made in all the previous years put together so the industry has to find additional markets each year as large as the sum of all the previous markets. To do it, prices have to fall. They have – by a million times. Offsetting that fall to some degree is the unit price for manufacturing equipment such as a lithography machine or an evaporator, which used to be about $12,000. Unit prices are now about $55 million.

Machines which handle multimedia data must do so at the speed required by the machine user. In general, a user issues a command such as 'display a motion video clip', and expects to start seeing the clip within a few seconds. In many cases the command which provides the end-result may be preceded by a sequence of commands such as 'display indexing ikons of the available motion video clips'; 'move video clip 507 to the time line'; 'move sound clip 918 to the end'; 'run clip 507 with sound clip 918 together on display and loudspeaker' (end-result).

In this and many other similar cases the volumes of data which must be handled to provide the end-result are very large. In a sequence of commands where a result simply indicates that the machine is ready for the next command, a result should ideally be available almost instantaneously. In cases where the user must think before issuing the next command, a few seconds or longer between command and execution is acceptable. The volume of data to be processed in response to a command may be enormous compared with similar processing two or three years ago.

Some of today's software packages are well ahead of the capability of the usual hardware to deliver results in an acceptable time. A user must know how long the software/hardware will take to complete a given process – it could be unacceptably slow. Clearly the value of a system which takes five minutes to complete a common task must be greater than one which performs the same task in five seconds. However, a supplier cannot be expected to know the duration of all possible combinations of hardware, software, and tasks, so elapsed time is rarely specified. Benchmarks providing general indications of speed for common operations would be very useful.

Considerable efforts have been made to measure and express speeds, primarily for the purpose of comparing the performance of one system with another. 'Benchmarks' have been defined but in spite of that: 'The only true evaluation of performance is to actually run the applications which you intend to use in the environment which you intend to use them with the data that you will be handling,' says Ben Smith, the technical editor of *Byte* magazine.

Measurement problems lead to arguments between manufacturers about speed. DEC argued that IBM's claim for its 9377/90 speed was three times more optimistic than DEC's own measurements. Borland claimed that its Paradox 4.0 database outperformed the supposed fastest PC database – FoxPro 2.0.

Megaflops, or Mflops – Millions of Floating Point Operations per second – has a majestic ring to it, and provides an idea of the capabilities of a large machine. A procedure for measuring the CPU's floating point performance in Mflops is called Linpack. Mips – millions of instructions per second – a measure of the CPU's ability to process integers (whole numbers) – is sometimes used with the DEC VAX 11/780, rated at '1 Mips' as a reference point.

Among the many benchmarks of the past, now largely discarded, are the Dhrystone, a measure of integer performance expressed in Dhrystones/sec or Mips, and the Whetstone, an NPL test to measure floating point performance. For example, the original PC's performance was stated to be 400 Dhrystones/sec, the PS/2 80 3707, and the Acorn Archimedes 4900.

In 1989 a consortium of manufacturers called the Standard Performance Evaluation Corporation developed the SPEC suite of benchmarks (Sharp and Bacon 1994). This measure now seems to have become generally used, particularly SPECfp92 as a measure of the speed and throughput of technical or scientific programmes, and SPECint92 for commercial and business applications.

Egal Juliussen, writing in *IEEE Spectrum*, April 1994, states that workstations using DEC Alpha processors are fastest with SPECint92/SPECfp92 values of 85/100, followed by PA-RISC (Precision Architecture – Reduced Instruction Set, e.g. Hewlett Packard) at SPEC 60/80, Power PC at 50/80, RS/6000 at 50/80 and 66 MHz Pentium at 60/55.

A list of processors with their Spec data is given in Table 5.1.

Table 5.1 Processor performance data

Type	SPECint92	SPECfp92	Processor clock		No. trans
Intel Pentium 100	100	80.8	100	MHz	3.1M
AMD K5	?	?	100/150	MHz	4.1M
Sun UltraSPARC	250/300	?	200	MHZ	?
Apple/IBM/Motorola Power PC620	225	300	133	MHz	7M
Mips T5	250	350	200	MHz	6M
Alpha 21164	300	500	266/300	MHz	9.3M

In October 1994 the author attended a session arranged by Times Graphics Systems (Kendall Avenue, London, W3) to assess an Apple 8100/80, fitted with VideoVision boards, 32 Mbytes of RAM, and a 2-Gbyte disk, running Premiere multimedia authoring software. Full-screen PAL motion video previously recorded on the disk was played back, providing pictures of very good quality. The speed of the system is entirely adequate for operations on motion video clips. This kind of performance is extraordinary considering the struggle there has been until now to display high-quality full-screen motion video. This subjective judgement on one application is a far cry from a general performance assessment, which is what this section is about. From recent comments about Power Macs we may conclude that it's too early to make a useful general assessment.

According to Thompson's tests on Apple Power Macs reported in *Byte*, April 1994, the 8100/80 and 6100/60 performance was well below the Apple Quadra AV. Thompson used a performance measure called Byte's benchmarks, not SPEC. The Power Macs performed fairly well when compared with some powerful RISC machines on 'Spreadsheet and word processing indexes under emulation'. But Thompson included so many 'buts' about emulation testing, absence of caches, etc., which weighed against the Macs, that these tests are unconvincing.

Comparisons should be made on a level playing field. Macs tested using emulation rather than native code are disadvantaged. Sharp and Bacon (1994) write about benchmarks and SPEC in particular. They include so many caveats that Ben Smith's remarks, quoted earlier, seem to be applicable. Sharp and Bacon point out that it would be disastrous to replace large machines optimized for transaction processing with workstations having a higher SPEC rating. CPU performance is less important than input/output capacity for some operations, the display adaptor of a PC 'may have most effect on the user's perception of performance', and so on. 'Seemingly authoritative measurements such as SPEC values are seductively tempting.'

The speed of the CPU is a necessary but insufficient ingredient among the factors which make a microcomputer work faster. The frequency at which the clock in a microprocessor operates dictates the speed at which a micro-computer will execute instructions but this is far from being the only factor which affects speed. Other factors which affect speed include:

Processor architecture

RISC architecture reduces the number of cycles per instruction and the need for memory accesses since some instructions can be executed by register-to-register communication only. In 1987 Acorn announced the Archimedes machine using its own 32-bit RISC chip. The machine outperformed many competitive machines.

Word lengths

In the last few years word lengths have become longer, leading to faster speeds for arithmetical processing, a near doubling of speed for some graphics operations, and the ability to address the very large memories now being used for video and image applications. Integer registers in 1994 are now usually 32-bit, whereas a few years ago they were 16-bit. A few machines have already moved on to 64-bit words.

Wait states

Wait states are non-operational clock periods, often necessary to accommodate relatively slow memories. Faster memories are gradually reducing them.

Cache memories

Large, fast cache memories can considerably increase processing speeds. The data most likely to be needed next are fetched from main memory into cache. The objective is to obtain a high 'hit rate' – i.e. to make as many accesses to cache and as few to main memory as possible. A '92 per cent hit rate', for instance, means that the design of the cache is such that on average only for 8 per cent of the time must it fetch data from main memory because it does not contain those data within itself.

Pipelining

Pipelining is a technique for overlapping operations normally taking place at different times, or to arrange for the simultaneous occurrence of operations otherwise occurring in successive clock cycles.

Co-processors

Co-processors, some of which are equal in power to the main processor (CPU), supplement the capability of the CPU by handling floating point arithmetic, database management, graphics, etc. These tasks would otherwise slow down CPU operations. Digital Signal Processors which are largely autonomous computers in their own right, are often used in multimedia machines for graphics processing.

Memory size

Larger memories provide more space for large files such as image files, with consequently fewer disk accesses.

Disk drive interface

The data transfer rate depends on the type of interface, type ST506 being the slowest, through SCSI, ESDI, to SMD, which is the fastest.

Data transfer method

Differences between the way memory is handled by the processor affect the transfer rate of files, particularly large files.

Semiconductor memories

There are several types of memory for different applications. A RAM usually consists of a large number of transistors, each charging or discharging an associated capacitor to store one bit. Dynamic RAMs (DRAMs), widely used for main memory, are cheap but 'volatile' – the capacitor charge leaks away so they need periodic 'refreshment'. CMOS Static RAMs (SRAMs) require less power, are non-volatile, but are more expensive. Memory speeds have lagged behind CPU speeds with the result that the CPU has had to wait until memory transfers have been completed. In June 1994 IBM announced 1 Mbyte SRAMs with an access time of 8–12 ns planned for general availability at the end of the year.

DRAMs are very widely used and US manufacturers abandoned the market in the mid-1980s when the Japanese jumped to 256 Kbit and then to 1 Mbit DRAM mass production with substantial price cutting. One company, Toshiba, makes one third of the world's consumption.

Other types in major use include Erasable Programmable Read Only Memories (EPROM), erasable by exposure to ultraviolet light for 20 minutes, and Electrically Erasable PROMs (EEPROM). These memories are used to retain data programmed into them ready for use when the equipment is switched on – for instance, for 'Booting', that is, to load sufficient software from disk to make a computer ready to use.

In 1989 a new kind of memory resembling an EPROM called a flash memory appeared. A flash memory may displace EPROMs, EEPROMs, or SRAMs. Flash memories offer storage which does not need an applied voltage (as do SRAMs) to retain data, they may be partially or completely reprogrammed within the host machine (EPROMs must be removed to be erased by 20 minutes UV exposure), and they cost much less and are smaller than EEPROMs (although they cannot be reprogrammed at the individual byte level). One application is as a 'solid state disk' on portable computers – as in the Psion Mc400 machine.

Other semiconductor types and applications

The size of the market for chips is now so large that it has been feasible to progress from the processor, through the processor plus co-processor stage, to the 'embedded' processor. A sufficient number of machines is required for special applications to justify a purpose-designed but mass-produced chip 'embedded' to handle just that one application.

Electrons move faster through a Gallium Arsenide (GaAs) crystal lattice than they do through silicon and GaAs transistors will operate at up to four times faster than the fastest silicon devices. Several manufacturers can now supply relatively expensive GaAs gate arrays for use when very high speed outweighs price considerations. GaAs devices operate at lower voltages and lower powers than silicon – up to five times less power. They will switch at much higher speeds, and will work over a wider range of temperatures. A GaAs circuit has the theoretical potential of being clocked at about 8000 million times per second (8 GHz), compared to about 200 MHz for silicon circuits. In April 1993 it was discovered that a gallium–sulphur compound can be used to add a layer to GaAs devices which increases their performance by at least six times. The process can be accomplished with little increase in production costs.

A transputer is a semiconductor device manufactured by an English (or more correctly ex-English when it was sold to the French company SGS-Thomson in 1989 for about £800 million) company called INMOS, founded in 1978, mainly on government money. Its first products appeared in 1984. A present generation transputer is a chip containing a CPU, some memory, a scheduler for changing on-chip links, and four serial communication channels. The arrangement is designed for the implementation of Communication Sequential Processes (CSP), in which one or more transputers run a number of sequential programs concurrently, exchanging messages over the communication channels, thereby providing parallel computing.

The H1 transputer embodies 8 channels using 1 micrometre spacing on the chip. It will process at over 100 million instructions per second. The transputer was designed for multiple-transputer parallel processing and in this form provides the cheapest, fastest form of ready-made parallel processing available. A company called Parsys sold machines working at 400 Mflops back in 1988.

An Application Specific Integrated Circuit (ASIC) is a chip designed for a specific application, sometimes available as a standard take-it-or-leave-it product, but usually made in small quantities for people who cannot get a standard chip for the job in hand and cannot justify the costs, or require the quantities, associated with tooling up for mass production.

In the US a semi-standard ASIC gate array would cost about $15,000 to modify for a specific purpose, and somewhat less to produce the first 1000 items. The total time for the job would be a few months.

A chip completely purpose-made from scratch would cost at least $250,000 to develop, would take more than a year, and would require a production run of an least 75,000 to be worth doing. Moreover, the 1994 cost of building the plant for chip manufacture is about $1 billion.

MULTIMEDIA COMPUTERS

Introduction

'Hypertext', described later in this chapter, has been described as a medium to support the writing process and to provide readers with search strategies and browsing facilities unavailable in 'linear text'. The word was coined by Ted Nelson (1981) and hypertext was mainly confined to academe. Later versions of Apple's Hypercard hypertext software include sound and images, so the word 'Hypermedia' became more applicable. More recently 'hyperlinks', an important part of hypermedia, have become the means of automatically connecting to different files in the Internet's World Wide Web system.

'Desktop publishing' – preparing pages for publication using inexpensive equipment – took off from about 1985 onwards. By then the development and production of low-cost component units using complex circuit semiconductor chips had advanced to the stage when entirely new microcomputer-based applications could be introduced.

Ongoing developments in video technology and CD data storage extended the possibilities from page presentation into sophisticated visual presentations. The processing and presentation of information in two or more media – multimedia – arrived in about 1988 and methods of adding video and motion video were developed soon afterwards.

In computer systems, images are represented as an array of picture elements (pixels). Until they are translated for display on the CRT, colours are represented by bit codes. Consequently a number of imaging requirements require consideration.

- Incoming data must be digitized if they are to be processed by the computer user;
- If not digitized and not processed, data must be synchronized so that, combined with any internally generated data, they may be viewed as a stable display;
- Considerable processing power must be available to move very large numbers of bits if image changes produced by the user's processing and editing commands are to be viewed without delay;
- A monitor with appropriate resolution, scanning rate, and colour capabilities must be used for viewing the work. The presentation may be edited and recorded for repeat performances.

Motion video

Although the Mac II has been superseded by improved machines, it is still in wide use. The main video and motion video functions which can be handled using a Mac II or more recent machines having 4–8 Mbytes of RAM, at least 80 Mbytes of disk, a colour monitor, and a variety of third-party plug-in boards and software are to:

- Capture and digitize video frame-by-frame with a 'frame grabber', and output frames with added animation frame-by-frame under Hypercard control;
- Replace video data in a given colour (the 'key' colour) with a different set of video data if you want to add special effects;
- Import TV-standard NTSC or PAL motion video from a Hypercard-controlled videodisk player or a camera, and display it in real time in a window on the Mac's screen or on a separate monitor. A Mac II system used not to be fast enough to allow full-screen colour at TV resolution;
- To overcome speed constraints connect the monitor directly to the video source, such as a videodisk player, for the direct full-screen colour TV resolution display of motion video, and control the videodisk from Hypercards to display a wanted picture; present other material, for instance text, synchronized with a picture on the Mac's screen;
- Overlay and synchronize ('Genlock') Mac text and graphics non-interlaced picture data with the imported interlaced composite TV signals (which contains all the synchronizing and picture data within the signal); record the composited pictures in NTSC or PAL format on VHS, or better S-VHS videotape for presentations elsewhere;
- Use the tape for mastering videodisks for interactive presentations. The

random access seek time for Level 3 Laservision-type Constant Angular Velocity (CAV) videodisk players with Hypercard control via an RS232 connector, ranges from 3 seconds, to 0.5 seconds for more expensive models.

A separate good quality monitor is desirable for these operations and essential for some of them. Monitors, or more particularly the CRTs inside them, continue to improve. Those currently most popular are probably the 14" and 17" (screen diagonal) 640×480 pixel (IBM VGA resolution) monitors. The colour tube alone costs about $300. By the time LCD display panels get to this stage, CRTs will probably have been improved to 1000×1000 pixels and will cost $100, so the CRT will be around for some years yet (see chapter 2).

The line-scanning speed of Mac II's normal 640×480 display is fixed but third-party video adaptors offer alternatives, such as rates between 800×560 for the 37" Mitsubishi monitor (at £6000), up to 1365×1024 pixels. Scanning speeds and frame rates are likely to be different in the various adaptors available. An auto-tracking monitor, where the scanning rate automatically synchronizes, is the best choice. Typical ranges are 30–57 KHz horizontal and 40–75 Hz vertical. Another desirable feature in monitors is the capability of running from NTSC or PAL composite video signals, RGB analog, or RGB TTL. With these alternatives the monitor should cope with almost any requirement.

Motion video, usually in either NTSC or European PAL analogue form, may be imported from TV receivers, cameras, videotape, or videodisks. Data are displayed on a TV CRT by smooth pixel-to-pixel changes of brightness and colour in direct proportion to the light reflected from the original objects. The NTSC system uses 525 scanning lines per frame repeating 30 times per second. PAL uses 625 lines repeating 25 times per second. Both systems use interlaced scanning in which the frame is divided into a field of odd-numbered lines followed by a field of even-numbered lines, providing 60 and 50 fields per second respectively, reducing the flicker, which would otherwise be noticeable.

Computers, or boards plugged into them, able to accept interlaced TV signals, include circuits for producing synchronized non-interlaced frames from frames containing interlaced fields.

Hypertext

The word 'hypertext' was coined by Ted Nelson and discussed in his privately published 1981 book *Literary Machines*. It was said that 'from the writer's point of view, hypertext systems are the next generation of word processing' and 'from the reader's point of view hypertext systems are a new generation of database management'.

Hypertext became widely known in the late 1980s because Apple supplied a free copy of Hypercard software with its machines. Academics latched on to it as it encouraged a breakaway from linear text and encouraged browsing by linking related parts of a document without the need for footnotes or 'see' references. One curious outcome was that certain problems associated with indexing, described as 'navigating' to evade the boredom engendered by that word, could result in a user getting lost in a network of interlinked items.

Hypertext was later pressed into service as a convenient form of multi-media control for the presentation of text, sound, music, voice, graphics, pictures, animation, or motion video. Simple programs using English words may be used. Hypertalk Script writing, composition in a standard form, but consisting of English words and phrases arranged and used in order to create a command protocol, requires a longer learning commitment but is still relatively easy.

Multimedia interest in Hypercard centres on access to third-party software. A command is a message containing a keyword which will cause the script for an object containing that keyword to be executed. A function is some kind of instruction. External Commands (XCMD) cause a 'resource', or code module, written in Pascal or Assembly language, to be executed by a command message. An XCMD may be used to control driver inter-operable software associated with an external device such as a videodisk player.

A resource has to be written by a programmer, but when Hypercard-compatible devices and software or special-purpose software are used, this is not necessary because the software includes ready-made resource code and driver, and the XCMD can be installed in a Hypercard stack. The user may then create a button, labelled appropriately, to execute a script containing the XCMD.

Client-server

The phrase 'client-server' occurs all the time in the multimedia world. It is frequently used in chapter 8 because it is the 'servers' which store and distribute the very large quantities of data which are transported in distributed telecommunications systems.

Client-server computing started when personal computers (that is 'PCs', 'Macs', or any other type of personal computer) became almost as powerful as the mainframes used a few years earlier and when LANs came into use. The 'clients' – that is, the personal computers, each with its user, contain a variety of software, particularly the software for handling the user's applications; it has become much more than a 'dumb terminal'. Many of the functions previously performed by the mainframe are now performed by the client computer. The LAN was used for retrieving data from the 'server' connected to it, as well as for client-to-client communication. The server is a computer which manages a store of data maintained for the benefit of clients, dispatching it to a client when requested.

A client-server arrangement is now widely used for corporate and Internet purposes. A company maintains files of data in its server for the use of its clients – i.e. company employees with LAN-connected personal computers. Internet hosts act as servers with their clients using software designed to connect a client to a host, search its data, and download the results.

MULTIMEDIA PROGRESS

Figure 5.1 shows a multimedia system conceived in 1977, although the word had not yet been invented, or perhaps it was an early attempt at Virtual Reality. It was called a Spatial Data Management System (SDMS) and was used for research and experiments at the Massachusetts Institute for Technology (Bolt 1977). The user sat in a special chair and used joysticks to control a back-projected picture, listening through multiple loudspeakers.

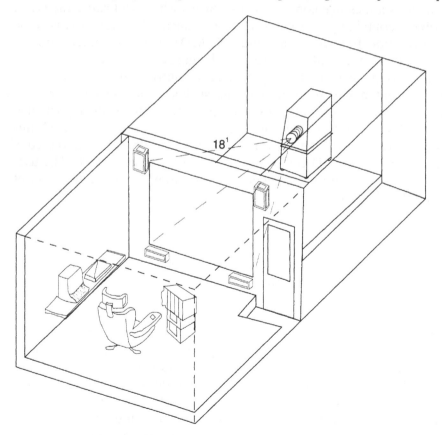

Figure 5.1 The MIT multimedia room
Source: AEC

Many years later an increasing number of CD-ROM disks began to appear on the market. CD-ROMs have become widely used vehicles for software delivery and for storing 'publications'; CD-ROM drives are now included with multimedia machines.

A multimedia PC is an ordinary 386/486 PC with a high-resolution colour display, a sound card, a CD-ROM drive, and a sufficiently large amount of RAM and hard disk memory, as specified later in this chapter. The first addition needed to convert a PC into a multimedia PC is a sound card. There are a number of different types on the market today, but the most widely used, compatible with most CD-ROM multimedia disks, is probably the Sound Blaster from Creative Labs. This card will enable the system to generate high-quality music and sound effects, as well as offering a digitized voice channel and a text-to-speech synthesizer. Output is of FM quality with up to 11 voices. The output power of 4 watts per channel is sufficient to run loudspeakers.

The next requirement in a multimedia system is a suitable user interface program. Here the choice is simple since the most suitable product if you have a PC is Windows 3.1. This version is a considerable advance on version 3.0 and includes support for both CD-ROM drives and sound cards. The interface is compatible with many of the disk products from CD-ROM publishers.

Until 1991 the equipment needed to provide a fully fledged multimedia show was untidy and could be expensive. For example, it might have included a Mac II with additional boards, CD-ROM player, videodisk player, videotape player, external sound amplifier, and loudspeakers, with assorted software, interconnecting cables, and the space to accommodate it all. That was the penalty for using a cobbled-together rather than a purpose-designed solution, although most of the individual units were already being mass-produced. Such a multimedia platform would look something like the equipment shown in Figure 5.2.

The outlook for multimedia changed in 1991/92 when it started to move out of the new toy syndrome into an era of useful applications. Purpose-designed equipment started to appear in anticipation of a large enough market to recover costs, as opposed to an emerging market coverable with cobbled-together equipment already in production. The industry became convinced that the market warranted the manufacture of both 'Up-Grade' kits to convert a micro into a Multimedia PC (MPC), as described later, and purpose-designed multitimedia system. Up-grades and complete systems are usually supplied with a range of software, authorware, and sounds library, with several CD-ROM titles such as *Grolier's Encyclopedia*, *Microsoft Bookshelf*, *Sherlock Holmes*, etc. included in the price. Current activities by IBM and Apple indicate that multimedia is now regarded as serious business and optimistic growth forecasts (see chapter 1) tell the industry what it wants to hear.

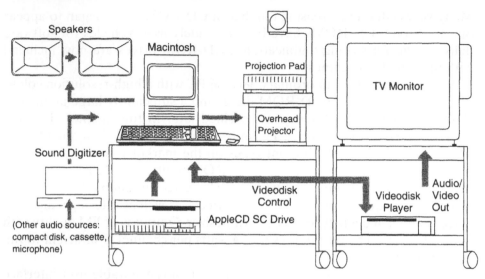

Figure 5.2 A pre-1992 multimedia platform

Source: AEC

MULTIMEDIA PLATFORMS AND THEIR SOFTWARE

Apple multimedia systems

The Apple Macintosh microcomputer, introduced in 1984, was noted mainly for its high-resolution 512 × 384 pixel screen and excellent graphic user interface. It had an 8 MHz processor, 16/24-bit data path/bus, 400K floppy drive and 128K memory. Its integrated design and lack of slots for cards provided little scope for third-party developers. The Mac II, which came out in 1987, became one of the leading machines for multimedia applications. In 1990 Apple introduced the Mac IIfx with a 40 Mhz 68030 processor and 68882 co-processor, cache memory, and three auxiliary processors. This made the machine up to four times faster than the improved Mac II (the Mac IIx). The US Mac IIfx price was originally $12,000 – about £7500. An equivalent Apple machine today costs very much less.

Apple also introduced the 20 Million Instructions Per Second (MIPS) 8/24 GC display card, with a 30 MHz RISC processor on board, providing 8-bit colour at 640 × 480 pixels, or 8-bit (256 level) grey scale at 1152 × 870 pixels. The price was about $2000.

A major reason why the Mac II became one of the multimedia leaders was that its innovative simple user interface, descended from the Xerox Star, was now accompanied by the slots which enable third-party suppliers to offer supplementary hardware. A huge range of add-on hardware and software became available. As someone said in regard to multimedia applications: 'The Mac is doing what it does best – providing a consistent user interface, seamless data exchange, and gorgeous 24-bit colour graphics.' According to Dataquest, in 1995 Apple was the world leader for multimedia machines with 23 per cent of the market.

In 1992 Apple reorganized its range to consist of the Classic, Powerbook, the powerful Quadra, and the improved Macintosh II models. The Quadra 840AV runs on a 40 MHz MC68040 chip. The Quadra includes SCSI and Nubus ports, an Ethernet adaptor, and a video system incorporating a VRAM. It uses dedicated I/O processors and provides mono and stereo output. A 4 Mbyte RAM is expandable up to 128 Mbytes, and a 230 Mbyte hard disk drive is provided. The Quadra 840AV's specification includes:

68040 40 MHz processor
3210 66 MHz Digital Signal Processor (DSP)
8 MByte RAM expandable to 128 Mbyte
1 MByte Video RAM (VRAM) expandable to 2 Mbyte
230 Mbyte hard disk

In 1993 there were further major changes and more price reductions. Apple's machines are now competitive and their relatively high cost has virtually disappeared as a reason for not buying one. The Quadra is particularly suitable for business and multimedia use. The Quadra 840AV model, AV meaning 'Audio Visual', sells in the UK for around £2000 (December 1993).

A 21" colour monitor would cost £2500 and a keyboard £145. A Cannon colour laser printer/copier/scanner would cost about £5500 including software. A special disk array for motion video with the interface would cost about £3000. Application software to mount multimedia presentations could cost another £1500. An associated Power CD-ROM drive will play CD-ROM, photo-CD, and audio-CD disks. Today's prices are much lower.

When plugged into a television receiver, photo-CD 35 mm colour photographs may be viewed. The drive with SCSI cable costs about £365. Other boards may be needed, as discussed below, so a very comprehensive 1993-technology multimedia system could cost £10,000 or more, while a system adequate for many purposes would cost about £3000.

The Quadra 840AV integrates telephone, modem, and fax into a single desktop system. It also includes Apple's new speech recognition system known as Casper. The system needs to be trained and includes a 60,000 word dictionary. The recognition software has been compiled with reference to a large number of speakers with various regional accents from all parts of the United States. Appropriate dictionaries will be needed for foreign countries which will require a similar compilation effort. Text-to-speech software for translating text into synthesized speech is included. The effectiveness of speech software is notoriously difficult to access. Its applications range from

the management of routine commands to conversational dictation. This
system will operate somewhere between these extremes, requiring subjective judgement on whether it will handle, reasonably effortlessly, the application the user has in mind.

The Apple Quadra 840AV, running System 7.0 with Quicktime software,
16 Mbytes of memory, and a 1 Gbyte disk, received *Byte* magazine's award
of excellence in January 1994 as 'the most fully featured personal computer
ever made . . . the premier computer for multimedia authors'. The UK price
was then £3575. The machine will support 16-bit colour on a 21" 1152 × 870
pixel monitor. It has reduced the gap between 'standard' and 'special' hardware for managing still television pictures and motion TV. The Quadra will
accept PAL or NTSC signals from, say, a video camera. The machine comes
with system 7.0 and Quicktime software and live video can be dragged to a
re-sizable window anywhere on the screen. A video clip to be captured
and run as a Quicktime movie provides a window of about 4" × 3" at 320 ×
240 pixels in colour.

The standard arrangement just described will record motion video pictures
of limited size and resolution, but adequate for many purposes at about
1.5 Mbytes per second, with storage on the 500 or 1000 Mbyte disk provided
with the system. Video will rapidly fill storage space.

In order to run and record a significant length of 24-bit colour motion
video in PAL format, full screen, some extras are still needed like an extra
plug-in board and a faster disk with improved compression software. The
disk will be a disk-array with JPEG compression software, delivering data
under these conditions, at about 100 Mbytes per minute. Thus a 1 Gbyte
disk system will provide storage for 10 minutes of video, said to be 'as good
as VHS reproduction', although the JPEG compression ratio must be fairly
high. A special card and SCSI/2 interface are needed. A user may require
other peripheral units to handle inputs and outputs to make the most of its
performance.

Quicktime software

Quicktime software is included with the Quadra. It is an extension of the
Apple 7.0 operating system originally used on Apple Mac microcomputers,
introduced to handle animation and video including motion video with
sound. It enables a picture or motion video to be displayed in a window on
any Mac with a 68020 or later processor running system 7, preferably with
at least 4 Mbytes of memory. Quicktime has four major components –
system software, file formats, compression, and interface with utilities. Its
design is such that it will support many different kinds of data. Routines in
the 'movie toolbox' control the formation of movie tracks as described
below. Quicktime includes an Image Compression Manager (ICM) which
controls the opening and closing of different kinds of image compression

algorithms – for example, JPEG. It also includes a Component Manager to provide the user with a service to manage data of various kinds which constitute the components for a movie. The Sound Manager is not included in Quicktime but it is available for sound control.

Soon after it was introduced in 1991 a number of suppliers advertised cards for Macs running Quicktime. For example, a board may be used to capture live video and convert it into Quicktime format, enabling a 'movie' to be edited and merged. A board of this type from VideoSpigot will continuously process NTSC or PAL motion video into 24-bit colour digital data.

A Quicktime 'movie' file may contain sound, video, or animation in any combination stored on appropriate media. Data from the media are controlled by signals from separate tracks which are run together and synchronized. Additional boards may be needed for capturing and digitizing video or audio. The movie file may be assembled and edited in order to create a complete multimedia presentation using editing software such as Adobe's Premiere (see chapter 6). When Quicktime is associated with Premiere software (see chapter 6), the user is presented with a display for assembling a multimedia programme showing several horizontal time-calibrated tracks (to specify the duration of component sections of the movie), each of which displays a series of user-selected miniature digitized video frames or representations of audio sequences. Candidate video or audio frames displayed on other areas of the screen may be dragged into the correct time-sequence position on a track. Various facilities for mixing, fading, alignment, superimposition, etc. are provided. With this system, frame-by-frame digitized video and sound frames, or motion video clips, may be imported, assuming that associated boards for data capture and compression management have been installed. Finally, the completed tracks for a movie may be viewed and stored ready for export on suitable media such as videotape for presentation purposes.

A Quicktime movie must have the necessary memory, disk, videotape, CD storage on hand ready to supply movie components, as they are called; pathways with the necessary bandwidth for transporting the data must be available. Compression is used to limit the number of bits of video data which must be moved.

High-quality full-screen colour motion video of PAL TV standard needs to be transmitted at a rate of over 200 Mbits/second (see chapter 2). One minute of such video would require 12 Gbits or 1.33 Mbytes of storage. Compression ratios must be an appropriate compromise for providing acceptable quality while requiring an acceptable amount of storage. Thumbnail and small-window images may be used to reduce the problems of bandwidth and storage.

Quicktime 7.0 was updated to Quicktime 7.5 in due course which was in turn updated to 7.5.1 embodying further improvements.

A new Apple operating system to be called Quicktime 8.0 or Copeland is under development. It includes the following features:

- Has 32-bit memory with an address space of 4 Gbytes with 1 Gbyte allocated for OS and buffers;
- Requires 8 Mbytes of memory and 40 Mbytes of disk inclusive of 20 Mbytes swap space;
- Embodies 'pre-emptive multitasking' which switches between tasks to provide sufficient time for each and isolates each program;
- Uses disk as virtual memory by switching parts of programs into disk, restoring them to memory when needed automatically;
- Includes rewrite of file systems and I/O and SCSI manager as native code which was previously performed as slower emulation;
- Increases drive partition size to 256 terabytes to accommodate very large multimedia files;
- Offers 'open transport' to cover major network protocols including Internet access;
- Has full complement of e-mail features.

It will include a number of improvements but will work with existing Mac software. When introduced it will be competing with Windows 95, Windows NT, and Warp/OS/2. The final Copeland system is due to be released in late 1996.

The latest Apple hardware

On 14 March 1994 the Power Mac 7700–66 was introduced in the UK. It uses a RISC processor and provides a general improvement in speed and performance of about three times compared with the Quadra 840AV. It comprises MPEG motion-video compression, 8 Mbytes of memory, and 500 Mbytes of disk at a price of £3000. Reduced memory/disk capacity is partially due to more effective compression.

By mid-1995 a series of five Power Macs had been released, starting with the 6200/75, a 75 MHz 603 processor, 8 Mbyte RAM, 500 Mbyte hard disk, CD drive, and 15" colour monitor, listed at £1475 in the UK (July 1995). The four other models embody the 601 processor. The UK price ranges from £1299 to £4477; as the price increases, more facilities and a higher performance are offered.

The specification for the top of the range 8100/110 is as follows:

CPU	Power PC 601
Speed	110 MHz
Floating Point Unit (co-processor)	Yes
Nubus slots	3
SIMM slots	8
RAM range	16–264 Mbytes

| Hard disk | 2 Gbytes |
| CD-ROM drive | Yes |

In July 1995 Apple launched its second-generation Power PC, the 9500, using the Motorola Power PC 604 chip and PCI Bus MacRISC architecture, claimed to provide double the speed of the 8100/100, and six times the speed of the Quadra 950. Currently running at up to 132 MHz, the processor's speed will be increased to 150 MHz later in the year. With this machine, Apple has moved away from its unique Nubus into the more widely used Peripheral Interconnect Bus and the PCI world in general. The quantity production of PCI boards by third-party manufacturers makes them available for less than half the price of Nubus boards. There are three machines in the range as at July 1995 – the 9500/120, /132, and /132 with video card. All models have quad speed CD-ROM drives and have Ethernet 10-base T connections. UK prices are in the range £4000–£5000.

These machines represent major changes in Apple's policy. The machines now look much more like competitive products and will be compatible with many of them.

Commodore Amiga

The Commodore Amiga microcomputer was noted for its colour before the Mac. It could also display video images from an external source synchronized to on-screen effects produced by its user ('genlocking'). Although it might be the first machine to include most of the features needed for multimedia, for several years it was eclipsed by Apple. In 1990 Commodore made a strong bid to catch up with a new machine – the Amiga 3000 – having a performance nearly matching the Mac II at half the price at the time (£3160 with 2 Mbyte memory, 40 Mbyte drive, £3610 with 100 Mbyte drive). The 3000 is a 32-bit machine with the same processors as the Mac IIfx – 68030 and 68881 co-processor – running at up to 25 MHz. The machine includes an enhancement of the Amiga special set of three controller chips which provide much of its multimedia capabilities. Memory is from 1 to 16 Mbytes, with internal hard disk up to 100 Mbytes. The screen displays a choice of 16 out of 4096 colours at 640 × 400 pixels. Colour selection includes a unique 'hold and modify' feature permitting 4096 colours to be displayed at one time with certain limitations. The chip arrangements, including a separate chip for graphics control, are one of the reasons why the machine acquired such a good reputation for video.

In August 1990 Commodore introduced what was arguably the first complete purpose-designed multimedia system, anticipating systems from other suppliers. The CDTV interactive graphics CD-ROM player/microcomputer was demonstrated at the November Computagraphics show at Alexandra Palace, London. Commodore expected numerous disk titles with

CD-I-like presentations, intending to make its mark well before CD-I got going. It was believed that CDTV 'user authoring' would soon catch on and that suppliers would produce ready-to-use entertainment disks, using conventional mastering processes. The machine includes a 64 Kbyte card memory slot, but no floppy disk drive. Unfortunately the CDTV was premature. Commodore's reading of the market was mistaken and the machine was withdrawn soon after its launch.

The company launched the Amiga A4000 in 1992 based on the Motorola 68040 processor and a new graphics chipset, providing a display of up to 1280×400 pixels with 256,000 colours from a 16.8M palette. It uses the 'AmigaDOS' operating system and a 'Cross DOS MS-DOS' file transfer utility for PC file exchange.

In 1994 the company got into difficulties and its US operations ceased. As at January 1995 a management buyout of Commodore UK was being attempted. Supposedly the A4000 can still be purchased in the UK. In fact, neither of Commodore's two distributors stock any. It is hoped that UK manufacturing will recommence this year.

IBM Ultimedia

The huge installed base for IBM PCs and compatibles encouraged other manufacturers to supply add-ons to provide machines with multimedia capabilities. For example, improved versions of VGA cards became available, sometimes almost establishing their own *de facto* standard (for instance, TIGA cards), to give a wide choice of improved colour and resolution. Add-on sound cards became available, again establishing their own *de facto* Standard (for example, Sound Blaster).

Microsoft's Windows, and later Multimedia Windows, became available providing a user interface similar to Apple's, if more difficult to operate. IBM itself came out with multimedia hardware and software for PS/2s which use an improved bus called Microchannel Architecture (MCA).

IBM introduced a range of PS/2-based 'Ultimedia' systems in 1992 with the top of the range Ultimedia M77 486DX2 model selling at $3355. The software is called Multimedia Presentation Manager (MMPM/2), an extension of IBM's OS/2 operating system. All models include 8 Mbytes of RAM, an SSCI 212 Mbyte hard-drive, MCA, and a Kodak Photo-CD/XA CD-ROM drive. Considerable attention is paid to sound quality – CD 32-bit over-sampling running at over 80 KHz is used (see chapter 11 under CD-DA). Action-Media II DVI boards using the i750 chip-set are available for Ultimedia models. They will play 30 frame per second 64×480 pixel motion video pictures in a $4" \times 5"$ window. An IBM PS/2 Ultimedia machine includes audio adaptor and microphone, internal speaker, CD-ROM/XA drive with CDs, tools, and application samples. Many Ultimedia tools are becoming available from a number of associated companies such as Macromedia,

Vision Imaging, and others. The tools offer authoring, creation, capture and editing facilities for providing video, audio, animation, music, etc.

IBM have also developed a number of Ultimedia units and software for their AS/400 series of machines. For example, the system/400 package enables application programmes to control video devices and windows.

In May 1993 IBM launched its PS/1 low-cost multimedia PC called the PS/1 Multimedia System. It includes a 386 processor, 85 Mbyte disk, Philips CD-ROM drive, and audio adaptor. It is suitable for playing family and educational CD-ROM disks, and will read Kodak photo-CD images.

Silicon Graphics

Silicon Graphics' arrival in the multimedia marketplace has been brought about by an extension of their range downwards from computers such as the Iris Indigo and the Indigo$_2$, designed for 3D graphics work. The basic Indy multimedia machine sells for about $5000 in the United States. The price includes 32 Mbytes of RAM but no disk. The emphasis on video applications, including videoconferencing, is evident from the digital video camera and microphone mounted on the top of the machine (Figure 5.3).

The Indy, at a relatively low price for what is included, is probably the

Figure 5.3 The Indy machine
Source: Silicon Graphics

fastest, most comprehensive microcomputer multimedia machine available at the time of writing. However, if extras – for example, CD-ROM and hard disk drives, 24-bit colour graphics, etc. – are added, the total price comes to over $20,000. The operating system is IRIX, based on AT&T's UNIX system, with X Windows and the Indigo Magic interface; the screen presentation includes the usual features to be found on Mac or PC/Windows interfaces. The Indigo Magic software controls the screen appearance and includes electronic mail. The basic specification includes:

Mips/NEC R4000PC RISC super-pipelining 64-bit 100 MHz CPU with cache module
32 Mbyte RAM optionally expandable to 256 Mbyte
$4 \times 256K \times 16$ VRAM
Video, audio, and graphics subsystems with special ASICs
Data bus transfer peak burst-mode rate at 267 Mbytes/sec (2136 Mbits/sec)
Indycam digital colour video camera
Optional extras: internal hard disk drive up to 1.05 Gbyte and 20 Mbyte floptical drive.

The sections of the machine – CPU, memory, input/output (including video), and graphics – are shown in Figure 5.4. Shaded sections are Application Specific Integrated Circuits (ASICs) made for the Indy. The CPU may be upgraded to include a 1 Mbyte secondary cache.

An instruction-cache is a small, fast memory, storing the data most likely to be required so that accesses to main memory are much reduced. When a secondary cache is added, it is likely to contain frequently used data moved into it from the main cache; the net result is still fewer accesses to main memory and much faster operation.

Pipelining means that the instruction stages (e.g. fetch, read, execute, memory) overlap, taking between one and two clock cycles instead of several. In super-pipelining, instruction stages proceed at one per cycle to provide still faster throughput. The small figures on the lines connecting to the buses indicate word sizes.

Data may be exchanged with external devices via the standard serial and parallel ports on the input/output section, or via the Ethernet, ISDN, SCSI peripherals and stereo digital audio ports. Digital camera video, NTSC or PAL composite analogue or S-video analogue video sources are connected via the video subsystem.

The Iris Showcase package provides for the management of interactive multimedia presentations using text, raster images, digital audio, and live video. The presentation may be viewed on the screen or edited for transfer to videotape. Also 24-bit colour Display Postscript is included so that there is little delay in displaying special fonts or artistic designs.

The graphics subsystem is designed to be used with the Iris Graphics Library for polygon processing with clipping, lighting, rendering, and Gouraud shading with a 24-bit colour 1280×1024 pixel display.

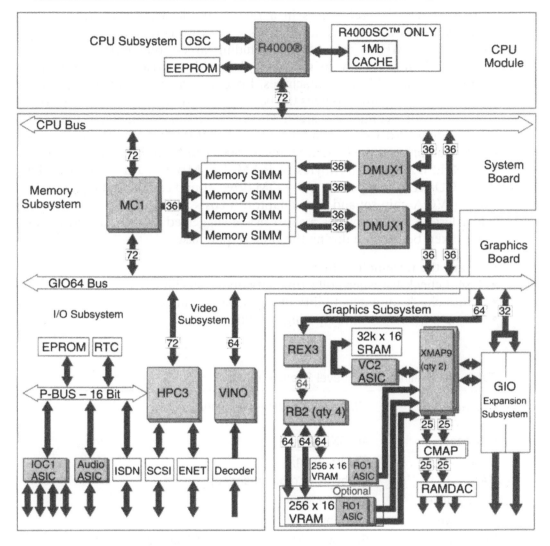

Figure 5.4 Diagram of the Indy machine

Source: Silicon Graphics

MULTIMEDIA PERSONAL COMPUTERS (MPCS)

A new generation of machines, called MPCs (Multimedia Personal Computers) by the Multimedia Council, are supposed to include at least a PC, CD-ROM drive, audio adaptor, Windows with multimedia extensions, and speakers or phones. The Council announced its MPC Level 2 specifications in May 1993. Level 2 represents a substantial upgrade of the original 1991 MPC specifications, reflecting the need for improved performance and the development of the hardware and software to supply it.

Loveria's (1993) preferences in a review article are Creative System's MPC upgrade for 'add-ons' and NCR's 3331 MLS complete system based on a 86DX 33 MHz micro at $4294 including large-screen monitor.

Tables 5.2 and 5.3 show the general and the video and audio requirements for multimedia PC Level 2 machines. Loveria concludes that the upgrade kit from Creative Labs provides the best value, and that the NCR 3331 MLS is the best value complete system. The Creative Labs kit includes a Sound Blaster audio Pro 16 board, a Panasonic CD-ROM drive, and other accessories. The price in the United States is $800. The NCR 3331 MLS includes a 33 MHz DX micro, 8 Mbytes of RAM, 240 MByte hard drive, Toshiba Photo CD/XDA compatible CD-ROM drive, sound card, and it comes with a super VGA chip-set and DVI adaptor. It costs $3805.

Nordgren (1994) provides a short list of suggested elementary measures to be taken before and during the time of purchase:

- Learn the terminology first
- Use a check-list when collecting data about machines
- Cross-check for compatibility of any separate units
- Compare the cost of competing systems

Table 5.2 Multimedia PC Level 2 requirements

Characteristic	*PC Level 2 recommendations*
Processor	486SX (min)
Clock	25 MHz (min)
RAM	4 Mbytes (8 recommended)
Floppy drive	3.5" 1.44 Mbytes
Hard drive	160 Mbytes (min)
Keyboard	Standard 101 key IBM style with DIN connector
Mouse	2 button
Mouse connector	Bus or serial with at least one additional COM port free
Serial port	9 pin or 25 pin synchronous Programmable up to 9600 baud Switchable interrupt channel
Parallel port	25 pin bi-directional with interrupt capability
MIDI port	In, Out, and Thru with interrupt support for input and FIFO transfer
Joystick port	IBM-style analogue or digital
Expansion slots	Not specified
CD-ROM drive	For CD-ROM XA

Table 5.3 Video and audio specifications for multimedia PC Level 2

Characteristic	Major multimedia PC Level 2 specifications
VIDEO	
Colour monitor	Required
Display resolution	640 × 480 pixels (min)
No. of colours at 640 × 480	65,536 ('64 Kbytes')
Performance goal for VGA with adaptors	Able to blit 1, 4, and 8 bits per pixel Device Independent Bit Maps (DIBs) at 1.2 Megapix. per sec, given 40% CPU (Supports delivery of 320 × 240 pixels, 15 frames/sec, 256 colours)
AUDIO	
16-bit D/AC:	
Linear PCM sampling	Required
DMA or FIFO buffered transfer	Required with interrupt on buffer empty
Sample rates	44.1, 22.05, and 11.025 KHz
Stereo channels	Required
CPU bandwidth needed to output 22.05 and 11.025 KHz,	Not more than 10%
and to output 44.1 KHz	Not more than 15%
16-bit A/DC:	
Linear PCM sampling	Required
Sample rates	as for DAC
DMA or FIFO buffered transfer	Required with interrupt on buffer full
Microphone input	Required
Multi-voice multi-timbral internal synthesizer	Required,with 6 simultaneous melody notes plus 2 percussive
Internal mixing: 4 sources presented at output as stereo line-level (CD Red Book, Synthesizer, DAC waveform, and aux.)	Required (aux. is optional)
Input source volume control	Required (as specified)
Clipping	Required (as specified)
Individual source vol. reg. and Master vol. register	Recommended
CD-ROM XA audio	Recommended

Portable notebook-size multimedia machines

Battery-operated, small lightweight multimedia machines (the smallest are now called 'sub-notebooks') with LCD displays have been developed to provide most of the facilities of the larger machines but are usually more expensive on a like-with-like comparison basis. Notebooks normally weigh about 10 pounds and have a 10" colour screen. Sub-notebooks weigh 6 or 7 pounds with usually a mono 8" screen. They usually include a 'trackball' – a small ball inset into the surface and moved by a finger to move the cursor in a similar way to a mouse. Batteries make a large contribution to the weight, so rechargeable batteries of very light weight to give the longest possible life between charges are essential. In order of preference, lithium-ion, nickel-metal-hydride or nickel-cadmium batteries are used. Lithium-polymer batteries which may be moulded into any shape may become available in a few years' time. The circuits of these machines, reliant as they are on battery power, embody arrangements for automatically reducing power or shutting down those parts not in use.

Byte magazine reviewed 486 portables in 1994 (Lennon 1994) and considered that the Zenith Z-Star 433 VL model 200 was the best monochrome machine, while the best colour machine was the Sharp PC 8650. The Sharp 8650 has a 33 MHz processor and an active matrix 8" colour display. Maximum RAM capacity is 20 Mbytes. Its battery provides just over 3 hours of operation between charges and its weight is 6.4 lb.

Since the *Byte* review portables have progressed in an active competitive market. IBM ran an advertisement on UK national television during July 1995 promoting its Thinkpad 710 notepad. When the lid is closed the keyboard is in stowed in two sections. Opening the machine causes the sections to click together alongside each other to form a wider, more easily used keyboard.

In June 1995 IBM introduced its 755 CDV multimedia Thinkpad. The machine incorporates a dual speed CD-ROM drive and a 10.4" see-through colour screen. When the screen is mounted on an overhead projector, its contents may be projected for viewing by a large audience. The Thinkpad processor is a 486 DX4/100 upgradable to a Pentium. A nickel-metal-hydride battery is fitted which may be upgraded to a lithium-ion. The operating system for the 755 CDV is OS/2 Warp and Windows 3.11. Fifteen software applications are supplied with the machine. The UK price for the Thinkpad with 8 Mbytes of RAM and a 540 Mbyte hard disk drive is £5585.

The latest Panasonic multimedia notebook (July 1995) is the CF-41 which comes with a CD-ROM drive and storage space for a second, and a 10.4" active matrix colour display with a resolution of 640×480 pixels. This machine includes a Soundblaster Pro with stereo speakers and a nickel-metal-hydride battery. The CF-41 contains two slots in its side for PCM1A cards. A photograph of the CF-41 is shown in Figure 5.5. Other features of the CF-41 include:

CPU   Choice of DX4 100 MHz
                        DX2 50 MHz
                        Pentium 75 MHz
Hard disk   260, 450, or 680 Mbytes

RAM   8–32 Mbytes
VRAM   1 Mbyte
  Pointer   Trackball
  Software   MSDOS 6.2; Windows 3.11
UK price   Pentium/16 Mbytes/680 Mbyte £4799

Figure 5.5 The Panasonic CF-41 multimedia notebook machine

Source: Panasonic

MULTIMEDIA COMPUTERS AND SYSTEMS – FUTURES AND CONCLUSIONS

The business market for multimedia software and systems in the US and Europe will grow from £500m in 1991 to £9bn in 1997, according to one early forecast. In 1991 there were only two significant uses for business multimedia – interactive computer-based training systems and point-of-information/point-of-sale kiosks.

Nordgren (1994) makes a number of other points to consider when buying:

• Is an interface card needed for the CD-ROM drive? If possible select a non-proprietary SCSI II card;

- Note the requirement for MIDI and joystick ports;
- To be fully XA compatible, drives may need additional circuits to decode interleaved channels of audio and to perform ADPCM decompression;
- Video boards should preferably be SVGA compatible, preferably with 1 Mbyte of memory.

By 1994, a survey based on detailed case studies of 25 systems suppliers, software developers and users reckons that there will be four main products with operating system extensions that support multimedia – multimedia enhancements to spreadsheets and wp packages; business presentation packages, and information access packages that include publications, databases, and tools. By 1997 the survey adds two new categories which will extend the market still further – multimedia-enhanced electronic mail packages and group-ware, including videoconferencing facilities.

An organization called First Cities intends to create a significant market-place for networked multimedia information and entertainment products and services by accelerating developments of a national infrastructure for entertainment, distance learning, health care, and electronic commerce.

An even more ambitious future is planned by the Microelectronic and Computer Technology Corporation, whose 'ultimate goal is the creation of a seamless environment for the spontaneous use of integrated interactive multimedia services in the home, the community, or on the move'. MCC will provide:

- software that will enable individuals to connect their homes to the interactive multimedia services networks;
- software to enable communication delivery organizations to provide a gateway through which customers can connect;
- applications servers that will enable distribution of a wide range of services through the gateway and into individual homes.

The companies joining MCC in the initial phase of a national multimedia testbed are Apple Computer, Bell Communications Research (Bellcore), Bieber-Taki Associates, Corning, Eastman Kodak, Kaleida Labs, North American Philips, South-Western Bell Technology Resources, Sutter Bay Associates, Tandem Computers, and US West. Discussions are under way with many other companies.

Some more opinions about multimedia are included in a Frost & Sullivan report (Clark 1992). In the US, DTP was worth $3868 million in 1992 and about $3000 million in Europe. Multimedia was worth about $7000 million and £2178 million respectively. The expected expansion in the US is enormous – an increase to over $25,000 million by 1995, but the European expansion rate is much slower – to $3066 million by 1996. In the US, Multimedia is said to have 'attracted much attention and generated great excitement throughout diversified sections of business, industry, government and academe'. Apple had 40 per cent of the US 'multimedia basic systems' market in 1990, but in Europe it was dominant (1991) with 58.5 per cent of the 'multimedia market', the next contender being Acorn with 4.1 per cent.

A staff member of the Getty Conservation Institute, Marina del Rey, California believes that photo-CDs have 'a great deal to offer conservation'. Photo-CDs created from ordinary 35 mm film shots can be obtained with images at five different resolutions. The appropriate resolution may be selected for conservation records. The Kodak photo-CD maximum resolution is 2000×3000 pixels with 24-bit colour – a total of 96 Mbits (12 Mbytes) of data. Compression without much loss reduces this to 4.4 Mbytes. Accordingly compressed high-resolution or an alternative lower-resolution picture may be chosen as required.

Marcus and Van Dam (1991), discussing the evolution of modern Graphical User Interfaces (GUI), say that they have been made possible by developments in dedicated computers, bit-map graphics, and the mouse. Further advances will include gesture recognition for character and command input, real-time 3-dimensional animation, sound and speech with combined modalities – for instance, visual and acoustic cues to improve comprehension and retention.

According to Alan Kay and Raj Reddy, leaders in the art, say Marcus and Van Dam workstations will execute 1 Giga-instruction per second, have 1 Gigabyte of memory and a Gigabyte bus, and will cost less than $10,000. They will support real-time dimensional graphics with transformation and smooth-shaded rendering at about 1 million triangles per second. A gesture translation, for example, will change 2-dimensional mouse movements into 3-dimensions. For instance, if a user adds a propeller to a computer model of an aircraft, the object will be projected into screen space and the axes compared to the vector formed by the cursor's start and end positions. Translations will automatically display a 2-dimensional shadow in three perpendicular planes on to a 'stage' setting, including the newly added propeller, in order to aid spatial perception.

The problem of authoring for multiple media is far greater than the sum of the authoring problems in the individual media because it is necessary to co-ordinate and synchronize the media into a coherent presentation. Video and sound materials are especially demanding, since few users have experience in video editing. Skilled interdisciplinary teams of cognitive psychologists, user-interface designers, graphic designers, and content-area specialists will be required to produce user interfaces that help users do useful work and produce material of lasting value. It will become possible to direct a design assistant, for instance, to alter the shape of the corners on the dinner plates designed last week so that they fit production methods for special china and meet hotel restaurant durability requirements.

Note that some parts of this directive can be expressed by natural language, some by pointing, some by sketching, and that feedback in the form of a realistic pictorial display is essential. Some of these technologies are within our grasp but fully general natural-language understanding will take considerably longer.

Chapter 6

Planning and preparing multimedia presentations: authoring systems

INTRODUCTION

It has been said (Anon. 1992b) that:

> Although complexity is being steadily eroded by the rise of sophisticated authoring programmes, it is safe to say that for any ambitious CD-I project (as for any other multimedia product) the designer/publisher will need to have access to both production talent as well as the skills of an experienced software specialist.

Authoring for CD-ROMs, CD-Is, etc. will not be successful unless the author understands the possibilities and constraints of the media. For this reason technical aspects of commonly used CD-based media – one of the most widely used – are discussed at the end of this chapter, followed by some information about CD-specific authoring software, and examples of CD publications. An attempt is made to confine all other technical matters to other chapters.

To exploit media properly and to provide a professional presentation, an appropriate authoring effort supported by the necessary hardware and software will be needed. Some typical costs will be given in this chapter. Multimedia presentations may be provided by using the presenter's own composition, or by using a purchased multimedia product stored, for example, on a CD-ROM.

HYPERTEXT/HYPERMEDIA

Hypertext was briefly discussed in the previous chapter, but hypertext-based systems are still so widely used that they will be considered here in more detail. Hypermedia is a similar arrangement of interconnected information from two or more media. Hypertext systems were among the earliest forms of multimedia. They have endured mainly because hypertext software is relatively simple and provides for a degree of user interaction.

The extension of hypertext to hypermedia followed once computer systems were able to handle both text and other media. While still used for their original purposes, hypermedia-like systems and controlling actions are often used in multimedia authoring, but a different aspect has suddenly become of major interest. Retrieval on Internet's World Wide Web is aided by hyperlinks between information entities (nodes). In fact the wide reach provided by this facility is probably the reason for the Web's success.

Hypertext is a class of software for exploring information, usually mainly text, by alternative paths as opposed to the fixed path or structure found in conventional printed systems. In its simplest form, text is split up into small chunks, each displayed on what appears to be a card. The linear arrangement of information, as in a book, is not always the most convenient to use. A feature of hypertext is the provision for jumping from one piece of information to another. As mentioned in the previous chapter, a user could instantly jump from a cited item to a complete reference or from a word to its definition.

The content of a card is indexed, usually manually. The best known hypertext system is Apple's Hypercard, designed to be used by non-programmers. Hypercard's fields, cards (maximum size a 'screen-full' with a bordered edge looking like a card), and stacks roughly correspond to the fields, records, and files of a database. Cards are organized into a tree structure – a hierarchical data structure. There must be a vocabulary from which a card is labelled/indexed with at least one term, and ideally there should be a relatively uniform distribution of classification terms among all hypertext cards.

Hypercard was preceded by and co-exists with a number of older systems which are broadly similar. Hypercard, or one of its more recent alternatives such as Supercard or Hyperdoc, is a convenient method to control multimedia material such as text, sound, music, voice, graphics, pictures, animation, or motion video. Hypercard, which started as a hypertext system, soon became a hypermedia system with version 1.2, introduced in late 1988. This version included some improvements taking it into the multimedia area – for instance, for using data from a CD-ROM drive connected to the Mac, with disks which included text, sound, and music data.

Hypercard was originally developed for the manipulation of cards containing text. The control of other media came as a bonus. It may be used to manage images, diagrams, etc. Facilities for controlling peripheral equipment on which other material is stored make Hypercard or one of the other competitive hypermedia products a convenient and frequently chosen way of retrieving and controlling the material in multimedia systems. One of the most interesting features in Hypercard is a button. A button is a small, labelled rectangular area. When the cursor is directed over it with the mouse and the mouse is clicked, the button is 'pressed' and a script is executed to perform some kind of action. A button may be on the card's background, in which case its action is the same whatever the overlaid card, or it may be on the body of a card, in which case its action applies to that card only. When 'pressed', a button may execute an external command or XCMD, routed through the appropriate 'driver' (software compatible with particular external peripherals such as a videodisk player, CD-ROM, etc.) to a peripheral unit. For example, Macromind Director multimedia presentation software (described later in this chapter) displays frames of information, corresponding to cards, with the means of controlling both external equipment and objects within a displayed frame. The role of Director's 'XObjects' is to a frame what Hypercard's XCMDs are to a card.

A statement called a script in Hypercard's Hypertalk language (with words in English) is associated with 'objects', such as a word or a button on a card. When the cursor is placed over a button, which will normally be captioned, the mouse is clicked and a message is sent to a script for it to be executed to perform some kind of action. The action might be to activate a link to another card in the same or in a different stack, to retrieve that card. It is relatively easy to create a simple Hypercard system using the wide range of ready-made facilities provided. Writing Hypertalk scripts, which consist of standardized English phrases or words in order to create more elaborate schemes, requires a longer learning commitment but is still relatively easy.

A card is Hypercard's smallest unit of information – the minimum amount of displayable information is one card. Hypercard fields of information are displayed on a 342×512 pixel size numbered card – a Mac screenful. The field for editable text is displayed in a window which can occupy most of the screen. It can contain up to 30,000 characters and graphics in within-window scrollable lines; the text is in a font selectable from a number of alternatives. A 'find' command will search through all cards in a stack for a character string in a named field. A card actually overlays a background, which may be invisible if the card completely overlays it. Usually a background is visible and contains information common to a number of cards, or to all the cards in the stack. A Hypercard system may contain many or no 'information' stacks, but it must contain a special stack called the home stack used for 'house-keeping' purposes. A card typically contains up to about 100 Kbytes of data plus its associated script. Stack size may be up to 512 Mbytes. Two Mbytes of RAM is recommended for Hypercard on a Mac, with hard disk space of, say, 20 Mbytes.

Hypercard activities are initiated by messages, which may be commands such as 'find', or within-system descriptive messages such as 'mouse is within button area' or 'mouse up' when the mouse is clicked. A user can send a message, which must include a keyword, to the current card, or to an object by typing it into a special area called a message box. Messages are routed to objects such as buttons, fields, background, stack, home stack, and Hypercard in that order. Each object has an ID number. A stack must have a name, and other objects may be given names by the author. Each of the above six objects has a handler attached to it. A handler comprises statements in the Hypertalk language collectively called a script. The keyword of a message in transit is matched against the keyword in the script associated with the first object it meets. If there is no match it goes on to try a field, then background for a keyword match, and so on through the hierarchy. When a match is found with an object a script is executed.

POSTSCRIPT, ILLUSTRATOR, AND ACROBAT

These Adobe products represent an extension of ideas which were first used in desktop publishing systems for text and graphics. Since then they have been steadily improved and now dominate the text/graphics end of multimedia.

Postscript and Illustrator are software packages for a printer programming language, and typeface and artistic effects respectively, both devised by Adobe Systems. DTP systems were made possible by the arrival of the Apple Macintosh machine and laser printer, enabling substantial advances to be made in the reproduction of printed typefaces and printed artistic effects. Postscript and Illustrator were the most outstanding of the corresponding software packages needed to effect that reproduction. Both are now widely used in multimedia systems.

Postscript controls the beam of a laser printer to print almost any kind of symbol or illustration. Image dot structures are changed into vectors. The benefits are economies in data, versatility, and resolution limited only by the printer in use. The amount of data required to represent an image in Postscript is usually far less than in a bit-map. It is only necessary to store the description of a font in a single size. To call up the font in a different size, only a simple Postscript scaling instruction needs to be executed. An early disadvantage was that the time taken to print a Postscript page could be much longer than the time taken using other methods. This disadvantage has now largely disappeared. Plug-in cards and software are available to convert a non-Postscript printer into a Postscript printer. Postscript changes the dot-structure description of text, graphics, and illustrations in a file – for instance, a Pagemaker or Ventura DTP file into a vector description. A vector is a quantity which has magnitude and direction. The instructions are coded in ASCII code. Postscript describes every item on a page in terms of its constituent lines, curves, polygons, etc.

For example, in bit-map format – as commonly used in a CRT display – a ruled line 20 pixels wide and 1500 pixels long requires 30,000 bits to describe it. In Postscript the description would be in the form 'Start in position X and perform a 20 point line from A to B'. This instruction would require perhaps 200 bits of code. A rectangle in Postscript would be described by a co-ordinate representing the position of a starting point on a page, the co-ordinates of its corners, the thickness of a line, and the instruction 'move to'. The printer then draws the rectangle. These instructions are coded in ASCII code. The ASCII code is then sent to the printer's Raster Image Processor (RIP).

Postscript describes every item on a page in terms of its constituent lines, curves, polygons, etc. To execute such operations two main processes are required. First, the bit-map has to be converted into ASCII-coded vector form. The ASCII code is then sent to the printer's Raster Image Processor. The RIP changes it into the line-by-line form required by a laser printer. The printed resolution is then limited only by the printer, not by the file format. Thus the result of sending a disk containing material in Postscript to, say, a bureau with a page-setter will be printed material of typeset quality. While a displayed 'coarse' version of a page may be good enough for checking purposes, a disk containing page data may be sent to, say, a bureau with a 1200 dpi Linotype page-setter for quantity printing. The printed resolution will then be 1200 dpi.

The amount of data needed to represent an image in Postscript is much less than in bit-map, and font size may be scaled up or down with only a simple Postscript scaling instruction. Originally, Postscript printing was much slower than most other methods.

Plug-in 'go faster' boards are available. But 'Display Postscript', first supplied with the Apple NEXT computer, is much faster so that display delay is no longer a problem. Screen conversion does not have to be done again for printing, so printing delays are much reduced.

Illustrator provides for enhanced typographic and artistic effects. For example, the cursor may be moved to any point on a curve displayed on the screen and a tangential 'handle' may be pulled out from the curve; by dragging the handle with the mouse the user may change the curve into a different form – for example, into a sinusoidal waveform or an oval shape. An image may be moved bodily to any location on the screen by dragging it with two crosshairs intersecting at its bottom left. That part of it lying above and to the right of the crosshairs will appear in the new position on the screen and in a corresponding position on a printed page.

When Postscript and Illustrator are used together, virtually any shape can be designed by a user who knows the Postscript language. Alternatively, a library of ready-made designs may be purchased on disk ready to be called on to pages. The value of this aspect of these packages depends on the application. The 'stunt-images' shown in publicity leaflets may or may not be needed. A selection of the fonts supplied with Illustrator are shown in Figure 6.1.

Illustrator may be used as an aid for the professional artist. For example, it will provide a faint displayed image, of, say, a scanned-in sketch so that the user can trace over it in bolder lines, modify it to produce a radically different sketch, augment it, in-fill it, or change details. Alternatively, Illustrator may be used to ease the creation of an own-drawing.

Courier
ITC Cushing*
Dorchester Script*
ITC Eras*
ITC Esprit*
ITC Fenice*
Friz Quadrata
ITC Galliard*
ITC Garamond Condensed*
ITC Garamond*
Gill Sans*
ITC Giovanni*
Goudy Text*
Helvetica*
ITC Isadora*
ITC Kabel*
ITC Korinna*
ITC Leawood*
ITC MACHINE*
Madrone*
ITC New Baskerville*
Nuptial Script
Pepita*
Ⲣ︱︱︱︱︱︱︱*
Poplar*
ITC Officina Sans*
ITC Officina Serif*
ROSEWOOD*
Russell Square
ITC Slimbach*
ITC Souvenir*
STENCIL
Symbol Σ ψ μ β ο λ
ITC Tiepolo*

Figure 6.1 Illustrator fonts
Source: Adobe

Illustrator 5.5 for the Power Mac was introduced in 1994 with a variety of improvements and the inclusion of Acrobat (see below). It comes on a CD which includes 'Collector's Edition' of 200 patterns, the Illustrator 'Art Gallery', with a large number of images by leading artists, and 146 files of clip-art. Figure 6.2 shows a facility being used for editing a Portable Document Format (PDF) file produced on Acrobat and imported into Illustrator. The picture is taken off a screen from the latest version of Illustrator – 5.5. Figure 6.3, from the same version of Illustrator, shows an operation in progress where adjustments are being made to the colour change gradient in an area filled with different colours.

Figure 6.2 Illustrator PDF for editing

Source: Adobe

Acrobat is a software product first announced by Adobe in November 1992. It amounts to an attempt to introduce a universal document communication language for viewing or printing. Acrobat is said to be able to provide a portable document which can be run on any computer, operating system, or application. With Acrobat the evolution of the Postcript/Illustrator/ Acrobat software has moved the system right into the multimedia arena – if the first two products had not put it there already. The reason is that it supports structured documents such as SGML, and provides functions similar to ODA (see chapter 9).

Acrobat embodies a Postscript-like format called the Portable Document Format (PDF). A PDF file can describe documents containing any combination of text, graphics, and images of any complexity, independently of their resolution. Adobe has published PDF as an open Standard so the format may be supported by third parties. A PDF file can be created from any application program which supports Postscript, and which started as a word processing file, illustration, worksheet, or graph from a spreadsheet program. JPEG compression is used for compressing colour and grey scale images with ratios varying between 2:1 and 8:1. Adobe claims that PDF is the first universal alternative to ASCII. It is claimed that it works equally well on Macintosh, Windows, Unix, DOS, and other operating systems. The

Figure 6.3 Illustrator gradients
Source: Adobe

Acrobat Distiller, which is a part of the system, is a software program which translates Postscript files into PDF. The Acrobat PDF Writer is a printer driver which converts PDF files from applications.

A part of the software called Acrobat Exchange creates electronic documents on a Mac or PC which may be viewed, searched, or printed. Annotations and hypermedia links may be added.

In 1994 Adobe purchased Aldus, producers of a number of software packages, which together generate revenues of over $500 million. Adobe's Postscript licences alone are said to produce a revenue of $150 million per annum.

AUTHORED PRESENTATIONS

Types of presentation

Authored presentations seem to be of three different kinds with an ill-defined boundary – computer-composed slide presentations, computer-projected slide presentations, and multimedia presentations.

A computer-composed slide presentation is an up-market slide show composed with the aid of a computer, usually for 35 mm slides, the slides being designed and used mainly for business purposes, especially sales presentations. The major benefits are the impact of text in a professional font with special designs in colour, diagrams, and illustrations. You will recognize a computer-composed slide presentation from the characteristics of the first slide presented. Typically it will contain a few lines of text in a large, clear typeface, readable by the back row of the audience, with each line preceded by a 'bullet' on a background which may be patterned or composed of several different colours merging into each other. The company's logo will appear in the corner, and the text in each slide will be a terse sales message which the presenter will discuss. Such a slide may be produced by a non-professional using a multimedia system who is not an artist, but who knows how to put its facilities to good use. It is claimed that the machine and its user should be able to produce a result which looks as if it was the work of a professional artist. In practice a user without any artistic talent – a talent which cannot be supplied by a machine – cannot match the work of a professional.

If the author has completed the slide design using a computer and wants to have slides made for projection by mean of a conventional slide projector, the data will probably be sent on disk to a graphics bureau, which will make the actual slides – usually 35 mm slides. In-house slide production requiring a high-resolution CRT with built-in recording camera will be used when the volume of slide production justifies it.

A second, more elaborate, kind of presentation using successive slide-like frames, must be computer-projected using appropriate software. If it is to be viewed from the display directly, the audience will be limited in size. A device such as a Proxima or Visualex active-matrix projection panel can be obtained to project an image on to a lecture-room screen which should be visible to a large audience. Visual presentation techniques are discussed in more detail later in this chapter. Computer-projected hardware/software usually provides output in the form of a screen display, as printed audience handouts and speaker notes, and (indirectly) as 35 mm slides. Screen-presented computer-driven reproduction enables special effects to be included which are impossible when fixed-format 35 mm slides are used. For example, inter-slide transitional effects may be introduced with wipes, blends, or dissolves instead of the usual abrupt changeovers. 'Layered pages', where lines are gradually revealed – a more sophisticated procedure than moving an opaque sheet down an overhead projector transparency – may be presented. The order of the slides may be altered as required.

Software for the first and second types of presentation just described is likely to cost from £150 to £400 and will run on modestly powerful Macs or PCs. In 1991 Diehl (1991) described trials of presentation software used to prepare a 'multiple-level bullet chart, a pie chart with exploded slice, two bar charts . . . etc.'. Twelve packages for DOS windows and Mac operating systems were tested. The author's choices were Harvard Graphics for DOS, Persuasion 2.0 for Windows, and Move 3.0 for Macs. Several of these 1991 packages include 'Outliners' – that is, the means of manipulating and editing the contents of a box representing the slide. Facilities vary but most packages provide scalable fonts, drawing tools, chart designs, files of clip art, and numerous other features. New software packages for preparing more sophisticated slide-based presentations are still in demand in 1995.

Harvard Graphics continues to be successful, the latest version being 4.0. This package for Windows was reviewed with others for Windows, including Charisma 4.0, Lotus Freelance Graphics 2.1, and Microsoft Powerpoint 4.0 by Yeaton (1995). The reviewer considers that the creation of slides is the core of the presentation process. The range of facilities in these packages, each in the $400–$500 price range, is enormous. Each includes a large number of clip-art symbols and Charisma has more than 7000 on a CD-ROM. Charisma and Freelance Graphics have sound-clip libraries. All provide numerous slide transition effects and the means for drawing on the screen during a presentation. All manner of charts and a whole range of drawing tools such as freehand shapes, bezier curves, object rotation, and adjustable shapes are provided. A range of outliner templates are available which provide a background design for a slide. Powerpoint was considered to deliver the highest quality.

Processes in slide creation carried out by RCW Ltd are shown in Figures 6.4 and 6.5. The text in Helvetica under 'Financial Summary' is moved into the slide outliner using Microsoft Powerpoint software. The font is changed into Times Roman and enlarged and colour is added. Finally, the slide in Figure 6.5 is created.

For its Hollywood software, IBM claims that it is 'a powerful presentation graphics software product which allows business professionals to easily create high-quality hard copy, transparencies, slides, and on-screen presentations'.

In the third type of authoring – the 'multimedia presentation' – the slide metaphor is usually abandoned and music, motion video, and high-quality pictures are included. The result is a full-scale multimedia show, designed, produced, and delivered with the aid of a powerful computer and sophisticated software. The development of much improved authoring software of this kind took place during the same period as the hardware developments described in chapters 2 and 5. In 1990–91 nearly all the available software was for slide presentation. The introduction of still and motion video and Apple's Quicktime in 1992 was accompanied by a move towards authored production multimedia with higher performance.

The single most important requirement for a multimedia presentation is good authoring. Authoring means the writing of a script by an author who understands the potential and mechanisms of the technology. The author will then be able to extend the scope of his or her ideas beyond print-on-

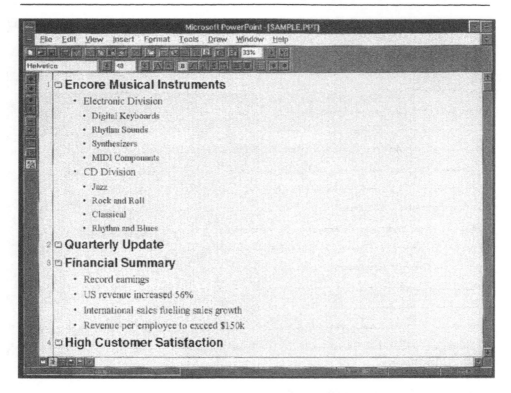

Figure 6.4 Slide making with Powerpoint

Source: RCW Ltd

paper by including sound and visual effects. The term 'authoring' usually also covers the preparation of a storyboard and may cover the whole production process.

'Storyboard' is a term borrowed from the film and TV world. A storyboard will probably be divided into modules and will be based on a script. It may be associated with a flowchart and production schedule, with notes about sequences and an inventory listing the video stills, motion video clips, sound clips, and the text and graphics to be used. Account must be taken of continuity and timing, and interactivity options must be described for a presentation where the software provides for it. The producer of a modest programme may take responsibility for all the creative aspects; for more elaborate productions the expertise will be distributed between script writer, programmer, engineer, artist, animator, etc.

For non-commercial products a multimedia program may be stored on videotape compiled from a range of source material and edited with the aid of appropriate software. If the end-product is to be sold commercially, the storage media may be videodisk or – more likely these days – a disk from the CD family.

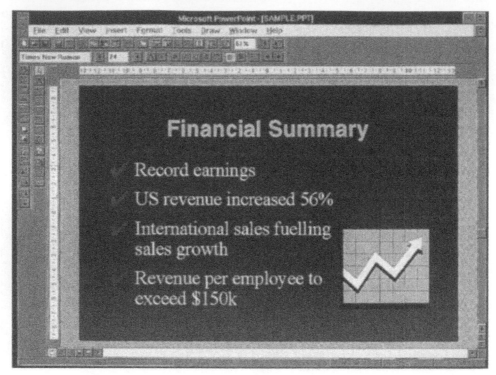

Figure 6.5 Slide making with Powerpoint
Source: RCW Ltd

The difficulties of good authoring

Larry Friedlander (1993), who is associated with the preparation of a multi-media system for the Globe theatre, says (describing museum multimedia):

> In multimedia the designer must shape a unified focused meaningful experience, moment by moment, out of the richness and potential of the medium. Museum programs often confront the user with an overwhelming onslaught of pictures, texts, diagrams, and audio which have not been adequately formed and selected . . . overwhelmed by the sheer mass of information, the visitors were reluctant to continue accumulating more facts, when, indeed, they seemed not to know what to do with those which they had already collected. After a while they stopped engaging with the experience and simply gave up.

Sayre (1993) comments: 'Gathering images and digitising them may be a huge and expensive task.' In fact, this task is also likely to be the most costly part of the preparation of a museum multimedia presentation, exceeding even the authoring costs.

Hemsley (1993b) considers that:

> In certain types of computer systems work it is the *content*, not the hardware nor the software, which constitutes the biggest single cost component. In the Geographic Information Systems area for example, figures for content costs as high as 70% of the total cost of the project are sometimes quoted.

Hemsley quotes from the Philips's IMS CD-I Design Handbook:

> Most CD-I designers agree that, while it might be tempting to exclude programmers from early stages of design and development, it's a good idea to have someone around who thoroughly understands the technical aspects of CD-I and can quickly spot any potential pitfalls before effort has been wasted on designing something that can never work.

With regard to computer problems, Hemsley considers that computer systems are risky and accident-prone, and he cites

> a space-shot aborted because of a missing comma in the code, malfunctioning of medical equipment due to software errors leading to human injury and death, and financial failure/disruption of companies due to software difficulties both at operational and development phases.

Hemsley thinks that a skilled multidisciplinary team is needed whose skills include researchers and writers specializing in content, graphic designers, user representatives – for example, curators and educators – human factor specialists, software and other technical staff, photographers, sound and video staff for new materials, project management staff, creative directors, and marketing people for products.

The need to take the operation of designing and laying out an authored item through to comprehensive testing on users is emphasized by Hirumi *et al.* (1994). They report on a system for public access installed at the San Diego Natural History Museum about deserts and desert life. Storyboards and flowcharts were used in the initial design to work out the program structure, but 'curators and other reviewers could not assess the feel of the attraction sequence or evaluate how users would proceed through the program'. The attraction sequence refers to a continuous show of images with button-selected options for more, and the playing of recordings of sounds made by desert animals. Accordingly, a working prototype of the complete system was tested, changes were made and tested, revised, and tested again. This was followed by a field evaluation in which the behaviour of a sample of fifty visitor-users was observed, attention being focused on the ability of the program to attract and hold visitors' attention. The comments made by Hirumi *et al.* emphasize the need for what may be a time-consuming but essential task which is never mentioned by multi-media enthusiasts – the assessment of the effect of a presentation upon the people it is designed to affect and the incorporation of improvements as necessary.

In August 1989 an article in the *Financial Times* said that the 'Desktop Publishing boom is over . . . a main weakness of DTP is the lack of skilled personnel. Realistically it takes six to nine months to become effective.' It was suggested that perhaps Presentation software might be developed from DTP techniques, implying a reduction in skills. Although the skills reduction comment is entirely mistaken, the possible growth of Presentation software was hinted at. A software package called Persuasion, destined to become one of the most popular, was mentioned.

According to a 1994 US forecast, the business presentation software market will grow from about $1 billion in 1993 to over $2.4 billion by 1999.

MULTIMEDIA TOOLS

An article appeared in *Electronics*, in May 1991, entitled 'The birth of an industry: a multimedia infrastructure begins to take shape'. The author was talking about the multimedia presentation 'industry'. He described how organizations were overcoming authoring and copyright problems. Microsoft invested in the UK CD-ROM publisher Dorling-Kindersley because it *was* a publisher and owned all the intellectual property rights to its illustrations, photographs, and text.

A number of authoring tools have become available. They usually include a means of controlling program flow and timing, and they handle animation, voice, motion and still video, graphics, text, and audio. They have been developed for running principally on PCs and Macintoshes.

Rash (1992), under the heading 'Real products for real users', says that

[the] IBM/Intel *ActionMedia II* supports high quality full-motion video at 30 frames per second, VGA and XGA images, and digital audio. It conforms to a series of de facto multimedia standards to ensure inter-operability. . . . Instead of the usual still images, IBM and Intel used full-motion footage . . . more important, *ActionMedia II* stores the video images and digital sound on a standard Netware file server hard drive instead of on a slower CD-ROM drive.

Referring to another product, Curtain Call, Rash says:

Imagine how powerful your presentation would be at the next meeting if you could mix your slides with photographs and recorded sound. Imagine presentation text and drawings other than the usual Times Roman, Helvetica, and black line art that you usually see . . . full-motion animation and video will be coming shortly.

The unanswered question is the cost of gaining the authoring experience, preparation time, artistic design ability, source material acquisition, continuity editing, etc. required for such a presentation.

A system for developing a multimedia presentation really needs to include a powerful microcomputer with a large-screen monitor, a CD-ROM drive, a large hard disk – with a capacity of, say, 600 Mbytes – stereo loudspeakers, a microphone, and mouse (see chapter 5). Suitable input devices would be a video recorder or videodisk drive. The system should accept 16-bit stereo sound with a high sampling rate – at least 44 KHz. Adaptor cards may be needed for compression, MIDI interface, and video.

The choice of multimedia equipment and the variety of possible endproduct program storage/reproduction media are enormous. The producer of a modest program may take responsibility for all its creative aspects. For more elaborate productions the expertise will be distributed between people with a range of different abilities, as already mentioned. There is general agreement that, while the choice of a suitable hardware 'platform' and software is important, authoring is by far the most important and most difficult part of producing a multimedia product. Remarks made about this subject include: 'it is easy to become overly concerned with the technical aspects . . . the development of appropriate effective content is still the most difficult part of the process'.

For non-commercial products a multimedia program may take the form of a videotape compiled from a range of source material and edited with the aid of a software package based on the Mediamaker principle as described below. As a product for general sale the storage media may be videodisk or – more likely these days – a disk from the CD family.

VISIBILITY FOR THE AUDIENCE

Considerations of the visibility, mobility, and legibility of a multimedia show of whatever kind raise the question 'How are you going to show it to audiences of various sizes in different locations?'

Media suitable for storing and providing vision and/or sound include, for slide presentation shows, 35 mm slides with an optical projector or computer with monitor if motion effects are included. For fully fledged authored shows, videotape with TV or computer display, or CD-ROM and computer display are required as well. But shows presented on a CRT monitor can only be viewed by a small number of people.

The common problem that slides, or for that matter any kind of visual presentation, are legible only to the lecturer and the front of the audience cannot unfortunately be solved by multimedia. The lecturer needs to know the length of the hall, the area of the screen filled by a slide, and the maximum number of lines of type permissible per slide for the type to be readable in the back row under these conditions. Unfortunately, this information is not usually available in advance. The question of the distance viewing of images and text and the design of screenfuls of multimedia data does not yet seem to have received much attention. It has for text. The author of an article written twenty years ago about this topic criticizes presenters who say: 'As you can see from this chart . . . ' when 'they know that nobody beyond the front row can make it out'. The article is by Gould (1973).

Data from a small computer display may be projected on to a screen large enough to be seen by a larger audience. The simplest and cheapest device is an LCD panel laid over an overhead projector in place of the usual acetate transparency. The panel is plugged in to a computer and behaves like a transparent computer screen, an image of whatever is displayed being projected with the aid of the overhead projector's light source. A monochrome panel costs about £1300 in the UK and a colour panel £2500.

A brighter, larger image can be produced with an LCD projector comprising (for colour) three LCD panels with colour filters, typically providing 640×480 resolution with 24-bit colour. The Proxima (San Diego) 8300, for example, is compatible with PC and Mac micros, and supports PAL, NTSC, and SECAM video standards. Together with Cyclops, a device for providing the presenting speaker with an interactive pointer, it costs £9500 in the UK.

To provide yet bigger, brighter pictures from a computer, light valve projectors which use a combination of CRT and LCD panels permitting a more powerful light source, or projection CRTs, may be used but they are much more expensive. All types of machine may be purchased or hired from GB International, Milton Keynes, UK.

For easy portability CD-ROM or CD-I storage is convenient. CD-ROMs may also be used for 'own design' general presentations; prices for 'do-it-yourself' CD-ROM preparation have dropped substantially. CDs are discussed later in this chapter. Portability meaning (as just used) easy to carry is one thing; portability meaning compatibility between one or more systems is another.

We have not yet got to the stage, as we have with 35 mm slides, where lecturers can take their own stored presentations, knowing that they can use them on the system provided by the host without any problems. On the contrary, unless they have previously arranged a successful rehearsal, the chances of a problem-free multimedia presentation are remote.

ARRANGING FOR INTERACTIVITY

With interactive multimedia the user becomes an active communicator with the machine. Since the days of cumbersome hard-to-use arrangements, much attention has been centred on the man–machine interface and on the provision of more convenient interactive controls such as touchscreens, trackballs, joysticks, mice, and the CD-I 'thumbstick' controller.

On-screen interactive features include menus, buttons, and hotspots. A menu usually causes a program to stop until the user has acted to force it to resume in a particular direction; several choices are offered, the user selects one, and the program continues along the path dictated by the choice. A hotspot usually produces the same effect as a hypertext button but its presence on the screen may not be indicated; for example, if a child is asked to use the control device to point to a particular kind of animal in a picture, a 'yes' indication comes up when the pointer touches the right animal.

Burger (1993) provides some good advice:

> Capitalize on the fact that people love to explore. Provide a framework for interaction that fires the imagination and the desire to learn. An educational program might be framed as a treasure hunt, or a corporate training program can be framed as a mystery to be explored. . . . Delays should be avoided whenever possible. . . . When delays are inevitable the first rule is to let the user know that something is happening.

Burger continues: 'Don't make people read . . . society in general is accustomed to being spoon-fed information on television. Even viewers who enjoy books often find detailed reading on a CRT or video monitor to be tedious.'

Burger's remarks about delays are important because multimedia software's speed requirements have progressed faster than hardware's ability to supply them. The delay in executing a user's command should take no longer than it takes the user to decide on the next action. Sometimes this means that a delay in excess of a second may become frustrating. At other times the user requires time to think, so a longer delay is acceptable. To fill a screen almost instantly with the amount of data contained in a high-resolution full-colour picture, for instance, requires a very high bit rate. The user may need to see the picture before making the next decision but inadequate hardware forces him or her to wait. Waiting time for particular operations is difficult to specify because it varies according to the amount of information being processed and suppliers are unlikely to draw attention to slowness. Inter-activity is further discussed in the CD-I section in chapter 11.

SOUND

Sound digitization

In this section more specialized aspects of sound are covered. Surprisingly, some features such as synchronizing control and sound editing may not be available with supposedly comprehensive sound systems. Some comprehensive general-purpose authoring software packages which have been briefly mentioned earlier do include these facilities. More detailed information about them is provided in this section.

Voice, music, or sound special effect sources include microphones, keyboards, musical instruments, CDs, CD-ROMs, self-created Midi files, and professionally made Midi files recorded on CDs. Music is widely used in multimedia presentations for the same purposes as it is used in films and television – as a background sound or to act on the emotions of an audience watching a presentation. Sound is usually digitized so that it may be computer-processed; sound passages of speech, music, or effects of any length may be represented on the screen as 'frozen waveforms', or as MIDI data, and all kinds of control and editing functions then become possible. The real, playable sound behind the screen representation of it, eats up computer storage space (see chapter 3 for information about audio compression).

Digitized sound is represented as a smooth waveform for editing when displayed. For instance, silence occupies storage; long pauses between speech sentences may be removed. Special effects such as reverberation or echo may be added. Sound mixing between different sound tracks can be arranged. Sound may be stored as an Audio Interchange File Format (AIFF), which is a standard audio file compatible with most multimedia systems. As explained in chapter 2, to digitize the volume or, as subjectively experienced, the loudness of a sound, the value (level) of the amplitude of the sound waveform is periodically sampled. A 4-bit sample, providing 16 different values, would provide poor quality since there are insufficient data to reconstruct the waveform properly. At least 8 bits (256 levels) are needed to provide a proper represention of a soft-to-loud wide dynamic range.

Samples must be repeated often enough to preserve information about the highest frequency components of the sound, otherwise those frequencies will be lost when the sound is converted back to its analogue form and reproduced. Sampling 22,000 times per second with 8 bits (256 levels) per sample produces digitized sound of reasonably good quality. The sound playback duration for different digitizing conditions is shown in Figure 6.6.

Some computers now include facilities for handling sound; plug-in boards for the purpose are described in a later section. Speech and music are reproduced through headphones or through a small loudspeaker or loudspeakers for stereo sound. For an audience, the computer's output may be connected to an amplifier with larger loudspeakers, this part of the equipment then being subject to the usual 'hi-fi' considerations.

If good quality equipment is used in order to reproduce music that is also of good quality, an increase of the rate to 44K per second 8-bit samples may be needed, as normally used for CD recording; 1 Mbyte of storage for a recording will then last for 22.7 seconds. Figure 6.6 shows the duration of a sound track and the storage space it occupies for several different values of the number of sound samples taken per second. The greater the number of samples per second, the better the quality up to about 44K, above which there will be little audible improvement.

There are other constraints when storing digitized sound in RAM memory

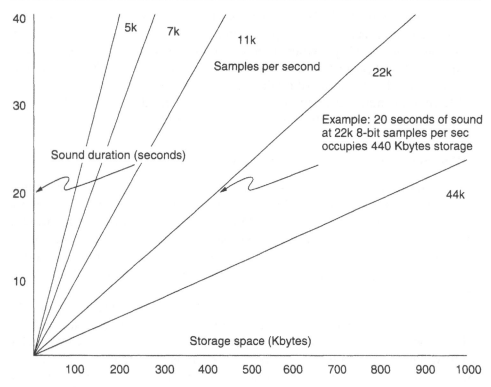

Figure 6.6 Sound sampling conditions
Source: AEC

or on disk. The uninterrupted duration of a passage of sound stored in memory is proportional to memory size. If the memory is too small and must be filled from disk during a sound passage, there will be a break in the sound unless special measures are taken. The 'special measures' are to add processing power with appropriate software to reload memory almost instantaneously. This may require a plug-in card with its own digital processor.

One way of adding sound to visual material is to use an Apple CD-SC drive, which plays CDs or the audio tracks from CD-ROMs, in conjunction with Apple Hypercard CD Audio Toolkit. The toolkit provides XCMDs for a stack to control the player by accurately selecting passages of speech or music from the disk. This is not only convenient but it has the great advantage that the stored music consumes no microcomputer memory or hard disk storage because it remains on the CD until required. The CD-Audio Stack from Voyager (Santa Monica, USA) will select tracks and automatically generate buttons for selection purposes.

A simple sound package is available from Farallon Emeryville, California, USA – the MacRecorder Sound System 2.0 outfit. A small electronic digitizing box plugs into the serial port of a Mac for voice, sound effects, or music input. Farallon's Hypersound software creates a stack requiring XCMD commands to record or play sound. Sound Edit is an associated software package which provides a range of facilities including compression options, cut and paste sounds represented as waveforms on the screen, mix sound channels, alteration of quality, and so on.

Multimedia machines usually contain a small loudspeaker and a stereo output socket for connection to an external amplifier and loudspeakers.

MIDI, music synthesizers, and multimedia

The computer music business is a field of its own headed by the pop groups, who have the money to buy all kinds of equipment to make unusual sounds – the more unusual the better. Major MIDI hardware and software suppliers include Roland Yamaha and Korg. Linear recording takes music in its natural sequence; sequencing is a method of putting music together by dragging, copying, cutting and pasting together patterns of displayed previously stored music.

The Musical Instrument Device Interface (MIDI) started as a system to be used by a musician playing music from a piano-like keyboard connected to a MIDI controller. Subsequently the General MIDI Specification was added to it which specifies a list of numbered programs. The music is recorded as MIDI instructions on up to 16 parallel channels. The instructions, conveyed as a 31.25 Kbps stream of data, are used to switch on and control the sounds produced by a synthesizer – capable of reproducing sounds which simulate a variety of different musical instruments. MIDI interconnections are made with cables and standardized DIN 5-pin plugs.

A list of MIDI jargon follows:

Multi-sampling

A technique used in wave-table synthesizers where samples of the sound of an actual instrument are taken at different intervals and stored. When reproduced, the resulting sound embodies the timbre of an instrument by properly reproducing its overtones.

Multi-timbral

The number of different tone colours that an instrument can play at the same time. MIDI instruments are often 16-part multi-timbral.

Patch

A number identifying the instrumental sound that data from a MIDI channel will cause a synthesizer to simulate. The general MIDI Standard specifies 128 patch numbers, each always providing the same instrumental sound when produced by MIDI-compatible equipment. For example, patch 20 is a church organ, 22 an accordion, 60 a muted trumpet and 106 a banjo.

Polyphony

The number of different notes that can be reproduced together from an instrument. MIDI instruments are usually at least 24-note polyphonic.

Sequencer

The hardware and software which provide the means for recording and editing MIDI data, usually on 16 separate tracks ready for conversion into sounds from a synthesizer. Some sequencers handle digitized audio data and voice as well.

Timbre

Tone colour or quality.

In 1983 Casio introduced the first fully digital instrument. The Moog analogue synthesizer developed by Dr Robert Moog, was the first widely used device (Moog 1986). Subsequently Moog became vice-president of new product research at Kurzweil Music Systems.

Synthesizers, such as the Yamaha DX series, used to be based on FM synthesis, an inexpensive technology invented at Stanford University. Complex sounds are constructed by combining waveforms of different audio frequencies. An improved technique called wave-table synthesis is used on some synthesizers; sound wave-forms from actual instruments are sampled, stored, and played back after processing. Wave-table synthesizers produce higher quality sound but require more storage space – up to 4 Mbytes of Read Only Memory (ROM) storage in which the wave-tables are permanently stored. Wave-guide synthesizers, also invented at Stanford University (Shandle 1993), may replace wave-table machines in due course; mathematical models of circuits which generate waveforms simulating acoustic instruments are used.

Under MIDI data control, a synthesizer generates sounds – if required, several instruments of an orchestra playing together – with each simulated instrument producing a note or notes in the range of timbres and styles of which it is capable. For example, a piano can be made to sound like an acoustic piano, an electric piano, a honky tonk piano, a chorus piano, etc., at the choice of the controlling 'musician'. Simulated percussion instruments may include a pedal hi-hat, Chinese cymbal, maracas, splash cymbal, tambourine, etc.

The music is recorded on sound tracks which may be edited and synchronized with video tracks in a multimedia authoring system, and played back through amplifiers and loudspeakers during the preparation of a presentation, or when the presentation is given to an audience.

To create music from a keyboard the user has to be a musician, but with the arrival of a range of competing software packages, control can be exercised over already recorded MIDI data files using ikons and other symbols displayed in a screenful of graphics. The controlling 'musician' with his MIDI software package is behaving rather like a microcomputer operator using a desktop publishing package to create page layouts and coloured designs. Neither will do it as well as a professional but something acceptable will be created. A person who is not a musician can buy a music score canned as MIDI data, ready to produce music from a synthesizer, some of which (it is claimed) has licensing and copyright already arranged (see chapter 7).

MIDI has the considerable benefit of dispensing with the need to use a large amount of storage for digital music since only a limited range of instructions is stored. The instructions are translated into music by the synthesizer.

The Korg company, previously one of the leaders in the electronic music business, moved directly into the multimedia business during 1994 with their Audio Gallery Multimedia Music System for PC Windows or Macs. The major function of the PC or Mac is to display recorded information to enable a user to control or edit it from the computer's keyboard. The Audio Gallery, which includes the Korg AG-10 synthesizer, is priced at about £400 (including VAT). The software which comes with the AG-10 includes 128 General MIDI sound programs, 4 special drum programs, reverb and chorus effects, and sound editing software. The system, in effect, contains its own time code because it provides 240 clock pulses per quarter note. Its 16 channels of audio data can control the synthesizer to play 16 independent parts. The data may be edited using tape recorder-like controls for functions like record, play, stop, fast rewind, fast forward, etc. The data may be displayed in MIDI format or in conventional musical notation format. The package is completed with a song library of directly playable tunes. The package may be used in conjunction with MIDI-compatible general multimedia software to add, edit, and synchronize multi-channel music with visual data channels.

Sound authoring

With most multimedia hardware and software the information available about products usually leaves a number of questions unanswered. Unfortunately, unless a prospective purchaser knows something about systems the right questions cannot be asked until after a purchase. The previous section should provide enough information for a reader to make an informed choice of a sound board.

'Cut and paste' sound editing may be performed with the aid of a display of either digitized sound represented by the software as a sound waveform, or on MIDI data. Editing is carried out by 'cutting out' the section of sound to be used and dragging and dropping it in front of the sound representation on another track. See also the synchronizing section of chapter 2.

Some computers suitable for multimedia work have facilities for managing audio, and general authoring systems such as Premiere include software for sounds and music. However, 'sound system' boards with facilities for digitizing several different sound sources and for handling MIDI data are a relatively inexpensive way of improving inadequate sound management. They often include software for compression and for editing music or speech. Some examples follow.

SOUND AUTHORING SOFTWARE

Ballade

Ballade for 286 PCs first appeared in 1990. In the UK the price was around £200 and when used with the Roland MT-32 or CM32L it catered equally well for musicians and non-musicians. Ballade is still available from Roland. Ballade is a sequencer – its major purpose is to handle MIDI messages created with a keyboard. The MIDI data can be fed into any MIDI-compatible computer. A complete system would consist of a keyboard and an MT-32 with a MIDI interface, amplifier, and loudspeakers. If, for example, it is required to play up to 8 of the 128 sounds available in Ballade, MIDI messages would be sent to, say, channels 3 and 6 controlling piano and saxophone, and the MT-32 would play sounds simulating those instruments together.

The Ballade editing screen displays the conventional musical notation of notes on treble and bass staves. The notes may be entered by positioning and clicking a mouse – users can write their own music in this manner and play it back during composition. Alternatively, the notes may be entered from a keyboard and the software will convert MIDI data to musical notation. Ballade comes with some samples of music – for example, 'Spring' from *The Four Seasons* by Vivaldi. Once loaded, the selected music will be played by the synthesizer, which produces sounds from the eight instruments previously programmed.

Producing your own music is laborious. Schifreen (1990) says: 'Unless you are fairly experienced, expect to take at least 20 hours to write, record, and edit a four minute piece of music.'

Windows sound system

In view of the widespread use of Windows, some of the features of the Microsoft Windows Sound System (MWSS) will be used as an example of a board-based sound system. This system is good value at £115 in the UK. It is supplied as a kit consisting of a board (preferably plugged into a 16-bit socket in the computer), microphone and headphones, and five 3.5" disks containing the software. A suitable computer should include at least an 80386SX 25 MHz processor, VGA monitor, 2 Mbytes of RAM, and 10 Mbytes of hard disk capacity.

MWSS includes a voice recognition and synthesis system. The recognition system can be used to add words to the stored vocabulary of words available for computer voice control – e.g. 'Enter', 'Find', 'Help', 'Menu Bar', etc. The system requires 'training' to a speaker's voice by the repetition of words to be used in the software's voice acoustic model. The synthesis system may also be used to 'proofread' data using words in its vocabulary from text filed for any Windows application. Voice recognition and synthesis are outside the scope of this book. Suffice it to say that a tremendous research effort has been made in an attempt to enable a computer to recognize continuous speech by any speaker. MWSS represents what can be done today at low cost for speech recognition with a limited vocabulary, distinct separated-word speech, and after being trained by a particular speaker. For more information see Roe and Wilpon (1993) and Picone (1993).

A major function of the MWSS board and software is to digitize incoming voice or music from sources such as a microphone or CD drive connected to its input sockets, compress or process it, and output it after digital–analogue conversion, to headphones or loudspeakers. 'Processing' means create, edit, play, and add special effects to a sound recording, or add or include sound with picture or motion video presentations.

Alternative MWSS compression schemes include 'True Speech', which compresses speech by about 80:1, resulting in adequate quality, or Interactive Multimedia Association Adaptive Delta Pulse Code Modulation (IMA ADPCM) – a variation of PCM, widely used for analogue to digital conversion (see chapter 2); ADPCM provides about 22:1 compression. For music, ADPCM provides a compression of 16:1. Uncompressed 16-bit music occupies over 5 Mbytes of disk per minute.

MWSS can be used to control the playing of tracks on a CD in a CD-ROM drive attached to it. It will also display a menu of windows files and a menu of sound files so that a user may designate a chosen sound file to start playing sound when a windows file starts.

Sound Blaster CD16

Sound Blaster CD16 Discovery from Creative Technology includes some extra facilities. MWSS may be good value but CD16 provides extraordinary value. A plug-in board and software on 3.5" disks, two loudspeakers, a double speed Panasonic CD-ROM drive supporting photo-CD multi-sessions, CD-XA, and MPC Level 2, and a selection of CD-ROMs such as the Grolier Encyclopaedia is priced at £270 inclusive. CD16 computer requirements are similar to the MWSS, and the software includes similar features. It also includes the means of controlling a music CD played on the CD-ROM player, and displays a track selection menu. It claims to support MIDI but does not display audio waveforms for editing.

Synchronization (see chapter 2) is an important aspect from the viewpoint of a user who wants to make the most of multimedia music, but this is not included either.

Sound Edit Pro

Sound Edit Pro for Apple Macs from Macromedia is priced at about £250 in the UK. It will enhance the sound facilities of packages such as Premiere when used with them. For digitizing a sound source such as a microphone, SEP allows the user to select the sound sampling rate. As average quality sound uses up about 1.3 Mbytes of storage per minute, the rate can be selected accordingly for speech or high- or low-quality music.

A variety of music clips is available from Macromedia on their Clip Media series of CD-ROMs. The music is recorded in various styles and formats and at different digitizing rates.

PICTURE AUTHORING SOFTWARE

Introduction

The first real impact of authoring systems was felt at the 1989 MacWorld show in Boston. In the same year a similar show was presented at Apple's offices in Stockley Park near Heathrow Airport. A software package called Mediamaker written by the BBC Interactive Television Unit at Boreham Wood was used. What it does is described by Cawkell (1989). It provides for multimedia authoring on a Mac IIx.

The major sources of still graphics or full-colour illustrations are scanned items, computer-generated graphics and art of various kinds, either user-created or imported from other software. Hypercard, or similar software, is often the basis for storage and retrieval. A Hypercard can contain graphics and illustrations in colour up to a size of 18" × 18", 1280 × 1280 pixels. If parts cannot be seen because the screen is too small, those parts may be scrolled on to the screen.

The most common format for graphics or illustration files is the Tagged Image File Format (TIFF). Each image contains a header directory specifying its colour, resolution, grey scale, etc., details which are read and suitably handled by the processing software. TIFF was introduced by Aldus and has been adopted by many other organizations.

Simple animation – meaning usually relatively unsophisticated motion – may be created without excessive cost or effort. Greater realism requires more expense and professionalism. One way of making animation sequences is to create a picture, copy it on to a second card, alter it slightly using Apple paint, copy the altered picture on to a third card, and so on.

For example, Studio One software from Electronic Arts provides animation control from Hypercard stacks with XCMD driver control for loading and playing sequences. It includes the automatic creation of inter-mediate stages of smooth animation ('tweening') between two different scenes – a facility saving an enormous amount of time.

A very large selection of software packages for PC or Mac machines is available. Some of the better known ones are described here as typical examples of the kinds of preparational facilities that are now available for multimedia presentations. Most packages will run either on fast Mac or PC machines unless stated otherwise.

Supershow and Tell

Supershow and Tell (from Ask Me Multimedia Centre), which costs $150, is a relatively simple and easy-to-use package for Windows for preparing what the suppliers call 'super slideshows'. The data are packed into a single window showing the current scene. Navigation controls and a Draw Editor are included. The package also contains thumbnails of other scenes com-pleted or in preparation. A single-colour or tiled background may be used and MIDI files are supported for sound. Every object in a scene is also an interactive button so that when the button is pressed modifications can be made to it.

To create a slide, ikons representing text, images, sound, drawings, or movies are dragged on to the slide. The arrangement may then be edited – for instance, to attach sound to a movie, to change fonts, change colours, etc., and finally to add action to the contents such a scrolling text, altering shapes, etc.

A suitable machine for running SST would be a 486/50 with 8 Mbytes of RAM, 100 Mbytes of hard disk, and a video and Sound Blaster card.

Compel

Compel, from Asymetrix and listed at $295, contains features similar to Supershow and Tell with some additions. It runs on MSDOS with Windows 3.1 operating system on a 80386SX machine or higher and needs 4 Mbytes of memory. It comes on floppies or CD-ROM. The CD-ROM comes with graphics, video, and sound clips, so to play them the host machine also needs multimedia capabilities. The software is based on a large number of slide templates suitable for making 35 mm slides or for directing the display straight on to a screen. The templates provide a choice of different design features and a choice of colours and fonts. Each template contains designated areas into which objects chosen from the CD-ROM selection or created by the user, such as text, graphics etc., may be placed. Various inter-slide transitional effects such as fades and wipes are included.

An advanced feature of this system which requires mouse operations by a lecturer, is the use of slide-to-slide hyperlinks. Words shown as being, in effect, 'buttons', may be clicked with the mouse, and a connected slide is displayed. For example, the words 'piano tuner' could be clicked to a slide containing a video clip of a piano tuner at work with sound. Numerous drawing aids are included and sets of up to six thumbnails may be displayed at a time on the screen during slide preparation for a quick check of the presentation. If necessary, the slides may be reordered. Slides may be printed on to transparencies and lecture notes may be printed for distributing to an audience. The software comes with a comprehensive instruction manual which includes hints and tips about slide design.

Mediamaker

Mediamaker suffered from being a mainly analogue system. Changes in this field were rapid. A US company called Macromind took over Mediamaker (still available as Mediamaker 1.5 at £649) as an alternative product to Macromedia Director, an improved product handling digitized data. However, Mediamaker pioneered presentations using a 'time line', an idea which has been often followed since. A time line track, calibrated in minutes, appears across the bottom of the screen for assembling data into a presentation programme. The data are indexed by 'picons' (ikons), previously retrieved on to the main body of the screen, describing clips of sound, graphics, text, or motion video. The picons have been retrieved from various peripherals such as videodisk, video-8 tape, Mac files, etc. For motion video a picon is a single picture acting as an indexing term for the clip. A sound picon is usually a small box containing a description in words.

To assemble a program a picon is dragged from the screen on to the assembly track in the required order of play. Once on the track, the length of the picon automatically changes to occupy a length of track corresponding to the actual playing time in minutes of the data associated with it. The track can be edited and recorded as a videotape programme for presenting to an audience with the playing time corresponding to the total track time. The arrangement is impressive and was way ahead of anything else available at that time. In 1991 Mediamaker was followed by an IBM authoring package called *Storyboard Live!* for PCs, providing rather similar facilities. The interface was considerably less friendly than Mediamaker's.

Macromedia Director

Mediamaker's time track principle has been adopted in more recent multi-media authoring packages. One of the most widely used is Macromedia Director; the suppliers claim that there are over 100,000 users of the system. Director received its most recent upgrade in 1994 as Director 4.0, and became available at about £1000 in the UK in 1995. It will run interactive applications on Macs or PCs. Director's display consists of a time line calibrated by frame number, 48 channels of 'score' assembly including two sound channels, and a resizeable scrolling area for displaying a database of up to 32,000 'cast' elements or thumbnail ikons each representing a data file which may be dragged and dropped on to the score line. The score may contain text, graphics, animation, digital video, and sound. Interactivity may be added using the Lingo scripting language.

Director will control videotape recorders, laserdisk players, CDs, and external sound files. PAL, TIFF, Photo CD, Video for Windows, Quicktime for Windows, Quicktime Movies, MacPaint, animation, and other files may be imported depending on the PC or Macintosh machine being used. Director will run on 486/33 or more powerful PCs with 8 Mbytes or more of RAM, Windows 3.1 and DOS 5.0 or higher, and 40 Mbytes of free space on a hard disk. Alternatively, it will run on a Mac with at least a 68030 processor and System 7.0 software. For digital video support Microsoft video for Windows or Apple Quicktime extension are needed.

Figure 6.7 shows progress in preparing a presentation using the Overview window in the original version of Macromind (now Macromedia) Director (Macromind Inc., San Francisco, by courtesy of the Que Corporation (see Bove and Rhodes 1990)) – a software presentation program which includes the various functions provided in Mediamaker. In Figure 6.7, event sequences including text, graphics, sound, transition effects, and animation are being controlled with the aid of selection ikons and a display of the complete sequence. The Lingo scripting language is used for various purposes – for example, for creating external links and adding interactive features. Director files may be saved as Quicktime movies.

Authorware Professional

A more recent product from Macromedia called Authorware Professional comes with an interface which looks like a flowchart. It provides storyboard visual construction facilities for designing an interactive programme, for instance, an interactive training programme. No computer program writing is needed. Ikons are dragged-and-dropped into position, one beneath another on the flowchart. A vertical connection line between ikons indicates the presentation sequence. When the user is to be offered choices, the line is divided into a number of vertical parallel lines, each connecting to an ikon, representing an alternative sequence to be chosen by the user. Facilities are

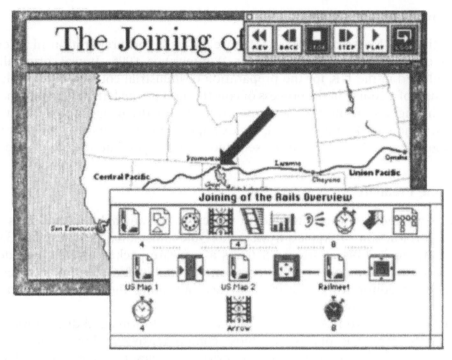

Figure 6.7 A screen from Macromind Director
Source: Que Corporation

included for displaying an ikon representing an imported file of graphics or text. Either may be edited. These ikons are fitted into the flowchart, eventually becoming the software for an interactive training course.

Authorware Professional supports various graphics, different types of sound, animation, etc. It requires (at minimum) a 20MHz 386 machine with 4 Mbytes of RAM, 16 colour VGA, and 40 Mbyte hard disk. It supports Macromedia Director, so files from that software may be called on to the flowchart.

Schorr (1993) describes a kiosk application of Authorware Professional 3.0 called 'town guide'. For instance, a user may choose from a selection of restaurants and view more details by clicking on a button. Authorware Professional uses Hypercard XCMD commands for control purposes. Authoring software with as many features as Authorware Professional may take a designer 'three to six months full-time ... before feeling truly proficient', according to Schorr. Numerous facilities are provided for capturing, manipulating, and displaying data. Animation facilities include control of timing, speed, and multiple layering so that animated objects may be overlapped. Digital and analogue video facilities are provided including start control, freeze frames, etc.

Masterclass

Multimedia Masterclass 2.0 is software to assist the preparation of interactive presentations. The cost (for Windows) is £995. It was originally
developed in the UK for the preparation of industrial courses. The display
consists of a course in the process of construction on the left, and an ikon box
on the right showing the elements available for dragging into the course
area. When an ikon is selected, for example, 'graphics images', the files of
images may be browsed and the selected item dragged into the course area.

Adobe Premiere

Premiere looked promising when it came out but was held up by delays in
the introduction of Apple's System 7.0/Quicktime software. Premiere 3.0,
introduced in 1994 at around $700, is a software package which provides
improved Mediamaker-type programme assembly facilities. It has been
called an editor for Quicktime Movies, indicating the close Quicktime/
Premiere association.

Premiere 3.0 from Adobe (Mountain View, California and distributors in
other countries) is one of the most comprehensive authoring packages
available at the time of writing. The price, for Macs, is around $1000 (CD-
ROM deluxe version). Premiere 3.0 is well described by Lindstrom (1994).

Premiere 4.0, embodying additional improvements, became available in
late 1994. Lindstrom recommends the fastest available Mac with 16 Mbytes
of memory and possibly several Gigabytes of hard disk capacity. A buyer
needs to consider whether he needs Premiere's sophistication or whether a
system nearer 'entry level' would provide all that is needed.

How many of the new features and facilities requiring new hardware and
software are likely to be used, and how much learning time will be required
to use them effectively? The purchase of Premiere 4.0 and associated
equipment may or may not be considered as being well justified for preparing a state-of-the-art multimedia presentation. The software resembles
Mediamaker. The required collection of objects such as digital still and
video motion clips, graphics, animation clips, and digital audio are retrieved
and displayed thumbnail-size on the screen. They are selected, dragged
and dropped into the 'construction window' area using similar but more
sophisticated facilities and with the same objectives as in Mediamaker. The
construction window is shown in Figure 6.8. On the right the software is
being used to set up an image correctly.

Clip lengths are identified with the SMPTE time code. The need for
computer power is obvious from Lindstrom's comment about integrating
various effects into a complete presentation on videotape: 'generating even
a relatively brief Quicktime movie will take 15 to 30 minutes or more
even on a fast Mac'. Premiere includes a range of transitional effects which

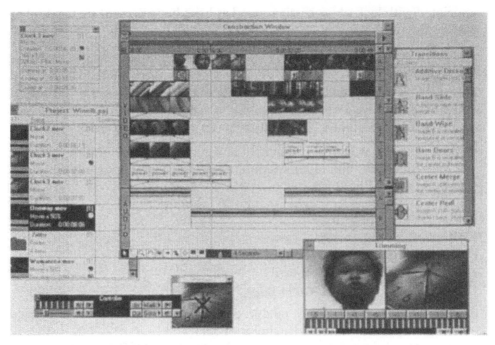

Figure 6.8 Premiere construction window
Source: Adobe

are frequently included in TV commercials. For example, Scene A may be represented on one face of a rotating cube, while Scene B appears on another face as A disappears.

Premiere can handle three-track sound recordings with fade and adjustable level control for sound or music. Music from one track can be faded into music on another, or music can be reduced in volume as speech is introduced on another track.

With even more extra facilities provided by plug-in boards, advanced presentations can be produced with Premiere. Lindstrom says: 'Premiere performed superlatively well using video clips that I captured with New Video's high-end Eye-Q system – a full screen full-motion audio-video capture and compression set-up.' The refinements added in Premiere 4.0 include a trimming window where the head and tail of adjoining clips may be viewed and edited. Many other special effects are available. For example, moving images may be twisted, zoomed, rotated, or distorted.

In October 1994 the author tried out Premiere with extra boards resembling Lindstrom's (by courtesy of Times Graphics Systems, Kendall Avenue, London, W3). The hardware consisted of an Apple 8100/80, fitted with VideoVision boards, 32 Mbytes of RAM, and a 2 Gbyte disk. Full-screen PAL motion video previously recorded on the disk was played back, providing pictures of very good quality without any of the problems associated with lack of processing speed as have been present on most other systems up until now.

Media Suite Pro

This package from Avid (UK) at around £20,000 is a complete hardware/software outfit designed for professional video productions to be used with Apple Quadra machines. The outfit includes the following units.

- MSP software with frame digitization options, timeline editing, picture-in-picture effects and Open Media Framework system compatibility
- Quadra 950 with 32 Mbytes of RAM, 2 Mbytes of VRAM, 230 Mbyte disk, Apple extended keyboard, and 20" monitor
- Avid 4 Gbyte disk drive
- Digidesign Audiomedia 2 card
- Truvista NuVista video digitizer card
- Avid JPEG5 compression card
- Atto SCSI II accelerator board

It will digitize video sources, enable comprehensive editing to be carried out, and output the results to a chosen media.

Apple Quicktime files are converted into Avid MSP format enabling Quicktime movies to be used in other programs, which may then be compressed and moved into MSP to be edited and output on to, say, videotape. Alternatively, appropriate MSP files may be converted into a Quicktime movie which may then be moved into any Quicktime-compatible programs.

The system could form the major part of a video and film editing suite.

Asymetrix Toolbook

Toolbook has been described as a Windows' version of Apple's Hypercard. It is associated with Microcosm in a teaching application and is further discussed under the teaching section in chapter 15.

Media Mogul

Unlike the packages described above, Media Mogul is specifically CD-software. It includes formats of up to 768 × 560 pixels in 24-bit colour using two graphic planes with certain limitations on scene-to-scene transitions, run length encoded animation, and part-screen DYUV images running at up to 25 frames per second to provide limited motion within a small area.

Embark

Embark is also unlike the previous packages because it is designed for a specific type of user – a museum. Moreover, it embodies the experience of at least nine major museums in the United States. It has four components – image management integrated with collections management, kiosk for public access, and exhibition management. Embark is something more than an authoring package – it is a museum object management package.

The system is available from Digital Collections Inc., Berkeley, California. It runs on a 68040 Macintosh such as a Quadra 650 with 24 Mbytes of RAM and 250 Mbyte hard disk, using System 7.0 and Quicktime. Price depends on the number of users. The design for a kiosk in the public access part of the system includes provision for a multimedia tour of a museum, audio messages, index for searching for particular items, and so on. Embark has been favourably reviewed by Jones-Garmil (1994).

The public access feature is independent of collections management. It includes a Quicktime movie about the museum, and an audio commentary may be added if required. An index tree is provided into which may be fitted the names of objects or artists. Sets of thumbnail-size images may be retrieved, and full-size screen expansions with zoom-in for examining details may be requested.

In the collection management package provision is made for 1200 customizable fields in four groups: Descriptive, Historical, Management, and Documentation. High-quality images in 24-bit colour are supported and in the next version the Art and Architecture Thesaurus (AAT) and the Union List of Artists' Names (ULAN) will be included. Jones-Garmil says: 'Embark is one of the finest collections management systems that I have seen and I would use it without hesitation.'

Other systems

As well as the high-performance systems just described, there is a range of less expensive software packages from which to choose in order to make the most of the increased power of the hardware without adding expensive boards.

Cryan (1994) shows the difference when the presentation runs as a series of timed activities. The seven packages which he compares are 'to show slide presentation on your computer screen . . . with fancy slide transitions', but including 'the added element of time'. Cryan says that these packages are aimed at 'the general business presenter'. In fact they represent the 'low end' of a range of current products for helping the author with the creation of a presentation containing all the bells and whistles made possible by the increased power of multimedia computers.

The least expensive of the seven – Q/Media (Vancouver, Canada) 1.2 at $99 – includes provision for importing CD audio and a wide range of image formats. The author's choice is Astound for Windows or Macs at $399 from Gold Disk (Santa Clara). Astound includes the 'outliner' facility present on the 1991 packages, but there are numerous added facilities such as drawing effects, twenty-two different ways of representing scene transitions, dropping text letter by letter, and a CD-ROM with 1300 items of clip-art including graphics, art, sound, music, digital video, and animated sequences.

VISUALIZATION

Visualization is a technique which came to the fore in the 1980s with the arrival of sufficient computer power to process very large amounts of data. A huge mass of scientific data may be better understood when presented in compact pictorial form rather than as mathematical expressions, numerical data, or graphics. According to Arrott and Latta (1992), the origins of visualization lie in the special effects which were first seen on television in the early 1980s, later adapted by engineers and scientists, allowing them to explore volumes of data in ways which were not previously possible. The objective of visualization is to 'provide tools and a system which allow the user to extract information from the data'. This involves a diverse set of tasks: data formation and management, 2D image processing, display of 3D data, user interface design, visual representation (opaque, transparent, colour map, etc.), animation and computation system (Farrell 1991).

A good example of identifying and analysing patterns of data is provided by Weber (1993): 'Convert the prices of individual stocks into the motion of vertical stalks, plant several hundred of them on a computer screen, and watch as market trends are revealed in the shimmering crop before you.'

It may be necessary to apply large amounts of computer power to produce the desired effects. The IBM Power Visualisation System (PVS), for example, uses a 'visualisation server containing 32 i860 RISC processors and . . . a parallel disc array of linkable 170 Gbyte units' (Foster 1992).

However, a range of visualization software has been developed for PCs and workstations capable of dealing with smaller requirements. For instance, Advanced Visual Systems (Waltham, Mass.) offers its Developers AVS Unix software for $25,000. It provides visualization techniques for geometry, volumes, numerical data in arrays, grids, and finite element formats.

A whole issue of the *IBM Journal of Research & Development* is devoted to papers on the visual interpretation of complex data. A good example of a practical application of an IBM software package called GALAXY is provided by Barberi *et al.* (1991) in the issue. The article describes how the package is used to process data collected by sensors aboard the Landsat 4 and Landsat 5 satellites. Terrain elevation information can be obtained from stereo digital images of the earth photographed from a satellite to an accuracy of between 3 and 10 metres. Figure 6.9 shows a set of scientific data which has been transformed into 'visualization' format.

In July 1994 another journal, *Computer*, devoted an entire issue to visualization. All the authors are based in universities. This issue covered similar ground to the special issue of *IBM Journal of Research &*

Figure 6.9 Scientific data visualized
Source: IBM

Development referred to above. The 8 articles in *Computer* contain 82 references but not one of them cites any one of the articles in the IBM journal published only three years earlier. This says something about visualization's rate of progress. Kaufman (1994) writes that the field is growing rapidly. He believes that expenditure on hardware will increase from $1 billion in 1990 to $3 billion in 1995. Judging by the lack of reference connections between the journals just mentioned, a core of 'milestone' articles has yet to be formulated.

Chapter 7

Multimedia, copyright, and patents

COPYRIGHT

Introduction

Copyright protection goes back to Queen Anne's Statute to protect the rights of book authors in England, introduced following pressure from the Stationers' Company in 1710. Similar laws were enacted in many countries according to the local background – whether based on Roman or Anglo-Saxon tradition. International agreement came with the Berne Convention of 1886. Since then there have been many changes, notably at the Universal Copyright Convention, Geneva, 1952, at the Paris 1971 revisions, taking special account of the needs of developing countries, and in the UK with the repeal of the 1956 Act and the Copyright Designs and Patents Act 1988.

In the US a copyright subsists in an 'original work of authorship fixed in any tangible medium of expression' (US Copyright Act 1976), extending for the life of the author, usually plus fifty years, the same term as in the UK. Items subject to copyright include the following:

Text	Exclusive rights
Graphics	Copyright when fixed in a medium
Source and object code	Usually covered by program's copyright
Composer's music	Recording company, and musician rights over a recorded program
Film	Every frame copyright

Areas of abuse for a number of products include the following:

Books	Photocopying, translating, reprinting
Journals	Photocopying
Computer programs	Copying, cloning, translating

Machine-readable activities	Copying of citation records, abstracts, data, full text articles, CD-ROM data and software copying
Cassettes	Duplication for sale
Trademarks and patents	Counterfeiting, copying

Two documents proposing reforms were published in the UK – the Whitford Report (Anon. 1977) and the 1981 Green Paper (Anon. 1981). Whitford was in favour of blanket licensing for photocopying, whereby an organization like the US Copyright Clearance Centre (CCC) would collect royalties and distribute the proceeds to publishers with no such exceptions as are now provided for research purposes. But the Green Paper proposed that the exceptions should be retained 'with some tightening to control abuse'. Neither the British Library nor the publishers were happy with the Green Paper, the publishers considering that the approach to photocopying was inconclusive.

The UK Copyright, Designs, and Patents Act 1988 became law on 1 August 1989, replacing the 1986 Act. Comments about it appear later in this chapter.

Fair dealing (fair use)

Fair use, the more specific US equivalent of fair dealing, is an important concept which has been well described by Wilson (1990). Wilson quotes the US 1976 Copyright Act, although his remarks could probably equally well be applied to the situation in the UK. The Act says 'the fair use of a copyrighted work for purposes such as criticism, comment, news reporting, teaching . . . is not an infringement of copyright'. Wilson continues: 'there is no precise rule for determining Fair Use'. Some of the factors to be considered in deciding fairness of use include purpose, the nature of the work, the amount and the substantiality of the portion used in relation to the whole work, the effect of the use on the potential market for, or the value of, the copyrighted work, 'but it is generally agreed by commentators, and recently by the Supreme Court, that the effect on the market for the copyrighted work is undoubtedly the single most important aspect of Fair Use'.

In the UK, fair dealing continues under the 1988 Act with a tightening up of certain aspects of photocopying in libraries such as 'one copy of the same article per person' and 'allowing photocopying of no more than a reasonable portion of a book'. In view of the difficulty of policing self-service photocopying machines to be found in all libraries these points seem unrealistic.

Martin and Cowan (1994) quote the opinions of a lawyer specializing in image copyrights: 'Borrowing a small portion of someone else's image and using it in your own represents what is the ultimate grey area in copyright law.' Borrowing all or a small part of an image created by somebody else is a copyright infringement. Fair use applies, since it is debatable how much of a picture can be borrowed without infringing.

Martin and Cowan quote the case of one Fred Ward, a magazine photographer. Ward noticed that a small photograph he had taken of fibreoptic wires had been reproduced on a computer screen within an advertisement in a computer magazine. He had not sold the rights and when his lawyer approached the advertiser, who had used an agency to produce the advertisement, the advertiser had assumed that permission was unnecessary. Ward says his lawyer sent the advertiser a bill for as many times as the advertisement had been used, and they paid for each use. Most works of art, owned by museums, collectors, or art galleries, must not be reproduced and their permission must first be obtained.

Further examples of copyright infringement are provided later in the chapter.

Copyright and new technology

The advent of technology enabling text and images to be electronically created, easily reproduced, and then copied with a quality quite closely approaching the original, introduces many new copyright problems. The superhighway increases the threat to an author's ability to exploit rewards for his work. This aspect of it is discussed briefly in chapter 8.

New problems were perceived in the 1970s. Exclusive rights were extended in a 1980 Amendment to the US 1976 Copyright Act. After a description of 'derivative works', the following phrase was added: 'or any other form in which a work may be recast, transformed, or adapted'. Ownership, rights, and 'enforcement in cyberspace' in the United States are discussed at length by Ginsburg (1995), a professor at Columbia University. The Amendment is intended to extend protection from the print-on-paper medium to any form of media – notably current and future media enabled by new technology. There have been a number of image-related examples illustrating the point.

The European Commission has been active in this area recently. Its paper-work includes Green Papers (discussion documents), Draft Directives (for comment), Directives (passed by the Council of Ministers, for implementation). Ambiguities suggesting that a database might be a cable program, for instance, have now been removed. Other items in early draft proposals did not satisfy the information community, with whom, it was suggested, there were inadequate consultations. A Draft Directive concerning database copyright in 1992 was clarified in a 1993 revised EC Draft Directive. A database is defined as 'a collection of data, works or other materials arranged, stored and accessed by electronic means, and the materials necessary for the operation of the database such as thesaurus, index, or system of obtaining or presenting information'. Databases may be protected by copyright as 'collections' within the meaning of the Berne Convention protecting literary works. Oppenheim (1994), among others, comments on this draft, say that 'fair dealing will apply to databases'.

Sui generis (unique) protection is accorded to films, which are regarded as 'something complete and independent'. Multimedia receives piecemeal attention under books, databases, software, etc. A database – 'a collection of works' – is accorded *sui generis* protection in an EC Directive proposal of July 1995, and licences are compulsory.

The EC Commissioner Mario Monti believes that copyright as it now exists will encourage the formation of a critical mass of services justifying investment in the Information Superhighway infrastructure.

The Trade Related Intellectual Property (TRIPS) agreement, a US-sponsored component of the GATT agreement, also covers compilations of works. It is hoped that TRIPS will help to ensure that all participating countries comply with copyright protection.

The anxieties of publishers and recording companies, art galleries, and museums with regard to infringements of their copyrights could be reduced if they grasped the opportunities for promoting their holdings and their revenue-earning possibilities. 'Obtaining rights can be extremely difficult for potential developers unless the collecting societies respond to new needs and find mechanisms for licensing an adequate volume of material,' says Nicholas Higham, a London solicitor. 'If they do not do so, then the voices of those who already call for compulsory licensing, or for an emasculation of rights of copyright into a mere right to economic compensation for the use of a work, will be increasingly heard.'

A book governing the copyright situation in the UK has been published by Raymond Wall (1994). Much of it covers aspects of the UK Copyright, Designs and Patents Act 1988, but there is a chapter of particular interest covering multimedia aspects, entitled 'Audiovisual media and electronic copyright'. Wall says that although databases are not mentioned, 'it should be quite clear that online electronic databanks whether of pictures or text, are cable programme services'. A cable program means 'any item included in a cable program service', and cable program service means 'a service mainly for sending visual image sounds or other information via a public telecommunications system otherwise than by Wireless Telegraphy for reception at two or more places'. CD-ROMs, diskettes, or tape are not included in the definition of a cable program service and Wall suggests that a CD-ROM should be treated like a book. Wall provides some examples of infringements in respect of electronic databases, including: 'making multiple copies of a printout . . . supplying a copy to an enquirer . . . supplying large segments of a compilation . . . and downloading for input to another database'.

Special conditions in the United States

Copyright protection in the US extends to collective works – that is, where a number of independent works are assembled into a collective whole. This is thought to cover full text databases such as Lexis even although this database is a compilation of public domain material. If this kind of information is, in fact, protected, databases containing the full text of articles not in the public domain, and contributed by separate authors, would also seem likely to be covered.

International copyright issues are becoming increasingly important in view of the use of international networks like the Internet, and the trend to ease 'collective copyright' royalty problems by international services like 3DO, Andromeda, Dialog, and others.

In the US a unique factor affects attitudes towards national copyright which also affects within-US activities of foreign origin, which are, of course, subject to US copyright law. While major countries might be expected to act similarly because they all belong to the Berne Convention and the Universal Copyright Convention, the unique influence in the United States is the effect of the First Amendment to the Constitution. The Amendment says that the Congress shall 'make no law . . . abridging the freedom of speech, or of the press'. The effect of the Amendment used to be clear from a case cited by the late de Sola Pool (1983) when telephone service was denied to a subscriber in 1885 after he had used bad language. Denial of a printing press to a publisher because of obscenity in his publications would be unconstitutional.

Miller (1993), in tracing the ancestry of electronic information services back to the telegraph system, quotes a comment from another publication (*Technologies of Freedom*) by Pool:

> Courts like to treat new phenomena by analogy to old ones . . . it may seem odd that when a new technology came into existence the courts did not perceive it as an extension of the printed word sharing the same significance, the same infirmities, and the same need for protection as the press whose liberties the courts had so sedulously guarded.

The reason for this dim perception of telegraphy was that the early telegraph carried so few words at such a high cost 'that people thought of it not as a medium of expression but rather as a business machine'.

Coming to the thrust of his long article, Miller considers that for electronic information services, analogies with other communications media are strained. Moreover, the status of new services with respect to government intrusion must be determined in respect of the so-called 'Fairness Doctrine' restriction of freedom provided by the First Amendment. The Fairness Doctrine allows government intrusion into constitutionally protected services when the rights of listeners override the inviolability of the freedom rights of those services.

Miller discusses two cases – *Telecommunications Research and Action Center (TRAC)* v. *Federal Communications Commission* (1986/87) and *Cubby Inc.* v. *Compuserve Inc.* (1991).

In *TRAC*, the FCC concluded that its teletext service resembled print media. However, the Court of Appeals disagreed with this reasoning and focused on the technology most nearly analogous to teletext. It concluded that it was similar to broadcasting so the Fairness Doctrine applied; accordingly, it was effectively a common carrier and so would have no editorial control, being required to make any third-party service available.

In *Cubby* – a case brought to determine whether Compuserve was liable for defamatory statements made on one of its third-party services – it was concluded that Compuserve had no duty to monitor each issue published. It had assumed a role similar to that of a common carrier, and so was not liable for statements made on one of its third-party services. However, as a distributor it could decline to carry a given publication.

Miller asks whether, if an electronic information service does exert control (as did Prodigy in its electronic mail services), it would be liable for actionable content. 'Such a result would be somewhat ironic,' continues Miller, 'since it would effectively punish operators who attempt to take an active editorial role and reward those who simply sit back and assume the role of passive common carriers.'

The uncertainty created by these cases relates to the notion in the *TRAC* decision that a service 'picks up' the regulatory traits of its transmission medium. But it was also concluded in *Cubby* that Compuserve was acting as a distributor/carrier and so would not be liable, for example, for copyright infringements – we are back to the unique effects of the First Amendment on copyright; in the US, is or is not an electronic information service liable for an infringement? Miller considers that outdated analogies, as made in *TRAC*, are inappropriately burdensome. But until the matter becomes clearer as a result of more court actions to which the US is prone, the liabilities of UK information carriers or providers operating in the US remain in doubt.

In many countries provision is made for taking a copy of a journal article for 'research or private study' which is considered to be fair dealing (UK) or fair use (US). Copying may be done provided that the person taking the copy signs a declaration that the copy is for this purpose only.

According to Wall (1993) the amount of material considered reasonable to copy in the context of fair dealing varies according to circumstances. It may be 'One copy of a complete chapter in a book . . . a maximum of 5% of a literary work . . . up to 10% of short books, reports etc.'. For other kinds of publication different criteria may apply.

Collective works

There is a quite a different aspect which affects the earnings of museums and art galleries. How can museums and art galleries earn revenue by selling reproduction rights for multimedia products containing thousands of images without hampering the market? They currently earn up to $500 per picture for allowing reproduction in commercial publications. These kinds of prices per image applied to multimedia would encourage infringement. In 1991 an informal meeting between several major museums was held and a 'Model Agreement' was proposed to cover conditions of use and royalty payments for multimedia usage.

The same principle applies in general commerce. The *Sporting News* wanted to purchase the rights to cards owned by the Topps company (Shandle 1991), showing football players. They wanted to publish a CD-ROM about football. This would involve negotiations with up to 1000 players' lawyers so the idea was abandoned; project viability required a royalty not exceeding 0.15 per cent.

Breward (1993) and White (1993) discussed social and regulatory issues, property rights, copyright, and standards at the London Online meeting. White says:

> Copyright law protects the interest, first and foremost, of the creative community; writers, artists, photographers, musicians, computer programmers, film makers, etc. Whenever a new medium emerges for creative works, this is liable to put pressure on copyright and perhaps bring about amendments to the law.

They continue with a general review of copyright law, and among other matters discuss 'collective copyright licensing' – an area which is currently presenting severe practical difficulties to people involved in multimedia. The basic problem, typified by the Topps company's problem just described, is explained by White:

> At present a person wishing to use works for a multimedia product has to make an individual approach to each rights owner for permission, and clearly this task can be an enormous one.
>
> There are, at the time of writing, no significant mechanisms for the collective licensing of works . . . the inconvenience, delay and expense involved in gaining individual licences of so many rights owners are reported to be having an inhibiting effect on the growth of the industry.

Bearman (1994) suggests that Museums and Art Galleries should collectively organize themselves to create a market for their collections. He discusses a number of steps that should be taken to safeguard protection, mainly by making it clear in notices and general publicity that reproduction of objects in any form infringes the museum's or gallery's copyright.

Solving the collective works problem

Attempts are being made to deal with copyright problems by companies which offer large amounts of data which may be used without copyright restrictions within certain limits.

A company called 3DO in San Mateo, California, is making available a very large database containing music, sound effects, and thousands of photographs, footage, and clip art, available to licensees without copyright restrictions. By March 1993 nearly 100 publishers had become licensees. The database comprises over 100 Gigabytes on 170 CDs containing a clip art library, 20,000 still photographs, 60 hours of music, and 20,000 sound effects, together with a quantity of film footage and numerous texture effects. The database is available to software licensees without copyright restrictions. The deal includes the supply of hardware, and although the 3DO is associated with Matsushita, it does not seem to have lived up to the hype surrounding its launch at the beginning of 1993. But in 1994 Matsushita was said to be putting in a big effort to market a 3DO hardware product called The Real.

Another company, Andromeda (Abingdon, UK), offers a product called Resourcebank which it claims is 'one of the largest high quality illustrated encyclopaedic databases in publishing' (to quote from the sales data). Andromeda says that it has 'open access to tens of thousands of different media material from key copyright holders throughout the world'. It includes professionally created sound effects, 50 hours of varied music, and 20,000 photographs.

The data come on CDs, CD-ROMs, or photo-CDs and the catalogue is large. For example, there are at least 14 CDs entitled 'Artwork-birds'. Numerous other artwork disks cover, for example, mammals, prehistoric life, the earth, Romans, transport, and so on. There are nearly 100 photo-CDs covering individual countries, space, etc. A separate disk called CD-Index is supplied which embodies search software, enabling a subscriber to order the appropriate CD. The Resourcebank has negotiated reproduction rights with the suppliers of the data. Andromeda states that so long as the material is used solely for electronic publishing, it may be resold publicly on a 'copyright-paid' basis – that is, no additional permission to publish or copyright fee is required.

To join Resourcebank you pay £7500, entitling you to access all its material, and its search and retrieval software. You can buy a disk from the databank for £50 but you may not use more than 20 per cent of the content of any one disk in a single publication unless you negotiate an additional fee. Further enquiries in December 1995 reveal that the system is unavailable pending an online relaunch expected early in the new year. Details should be available shortly but it is not known whether file content and prices will be similar to those mentioned above.

In April 1994, Dialog – a major operator of an electronic information system supplying data from a database in the US – provided the means for a subscribing organization to make copies or to store downloaded results, priced on a scale depending on the number of copies or users.

Several large database providers have agreed to allow their records to be used in the scheme, including Predicast, Inspec, Derwent, ABI/Inform, and Chemical Abstracts. However, some database providers have refused to participate.

Multimedia music copyright

As stated in the UK Copyright Designs and Patents Act 1988, copyright subsists in original literary, dramatic, musical, or artistic works. These copyright works include computer programs, sound and video recordings, films, cable-TV, and publicly accessible databases, all of which are protected for 50 years. Permission must be obtained from the copyright owner before a copyright work may be publicly performed. Permission is required by companies recording or re-recording music, by a recording company which wants to use the music in a public performance, or by a person or organization wanting to use live or recorded music in a public performance. Licensing and fee-collecting agencies act on behalf of their members in each of these three categories.

The major agencies are shown in Table 7.1.

Table 7.1 Licensing agencies

Organization	Function
Performing Right Society	Licenses the public performance of live or recorded music. Acts for composers and publishers
Phonographic Performance Ltd	Licenses the public performance of sound recordings. Acts for recording companies
Mechanical Copyright Protection Society	Licenses the recording of music. Acts for composers and publishers

Royalty collection realizes large sums of money. For example, in 1993 the gross revenue of PRS was over £156 million. The BBC alone was a source of over £27 million. Other royalties came from cinemas, concerts, hairdressing establishments, public houses, shops, restaurants, etc.

Music is used in multimedia presentations for enhancement purposes just as it is used in films or television programmes. Apparently 'canned music' in the form of 'buy-out CDs' may be purchased in the United States. It may include performances totalling an hour, split up into sections lasting for 15, 30, 120 seconds, etc., suitable, say, for playing as background music in a multimedia presentation.

Disk purchase includes a user's right to reproduce the music privately or in a public performance without infringing copyright. Presumably fees covering a 'blanket reproduction licence' have been paid by the disk publishers to the music publishers unless both parties work for the same company.

Andromeda's Resourcebank offers a large amount of media material as already mentioned and a second enquiry revealed that they will also supply music. Having been established to become (as stated in its publicity material) 'the principal provider of background material for electronic applications worldwide . . . all material in Resourcebank is available to subscribers for use in any electronic application (excluding broadcast and bulletin boards) royalty free'.

The music is generic, and for its other material the company either owns it, or acts as a 'seller-on' for material owned by others who have agreed to Andromeda's resale activities. Presumably these others have paid royalties to authors of the material. It is not clear why the Resourcebank excludes its customers from royalty-free broadcast and bulletin board applications, but does not exclude any other kinds of public performance.

Multimedia software often provides facilities for processing imported music, images, video, etc. The processing may consist of dragging 'clips' from the imported material into an assembly area, the assembled material being stored on, say, videotape for future presentation purposes. If the imported material originated from owners entitled to a royalty, it appears that in the event of a public performance, whatever the degree of electronic processing, editing, modifying, etc., their rights would remain unaffected. However, in view of the extraordinary effects that may be produced with multimedia software, an owner's material might or might not still be identifiable.

Copyright infringement cases

The 1972 *Williams & Wilkins* v. *United States* case is a copyright landmark. The US Court of Claims commissioner recommended that a publisher, Williams & Wilkins, was entitled to compensation for the photocopying of its journal articles by the National Library of Medicine (NLM). In 1970, NLM handled 120,000 photocopying requests. Eighteen months later, in a 4 to 3 decision, the court rejected the commissioner's recommendation, finding no evidence of economic harm to Williams & Wilkins. This decision was upheld by an equally divided Supreme Court in 1975.

One consequence of this decision was a redefinition and formalization of the manner and extent of photocopying in libraries, introduced in the US 1976 Copyright Act. In 1978 the Copyright Clearance Centre (CCC) was set up to handle royalties accruing from library photocopying in excess of the permitted quantity. Journals print the royalty due on the title-page of each article. The CCC soon ran into difficulties because the royalties collected did not cover the processing costs. However, things improved in 1980 when royalty collection increased to $300,000 compared with $57,000 in 1978.

In a 1977 US case, *Wainwright Securities* v. *Wallstreet Transcript Corporation*, Transcript wrote an abstract of an item from a Wainwright report, appropriating almost verbatim original aspects of the report. It had the obvious intent, if not the effect, of fulfilling the demand for the original work. This was considered to be not legitimate news coverage or fair use but rather 'Chiseling for personal profit'.

In June 1990 a judge found in favour of Lotus against the VP Paperback Planner because of similarity between a Paperback and the Lotus 1–2–3 spreadsheet interface. In 1–2–3 the choice, structure, and presentation on the screen were found to be original and non-obvious and therefore copyrightable. VP-Planner had been deliberately copied from 1–2–3.

In March 1991 there was some further support for the idea that 'look and feel' could be copyrightable in the well-publicized case of Apple versus Microsoft and Hewlett Packard. These companies claimed that Apple's iconic interface infringed Xerox's copyright covering, for instance, features in the Star machine which caused a sensation in the late 1970s. A judge gave Apple permission to pursue its copyright suit, considering that there was no evidence of Apple's infringement of Xerox's 'look and feel' copyright. In regard to Apple's claim that Microsoft and Hewlett Packard were infringing Apple's own look and feel copyright, the judge obviously thought that this was too wide a concept. His permission to allow Apple to proceed was based on the point that there could be specific features of the two companies' software which infringed.

In June 1991 there was a case of copyright infringement which was so evidently blatant that arrests in the United States followed an investigation. Those arrested were employed by a number of Taiwanese companies making or using copies of Nintendo's chips for computer games.

Fair use infringement considerations were considerably muddied by the Texaco case. In 1992 a scientist within Texaco had been routinely photocopying articles from a particular journal (*Journal of Catalysis*, published by Academic Press) for personal retention and use as part of his duties as a research scientist. The question raised in the case was whether R&D scientists can, in general, routinely photocopy articles of interest to them and keep them in a personal file if they work in a commercial company. The court concluded that such photocopying was not fair use and that Texaco was guilty of copyright infringement. The reasoning centred largely on two arguments, namely that:

1 Texaco was a company which is making profits, weakening the fair use doctrine which is strongest when the copying is intended for research and private study in the not-for-profit sector;
2 There were clear alternative ways in which Texaco could have provided the extra copies to its scientists, such as ordering more copies of the original journal, or ordering phototocopies from a Copyright Clearance

Centre-registered organization, which would charge more but which would pass on a portion of its charges to the copyright owner.

The case will go to an appeals court.

At the Multimedia and CD-ROM conference in March 1993, exhibitors claimed they were warned by the American Society of Composers, Authors, and Publishers (ASCAP) that 'spotters' would be at the show listening for copyrighted music in multimedia presentations.

Keates and Cornish (British Library) raise the problems of access and protection in terms of copyright at the EVA 1993 conference (Hemsley 1993a). 'The intellectual property industry cannot afford to allow its products to be copied, packaged, pirated or distributed without ensuring adequate economic compensation,' they say. They propose a system called CITED to list and standardize a number of aspects and to deal with the relationship established by the actions taken by people such as owners, distributors, and end-users.

A number of organizations involved in teletext broadcasting, including the BBC, ITV, Sky Television, CNN, Intelfax, and the Press Association, are discussing the question of taking legal action against several companies which they consider are infringing their copyright. Evidently some information providers are downloading information from one of these services and selling them as part of a database package.

Fred Ward's successful action against infringement was described earlier. Most works of art, owned by museums, collectors, or art galleries, must not be reproduced until permission has been granted.

PATENTS

Introduction

There is rather less patent than copyright activity in multimedia and related fields.

International patent law was harmonized in the 1978 Patent Cooperation Treaty which sixty major countries joined. If one patent application is made for a patent to be recognized by all these countries the total cost would be about £2276. That does not include the cost of drafting the patent, lawyers' fees, etc. It would cost about £1172 to take out a patent covering only European countries. A UK patent costs about £285.

In the EC, Article 85(1) of the Treaty of Rome has the effect of prohibiting restrictions in patent licensing, except when certain market thresholds are not exceeded. In 1995 a commission proposal to withdraw this exemption met strong opposition from industry.

Patent infringement cases

Patent infringement lawsuits occasionally occur in the multimedia and computer industries.

In February 1994 Microsoft lost an infringement lawsuit brought by Stac Electronics, and had to pay them $120 million.

A second, major patent issue, directly concerning multimedia, is associated with US Patent no. 5,241,671, awarded to Comptons New Media. The patent covers retrieval methods from a multimedia database. Comptons New Media was sold to a major organization, the Tribune Company. The patent was filed in 1989 and Comptons expected to receive royalties of up to 3 per cent from companies offering software capable of searching multimedia databases. Following complaints that the patent had been anticipated, it was re-examined by the US Patent Office in February 1994. After the Office had considered the complaints, the patent was revoked and royalty payments were stopped. In March 1994 Comptons New Media was given two months to appeal.

A case in the United States is being pursued by an inventor, Roger Billings, who is suing Novell for $200 million, claiming infringement of his distributed database patent. Novell claims that Billings's patent is invalid.

Chapter 8

Transmission systems and multimedia

DATA TRANSMISSION

Analogue and digital data were discussed in chapter 2. The transmission of digital data has a number of advantages. For example, each amplifier in the succession of amplifiers needed to boost analogue signals generates additive 'noise'. Not only can digital impulses be noiselessly boosted by regeneration, they are also in a form which may directly stored, processed, etc., by a digital computer.

Alec Reeves was among the first to utilize these advantages. In his 1939 British Patent 535860 (Reeves 1965) he specified a transmission method called Pulse Code Modulation in great detail – a system still in wide use today. In PCM circuits a smooth analogue waveform is sampled by an electronic device at fixed intervals to determine its height. The numerical value of each step corresponds to the value of the analogue waveform at that instant. This value is transmitted as binary code – thus if there are, say, 16 steps, each step may be represented by a 4-bit code ($\log_2 16 = 4$). If the waveform samples, now represented as values, are taken, say, 10 times per second, 10 4-bit codes, that is 40 bits per second, will be transmitted. During conversion, the level of the analogue signal may be measured with sufficient accuracy at the sampling instant by comparing its value with a staircase waveform containing steps of known values. There have to be enough steps for the digitized representation of the waveform to be good enough for a particular application: 256 different levels is usually considered sufficient for most purposes. Thus if the level of the analogue waveform corresponds at the sampling instant to, say, step 102 in the staircase waveform, that number must be transmitted.

DATA TRANSMISSION SPEED CONSTRAINTS

Multimedia information in image, sound, and other formats is described by a large number of bits. When it is electrically communicated, the bandwidth of the telecommunication channel must be wide enough to transport it at an acceptable transmission rate, even when efficient data compression is used. The cost or unavailability of suitable links is a severe constraint.

If an 'on–off' pulse representing a symbol, signalling element, or bit, is transmitted once per second, the signalling rate is said to be one baud. The greater the number of steps or levels per baud, the larger the number of bits per second transmitted: 256 steps (8 bits) is sufficient to make the 'staircase' waveform described in the preceding section closely resemble the shape of the original waveform. It is also necessary to ensure that a waveform sample is taken often enough to describe the levels of its highest frequency component. Harry Nyquist made the remarkable discovery as far back as 1928 that all the information in a smoothly changing analogue waveform can be extracted by measuring its value at least twice per cycle of the highest frequency component. For instance, if you want to digitize a PAL television waveform, you must sample its highest frequency component at least twice per cycle and transmit its digital value at that rate.

The great benefit of digitization, whether for data transmission or computer processing, is partially offset by the disadvantage that the band-width required for a communication channel satisfactorily to 'transport' the burst of pulses representing values at each sampling instant is about ten times more than the bandwidth required to transport the analogue signal representing the same data. If the signalling rate (frequency) is increased, a wider bandwidth may be required so there is an incentive to transmit as many bits per signalling element as possible.

It would appear that to send large volumes of data through a narrow band channel it is only necessary to make each baud represent a large number of bits without increasing the baud rate.

But if a signal being sent at the maximum permitted level is increasingly subdivided to provide more levels, eventually the small level changes will be comparable to the level of channel noise impulses. The receiver will then provide erroneous information, being unable to distinguish between signals and noise.

C is the maximum theoretical rate for data transmission through any channel – a target rate which may be approached by a highly efficient system but never reached. Since speeds and costs are the most important factors in today's telecommunication networks such a yardstick is extremely valuable. This equation was one of the major findings of C.E. Shannon as described in his famous paper (Shannon 1948):

> The maximum rate that information may be sent through a noisy band-limited communication channel using ideal coding, expressed as the channel's 'information capacity', C, is:

$$C = 2W \log_2 n \, (S + N) - 2W \log_2 n \, N$$
$$= W \log_2 (1 + S/N) \text{ bits per second}$$

where C = channel 'information capacity'
    S = average signal power
    N = average gaussian noise power

In practice a variety of methods which are much more ingenious than the simple method of 'voltage level coding' are used to add data without increasing the signalling rate. The phrase 'ideal coding' means that the rate C can never be reached, but recent developments in codes approaching the 'ideal' have enabled speeds to be increased considerably.

The problems of transmitting multimedia pictures constrained by channel bandwidth will be evident by considering the data volumes which might need to be transmitted, as shown in Table 2.2 in chapter 2. The top four rows of the last three columns show the Mbit totals for CRT 'picture frames' at 1, 8, and 24 bits per pixel. Table 2.3 shows that the volume of data contained within most multimedia pictures lies within this range – from the 512 × 342 screenful of the early Apple machines, through television frame screens to the Nokia monitor.

For a monitor like the Flanders, 24-bit per pixel operation is unlikely. But the Nokia monitor requires 200 Mhz bandwidth digital/analogue convertors and driving channels when the signal has been decompressed to be applied to the tube.

If a user wants to transmit pictures for full-screen reproduction somewhere within the range covered by Tables 2.2 or 2.3, the additional factors to be considered are the availability and cost of a channel with a given bandwidth, the compression ratio, the acceptable response time, and the correct synchronization. Consider, for instance, the transmission of 46 Mbits – the data volume representing a 1600 × 1200 24-bit colour picture corresponding to the screen capacity of the Nokia monitor. The result of transmitting and displaying these data at 24-bit per pixel (Table 8.1) display on the Nokia would be a picture of excellent quality and colour. The quality after, say, 20:1 compression/decompression equivalent to sending only about 2.3 Mbits, depends on the method used but it would still be good.

Table 8.1 Transmission times for a 1600 × 1200 24-bit picture

Channel		Duration including 20% OH			
Speed	*Type of line*	*Uncompressed*		*Compressed 20:1*	
64 Kbps	ISDN B	12	mins	36	secs
128 Kbps	2 × ISDN B	6	mins	18	secs
1 Mbps	leased	46	secs	2.3	secs
25 Mbps	leased	1.8	secs	0.09	secs

The bandwidth for occasionally or routinely transmitting data for such pictures depends on today's availability of the ISDN between stations, or on the economics of renting special lines, or using a suitable network. Transmitting at, say, 25 Mbps or more would be feasible for organizations sending large numbers of multimedia pages or pictures. There are a few practical examples today such as station-to-station satellite or wideband cable press links. The transmission speeds required over future super-highways for services such as Video on Demand are another matter. An idea of the possible compromises suitable for managing the delivery of this type of data is provided in the VOD section of chapter 2.

MODEMS

The part of a telecommunications system which an average user is most likely to meet is a modem. A modem will usually be within the user's premises or attached to or within a multimedia computer. Signalling at either end of a telecoms channel is performed by modems (MODulator DEModulators), which exchange data in a form suitable for transmission in the channel. The modems are connected to machines – data terminals, computers, workstations, fax machines, videotex terminals, etc., which generate and receive signals in machine format. The modem converts machine format signals to channel format signals or channel format signals to machine format signals.

Data signalling may be carried out on the Public Switched Telephone Network (PSTN). In the UK the cost of a 'data call' is the same as the cost of a voice telephone call according to the duration, distance, and time of day. On a data network, such as PSS, the connection to a 'node' or interconnection point, will normally be made via a PSTN or special analogue line.

A modem is usually packaged in a box with front panel controls and plug and socket connections, or it may be constructed on a board to be plugged into a socket within a microcomputer, in which case control and indicating functions will be displayed on the screen. The modem–computer and computer–telecoms channel connection normally handle data serially.

The advent of liberalization or privatization brought with it the removal of the PTT's modem monopoly in many countries. The modem market became highly competitive so there is now a very large choice and modems are available for a wide range of speeds. At one time it was thought that the PSTN could be used at speeds up to 2400 bps. Faster modems were available for better, more expensive, analogue leased lines. However, the size of the market has prompted some ingenious ways of getting the most value out of PSTN signalling using modems working at speeds thought to be impossible a few years ago.

The simplest type of modem – an Acoustic Coupler – is a small box connected to a terminal with a cable, and to the telephone line via the telephone handset which is inserted into a shaped receptacle on the Coupler. The receptacle contains a microphone to pick up incoming telephone line tones from the earphone fitted within the handset; the tones are converted into digital signals. Outgoing digital signals from the terminal are converted into tones fed into a small loudspeaker picked up by the microphone in the telephone handset. The use of Acoustic Couplers has declined because of their susceptibility to acoustic noise, the now widespread use of plug-and-socket telephone connections, and the arrival of cheap directly connected modems.

Modems on a plug-in board to be used in a PC slot are convenient and popular. Standard modem circuits are available on chips and a modem board usually contains two or three chips with a few separate components also mounted on the board. Alternatively, modems are supplied in free-standing boxes with cable/plug-and-socket connections.

Modems usually conform to 'V series' CCITT Standards so that any pair of modems having the same V number should work together. Performance advances include higher speeds (over the PSTN in particular), compression, error correction, and lower prices. Higher speeds are mainly achieved by data compression and working at more bits per baud; susceptibility to noise increases accordingly. Error correction reduces the effects of noise. Compression enables more data per bit to be transported.

A form of compression was introduced by Samuel Morse, who noted the size of the stocks of letters and hence their frequency of occurrence, when visiting a local printing house. He designed the Morse code accordingly with E as ".", and Q as "_ _ . _". This general principle is still used, but the modern equivalent is 'run length coding', where long strings of binary noughts and ones are represented by short codes.

Added improvements and the necessary complexity are enabled by cheap storage and processing power. In the BTLZ method, frequently occurring character strings are stored as a dictionary of short, fixed-length codewords. When a listed string recurs, a short codeword is automatically substituted for it.

Most error-detecting/correcting systems are based on the automatic addition of extra bits to a block of a given number of data bits at the trans-mitter to enable a checking procedure to be carried out at the receiver. A repeat of erroneous blocks is automatically demanded. In some modems the quality of the line is monitored and blocks of characters are retransmitted if erroneous.

Current modem developments have been towards new compression systems, sophisticated modulation schemes with more bits per symbol, improved methods of error correction, and the addition of functions such as telephone answering machine control. The complexity required for these functions is embodied in mass-produced chips so prices have not increased much. Modem chip sets are now available to provide a wide range of performance alternatives and different functions. Slightly increased prices have been accompanied by far higher speeds so transmission time costs have dropped substantially.

The most recently introduced type of modem – to the CCITT V34 recommendation – first checks the characteristics of the channel and chooses the most suitable carrier frequency – the optimum centre frequency that will support the maximum number of symbols. A good example of a V34 modem is the Hayes Optima priced at $579. It enables files of facsimile data to be sent from a PC to a fax machine. It includes a 16 Kbyte data dictionary for short code look-ups to increase transmission speeds.

VIDEO DATA TRANSMISSION

In order not to make existing black and white receivers obsolete when colour TV was introduced, it had to be possible for a B&W receiver to provide B&W pictures from colour transmissions. A rather complicated arrangement was devised whereby chrominance (colour hue and saturation) data providing the extra information about colour for the new receivers would be included. These data would be discarded by B&W receivers. Chrominance data are sandwiched between luminance (brightness) data elements so the new transmissions occupy a transmitted frequency band no wider than before.

The Nyquist sampling rate still applies to the digitization of television signals without loss of information, and needs to be considered in conjunction with the 1986 CCIR recommendation 601. The recommendation attempts to provide some common ground for 625 line/50 Hz (PAL) and 525 line/60 Hz (NTSC) systems.

TV signal sampling is specified as '4:2:2', meaning that digitization is carried out by using 4-bit luminance sampling done at 13.5 MHz, plus two 2-bit colour-difference samples each done at 6.75 MHz. Thus the transmission rate for the 8 bit total without information loss will be:

$$(13.5 + 6.75 + 6.75) \times 8 = 216 \text{ Mbps}$$

One way of achieving modest compression is by sampling at lower rates than those just specified, using data interpolation methods for the partial restoration of missing data, and including comb-filtering in the processing circuits to removing 'aliasing' (distortion) effects produced in the process (Sandbank 1990).

The above considerations are likely to be the starting point for the various compression systems used in multimedia systems, such as those described in chapter 3 under 'video'. More information about compression is provided in chapter 3.

For HDTV the bit rate using similar sampling methods would be over 2 Gbps – i.e. 20 times greater than PAL bit rates – requiring a far greater channel bandwidth than is needed for the current PAL service. For digital PAL or HDTV, special coding techniques could reduce these rates substantially – perhaps down to 70 Mbps for HDTV.

LOCAL LOOP ALTERNATIVES: FIBRE

The wires between telephone exchanges and homes are a narrow-band bottleneck limiting the flow of information to ISDN rates, assuming a home can afford ISDN. How long will it take before something better and cheaper arrives? When it does, will unlimited information arrive for home users?

Perhaps fibre will be the medium of the future. Fibre might be the solution to a major end-to-end wideband connection. The 'fibreoptics to the home' idea has been in the air for many years. Charles Judice of Bellcore (*IEEE Transactions on Communications*, May 1992) thinks it will remain there. 'Substantial penetration will not occur for at least twenty years,' he believes. Others disagree. KMI, a US forecasting company, thinks that 'Europe's fiber-in-the-loop market will skyrocket from its current $60M level to $4 billion in eight years' (*Photonics Spectra*, February 1993).

Several recent media events are likely to hasten the arrival of information into the home although little is discussed about demand and costs. Speculation about wide bandwidth via fibre into the home has been rife for years but not much has happened recently to raise hopes in Europe.

In July 1991 a major study in the EC's RACE programme concluded that fibre to the home should be delayed until costs fall or until the volume of telecommuting or HDTV sufficiently increases the justification for it. The study concluded that a fibre shared between 32 subscribers would cost ECU 1200 per subscriber – 30 per cent more than copper. The cost would increase to ECU 2000 shared among 8 subscribers, and ECU 2500 for fibres for individual homes. Much of the cost lies in the associated electro-optical components, which can only be reduced by quantity production.

An alternative technology is being developed by Ionica, which received its licence in February 1993 – a consequence of UK deregulation policy. It proposed launching a service competing with Mercury and BT, bypassing the local loop with a home-to-exchange wireless connection. It hopes to offer equal service at lower cost.

In the United States, methods of overcoming the local loop problem – called 'bypassing' – have developed into an industry. Fibre may still be a possibility thanks to further deregulation which took place in July 1992 allowing the Bell companies to provide means for subscriber selection of video programmes.

Cable-TV in the United States is transported mainly by coaxial cable carrying 155 channels of 6 MHz analogue television. All of the Bell companies are testing new systems in conjunction with cable companies. Estimates for the cost of installing fibre nationally have been up to $400 billion. Bell companies have made a substantial investment in deregulated British cable companies.

In 1991, C. Valenti of Bell Communications suggested that ADSL technology should be feasible. Since then it has progressed to the trials stage. ADSL is discussed in the 'Methods of transmission' section which follows. With regard to information to be delivered by ADSL the Bell researchers suggest that authors would be expected to index articles and users would submit interest profiles for matching against their needs. Unfortunately, say the researchers, 'the current state of the authoring art for multimedia is inadequate . . . authoring of an article frequently requires the services of a programmer and several weeks of effort'. They express the hope that it will improve. Interaction must be simple and 'it must be possible to economically deliver information'.

TELECOMMUNICATION CHANNELS FOR WIDEBAND MULTIMEDIA DATA

The advent of wideband nationwide networks running at speeds of up to 1 Gigabit per second or more will eventually reduce the telecoms bottle-neck – a bottleneck created because existing networks, representing an enormous amount of invested capital, have been pressed into service for transmitting data at speeds for which they were not designed. In the UK, the ISDN provides relatively fast data delivery; the purpose-designed SuperJANET nationwide inter-university wideband network capable of running at speeds of over 600 Megabits/second started operating in 1993.

Loeb (1992), from the Bellcore Laboratories, discusses problems of sending large files over networks and concludes that 'very little effort has been made . . . to examine the network aspects of hypermedia applications'. After providing some tables showing the order of magnitude of 'P-objects' – that is, a range of items from magazine articles to motion video frames – Loeb concludes that large amounts of information would be delivered unnecessarily. Fast, unpredictable shifts in end-user requests for service would be very hard to fulfil.

It is worth while quoting another of Loeb's conclusions, although they are already well known, namely that studies show that for response time, tolera-tion of delays depends on how the user perceives the communication. If the user expects the system to be of a type that has no internal complexity (one which responds to stimulation without going through computational states) then the response time expected is in the order of 0.2 seconds.

Transmission protocols and standards are a very important part of attempting to ensure that multimedia data may be exchanged and repro-duced by a receiving machine exactly as intended by the sender regardless of the machines being used or the route taken by the data. This subject is discussed in chapter 9.

Methods of transmission

STM

Synchronous Transfer Mode (STM) is a method which is widely used for wideband signal transmission. It is gradually being replaced by more efficient methods. The signalling elements used in STM wideband transmission are 'framed' by timing impulses from which terminals can also derive their synchronization. The supposedly synchronous bit rates are not in fact exactly synchronous and have to be brought into synchronism by bit stuffing, or 'plesiochronous' methods. Dummy bits have to be added in order to make up elements of the right length to ensure synchronization. STM is associated with Synchronous Time Division Multiplexing (STDM), where signalling elements from multiple sources are accommodated in a single circuit by being allocated specific time slots in the multiplexed stream from each data source. STDM is inefficient for sources which send data intermittently because some time slots will then be unoccupied. STM is likely to introduce delays into transmissions caused by error correcting or other procedures.

Packet Switching: ATM

Circuit switching means that users are interconnected by a channel – for example, a telephone line – via conventional switches which make the user–line–user connections. It is a physical path set up for the duration of the call for the sole benefit of its users.

In Packet Switching (PS), switches of the kind that are easily visualized are not used. Messages are split into a number of packets and are dispatched from a network node independently through any available network path. Upon arrival at the node to which the addressee is connected, the packets are assembled into the original sequence and presented to the addressee as a complete message. The net effect is that the same amount of data is transported over a network of much smaller capacity than is possible in a circuit-switched network. Computer-controlled store and forward nodes ensure efficient error-free transmission. Nodes are usually interconnected by at least two telecom channels.

A gap in PS transmission may be relatively short – for example, a gap during a telephone conversation – but it is immediately occupied by as many packets from other users as there are time slots during that gap. Consequently the data occupancy of the network is considerably higher than in a circuit-switched network where a fixed channel is available even when it is empty of data for most of the time.

PS includes other advantages such as error correction and multiple-route availability – if one route fails, another is instantly available.

The Asynchronous Transfer Mode (ATM) protocol has been agreed between the CCITT and ANSI for future wideband networks. ATM is not based on element timing so it does away with the STM system's synchronizing problems. Error correction, which causes delays, is not needed. ATM embodies the advantages of both circuit switching and packet switching. This makes it attractive for network providers and users.

So-called 'ATM switches' are very important. They do not consist of contacts or semiconductor on–off switches. An ATM switch would be interposed between a LAN and, say another LAN, each LAN being configured as a 'hub' serving a number of workstations. Instead of the workstations being connected directly to the LAN, where intercommunications are restricted because of shared bandwidth, each workstation has a line direct to a switch port in the hub, capable of full bandwidth rates regardless of the other LAN traffic. A large hub by LANNET is shown in Figure 8.1. The controlling ATM switch runs at 1.28 Gbps, permitting up to 128 stations to communicate, each running at 10 Mbps as if they were connected to a line capable of that rate, regardless of the traffic from other stations.

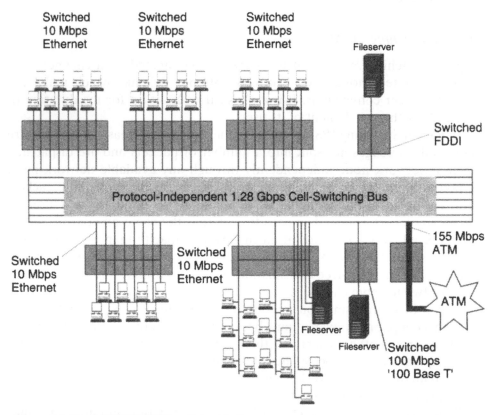

Figure 8.1 The LANNET ATM switched hub
Source: LANNET

A problem with Packet Switching is that it may increase the length of an already long message, say in videoconferencing or multimedia, to an unacceptable length because of the random occurrence of time-slots and waiting times for the next empty slot. With ATM, timing is arranged in such a way that when a packet (called a *cell* in ATM) is transmitted, the next packet is sent after a very short time interval – usually a few microseconds long – compared with milliseconds for packet switching. ATM is 'scalable' because its format is independent of transmission rate. It may be used in LANs, WANs,. etc., at whatever data rates may be dictated by the available bandwidth, ranging from 10 megabits to hundreds of megabits per second. Because users pay only for cells dispatched, not for bandwidth which is available but which may never be needed, it is versatile and relatively cheap.

ATM transmission speed depends on the method of transport, for instance a system called FibreChannel will run at several speeds in the range 100 Mbps to 1600 Mbps. ATM is expected to be used in a Synchronous Digital Hierarchy (SDH) system based on the American SONET. SONET is an ANSI interface standard for synchronous data transmission at a hierarchy of speeds commencing at 51.84 Mbps and going up to 2488.32 Mbps. SONET will probably also be used as the transport layer in the B-ISDN. SONET uses SDH channels to carry ATM-based data – which embodies the several advantages discussed above, replacing the existing Synchronous Transfer Mode (STM) system used in trunk networks. SDH is controlled by accurately synchronized timing impulses and is based on multiples of the CCITT-recommended bit rate of 2.048 Mbps ('Megabits') in Europe and on 1.544 Mbps ('1.5 Megabits') in the US. SDH will be based on a 'harmonized' 155.52 Mbps. A SONET frame carrying ATM-based structures consists of an 'overhead' section, and a data load section within which the ATM-based data is carried. User network interfaces are provided for data running at 155 Mbps or 622 Mbps (approx.) or faster, over SONET fibreoptic channels.

ADSL

Asymmetric Digital Subscriber Line (ADSL) is a new method devised to transmit data between the local public telephone exchange and a subscriber over an existing twisted pair telephone cable. The rate can be 2 Megabits per second or more for over 90 per cent of the 'local loop' in the UK. A page of text produced on a word processing machine is coded as about 6000 Mbytes or 48 Kbits, so 42 pages per second could be transmitted at this rate, compared with about 1.35 pages/second over a 64 Kbps ISDN channel. A 16 Mbyte high-resolution colour picture compressed by an attainable 10:1 would take about 6 seconds by ADSL.

ADSL was proposed by the Bell research workers Lechleider and Valenti in 1991. It has since been tested and an international standard is in the process of being agreed. A telephone twisted pair designed for speech in the frequency range 400 to 2800 Hz should support a bit rate of up to some tens of kilobits per second (assuming 'ideal coding') according to Shannon's criteria for channel capacity, so how can an ADSL bit rate of 2 Mbps be accommodated?

The answer is by 'automatic equalization' and special coding. The frequency response is flattened by filters to compensate for the enormous high-frequency loss, and 'ideal coding', or something approaching it, is achieved by dividing the channel into numerous sub-channels, each automatically accommodating as many bits as noise allows in that channel. The complex circuits needed are once again enabled by the astonishing advances in microelectronics.

ADSL was tested by BT on the lines of 60 of its employees and is now being tried out on 2500 members of the general public. Oracle software will be provided for BT to test interactive TV over copper phone lines in Colchester using up to a 200:1 compression ratio. A massively parallel computer and server will be installed at the local telephone exchange – but what will be the cost of ADSL coding and decoding at the exchange and at a subscriber's premises? More information is awaited.

NETWORKS

Introduction

A telecommunications network consists of communicating devices, such as terminals, an inter-communicating medium, such as cable, and a means of establishing communicating paths through the media. Networks cater for the needs of people with information-intensive occupations, mainly in the business area; they are steadily increasing in importance for multimedia data transmission and may culminate in the widely publicized 'Information Superhighway' – the last network to be discussed in this chapter.

A Managed Network is a network directed and maintained by a telecoms organization on behalf of a client. A Metropolitan Area Network (MAN) is a 'Super LAN' fibreoptic ring operating at 150 Mbps or more over an area of about 50 m. More efficient within-site, short-distance private networks designed for data exchange between terminals and computers called Local Area Networks (LANs) are now widely used.

LANs (described below) set up in different parts of the same site may be interconnected, so a station on one site may exchange messages with a station on another. A LAN group on one site may be connected to a LAN group on a distant site by a suitable link able to convey messages satisfactorily over long distances. The arrangement is then called a Wide Area Network (WAN) – a label also applied to almost any type of long-distance network.

MANs and LANs do not usually use switches to make fixed connections between stations for the duration of a message; instead, messages passing along the network contain address headers which are recognized by the addressed station, which then captures the message.

Specialized types of network have been developed in the last fifteen years, although WANs, based on lines leased from the telecoms authority, came into use earlier. The main driving forces have been the arrival of compact, powerful, cheap technology and the need for business 'communications'. Telephone systems used to be run by a public authority, except in the United States. After arguments about the virtues of state-run monopolies versus privately owned networks, the latter have steadily gained ground. However, the rate of change has been slow.

Vested interests have frustrated the efforts of the European Commission, who believe that some kind of unified European system is essential. In many other parts of the world, safe, phlegmatic state-controlled monopolies are still preferred. The upheavals and uncertainties following a change to private operations are unwelcome.

Private telephone networks consist of an internal exchange for interconnecting telephones within one site, and lines leased from the authority to interconnect exchanges on different sites. This arrangement has become used for data transmission, perhaps based on a Private Automatic Branch Exchange (PABX). More recently still, Metropolitan Area Networks (MANs) have been developed to convey messages over intermediate distances – for example, between LANs linked to other LANs in the same city. A major objective in these various types of network is first, to make the system transparent to the user. This means that a user sends a message to another, unaware of the complexity of the intervening media and of the routing procedure. A second objective, particularly important when one user communicates with another in a different organization, say overseas, using equipment and networks supplied by a different manufacturer, is that in spite of these differences, messages may be satisfactorily exchanged. The objective of the international OSI standardization effort, described in chapter 9, is an attempt to make this possible.

The phrase 'Enterprise Network' describes a network providing access to all kinds of information via an organization's all-pervading network. For large organizations this means the provision of LANs on different sites in the same or in different countries interconnected by a Wide Area Network. According to a KPMG Peat Marwick report: 'although 50% of IT investment goes on the desktop, less than 5% of the top 1000 UK companies have achieved complete integration of their computing environments'.

LANs have been widely adopted in libraries. There will be a LAN in the British Library's new building at St Pancras, London, for about 1300 users costing about £1.5 million including the cost of the fibreoptic backbone. It will include twisted pair spurs for Ethernet LANs, and Novell's netware will be used.

So-called distributed computing, meaning decentralizing by using networked computers, is now widely used. Taking account of this trend, new generation operating systems will include networking facilities which previously were only supplied as separate packages. Windows for Workgroups (WFW) is a self-explanatory title of a networking application which will be incorporated in Microsoft's 32-bit Chicago, otherwise known as Windows 95, and Daytona, a 1995 successor to Windows NT.

The commercial linkup between Novell and Microsoft has prompted Chicago's easy access to Netware. According to Udell (1994), Chicago 'enjoys access to WFW, NT, and Netware resources, including redirected drives, printers, and file-based and client-server network applications'. Chicago and Daytona can run NETBIOS networking using TCP/IP protocols.

Microsoft is also working on software called Dynamic Host Configuration Protocol (DHCP) to overcome the network address problem for people who want to plug in a portable at different times and at different locations. Running with a server, it maintains a collection of addresses allocated to users as they appear, usually for a limited period of time. With DHCP and the Windows Internet Naming Service (WINS), another new development, it will be much easier for machines running them to communicate over Internet using the TCP/IP protocols.

IBM has also launched a new 32-bit operating system called OS/2 Warp which will work with 4 Mbytes of memory – smaller than is needed for Windows 95. It includes built-in arrangements for Internet communications. OS/2 Warp is priced at a low £70 and is aimed to increase the 6 million customers for existing OS/2 software as against the 60 million users claimed for Windows.

Local Area Networks (LANs)

In a LAN a cable spur from the network connects to an adaptor card plugged into a computer. The card contains the necessary intermediate components which handle 'driver' software – that is, software designed to communicate with the network being used. Widely separated LANs may be interconnected by leased lines such as those available in the UK from BT, Mercury, and Cable companies. in the US a T1 1.544 Mbps link is often used.

The major types of LAN protocols are Contention and Token Ring. The first Contention LAN, called ALOHA, was developed at the University of Hawaii around 1972. Ethernet, developed by Robert Metcalfe at the Xerox Palo Alto laboratories in the mid-1970s, became a leader. It was first used for interconnecting Alto computers – precursors of the Xerox Star from which was descended the Apple Macintosh. The Ethernet Contention system uses Carrier Sense Multiple Access with Collision Detection (CSMA/CD). All stations listen and wait to transmit a packet message addressed to another station when the cable is clear. In the event of two stations transmitting at once, one or other jams the network, waits for a period of time of random length, and then tries again.

Token Ring or 'Token Passing' systems were developed at the University of California at Irvine and at Cambridge University. Empty data packets circulate and a station wanting to transmit detects a 'token' empty packet, enters an address, and adds a frame consisting of a header followed by a message of up to 4500 bytes. The station empties the packet when it next comes round. All stations examine all packets, accepting only those addressed to them.

Low and medium speed *wireless* LANs get rid of the cabling problem and enable workstations to be easily sited in the most convenient positions. *Radio* LANs may require a licence and are liable to interference, but are better for the higher speeds. *Infrared* LANs are less expensive, but are obstructed by line-of-sight obstacles.

There used to be considerable controversy about the merits and capacity of competitive LANs and they were classified according to topology or protocol. Now that data rates have become faster they tend to be divided according to speed – low/medium: 10–20 Mbps; high: 50–150 Mbps; super-computer: 800 Mbps (proposed), and Ultragigabit (proposed): 1000–10,000 Mbps.

As speeds have increased there has been a strong trend towards the use of fibreoptic interconnecting cable. A Standard for FDDI, the Fibre Distributed Data Interface – was agreed in 1990 (see chapter 9). FDDI stations use cheap Light Emitting Diodes (LEDs) for the transmitting element and PIN Field Effect Transistors (PINFETs) for reception. An FDDI network consists of two contra-rotating rings for increased reliability.

LAN networking, or any kind of networking for that matter, introduces several new considerations. A fairly heavy memory overhead is added to participating micros and, unless they are sufficiently powerful, operations are likely to be slow. For accessing databases outside the networks a shared gateway is required with enough ports to provide adequate service per user, assuming that only some fraction of users will require simultaneous service.

Apple has its own protocol called Appletalk for inter-communication over a LAN. Each computer on an Appletalk network is allocated a network number. Appletalk consists of three elements – the Link Access Protocol which controls the mechanics of the CSMA/CD network, the Datagram Delivery Protocol which manages the communications between stations, and the Appletalk Transaction Protocol which controls the dialogue – for instance, a file transfer request – between Appletalk stations. Appletalk runs on an Ethernet CSMA/CD network or on Token Ring. Novell and 3 Com provide compatible networking systems so that Macs can be used as work-stations and share data with PCs, Unix, DEC, and IBM minis/mainframes.

The most popular data rate for LANs is nominally 10 Mbits per second, but the rate decreases appreciably when a number of users are exchanging data – the bandwidth is shared by the users. LANs work perfectly well in most cases when short bursts of data, such as electronic mail messages, are being exchanged. However, the maximum speeds for LANs are on the increase and existing LAN users do not have to change the cabling or the software to use them. These faster systems, which run nominally at 100 Mbytes per second, are more expensive than ordinary LANs but much less expensive than FDDI optical networks (Clarkson 1993).

LAN operating systems

IBM's NETBIOS was the first network operating system and was designed primarily to enable DOS-based PCs connected to a relatively small LAN to access printers or file servers. Two types of operating system dominate the market – Novell, who recently bought in to Digital Research for £72 million, are alleged to have 75 per cent of it with its Netware operating system – version 4.1 was introduced in December 1994. Microsoft's Lan Manager 2.0 has most of the remainder.

Most operating systems run on a server and arrange for users to access network resources in such a way that the access mechanism is 'transparent'. It appears to the user, working on his own application with his own computer operating system such as MS-DOS, OS/2, etc., that he or she is accessing files, databases, etc., in his or her own machine.

Operating systems are able to connect to equipment on the network made by various manufacturers using various protocols as they are added to the network, and support the major transmission standards such as Ethernet and Token Ring. A user is able to do much more than simply exchange files. Traditional 3270 terminal emulation and basic file transfer are replaced by arrangements where the mainframe looks after the corporate database, and networked workstations provide user-friendly information presentation.

When users try to access the same file, all users except one are locked out until any changes made by that user are completed. In the case of shared access to a database, special arrangements need to be made if lockouts are not seriously to slow down access. Methods include locking out on an individual record basis, read locks for queries and write locks when the database is being updated, or better still, lockouts on a row-by-row basis. Such arrangements require database reorganization – for instance, the database and the database management software reside in a server, while each PC contains a database user interface.

Peer-to-peer LAN operating systems are widely used for implementing these facilities. Nance (1994) reviews four such operating systems where users can share each others' files. They all use DOS to access files on the hard disk of a server but this is expected to move on to improved arrangements with Windows 95, OS/2, and others. Nance considers that of the four systems tested – Artisoft's LANtastic 6.0, Microsoft's Windows for Workgroups 3.11, Novell's Personal Netware 1.2, and Performance Technology's PowerLAN 3.11, LANtastic ($119 per node) is the best. A LANtastic server requires memory of 45 Kbytes per client, runs a cache, and will support an unlimited number of nodes. It includes various security precautions, E-mail, and fax software.

The Integrated Services Digital Network (ISDN)

The CCITT's definition of ISDN is 'a network evolved from the telephony network that provides end to end digital connectivity to support a wide range of services, including voice and non-voice, to which users have access via a limited set of standard multi-purpose interfaces'. It is a digital transmission system able to handle digitized voice and data on an 'end-to-end' (subscriber-to-subscriber) basis. Preliminary world standards were set in 1984. It took until 1992 for its slow development to lead to many applications, controlled as it is by the policy of the PTTs, not by market demand.

The public ISDN network represents a transformation in stages of the telephone system into a wider bandwidth data network, where the data may be speech, text, graphics, halftone or colour images, or motion video. Several of the world's major PTTs are in the process of converting the telephone system into a subscriber-to-subscriber ISDN data system without interrupting existing facilities.

The Plain Old Switched Telephone System (POTS) is by far the most universally available communication channel into homes and businesses. The frequency band of POTS is just about wide enough to transport data up to 140 Kilobits second (Kbps) – the speed specified for the ISDN primary data rate. A 64 Kbps circuit may be used for either digitized speech or data. A typical domestic terminal consists of a PC with special plug-in card or a purpose-designed terminal which will use one circuit, and a digital telephone which will use the other. Two subscribers can talk to each other and at the same time exchange diagrams, illustrations, etc., between their terminals, the necessary control signals being exchanged over the signalling circuit. ISDN subscriber options are as follows:

- Basic rate access: 2 64Kbps 'B' channels for data or voice, and a 'D' signalling channel. Typically one B channel would be used for digitized voice and the other for data.
- Primary rate access: 30 B + 1 D channel (Europe), 23 B + 1 D channel (US). Typically for the connection of Private Automatic Branch Exchanges (PABX) for integrated digital access.

The ISDN, if used at the 2 × B channel = 128 Kbps data rate, could deliver quite a good picture in about 36 seconds. If 30 × B channels are made wholly available for multimedia, the transmission rate would be about 2 Mbps, reducing picture delivery time to less than 2 seconds. Transmission duration could be decreased in both cases by data compression. Thus 40:1 compression for a $2 \times B$ channel would enable a picture to be delivered in less than one second, which would be acceptable for many applications.

A number of different devices are available for ISDN ranging in cost in the UK between about £500 and £1500. Some come as cards enabling a PC to be used for ISDN work; others are in self-contained boxes.

Diverse opinions are expressed about the ISDN. Inoue from NTT thinks that 'ISDN will be an indispensable means to business activities in the 1990s' and Temime from France Telecom forecast that 'half of all French companies will have an ISDN PABX by 1995'. Lowenstein, commenting about the ambivalence of phone companies, considers that 'connectivity is simply not there', while McClelland, editor of *Telecommunications* magazine, thinks that 'many countries are simply disinterested, despite useful initiatives'.

The ISDN may be too slow for effective multimedia communication, but in a recent report (Stevenson and Howard-Healy 1993), the authors believe that even its much faster proposed successor will be a non-starter. They say: 'B-ISDN is dead' and 'Perpetuating it for a new technology is a grave mistake. . . . ATM is the only technology which supports real-time voice and video'. Katsuyama *et al.* (1993) from Fujitsu's Laboratories (*IEICE Trans. Comm.*, March 1993) forecast success for 'ATM-based B-ISDN', but as ATM is not mentioned in the rest of the article, this is rather confusing.

There is a severe 'critical mass' problem which inhibits the widespread adoption by business users, the information-conscious section of the public, or by the public at large, of any new 'information network' which somehow has to get itself into a 'take-off' situation.

The critical mass has long been surpassed by the telephone system, where the number of telephone subscribers far exceeds the number needed to encourage new subscribers to join. Potential subscribers know that they will be able to talk to a significant fraction of the world's population should they install a telephone.

The ISDN is ultimately supposed to become a national and international network. The general opinion of non-PTT commentators seems to be that it has been developed too slowly, that little attempt has been made to market it, and that its supposed virtues are inadequate and may be overtaken by other schemes able to work at the higher speeds called for today.

However, a CEC-sponsored European ISDN users' forum, which first met in September 1990 in Brussels, appears to have got off the ground. The ISDN cannot live without users. 'Until the equipment suppliers and public network operators that have driven ISDN developments for the last two decades realise this and ensure an adequate role for users in standards, applications, and tariff definition, the market uncertainty that has dogged ISDN will not end,' says a commentator.

The next stage – the Broadband ISDN – was confidently forecast in the United States. 'I expect Broadband ISDN to be economic on a parity basis probably around late 1993,' said a Bell South spokesman. In reality it seems as if the ISDN may arrive in the late 1990s if it is not overtaken by something better, and the Broadband ISDN early in the next century. The B-ISDN will require a much larger investment than the ISDN. It is expected to provide integration of multiple electronic media which will allow for the full range of communication capabilities ranging from telemetry and voice at the low end to HDTV at the upper end, stimulating the extensive use of high-resolution image communications and high-speed data exchange between computers. The most likely protocol will be ATM. The B-ISDN will probably require interconnection via a Network Node Interface (NNI) to a SONET-type monomode fibreoptic network with special switching. Subscriber rates will start at 155 Mbits per second. The availability of such speeds depends on the time it will take for the existing narrow-band copper subscriber loops to be replaced by fibreoptic or other wideband transmission links.

THE INTERNET

Introduction

> O what a tangled web we weave
> When first we practise to deceive!
> (Sir Walter Scott, 1808)

The Internet is a large network formed of interconnected networks in the United States some time after Scott's demise, and later extended to other countries. The World Wide Web is a bit tangled, but, so far as I am aware, no deception is intended.

As the Internet is becoming so widely used for transporting multimedia data, some basic information about access, services, and functions is provided here. Many books have been published about it, such as Krol (1994). Information about getting connected and access is given by Smith (1994). In-depth information about Internet's TCP/IP protocol and its relationship to the OSI protocol is provided by Black (1995). Care is necessary in choosing the right book; it may well be already out of date.

In 1969 Internet's precursor ARPAnet (Department of Defense Advanced Research Projects Agency network) was designed for communicating information about military research and for withstanding damage from an enemy; it used multiply connected pathways. Later it connected to NSFNET, funded by the National Science Foundation, in order to interconnect academic researchers via five large computer centres. NSF sponsored the development of the Transmission Protocol/Internet Protocol (TCP/IP) – a communication protocol enabling messages to be understood by different kinds of interconnected machines. Internet's wide usage has made TCP/IP a very widely used protocol at the expense of OSI, a more systematic attempt to create an internationally agreed Standards model. Internet became used for commercial purposes as an extension of its use by the research departments of corporations under the general agreement of use for research and educational purposes. The academic/military research requirement has become steadily more relaxed and many other kinds of users are now connected to it.

Several other large networks, built for different purposes, are also connected to Internet to form an enormous intercommunication highway. These include the National Research and Education Network (NREN) established by Act of Congress in 1991, SuperJANET, the UK academic network developed from JANET (Joint Academic Network), and the European EUnet network. In due course the OCLC network and Performance Systems International (PSI) cable TV network will probably be connected as well. Internet provides access to thousands of databases and intercommunication for millions of people the world over.

Schwartz (1993) reports that by using a research algorithm called NETFIND he can search domains, such as departments within a company containing 5.5 million people who have electronic mail addresses. Examples of domains include over 3000 educational and nearly 1000 commercial domains in the US, 836 domains in Germany, 360 in the UK, 184 in France, 18 in Iceland, and 1 in Antarctica. The total number of different countries on the Internet system at the time of writing is 53. It was suggested in a late 1994 news items that there were 20 million Internet users and that the growth rate was 10 per cent per month at that time.

Gates (1993) divides Internet activities into three phrases – the research phase up to the mid-1980s, the academic club phase (mid-1980s to early 1990s), and the communicating phase (early 1990s onwards). The fourth phase is approaching – the process of making the Internet self-supporting has started. A principal funding agency, the National Science Foundation, is moving its support from the Internet to the experimental very high speed Backbone Network Service (vBNS), which will be used for research purposes. The objective is to develop a network able to run at 155 Mbps, and ultimately up to 622 Mbps.

The main Internet backbone (NSFNET), operated as a non-profit service since 1990, was sold to America Online in 1993 with maintenance by MCI, Sprint, and others. Accordingly 'The Internet will go where private money sends it' (*Byte* 1995).

Services

Introduction

As at September 1993, Obraczka *et al.* (1993) described a number of 'Resource Discovery Services'. A selection is shown here.

- WAIS
  (The Dow Jones, Thinking Machines, Apple, KPMG Peat Marwick, Wide Area Information Services Project). WAIS provides access to over 300 databases.
- ARCHIE
  A system developed by McGill University which runs database servers and interfaces to other systems. It offers access to over 2 million files and 3500 software packages accessed from 47 countries about 50,000 times per day.
- PROSPERO
  A system of Internet directory registrations with their contents, run with the aid of 50 servers, and with clients from 10,000 systems in 30 countries.
- WORLDWIDE WEB (WWW)
  A system for full text document searches using hyperlinks to interconnect documents. Developed at CERN.
- INDIE
  (Distributed Indexing) developed at the University of Southern California which enables users to search all participating databases.
- GOPHER
  Developed at the University of Minnesota, Gopher contains indexes to documents accessible via Internet held by university, government and corporate organizations.
- MOSAIC
  A collection of Web browser client software versions for a number of different computers, so that a user may connect to a Web server for browsing purposes.

There are many others. Some say that it is easy to become 'hooked' on Internet, but others find that some searches may take a very long time. Client-server operations will work with a range of popular operating systems such as MS DOS, OS/2, Unix, Apple Mac, and others. Client users are presented with menus showing the availability of 'nodes' – documents or items containing chemical, mathematical, or other data collections. Nodes are sometimes arranged hierarchically.

Gopher offers services to Internet clients by connecting them to a Gopher server – that is, a computer controlling a large volume of stored data of various types such as text, images, sound, etc. The Gopher + Protocol is a method for retrieving the attributes of a node rather than its contents. An attribute contains information about the Node such as a particular aspect of it, like TIFF data, or an abstract of its contents. Gopher servers are very widely available.

But the World Wide Web (WWW) is the service mainly responsible for the recent rapid growth in the numbers of hosts and users. A major feature of it is the improvement in search facilities since searching was done using ARCHIE and Gopher.

Subsequently, search software was introduced by a humorist who called it VERONICA, meaning Very Easy Rodent Oriented Netwide Index to Computerized Archives. After these various attempts to make searching and retrieval easier in a rapidly growing system, the people at CERN, the research establishment in Geneva, decided that something better was needed. A client-server system, HTML, with hyperlinks was introduced, as described below.

A useful information source for Internet services and Standards is provided by Adie (1994).

Access

Alden discusses three ways of accessing the Internet:

- Gateway access
  Accessing via another network to which your computer is connected. The network/Internet gateway may limit activities.
- Remote terminal access
  Access using a PC connected to an Internet host via a modem. The host will be running e-mail, Gopher, etc.
- Full access
  Via a PC which is an actual Internet node, using for instance Serial Line Internet Protocol (SLIP) or Point to Point Protocol (PPP).

Blakeman (1993) considers that there are two major reasons for using Internet – for electronic mail or as a subscriber to a general facilities gateway. In the UK, Geonet offers electronic mail at £12 per month minimum fee with connect rates at 16p per minute during peak hours. Compulink Information Exchange (CIX) provides full access at £3.60/hour peak rate. Access to BRS, Dialog, Dow Jones, RCIN and other databases is available, assuming prior arrangements with suppliers.

Most information about the Internet assumes that a PC will be used as the access machine. Some useful information for Apple users is provided by Elliott (1995). He points out that there are 35,000 servers on the Web and claims that 100 new sites are added every day. Elliott considers that WWW is 'the information vehicle of the decade'. The way a user obtains access to the Internet in the UK is typical and is described here: user may connect a personal computer to an Internet provider who is operating a log-on, sometimes called a shell, account with an access provider. The simplest connection is machine–modem–dial-up telephone line using SLIP (Serial Line Internet Protocol) or a later version of it PPP (Point to Point Protocol). Data generated by the machine or received from the provider will be in packets managed by the Internet Protocol (IP), which assembles machine data into packets and disassembles packets from the Internet into machine-readable data. Other ways of connecting include the ISDN, X25 (see Glossary) if an intermediate packet-switched network is being used, or leased line if heavy usage is expected.

Access providers usually provide not just one POP (Point Of access Point) at some central point, but several around the country. This enables a user to select the nearest POP for connection in order to minimize telecom fees. In major countries the collection of POPs operated by a number of access providers enables most people to find one which is close to their address. In the UK, for example, Demon has 9, Pipex 5, and EUnet 6.

Browsers and search tools

A server may be browsed by any user who has the associated client browser program. For example, to connect to a World Wide Web server the server's address should be prefixed with the letters HTTP (HyperText Transfer Protocol). This negotiates admission for the browser and initiates the use of HTTP for message control. Browsers usually contain search tools, which range from the crude to the moderately effective. The tools enable a user to search the material which is available to that browser. Searching for information from a well-organized information database is an unequal struggle, which was the founding problem of Information Science (see 'Indexing' in chapter 4). Searching the Internet adds further dimensions and greater difficulties which, by and large, remain to be tackled.

Because of the specific problems of searching rather than browsing, the former is described below in a separate section.

The World Wide Web

The WWW is the Internet service mainly responsible for the recent rapid growth in the numbers of hosts and users. In some useful information provided for Apple users, Elliott (1995) points out that there are 35,000 servers on the Web and claims that 100 new sites are added every day. Elliott considers that WWW is 'the information vehicle of the decade'. A good information source for Internet Services and Standards is Adie (1994).

An Englishman called Tim Berners-Lee and his colleagues, working at the CERN Physics Laboratory, developed Web protocols Hypertext Mark-up Language (HTML) and the Hypertext Transport Protocol (HTTP).

HTML is like a simplified form of the Standard General Mark-up Language (SGML) used for defining the format of technical documents and manuals. HTML includes the interlinking ('hyperlinks') of separate but related items as used in the original Apple HyperCard software. HTTP moves data quickly from point to point using Internet's TCP/IP transmission protocol. HTML includes the Internet's name of a server and the name of the file on it holding data hyperlinked to the source document. Comerford (1995) provides an example describing a video clip in a remote computer using a string of symbols called the clip's Universal Resource Locator (URL):

Click <A HREF="http://www.noware.com intmovie.mpeg">
for an interesting movie.</A>

"www.noware.com" is the address of a computer containing a file called "intmovie.mpeg", "mpeg" meaning that the file is mpeg-compressed. A Web browser on a user's client computer which has downloaded a document containing this URL will contain the phrase 'click for an interesting movie'. When this phrase is pointed to with a mouse and clicked, a copy of the video clip will be transferred from the server to the client machine and the file can be viewed as long as the client computer contains the appropriate decompression software.

The Web is arranged in client-server form. The server stores data, and provided a client computer contains compatible browser software, server data may be read on the client via the network. Web servers store documents containing pointers linking an object in a document (e.g. a word or phrase) to other documents on the same or a different server. HTML enables pointers to be inserted and HTTP handles the linkage mechanism. Hopefully the association between the source object and the destination object will reveal another relevant document, or a relevant part of it.

The Hyper-G browser (according to Flohr 1995) 'supports tools for structuring, maintaining, and serving heterogeneous data. It guarantees automatic hyperlink consistency, and supports hyperlinks among multimedia documents, full-text retrieval, and a Unix-like security system.' Hyperlinks are indicated in a document as 'anchor' items – for instance, a highlighted word. Hyper-G will also support anchors in graphics, sounds, 3D objects, Postscript documents, or video clips. The author of a document must indicate which items within his or her material should be designated hyperlink anchors – for instance, a word might be highlighted. The anchor may indicate a hyperlink connection to a relevant part of the same document, a different document on the same site, or a document on another site. The author becomes involved in a kind of indexing operation. The effectiveness of information retrieval by searching carried out by hopping from an anchor to other documents and, in turn, from those documents to further documents, depends on an author's earlier activity as an 'indexer'. As just mentioned, the existence of such connections is at the discretion of authors.

A cross-platform language called Java was developed by Sun Computers in 1995. If an HTML tag called an <applet> is used on a page being run on a HotJava browser, the referenced URL is read and some byte code is transferred to the client page. A Java virtual machine (a small package of software associated with the user machine operating system) will execute an application at that position on the page. For example, a weather applet devised by Sun (Anon. 1996a) has its own URL. When a HotJava browser comes across a page containing that applet, it reads the URL, transfers a weather map on to the page, and provides for an interactive application – if the mouse is moved on to a city and clicked, the current temperature, wind speed, and humidity of that city appear at the top of the screen. Note that this idea greatly increases the information content of a page, with more information being released when a user interacts with it.

Java is an object-oriented programming language which will run on any machine provided that it contains a Java virtual machine compatible with its own operating system. Major Web browsers are available in alternative forms for major machines, and the latest versions of them will adopt Java. In December 1995, Microsoft, Lotus, Borland, Silicon Graphics, and Netscape announced that they would adopt Java tools for applications. IBM will be using Java to enable objects to be sent to and retrieved from client machines (Johnson 1996).

Setting up your own service on WWW

If you wish to set up a Web site, space may be rented on an access provider's computer, or your own site with its server may be connected to an access provider company via a dedicated line of adequate capacity. Server software may be downloaded from the Edinburgh or other Web sites. Your site needs to be named and registered with the CERN laboratory and major search engines. Pages of text need to be converted into HTML form. Creating and maintaining a Web site is a job for professionals. Most people will access the Web via a dial-up telephone line to the computer of an access company or by hiring a dedicated line according to how much they want to use it.

If most of the people for whom you wish to set up a service are already Internet users, setting up your own service with the Web for interconnections may be a net benefit. Required frequency of use will determine one major component of the cost, ranging from hiring space on the computer of an access company using dial-up access to leasing a dedicated line.

The other major cost is organizing your data into a suitable format and ensuring that your service enables others to find the information they want easily when they use it. If advantage is to be taken of hypertext links enabling a user to hop from one place to another, then you will need to know about HTML described above. The right person to set up a service is a librarian or information scientist who knows how organize a search and retrieval system.

No doubt many people set up a service because they cannot resist the new toy or because of the keeping-up-with-the-Joneses syndrome, with the value of rapid communication and the ability to change it on a daily basis as a secondary consideration. But unless the service is easy to use and accommodates information that users need, the novelty will wear off and so will usage.

Searching and data delivery

To quote one librarian: 'Finding what you want may be difficult. Internet is like a library where all the books are piled on the floor in disorganised heaps with no organisation or indexing . . . except that lots of little gnomes throw the books around so they're never in the same place next day.' If there are 4 million hosts – and no centrally organized method for finding one wanted item out of, say, at least 100 million in total, it is hardly surprising that finding what you want is a difficult, sometimes impossibly difficult, task.

The scale of the Internet and the fact that it was developed without plans for searching has prompted the development of several 'search engine' facilities associated with browsers as shown in Table 8.2. ARCHIE, Gopher and VERONICA (Very Easy Rodent Oriented Netwide Index to Computerized Archives) were followed by the WWW containing hyperlinks which act as a search aid. Hyperlinks are used in search engines developed for use with the Web such as Web Crawler and Lycos. Other newer search tools include Yahoo and IBM's QBIC search system (see chapter 10). QBIC enables searching for images by colour, texture, pattern, or shape, or combinations thereof. Shape questions may be devised like 'Are there any pictures of red cars with six wheels?'

In addition to search tool effectiveness a user must consider the volume of information available to a browser's search tool (see Table 8.2). This table comes from Bell *et al.* (1996).

Table 8.2 Browsers and searchable documents

Tool name	Number of documents
Lycos	11M
Excite	1.5M
Open Text	1M
Infoseek Net Search	1M
Web Crawler	250,000
Yahoo	85,000
Galaxy	55,000

Yahoo (Yet Another Hierarchical Officious Oracle) was reintroduced in July 1995 following a survey of 67,000 users (Lester 1995) by Jerry Yang and David Filo, students at Stanford University. Later they formed a business, earning revenue by advertising, and maintaining and improving the system. This browser is exceptional because it includes a search screen showing fourteen major subject categories in hierarchies, each with up to nine sub-categories, for example:

Regional
US states
Idaho
Boise
Education
Colleges
Boise State University
Departments and programs
History of Western civilization

Hyperlinks are included at all levels. Yahoo's entries are found by starting at its home page; searches may include Boolean AND and OR logic. Yahoo searching is believed to be at present the only system providing facilities based on library practices. Yahoo grew rapidly during 1995 but its weakness at present is it that it contains a relatively small number of searchable documents.

The impression may be given that indexing and searching are a simple business. In an article entitled 'Web Search', under the heading 'Basic Indexing', Udell (1995) talks about WAIS: 'Once you've got the index built it's a snap to connect Web clients to it.' The essence of the system – the indexing arrangements themselves – is not discussed.

George McMurdo (1995) describes several search engines, Lycos in particular, showing a search using the phrase 'Turing machine'. Lycos uses 'a probabilistic technique to skip from server to server catching URL's'. The results are not described in enough detail to assess the effectiveness of the search.

Cronin and Hert (1995), mention the Web's 'free-wheeling . . . largely uncommercial nature . . . analogous with a library where all the books have been donated by patrons and placed randomly on the shelves'. The authors describe a search using the Web Crawler Index 'covering more than 50,000 documents on 9,000 servers . . . constituting a credible test site for assessing the utility of network discovery tools as foraging facilitators'. Using the phrase 'citation analysis' for searching, they consider the results to be 'strikingly idiosyncratic'. With the exception of the first hit, 'it is not at all clear how any of the others might relate, directly or tangentially, to the topic of "citation analysis".'

Betsy Anagnostelis (1995) lists URLs for a number of medical servers and comments on Web search engines, which she considers 'offer high returns in the quantity of resources yet low discrimination in terms of the relevance and quality of information delivered . . . traversing links can be time consuming and sometimes fruitless'. She goes on to describe several organizations which are currently assessing the usefulness of Web sites. A new service called OMNI will provide UK access to 'high quality biomedical resources that are filtered, evaluated, described, and classified'.

Internet files, containing diverse unstructured texts covering all aspects of human endeavour (of which science forms a small part) have become searchable during only about the last three years. Moreover, the Internet was evolved from a system for academic information exchange rather like a glorified bulletin board. Its files were not designed to be readily searchable, although the Yahoo browser/searcher mentioned above should help.

This situation may be compared with systems for the online searching of databases covering the scientific literature. In the three hundred and thirty years which have elapsed since the *Journal des Sçavans* [sic] and *Philosophical Transactions* were first published, numerous databases and methods of retrieving information from a structured scientific literature have been developed for searching thousands of scholarly journals. Searches for scientific information are still usually carried out by intermediaries but the ubiquity of the Internet encourages the efforts of naive users to search it. The Web has acquired a bad name, reflecting poor search results obtained by over-expectant searchers. It would seem to be even more necessary, whenever possible, to get an experienced searcher to search the Internet on your behalf. You may want to enjoy the serendipity, if not the noise, or a searcher may not be available. In these cases be prepared to spend a very long time doing it yourself while your telecom charges mount up. The amount of traffic and the size of the files being moved may exceed the network's ability to transport data within a reasonable period of time – a symptom of the Web's growth rate. The Web's servers and its client browsers can handle bit-intensive multimedia. When network use increases unaccompanied by an appropriate increase in channel bandwidth, it takes longer to transport a file. Things will get worse before they get better.

Karen Blakeman (1995), an experienced Internet user, has described frustration caused by network limitations:

I have given up using ftp after mid morning because the transfer rates that I achieve are impossibly slow, simply because of the number of users on the networks. Add to that the videoconferencing and broadcast systems that can now be used over the Internet, and you will end up with a network that is next to useless for communications and information retrieval.

Throwing a question at the system without regard to necessary preliminaries is more likely to generate frustration than answers. It will pay off to find out more about sites likely to contain information of the kind which is required. Start with a known URL if possible. Using Hyperlinks in a search tool such as the Web Crawler may produce some results. Choose local sites containing indexed information which will not include the delays inherent in using remotely stored files or search engines. Accumulate search notes during every search for future use. There is a huge amount of literature about the Internet but not much about effective search procedures. Some work needs to be done on how specific items of information may be located and retrieved from the huge volume stored on Web servers without consuming large amounts of time.

Workstations in the computer department at the University of Southampton are on the university's network, itself connected to the Internet via SuperJANET. At 14.30 UK time I asked a user to retrieve a picture using the World Wide Web. He was unfamiliar with the availability of picture files and eventually found a database about the Vatican library which contained pictures and retrieved a picture of unknown resolution and colour fidelity. After 10 minutes a small part of it had been scanned out at the top of the screen. It was going to take perhaps an hour to be delivered but we did not wait. The user said that the net slowed down considerably during peak periods, but allowing for that it was obvious that the delivery period for a picture file over the connection route picked up on this occasion was unacceptably slow although compression/decompression was being used.

The Internet: commercial activity, payments, security

Expansion of business applications on the Internet is restricted by security considerations. Many people seem more relaxed about security than they used to be – for example, they will quote their credit card number over the telephone. Compuserve's 'UK shopping centre', in association with W.H. Smith, Interflora, Virgin, Tesco, and others, arranges payment by asking customers to key in their credit card number.

Evidently this procedure is considered to be unsatisfactory. Visa and Mastercard, with their partners Microsoft and Netscape respectively, tried to arrange better security, but in late 1995 they announced that they had failed to reach an agreement. A group of 65 banks, companies, and government agencies called the Financial Services Technology Consortium (FSTC) is now trying to establish a standard for electronic commerce (Anon. 1995k).

Academic researchers have a natural bias to the open exchange of information; for business, however, secure communications is a basic requirement. Also no business is going to make a serious commitment to the Web, possibly risking its commercial future, unless it has confidence – and ideally, some say, in the Web standardisation process.

(Dettmer 1996)

Dettmer says that a new business organization has been formed called the World Wide Web Consortium (W3C). As at October 1995 there were 50 US members, 37 European, and 8 Asian. Secure communications and other Web issues are being worked on.

Pichford (1995) believes that Internet is an 'electronic toolbox of business functions'. File Transfer Protocol may be used for 'fast easy and cheap office-to-office file sharing'. A UK manager is quoted as saying that the Internet is heavily used for communicating with the head office in the States.

However, two UK companies, Forrester Research and Phonelink report a very different picture from their surveys. Barriers include lack of widespread reliable network access, low access speed, and lack of security. Only 27 per cent of 211 executives surveyed said that it contributed to their business. 'The undoubted potential of the Internet has not yet been matched by its ability to deliver practical business benefits,' say Phonelink.

By contrast, Riezenman (1995) reports that the chairman of the FCC believes that computer networks are the single biggest factor behind restoring productivity in the United States economy. Referring to the Internet in particular, he thinks that

> the government should intervene as little as possible except to ensure competition . . . competition will sort out such issues as how much bandwidth should reach every home, what sort of interfaces customers prefer, and the content that should be drawn down different pipes.

Security is unimportant for Internet academic communications, but that is not the case for the large amount of business and commercial data now passing round it. Security may be obtained with routers and 'firewalls'. Firewalls include the use of secure application gateways requiring user indentification and password; packet filters allowing only specified access and capable of coping with certain security flaws may also be used.

Payment for Internet services is an interesting topic. Vaughan-Nichols (1995) says that people who think that the Internet is free are mistaken. Some costs, such as network costs, can be hidden from users because their employer pays for them.

Those who cannot afford to wait for the half hour which it may take to carry out a search during busy hours may have to turn to charged services. Unisys has started to charge licensing fees for certain compression algorithms; consequently Compuserve will probably start charging for programs which use that algorithm.

Security is important in financial transactions involving, for instance, payment mechanisms for goods in home shopping, and those which need personal or business privacy. A big effort is in progress to perfect secure electronic payment systems and they are gradually being introduced. Ghani (1995) reviews the requirements and options available for making secure payments. He concludes that interest is growing rapidly and a number of trials are in progress, particularly by suppliers of Web software.

Pipex, one of the largest Internet service providers in Europe, was testing its newly installed security system in May 1995. It will provide a service for the end-to-end encryption of credit card details with authentication and clearing for cards used by home shoppers.

Netscape started a new service at the end of 1995 using a Secure Sockets Layer (SSL) for its Netscape Navigator Browser. When they are connected to a Netsite Web server all data exchanges are encrypted (see the super-highway section at the end of this chapter). A key in the corner of the screen shows that data are being transferred securely; a broken key indicates that SSL is not being used. Otherwise a user will not know whether or not a transmission is secure.

For organizations using Internet as an inter-site network, a US company, Raptor, will set up the sites as a virtual private network with message authentication, encryption, and access rules. In June 1995 IBM announced that it would now provide connection-secure Web browsers and servers for its OS/2 and Aix-based systems. It also offered Secure Hypertext Transfer Protocol (S-HTTP) and SSL. IBM's secure browser called the Web Explorer for OS/2 provides drag and drop and graphic streaming facilities.

In a *Byte* review Singleton (1995) mentions two secure electronic payment systems to be introduced by Visa/Microsoft and Master Cards/Netscape. Singleton also describes six different existing commercial secure electronic payment systems. In June 1995, First Data, the largest company processing bank cards in the UK, merged with the First Financial Management Corporation which owns a subsidiary called Nabanco dealing with card settlements. Nabanco will be using a secure payments system developed by Microsoft for its proposed new network, a deal between Microsoft and Intuit for a similar purpose having been called off. Sun is also considering a secure payments system. Large companies are taking a growing interest in secure payment systems for networks. Their use in financial transactions looks like becoming the norm before long.

The Internet: making telephone calls

Internet phoneware software can be purchased from several vendors such as Camelot (Dallas, Texas) at $150 to $50 for Webphone (Miami, Florida). When a call comes in, a tone sounds on the user's computer; the user then clicks on an ikon contained in the phone software and this displays the caller's name.

The quality of speech depends on the type of compression used, the speed of the modem, the sampling rate, and certain other matters. At 9.6 Kbps the quality is poor; at 28.8 Kbps it should be satisfactory. If the machine is not connected to the Internet at the time, the caller is informed. If the recipient accepts the call, it is routed to the other party via each party's connection to their local Internet service provider. The phone software vendor will operate directory services of various kinds, accessible through the vendor's directory server. Directories will probably be regularly updated. You can download a directory and edit it to provide your own telephone book.

The Internet: broadcasting (sound)

Dejesus (1996) points out that 'becoming an audio broadcaster on the Internet requires far less sophisticated and less costly hardware' than is required for multimedia or video activities. Organizations like ABC and others are already providing news broadcasts. The World Radio Network repeats its short-wave broadcasts over the Internet using a 45 bps line to connect its server to the M-bone. Browsers will soon be expected to support Multipurpose Internet Mail Extensions (MIME), which includes the provision for handling audio streams.

The Internet and multimedia

Since 1991, traffic running at 45 Mbps has become possible at 16 major sites on the NSFnet part of Internet. The use of cable-TV as a wideband network connected to Internet was scheduled to be introduced during 1994. The idea is to connect organizations using 10 Mbps Ethernet to a 100 Mbps Metropolitan Area Network (MAN), itself connected to Internet via Performance Systems International (PSI) cable-TV channels.

The possible exchange of multimedia data over the Internet is discussed by Worthington (1994). Worthington considers that USENET, which offers network news, is a good source of information about images via Gopher. There are also some actual image files available such as weather maps, geological survey pictures, and satellite images, to be retrieved from the TELNET archives, or, using a special File Transfer Protocol (FTP), from various other sources. A version of FTP called Anonymous FTP does not require a user ID or password for publicly available files. You may use your e-mail address as a password. A huge volume of data exists on these files.

E-mail over the Internet is now used by many organizations. With low cost and fast delivery it is believed to account for much of the Internet's traffic. At present security is inadequate unless special measures are taken. Internet e-mail suffers from the usual e-mail problems, summarized by Hayday writing in *Business & Technology Magazine*:

- Uncertainty whether the message has reached its destination
- Uncertainty about delivery if addressed to an organization rather than an individual
- Doubts about compatibility if spreadsheets or other document types are e-mailed

- Doubts about recipient's ability to decompress if compression is used
- Lack of sophistication of people using the system.
- Clogging up systems with junk e-mail
- Necessity to take special security measures

Froment *et al.* (1993) claim that 'Telecommunication administrations are willing to provide new interactive services' but they do not cite any evidence for that claim. Instead they discuss the need to standardize elements of 'Multimedia and hypermedia information retrieval services' and Audio-visual Interactive Services (AVI) in particular. Froment *et al.* discuss the requirement for standardization in terms of 'scriptware' considered 'as a view on a set of objects assembled for a particular usage'.

The progress of these ideas within the CCITT and ISO committees mentioned by Froment *et al.* will show whether such work is too far ahead of the market and whether attention will be concentrated on real needs. For general communication over Internet between any two users, the maximum bandwidth, and so telecoms speed, is that of the link in the chain with the narrowest bandwidth. In practice this is about 128 Kbps, meaning that such a link could carry data at about 5 Mbps if compressed by 40 to 1. This is satisfactory for many data types but is inadequate for television and multimedia.

The Internet: problems

Traffic problems on the Internet have been described by Vaughan-Nicols (1994): 300,000 files, many of megabyte size, were downloaded from a NASA server during one week in July 1994. In a peak hour 6000 requests were handled. The possibility of having to close down the service was considered.

The Internet needs better addressing facilities. They will be incorporated in a new version of its TCP/IP protocol to be called IPng or IPv6. The draft protocol calls for a 16-byte address field – more comparable with the OSI 20 byte field. Its present field can contain only 4 bytes. Sooner or later Internet will be improved, presumably by installing adapters, switches, routers, and hubs so that versions of Fast Ethernet may be used.

Acceptable quality for digital television services, the basis for public entertainment, is hard to specify. At present the 128 Kbps M-Bone limits quality to small frames in a window recurring at from one to four frames per second. But 5 Mbps data compressed by 40:1 are 129 Kbps – a quality adequate for some purposes. It seems likely that a 200:1 ratio will become usable without too much loss of data enabling pictures to be transmitted at 25 Mbps – still well short of good full-screen motion-picture reproduction.

The Internet protocol TCP/IP is also a constraint for some applications, particularly entertainment. But for many purposes, relatively poor-quality low-cost Internet videoconferencing may be preferred to a more expensive, specially leased wideband line. A distance learning project at a US naval school and an underwater science scheme developed by Woods Hole, using Internet as a videoconferencing link, have been described with enthusiasm.

John Murray (1995) compliments Martha Siegel, a lawyer, for drawing attention to regulation on the Internet. 'Most of the media's concerns,' he says, 'have been with hyping on-line shopping and video on demand rather than discussing the necessary liberties and legal frameworks for cyberspace.' Murray also raises the well-known argument about whether information providers should behave like common carriers who accept responsibility for the delivery of a message but not its contents. Siegel complains that the Internet is not a good medium for commerce, but at the same time aroused controversy by advertising on the Internet the fact that her law company would help people to enter a US immigration lottery. It turned out that the company was 'charging $95 to submit a name and address to the Immigration Service whereas anyone could do it simply by mailing a postcard to the local US consulate'.

Murray can't see how freedom to advertise on the Internet can be easily restricted: 'all data looks the same'. He asks how a node can be expected to differentiate between data packets originating from 'Siegel's advertising mill' and advertising coming from an anonymous mail server in Finland.

It is difficult to find out about the usefulness of Internet for particular requirements because there is no consensus. In the heading of an article by Looms (1995), the author says that 'Bringing the Internet to today's business environment is crucial for companies keen to exploit the opportunities for economy and better customer service'. The article extols the virtues of Lotus Internotes and the Electronic Embassy for providing information about foreign embassy services on the WWW.

But according to the Aslib (London) publication *IT Link*, the World Wide Web seems to be 'stuck in a rut producing a plethora of rather pointless self-publicity material for individuals and institutions, together with some interesting, but hardly useful, multimedia tasters'. Blakeman, also writing in *IT Link* (Blakeman 1995), says that she is beginning to wonder 'if it is worth all the hassle'. These words come at the end of article which starts with 'If anyone tells you that surfing the Net is a piece of cake, point them in my direction and I will convince them of the error in their ways.' She particularly recommends something called Netdial, which provides connection to five different services and provides a log of your activities. The trouble is that to find Netdial, Blakeman must first type 'ftp.sunet.se/pub/pc/windows/winsock-indstate/netdial/nd250s.zip'.

OTHER NETWORKS

The JANET and SuperJANET networks

The Joint Academic Network (JANET), an X25 packet-switched network interconnecting several major Packet Switching Exchanges in the UK, is in turn connected to a number of universities and research establishments. X25 is the CCITT recommendation for the interface between asynchronous Data Terminal Equipment (DTE), and the point of entry to a packet-switched network (Data Circuit terminating Equipment (DCE)). The JANET network has been upgraded to work at 2 Megabits per second (Mbps) over most of its links. JANET was established by the Computer Board in 1984. By 1990 over 130 institutions were connected to it. JANET is connected to Internet, using the TCP/IP protocol. JANET users are not charged, but the suppliers of some services may charge. A project called SuperJANET was first discussed in 1989 and in 1992 British Telecom was awarded a contract for £18 million to provide and operate this new fibre-optic network working at up to 622 Mbps. The operation is breaking new ground, and may encounter fewer regulatory constraints since it is a 'private' system not publicly available and so not subject to regulation politics. Whjen the project started in 1993 it ran at 34 Mbps, with six sites interconnected.

SuperJANET uses Switched Multimegabit Data Service (SMDS) under its immediate future telecoms regime until it changes to Asynchronous Transfer Mode (ATM) protocol. SMDS is a 'bandwidth on demand' system enabling what amounts to 'closed user group' transactions to be processed. The network will also incorporate a billing system so that, if necessary, charges may be made for services. SMDS is a 'cell based' not a 'packet based' system (Cawkell 1993b), so picture data are transmitted as a virtually continuous data stream to arrive in one piece. Under SMDS, 'user channels' may, in effect, be set up between a terminal on a network and the server at the database end. It will appear to the user as if he has a dedicated line to the database.

'Intelligent' Networks (IN)

This term, coined by the Bell Organisation, implies that a range of easily selectable services will be available over a network. The network may include the provision of a Private Virtual Network, that is, a switched network of the type normally only available in a private line system, but whose costs are closer to the costs of a public network. Such a network would include the facilities of an ISDN network, with enhancements. The phrase has come into use to imply certain facilities which are expected to evolve with these networks. Networks will embody the necessary circuits and software needed to control and deliver the kinds of services permitted by the much wider bandwidth.

Central databases will control a wide range of network services such as billing and credit card payments. When a customer initiates a toll-free or credit card call, it will be intercepted and managed by the signalling network, which directs it to a centralized database. The database handles the call and returns it through the network to the appropriate switch for completion. The network provides 'intelligence' centralized in databases and its features are no longer solely dependent on resident network hardware and software.

Abernethy and Munday (1995) make several points:

- It may take a considerable time to install switch-based new services.
- A key requirement is to separate basic functions such as path switching, from the software controlling new advanced features.
- The requirements for the rapid introduction of new services are driving developments.
- Reliance on switch manufacturers for new services needs to be reduced.
- The ability to offer integrated service packages must be improved.

'Intelligent Peripherals' which would provide additional functions needed could be:

- Special voice announcements
- Synthesized voice or speech recognition
- Audio conference bridging
- Information distribution bridging
- Protocol conversion
- Text-to-speech synthesis

They remark on the importance of IN Standards (see chapter 9). Their comments fall short of the comments quoted earlier, about the expected benefits of Intelligent Networks. In an article by Willis and Dufour (1995) about future possibilities rather then current Standards, three kinds of network are envisaged: interactive cable-TV networks, packet data networks, and multimedia networks. 'The suppliers of multimedia services information will become utilities.'

'Information appliances' will plug into utilities as today's domestic applicances plug into the gas, communications, or electricity utilities.

'Intelligent Agent' is a phrase gaining ground to describe a chore executed by software embodying artificial intelligence functions. Both IBM and AT&T are reported to be developing networks with agents. An agent stands in for a subscriber as a proxy.

According to Reinhardt (1994), IBM's Alter Ego, for example, will undertake an instruction such as: 'If I get mail from the CEO, page me. If I get any faxes from Finland, forward them to my hotel in Orlando; send all other mail to Murray.'

Personal Communication Networks (PCN)

PCN is intended to provide communications over a wide area. Accordingly the access network of fixed radio stations are placed in cells in a similar manner to existing cellular radio systems.

A new generation of cordless telephones called CT2 was developed in the UK and later the idea spread to the United States, where there were a large number of applications to the FCC for licences. A user would be connected to the public network via antennae (aerials) along major highways and his portable radio-telephone, providing wireless access to the PSTN.

Later, Ericsson introduced a third-generation system called CT3 which included two-way calling. In 1991 a UK licensee called Unitel estimated that there were nearly 8 million households as potential users, and trials indicated that there could be 1.8 million households who would actually use the system.

The Digital European Cordless Telecommunications (DECT) system is a development of CT2 able to run on the ISDN and working in the 1880–1900 MHz band. The DECT standard was finalized by ETSI in July 1992. Each European country which is a member of the EC must make the frequency band 1880 to 1900 MHz available for DECT systems. These could include business or residential applications, mobile radio or personal communication services.

GSM 900 is a complete network system for a Pan European Digital Cellular network operating on a 890-915 MHz band uplink, and 935-960 MHz downlink. The appropriate Standards for GSM were approved by ETSI in 1990 and incorporated in the DCS 1800 Standard. The Standard provides various options and design alternatives.

Personal Communication Networks will fit in somewhere between Mobile Cellular Radio and Telepoint. Telepoint's success will be badly affected unless it is well established before PCN arrives. In fact PCN appears to be a much improved Telepoint. The system will be quite similar to Mobile Cellular – radio handsets, base stations in cells, and network accessing and interconnecting services. The range of the pocket-size radio handsets will be shorter so there will be more cells – perhaps including individual short-range cells covering a household or a farm. Personal Communication Networks progressed from idea to development work to service licensing in a remarkably short time. In January 1990, the UK Department of Trade and Industry (DTI) awarded PCN licences to Mercury/Motorola/Telefonica, British Aerospace/Matra/Millicom/Pacific Telesis/Sony, and Unitel formed by STC/US West/Thorn EMI/DBP Telekon.

PCN users will carry cheap portable radio telephones communicating via the PCN base-stations. However, the companies just mentioned reconsidered their positions because of slow take-off. The technology has not yet been fully worked out – but that does not deter the forecasters. It has been estimated that the European market will be worth £635 million by 1996, with the UK taking 43 per cent, France 11 per cent, Germany 8 per cent, and others 38 per cent.

Cable-TV networks

Cable-TV networks are the odd man out in the categories of network here described because they were originally developed for one purpose only – the distribution of television data to viewers who were outside the range of television broadcast stations. Later they became the means of providing a large choice of stations regardless of geographical location, from a single multi-channel cable-TV connection.

In the United States, satellite links with the necessary bandwidth for interconnecting widely spaced centres of population with local cable TV centres became available in the late 1970s. First Amendment considerations restricted such systems until the Nixon administration reversed the Johnson decision by introducing an 'open skies' policy. Plurality of choice then removed the need for FCC regulation. By 1982 there were estimated to be 25 million subscribers in the US, but today about 65 per cent of all US homes are connected.

In Belgium over 80 per cent of homes are connected while in the UK the number is about 600,000 connected, although growth is rapid.

The case for considering cable-TV for multimedia transmission in the United States is twofold. First, it is second only to the telephone network as a ubiquitous telecoms media, and second, being designed for television signals, it is wideband.

The performance of cable systems depends on layouts. With 'tree and branch' the main supply line splits off to separate cables for delivery to households, where a desired channel is selected. With 'star' networks – an arrangement amenable to interactive two-way services – cables radiate out to local distribution boxes from which channels are switched into the cable for each household as controlled by the cable operator according to the customer's subscription schedule.

Most cable-TV network systems in the US provide a choice of 110 channels, each occupying a band 6 MHz within a cable with a 54–750 MHz bandwidth.

The American Television & Communications Corporation (ATC) – a cable company with 4 million subscribers – has provided some information about its technology, particularly in regard to the feasibility of wiring homes with fibre. ATC are running fibreoptic cable from the head-end at the cable control centre along the existing coaxial cable ducts to distant network nodes, the coax having been disconnected. The existing coax from nodes to subscribers completes the network. Consequently the noise generated by, and the power supply and maintenance required by, the amplifiers at intervals along the disconnected coax are no longer a matter of concern. ATC consider this evolutionary 'fiber backbone' approach and the introduction of other necessarily gradual pay-as-you-go measures to be appropriate because 'the enormous investment in completely new plant necessitated by a radical change to new architecture would be highly imprudent unless set-off by huge new revenue streams'.

The implication is that all-fibre systems are going to be slow in arriving in the US and even slower in other countries.

Figure 8.2 (after Large 1995) shows how the frequency spectrum in a cable for supplying 500 homes in a US system for new markets might be used. The arrangement would provide 62 channels of analogue and HDTV video, and 330 switched digitally compressed program channels shared with others. The 'upstream' spectrum is reserved for signals originated by users.

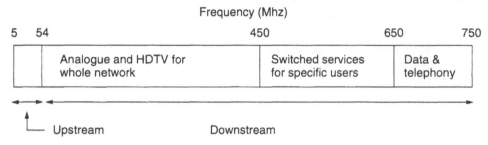

Figure 8.2 Multiservice CA-TV cable spectrum
Source: after Large (1995)

Such a cable with this bandwidth in a modern system would consist of a fibre 'backbone' from the head end to a local node with coaxial cable from that point to each of 500 households.

A Video Dial Tone network (Dixit 1995) is a relatively new idea for organizing a joint wideband cable-telephone system for VOD and interactive TV services. It provides equal access for multimedia providers and dial-up services for users. Audio, video, and data streams are multiplexed into each 6 MHz channel. Control and management functions and signalling are handled by a separate network which connects to users and providers. The arrangement allows for any number of servers from different information providers to be connected to users for 'near VOD' services for movies with a maximum waiting-to-start time of 15 minutes for any movie selected. ATM switching is used to switch movies from one channel to another.

According to Halfhill (1994), the Oracle company has already supplied a storage unit to one of its customers with a capacity approaching one terabyte. A future requirement for a library holding the world's estimated 65,000 films compressed to 1.5 Gbytes per film would be for 95 Tbytes of storage.

Synchronization and timing

McLarnon and Muxie (1994) review some of the problems that may arise in synchronizing sound to video. The authors describe the SMPTE time code described below and the Vertical Interval Time Code (VITC), recordable within the vertical interval between video frames. The authors emphasize the importance and difficulties of synchronizing sound when video compression and non-interlaced frames are used.

Continuous synchronization refers to lip sync, music-video sync, etc. *Event driven* synchronization may be fixed by a user, or by the reaching of a particular point in a presentation. Both types are particularly important in distributed multimedia applications where a number of computers are interconnected by one or more networks and may be accessing different information sources. The most obvious multimedia requirement for synchronization is 'lip sync' – audible speech correctly synchronized with visible lip movements. Another is the need to synchronize audio clips with video clips during an authoring/ editing session. Yet another occurs during the transmission of data of different kinds to a remote location via networks using different protocols. The transmission needs to appear to be 'seamless' and synchronized.

In a presentation to be recorded on, say, videotape, a passage of music or speech must start and end at the same instant as the related sequence of video frames, and remain in synchronism for its duration. Presentation software incorporating a 'time line' or 'construction window', as in Adobe Premiere or Macromind Director, makes the editing process easier. Editing is carried out on either MIDI data or a sound waveform (see chapter 6, pp. 157–9). In Premiere, for instance, a video clip and the audio data which were recorded with it are locked in synchronism. However, you may want to accompany a motion video clip with background music recorded separately. In this case the video clip, represented by an ikon, is dragged on to the video track on the time line and the first frame of it is displayed; the named sound recording, represented as a 'frozen waveform', is dragged on to the audio time line and positioned to correspond to the starting point of the video frame. When recorded for presentation, the music will be heard at the right time to accompany the video.

A way of dealing with synchronization more precisely is to use the Society of Motion Picture and Television Engineers (SMPTE) time code – widely adopted for audio and video synchronization purposes; it may be used for finding a particular video recording. Each frame in a TV programme can be individually identified and located by the SMPTE hours/minutes/seconds/frame code. For example 01:18:39:3 means 1 hour:18 minutes:39 seconds: frame 3. For videotape these data are recorded as an 80-bit word on every frame by a time code generator in a process called striping. The code is recorded in the vertical blanking interval and is then known as the vertical interval time code.

For other media it may be recorded on a track such as an audio track, and is then known as linear time code. Time codes are written on to tape by some camcorders, or may be recorded using a Time Code Recorder. For sound a similar technique is available called the MIDI time clock, which sends MIDI time code (MTC) down the MIDI cable connection.

For serious work, machines are available, such as the Timecode Machine from Opcode (California, USA), which enables MIDI data to be timed with the SMPTE time code and synchronized with SMPTE-encoded video frames.

Alternatively, a general way of implementing sound/visual sync is to arrange for a visual cue to pick up the appropriate instant on the music track by aligning the audio track with the visual cue – for instance, a video frame. The alignment of visual to audio is done against the displayed MIDI time code track.

Distribution and synchronization in multimedia networks

Requirements for multicast networks capable of transporting multimedia data are of particular interest because such networks will be required for the Information Superhighway, assuming that the ideas of its more ambitious supporters come to fruition.

For example, Marshall and Bagley (1995) discuss service control and management of a broadband network conveying information from a large number of third-party interactive and distribution services. A consortium called TINA-C of about 40 telecoms companies is attempting to define an information networking architecture for the purpose.

Parts of a distributed system which may cause transmissions to become asynchronous are discussed by Furht (1994) – see Figure 8.3. Fuhrt points out that the end-to-end delays in multiple data streams include skew (difference in presentation time between supposedly synchronized objects), jitter, utilization (for example, duplication or dropping of video frames), and speed differences.

The proposed method for eliminating asynchrony consists of introducing controlled buffer storage large enough to smooth out the maximum end-to-end or latency delays. Extra delay is introduced by controlling the rate at which a buffer releases data in order to bring about synchronization. The control techniques have been described by Little and Ghafoor (1991).

Synchronizing sound and vision with the aid of authoring software for a presentation was described in chapter 6. The process of actually ensuring that it is done effectively has not been very well covered in the literature. Synchronizing in distributed multimedia network systems – an essential requirement for the Information Superhighway – is still being researched.

Most people working in this field consider that users will demand a certain Quality of Service (QOS), mainly in regard to delay-sensitive data and

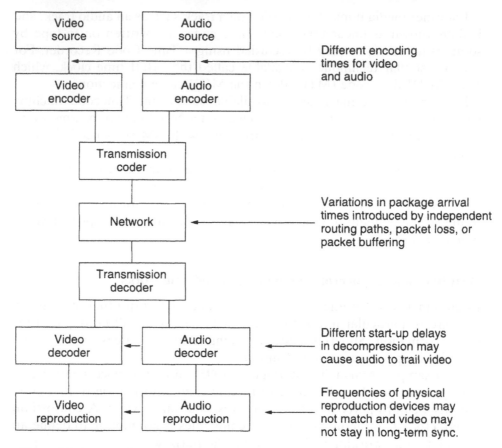

Figure 8.3 Causes of asynchrony in a distributed multimedia system

Source: after Fuhrt (1994)

freedom from errors. Because of the different kinds of errors and timing in different kinds of data, for instance, between video and audio, the usual way of dealing with the problem is to separate data into different major categories and arrange to control them separately to bring about synchronization.

Aspects of the problem confined to a database system rather than to those introduced by networked transmission are considered by Saiedian and Awad (1993). The database is imagined to be divided into media-specific sections such as voice database, visual database, etc. Each section has its Media Specific Synchronizer (MSS), with all MSSs controlled by a Global Sync Manager (GSM) which receives messages from the Database Management System (DBMS). When a user sends in a request, the DBMS sends it to the GSM, which breaks it down into parts to be sent to a media-specific section and to provide processing information regarding start, pause, resume, etc. For example, if a user viewing already delivered video requests it to stop, the GSS ensures that associated voice or music also stops.

Networks may be of the 'one-to-many' or 'many-to-many' types, but a large public system is likely to be of the 'several-to-many' type. Ramanathan and Rangan (1994) propose a large public system to serve the San Diego area in southern California and include a description of a proposed synchronizing technique. The scheme consists of a number of information providers connected to a hub operated by a metropolitan areas provider such as Pacific Bell. The hub contains a server with numerous disks, distribution being controlled by an ATM switch. The metropolitan hub connects to a number of smaller hubs, each with an ATM switch, which handle local requirements such as the university library, the La Jolla residential area, etc. The authors provide an unrealistically small example of a 100-client system in a residential neighbourhood capable of supplying a service of 100 video programmes, each one hour long. The suggested storage requirement for MPEG-2 compressed data to be delivered at 4 Mbps is $4 \times 100 \times 60 \times 60/8 = 180$ Gbytes.

To carry the data for switching, and assuming that nearly all the data are downstream, the switch needs to handle 100 clients all looking at different programmes, so its maximum requirement is data handling at 400 Mbps. Note that the scheme provides only one type of service for only 100 users. If the service managed 1000 users, the switch's capacity would have to be 4 Gbytes.

The authors point out that while intramedia synchronization is important 'synchronisation is mainly an inter-media requirement . . . playback of higher level components of a document may be temporally related as in sequential or partially overlapped playback of two video programmes on a personal channel'.

The proposed technique is to deal with sync hierarchically in three levels – 'strands', 'rope', and 'chains', where a strand handles audio and video stored on different disks in the same server, ropes tie strands together, and chains tie ropes. The procedure is complex: 'For continuity-guararanteed servicing of multiple clients, storage servers employ the optimal Quality Proportional Multi-Client Servicing (QPMS) algorithm' developed for HDTV multi-user storage. Rope control involves 'relative time stamps' in each strand.

Yavatkar and Manoj (1994) also discuss one-to-many multimedia distributed systems, providing as examples 'remote visualisation, distributed simulations, media storage services, and on-demand multimedia services such as accessing CATV or an on-line video rental store across a network'. Moreover, they say that research issues must be solved *before we can realise large-scale dissemination services across a high-speed Wide Area Network* (my italics).

Yavatkar and Manoj continue:

A multimedia dissemination service must provide service to a large number of subscribers at the same time. Because end-to-end delays and loss characteristics of the WAN differ vastly at recipients dispersed across it, the problem of meeting QOS requirements at a large number of receivers is much harder.

Their proposed remedy is a system called Quality Management Transport Protocol (QMTP), which 'uses a combination of rate-based flow control, redundant transmissions, and occasional feedback messages (Negative ACKs) to deliver QOS within an acceptable range at each recipient'.

Ghassemzadeh and Regan (1994) address a further complication in their paper about user interactivity in distributed multimedia systems. Their proposed Timed Interaction Policy Server (TIPS) system is about tele-conferencing and Computer Supported Cooperative Work (CSCW) where synchronization during interaction between each teleconferencing group is needed. 'Interaction in terms of a working application is often an error prone and labour intensive task. . . . Minor changes to the intended structure can require a major rewrite of the application,' say the authors. Their proposal is to separate the synchronization structure from the rest of the application. Each application has its own 'TIPS service agent' containing a description of application events in a formal language. This is regarded as the defined local 'policy' for that application. Each service agent communicates with the service agents of other applications in order to effect synchronization.

Network management

Network management usually means the inclusion of the necessary monitoring facilities to enable faults to be diagnosed and reliability maintained. It can also mean controlling other machines or facilities on the network from a 'host' machine for 'one-to-many' (or vice versa) sessions such as teacher control of machines in a class of pupils.

The most well-known management system is the Simple Network Management Protocol (SNMP) developed for the real world of TCP/IP networks. OSI people are beavering away at the OSI-compatible equivalent CMIP (Common Management Information Protocol) but it will be a long time a-coming. At least 30 different SNMP software packages are available. Each arranges for a dedicated machine, which must include a good GUI (Graphics User Interface), nominated the 'Network Management Platform', to be used by the manager for monitoring the state of the network.

The software arranges for data like network topography, traffic levels, errors, faults, etc. to be displayed. The human manager can customize display modules to include, for instance, a building plan showing wiring and stations.

APPLIED TELECOMMUNICATIONS

Library networks

A 'library network' often means a library resource-sharing co-operative, not necessarily a number of libraries connected to a computer network. Library networks in the general sense have been functioning for many years simply because few libraries can supply the needs of clients from their own stocks and it makes sense for several smaller libraries to make their combined stocks available to all their clients.

Computers were adopted by library networks to make their task easier and in due course enabled other resources to be shared as well as book or serial stocks. A small network, NELINET, was operating between five New England university libraries in 1968. Requests to computers in a central office were made from terminals in outlying libraries for catalogue card production, book labels, etc.

The Library of Congress has been a library-system leader in the US, but its activities were matched by the Ohio College Library Center, which became the Online Computer Library Center (OCLC Inc.) and aggressively introduced several innovations. Another leader in the US was Research Libraries Information Network (RLIN). Both these organizations have been active in developing library systems and networks.

The US National Science Foundation is considering the promotion of multimedia libraries for supporting research, education, and commerce, together with a 'libraries without walls' project for an online system of at least 100 million items including books, maps, cartoons, photographs,. etc. This scheme may be related to the distributed Internet digital library, which is, or will be, available via World Wide Web. It is a project sponsored by ARPA and devised by a consortium called CNRI composed of MIT and the University of California at Berkeley, Carnegie Mellon, Cornell, and Stanford.

The UK JANET network described earlier is used by libraries mainly for calling up someone else's Online Public Access Catalogue (about 50 OPACs are connected), for document requests via the British Library's ARTtel service, or for connecting to the International Packet Switched Service (IPSS) and accessing online databases. UK library networking is becoming widely used, encouraged by the UK Office for Library Networking at the University of Bath.

The British Library operates a CD-ROM network for the benefit of clients using its Science Reference and Information Services at Holborn and Aldwych, London. A total of 28 CD-ROM products may be accessed from nine workstations. The system uses CD Net with the disks held in 3 Novell Netware 3.11 file servers each containing 28 drives, so there is plenty of room for expansion. Any user may search any disk with very little delay due to disk-to-disk transfers.

The arrival of computer-based integrated library systems encouraged the use of within-site LANs for sharing various resources, and the use of LANs in a small number of libraries in the UK and US was reported. See also CD-ROM networks in this chapter. Other applications include the support by a large public library of its services at its branches, the provision of special software access for clients, and arrangements for access to a catalogue from networked microcomputers.

Virtual Private Networks

A Virtual Private Network (VPN) appears to be the brainchild of the US Sprint Communications company, which runs a long-distance fibreoptic network in the USA. They have teamed up with Cable & Wireless, owners of the North Pacific and PTAT Atlantic cables, to offer a 64 Kbps ISDN-like service, aimed at multinationals. One-stop billing and integration with private networks will be included, and users will appear to be using their own international network.

Many businesses already have extensive private networks. The requirement of a Virtual Private Network is to obtain at least the facilities currently obtained by using leased lines but at a lower cost. A VPN includes dynamic bandwidth allocation purchased on a 'pay as you use' basis as an alternative to paying for dedicated lines which are only occasionally used at full capacity.

CD-ROM networks

Heavy usage of several CD-ROMs in one location can be managed by buying extra drives and subscribing to several copies of the same CD-ROM. In 1989, by which time LANs, particularly in libraries, had become commonly used, the idea of enabling several users to access one or more drives using LAN interconnection was introduced. Either PCs or Apple machines may be used for CD-ROM networking.

Most of the information which follows applies to PCs, an application which is not as easy as networking with Macs. For Macs on an Appleshare network the CD-ROM drivers are installed in the 'server folder' and CD-ROM players on the network become available to all users. The following list explains some of the acronyms and jargon in use in this field

- BIOS
  Basic Input/Output System. Software designed for IBM PCs and stored in ROM for controlling input/output functions and screen data.
- CD-ROM driver
  A software package which enables a computer to control an attached CD-ROM drive.

- MSCDEX (MS dos CD rom EXtension)
  An MS-DOS extension enabling a CD-ROM disk to be accessed like a hard disk, overcoming the inability of DOS to recognize a disk capacity exceeding 32 Mbytes. MSCDEX redirects BIOS CD-ROM read or write requests to itself.

- NETBIOS (Network Basic Input/Output System)
  A PC telecom protocol/interface for connecting IBM PCs, PS/2s, and compatibles to each other via a LAN. It establishes a communication session between named stations. It was the first network operating system and was designed primarily to enable DOS-based PCs connected to a relatively small LAN to access print or file servers.

- NLM
  Network Loadable Module. Software used when a network does not have a CD-ROM file-server installed. One module per installed CD-ROM drive is included in the network file server.

- Peer-to-peer operation
  Access to a CD-ROM drive attached to a particular computer by other similar computers on the network using inter-computer commands.

- Pre-caching
  Writing a CD-ROM on to a hard disk of equivalent capacity so that a computer can access and transfer data at hard disk speeds which are much faster than CD-ROM access and transfer speeds.

- SCSI
  Small Computer System Interface.

- Server
  A dedicated server (file-server) is a fast microcomputer with large memory capacity connected to a network acting as the controller of a CD-ROM drive or drives for the use of network clients using their own machines.

With reference to the server – the last item in the list above – a shared resource of this kind is likely to be less costly than the possession of comparable facilities by individual users. A non-dedicated file-server is a lower cost alternative where a workstation acts as a server as well as functioning as a user's workstation. If the file-server PC is sufficiently powerful, a number of users can access it at the same time with some degradation of performance. For example, in throughput tests of a Storage Dimensions Filemaster II machine, the speed degradation when there were 4 users instead of 1 was 41 per cent. The Filemaster II contains a 33 MHz processor and 4 Mbytes of memory with cache and two 150 Mbyte disks.

Opti-Net file-server software was one of the first for CD-ROM control. It enables up to 100 users to control up to 32 drives. Fairman (1991) describes how it was used with six workstations accessing 16 drives. Simpson *et al.*

(1994) describe a networking system using Novell Netware LAN software and a 486 microcomputer as a file-server.

Van de Sompel (1994) has organized a client-server network at the University of Ghent capable of managing up to 2000 workstations connected to a TCP/IP 2 Mbps fibreoptic network. Users may search all servers and will be supplied with data from whichever server is running the disk containing the required data. Inter-campus operation can be provided using Internet with TCP/IP protocol as if it was a WAN.

A comprehensive CD-ROM networking system enabling up to 100 users to access any number of servers on a network is described in Fenwood's (Guildford, Surrey, UK) specification. They offer two types of network called Ultra*Net and Ultra*Net NT. Both are designed for DOS-based networks but Ultra*Net NT includes several improvements including Internet-compatible protocols for searching Internet-connected players by arrangement with their owners/publishers. They recommend the Toshiba 4101 dual-speed or the 3501 quad-speed player for SCSI MPC computers.

Ultra*Net includes the means of pre-caching the contents of a CD-ROM on to a 9 Gbyte hard disk. The disk will hold up to about twenty titles from nominally 640 Mbyte CDs depending on contents and compression method adopted. To the user, the disk will appear to be a normal CD-player except that it will be much faster. Fenwood claim an improvement of between 2 and 5 times for a single user, but for five or more users performing different searches a performance improvement of up to 200 times is claimed. Up to eight 9-Gbyte drives can be accessed via their servers.

Fenwood can provide installation, training, and support. Complete systems range from server, 7 players, and licence at a total cost of £7405, to their most comprehensive server, with 4 quad-speed players, two 9 Gbyte drives and a licence for an unlimited number of users at £24,000. The server in the larger system includes a Pentium processor with 32 Mbytes of RAM and a one-Gbyte hard disk.

In February 1995 the British Library announced that it had been using a CD-ROM network in its Science Reference and Information Service at Aldwych and Holborn, London, since August 1994, as explained earlier.

Other network applications

Mumford covers a number of aspects of multimedia networking in Mumford (1996). She makes a number of points with educational applications in mind:

- Multimedia makes heavy demands on storage and transmission.
- Predictable transmission according to the application is needed.
- Data compression reduces demands usually at the expense of some loss of detail.

- Methods of access and interconnections have important consequences.
- Costs of transmission will determine the pace of networked applications.
- Standards for networking are essential.

In addition to numerous military applications, much of the activity in this rapidly growing field is centred on medical imaging, museums, art galleries, and photographic archives. This area is covered in chapter 14.

High-resolution 2560×2048 8-bit ($= 42$ Mbits) radiographs viewed on the UCLA medical network are displayed on Megascan 300 dots per inch monitors. Bits are delivered to the CRT at 8 Mbytes/second ($= 64$ Mbits/sec) from buffer storage. A speed of 4 Mbytes/second is considered necessary in the supply network so that a radiograph that has been called up will appear in two seconds. UCLA found that a 1000 Mbps network from UltraNet met their requirements for many simultaneous wideband imaging processes.

THE INFORMATION SUPERHIGHWAY

Introduction

If the ISDN is too slow and its implementation is lethargic, and if fibre may not be arriving yet, why is there new optimism about the nationwide delivery of multimedia entertainment and other programmes? It seems that a complex combination of cable/Internet, deregulation politics, or new methods of overcoming the constraints of the local loop could enable online wideband communication to arrive sooner than expected. Extraordinarily sophisticated low-cost chip-based high-speed processing has become available to distribute and select data.

The 'arrival' of an Information Superhighway (IS) could mean usage by 5 per cent or 25 per cent of major organizations or by some percentage of the whole population. The phrase 'universal wideband service' which is being discussed, of course means availability to the whole population. The idea has not always met with approval. One critic, Michael Sage, suggested that:

> Since half of American adults are illiterate [if that is true for the US it applies equally well to Europe] it would be far more logical to give people subsidies for newspaper and magazine purchase and keep the public libraries open longer than to subsidise superhighway development; nothing is more misguided or misleading than to suggest that access to it is somehow central to determining wealth or poverty in the information age.

The increasing disparity between the 'information rich and the information poor' introduces another discussion. Jacobson (1994) considers the global distribution of wealth and network density. The figures (1990 data, from a World Bank report) in Table 8.3 speak for themselves. Table 8.4 shows the number of Internet hosts per selected country in 1992 – by 1996 the number will have doubled (at least). Jacobson quotes the remarks made by the Tanzanian prime minister at an international telecommunications conference: 'It is insensitive to talk about new broadband and mobile networks that would provide multiple new services to wealthy countries when 25% of the world's population lacks access to an adequate basic telephone and millions have never used one.' 'Have-not' considerations may be 'insensitive' but they have not reduced expansionist talk at current telecoms conferences. Jacobson suggests no remedies.

Table 8.3 Development indicators

	Country income levels			
	Low	*Middle*	*High*	*US*
Population (in millions)	2948	1104	830	249
GNP per capita ($)	350	2220	19,950	21,790

Table 8.4 Internet hosts per country

Country	Hosts
United States	591,049
Australia	43,262
Germany	42,486
Canada	37,021
UK	32,843
Sweden	20,321
Netherlands	20,255
France	18,508
Italy	7458
Portugal	1291
Mexico	776
Chile	146
Tunisia	25
India	6
Thailand	1

Yet another objection to the IS is lodged by Snider (1995). He thinks that the Information Superhighway is nothing less than an 'environmental menace'. The coming information superhighway portends 'an environmental disaster of the first magnitude'. Because people will be able to live and work in rural America and having open space round your house is equated with a high standard of living, dream homes with several acres of land 'will require the destruction of forests and open land across the country'. An apartment building with 200 families will become 200 five-acre homes occupying 1000 acres. 'The best and the brightest will leave the urban blights' and blight, for instance, 'that little gem of a state' – Vermont. Since 1950, Vermont's population has increased by 50 per cent. Its few suburban areas are 'chock full of expatriates from nearby metropolitan areas such as New York City and Boston'.

To return to the question of network capacity: there is no data speed limitation problem with cable, which was designed to transport television signals. The speed of any route through the Internet network available to the average user depends on the speed of its weakest link – about 128 Kbps.

The ultimate objective of the IS is to provide a global universal tele-communication network to deliver entertainment and information. It is potentially one of the most important developments in telecom services ever considered.

Regulation

The United States

General regulatory conditions in the US are gradually being relaxed. The FCC has removed restrictions stopping local telephone operators from offering home entertainment over their networks. Bell Atlantic is reported as being almost ready to provide such services.

In spite of the relaxation, Egan (1994), a recognized authority working at Columbia University, introduces a telling discussion. He states that because of the inadequacy of public finance, regulations must be arranged to stimulate private investment. The business objective is high profits and competitive advantage, but existing regulations are designed to limit earnings and market power and 'represent a formidable roadblock to increased private investment'. Egan argues that flawed regulations may not slow down the development of the IS, if the government does not over-regulate and so discourage the entry of new players into the market. 'Herein lies the most pitiful irony of the situation,' says Egan. 'The most fundamental drivers of private market investment incentives are exactly the opposite of what government authorities are prepared to adopt.' He recommends 'doing it the old-fashioned way' by·removing market entry restrictions, profits, and operational scope.

Existing regulations are an example of the politics of 'turf regulation'. The turf in a given region is allocated to monopoly providers of cable-TV, telephone, broadcast, and often newspapers (in the US). Significant cross-market ownership is not authorized to any extent. Investment in public networks outside the established core is stagnant in spite of industry buzzwords like 'seamless nationwide', 'high speed digital', and 'information superhighways'. Meanwhile, a 'cornucopia' of alternatives is filling market niches. They include private satellite systems, cellular networks, 'wireless' cable, packet data radio, etc.

Egan considers that the argument for a best case return on capital indicates that for every $1000 invested per subscriber for access purposes, $14 of additional revenue per month per household would be required for capital recovery over a 10-year discounted payback period at a 12 per cent return rate. Most types of service require considerably more than a $1000 investment. Consequently, 'unless an integrated network operator is allowed to freely pursue all revenue opportunities . . . it is very difficult to justify mass deployment of the new broadband to the home technology'. Finally:

> Nowhere in the most basic of economic principles is it clear that two or more local media monopolies is better than one . . . the choice for a broadband infrastructure network may be one provider or none. . . . Why would policy makers want to prevent companies from investing to modernize parts of the infrastructure, like household lines, that everyone wants to use but no one company can afford to build on its own?

The year 1934 was a milestone for telecommunications in the United States. In that year the Telecommunications Act became law; it has survived with some amendments ever since. The Act brought in a supervisory agency for regulation, the Federal Communications Commission (FCC). ARPA-NET, the Defense Department's Advanced Research Projects Network, which developed into the Internet, was founded in 1969.

In the late 1980s several computer companies formed the Computer Systems Policy Project to consider their options. In 1990 the High Performance Computing Bill was introduced, directing the National Science Foundation (NSF) to develop the National Research and Education Network (NREN) and to provide $400 million to develop a 3 gigabit/second network. The High Performance Computing and Communications initiative, covering advanced systems, technology and resources, became an Act in 1992, authorizing the extension of Internet by connecting the NREN network to it. A National Competitiveness Act covering an information superhighway infrastructure was proposed.

In mid-1993 an example was set by the White House and other agencies. They initiated a public information service by enabling certain files to be accessed via Internet, issuing e-mail addresses for the purpose. McMurdo and Simpson (1994) drily comment: 'In view of the recognised differences between the UK and US government cultures of access to information there is little for the UK public to compare with the White House information dissemination initiative.' In September 1993 the Clinton administration published a nine-point agenda to encourage the construction of the highway. This White House agenda aimed to ensure that it would be available to all at affordable prices. Al Gore, the Vice-President, said that the federal government would act as a catalyst for a National Information Infrastructure (NII) to be built by the private sector. According to one observer:

> The NII is imagined to consist of a network of competing networks made seamless and transparent by government standards and operated and maintained by private industry. This competitive marketplace will benefit consumers small and large by yielding better services at lower prices. The phone companies can compete and win in that environment and so can the cable companies, wireless companies, long distance providers, and many others who have the know-how to give consumers what they want.

Subsequently Gore broadened the concept to a Global International Infrastructure in the hope that all governments would join in (Gore, October 1994a). The message was reinforced at the end of the year (Gore, December 1994b) with the announcement of a 'Telecom Summit' in early 1995 and promised legislation to open markets. We must 'work toward our goal of connecting every classroom, library, hospital, and clinic to the NII by the year 2000', said Gore.

A far-reaching attempt was made in late 1994 to introduce a Bill to amend part of the 1934 Communications Act which would drastically alter the rights of communications companies. Telephone companies would be allowed to enter cable-TV and would probably be allowed to enter into manufacturing, electronic publishing, and security services as well. Cable-TV would be allowed to provide phone services. Having passed the House of Representatives, the Bill, sponsored by Senator Hollins, was blocked when it reached the Senate. It was thought to provide too many advantages for the Bell companies. Meanwhile, the FCC authorized the first video dialtone service for New Jersey Bell to supply service to homes in Dover Township, New Jersey.

A major change in regulatory conditions in the United States finally occurred when President Clinton signed the Telecommunications Act on 8 February 1996. Wiley (1996) summarizes the major issues being discussed at the end of 1995 when two different versions of the Act were passed by the House and the Senate followed by attempts to draft a single compromise version. The major issues were:

- Allowing competitive entry into the local telephone market.
- Removing the remaining restrictions on the Belcos except for rights of competitors to use their transmission facilities.
- Allowing telephone companies to provide video programmes to subscribers in their area.

The imminence of the Bill prompted a merger between Bell Atlantic and Nynex which would have been worth $25 billion. In spite of the passing of the Bill early in 1996, these two companies changed their plans and now intend to launch a long-distance telephone venture.

Cable-TV plus Internet already have a customer-base large enough for multimedia entertainment/information service viability. The cable-TV operator Telecommunications Inc., Denver, alone has 10 million subscribers out of an estimated US total of over 50 million. However, the technical problems of the cable to Internet interconnection, and Internet's bandwidth limitations must first be solved.

Europe and the Union

In Europe about 30 million homes are connected to cable but connections are patchy. Germany has about 13 million subscribers. It is not clear whether these figures refer to 'homes passed' by cable, households actually connected, or the total number of viewers in connected households. However, this is a fairly large base from which something like a super-highway might emerge.

Carlo de Benedetti (1994), chairman of Olivetti, thinks that 'Conflicts of interest paralyse the decision-making process or spin it out to such extremes that European markets, industries, and institutions often give the impression of unchangeable, immovable objects in a highly fluid world. A lot of chat and no action turns information highways into information hypeways.' The Commission of the European Communities has had an uphill struggle against vested interests when trying to establish some kind of unified European telecoms system. It decreed an open market for certain services by the end of 1989 and free competition for terminal purchases by 1990. In July 1990 'framework directives' for competitive services were proposed, backed by the force of Article 90 of the Treaty of Rome. They 'would herald the dawn of a new era', said the commissioners. If not by 1992, then perhaps by 1995, they would 'open up unlimited opportunities for the telecommunications industry, for business users and for the individual consumer'. In April 1993 the EC ministers voted with 'Decisive indecision' (in the words of the journal *Telecommunications*) to delay full liberalization of public voice telephone services until 1998. In August 1993 there was a White Paper for Growth, followed by plans submitted in June 1994 by Commissioner Bangemann to liberalize telecoms by 1998.

It is believed that the Commission may attempt to break up media monopolies by introducing new publishing and broadcasting regulations to guarantee pluralism.

The current progress of European telecoms in regard to coping with the success of the Internet, and the merits of OSI and TCP/IP protocol Standards are discussed under 'Protocols and Standards controversy' later in this chapter.

Japan

In 1985 the NTT monopoly became a private company and the market was opened to competition. A number of international, national long-distance and local, and mobile services soon became established. NTT plans to make its backbone trunk a terabit fibreoptic highway with loops round Tokyo for through traffic. It already provides ISDN services and plans to start installing broadband ISDN with ATM protocols in 1996 using optical fibre in local loops. Toda (1993) from NTT describes the company's telecom plans in some detail and suggests that entertainment, business, conference, health care, library, education, and other services are likely to be expanded.

The UK

UK cable received considerable government publicity in the long-forgotten days of 1982 when it was thought that all technology was a Good Thing. Development was slow, but in 1990 26 new cable franchises were offered to bidders and government policy was changed, lifting the ban on foreign ownership. US telephone companies, unable to enter the cable business under existing regulations in their own country, invested heavily in UK cable, believing that this was the way to enter the UK telephone business. Additional franchises have increased the total of homes passed to at least 9 million, but only about 600,000 households are actually connected. However, there were 50,000 new connections in the last two months of 1993 so growth is rapid. About half of all the subscribers have also opted for cable-telephone services. There is no apparent difference between a cable-telephone and a conventional telephone call. Your telephone number is allocated at a BT exchange.

The Department of Trade and Industry (DTI) 1987 broadband highway report contained a classic bureaucratic killer phrase: 'We did not presume to consult potential users' and 'technology continues to advance very rapidly. The UK might end up by locking itself into a sub-optimal technical infrastructure.' This excuse for doing nothing is, of course, applicable to all new technology at all times.

A 1994 report (Anon. 1994b) from the same department came to exactly the opposite conclusion. The UK has 'an opportunity to develop a communications infrastructure that is at least as good as any in the world. It is an opportunity that the UK cannot afford to lose,' it said.

On 22 November 1994, the government decided not to lift the 'entertainment' ban on BT, imposed earlier to encourage cable start-ups. BT's plans to spend £15 billion on fibreoptic cabling have also been abandoned. Reguly (1996) quotes a broadcasting research group who say: 'One has to look at cable as the channel tunnel project of the TV industry. The payoff might not come until the next millennium.'

American investment in the US cable network is declining and 'Since cable companies (in the UK) have no earnings, pay no dividends, are less than halfway through a £12 billion construction programme, and are pioneers in a new industry, the City has had a difficult time valuing them.' Only one in five of the 6 million homes passed by cable subscribe: 'There is talk that some American and Canadian groups have read the riot act to their cable subsidiaries in Britain.' Reguly, quoting David Miller of General Cable, says:

> In the coming years they will try to introduce VOD, home shopping and banking ... but there's a good chance this extra effort won't give the cable industry star status – BSkyB is getting bigger, a fifth terrestrial channel is coming and so is digital terrestrial TV.

In October 1994 the DTI reached a telecommunications agreement with the United States in order to encourage competition with existing carriers in transatlantic services, and to allow other organizations to lease lines to interconnect the telephone networks of the two countries.

The BBC intends to install up to seven compressed 5 Mbps PAL digital TV channels on a single satellite transponder. It is currently considering whether it should use the potential of this new digital TV system to offer more than conventional entertainment services. It could become a lumbering but formidable provider. Its erstwhile Deputy Director of Engineering wrote the standard 650-page work about Digital Television (Sandbank 1990). The digital TV timetable is supposed to be: services in the US to start during 1995, finalization of a European Standard at the end of 1996, and the first European services to be launched in 1997 on channel 35. European progress crucially depends on completing the Standards on time. The BBC will also be starting up twelve national digital audio broadcasting services with the assumption that the majority of listeners will be using portable and mobile receivers.

Mansell (1994), at the Science Policy Research Unit, University of Sussex, UK, covers similar deregulatory topics for the UK as Egan did for the United States (p. 233). His advice is a little different. Instead of allowing private industry full rein, he advocates redressing imbalances in network access: 'Regulation in the name of public services is not only possible; it will be essential in the future ... regulation, imperfect as it is, will play a crucial role in monitoring and guiding decisions by the players in the market.' 'Network openness' is the key factor, according to Mansell. The terms for network interconnection – so that new entries can gain access to the networks of the Incumbent Dominant Operator (IDO) with the consequent access to businesses and households – are critical. They depend on the degree to which the IDO will unbundle and provide access to service functions and on an agreement for reasonable charges for the use of the IDO's network by new entries. He considers two possibilities – separate the global and domestic services of the IDO; the domestic offshoot would then negotiate connections between the global IDO and new entries. Alternatively, use cost accounting mechanisms to achieve network openness.

An organizational environment is needed for an ongoing debate about changing technology and markets. Regulatory activity should be directed towards a minimum set of essential and manageable tasks.

Copyright

In the *Peggy Lee* v. *Walt Disney* case in the United States the assumption that a film distributor can exploit a film by 'all means known or hereafter devised' may have to be changed. In the case brought about by a video re-recording of Lee's earlier recording of *Lady and the Tramp* without permission, a court ruled that video could not have been anticipated at the time of the first recording. There are some unique aspects of copyright in the United States when the Fairness Doctrine occasionally overrides the Third Amendment, as discussed by Cawkell (1994) and Wall (1994).

The anxieties of publishers and recording companies, art galleries and museums with regard to infringements of their copyrights could be reduced if they grasped the opportunities for promoting their holdings and their revenue-earning possibilities. 'Obtaining rights can be extremely difficult for potential developers unless the collecting societies respond to new needs and find mechanisms for licensing an adequate volume of material,' says Nicholas Higham, a London solicitor. 'If they do not do so, then the voices of those who already call for compulsory licensing, or for an emasculation of rights of copyright into a mere right to economic compensation for the use of a work, will be increasingly heard.'

See also chapter 7.

Competition, demand, and company shakeouts

The progress of technology is far easier to forecast than its social effects. The behaviour of people when confronted with a digital information super-highway is uncertain. What information will customers perceive to be of value and what will they be prepared to pay for it? We know that certain kinds of information delivered without delay are considered to be valuable. Information concerning the money market, and the rate at which it is up-dated, are a rare example where value may be assessed. Other occupational information has often not survived the test of profitability in the market-place. The idea of trying to establish a monetary value for information has almost been abandoned (Repo 1989).

The probability of success for a profitable consumer information service is hard to predict. For example, what would a consumer be prepared to pay for the convenience of a Video on Demand Service and associated costs in competition with a video hire service currently charging about £1 per day in the UK?

In the United States the players in multimedia markets feel that if you want to succeed on a future information superhighway you need to be master of the technology, telecoms, and information content; if you own a big network you must have some material to send along it. The hardware people see the benefit of owning a complementary company to supply the 'software'. Copyright is not viewed as a serious problem. If you want a chunk of material, you take over the company that produces it, together with its copyright, or you set up some kind of joint operation. The early battles between VHS and Sony's Betamax recording systems might have gone Sony's way if VHS had not been able to supply a volume of VHS consumer tapes. Sony soon recovered and was one of the first companies to pursue this policy. They purchased CBS records back in 1987 for $2 billion. In 1989 Sony bid $3.4 billion for Columbia Pictures, whose library of 2400 films included *Lawrence of Arabia* and over 20,000 TV shows.

The race started in earnest in the 1990s. According to John Maney, as recounted in his book (Maney 1995), 'No set of companies ever changed so much, so fast' – and they were triggered by a single event. In August 1993 a court in Virginia ruled that Bell Atlantic could operate a cable-TV network. The eight Bell telephone companies, spun off when AT&T was broken up in 1984, were prevented from such operations until then by the 1984 Cable Act. In November 1992 John Sculley, Apple's chairman, had predicted that by 2001 the global megamedia industry would be worth $3.5 trillion – i.e. 3.5 million million dollars. Following the court decision a deal was agreed between John Malone, Chief Executive Officer (CEO) of Telecommunications Inc. (TCI), the country's biggest cable-TV company, and Ray Smith, chairman of Bell Atlantic, the second largest of the eight Belco telephone companies, spun off when AT&T was broken up. They agreed to merge their two companies in order to deliver interactive 500-channel TV and two-way video communications. The other Belcos filed similar suits in their regional territories and embarked on various other manoeuvres.

The Atlantic Bell–TCI deal fizzled out later for various reasons but that did not affect the general momentum. Southwestern Bell took over two cable networks in Washington D.C. and paid $650 million for them. 'Many executives in both industries saw the beauty of combining rather than battling,' observes Maney. This deal was immediately followed by another – US West (another Belco) offered $2.5 billion for 25 per cent of the Time Warner cable system. It would help Time Warner build the fibreoptic network for trials in Orlando, Florida.

Maney's book is about the 'key players' who are trying to control the industry. 'This gives you a picture of the leaders of the companies because strong leadership and vision seem to be keys to success in megamedia.' He thinks that Wall Street's focus on the next quarter, and success as judged by the price of a company's stock is inadequate. 'My focus is overwhelmingly on U.S. companies. The reason is that the United States, in general, is far ahead of the rest of the world in megamedia.'

Sony owns Columbia/Tristar, which has a library of 3400 films and 25,000 TV episodes, Disney and TCI have an agreement for a new compressed digital-cable TV channel called Starz, running until 2004 for access to Disney movies, and IBM and Sears offer the Prodigy home shopping service. Disney's Paris theme-park may be a doubtful investment but *Aladdin* has earned $440 million so far and revenues from *The Lion King* will probably exceed it. Disney is the biggest movie producer, making about 60 films every year; it is planning to build 500 stores world-wide selling Disney character-branded goods. If Disney was taken over it would cost the acquirer about $35 billion, says Maney.

Two important factors not mentioned by Maney contribute to the potential success of megamedia in the United States. In past years the US Department of Defense has been a huge customer for IT products and the US government has provided a mammoth network, the Internet – a superhighway precursor – for nothing. Much will be learned from its inadequacies.

Servan-Schreiber was alarmed when he wrote *Le Défi Américain* back in 1967. At that time he pointed out that US industry produced more than twice the goods and services of Europe, including the UK. He noted that American society gambles much more money on human intelligence than it wastes on gadgets.

The personalities of CEOs provide one viewpoint, but their permanence and the effects produced by their successors are unknown. Doubtless the CEOs of Xerox, which failed to capitalize on inventions from its PARC labs, Commodore with its pioneering but unsuccessful Amiga machine, and of KSR and Thinking Machines, had ebullient confidence. Commodore had nearly 20 per cent of installed microcomputers in Europe at one time. Inmos (now French), Sinclair, and Nexos are examples of companies which seemed destined for success. David Kaye (1994) had something to say about operations of these kinds:

> Leaders in revolutionary times tend to have uncertain careers. Some fail because they are too slow to embrace revolution's possibilities and promises. Some fail because they cannot manage expectations. Some succeed either through a mixture of luck, energy and ability, or because they know how to make the many facets of inertia and change work together to their advantage, having the position, resources and commitment to make this happen.

Takeovers and mergers continued after the period covered by Maney. In 1995 MCI Communications and the News Corporation, chaired by Rupert

Murdoch, agreed a $2.4 billion deal; their first project would be an electronic newspaper. MCI owns Internet MCI, which provides services such as electronic shopping, while the News Corporation runs Delphi Internet Services.

Lewis (1995) discusses 'Gilder's Law', which postulates that the price of a service, product, or idea decreases by 30 per cent each time that production doubles. The extraordinary success of Netscape is a case in point. Netscape was valued at $2.8 billion when it came to the market in August 1995, 16 months after it was founded. It introduced Netscape 1.1 with HMTL before it was agreed as a Standard, did deals with Macromedia, Adobe, and Sun (Java), and very rapidly established itself as a major force on the Internet, believing that in due course it would be in a position to take advantage of a huge expansion in interactive multimedia operations.

It looks as if the UK will follow the trend in the United States of media mergers and takeovers. The Broadcasting Bill, referred to in the regulation section in this chapter, is accelerating the progress. According to Reguly and Tieman (1996):

> The merger of United News & Media, a vintage slow moving newspaper company, and MAI, an aggressive television and financial services group, is expected to be the first of many such deals in Britain . . . the age of the media conglomerate is here.

UN&M own the *Daily Express* and the *Sunday Express* while MAI's major interest are in Meridian, Anglia, and the new Channel 5 television. The value of the merged company is nearly £3 billion. The merger took place in April 1996.

AT&T is planning to build a business in the UK worth $1 billion within five years provided that OFTEL relaxes its regulatory conditions. In particular AT&T wants OFTEL to guarantee that customers could change their telephone company without changing their telephone number, and without adding an additional code in front of it. AT&T, having itself been split in 1984, is planning to split itself into three parts by the end of 1996.

It is as well to bear in mind some remarks made by John Priestley (1995) about the information superhighway; they are equally applicable to multimedia/megamedia. He says:

> We have never been very good at predicting the future use of technology, even when we have had some success in predicting technology changes themselves. We may, by now, have a shrewd idea about some of the new tools that will be available to us, but we should be very wary indeed about assuming we know how they will make their impact.
>
> We know that we will have much more powerful and cheaper computing . . . we know too that we can bank on having a lot more communications

capacity – and that an unstoppable combination of technological progress and political liberalisation will ensure lower prices, [but] we really should have learned by now that the availability of technologies is only one surprisingly small factor in a range of influences that determine social and behavioural change.

The conclusions reached following a survey in Europe are listed in a CEC 1993 report (Anon. 1993d). They are rather mundane. Residential needs are reported as first, access to quickly changing information such as news, stock prices, and the weather, already adequately supplied by existing media. A second need is transactional support for home banking, travel reservation, and teleshopping. Nothing is said about new forms of entertainment.

In Anon. (1994d), the CCTA suggests that the government might use an information superhighway for:

- Tax, social security, vehicle registration, and other official correspondence;
- Information such as school prospectuses, job vacancies, etc.;
- Electronic mail;
- Appointment booking – e.g. at hospitals.

Changes in lifestyle spending are slow – leisure spending in the UK has remained at about 8 per cent of GDP for some years, and TV viewing has stayed at about 26 hours per week since 1985 – this is one aspect of use which needs close attention. Set-top box information/entertainment providers will need to obtain a larger slice of a cake which remains about the same size.

The development of set-top TV media selection superboxes

A 'first generation' set-top box manages the decoding of incoming data from a media channel and reconstructs it in a format for human assimilation – for example, as a television programme to be viewed on the associated TV receiver. It also enables the user to request information – for example, the title of a film to be viewed on the receiver.

For the developed information superhighway a 'second or third generation' 'superbox' may have to accept data from one or more channel types – for instance, cable, broadcast television, satellite, radio link, mobile station, telephone line, etc. – and may also have to be able to send information, such as a tape recording from a camcorder, to another subscriber.

The first stage in this process is likely to be a box capable of receiving data from one channel type, decoding and reconstructing it, and also capable of sending user's instructions for a selected programme. The ubiquitous TV set, acting as the man–machine interface, will be surmounted by a set-top box. The viewer will choose information to come back down the line to be displayed and printed as required. The information which the system handles may arrive via one of the numerous channels just listed. Several questions need resolving. Is there a channel/services leader which will become dominant? Will all providers supply information using their own channels? Will they interconnect or combine to share a single channel in some way? The form of the superbox will presumably be dictated by the type of the dominant channel – or will it be required to handle several different types of channel? The success of a channel will depend on the faith and finance of its owner, the date by which it becomes widely available, and the perceived success of its services.

ATM switches are of special importance for superboxes. Various types are becoming available. In this application they are used for a different reason from methods described earlier in this chapter. The switch multiplexes a number of channels, and switches at a bit rate of at least n times the bit rate of each channel where n is the number of channels. Thus if 100 data links to set-top boxes in homes are each to receive a 2 Mbps service from a central point via an ATM switch, the switch must run at least 200 Mbps.

Superboxes are being developed in the United States. For example, US Philips and Compression Labs are reported to be supplying Bell Atlantic with an ADSL (discussed earlier) or fibre system capable of showing MPEG compressed movies with a good quality 720×480 display. Movies, health care, education, and children's shows are said to be available. Microware's OS/9 operating system and MPEG compression/decompression will be used in the 'Stargazer' Video On Demand (VOD) service.

See chapter 9 covering the question of Standards which are currently being discussed in the United States.

The development of at least two types of box is well advanced in the UK – designed to make use of the potential of their owners' channels – for BT it is the public telephone network, and for the Cambridge Cable consortium the cable-TV network.

BT owns most of the telephone network in the UK. In 1990 it carried out trials with fibreoptic lines to households at Bishops Stortford with GEC Plessey (GPT), BICC and Fulcrum, for multi-channel TV, access to a videodisk library, and teleworking. The trials ended in 1992. In November 1994, BT dropped its plan for a £15 billion fibre information superhighway after the government refused to lift the ban on BT's entry into TV broadcasting.

BT will make the most of the enormous investment in the 'copper loop', which provides it with an entry to businesses and homes. Regulatory legislation does not appear to prevent it from offering services such as VOD. It started trials in the spring of 1994 although OFTEL warned it in November 1994 that a full system must be consistent with UK policy. The trials are mainly based on DMT ADSL (Discrete Multitone Asymmetric Digital Subscriber Loop), in which the maximum bit rate of the PSTN, nominally about 140 Kbps, is extended by equalization and the selective use of frequency bands within the channel, to up to about 2 Mbps. 'Asymmetric' means that the return path from a subscriber works at the lower rate of 64 Kbps. Acceptable television pictures from, say, an 80 Mbps service, compressed by 40:1, could be delivered and viewed over such a system. In these trials, supplying about 2000 households in Colchester, Essex, BT is using material from the Sears group and W.H. Smith for home shopping, Thomas Cook for holidays and travel, the BBC, Carlton, Kingfisher, Granada, and Pearson for TV programmes, sport from BSkyB, and music from BMG Video, EMI, Polygram, Sony, and Warner. A massively parallel computer with an Oracle media server and nCube software is used at the head end. Set-top boxes supplied by Apple consist of LC475 machines with MPEG decompression and Quicktime, receiving data at 2 Mbps. Viewers' requests, sent at the 64 Kbps rate, are received at a central point via an ATM switch.

A different approach is being used in a trial started in 1994 by a group composed of Olivetti, Online Media, Acorn, Cambridge Cable, ATM Ltd, Anglia Television, and BNR (Europe), a subsidiary of Northern Telecom. An interactive set-top box will handle bidirectional ATM MPEG-1 compressed television data running at 2 Mbps. The superbox is based on Acorn's 32-bit ARM610 chip, a version of the Advanced RISC machine's chip designed by ARM, an Acorn Computer subsidiary, being manufactured by Texas Instruments, VLSI Technology, and others. The chip's speed is claimed to be 140 Mips/Watt (a measure of integer processing performance) compared with the latest Apple/IBM power processors rated at 35 Mips/Watt – far slower at a given power dissipation. The ATM network associated with the superbox has been described by Wray et al. (1994). Each component such as a camera, audio system, display, etc. is treated as an 'ATM direct' module controlled by an ARM RISC processor, each module being directly connected to the network. The network will convey 'many streams of multimedia data, perhaps thousands, which are active simultaneously'.

In November 1994 I was informed that this superbox should be available next year at about £300 giving plenty of room for reduction if mass-production is put in hand. Will the general public be able to cope with the potentially much more complex set-top box interface? That depends whether system designers make time to try it out on average members of the public before releasing it.

Protocols and Standards controversy

A protocol is a set of rules governing the exchange of data. A controversy has developed which could seriously upset the idea of a global information superhighway, so it is a matter of some importance. In the protocols of interest here, OSI (an internationally agreed protocol supported by the EC), and TCP/IP (of American origin) control the several functions requiring attention when two terminals intercommunicate over a network. Separate rules are applied to each function. The rules enable all kinds of incompatible network, equipment, software, and interface functions to work together in order to present information on a recipient's terminal in exactly the way that the sender intended.

The EC introduced a series of standardization measures in the period 1977 to 1989. In 1990 the European Standards Organisations had at least 3000 items, worked on by 250 technical committees, which they were required to digest by January 1993. They would then have to be agreed, tested, and eventually incorporated into products – a far distant prospect. However, the idea that the European Committee for Standards (CEN), on which US interests were not represented, could become 'adjudicators of the IT industry in Europe . . . had the American manufacturers up in arms' (Frenkel 1990). Most of the new Standards would be accommodated within the European-supported OSI model. For a time there was much US activity and expressions of intent to become OSI-conscious. The Department of Defense published the GOSIP report specifying that US telecoms products should support OSI. Meanwhile, the Internet, using TCP/IP, was growing and TCP/IP had become virtually the *de facto* protocol. Recognizing the inevitable, in 1994 the Federal Internetworking Requirements Panel (FIRP) proposed a change in the GOSIP policy, relaxing its OSI preference and recommending that TCP/IP should receive equal support.

The way in which the TCP/IP protocol handles the *en route* functions differs from the way OSI handles them. Their design philosophies are different. OSI and its family of Standards are carefully considered and agreed. You cannot rush the careful attention and inter-country agreement which must be given to processes intended to endure. TCP/IP protocols were developed by a single organization – ARPA – for a single country – the United States. The ARPA control software became TCP/IP in the early 1980s. Both the popular and erudite literature about OSI and TCP/IP present pictures of two protocols influenced by nationalistic, *fait accompli*, alleged weaknesses and strengths, interlinking ease or difficulty, general complexity and state of implementation, or *deuxième défi Américain* viewpoints, depending on the source of the literature and the author's prejudices.

In September 1994 an EC paper (Anon. 1994f) pointed out that the Internet has 2 million hosts in the US and nearly a million elsewhere. EUnet GB is the largest European commercial provider operating in 25 countries. The paper continued with a discussion of Internet problems and opportunities.

In December 1994 the EC launched its Information Society Project Office to 'help promote international cooperation by aiming to build a global information infrastructure', among other objectives. It also issued a proposal to 'lift restrictions on the use of cable TV networks for the carriage of all liberalised telecommunications services'.

A 'Working Paper' (Ameil 1995) was published by the Directorate General Research of the European Parliament, presumably in anticipation of the February 1995 DG7 conference in Brussels. Apparently an 'official' document, it carries a disclaimer saying that the opinions expressed are 'not in any way those of the European Parliament'. It calls for action by the European Union and quotes an article from *Le Monde Diplomatique* entitled 'Qui tirera profit des autoroutes de l'information?' in support of a 'What's to be done about Internet?' argument. The paper, translated from the French, was published ostensibly to discuss Standards. Internet's TCP/IP protocol is 'an essentially monocultural model', whereas OSI is 'polyculturally inspired', says the paper. A quotation from *Le Monde Diplomatique* is used to support criticism of Internet: 'The concerns of the public are being disdainfully disregarded as greater support is given to the objectives of the giant cable, telephone and leisure companies.' The paper concludes that 'a specifically European Internet' should be developed 'as a support for the Standards chosen by the Europeans'. It says:

> By allowing the other side to choose the playing field the European Union is obliged to leave everything to their initiative, to move forward at the pace they impose, to play on unequal terms, and ultimately to retreat on other fronts.

Having discussed the merits of OSI standards versus Internet's TCP/IP protocol, the paper continues:

> By forcing the market to give up the immediate advantages of marketing the first available standard instead of collecting information about existing standards and the structure of potential demand, the political authority has the possibility of increasing the probability that the final choice will be a more sophisticated standard offering better prospects. ... [The EU should] develop a specifically European Internet as a support for the standards chosen by the Europeans, both for equipment and for services (applications) and by means of tax incentives.

The probability that the EU could introduce measures to successfully defeat *le deuxième défi américain* seems remote. This phrase comes from Servan-Schreiber's book *Le Défi Américain* (1969) describing what he considered to be the decline of Europe in the face of an American economic invasion. It inspired Nora and Minc's report (1978) presented to the President of France, which prompted substantial changes in French policy.

In market forces versus governmental action contests, market forces usually win. The lessons of history are clear. The need for standardized protocols cannot be denied but if you are successful (e.g Japanese Group 3 fax, and IBM's SNA) you can get in well ahead of the competition. Your equipment generates a *de facto* standard. The official Standard which arrives five years later – a typical time lag – may well be different from your system but it need not concern you. Your updated system is still better than your competitor's which conforms to the new Standard, probably already out of date. OSI versus TCP/IP is a somewhat similar higher level contest.

Summit-type conferences are now commonplace. *The Times*, in reporting such a conference in its 30 March 1995 issue, said on its front page that you can tell one by the presence of 'Marble, plate glass, Mercedes Benzes, Royalty, men with walkie-talkies, and women in hats'. If this conference marked a turning point it would 'only be for the quails' in the lunch provided.

It is hard to tell whether the G7 Information Society meeting in Brussels on 24–26 February 1995 will have been a turning point or not. The speeches made by the dignitaries reported in Anon. (1995b) are the usual expressions of hope, with the possible exception of some remarks made by Klaus Hansch, President of the European Parliament. Hansch said that information exchange should be 'on the basis of fair exchange and reciprocity'. 'For similar reasons of equity the Union supports the notion of international Standards laid down by International Standards Organisation should apply universally.' These Standards are those embraced by the OSI model, not TCP/IP.

If a confrontation develops, the supporters of one side or the other might back down. Alternatively, both sides might be obstinate and there will be some kind of face-saving fudge. Alternatively again, bridging of some kind might be introduced to make interconnection simple; this seems rather unlikely because the necessary gateway would be inconvenient, complex, and expensive.

Security

Good security practice must be applied in a variety of ways wherever confidential information is handled. The aspect of interest here is the security of the contents of a message during transmission. A message is a series of symbols representing text, graphics, sound, pictures, etc. A code is the substitution of codewords for plain language, while the two major types of cipher – transposition and substitution – are operations on individual characters. Ciphers and cryptography (from the Greek *kryptos*, hidden, and *graphein*, to write) are used to prepare secret messages.

One of the weakest parts of any telecommunication system is the area through which messages are passed outside the control of the sending and receiving stations. They may then be monitored by third parties; their contents should remain secure if the messages are enciphered. Ajluni (1995) describes several methods suitable for networks such as the Internet, and presumably for an information highway, by controlling access to routers – a key unit which allocates routes which are controlled by data contained in a message. A scheme called the Terminal Access Controller Access System

(TACAS) protocol, provided by Cisco Systems, is also described. It controls servers to which authorized users have access. Ajluni goes on to describe the DES and PKA systems (see below). The design background to such systems is discussed in a more advanced article by Zeng *et al.* (1991). A brief description of the background to enciphering methods is provided below.

A great deal of effort was devoted to devising supposedly secure encryption systems for messages transmitted by radio during the Second World War and at least as much effort to breaking them. The first, and possibly the biggest, code-breaking effort was made by the Government Code and Cypher School (GC&CS) at Bletchley Park.

An early system which endured was the 'one-time pad', invented by G. Vernam in 1917. As used in the war, a one-time pad contained lines of columnized randomly generated decimal numbers held by message sender and recipient. The letters of a message to be sent were first encoded into numbers, using a simple substitution code. The sender subtracted each number, without borrowing, from a one-time pad number, starting at a particular column and line on a particular page, and the result was transmitted. The message contained a group – the 'key' – at the beginning telling the addressee where to start on his pad. The recipient, starting at the place indicated by the sender on his copy of the same one-time pad, subtracted each received number from his one-time pad number without borrowing, thereby deciphering the message, and then changed the numbers back to the original letters, using the same substitution code as that used by the sender. Provided each new message was enciphered using a part of the pad never used previously, the method was perfectly secure.

This system is clumsy when a very large number of users is involved. The major alternative wartime system was for all users to have a machine containing rotating wheels. An input character produces an output character according to the positions of the wheels, which determine the path taken by an electric current. One or more wheels rotate by one position each time an input character is typed. The greater the number of wheels and the number of positions that each can take, the larger the number of alternative output characters that can be produced. Only if the positions of each of the identical wheels in a receiving machine are the same as those in the sending machine during the transmission of a message can the identity of each character be determined by the receiver. The 'key' is the starting position of each wheel. This was the basis of the 'Type X' and 'Enigma' machines. Unlike a one-time pad, the machines were automatic and the problem of distributing and stocking huge numbers of pads did not arise. Provided a one-time pad was used once only, messages could not be read without key and pads. The machine method was thought to be almost as good and much more convenient; the number of alternative output characters that the same input character could generate was so enormous that it was believed that it was impossible to read a message enciphered with a machine without the key. However, GC&CS did develop a method for reading messages enciphered with the Enigma machine.

The DES (Data Encryption Standard), RSA (invented by Rivest, Shamir, and Adelman), which is somewhat simpler to manage, and PKA (Public Key Algorithm) are probably the best known methods of encryption used to today.

The DES specifies an enciphering algorithm for the high-speed processing of data by computer hardware. A 56-bit key is used for multiple permutations of blocks of plain text composed of 65 bits inclusive of 8 error-detection bits. To decipher, it is only necessary to apply the same algorithm to an enciphered block using the same key. Everyone knows the algorithm but only the sender and receiver know the selected key.

RSA, based on factorizing large prime numbers, uses a 512-bit key, making it slow, although less slow than it may appear because of the development of fast, dedicated processing chips. It is considered secure because it would take a 1000 mips (millions of instructions per second) machine running for 2000 years to break it.

The PKA, however, embodies an additional factor to nullify the possible effect of the security risk inherent in the DES; with DES, information about keys could be intercepted *en route* to perhaps many correspondents. PKA uses two separate keys – a public enciphering key and a different secret deciphering key. The inverse of the enciphering functions cannot be derived even if the enciphering functions are known.

Netscape uses a 128-bit key for RSA encryption in the US. In August 1995 its RSA 40-bit encryption key, used abroad, was broken by French students using two supercomputers with 120 workstations. The version of RSA called RSA-129 was also broken in 1995 after an even larger effort.

The distribution of information about PKA keys to the message recipient is not necessary because of the so-called 'trap-door' method of using one-way enciphering and inverse functions. The PKA also embodies a signature to authenticate the sender as actually being the person he is purporting to be.

In a method invented recently by Robert Mathews, the inconvenience of distributing keys to intended message recipients in advance is overcome. It includes a device which causes the same set of random numbers always to be generated by a particular triggering number. Actually the system as just described could not work because a truly random number list cannot be repeated. In fact the numbers are 'pseudo-random', generated by electronic circuits capable of generating the same set of pseudo-random numbers when triggered by the same triggering number. Each set of pseudo-random numbers generated by a different triggering number is sufficiently different from all other sets to make cipher-breaking almost impossible.

The only way to determine the randomness, and hence the indecipher-ability of a message using a particular system design, is to subject messages to 'merciless attacks' using the armoury of known cipher-breaking techniques to see if the system can resist them.

A different solution is needed for the case when a large computer, connected to a communication network, contains files of different security classifications, and it is desired to make the installation available to a number of people who themselves are within different security categories. Machines can embody a security 'kernel' or interface between the operating system – that is, specialized software controlling computer functions – and the hardware. The function of the kernel is to check the access rights of each user to any information-containing system element. It may, of course, be necessary to encrypt data flowing through the network as well.

Hackers have successfully broken in to supposedly secure systems and have received a great deal of publicity. The wide use of the Internet and the need to make many types of message secure demands that users can send them knowing that they cannot be read by a hacker. The arrival of an information superhighway conveying a greater number of messages for a large number of different purposes makes message security essential.

Benefits and growth

In discussing the arrival of digital television, Netravelli and Lippman (1995) believe 'it can only be understood in the widest possible context, if at all ... we can only speculate about some of the possibilities ... many issues remain questions'. These remarks occur in a section of his article entitled 'Some imponderables and creative hurdles'. Although this part of his article is about the broad imponderables in digital television, I am giving Netravelli's list the new title of 'Evolutionary uncertainties affecting an information superhighway'. This title describes its contents equally well. A formidable list of questions is provided by the author.

1 How will computer architectures, operating systems, and databases change to encompass digital video?
2 Will advanced services such as HDTV, interactivity, and home information systems become commercial as the result of entertainment processors in every home?
3 Will digital video mature to become a software utility? What new algorithms will become part of the repertoire?
4 How will entertainment, information access, and home-office needs be satisfied by a customized integration of different video, networking, and service modules?
5 How will the competition in the local distribution of video emerge?

Telephone, satellite, cable, terrestrial broadcast, and package media may compete, combine, or divide distribution among them based on content. What impact will this have on the emergence of technology?

6 How will the diverse needs of commercial users merge with entertainment?

7 When will content-based browsing, filtering, and assembly of multimedia databases become practical?

Chapter 9

Standards

A considerable effort is in progress to introduce Standards by the CCITT (renamed ITU, which is also the name of the parent organization), ISO, and the industry. The composition of multimedia Standards is a highly necessary but very difficult topic emphasizing the usual Standards problems – how to fix the Standard on a particular date in the face of rapid advances, intense competition, the setting of *de facto* standards by fleet-of-foot entrepreneurial organizations, and the undesirable consequences of being quickly over-taken by events because the Standard is set too early. The likely result may be the setting of a Standard with so many alternatives and options that it is ineffective.

CD STANDARDS

CD Standards are defined in books identified by their colours and written by Philips, Sony, and, in the case of Video-CD, JVC, which specifies different CD formats (see Table 9.1).

More details about disk types and functions are given in chapter 11.

Once a production has been prepared for CD, the data have to be changed into a form suitable for their storage media – for instance, to conform with ISO 9660. An attempt is being made by a company called the Micro-electronics and Computer Technology Corporation (MCC) to bring a degree of standardization to multimedia interfaces. They have formed a consortium of industry members including companies like Apple, Bellcore, Kodak, Philips, etc.

ASSOCIATED CD STANDARDS AND SPECIFICATIONS

Balboa Runtime Environment

A program suite created by Philips consisting of a set of utilities to assist authors in CD-I programming.

Table 9.1 Compact disk specifications

Specification	Details	Player
Red Book	CD-DA 783 Mbytes audio data	CD
Yellow Book	CD-ROM Mode 1 680 Mbytes computer data	CD-ROM

	CD-ROM Mode 2
	  650 Mbytes of compressed
	  computer data. Additional error
	  correction
		CD-ROM

Yellow Book
  Extension
	CD-XA
	  Video and audio data are
	  interleaved
	    Mode 2. Form 1
	      Computer data
	    Mode 2. Form 2
	      Compressed video
	      Audio & picture data
		CD-ROM + XA card

Green Book	CD-I Forms 1 & 2	

Orange Book	CD-R
	  Part 1 (rewritable)
	  Part 2 (write once)
		CD-ROM

White Book	CD-Video	CD-I with TV receiver
–	CD Bridge	CD-I with TV receiver
Photo-CD		CD-XA player with a computer
Audio/CD-ROM mixed mode		CD

Frankfurt Standard (ECMA Standard 168)

A cross-platform Standard in preparation associated with CD-R Orange Book. It will include proposals for the retrieval of material recorded on CD-Rs.

Hierarchical File System (HFS)

A non-ISO 9660 CD-ROM proprietary format devised by Apple for Apple Mac machines.

ISO 9660

A Standard specifying how data should be stored on a CD-ROM, including disk volume number, Table of Contents, and Directory specifying file locations. CD-ROMs made to this Standard can be read by DOS, Apple operating system, or Unix when these operating systems include software included for this purpose. ISO 9660 is derived from and closely resembles the original Hi Sierra Standard which was agreed in a hotel of that name in Nevada. Hi Sierra is still occasionally used.

Rock Ridge Standard

A CD-ROM conforming to ISO 9660 Standard with a special data content of Unix files.

COMPRESSION STANDARDS

See chapter 3.

DISPLAY STANDARDS AND THEIR *DE FACTO* EVOLUTION

Eighty character × 25 line displays prevailed on microcomputers for some years but eventually a plug-in board was provided to generate a 640 × 200 (128 Kpixel) display for graphics. The display on the Apple Lisa 1 showed only half an A4 page but it did so with remarkable clarity on a screen 720 pixels wide × 364 high (262 Kpixels) considered to be 'crystal clear' at the time.

The Apple MacIntosh which displayed 512 × 342 (175 Kpixels) was soon topped by the Amiga's 640 × 400 (256 Kpixels). A considerably more expensive machine, the IBM 32700, became available in 1985 with a 1024 × 1024 (over 1 Mpixel) display on a separate monitor with a 19" (diagonal) tube, a very considerable improvement but still less than 100 pixels/inch.

A problem of which it is as well to be aware, is the range of 'standards' which has evolved as the technology has made increases in storage capacity and bit rates possible.

In general the total number of bits – the product of the total number of pixels and the number of bits per pixel – has been going up; each time it increases, new trade-offs for resolution against the number of displayed colours become available.

Some of the 'standards' (meaning, in effect, system types which have sold in appreciable numbers) are shown in Table 9.2. Note the resolution/colour trade-off at each advance, and how the screen resolution drops with the number of colours.

The advent of colour has produced controversy. Suppliers of Desktop Publishing (DTP) equipment would have us believe that DTP colour is here. In practice its adoption in actual DTP-printed material has been relatively small. The overall costs including inputs and printing are still too high, but will gradually fall. The choice lies in knowing just what machine with what amount of memory will work with what monitor driven by what software.

Table 9.2 CRT display types

Title	Screen resolution	On-screen colours/palette
CGA	640 × 20	Mono
	320 × 200	4/16
	160 × 200	16/16
EGA	640 × 350	16/64
Enhan.EGA	640 × 480	16/64
VGA (PS/2)	640 × 480	Mono
	640 × 480	16/256K
	320 × 200	256/256K

GRAPHICS STANDARDS

The Graphics Kernel System (GKS) standard, now an ISO Standard, defines drawing element 'primitives' from which a drawing may be constructed – lines, marks, text, polygons, raster images, and miscellaneous. Each has 'attributes' – for instance, the attributes of lines are type, scale factors, and colour. A 'GKS Workstation' with the appropriate software and power is necessary to run GKS.

The Computer Graphics Metafile (CGM) is associated with GKS. It provides for the encoding of GKS elements so that graphical information can be exchanged between different programs. An extension of GKS is being used called the Programmers' Hierarchical Graphics System (PHIGS) for describing 3D graphics by means of data arranged in a tree structure.

A number of multimedia Standards are briefly described in the Glossary and are mentioned elsewhere in this book. For further information see the 1993 issue of *Information Services & Use* (IOS Press, Amsterdam): Bryan (1993), Soares *et al.* (1993), Fromont (1993), Fromont *et al.* (1993), and Pring (1993), who summarize progress.

STRUCTURING STANDARDS – SGML, HYTIME, MHEG, AND ODA

SGML

The Standard Generalised Markup Language was introduced during the 1980s in an attempt to standardize parts of a document generically. SGML is covered in the Standard ISO 8879. It may be regarded as a formalized and greatly extended set of tags like the much smaller range of tags included in

Word Processing software. Without the tags in WP such as 'line end', 'super-script', 'italics', 'font Roman 12 point', etc., a document created on a WP machine would emerge as a featureless string of characters.

The structure of an SGML-tagged document is described in a formal DTD – Document Type Definition (or Declaration). Agreement on a common DTD for scientific articles has not yet been agreed. SGML tags enable different parts of a text's structure to be identified so that parts of it – title, author's name(s), author's address, references, diagrams, illustrations, headed sections, etc. – may be individually handled, or accessed. The layout of a document may be specified in various ways, or those parts of it to be retrieved for repackaging. An SGML document could exist in different media files on a network, in which case it could be reconstituted into its original form, and decoded as a single file.

HYTIME

A Standard called Hypermedia Time-Based Structuring Language, ISO/IEC 10744 (HYTIME), defines an integrated open Hypermedia document. It specifies how document concepts using SGML may be represented. According to Adie (1994), who provides a very useful description of multi-media Standards, these concepts include:

- Interconnection of objects in a document with hyperlinks
- Space and time object relationships
- Logical structure of a document
- Inclusion of non-textual data

HYTIME enables a web of data sources or *objects* to be created, the relationship between the hyperlinked objects being defined in an SGML encoded *hub document*. A HYTIME object may be video, audio, text, graphics, or a program, and the hub document may contain bibliographic references to documents outside the hub set. Music is handled in terms of MIDI playing instructions.

The functions of HYTIME are set out in six modules:

- BASE MODULE
  Facilities required by other modules. Management functions
- MEASUREMENT MODULE
  Location of object in a user-defined space specified by its co-ordinates
- LOCATION MODULE
  Named location address of an object to identify and refer to it
- HYPERLINKS MODULE
  Defined types of hyperlink
- SCHEDULING MODULE
  Specifies the sequencing of events

- RENDITION MODULE
  Allows for objects to be changed, e.g. audio channel volume

The base module contains elements and attributes used to identify objects and also includes options for managing objects in the set, which includes facilities for identifying copyright restrictions and for the enforced reporting of usage of any copyrighted objects.

MHEG

Multimedia and Hypermedia information coding Experts Group. A Standard which will provide the rules for the structure of multimedia objects in their final presented form – for example, an encyclopedia or an interactive home entertainment appliance. It will not be suitable for use during authoring. It will consist of two parts: (1) Base Notation defining objects in the Abstract Syntax Notation One and (2) in the SGML notation.

Open Document Architecture (ODA)

ODA used to be the acronym for 'Office Document Architecture' but was renamed by the CCITT. The ODA recommendation is related to X400 and is compatible with it. ODA caters for the efficiently coded representation of multimedia documents – that is, a mixture of text and raster or bit-map images such as graphics or illustrations. ODA software is used to format documents for transmission at the time they are created. To format a document already in page form, pages will have to be first presented in electronic form for format tagging. ODA defines:

- Characters representing written text
- Geometric shapes, lines, curves, etc., for drawings
- Raster graphics for facsimile or other images

The ODA Standard defines graphic element and control functions, and how elements are to be positioned. It also provides the means for transforming content into the correct layout structure by reference to a set of attributes.

ODA is going to be supplemented by an extension called HyperODA. Its objectives are to handle references to external documents, structures using hyperlinks and temporal relationships between components – i.e. synchronization.

TRANSMISSION STANDARDS

The CCITT division of the International Telecommunications Union (ITU) – known as the 'ITU Standardisation Sector' since March 1993 – and the Bell Telephone Company set up 'recommendations' or Standards independently in the early days, but latterly international Standards have been set by the CCITT/ITU. For many years a 'standard' called RS232 (adopted by the CCITT as V24) sufficed to describe the interconnections between terminal and modem. It is still widely used.

The CCITT 'V series' of recommendations includes modem and interface specifications. The major modem progressions have been V22 (300/1200), V22 bis (2400 bps), V32 (9600 bps), V32 bis (14,400 bps), V34 (28,800 bps). V34 has been finalized quite recently and modems conforming to it embody processing power of up to 34 Mips.

A few other standards may be encountered. V24/RS232, mentioned above, is the terminal/modem interface for serial data transmission at speeds up to 19,200 bps. Circuit/pin numbers for the interconnecting terminal to modem cable are specified but manufacturers may not use all the interconnections and may use different numbers.

Protocol Standards

A protocol is a set of rules governing the exchanges of data.

The CCITT 'X series' covers packet data networks. CCITT recommendation X25 for the interface and protocol between asynchronous Data Terminal Equipment (DTE) and the point of entry to a packet-switched network Data Circuit terminating Equipment (DCE) is the most widely used. Although an X25 link can handle hundreds of simultaneous connections, it can also be used for a single connection from a modem or PC with a Packet Assembly/Disassembly Device (PAD) interface board. The X25 protocol is used in packet-switched networks implemented in the lower three layers of the ISO seven layer model (see below). An X25 packet consists of a flag, header, an area for data, a frame check, and a terminating flag. The protocol, known as the Link Access Procedure Balanced Protocol (LAP-B), controls data errors and data flow rate.

The difficulties caused by incompatibilities between different computers attempting to inter-communicate, and the intervention of software-controlled protocol along chains of different interconnected networks, prompted further standardization discussions. A supposedly international but primarily European model, the Open Systems Interconnection (OSI), was agreed with great difficulty in the period 1976 to 1986.

OSI and TCP/IP protocols are given considerable space in this publication because their future is likely to be controlled by political controversy, as explained in the Superhighway section of chapter 8. Making the same point in a different way, global progress, or lack of it, of such a highway may depend on reasonable political decisions about communication protocols. Comments about some degree of technical reconciliation by Black (1995) are provided at the end of this section.

A hardware/software system manufacturer may claim OSI compatibility so long as the system performs the service described in the Standard, and so long as the protocols for communicating with adjacent layers are as described in it.

There are certain kinds of telecom system which will not benefit much from OSI, namely those in which the individual components were designed at the outset to work together. The public telecom systems come into this category, including those relatively unadventurous items in the 'terminal service' list which have been gradually introduced by the public authority. Private computer/telecom systems such as all-IBM SNA, and all-DECNET offerings will not intrinsically benefit much from OSI.

Transmission Control Protocol/Internet Protocol (TCP/IP) was introduced in the 1970s by the US Department of Defense for the same reasons that OSI was introduced internationally. The remarkable growth of Internet, with a very large number of users the world over, has resulted in the widespread adoption of TCP/IP.

The complexity of OSI compared with the availability of ready-to-use TCP/IP systems, the adoption of TCP/IP by the BBC and others, and the size of the TCP/IP CIX (Commercial Internet Exchange) in the US, have not contributed to the adoption of OSI.

Descriptions of OSI or TCP/IP protocols usually include a diagram similar to Figure 9.1. Recognizing that a series of operations or functions must be implemented when equipment users exchange messages via a network, the model separates and defines them. The two stacks on either side of the diagram represent protocol functions during a data exchange between two terminals. Ignoring the double line and the arrowed lines for the moment, the model shows service functions in seven idealized layers. There is a Standard specifying each function and a Standard describing the rules (protocols) to be used for communications between layers.

In OSI these functions are performed by various hardware/software systems, a number of them being already available. Two or more functions may be performed within a single part of a system, but even then the individual 'layer' functions will usually be recognizable.

The top three layers of the model are concerned with processing or application functions and should be present within the user's equipment. The bottom three layers are concerned with telecommunications and should be present in nodes (interconnection points) in the network. The transport layer, which is within the user's equipment, is a telecom services intermediary; for instance, it might be appropriate for a number of individual connections to be made to the network in parallel to increase traffic throughput.

The double line in the diagram indicates a message route down from a machine of some kind through the layers, along a telecoms channel, and up to a receiving machine. Alternatively, a message may be going in the opposite direction. An OSI 'layer' is a process through which a message

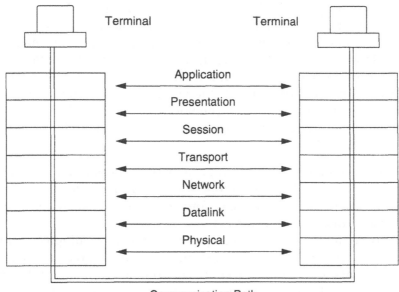

Figure 9.1 OSI protocol model
Source: AEC

passes at the sending end and is decoded and acted upon during its passage and upon arrival at the addressee. The action taken by an OSI layer depends on the 'header' at the beginning of every message. A header is a section containing control data which may be added by any layer through which it passes. The header includes the address of the corresponding layer at the receiving end. Accordingly, a message may contain up to seven header sections when it enters the telecom channel. As a message progresses towards a receiving machine, the first layer through which it passes, observing its own address, acts on the control data, and strips off its part of the header. Each subsequent layer does likewise. Eventually, all of the header having been stripped off, only the message arrives at the destination machine for the attention of the user.

A header inserted by, say, the presentation layer at the sending end, and addressed to the presentation layer at the receiving end, will be acted upon by that layer. This logical communication between sending and receiving layers of the same kind is called 'peer-to-peer' communication. The arrowed lines between the two stacks indicate that a particular 'sending' layer imparts information destined for the corresponding 'receiving' layer at the moment when the receiving layer recognizes a header addressed to it as the message 'passes through it'.

The disadvantages of OSI, apart from the complexity needed to deal with a complex problem, are not often spelled out. They include up to 400

Kbytes of memory for handling the layer-by-layer processing software, and added in-transit time of data. OSI is associated with ISO Standards with which the United States is active, OSI support has come mainly from Europe. However, the UK Government Centre for Information Systems (CCTA) runs its Government Information Service on Internet's World Wide Web using TCP/IP, saying that it has selected it because 'it is available now' and 'uses tried and tested technology' [Anon. 1995c].

Originally the United States was lukewarm about OSI and a warning comment was made in 1991:

> Given the immensity of the European market – larger than that of the US – vendors outside Western Europe will have little choice but to conform to EEC-sanctioned Standards. Enforcement will include requirements for product certification and warranty.
>
> Many countries and major computer vendors have adopted – or intend to adopt – some form of the OSI model ... yet a great many de facto standards based on existing technologies remain, despite rapidly growing interest in OSI, among consumers who have been captive to vendor-proprietary architectures and standards ... proprietary systems are not likely to disappear but the open systems concept is the wave of the future bringing vastly broader opportunities for competition in the development of software-based systems.

When the US Institute of Electrical and Electronics Engineers (IEEE) formed its 802 committee to consider Standards for Local Area Networks (LANs), it also considered how their Standards should relate to the OSI model. Five IEEE Standards define the protocols for the three major LAN types, for Metropolitan Area Networks (MANs), and for integrated voice and data communications. They reside at the physical layer.

There is one anomaly: 802.3 specifies a version of CSMA/CD transmission. In fact most people use the Ethernet *de facto* version, which is slightly different and incompatible with 802.3. 802.2, at the OSI data link level, defines the functions of Logical Link Control for two types of service provided by the 'lower' systems – first, 'connectionless', without provision for a receipt-acknowledgement procedure, and second, 'connected', with a procedure for the establishment of a 'connection'. A 'connection' in this context means the temporary establishment of a message exchange procedure between two users, not a switched connection as in the telephone system.

802.1 specifies how other IEEE 802 Standards relate to each other and to the OSI model. The reason for this special IEEE effort was the urgent need to get LANs under control before they followed the usual path of competing proprietary systems, each attempting to become the *de facto* standard.

Private systems created by assembling parts selected from different vendors as being the best for the job currently require a budget which includes generous provision for resident purchasing, fitting-together, and maintenance expertise. Small organizations unable to marshall such resources and who do not adopt a single vendor purchasing policy will almost inevitably run into horrendous making-to-work time-wasting. Both of these scenarios will benefit from TCP/IP or OSI.

When two people communicate face to face, their brains size up a huge number of variables almost instantaneously. Circumstances, surroundings, other person's background knowledge and appearance, required language, conversational gambits, etc. are all processed in the wink of an eye and compared against a colossal fund of stored knowledge. If the first person, versed in a particular art, perceives that the other is not understanding a conversation using the usual jargon or 'coded short-cuts' of inter-communication, he or she will instantly (we hope) and effortlessly harness immense processing power and knowledge known as 'common sense' to adjust transmitted messages so that they *are* received and understood.

Machines don't know about French, English, or German, have no general knowledge background, cannot make appropriate adjustments, and have no common sense. Everything must be spelled out in fine detail. If a simple black and white sketch with a caption is produced on a terminal's screen and must be produced on a different type of remote screen in a different terminal made by a different manufacturer via international telecom links, an enormous amount of information must be conveyed.

To consider but one set of functions – data cannot be transmitted and correctly received via a Local Area Network, packet-switched public network, satellite link, and then through various links at the other end unless all the *en route* effects such as different transmission techniques, error creation, delays, code changes, machine variations, etc. have been taken care of.

In OSI, user's source data must be accompanied by control data put there (preferably automatically) in the first place, in the expectation of encountering a number of 'managing' devices along the way, each reading the segment of data addressed to it. Each takes the appropriate action to route the message onward. Finally, the terminating device must be able to interpret the instructions addressed to it so that the message is correctly reproduced.

The above explanation of OSI almost suffices for TCP/IP as well. The Transmission Control Protocol (TCP) is a Transport Layer protocol responsible for the end-to-end transport of data. The Internet Protocol (IP) is a Network Layer protocol; it routes traffic from one host computer to another via the latter's address by looking it up in a routing table. In the lower two layers shown in the diagram – the datalink and physical layers – OSI and TCP/IP use international Standards with relatively minor differences.

There are considerable differences between the upper layers, notably between X25 (see Glossary) in OSI's Network Layer and IP in the TCP/IP's Network Layer. There are also a number of differences between the two protocols in the upper three layers.

A number of points are made by Black (1995) in his chapter 14:

- Several major US organizations had planned to use OSI led by the US Government with its GOSIP policy. However, 'the use of Internet Standards has overwhelmed OSI but OSI is still hanging on'. Incompatibilities could be resolved by 'designing a product to have hooks into and out of the OSI and TCP/IP worlds'.
- 'It should be stated categorically that the OSI and Internet protocols perform similar functions but there is definitely not a one-to-one mapping of their services.' The mapping of X25 to IP 'would be horrendous'.
- 'Invariably a movement to OSI will require what is known in the industry as *transition aids* . . . which act as convertors between the different layers in the stacks.' This is a complex and costly business.

OSI accommodates a number of existing protocols and the model is arranged to accommodate any new protocol so long as it conforms with certain conditions. It is intended to ensure compatibility between systems by specifying conditions for physical connection to a network, data flow control and routing, data quality, user-to-user dialogue, and data presentation and the machine–human interface. The result is that information from a sender is presented to a recipient exactly in the manner intended by the sender, regardless of machines, software, or *en route* variations.

The changeover to OSI has been slowed down by already adopted *de facto* Standards. IBM's SNA (Systems Network Architecture), with at least 20,000 users – among them the largest organizations in the world – is a well-tested system for which many products are available. Most users did not want to move to OSI. The EC clashed with IBM, which was secretive about its SNA system and showed little interest in OSI, but in 1984 a deal was negotiated and IBM agreed to publish details of its SNA protocols. In 1988 IBM announced its support for OSI and later included OSI-compatible protocols within its Systems Applications Architecture (SAA).

Another Standard, FDDI, the Fibre Distributed Data Interface, an American Standard (ANSI) X3T9.5, was agreed in 1990 for operations at up to 100 Mbps. The Standard is comprehensive. For example, it specifies minimum signal levels for receiving units and the permitted attenuation of signals in the network in order that errors shall be kept to a minimum. It also covers reliability – for instance, 'self-healing' by automatically bypassing any faulty station. It includes a requirement for built-in network management. FDDI had some severe birth pains, mainly to do with reaching agreement over compatibility between systems. Systems were installed but network management Standards awaited ratification. This delayed the growth of FDDI networks. FDDI specifies that certain facilities be built in to the FDDI adaptor cards used on communicating stations. A form of automatic network management is used in FDDI networks; if a fault or discontinuity occurs, the ends of the contra-rotating rings are automatically connected together in a few milliseconds on either side of the fault.

INTELLIGENT NETWORK STANDARDS

The continuing development by Bell of Electronic Switching Systems produced the SS7 programmable switch for telephone exchanges. Software can be written to provide a range of services and billing arrangements. The SS7 has become a *de facto* Standard and Bell's experience with it makes them a major force in the IN field.

Following proposals for Advanced Intelligent Networks (AIN) from Bellcore a number of organizations discussed the idea in the late 1980s. The result was AIN 1.0 setting the target architecture. ETSI and ITU (ex-CCITT) in Europe produced IN CS-1. The harmonizing of these Standards will now be required – an incredibly time-wasting process which appears to be made necessary by European needs to be seen not be slavishly following trends in the United States. Alternatively, harmonization processes may be needed because organizations in the US wish to establish a lead which they would not have if they entered into global discussions in the first place.

The Standards are complex and the reader is referred to Abernethy and Munday (1995), who choose to discuss CS-1 which describes INs in terms of four planes:

- Service plane
  Deals with features of the service

- Global functional plane
  Describes service-independent building blocks which hinge upon a basic call process

- Distributed functional plane
  A traditional network architecture with functional entities performing actions

- Physical plane
  A model of the physical entities and protocols existing within an IN networks

These Standards are lagging behind today's requirements, which are referred to as 'The future intelligent network' by Abernethy and Munday. They say: 'IN concepts, although currently applied to telephony-based networks, are also applicable to other traffic types such as data, broadband, video and multimedia services. Over the next few years this area will see significant attention to development and growth.'

SUPERHIGHWAY STANDARDS

The information superhighway remains a concept rather than a system proposal, so while there is no proposed system there are unlikely to be any proposed Standards. The superhighway may consist of data distribution through one of several possible channels or through all of them, or even through one unified channel brought about by socio-technical forces and competition.

The Internet is often incorrectly called *The* Superhighway. If a period of time elapses during which the Internet is joined by other large networks – for example, cable-TV networks – capable of conveying information from a variety of sources on the scale of the Internet, then users will need to be able to receive either. If there is a period of time during which n networks compete in parallel, users' equipment will need to cope with n different channels.

Ness (1995) states that the Standards are being considered by the Digital Audio Visual Council, formed in 1994, to 'promote audio visual applications and services for both broadcast and interactive use'. He distinguishes between boxes designed to work with four different kinds of data channels – cable, direct broadcast satellites, the telephone network, and video-CD players. A 'mixed-signal' box – meaning the ability to cope with analogue or digital data – has been discussed, but not a matter of greater interest – a multi-channel box, i.e. a box able to cope with a mix of information received via different types of delivery channel. The Council is said to be considering assigning 'a reference model for each delivery system and all the interfaces'. At present the operative phrase for superhighway channels and multiple or unified all-purpose set-top boxes seems to be *vive la différence*.

Part II

Multimedia applications and markets

Chapter 10

Indexing

A good legible label is usually worth, for information, a ton of significant attitude and expression in a historical picture.

(Mark Twain)

A perfect picture, I say; for he yieldeth to the powers of the mind an image of that whereof the philosopher bestoweth only a wordish description which doth neither strike, pierce, nor possess the sight of the soul so much as the other doth.

(Sir Philip Sidney, *c*. 1575)

FINDING WHAT YOU WANT

Multimedia technology is mainly confined to chapter 2 of this book and authoring to chapter 6, but for the CD family it would be inappropriate to place technical aspects, authoring, and products in different chapters. CD matters are best discussed in one place. In effect they are considered to be a multimedia application so all aspects are discussed in this chapter.

Later in the chapter many different kinds of application will be described but to start with, a topic more usually of interest to librarians, but essential for finding multimedia data, will be introduced – indexing. For example, multimedia databases are likely to include pictures, and pictures indexed by descriptive words can only be retrieved if the indexer has anticipated the possible indexing words that could be used by any user. Indexers and users have to get to grips with a serious problem – meaning. New advances enable pictures to be retrieved with picture content queries like 'Find all pictures containing babies' prams'. There has been some disagreement about the descriptive power of words and contents as the quotations at the beginning of this chapter show.

INDEXES AND INDEXING IN MULTIMEDIA

Broad as the multimedia field is, indexing is something that might be considered to fall well outside its borders. However, finding information is often the objective of a multimedia system. You could certainly find a wanted video-clip in a collection of 10,000 of them if you looked at every one. But if the clips were appropriately indexed, looking up 'George VI Coronation Procession (3987)' and getting clip number 3987 would be far quicker.

In some kinds of large collections of items of textual information the selection of a single wanted item is easy if the collection is arranged in alphabetical order. The indexing problem is immediately revealed, however, if you are interested in 'vintage car models'. The 1910 coronation procession might be an ideal place to see a number of them in action, but would the indexing terms chosen by an indexer enable you to find them in that clip?

An index is an ordered list of descriptive terms. The nature of the items retrieved from an indexed collection depends on the indexing language and method, and the objectives of the searcher who frames the search questions. In a typical computer-based search and retrieval system each item, such as a scientific article, an artist's drawing, or a museum object in a collection, is indexed with descriptive words (terms) by an indexer. The indexer chooses those words which he or she believes are most likely to be chosen by a person searching for the item. Matters of importance are the area or field covered by a collection, the time and convenience of searching, the retrieval performance, and the response time – that is, how long it takes to search the collection once the questions are posed.

The degree of success achieved when a searcher retrieves relevant documents is called the recall ratio – the percentage of relevant documents retrieved out of the total number of relevant documents in the collection. In a collection of articles, if 10 are retrieved out of 20 known to be relevant, the recall ratio is 50 per cent. The precision ratio is the percentage of relevant documents retrieved out of the total number retrieved – a measure of whether unwanted documents were effectively ignored. If 50 images are retrieved, of which 10 are relevant, the precision ratio is 20 per cent. If a searcher asks a broad question in an attempt to ensure that he or she retrieves all relevant documents, an increased number of unwanted documents will be retrieved – precision will decrease. If a narrow question is asked in an attempt to retrieve only relevant documents, some will be missed – higher precision is accompanied by lower recall. One hundred per cent precision with 100 per cent recall means that every relevant document is found unaccompanied by any unwanted documents – a possible result for a collection of factual documents. In a collection of records about employees a question like 'Who speaks French?' might be asked. Errors excepted, only the names of all French-speaking employees should be retrieved and none should be missed.

Indexing is an attempt to describe an object unambiguously in the face of the variation of opinions in regard to meanings and descriptions. To reduce ambiguity a thesaurus is sometimes introduced. It contains lists of synonyms and other words, referring the indexer and the user to the preferred words which must be used. For example, a thesaurus covering drugs would need to take account of the equivalence of chemical, generic, and trade names on the assumption that different searchers might use different alternatives when searching for the same item.

A very large alphabetically ordered printed index, such as a telephone directory, may often perform very effectively in isolating a single item from a million others. There are problems even in such a basic system. The London telephone directory uses the arrangement shown here.

S.W. Trading
Sacre K.J.
Sacred Heart Convent
Saint G.V.
St. Agnes Youth Centre
Society for Underwater Science
Society of Aviation Artists

However, it might be considered more helpful if the arrangement was as in the following instead.

Sacre K.J.
Sacred Heart Convent
Saint Agnes Youth Centre
Saint G.V.
Society (of) Aviation Artists
Society (for) Underwater Science
S.W. Trading

In a multimedia system, a simple alphabetically ordered word index may suffice. The major method used for image indexing is for an indexer to label (index) the image with terms (words) considered by him or her to be appropriate. The image is retrieved from, say, an image database, when the terms, chosen by a user, match the indexer's terms associated with an image.

We must turn to the scholarly and laborious work done in the art world to find systems which have gained some acceptance. Henri van den Waal from the University of Leiden invented a system for indexing pictures called ICONCLASS. He said: 'The material offered for consultation should always be visual. Any other reference – either verbal or by means of codes – can never be more than the first stepping stone.' The ICONCLASS code was such a stepping stone. The ICONCLASS thesaurus was published in the period 1973 to 1985. It consists of 17 volumes of hierarchically arranged codes associated with a textual description in English, designed for classifying the content and subject matter of fine art material.

The thesaurus is organized in a number of levels commencing with nine primary codes: '1. Religion and Magic', '2. Nature', '3. Human Being, Man', '4. Society, Civilization, Culture', etc. The first two characters of the code are digits and the third is always a capital letter, permitting 25 subdivisions (J is excluded) at the third level. To code the Van Gogh 'bandaged ear' painting, for instance, different sections of the thesaurus would be consulted. The indexer would find the notation for each wanted term (e.g. 'ear', 'easel', etc.) by looking it up in the alphabetical index. During thesaurus composition the words 'easel' and 'ear' would have been allocated codes determined from the level they occupy under the appropriate primary headings. Thus 'easel 48C5151' is a subdivision of 'Tools of the painter 48C515', descended from '4. Society, Civilization and Culture'.

A somewhat similar system called *The Art & Architecture Thesaurus* (AAT) originated at a meeting called by Professor Dora Crouch, a historian at the Rensselaer Polytechnic in 1979. Crouch was motivated by her need to select slides from a large collection for lectures. The result was an on-going project involving a number of people and eventually the publication in 1990 by Oxford University Press of the *Art and Architecture Thesaurus* (AAT) in three volumes and a floppy disk edition (Petersen 1990). The AAT contains about 40,000 terms 'Hierarchically arranged according to a rigorously constructed, internally consistent structure', using standard thesaurus conventions, modelled on the National Library of Medicine's MESH (Medical Subject Headings) thesaurus.

The AAT is used for the records of the publicly searchable INFOTRAX slide database of the Rensselaer slide collection. It took several years to refine. Indexers needed an initial training period of at least 3 months. It takes over 40 minutes for a trained indexer to complete a slide worksheet and enter the details into the database. It is believed that it will take 17 man-years to index the 50,000 slides in the collection. The second edition of the AAT, expanded to include 90,000 terms, was published in 1994 (Petersen 1994).

Evidently labelling an image for retrieval purposes is a time-consuming process to be carried out by subject experts. In addition to the investment made in compiling a thesaurus, there will be an on-going investment to update it. One might expect that this type of system would be able to manage a very diverse collection. However, the AAT is designed only to handle Western art and architecture out of the totality of art and architecture. ICONCLASS covers art with a difference in emphasis. Objects within the totality of art and architecture represent only a minute fraction of all possible items. A very diverse range would be encountered, for instance, in a newspaper's library, usually known as a morgue.

PICTURE INDEXING

Some years ago a survey of the image database literature was performed and it was concluded that, while the development of image database systems represents a huge amount of thought and effort, few, if any, databases were approaching the critical size necessary for operational application. The developers devoted insufficient resources to the user interface, to maintainability, reliability, data integrity, device independence, and certainly to indexing. The larger a collection, the more necessary does the discriminating power of the indexing system become.

In the last few years attempts have been made to break out from the restrictions of indexing pictures by words only. An image might be described, preferably automatically, in terms of its elements or constituent parts, and retrieved when a user's choice of descriptive picture elements matches those associated with an image in the database.

Special languages may be developed for the purposes of reducing the indexing effort, or making it more amenable to computer operations. They include various kinds of machine-processable data with which to describe the structure of an image. Picture Description Languages have been discussed for the co-ordination of terms, object descriptions, object attributes, relationships, and events. The eye–brain can recognize objects with such ease that, by comparison, systems of this kind seem to be crude and cumbersome.

Other more promising methods of retrieving a graphic would be to describe it in your own words, or provide a sketch, and the machine would translate that description into a representation which it would match against all graphics in the database and retrieve the ones most closely resembling your description.

A computer is unable to recognize the similarity between two quite simple objects when one of them is viewed from a different angle. The ease and speed with which a human accomplishes this task and can deduce the appearance of a complete object from a single viewing are unlikely to be matched by a computer in the foreseeable future. The following quotations capture the essence of the problem.

'The delight and frustration of pictorial resources are that pictures can mean different things to different people.'

'The content of a picture, whether from the realm of fine art or commercial photography, presents some potential difficulties. Since there may be a multiplicity of entities within a single image, and a multiplicity of attributes associated with any one of the entities, it is contended that the subject requests for which a given image may be deemed relevant, appropriate, or interesting, are much less predictable than is the case for textual material. A small-scale survey has been undertaken with a view to providing some experimental evidence in support of this contention.'

'It would seem unlikely that indexing could produce an appropriate key by means of which more than a small proportion of the multi-faceted information stored within a given image could be unlocked.'

'In the case of images, the use of thesauri to control inconsistency is not effective due to the individual responses prevalent in human reactions to visual materials. That inconsistency is a reflection of creativity and diversity of human interests, situations, and context. If inconsistency is to be overcome, system designers will need to relinquish the idea of the utility of using words to index non-verbal understanding.'

Not a great deal is known about the kind of questions that users are likely to put to a picture collection. What kind of users and what kind of collection are we talking about? There is virtually no analysis of the kind of questions asked or the success of any system in responding to those questions in any of the published papers, with the exception of the work conducted by Enser described below. However, we can imagine the range of queries that might be addressed to the picture in Figure 10.1.

This Belfast street picture, taken many years ago, shows men and women, taxis, cars, lorries and trams, buildings and shops. Information is contained in it about the transport, architecture, and fashions of the period, and about the appearance of the street itself. Any of these could be of interest to

Figure 10.1 A street in Belfast
Source: Queen's University, Belfast

potential users of the collection to which it belongs, but its contents remain potential information unless it is accessible via the indexing system. If the photograph is indexed by a human – the most likely way today of realizing its information potential – then that person must anticipate the range and manner of the questions that might be asked about it.

A good way of finding out about users' queries and the success of librarians in supplying answers is to observe clients' behaviour and retrieval performance in a large picture library. Enser (1993) carried out a study of usage of the Hulton picture collection in order to assess the effectiveness of the methods used to find the pictures requested by users. Retrieval problems are well illustrated by his comment:

> One of the many entities recorded was a perambulator; the photograph provides useful visual evidence of this seemingly bygone form of transport in ordinary use. All such information is lost, of course, when the picture is indexed by the caption such as 'market day in Kirby Lonsdale'.

The Hulton picture collection is enormous, and in Enser's words:

> such is the scale of the Hulton Company's operation, so varied is their customer base and so catholic their collection, that it would seem reasonable to expect the findings of this project to be generally applicable to non-domain-specific picture collections.

Enser's findings were, in fact, that in such an environment 'an extremely heavy dependency on the expertise and search time availability of the picture researcher in his/her role as an intermediary must continue to be the norm in the short-to-medium term' (personal communication).

Unfortunately, we do not have any results on 'failure analysis'. Users may not have always found what they wanted, or following a user-librarian dialogue and more searching, a user may have departed with a picture which was not a genuine response to his or her question.

Since then parts of the Hulton collection have become available, including events from five decades – the 1920s to the 1960s – and a 'people' section. They may be purchased on CD-ROMs with 'hit thumbnails' so that preliminary searching by the 'hit-screenful' may be undertaken.

Although the idea of inputting a query picture has much to recommend it, had such a system been available for Enser's tests, it would not necessarily always have been more successful than existing indexing arrangements. It would have been difficult to devise query-pictures for some of the questions asked during the test – for example, 'great personalities of the 20th century', 'street scenes in 1850', or 'smog/pollution in London'.

Systems for picture content indexing without words

Query-pictures do not always replace the descriptive power of words, which may be better for some abstract concepts. For instance, it is hard to see how a query-picture could be devised for 'great personalities of the 20th century'. How could such a question be posed without the use of words? In spite of that it is assumed that query-images could often be used for retrieval so that the enormous effort involved in creating, controlling, updating, and learning to use the thesauri and indexes will be reduced. The justification for this assumption is based on some remarkable recent advances.

Niblack *et al.*'s (1993) Query By Image Content (QBIC) prototype system runs on an IBM RS/6000 Risc machine. Queries may be asked in terms of full scenes or within-scene objects by using questions about colour, texture, shape, or by drawing an edge-sketch of the object of interest. A database of 1000 images and 1000 objects from a clip-art file has been used to test it.

The RS/6000 workstation called 'Powerstation 530' provides 10.9 Mflops and 34.5 Mips of processing power. It incorporates 128 Mbytes of memory and a 2.4 Gbyte internal disk; it uses Aix version 3 Unix-standard software. Its price is £42,747 with mouse, keyboard, and 3D graphics board. This board on its own costs £6731. A 19" colour monitor with 1280×1024 resolution and 24-bit colour is extra at £2350. This version was made available for beta testing as an OS/2 Ultimedia Manager/2 product called 'QBIC' requiring a far less powerful machine.

In the edge-sketch query method, the user draws a shape, however crude, on the screen, and the machine obliges by presenting as hits those thumbnails which most nearly resemble the sketch. The user may then narrow the choice if he or she chooses to improve the sketch in an attempt to reduce the noise retrieved by reason of the sketch's inadequacy. The system is used for approximate matching between an input query-picture and a database picture. It works as an information filter to eliminate pictures which do not match the input picture sufficiently well. The thumbnails are 100×100 pixel reductions of the main pictures.

When the database is loaded, objects within pictures which might be supplied as hits must be outlined. The indexer approximately outlines an object or a number of objects within a picture and the system uses Snakes software (chapter 4) to refine the outline so that it closely follows the outline of the required object. A choice of 256 colours is available to be used as a query, as is the texture of an object as described in an associated paper by Equitz (1993). The shapes of objects to be searched are assumed to be non-occluded planar shapes. Algebraic moment invariants are computed. For retrieving sketches, edge maps are created for all pictures and objects within them. 'Full scene' queries may be input based on colour and texture features, thereby avoiding the need to provide a sketch. Alternatively, a set of colours and textures in selected proportions may be input as queries.

A 'colour picker' screen with selection sliders is provided for colour selection. The method of retrieving 'hit' pictures from an input drawing is based on edges matching. A drawing is reduced to 64×64 pixels, partitioned into a set of 8×8 blocks, and each block is correlated with a search area of 16×16 pixels in the image. The result is scored for similarity. These 'fuzzy matching' arrangements are designed to reduce what may be hundreds of thousands of images in the database to a small number which are retrieved as thumbnail hits for browsing.

A query may consist of at least twenty separate questions. To identify and match objects in this type of question a method related to Quad-trees called R-trees is used. Computed values for objects and images are processed in a relational database called Starburst.

A range of drawing tools is provided. Perhaps the most useful is the polygon tool with Snake outlining. The desired object is roughly outlined and the Snake software provides a 'shrink-wrap' effect upon the outline. Any weighted combination of colour, texture, and shape may be used as a query and the results are displayed in order of matching commencing with the best match. Figure 10.2 shows a drawn shape question. 'Hit' objects which best matched the query shape are shown on the right. Holt and Hartwick (1994) describe the use of QBIC in the Department of Art and History at the University of California at Davis. A test base of 1000 slides was scanned at 1000 dots per inch with 8-bit colour using a Kodak RFS-2035 Professional Slide Scanner.

Figure 10.2 QBIC shape matching
Source: IBM

About 700 such images could be stored on a 1 Gbyte disk, uncompressed. The images were edited using Adobe Photoshop 2.5 on a Mac Cuadra 950 and saved as TIFF files. Objects within images were outlined as retrieval candidates. Searching could be carried out by words inserted by an indexer, colour percentages, colour chosen from a colour-picker menu, texture from a texture menu, drawn shapes, or from combinations of these items. Searching may also be carried out on a 'query by example' hit – that is, having obtained a hit, the system is asked to 'find pictures like this one'.

It was found that simple shape searching was satisfactory, but more complex shapes produced problems. Searches based on colour and texture gave quite good results. Holt and Hartwick state that 'we are continuing to refine our methods of image preparation and object outlining, and of image query, combining content-based queries with text. We are quite excited about the possibilities.'

In Hirata and Kato's (1993) system, the authors claim that the user has only to draw a rough sketch to retrieve similar images from a picture database. Similarities between the sketch and images in the database are automatically evaluated and the most similar candidates are shown to the user. A painting is reduced to a standard size of 64 × 64 pixels. Gradients for the RGB intensity values in four directions are then calculated. The database index is formed by inputting the RGB colour values of each painting. The gradients are used to generate edges in two stages – first to produce an edge-image for further processing and second to process the edges derived from the first process in order to produce an edge-image more suitable for representing the original picture. The thinned edges from this last image are used as an 'abstract' image in the 'pictorial index' against which input pictures are matched. Stages in this process are illustrated in Figure 10.3.

To search the database using an input sketch, both the sketch and all the database pictures are divided into 8 × 8 pixel blocks. Every picture so sub-divided in the database is then matched against the input sketch, but the blocks from the input sketch are shifted around the area of a candidate image to provide 'fuzzy matching'. In other words the sketch could be appreciably different from an image in the database, but the latter could still be generated as a 'hit'. The most similar are rank ordered and presented for 'hit' consideration. The permitted error between an input block and the database block of pixels may be up to about 12.5 per cent to be classed as a hit.

There are several processing stages to form an 'abstract image' for the 'pictorial index', which consists of an edge representation of an image. The processing simplifies the presentation; it appears to preserve all the essential features but eliminates some detail.

The system was tested using a database of 205 paintings of full-colour landscapes and portraits. A table is provided showing how well the sketches recall the best candidates from the collection. When eighteen different sketches were used as test pictures, the authors claim that the intended image was received as one of the five best candidates in 94.4 per cent of the tests. The authors also say that if the algorithms were to be applied to a large database, the time taken to retrieve images would become lengthy. The algorithms used are general enough to be applied to figures, diagrams, photographs, textile patterns, and artistic paintings.

Swain (1993) has described a tool called 'FINDIT' being tested at the

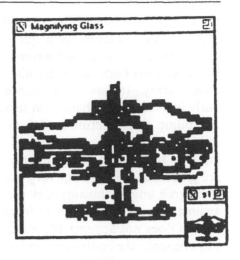

(b) Regular-sized image.

(c) Edge image of global edge candidates.

Image abstraction result.

Figure 10.3 Stages in image reduction (Hirata)
Source: NEC

University of Chicago. At the time of publication work in progress was based on the matching of a query image against a database image by the intersection of colour histograms. A histogram may be visualized as a bin whose size depends on the number of times a particular colour occurs in the image array. It has been shown that colour histogram intersection is fairly insensitive to changes in image resolution, histogram size, depth, and viewpoint. Each picture in the database is indexed by its characteristic set of histograms. These are matched against the histograms for a query-image input to the system. Some pictures of the results obtained with the system are given but they are not very convincing. Pictures of objects taken from a 45 degree angle, showing a degree of perspective distortion, are matched against objects photographed from the front. The degree of perspective distortion does not appreciably affect the shape of images in the photographs. Experiments are continuing on larger databases.

Dowe's paper (1993) describes a commercially developed system called Excalibur. Matching is described as a 'multiple layer neural net operation'. The neural net learning feature, managed by interconnected hardware nodes on other systems – is implemented solely in software. At an exhibition at the Wembley Conference Centre during June 1993, a prototype of the image-recognizing version of Excalibur was shown. Previously it had only been demonstrated on text recognition. Images were input to the system as photographs placed in front of a video camera. The database was searched, and if a matching photograph was found, it was displayed. In so far as one can judge the effectiveness of the system on an exhibition stand, it appeared to work satisfactorily, and should be recognized as an impressive achievement. This system is used for text pattern recognition by the British Library, but no software for picture matching is available from the supplier.

The papers by Samadani *et al.* (1993) and Shann *et al.* (1993) describe methods of selecting images within one domain – in the first case pictures of fossils in rock samples, and in the second case pictures of the Aurora. Since the curved structures of fossils in samples are fairly similar, the detection and characterization of such fossils are amenable to image filtering of a relatively simple kind because the system is only required to identify objects within a narrow domain. The same remarks apply to the system used for recognizing Aurora images.

There is some activity in work designed to match the similarity of images where different objects in the two images have similar spatial relationships. Graphical nodes can be used to represent the position of objects and the direction and length of their interconnections may be described.

In one case (Wakimoto *et al.* 1993) a method is described for recognizing similarity between diagrams or sections of diagrams of engineering plants. The same principle is mentioned in Ozsoyoglu and Wang (1993). Kitamoto *et al.* (1993) describe a graph-matching system where each graph describes the relationship between cloud patterns in photographs taken by a satellite. Oakley *et al.* (1993) describe a language or geometric construction to enable a user to specify groups of features of interest in an image.

This burst of activity from 1993 onwards as just described represents new methods at an early stage but looks rather promising.

Chapter 11

Business applications: CDs and CD authoring: publications

According to Thomasson (1994), business applications may be divided into training systems (39 per cent), point of sale and kiosks (28 per cent), videoconferencing, databases and networks (18 per cent), and corporate presentations (15 per cent).

The 1994 Touche Ross/FT review believes that the segments with the greatest potential in the next five years will be business and financial news, and messaging, travel, training, and intra-company briefings. However, 'Most respondents (75 per cent) believe that the market will be fragmented with many specialist applications.'

Scala (Herndon, Virginia, USA, and Ware, Herts, UK) specialize in multimedia for business and retail and can provide a system called Infochannel for distributing multimedia programmes from a central point to remote stations by a telephone line, LAN, satellite, or by data broadcast (using available space on a TV channel).

KIOSKS, RETAIL, AND SALES SYSTEMS

Woolworths

Woolworths have developed a point-of-sale system being tested since 1993 in the record departments of several stores in the UK including those in Hounslow, Norwich, North Walsham, and Surbiton. The system uses a 486 PC with Videologic board and touch screen. The company installed many more systems in 1994/95. The system is, in effect, a catalogue describing thousands of CDs, cassettes, and videos, together with an ordering system for handling a much larger selection of items than can be held in stock. Customers can hear tracks or clips and choose items which they want to buy. The choices are then printed on an order form which is processed by the store leading to home delivery the next day.

Co-op supermarkets

Four supermarkets in Leicester, UK, have installed interactive electronic cookery books. Choice is provided by touch-screen menus so customers may look up recipes and meal suggestions. A printout for any recipe is available and vouchers to be used at check-out points are provided. More stores are likely to adopt the system.

Trafalgar House property marketing

The Design Practice, Mill St, London, UK, provided special multimedia facilities for Trafalgar when the company wanted to make a presentation of its proposed developments at Paddington Basin. The presentation ran on a Mac machine with a large monitor for viewing by audiences of up to eight people with an Air Mouse for the presenter. The system was launched in 1993. Graphics and video were used as necessary.

Heathrow Airport shopping

Galleria 21 is a system becoming well known to the public passing through the airport. It is a product guide, ordering, payment, and delivery system supplied by AT&T Information Solutions. Customers may browse through items made by major suppliers at any time of day or night using a PC with animated joystick and keypad. Once chosen, any item may be paid for with a credit card, and will be sent to an address in any country.

EuroTunnel

An information and booking system for Channel Tunnel trains has been set up on the M25 orbital road at Clackett Lane. The system, provided by SVC Multimedia, Kent, UK, provides graphics, video impressions, times, and cost. The touchscreen, accessible from outside, is bonded to the shop's window so that information may be obtained when the shop is closed.

Ford

Ford provide on-screen information at 250 different sites in the USA and Europe using Scala Infochannel. In a newly opened Ford plant in Mexico City 128 screens are provided in corridors, cafeterias, and elsewhere for news in Spanish, updated several times a day. Systems provide for local news with pictures for 'making people local heroes'. When an employee receives an award he gets the multimedia treatment.

Esso

A system has been installed based on Oslo, Norway, with displays at Esso outlets surrounding the capital on a Scala Infochannel system. Advertisements and information about weather and road conditions are displayed.

Renault

Scala provided Renault with software for a system enabling customers to 'compose their own cars', according to a Scala leaflet. Information about the range of models with a video showing each in action, and a picture showing each in the colours available, is provided on a kiosk containing 60 Mbytes of information in French and Dutch. Kiosks are fitted on the premises of twenty dealers in Belgium and Luxembourg. A choice from the general to the particular is provided, starting with 'private car', 'van', 'price range', and 'special services'. A data broadcasting arrangement for updating the contents of kiosks is being considered.

Bovis Construction

Bovis Construction have acquired several Scala MM300 master authoring systems running on Amiga 4000 machines. The systems are used with large high-definition screens to provide customers with demonstrations of major successful building contracts using scanned photographs, cost breakdowns, etc., with animations and graphics.

Janssen Pharmaceuticals

Janssen operates an interactive mobile unit consisting of a PC with a Videologic digital video adaptor and Authorware Professional software for multimedia demonstrations using text, video, diagrams, etc., for describing new medical advances. The system uses a monitor or screen projector and includes the means for searching for information about particular subjects.

Miscellaneous applications

Thirty touch-screen multimedia kiosks were provided for the benefit of South African voters in the 1994 elections. The system was organized by Sandenburgh Pavon of Johannesburg using 486 computers. A development system was supplied by AimTech Corporation. Icons were provided for each of nineteen political parties which triggered messages and visual presentations. Simple design was essential for the many people who were voting for the first time.

Several companies specialize in large productions for conferences, roadshows, exhibitions, etc. For example, Face to Face Productions, Reading, UK, staged a special show for a Hewlett Packard European conference in March 1994 at the Intercontinental Hotel, Berlin. They used a mix of LCD screen projectors, live camera, videoconferencing, and a theatre set which ended by exploding into pieces. The show included a live videoconference with HP's Chief Executive in California.

Face to Face Productions set up a similar type of show at the London Mayfair theatre for the launch of IBM's OS/2 Warp software package. It included a large set with a 24-cube video display wall and flying logos.

Banks of CRTs arranged as a 'Videowall' is a multimedia application which is gaining ground rapidly. It is mainly used for retail advertising, leisure, and entertainment purposes. TheatreWall is a system using 2×2 or 2×3 54" diagonal CRT screens in a thin design only 21" deep so the system occupies only a small amount of floor space. The wall has a resolution of 800 lines and infrared remote control. Another system, called RamWall 1024 ID, can include up to nine screens and a wide range of effects can be produced on it. The Pixelite II is a large system which can handle up to 100 screens. A major supplier in the UK is Senelec which produces Videowall controlling software and provides a range of walls of different sizes.

VIDEODISK AND CD MULTIMEDIA INFORMATION SYSTEMS

Introduction

It is not possible to understand applications of CDs and videodisks without some technical knowledge. Technical functions and applications are difficult to separate. Accordingly, enough technical material is included in this section for a general understanding, instead of in chapter 2 in which most technical data are discussed.

Laser videodisks and the CD family of storage devices are plastic disks on to which patterns representing data are pressed. Philips Laservision was, and the Sony laser videodisk recording system still is, the major laser-based videodisk systems, but Philips no longer manufacture. The same two companies were the originators, with others, of the CD systems.

The master disk which makes the pressing carries a continuous spiral track of small pits formed by rotating it during a recording and periodically burning the pits into it with a laser. The pits and the unburnt areas between them represent coded data. In a 30 cm (12") laser videodisk, changes in a picture signal are represented as variations in the spacing between wave-form cycles provided by frequency modulation. The spacing between pits is proportional to that spacing. Additional pulse width modulation is used to convey audio data; the length of each pit varies between 0.5 and 1.5 micrometres to convey it. The laser is focused into a narrow beam. On a videodisk the burned-in pits are less than half a micrometre (0.00002 inches) wide. There are sufficient pits in one revolution of the track to carry all the coded data needed to represent one television frame. 50,000 frames are recorded on the whole of the fine-pitch track.

When a disk is played, the difference in reflected light from the pits and lands, using the same laser operating at low power, is read as '0's and 1's'. Since the reading laser is never in contact with the disk it does not produce any wear at its surface.

PAL television is reproduced at 25 frames per second, or if the system is used for NTSC television, at 30 frames per second. When a laser disk is rotated to deliver frames at either rate it will provide a TV programme whose duration depends upon the total number of tracks and the compression ratio of the TV data. A particular frame can be picked out by the retrieval mechanism which moves the reading laser over the selected track. If the laser is stepped back by one track once per revolution, the same frame is repeated 25 or 30 times per second and appears to be 'frozen'. In this mode the machine may be used for viewing data in a selected frame, instead of as a means of playing motion video.

In the CD family the general arrangement of laser recording, playback, and pits and lands, is similar to the arrangements in a videodisk. However, the diameter of the disk is 12 cm (4.72") and the pits and lands represent digitally coded data. Because the digital data can be made to represent virtually any type of information in the CD family, the CD capacity is usually expressed in Megabytes – usually in the range 500 to over 600 Mbytes.

The data to represent stereophonic audio in a CD-DA consist of PCM samples recorded at 44.1 KHz. An explanation of PCM is given in chapter 8. Reference to the findings of Nyquist, also explained in that chapter, show that this rate of sampling is more than adequate to provide high-quality reconstructed audio.

In a CD-ROM and other types of CD, the recorded information consists of data for the user, synchronization, error correction, and other kinds of support data. The coded representation of these data in terms of pit spacing and length is complex. A block is the smallest amount of addressable data and there is a total of 270,000 blocks in a CD-ROM, each block containing 2048 bytes of actual user data, making a total of 553 Mbytes of actual user data per CD-ROM disk.

Videodisks

A number of commercial recordings were produced in the 1980s including the Pergamon Patsearch system for displaying patent drawings. Patsearch was discontinued in 1984. In the Domesday disks describing people and places in the UK, some remarkable results were achieved with, by today's standards, low-performance computer equipment.

A large number of training disks have been produced covering finance, electronics, science, gardening, etc. The great advantage of videodisks is their large capacity for high-quality analogue pictures. Videodisks are still quite widely used, but CD digital disk systems introduced in the last few years now predominate; effective compression and the relative ease of digital processing have reduced the capacity advantage enjoyed by videodisks.

The decline of videodisks has been very noticeable in the museum/arts sector. In a sample of 40 projects from the IVAIN series (Pring, Isobel 1993–4), in April 1993 nearly twice as many analogue disk systems were being used than digital, but by November 1994 there were three times more digital systems than analogue – a remarkable changeover.

Video Compact Discs (video-CDs), quite different from videodisks, are described in a later section (see pp. 295–7).

CD SYSTEMS

Introduction: disk types and speeds

Various types of compact disk have been developed since audio-CDs, described in the CD-DA section below, were introduced in the mid-1980s. CD-DAs have now displaced vinyl disks, which reproduce music directly from undulations on the surface. CDs owe their success to relatively rapid agreements about standardization, high data storage capacity, low cost, and the robust mass-produced miniature laser systems used for data readout. The basic technology for CDs is the same regardless of the type – a factor contributing to successful mass production.

One aspect of CDs which is becoming important – networked retrieval – is not covered in this chapter; it appears in chapter 8 under 'Networks'.

Philips, Sony, and others were determined to lay down a degree of stand-ardization when they introduced CD specifications and Standards known by the colour of the books in which they appear (described in chapter 9). The CD-DA stores data on 98 tracks each with a number of sectors containing 2352 bytes with error detection and correction codes. All CDs are variations of the CD-DA format.

A new type of drive called a 'multispin' drive has been developed during the last two years. The first to appear on the market was the NEC InterSect CDR-74 – available in both Macintosh and PC versions. The drive speed is doubled and transfer times and search times are speeded up. The speeds of current CD-ROM drives are set to make CD audio play at the right speed for audio reproduction. Manufacturers have solved audio speed problems in the new drives by adding controllers that play back the audio tracks correctly. The NEC drive was soon overtaken because, starting in 1995, CD drives became available which run up to six times faster than the original single-speed disks. Single-speed disks read or write data at about 150 Kbps.

A number of quad-speed CD-ROM drives were available by the end of 1994. For example, Dynatek Automation's CDS654, priced at £399 in December, supports multi-session photo-CD and audio-CDs.

For CD-R use, a drive such as the Yamaha CR-R 100 writer will read in data at 600 Kbps. A 630 Mbyte CD can be written in about twenty minutes. A hard disk and drive such as the Micropolis AV, capable of providing a continuous stream of data, would be suitable for feeding data to a 600 Kbps CD-R.

In tests on quad-speed 600 Kbps drives it was reported that:

> The truest measure of multimedia playback performance is the through-put to the video display . . . which depends a great deal on the computer's processor and graphics accelerator . . . your system can play back video no faster than the data rate at which it was recorded . . . but if you play back video on a drive that's slower than the rate at which it was recorded you will get a slow, jerky, mess.

An important benefit obtained by quad-speed players is a considerable decrease in seek times.

Other benefits from higher speed recordings and drives are, if you are in the recording business, a higher disk production rate, and for playing, faster data retrieval (if that is the application) and display on a screen.

For recording and viewing continuous television data, if the TV bit rate (see chapter 2) is 165.89 bps and the data are compressed, say 150 times, and recorded on a single-speed drive, the played back decompressed data rate at the same rotational speed will be 165.89 bps. This statement holds good for dual or quad-speed drives – there is no advantage in storage capacity or bit rate delivery.

In 1995 a thin quad-speed drive together with a removable hard disk drive in capacities of up to 540 Mbytes was introduced by Teac at £650 in the UK. This combination enables a CD-ROM and hard disk drive to fit into a single PC bay.

Note that CD-ROM networking is described in chapter 8.

CD-DA

CD-DA, or just CD (Compact Disk Digital Audio) has 783 Mbytes of audio data on 99 tracks with a simple track directory. The Red Book Standard defines:

Physical characteristics: e.g. size, reflectivity

Encoding: method and error correction by sector (sometimes called 'frame')

Data type: audio.

Data organization: audio on up to 99 tracks

Data content: unnecessary – all audio

CD-DA (Compact Disk – Digital Audio), usually known as CD, is a magnetic disk medium which has now taken over from vinyl recordings. Sales of CDs, launched in 1982, are now over 800 million annually, with add-on CD players costing less than £100 in the UK. CD-DA is of passing interest here because it introduced the concept of CDs in all its forms.

The first player – the Sony CDP-101 – appeared in 1984. Players connect to amplifiers or hi-fi equipment. Certain aspects of CD technology have become the forerunners for the variations next described.

It seems not to be widely known that compact disc players do not necessarily reproduce the potentially excellent sound quality available from a CD. To digitize sound for recording purposes, 8-bit samples are generated by sampling the analogue waveform at 44 KHz. However, the process results in the acquisition of harmonic data which sound unpleasant. To get rid of them a technique called 'oversampling and filtering' is used in CD and CD-ROM players. The scientific basis for it is doubtful, but the improvement is undoubted. Bit rates are increased and if the discerning purchaser knows how to ask the right questions and the vendor knows the answers (which he may not), the purchaser will hear about '8 × 2', '16 × 4', etc. players. The first number denotes the number of bits per sample, and the second the pseudo-sampling ('oversampling') rate.

The best CD players, such as the Cambridge Audio CD3, embody '16 × 16' which means '16 bits with 16 times oversampling'. Oversampling is also used in the Amiga CDTV. Considerable attention is paid by Amiga, IBM, and others to sound quality. CD-ROM sound technology is the same as CD technology.

CD-ROM

CD-ROM (Compact Disk – Read Only Memory) has 680 Mbytes of computer data. The Yellow Book Standard Modes 1 & 2 define:

Physical characteristics: as Red Book
Encoding: Red Book method with advanced error correction
Data type: Mode 1: computer data; Mode 2: compressed audio, text, and
    image data
Data organization: to ISO 9660 Standard
Data content: e.g. Microsoft extensions, Apple Quick Time

A Compact Disk – Read Only Memory is a Constant Linear Velocity (CLV) 4.7" disk containing data recorded in a CD-like digital format. A CD-ROM drive comes in a separate box for connection to a microcomputer or as a unit which will slide into the drive aperture provided on the front of a microcomputer. There is a trend to connect a CD-ROM to the controlling micro through the Small Computer Standard Interface (SCSI) to increase data transfer rates. For CD-DAs, standardization and drive problems were minimized from the start and compatible disk players were manufactured thanks to the domination of Philips and Sony, and their specifications in the Yellow Book.

This was not the case for CD-ROMs. CD-ROM software formats must include uniform ways of describing and locating on a disk information about a volume set (collection of disks), a single volume (a CD-ROM disk), and a file. A file is any named collection of data. Each set or several sets of files could be a self-contained information product and a user could be allowed access to one or more products on the same disk. Alternatively, the product might be so large that the file for that product occupied a volume set comprising several volumes. Other aspects of interest include automatic error correction and file directory arrangements.

CD-ROMs are read-only disks, sometimes known as WORM (Write Once Read Many) disks; there is scope for optimized directory arrangements (to be achieved, perhaps, by a hashing algorithm) to minimize seek time, which is inherently slow. In the event, software formats were initiated by the High Sierra (HS) group – formed from a number of manufacturers in the US and including Philips and Sony. Successive attempts at finalization before the end of 1986 were unsuccessful, but agreement was eventually reached and HS became a *de facto* Standard with the objective of getting it through as an ISO Standard for universality and respectability.

Standardization enabled the industry to grow rapidly. Developments were remarkably quick since they were pushed by a relatively small number of organizations. HS duly became the basis for ISO 9660, independent of machines/operating systems, approved, again remarkably quickly, by late 1987. But the 'standard Standards' problem then began – how to actually develop and implement bug-free software conforming to ISO 9660. HS was not widely replaced by ISO 9660 because the former had been adopted and it worked. Suppliers either would not wait for the ISO software Standard or would not use it because their customers did not have version 2.0 of MS-DOS extended memory called for by ISO. However, ISO 9660 was ultimately adopted following special pleas by users who wanted hassle-free choices of applications which would work on any system.

Although 'making CD-ROM disks/players work' is relatively easy for the user, 'relatively' means compared with the other frightful hassles accompanying your average IT system. Many people will not find that installation is easy. The difficulties to be expected are sufficient to prompt numerous explanations telling you how to escape them. One particular problem was 'easily' tackled by *Byte* contributor Pournelle but Pournelle is a computer buff with very wide experience. Just how easy may be assessed from Pournelle's comments:

> Of course the solution was obvious. Access to CD-ROM drives requires two actions. First you have to load the CD-ROM driver with CON-

FIG.SYS. Then you have to execute the MSCDEX.EXE program which loads Microsoft DOS extensions that allow DOS to recognise disc drives large than 33 Mbytes. Then use LOADH1 to install the Amtek Laserdek driver with CONFIG.SYS and when I wanted to access the CD-ROM drive, open a window and execute MSCDEX.EXE command inside the window.

Easy for a computer buff, but for others?

Although CD-ROMs were not as successful at first as was expected by the ebullient forecasters, they have lately become successful enough to be well established in the 'information world', competing mainly against online searching. No telecommunication charges or long delays are incurred by their use. The capacity of a CD-ROM, at around 600 Mbytes, is sufficient to store quite a large textual database. CD-ROMs cannot be as easily and cheaply updated as online databases, so if there is a need for frequent updates, a CD-ROM may be unsuitable for the application. However, the price/update frequency difficulty does not disqualify CD-ROMs from medium-term updating or from being suitable for many other different kinds of application.

Ready-to-load software is now often supplied on a single CD-ROM as an alternative to supplying it on the numerous floppy disks required to store the larger and larger amounts of software required by complex programs. The fact that colour, graphics, illustrations, etc. can also be stored on a CD-ROM is an added bonus, although such additions eat up storage space. Data compression reduces this problem.

Most CD-ROM disks are 'transportable' – that is, they may be read using different microcomputers controlled by different operating systems. The micro is loaded with a driver program capable of dealing with all disks that will be used – provided they all have a standardized logical file structure. If that structure is known to the programmer who writes the driver, the driver will enable files to be opened and data to be interpreted. Not only that: only if the arrangement of data in the files is standardized will the user's application program be able to search the files and obtain results meaningful to its user each time he or she places a disk from a different information provider on the drive.

In January 1993 Nimbus announced that they could play two hours of video from a special disk run on a compact disk player. An ordinary CD player could be used for full motion video because the laser track used by Nimbus is only 1.2 microns wide and track read speed is reduced. The net result is a doubling of the data density. A 'black box' developed by Nimbus and C-Cube connected between the output of the player and a TV receiver contains a C-Cube chip which decodes the MPEG compression algorithms as the data are read off the disk. A double density 12 centimetre CD can contain over two hours of full-colour motion digital video with sound.

There are several CD-ROM points of interest in the Commodore CDTV described in chapter 5. A proprietary compression system of unspecified performance was adopted pending agreement on compression standards. The importance of effective compression can hardly be overestimated. The capacity of CD-ROMs for the CDTV may be increased by using the six spare 8-bit control channels for graphics.

Semi-standardized CD-ROM players have reached the critical mass needed to encourage the supply of a wide range of products for similar applications – for instance, for bibliographic database distribution.

CD-ROM drives come as internal units for a micro or they may be purchased in external separate boxes. NEC, Hitachi, and Panasonic are the major manufacturers. Storage capacities are either 630 or 560 Mbytes. The drive requirements for PC Level 2 machines are shown in Table 11.1.

Next Technology, Cambridge, England have developed a jukebox to hold 270 CD-ROM disks – a storage capacity totalling 175 Gbytes (1400 Gbits). It contains 8 drives, so more than one CD-ROM is accessible at one time. The jukebox is controlled by a PC; it takes 5 seconds to transport a disk on to a drive. The price is £22,000.

The Apple Perform 600 machine may be bought with a fast internal CD drive, the Apple CD 300i. The 300i provides a substantial price and performance improvement over Apple's external CD-ROM drive, the Apple CD 150. It also has full-blown support for Kodak's photo-CD system, and there is a direct sound connection from the drive to the Perform's internal speaker.

CD-ROM XA (Extended Architecture)

A CD-ROM XA disk conforms to the Yellow Book 2 format. The frames are read and synchronized in separate decoding channels but to a user they appear at the same time. Normal CD-ROM players require conversion to XA by adding an XA card with software to read the disk. XA Form 1 includes error detection/correction codes; XA Form 2 does not include them.

CD-ROM XA was announced by Philips, Sony, and Microsoft in September 1988. The format conforms to the ISO 9660 Standard. It provides some of the functions available on CD-I without departing much from established CD-ROM techniques.

The requirements for a multimedia PC which will handle the material on a multimedia CD-ROM are shown in Table 11.1

The main advance towards multimedia with XA is a new standard text/graphics format for microcomputers independent of operating systems, and a coding system for sound as specified for CD-I, but with disks playable on both CD-ROM and CD-I players.

A fully compatible XA drive incorporates Adaptive Differential Pulse

Table 11.1 CD-ROM recommendations for multimedia PC Level 2

Characteristic	CD-ROM spec. for Level 2 PC
CD-DA (Red Book) outputs	Required
Volume control	Required
Sustained transfer rate	300 Kbytes/sec (Min)
CPU bandwidth consumed during sustained 300 K transfer rate	Less than 40%
Average seek time	400 ms (max)
Mean Time Between Failures (MTBF)	At least 10,000 hours
CD-ROM XA	Mode 1, Mode 2 form 1, Mode 2 form 2
Multisession capability	Required
MSCDEX 2.2 driver or equivalent that implements extended audio APIs	Required
Subchannel support	Q required, P and R-W optional
Percent of sustained bandwidth consumed at 300 KByte/sec transfer rate	Less than 60%
Read block sizes/lead time for CPU utilization	Not less than 16 Kbytes. Lead time not more than time needed to load buffer with 1 read blk
Buffers	64 Kbyte (min) read-ahead

Code Modulation (ADPCM) decoding and decompression for separating interleaved audio channels. One application for CD-ROM XA equipment is to run Kodak photo-CD disks on it. A CD-ROM XA drive should also be able to cope with multi-session photo-CD disks where the disk contains several different batches of pictures.

CD-I (Compact Disc Interactive)

CD-I is a disk system specified in the Green Book in the same format as CD-XA, requiring its own operating system called CD-RTOS. A CD-I disk cannot be played on normal CD-ROM players but requires its own player and software connected to a TV receiver display. CD-I was developed from Compact Disc Digital Audio using the basic technique already described. It was launched in the US at the end of 1991 with 100 disk titles and players with interactive control software. For example, in a typical title 'A guide to photography' a user adjusts his camera settings to photograph a subject, takes the shot, and then looks at a 'print' to check the results. Another title displays 'pages from a colouring book'; a child can 'paint' in the colours. The CD-I idea requires special features in order to stretch the technique to produce the necessary performance. The scheme developed by the Philips/Sony team has been described by Preston (1988).

The data stored on the CD are audio, graphics, text, motion-video, etc. The picture on the screen usually consists of overlaid, separately controlled areas with *part* of each area sometimes containing motion video. All parts are controlled by software which also selects which data to shift periodically from the hard disk on to the screen.

A normal CD delivers data at 150 Kbytes/second and has a total capacity of up to 650 Mbytes. Such a disk could store about 650 PAL colour TV frames, each containing 1 Mbyte of data. If played back at TV rates it would provide a programme lasting about 30 seconds, but at the CD rate of 150 Kbytes/second the programme would be in slow motion and would last longer.

However, CD-I is organized to process data in a different way – quite different from the usual method of delivering data in a linear fashion, line by line and frame by frame. The techniques enabling a variety of programmes to be presented, getting round the refill-rate and other limitations are listed below.

- Reduction of the colour data in images by special coding schemes as described
- Provision for the coding of graphic images with text using colour lookup tables and run length coding
- Provision of the means for updating small areas of the screen at a rate acceptable to the eye normally at up to 15 frames per second
- Provision of 4 separate stores ('image planes') with a total capacity of 1 Mbyte, capable of storing four sets of data which may be scanned out in parallel to present four sets of information on the screen
- Provision for using the planes as overlaid 'matte' images. A 'front' image may be partially transparent allowing parts of a 'back' image to be displayed, or a solid small front image may have a transparent surround revealing a background image
- Provision for moving one image over another to provide full-screen animation requiring far less data than is required for a full-screen motion picture

CD-I formats include CLUT 384×280 pixels with 128 colours, DY UV 340×280 pixels, 24-bit colour and a 'high-quality' alternative called QHY with 768×560 pixels and 24-bit colour. With QHY both graphic planes are used simultaneously so transitions between the two are not possible.

Other formats include RL 7 (7-bit run length encoding) with 128 colours and reproduction at 15 frames per second for cartoon animations. A DYUV movie with a 100×160 pixels 24-bit colour partial screen image is reproduced at 15 frames per second to provide limited motion effects.

The eye is relatively insensitive to colour variations. A reduced-rate alternate line coding scheme may be used for the colour component signals (chrominance) version of DYUV producing 384×280 pixels – one-third of NTSC, i.e. a 3:1 compression ratio. With 8-bit colour, a frame is further reduced to $360 \times 240 \times 8 = 691$ Kbits = 86,400 Kbytes.

In a CD-I system the CRT is refreshed 15 times per second (half the NTSC TV rate), so with a bit rate of 150 Kbytes/sec, there are only 150/15 Kbytes = 10,000 bytes per 'screenful' of new data available 15 times per second. A full screen requires 86,400 bytes 15 times per second but it gets 10,000 bytes so only 86,400/10,000 = 8.64 per cent of its pixels can be changed and updated each second.

Other methods of compression are used in CD-I to eliminate all information that is not needed for a particular reproduced scene as described under 'Video colour compression' in chapter 3.

A CD-I player contains a store for holding a screenful of data – say, a picture of a bunker on a golf course. The disk delivers a small quantity of data once, representing the flight and the appearance of the ball when it arrives. Thereafter these data are stored and displayed by repetitive scanning. For an image of this kind which is displayed for seconds, or perhaps tens of seconds, the disk is required to deliver updating ball-flight data once only. CD-I programme content must be of a kind able to provide entertainment without the store refill rate exceeding 150 Kbytes/second.

The associated software provides the necessary control, such as that required for 'interactive play' routines. Thus, using the golf CD-I disk mentioned later, a user with a control device such as a 'joystick' may operate the figure of a golfer to play a shot towards what appears to be, say, the 18th hole at St Andrews, or possibly towards any hole on that course or on any other course of his choice.

Video-CD and Digital Video-CD (DVD)

CD-DA contains 99 data tracks with a simple directory. In a video-CD compressed data are fitted into the same number of tracks by using MPEG1 compression with a high compression ratio. A video-CD disk may be played on a CD-I player because it also includes data which the player recognizes as playback instructions. The data are formatted to comply with ISO 9660 and reproduction is VHS quality.

The new video-CD system was introduced in the UK in February 1995. A number of disks, many of them recordings of full-length feature films such as *Patriot Games*, *Slither*, etc., became available at about £19 each. Maximum playback duration is about 80 minutes so two-part disks are often supplied for films. For playing a disk a CD-I player with a film cartridge at a total cost of about £400 is needed.

Also in February 1995, Sony and Philips announced the DVD with a playing time of 135 minutes – sufficient for a feature film – while Toshiba said they will be able to supply two disks bonded together providing double that of DVD – a two-sided playing time of well over four hours. These advances are aimed to promote the wide-screen 'home cinema' – a TV receiver with a 32" wide screen rents for £40 a month in the UK. As at April 1995 some indication about the winner of this competition is awaited. Until then these developments are unlikely to prompt a move into the next wave of new products.

DV-I (Digital Video Interactive)

A system using a CD-ROM to Yellow Book Mode 1 specification requiring a compression/decompression chip set for handling audio and video files, DV-I is not in the Philips/Sony 'CD hierarchy' – it is currently an Intel product capable of playing full-screen VCR quality colour motion digital video.

Having started in 1983 at RCA's David Sarnoff research centre, DV-I work continued there under the control of GE, who took it over in 1985, and in 1988, when the GE operation was acquired by Intel, Intel introduced the Digital Video Interactive (DV-I) development system for CD media called Pro750 ADP in 1989, to be followed by a product called ActionMedia using a DV-I CD-ROM in 1990.

The major difference between CD-I and DV-I is that DV-I incorporates more efficient MPEG compression using inter-frame content comparisons so that only new data are supplied to a frame. The net data rate reduction enables over one hour of full-screen motion video to be stored and delivered from a CD-ROM, should that be needed.

DV-I builds on CD disk technology – a DV-I disk is basically a high-capacity CD-ROM disk running on a standard CD drive. Until recently, motion video had to be recorded on a DV-I disk via a mainframe computer to compress it to 5 Kbytes per frame. The disk will then play 72 minutes of full-screen colour motion digital video (VCR quality of 256×240 pixels). Alternatively, it will store and play 40,000 medium resolution or 10,000 high-resolution frames of 512×580 pixels, 750 Kbyte uncompressed still pictures, 40 hours of audio, 650,000 pages of text, or some pro rata combination.

Decompression is carried out by a 12 MIPS VLSI (Very Large Scale Integration) chip and a second chip handles the display. However, astonishing advances in compression techniques discussed elsewhere in this book enabled Intel to announce in November 1990 the availability of plug-in boards for microcomputers with 80386 processors, containing chips with on-chip proprietary microcode capable of 'mainframe' online compression rates. The microcode can be replaced so that DV-I compression/decompression algorithms can be made to comply with expected standards in due course. A DV-I player with a 30386 PC, keyboard, joystick, audio amplifier, and loudspeaker sells for about £5000.

One consequence of this development is that with an Intel TV-rate frame-grabber board installed in the micro, motion video from a camera or a broadcast TV signal can be compressed and captured on hard disk in real time, the disk removed, and the TV programme played back on someone else's micro.

Most disks have insufficient capacity so the most convenient removable 'disk' could be the removable cartridge on a Bernouilli drive external to the PC.

Elaborate compression methods have been developed by General Electric/RCA to enable data for one hour's motion video playing time to be stored on a DV-I disk – the same size as a CD-ROM disk. A compression ratio of up to 100:1 is obtained by a combination of several techniques. The data are compressed using a mainframe computer but in the DV-I player decompression is carried out by two Very Large Scale Integration (VLSI) chips. One runs the decompression algorithm at 12.5 million instructions per second (mips) and the other deals with the display format. A VLSI chip contains 100,000 or more transistors. The DV-I VLSI chips were developed at the Sarnoff Research Centre, but Intel has acquired the technology and expects to manufacture them.

The compression of a rapid succession of slightly different images enables different data between successive images to be coded and signalled. When a succession of very similar images is handled in this manner, huge compression ratios may result. Intel has announced several products – a plug-in board for PC AT computers for capturing and storing data in local storage, and a playback and decompression board at a total price of about £4000. A complete DV-I play back PC with monitor and CD-ROM drive could sell for up to £7000. IBM is expected to announce a DV-I workstation soon.

CD-Bridge

A disk format defining a way in which extra data may be added to a CD-XA track so that it may be played on a CD-I player with a TV receiver or a CD/XA player with a computer. This is the format used by Kodak photo-CD.

Photo-CD

A CD-ROM system devised by Kodak with Philips to CD-XA specification Form 1 (Orange Book specification, like CD-Rs) using the CD-Bridge arrangement. Photographs may be scanned and stored in multi-sessions – that is, different parts of a disk may be recorded at different times. Photo-CD disks are readable on CD-ROM/XA, CD-I, and special photo-CD players.

The Kodak company has been actively developing photo-CD and the whole or parts of it are being pressed into use for multimedia purposes. A Kodak photo-CD transfer station, which costs £85,000, includes a high-resolution film scanner, Sun workstation, disk-writer, and Ektatherm thermal colour printer. It became available in the UK in September 1992. It is used by photo-CD bureaux for the graphics industry. The London company Laserbureau, which installed the system in 1993, is believed to be first with a service in the UK. Efforts to extend the idea to the general public have not yet been very successful.

A client brings to a bureau a reel of exposed colour film containing pictures taken on an ordinary 35 mm camera, for conversion into a CD-ROM containing up to about 100 images for running on a CD-XA drive and displaying on a TV receiver. A print of thumbnail-size images, supplied with the CD, acts as an index to it. Alternatively, the image files from the CD may be input to a computer directly.

The processing equipment at a bureau includes a Sun workstation to receive images from a film scanner with three parallel CCDs, each handling one primary colour, and sends them to a printer to create a set of thumbnail-size pictures. A CD disk-writer developed by Philips makes the associated CD. For supplying colour prints, the CD runs on a separate system which applies the data to a thermal printer. The software provides for all the processing, and includes colour management and control to the Kodak PhotoYCC specification in order to provide consistent colour. Consistent colour reproduction has been a problem for years. PhotoYCC might be adopted as a *de facto* Standard. Adobe support it with their Level 2 Postscript.

Larger prints for customers are produced on a Kodak XL 7700 digital continuous tone machine which receives CD-ROM data and prints pictures by overlaying combinations of CMY (Cyan–Magenta–Yellow) colours from a three-colour ribbon. An A4-size colour print thus produced looks like a high-grade conventional colour print. The quality is quite remarkable for a printer of this kind. The complete processing /reproduction kit costs around £75,000. During processing a 35 mm frame film is scanned at very high resolution, generating 2000×3000 pixels with 24-bit colour – a total of 144 Mbits (18 Mbytes) of data. By compressing to 4.4 Mbytes, over 100 images may be stored on one CD-ROM disc.

The system could be used to provide an indexed thumbnail browser for displaying pictures by 'hit-screenfuls'. Sixteen pictures of 150×100 pixel size could be displayed on a 800×600 Super VGA screen, leaving enough room for short indexing keys. This size should be adequate for a user to identify any picture – to be subsequently supplied as a high-quality image – from a large collection. Each thumbnail would total $150 \times 100 \times 8 = 120$ Kbits or 15 Kbytes if displayed in 8-bit colour. Compressed by 10:1 each would occupy 1.5 Kbytes of storage. Thus $600/.015 = 40,000$ could be stored on a single 600 Mbyte CD-ROM. Compression/decompression of 10:1 using current methods should provide adequate quality for human recognition purposes.

Figure 11.1 (a) shows a full-resolution Kodak photo-CD photograph. The main body of the photo in Figure 11.1 (b) is an enlargement of part of 11.1 (a); a thumbnail small enough not to obscure the enlargement overlays it; the thumbnail contains a small, white-bordered area showing which part of 11.1 (a) has been enlarged. The point of showing the enlargement is to provide an idea of the latter's sharpness – even when enlarged by this amount. The motion by the riders in the original photograph is responsible for some of the slightly blurred reproduction in the enlargement rather than in adequate resolution in the original. It is hard to believe that it was produced on a thermal printer.

Table 11.2 shows the alternative resolutions which may be selected for reproducing images recorded on photo-CD. Although pictures are processed to provide a very high resolution, they may be retrieved at several different, lower, resolutions, as the table shows. For example, the reduction may be set to provide an image of, say, 128×192 pixels. A large number of such images takes up a file of easily managed size. A 720×480 VGA display, for instance, with 16-bit colour is composed with about 5.5 Mbits (less than 700 Kbytes).

If the images are being output to, for example, a Linotron printer capable of utilizing, say, 20 Mbytes (uncompressed) for high-quality images, lower resolutions would be selected for an acceptable cost/quality compromise. Photo-CD colour pictures would be obtained, with storage problems greatly eased.

Kodak also supply Photoedge with editing facilities, Shoebox, a picture database system with search and retrieval facilities, and a multimedia presentation system called Photo CD Portfolio.

McMahon (1994) reports on Laserbureau's service with thumbnails printed from a dye sublimation printer. 'Considering the scans came back in half the time at half the cost of conventional scanning, we were delighted with the results,' says McMahon.

A new phase for photo-CD is discussed by Steele *et al.* (1996) – the emphasis has changed from consumer to professional applications. Photo-CD did not have the expected impact on the amateur still picture market

Table 11.2 Photo-CD image file alternative formats

Image type	Pixels	Resolution	Compression
64 base	4096×6144	Full photo	Yes
16 Base	2048×3072	Full photo	Yes
4 Base	1024×1536	High	Yes
Base	512×768	TV	No
Base/4	256×384	Low	No
Base/16	128×192	Low	No

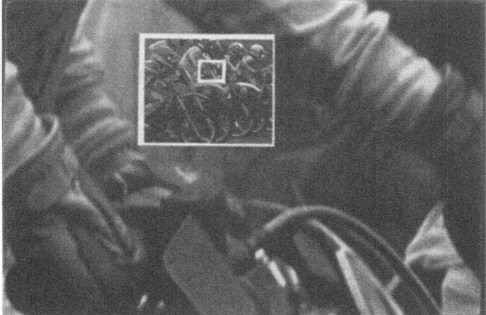

Figure 11.1 (a) and (b) Photo-CD resolution
Source: Kodak Ltd

because people would not spend £500 for a player which removed the portability appeal of snaps. You had to show them in the place where you kept the equipment.

Kodak tried again in April 1995 with more success in the professional market. Photo-CD will store images of high quality on a medium claimed to endure for at least sixty years. If the time comes for renewal they can be renewed with their original quality from digital storage. Applications are discussed in chapter 14.

CD-R and in-house production

A number of organizations will undertake to prepare a master disk from a customer's database and produce copies from it. A special tape must be prepared, together with the directory structure, ready for making the 'pre-mastering' tape, which will include synchronization bits, headers, error correction, etc. From this a master disk is prepared to produce copies – the CD-ROMs for customers. A specialized software house will prepare the pre-mastering tape, and the price for preparing a master disk from that tape will average about £2000 in the UK with the price of copies ranging from about £50 each for a small quantity, reducing to £3 each for large numbers (Philips' prices).

A CD-R (Compact Disk Recordable) is defined by the Orange Book 2 Standard covering physical and track formats for write-once CD-Rs used in personal ROM maker multi-session systems, enabling data to be added in separate recording sessions. CD-Rs conforming to this Standard will not play on normal CD-ROM drives. The system can be used for publishing because the CD can be written on. A disk has a polycarbonate substrate on which are deposited an organic die recording layer, a gold reflector layer, and a sealing layer. A recording laser cuts a bit pattern by melting pits in the die layer; the data are read by a laser of lower power.

Like most other IT systems, the cost of CD-R equipment has dropped to a level likely to make 'do it yourself' CD making feasible for some purposes. A CD-R drive and software now cost between £4000 and £6500. Disks cost about £20. According to O'Reilly (1994) CD-R recordings may be made in different ways, all in accordance with ISO 9660. In a multi-session recording containing a number of short sessions an overhead of 15 Mbytes per session is incurred. However, if each session is recorded on to distinct separated parts of the track an overhead of only 500 Kbytes is incurred. A small extra software package is needed to select the separate tracks.

Three systems for making a CD-R are reviewed by McMahon (1994) – the JVC Personal RomMaker, the Kodak PCD Writer 2000, and the Ricoh RS9200 CD at £6495, £3995, and £3995 respectively.

A 1.2 Gbyte disk is supplied with the JVC and the system enables a virtual CD-ROM to be tested. The systems include software for creating the pre-mastered data on a hard disk which is then burned into a CD-R on the drive, which may also be used as a player. According to McMahon, the JVC is the best system 'making a clean sweep of it in all departments'.

By 1995 the cost of CDs had dropped to about £5 each in quantities of 500, and to 75p each for 5000 in the UK. Using a quad-speed drive as described in a previous section in this chapter, recording time is considerably reduced.

CD Audio/CD-ROM mixed mode

A Standard specifying a track confirming to the Yellow Book Standard followed by Red Book audio tracks. This enables data, for instance audio instructions, directly readable via the audio jack on a CD player, to be heard as a preamble to, say, audio training information.

SYSTEM SIMPLIFICATION OR NEW INCOMPATIBLE SYSTEMS?

After agreement on the original Red Book Standard for CDs, the development of the variations described above followed, as did attempts to record and playback more data, particularly video data. The result is a situation where alternative formats and an understanding about what kind of software and drive are required to play what kind of disk are unclear. If today's choice works now, will it become obsolete within the next year or two?

It now seems possible that a multi-purpose CD may be introduced which will play on several different types of equipment. Instructions recorded on the disk will tell the playback system which of several programs stored in the system it should use, or will read the capabilities of the player before allowing that part of the disk within the system's capability to be played. Ideally, facilities within a single playing system should enable it to play existing types of disk as well, so that the user's existing collection remains playable.

In 1994 Philips/Polygram produced a disk which would play an audio recording on a CD player, but if played on a CD-I or a CD-ROM/PC/video decoder system, the same audio would be played accompanied by video pictures. Later in the year Philips brought out a CD which produced either sound on a CD player, video on a CD-I player, video on a PC with video board, or video on a PC in a window without a board. These ideas raise the possibility of one performance recorded on one multi-purpose disk, always assuming that performers will receive a royalty equivalent to the total royalty received per disk/performance when several different disks and performances were needed.

In 1995 the arrival of higher capacity disks has presented two possible alternatives for providing films on disk. Philips/Sony have developed the Digital Video Disk (mentioned above) which could also be used for providing improved multimedia since it can store 7.4 Gbytes of data. Recording time is doubled by incorporating two tracks recorded at different depths; a laser reads one or the other depending on its focusing. Meanwhile, Toshiba/Time Warner are developing a two-sided SuperDisc with 142 minutes of high-quality film recording per side. This idea is supported by Panasonic and Thomson.

Major computer manufacturers are interested but only if a single Standard is agreed.

Panasonic have also developed a rewritable disk drive combined with a quad-speed CD-ROM drive, which it says it intends to offer at a very low price. In short, it is starting to look as if extensions to the old Red Book as a means for preserving backward compatibility with a series of modifications have just about reached their limit. Further substantial improvements in performance may demand more radical changes making backward compatibility much more difficult to maintain.

CD AUTHORING

Authoring in general, discussed in chapter 6, contains information for people who may or may not end up with an authored CD. Some of that information will be of interest to 'CD authors'. This section relates to CD-specific authoring.

CD-ROMs may now be produced with do-it-yourself equipment at a price appropriate to non-professional producers. The Philips CDD521 drive is sold with an Adaptek 1542 SCSI-2 adaptor, advanced SCSI Programming Interface (ASPI) driver, software MSCDEX.EXE, and DOS utilities called CD-Write.

CD recording depends critically on an uninterrupted stream of data, particularly when – as with the CDD521 – the drive runs at twice the normal CD play speed, requiring a sustained transfer rate of better than 300 Kbps. The work space where the material is prepared ready to be written to the CD is usually a hard disk. CD-Write converts the data on the fly from the hard disk's DOS file system to the CD's ISO 9660 file system. The software will also redirect ISO 9660 images to a CD.

Tudor Grashoff (1993) discusses 'The pros and cons of producing your own CD-ROM'. Grashoff describes numerous functions which make up CD-ROM publishing including product design, data conversion from the source to files from which a CD-ROM can be mastered, and CD-ROM mastering and replication. He says that contracting out the CD mastering currently costs £1200 per disk, whereas if several CD-ROMs are being mastered it may be worth buying suitable equipment for do-it-yourself purposes costing about £5000.

Angela Ross (1993) expands on 'Making your own CD-ROMs – advances in CD recordable technology'. She claims that a CD-ROM can be created almost as easily as saving data on a floppy disk. Personal RomMaker software for the Macintosh costs about $13,000.

CD-I authoring

Some good advice is provided by Anon, (1992b), the Philips CD-I Design Handbook:

> In CD-I you should try to avoid designs that feel like a computer. For many people computers have negative connotations. By presenting people with a computer style interface, you may alienate them ... your viewers are much more likely to be familiar with television programmes and the graphic style used in that medium.

The Philips book recommends a flowchart, at least for planning the main sections of a CD-I multimedia program. To produce a CD-I an author must understand what can be done with each type of program element or medium. A CD-I player, if equipped with a plug-in digital video cartridge, can replay full-screen motion video for a total time of about 20 minutes either as one long clip or as numerous separate clips that may be accompanied by stereo audio sound. This assumes that an MPEG compression scheme is being used for video.

Ward (1994) describes the elements available for assembling a program using a tool such as Media Mogul. These include the preparation of formats of up to 768×560 pixels in 24-bit colour using two graphic planes with certain limitations on scene-to-scene transitions, run length encoded animation, and part-screen DYUV images running at up to 25 frames per second to provide limited motion within a small area. Media Mogul provides an on-screen interface to help an author define the order and duration of each audio and video segment in order to create a sequence with facilities for immediate playback. This software runs on a machine with development tools like a Philips CDI 605 machine with the CD-RTOS operating system. A complete system costs about £10,000.

In late 1994 Philips produced an authoring tool for interactive multimedia systems called Delta Vx designed for managing data produced on a Mac 33 MHz Quadra hard disk to be presented to the Media Mogul/CDI 605. The Mac should have 16 Mbytes of RAM and a 1.2 Gbyte disk. Delta Vx will also run on appropriate models of Sun or PC machines. Philips claim that it is 'simple and elegant' to use. It may be elegant but I have some doubts as to whether it is simple. It may be used to produce CD-I or video-CD disks. Delta Vx uses MPEG1 compression and disks made with it provide pictures of VHS quality from videotape output used for disk mastering.

A CD-I-based system was selected for the 'Lifetimes' project devised by Croydon (UK) museums with the New Media company, and installed in the town's central clocktower. The 12 CD-I consoles are the visitors' key to finding an exhibit of interest. Each acts as a catalogue to a particular class of exhibits. They are arranged in a gallery specially constructed above the museum. A visitor uses a touchscreen to select a photograph of an object of interest, and its selection leads to information usually supplied by its owner. The emphasis is on local history and images of a very large number of photographs and artefacts were selected after a period to test public reactions to the ideas.

Photo-CD authoring

The Kodak Photo-CD Access Plus software includes a program called Photo-CD Access for reading, displaying, and exporting photo-CD images at a number of different resolutions, and the photo-CD player software for playing back Portfolio disks with images, text, graphics, and sound. The software also includes facilities for editing printed images, and enlarging, or making them smaller, changing image formats, and other functions.

Photo-CD Access Plus is available for Macs with system 6.05 or higher and Quickdraw or 80386 or better PCs with Windows 3.0 or higher. In both cases 8 Mbytes of RAM is recommended or at least 30 Mbytes for full-resolution images. A CD-ROM XA drive is required.

Figure 11.2 shows a screen dump from the Access software in use.

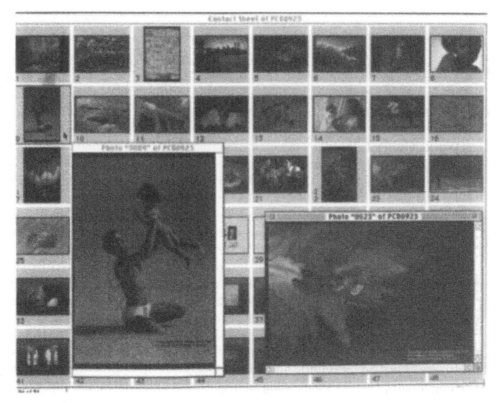

Figure 11.2 A screen showing Photo-CD Access software being used
Source: Kodak Ltd

CD PUBLICATIONS

Access

Networking for organizations requiring multiple accesses to a number of CDs simultaneously is discussed in chapter 8. For single-user applications where lookups from a number of different CDs otherwise repeatedly inserted and removed from the same machine are needed, there is a less expensive alternative – a CD autochanger.

A 1995 product, the MBR-7 introduced by Nakamichi, enables seven disks to be autochanged by pressing any of seven buttons. It connects via an SCSI cable and is CD-ROM, -DA, -XA, and photo-CD-compatible. The price which includes a boxed autochanger with drive, costs £285 in the UK.

Products

A 'CD multimedia publication' means a CD-ROM containing text, pictures, and sound. A very large selection in the area of learning, training, reference, and other subjects is available.

General publications

Some examples of CD-ROM publications are shown in Figure 11.3. There is a huge range of publications covering almost any subject but usually in those areas where the value of the hyper link 'non-linear text' presentation is useful. Several types are listed in the 'CD markets and growth' section below.

World Guide (Uppsala University Interactive Media Group, 1994) is a typical product which uses hyperlinks to advantage. It enables a group of countries to be selected, then a specific country, then a subject and a variable, and then a format. For example, for the subject 'Population growth in Benin' (formerly Dahomey) a user can go from a map and general history to life expectancy at birth versus a selected spread of other countries, to age distribution in Benin, as shown in Figure 11.3.

'Inventors and inventions' (from Interactive Multimedia and the British Library) is a CD-ROM designed for classroom use which covers textiles, power, communications, flight, and land transport. The material includes full-motion video, animated drawings, audio commentary and sound effects. The disk will run on Acorn machines which are widely used in UK schools, or on 386 SX PC with 4 Mbytes of RAM, CD-ROM drive, and Windows software. The screen dump shown in Figure 11.4 shows how the hyperlink arrangement provides for moving to other text, alphabetical lookup, etc.

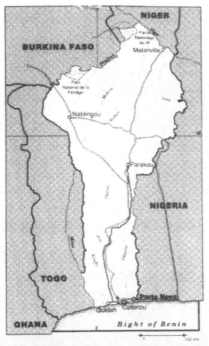

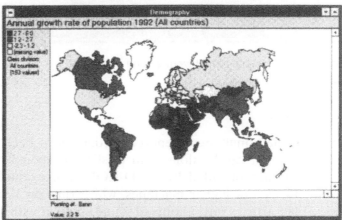

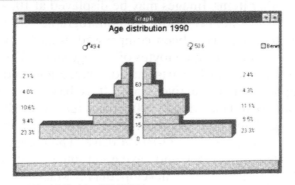

Figure 11.3 Entries in World Guide CD-ROM

Source: Uppsala University

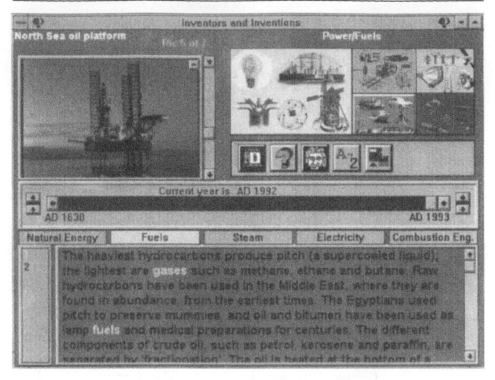

Figure 11.4 Screendump from 'Inventors and inventions'
Source: The British Library

Encyclopaedias

Several so-called 'multimedia encyclopaedias' have been published. They demonstrate what can be done with existing inexpensive software, hardware, and storage provided by a CD-ROM. For example, Encarta from Microsoft for 386 or higher machines, which runs on Windows, is said to include 21,000 articles with 7 hours of sound together with animations, music clips, and other items. Images may be displayed at 1024×768 pixels with 8-bit colour. The system contains 7000 photographs, charts, and graphics. All of the photographs have been compressed using Iterated System's Fractal Image Format into 105 megabytes of storage space. Encarta costs $395.

The 1994 edition of Encarta includes video and audio clips, animations, photographs, and interactive maps. It is based on the 29-volume *New Encyclopaedia* and includes 25,000 articles retrievable by keyword searching or browsing. Improvements mean that a faster system is needed to run it including a double speed CD-ROM drive. The computer should contain a 486SX processor or better, and have good sound facilities.

The Grolier Multimedia Encyclopedia for Macs sells in the UK for £99. It contains well over 30,000 logically arranged topics. It includes numerous still images, audio clips such as animal and bird sounds, historic speeches, and parts of musical scores and the sounds of individual instruments. Over 50 video clips include items like the *Hindenburg* airship disaster and the first moon landing. Text items include many maps and essays about a wide range of topics.

Census data

A CD-ROM would seem to be the ideal medium for providing access to census data. The 1991 census data have been published in this form by Chadwyck-Healey. They have been described by Rowley (1994). The data are said to come in different packages designed for different organizations such as government, public libraries, schools, etc.

A software package called SASPAC (from MVA Systematica) is available aimed at analysing small area, local, and special workplace statistics. Rowley provides a list of GIS software products because 'many organisations will seek to integrate census data into their GIS'. Rowley considers that libraries might mount disks on a jukebox linked into a network so that a number of users can exploit the facilities at the same time. Other libraries, starting to use a CD-ROM of this kind, might mount it in stand-alone equipment. Rowley discusses library applications stating that 'many academic and public libraries have made census data in printed form available to users. The availability of the data on CD-ROM facilitates much more imaginative and flexible application of the data.'

Rowley does not include any information about the marketing philosophy adopted by Chadwyck-Healey. However, their product is priced at £3000–£4000 for a set of up to nine disks, but to use the data a licence is necessary from the Office of Population and Central Statistics (OPCS). A licence will cost about £27,000 for a company but far less for a library, probably a few hundred pounds. The product became available to intending purchasers at the end of May 1994.

Museums and art 1: Treasures of the Smithsonian

Woolsey's idea that a videotape derived from the Globe system 'might be taken home for viewing' has been implemented in a different way by Hoekema (1990) and others. 'Treasures' was designed in 1987/88 from the data then available about CD-Is. CD-I players became available in the US at the end of 1991.

From the description of CD-Is given earlier it will be noted that inter-activity and motion are achieved by shifting relatively small amounts of new data on to the screen against a background of larger amounts of 'old' data which changes infrequently. This mechanism is not particularly useful for the 'Treasures' presentation. The CD-I facilities for combining commentary, music, and text as used here enable users to change a limited number of full-screen images but this is still a considerable advance on CD-ROM.

Hoekema says:

> we would try to give every treasure (about 150 are included) its due in
> the form of audio-visual presentations with the best images we could find,
> a lively narration marked by wit and personality, and a full soundtrack
> with music and sound effects which would reinforce the interpretation of
> the object being presented.

Another feature of the system is user selection of a treasure by date, by
museum, by category, or by associated person.

A 'tour' of several different sets of treasures connected by some common
theme may also be selected. The CD-I was published in October 1991, having earlier won an award from the American Association of Museums. The
price is $49.95.

Museums and art 2: Great artists

Attica Cybernetics (Unit 1, King's Meadow, Oxford, UK) and Marshall
Cavendish have authored a CD-ROM entitled 'Great artists' in association
with the National Gallery, London. The CD-ROM sells for £50 (VAT
included) in the UK.

The National Gallery themselves present their own system as described
in chapter 14. However, this version was compiled specifically for CD-ROM
presentation and was devised using information supplied by the gallery.
Marshall Cavendish is a well-known publisher so this version embodies
their expertise backed by Attica's technical expertise. The CD-ROM
includes a great deal of textual information about art and artists, as well as
numerous pictures, a 'workshop facility' for interactive analysis of content,
audio commentary, and twenty minutes of video for explaining painting
techniques, etc.

The CD-ROM also contains 40 fractal-compressed paintings from
selected artists reproduced at thumbnail or quarter-screen size within
descriptive pages. These pictures may also be reproduced full screen in 24-
bit colour at 640×480 pixels.

The disk requires a 486 or better PC operating with Windows software. It
is not available for Mac machines.

CD MARKETS AND GROWTH

In Armstrong's 1990 directory, 18 titles are selected for comprehensive
evaluation. Of these, 10 are bibliographic databases, 6 are directories,
dictionaries, or encyclopaedias, 1 includes full text abstracts, and 1 is a
numeric database. Libraries probably still form the main market, but
business applications are now showing the fastest growth.

By the end of 1991 there were believed to be 2.25 million CD-ROM drives in use worldwide, of which 1.44 million were in the US, and 200,000 in Europe. Stoneman (1993) from the CD-ROM publisher Silver Platter reports trends in CD-ROM publishing. The number of CD-ROM/multimedia titles has increased from 48 in 1987 to nearly 3600 in 1993. In a recent report it is claimed that over 1100 new titles were published in the first six months of 1993 alone.

Cambridge CD-ROM Ltd, of Stowmarket, Suffolk, UK alone list 130 new titles in their Autumn 1993 catalogue in the fields of arts and leisure, business and finance, computers and desktop publishing, dictionaries and encyclopaedias, earth sciences, education and teaching, entertainment and games, history, languages, life sciences, children's literature, library systems, medicine and health, music, science and technology, etc. In fact there seem to be few subjects which are not now covered on CD-ROMs. Specific subjects included in the Cambridge list include the 'EC grants and loans database', a 'gallery of dreams' said to have been created for 'the individual looking for a collection of images which are literally a breath of fresh air', EcoQuest, a saga about the adventures of a 12-year-old boy trying to save the environment, and the prime medical journal, *New England Journal of Medicine* updated every 6 months.

Hollis (1993) reports that a UK survey reveals that more people still use online information services than CD-ROM but the gap is narrowing. A major advantage of CD-ROMs is 'end-user enpowerment' – in other words end-user searching is often carried out directly, while online searching is usually done by an intermediary. Moreover, most libraries may not charge for a CD-ROM search, but they may charge for online.

At the end of 1993 Bowker Saur published a list of Russian books said to be the world's first Cyrillic CD-ROM. This publication lists 180,000 bibliographic records with the data listed both in Cyrillic and in a transliterated version. Bowker Saur's partners include the Russian Bibliographic Society and a Russian company called Vista-Dialog. The price of this disk is £995.

By 1993 there were over 2800 CD-ROM/multimedia companies, although the rate of formation of new companies has slowed down considerably. The fastest rate of increase in CD-ROM/multimedia publications by price has been in the range $100 or less. 'Acquiring data rights for electronic media will continue in importance but it is a huge task to convert existing print resources into electronic form. Safeguarding data rights during distribution will be a growing concern,' says Stoneman.

In early 1995 it was claimed that 27 million drives were shipped in 1994, of which it is estimated that about 10 per cent are used by companies. A drive may be purchased in the UK for less than £100.

From about 1985 onwards, CD-ROM versions of well-known databases such as ERIC, MEDLINE, Science Citation Index, etc. have become a viable complement, if not a replacement, for printed or online-searchable versions. At least two other major applications are of interest – selected data distribution (for example, the supply of census data to be selectively transferred to hard disk for specialized use), and 'smart disks' (where included software enables retrieved information to be further processed).

CD-ROMs have also expanded into areas beyond bibliographic data-bases. As early as 1987 the financial CD-ROM, Lotus One Source, sold 19,000 copies, followed by Microsoft's Bookshelf with 10,000.

Claiming to have sold 400,000 CD-I systems at the beginning of 1994, Philips expected to achieve a world base of 1 million systems by the end of the year with 200 titles available. Philips are competing with 3DO and in 1994 they launched the CD-I 450 player at £299, undercutting the 3DO machine by £100.

There were about 50 CD-I titles at the start of 1993. Combined sales estimates for CDTV and CD-I of about 400,000 units have been forecast for 1994. The biggest question is over the home market, says one observer. Can CD-I achieve all that Philips hopes for it or have they missed the boat, as some critics believe?

> Rumours of a DV-I unit targeted at the home cannot be dismissed, although software for it will be a crucial issue, and what impact will CDTV have? . . . Corporate communications, depending as they do on networking, will move with systems which support this need.

ELECTRONIC BOOKS

Origins and opinions

The term 'electronic books' was coined by Andries van Damm over 25 years ago, but it was Kay and Goldberg who first seriously considered the idea with their *Dynabook* (Kay and Goldberg 1977). Kay said in an inter-view (Press 1992):

> I started designing the machine in the late 1960s. I went to Xerox Palo Alto Research Centre with the explicit purpose to make it. As it turned out Xerox sort of punked out midway in the thing. All we did was to invent workstations and Macintoshes and stuff like that.

Kay suggested that 'future computers will let you move beyond McLuhan's individual'. McLuhan had suggested in *The Gutenberg Galaxy* (1962) that new media determines the nature of the social organization. Kay continued:

> The retrieval systems of the future are not going to retrieve facts but points of view. The weakness of data-bases is that they let you retrieve facts, while the strength of our culture over the last seven hundred years has been our ability to take on multiple points of view.
>
> The true significance of the *Dynabook* [will be] . . . the effect that intimate computing will have on our culture . . . five or ten years from

now we'll judge our AI systems not on how smart they are but how well they are able to explain themselves to us.

The *Dynabook* was intended to be a notebook with a 1-million pixel screen, eight processors, and both wireless and cable networking. Kay's estimation of what might become technically possible was not far wrong although his time forecast was incorrect.

The proposed electronic book was based on VLSI (Very Large Scale Integrated) circuits. It would be book-size with a flat screen display, the words being encoded as 12-bit numbers stored, together with coarse graphics, in a memory of about 14 Mbytes. The method of compression would enable the text of a novel to be stored. 'Books' would come in small plug-in memories, and an on-board microprocessor would handle decoding and presentation. The device would include a keyboard and string-searching capabilities for 'publications' requiring that facility. It was suggested that the electronic book would 'alter the nature of libraries, increase the efficiency of the scientific, legal, and medical professions, minimise information access time in industry, and modify the operation of the educational system'.

In 1993 Dr Frank Lukey, from Silver Platter, a CD-ROM supplier, said: 'The 500-year era of print is drawing to its close . . . In only 5-10 years a range of electronic books will be available of which the most common will be the portable book which will really sell the idea.' However, in the opinion of this author the demise of print is still a very long way off.

Information 2000, a multi-authored compilation, carries the imprimatur of the British Library (Martyn *et al.* 1990). It says about electronic books:

In order to become acceptable to consumers, the electronic book must have features which bring additional benefit over and above the experi- ence of reading continuous text from a printed book . . . . It is likely to be most effective as a reference work. This is borne out by early electronic books – they are dictionaries.

Sevonius and Witthus (1981) say:

A romantic quality characterizes the writing of many who depict the potential of the new technology for future information systems. A recurring theme is that of paperless information systems . . . . Lancaster epitomizes the paperless society in terms of an intelligent terminal located in one's home through which one can access, in interactive mode, books and periodicals, factual information such as airline schedules and football scores, and the information in one's personal files.

Goodrum and Dalrymple (1985) believe that 'The Electronic Book being talked about can either be one of the brief-case-sized computer screens that are increasingly seen on people's laps in airplanes, or the flat screens seen on designers' work benches.'

Fred Croxton of the Library of Congress, Ithiel de Sola Pool of MIT and Tom Surprenant of Queens College, City University of New York express concern about the effect of the on-demand book on libraries. All three express the belief that this innovation will come in the working lifetime of present library administrators and should be anticipated by present supervisors (Goodrum and Dalrymple 1985).

Blunden (1994) quotes some predictions about the potential European market for printed publications in the year 2000. It will be about 112,000 million ECU, while the electronic publishing market will be about 12,000 million. In the US the publishing industry's current revenues are currently about $55,000 million, and electronic publishing about 10 per cent of that. Blunden says: 'If one considers developments in speech input, super-highways, standardisation of imaging protocols, data compression, touch commands and iconographic language, then the suggestion that man's natural multimedia behaviour may be emulated in machine form within a decade is feasible.'

Doty and Bishop (1994) discuss the disappearance of familiar distinctions in publishing. For instance, single copies are no longer much more expensive than mass-produced publications. 'Previously unassailable and static arte-facts are now increasingly volatile . . . in museums multimedia information systems support the reconstruction of objects and their interpretation.'

A new kind of book is available from McGraw-Hill, which produces the Primis on-demand publishing product, allowing professors to select instruc-tional material from a large retrievable database, and integrate disparate subjects, ideas, and types of information.

A 'just in time' service is offered for printing, binding, and shipping 'customized books' direct to customers. In 1990 there were 7000 pages in the database and 30 user-institution customers. By 1993 there were 100,000 pages and 1000 customers.

Doty and Bishop believe that there are heavy costs to be paid for new and less tangible methods of publication. They cite lack of quality control, information liability, document authentication, and abandonment of the idea of 'having the literature' as examples. What will be the role of publishers, who currently act as 'value-added gate keepers' who evaluate, edit, produce, market, and distribute information? Doty and Bishop also believe that

> For the National Information Infrastructure and electronic publishing to reach fruition . . . present federal legal and regulatory frameworks must be changed . . . . Areas that need special attention include intellectual property, particularly copyright, antitrust . . . civil liability, free speech, privacy, information access, the status of proprietary information, the right of free association, and unreasonable search and seizure.

They consider that policy-makers should take advice about the matters listed below:

- Knowledge about the nature and use of information
- Skills in information organization and access
- Knowledge of users and their behaviour, especially information-seeking and use
- Knowledge of particular communities of information users
- Commitment to the preservation and dissemination of the cultural record
- An ethos committed to the user, whether an individual, an organization, or society at large
- Explicit and enabling links from large-scale public rhetoric, goals and initiatives to particular individuals and communities of users

Progress of so-called electronic books

In 1984 it was forecast that in the library of the future videodisks containing the digital text of reference books would be received from publishers. They would be consulted using interactive colour monitors 'permitting modes of access that are not possible today'.

Weyers' and Borning's (1985) model was the first serious proposal showing that at least one type of book could provide advantages in electronic format. They suggested that an electronic encyclopaedia

> should be as comprehensive and detailed as the best current encyclopaedias, but full advantage should be taken of not just text and static pictures but also video sequences, animation, simulations, music and voice . . . what the user sees would be custom-generated and based on the encyclopaedia's system model of the user's interests, vocabulary, knowledge of specific subjects and previous interactions with the system.

They provided an example of their intentions by showing a Hypercard-like access to an entry with interactive learning facilities: 'After specifying a load on a bridge we see the effect of forces transmitted to various truss members.' The bridge article might 'lead us to the collapse of the Tacoma Narrows bridge from movie footage available on videodisc'.

In 1987 two Australian companies announced a two-part 'Smartbook' with credit-card-like objects containing a micro-chip on which the text was stored, to cost about $50 each. It was said that by the time the device reached full-scale production there should be a reasonable library of reference works. Nothing has been heard of it since.

Another device called the Izon micrographics reader was developed at about the same time, supposedly to sell for about $100. It used an optical compression system with a form of Fresnel lens housed in a book-size box, with the expectation of breaking the portability barrier imposed by normal microfiche readers. Like the Smartbook it disappeared without a trace.

Publishing companies see electronic books as a way to save production costs and to improve accuracy and timeliness. The books most amenable to be changed into electronic form are engineering maintenance, instruction manuals, and encyclopaedias.

McGraw-Hill's 1992 Multimedia Encyclopaedia of Mammalian Biology is published on CD-ROM and runs on a CD-ROM drive compatible with Microsoft Multimedia Extensions to Windows 3.0. A DVI board is desirable for the full effect. It provides for text, sound, data, pictures, and motion video, with interactive software. The disk includes 300 motion video clips associated with selected text entries, each of which will provide about 15 seconds of full-screen motion video.

Weyer-like interaction is provided. Data display options are offered, and those data may be plotted graphically as demanded by the user. The encyclopaedia includes 3500 still colour illustrations as well as the motion clips. A major difference between this and alphabetically ordered encyclopaedias is that searches can be carried out using concept-based retrieval incorporating the BBC's TELCLASS classification system.

A product introduced in 1993 called *Financial Alert* represents a step towards a genuine electronic book. It combines a personal organizer to receive and display City information, stock market price changes, company news, etc. by radio. It consists of an LCD display, a touch keypad, computer, and rechargeable battery. It can work almost anywhere in the UK.

A 1994 microcomputer qualifies as a 'notebook' if it meets certain criteria. It must be about the size of an A4 notepad, thin enough to easily fit into a standard briefcase, weigh under 3 kg, be able to run under battery power for a least two hours, and perform most of the functions of a desktop machine. Many machines conform to these criteria, which fulfil the purposes of a paper notebook to some degree.

Electronic books versus printed books

Compared with a variety of objects labelled as 'electronic books' today, ordinary books possess overwhelming advantages, although there are a few promising specialized applications for electronic books which have some potential – for example, encyclopaedias, as just mentioned. We recognize printed pages bound between covers as a book, but the contents are often as variable as chalk and cheese – examples include novels, dictionaries, telephone books, textbooks, anthologies, instruction manuals, proceedings of meetings, and directories.

Information in print will endure for many years because, inefficient as the paper book or journal may be, the fact is that at the presentation interface the print–human match is far better than the machine–human match, in terms both of information transfer and of human behaviour. For general browsing, reading, annotating, scanning news items, appreciating pictures or drawings, and being generally entertaining, print on paper is superior. A screen still cannot compete with printed pages in terms of ease of annotation, portability, convenience, quality, colour, aesthetics, immediate availability of large chunks, and, at least as important, the ease and speed with which large chunks may be ignored. Numerous tests through to the late 1980s nearly always showed that reading from a screen was slower than reading from print, but Maurer and Williams (1991) state that reading from computer screens can be equivalent in speed and comprehension to reading from a book. However, approximately 30 per cent of the activity of skilled readers can be characterized as skimming and skimming book text was 41 per cent faster than skimming screen text.

Print can be written on, carried about, and digested in aeroplanes, on trains, or in the bath. It looks nice on shelves, and makes a very acceptable gift. In newspaper form it continues to be used, even when all its information functions are over, as a heat-retaining fish and chips container.

> There is simply no experience in life that matches silent reading . . . readers make everything happen just the way they want it to. The actions, scenes, and voices in a book come to life entirely in the reader's mind . . . . Sometimes when I can't go to sleep I see the family of the future. Dressed in three-tone shorts and shirts of disposable papersilk they sit before the television wall of their apartment; only their eyes are moving.
>
> After I've looked for a while I always see – otherwise I'd die – a pigheaded soul in the corner with a book; only his eyes are moving but in them there is a different look.

So says Jennings (1983). I don't suppose that much has happened since then to change her mind.

ELECTRONIC JOURNALS

'When there isn't an electronic journal that fits a need, starting one requires only a computer, access to a network, and the will to succeed,' says the editor of an electronic journal. 'Our publication *Unplastic News* is really only a silly magazine with no real writing in it, yet we have thousands of readers.'

'It seems likely that the electronic journal will not soon replace the traditional journal format, which has served us so well for these many decades,' says Freeman (1987).

> Rather, more likely it will carve out its own niche by providing those kinds of services unique to the electronic medium, services which emphasize interactive capabilities with databases and other colleagues, the communication of brief and highly current information, as well as the handling of large blocks of statistical information so valuable to the scientific community.

Electronic journals, usually scientific in nature, compiled, edited, and 'published' using a computer, and disseminated via computer terminals, have been much discussed. At least two large experiments have been carried out. The first was at the New Jersey Institute of Technology and was called the Electronic Information Exchange System (EIES); two actual journals were published called *Chimo* and *The Mental Workload*. The second was a scheme carried out at the Universities of Loughborough and Birmingham sponsored by the British Library called the BLEND experiment. Journals called *Computer Human Factors*, *References and Abstracts*, and *Annotations Journal* were published.

Information 2000 (Martyn *et al.* 1990) say that

> in some areas printed [scientific and technical] journals may disappear because the major product of the system is data, and the deposit of data in a data bank may be accepted as the equivalent of a journal article. ... The 'publish or perish' syndrome may change ... publication on CD-ROM with the end users paying for each contribution printed down or downloaded may also lead to the effective demise of the journal structure.

Although *Information 2000* devotes seven pages to the electronic journal, it manages to avoid saying that no such journal has yet turned out to be commercially viable, although journals on the Internet might change that.

Humans are conservative and don't like to see a serious disturbance of well-established customs which more or less ensure that ability is rewarded. The sociology of science, hinging on established publication practices, has been thoroughly researched (Cole and Zuckerman 1975).

A journal called *Multimedia Forum* has been started at the German National Research Centre for IT. The journal is at present used in-house so it is not subjected to the pressures of the open marketplace. *Multimedia Forum* uses hypertext links to connect highlighted elements on a page to other pages which expand upon those elements. The structure of documents is described by the Standard Generalised Markup Language (SGML).

Pam Wadell conducted a study of the potential for electronic journals in UK academia (Wadell 1993). She defines an electronic journal as a series of refereed articles available either online, as a CD-ROM, or in any other electronic form. 'Little short-term growth is expected, but predictions for the longer term vary from no change to electronic journals taking over.' According to Wadell, publishers and learned societies are cautious and are concerned about revenues, pricing structures, and loss of subscriptions. However, many librarians are said to be enthusiastic, foreseeing the saving of money and space.

Keating *et al.* (1993) from the University of Houston are more enthusiastic. They consider that electronic journals are the serials' equivalent of Detroit's concept cars: fast, flashy, and future-oriented. The Keating *et al.* article is really a guideline to libraries about handling electronic journals; they recommend that they should receive the same cataloguing and classification treatment as printed journals. They conclude that 'electronic journals are vehicles of immense power and promise which are revolutionizing the transport of ideas and transforming the landscape of scholarly communication. They offer thrills, chills, and spills to their riders.'

If Wadell and Keating *et al.* are representative of opinion in Europe and the United States, opinions, to say the least of it, differ. There are now a number of other electronic journals which are available on the open market. Several are running on the Bitnet and Usenet networks in the US and they will soon be joined by *Current Clinical Trials* published by the AAAS. A number of others are shown below.

Some electronic journal titles
Boardwatch
Czech Republic Business Bulletin
Der Spiegel
Early Modern Literary Studies
E Journal
Electronic Journal of Communication
Electronic Letters Online
Issues in Science & Technology Librarianship
Knowledge Synthesis for Nursing
MC Journal
Medical Sciences Bulletin
Oak Ridge Nat. Laboratory Review
Online Educator
Online Journal of Clinical Trials
Wall St News

ELECTRONIC LIBRARIES

An electronic library is another name for an image database or very large multimedia encyclopaedia. The potential convenience, time-saving, and travelling-saving aspects of easily accessing and reading online from a display of the material in a library are currently receiving some attention.

Professor Mel Collier, de Montfort University, UK defines an electronic library as 'a managed environment of multimedia materials in digital form designed for the benefit of its user population, structured to facilitate access to its contents, and equipped with aids to navigation of the global network'.

The disappearance of printed books has been forecast, but usually electronic libraries are considered as an operation which will take place in parallel with conventional libraries. The time factor – that is, when an appreciable number of electronic libraries might be expected to be in place for general or even for specific types of publication – is rarely discussed.

Some librarians are enthusiastic about the prospects. Professor Peter Brophy says that the electronic library is an unparalleled opportunity to transcend the barriers of traditional library services and deliver information where, when, and in the form in which it is needed. It offers us the scope to meet user needs in new and exciting ways. There is no longer any question: the electronic library is the future – and it works!

If libraries are ever completely eliminated in favour of an electronic equivalent, that situation is a far future concept. Spending on printed books in the UK more than doubled, from £755 million to £1590 million between 1985 and 1992. Library loans increase annually – for instance from 240 million in 1992/93 to 251 million in 1993/94 (Policy Studies Institute report).

The most likely successes of electronic libraries will probably come in the fast-moving scientific and technical fields. For other fields a Policy Studies Institute report stated that library loans exceeding 200,000 were made in 1992/93 for the works of a number of major authors including Jane Austen, Charles Dickens, Thomas Hardy, D.H. Lawrence, A.A. Milne, Daphne du Maurier, Beatrix Potter, J.R.R. Tolkien, and Anthony Trollope.

An electronic library requires that all material be in machine-readable form. It is possible that publishers will eventually provide material ready to use in that form. Until then the digitization of a part or all of the existing material is the first and usually the most laborious operation. Pages must be scanned and digitized using a scanning machine. Questions about this conversion operation and other electronic library considerations are shown below.

Electronic library considerations
- How time-consuming and costly would it be to convert printed material – that is text, 6 point references, halftones and illustrations into machine readable form?
- What are the storage implications?
- How would the material be indexed?
- How would copyright be managed?
- How could a system be assessed?
- What barriers, if any, are there in reading different kinds of material from a display instead of from a book?

If the pages to be digitized are separate and in pristine form, they may be managed like the paper in a copying machine.

Unfortunately, this ideal state does not normally exist in a library. Quite a lot of the material may be book pages and the pages must be turned over to scan both sides. If separate pages from reports and other easily separated material without a permanent binding are to be scanned, they may be of different sizes with edges which are not flat. Scanning procedure must be properly organized. The material to be scanned must be retrieved from the library, queued, scanned, indexed, and replaced on the shelves. Those involved in scanning operations are inclined to talk about simply the time taken by the machine, not the overall time for the complete operation. Arbitrarily assuming that the average overall scanning time is 1 minute per page, that a member of the scanning staff works 100,000 minutes per year, and that an average book has 300 pages, about 330 books could be scanned by one staff member per annum.

Some information is available about scanning operations. Galbraith (1993), in an article which should be read by anyone involved in this activity, does not provide any information about scanning rates, probably because of wide variations in scanning circumstances. Dale and Mitchell (1993) say that it takes an average of 1.18 minutes for the operations of filing a 'document' manually, but do not say what it takes with their scanning system. Ramsden (personal communication 1993) and Wu *et al.* (1995) claim to be able to scan (excluding associated tasks) single separate sheets of one size at the rate of about 5 seconds per page.

Several other projects are in progress to look at alternative methods for publishing and delivering full text possibly with $3" \times 2"$ 300×300 pixel 8-bit images (about 4.32 Mbits or 540 Kbytes) as quarter page graphics. Even full pages $8" \times 6"$ 300×300 in 24-bit colour (13 Mbyte) compressed 100:1 to 130 Kbytes are likely to become achievable. The EURILIA and DIADEM projects led by Cranfield University are of particular interest.

When you are confronted with information, the way in which it is presented is related to the rate at which it may be ignored – an important consideration. There is no screen-manipulating facility comparable with the rate of ignoring what you don't want out of the mass of information packed into, say, the *Financial Times*. There are some major aspects to be considered when assessing the feasibility of the idea, as listed above.

Storage requirements are also likely to vary greatly. Again taking an average, if a 300-page book contains 100 $3" \times 2"$ 300×300 pixel per inch 8-bit halftone illustrations and 250 pages of text, it will require about 60 Mbytes of storage. Some 5000 books in online storage would require 300 Tbytes of storage space. Good indexing is time-consuming, as already discussed. Wu *et al.* (1995) use Pixtex/EFS software for automatically indexing scanned images. Pixtex works by fuzzy-matching the pattern of a user's word question against the most likely matching text in the database. Most-likely pattern matching technique will still work in the face of errors. However, unless indexing terms are added to database text, 'automatic' means that an indexer's interpretation is absent, so the system is as good as matching query words against existing words in the text permits it to be.

The question of resolving problems associated with the use and payment for copyright material is discussed in chapter 7. Assessing the effectiveness of an electronic library is bound up with the provision of a large enough body of representative assessors operating under real world conditions to compare its effectiveness with that of a real library. The question of the acceptability of reading a book from a screen was discussed above in connection with electronic books.

Wu *et al.* (1995) provide some interesting information about the ELINOR electronic library at de Montfort University, UK – the major participant in a European research project. This project recognizes most, if not all, of the problems listed on page 320. For the moment it escapes most of them by working with a database of a limited number of course papers which can be conveniently scanned, rather than with books. Some books are also being used which are cut up for scanning purposes and rebound. Up to 3 Gbytes of material are stored. Line drawings but not material in halftones or colour are processed, and copyright agreements limited to material used for the research projects have been concluded.

User studies on a random sample of eight students have taken place at de Montfort. This sample appears to have been somewhat unenthusiastic about the system in comparison with a print library. Testing information systems always presents a problem. How comprehensive must a test be to truly represent the results which would be obtained on a scaled-up real world system? In spite of the problems we must assume that they will be overcome in due course and multimedia libraries will become common place. Information obtained from the ELINOR project will accelerate the arrival process.

Another form of electronic library – a pilot project arranged between Tilburg University in the Netherlands and Elsevier Science Publishers – is being tested using the full text of 114 Elsevier journals (Dijkstra 1994). Tilburg is also a partner in the ELINOR project discussed above. Dijkstra's definition of an electronic library is

A library which has the look and feel of a paper oriented library but where library systems have been digitized and archived.

It can be accessed in a networked environment, and where, in addition, users can obtain, even remotely, admittance from behind their desks, and which offers users advanced automated electronic services controlled by sophisticated and integrated automated systems such as open client-server architecture.

Tilburg adopted Carnegie-Mellon's MERCURY software, a standard interface for different databases, and converted it from Unix to PC use adding Z39.50 protocol in a networked client-server system. Over 2000 386SX or 486SX machines, of which 400 are in the library, are connected to a Novell LAN with an FDDI backbone. The full text of the Elsevier journals is scanned and digitized and users are offered a press-button page image ordering service following a database search. Additionally users may browse the tables of contents of the journals. Dijsktra describes the interconnection of this system with other systems in progress at Tilburg and discusses the availability of material from it via Internet's World Wide Web and Mosaic.

Olney (1995) reports progress at the Online Computer Library Center (OCLC – originally the Ohio College Library Center), where during daytime peak online transactions proceed at 100 per second with 4000 simultaneous users. A major project called GUIDON is a windows-based system for the delivery of electronic journals online. OCLC publish the *Online Journal of Current Clinical Trials* jointly with the American Association for the Advancement of Science – the first electronic journal to be included in the MEDLINE medical service. It is peer reviewed and uses the SGML format for typeset text and graphics. OCLC also publish a journal called *Knowledge Synthesis for Nursing* and *Electronics Letters Online*. The American Institute of Physics has agreed that OCLC should publish *Applied Physics Letters*.

The GUIDON system will shortly be able to deliver halftone or colour images. A somewhat similar project called RightPages has been announced by AT&T and articles published in Springer journals. In this system users are alerted by an e-mail message when an article matches their previously supplied profile of interests and page images are delivered from regional servers over the Internet.

Chapter 12

Home and consumer applications

PROGRESS OF SYSTEMS IN THE HOME

A recent article entitled 'Saturday night at the home cinema' implied that readers would have sufficient disposable income to be interested in grandiose hi-fi, perhaps motivated by the 'keeping up with the Joneses syndrome'. The article stresses the importance of Nicam (Near Instantaneous Companded Audio Multiplex) for TV sound, and 'An AV amp – a big bruiser of a machine with a rear panel which would shame a vintage telephone exchange made by the usual suspects' – together with numerous strategically positioned loudspeakers. Unfortunately, even a technically excellent home cinema is no substitute for the social pleasure of going out to the movies.

There have been several notable failures in home/professional multimedia-type offerings including the RCA grooved-capacitance videodisk, Prestel, the AT&T Knight-Ridder videotex service, and the AT&T Picturephone believed to have cost $500 million to develop; similar systems called Visitel and Phonovision also failed.

A BT engineer (although BT have just offered yet another similar device) commented: 'Few of us have total control over our appearance. We may be less attracted to the idea of a videophone since with an audio-only system we may cloak our advancing decay in the mystery of the disembodied voice.'

There will always be members of the public prepared to experiment with new gadgets and who have the necessary disposable income. But most people seem content with information systems which are adequate for their needs, involve no capital expenditure, no technical knowledge, and no making-to-work or maintenance problems. Why should they look any further than their newspapers and magazines? On the other hand, they have somehow afforded television sets and tape recorders so is there some gadget coming along which we will be unable to do without, which will both entertain us and raise our propensity to acquire information (effortlessly of course), as well?

A brief mention must be included about recent attempts within the general area of multimedia to extend information technology in the home. They include home banking, home networks ('buses') for domestic system control, general domestic technology, and the area where most progress has been made – home shopping.

'Home banking' describes a service for calling up a bank for information about a bank account, transferring money from one account to another, paying bills, etc. from a home terminal, using an interactive videotex or cable system connected to a bank.

In the UK the Nottinghamshire Building Society announced its Homelink service in 1982, believed to be the first in the UK of its type. By 1984 it was said to have several thousand users. In February 1991 the Bank of Scotland offered a lightweight portable terminal for its Home and Office Banking Service free if a minimum of £500 was kept in their account. Alternatively, the terminal could be purchased for £95. It plugs into a telephone socket. However, home banking does not yet seem to have been widely adopted.

A home bus is a within-home network to interconnect and control electronic devices usually from a central control point, and to enable users to control devices for delivering entertainment. Philips was a pioneer in the early 1980s with its 1980 D^2B bus, a simple interconnect and control scheme enabling a control device to manage other devices connected to a two-wire bus. Since that time work on developing buses has continued.

By 1985 the matter had become of sufficient interest to warrant a whole issue of the Institute of Electrical and Electronics Engineers magazine *Spectrum*. In that year engineers were starting to think about Standards. The cable and television industries had developed their products with little regard for interconnection.

By 1986, telecommunications for hi-tech homes were becoming more widely discussed. In Germany it was thought that broadband telecoms would start to be used in homes between 1990 and 1995. Restrictions on all types of service would largely disappear with the arrival of the broadband ISDN. Video communication would be the major home application. A number of remotely controlled services, such as meter reading, would be introduced.

In 1987 it was announced that Thorn-EMI, Philips, Thomson, Siemens, GEC, and Electrolux would get together to agree Standards on how signals would be exchanged between appliances connected to a home network. They planned to spend at least £12 million on the exercise during 1987/88, but there was not much to show for it.

At the Chicago 1987 International Summer Consumer Electronics Show, Mitsubishi demonstrated a home system controlled from touch-tone telephones or radio. Steve Wozniak's new company, CL9, showed a programmable master controller for most infrared controllable equipment such as stereo, tape recorders, TVs, and satellite receivers. By 1987 the CEBUS home bus Standard with a software protocol based on the 7-layer OSI model had been drafted.

In 1988 a CEC Eureka two-year programme was put in hand to define a European Standard by which domestic appliances could be interconnected by a common bus network. A similar Standard was being prepared by the electronic industry in Japan.

In October 1989 details of the Consumer Electronic Bus Standard for CEBUS were still being hammered out by a committee of the Electronic Industries Association (EIA) working groups in the United States. The Standard will count as successful only if people buy home-control networks and products. 'All that remains is to add the interface device that connects the appliance to the media and converts the incoming home-automation message into a code the appliance's microprocessor understands. It should cost $10 or less,' claimed an enthusiast.

In 1989 a company called AISI Research was marketing a $5 chip for controlling information transmission to devices connected to CEBUS. By 1992 the EIA CEBUS Committee completed its work on a Standard method for controlling and monitoring home appliances. The above brief review covers over ten years, but it is not at all clear whether the effort has produced any benefits.

Passing on to general multimedia-type technology in homes, in a 1980 home-computer survey of a university community's applications in the United States, 20 per cent of the 1313 responses received were for game-playing, 15 per cent for text creation, 10 per cent for record-keeping of various kinds, and 5 per cent for budgets. Among smaller usages were 2 per cent for keeping recipes and 1.5 per cent for other household applications.

In 1981 Warner-Amex Qube Cable inaugurated some special services for the home. The sensors in a home security system could be connected to the local police station, smoke detectors to the local fire station, and an emergency button to the local ambulance service. Furthermore, Qube ran a 'push-button voting system' to enable subscribers to provide yes–no answers to questions posed on TV followed by a display of the totalled results.

In the UK in 1984, it was estimated that about 3.5 million microcomputers were in use, of which about 90 per cent were used solely for games. 'It is hard to think of a single domestic application which can be cost justified,' said one observer. Another said: 'Educational software has performed solidly to the extent of accounting for half of all software sales into the home.' But a later report considered that 'a large number of consumers must have a basic level of computer literacy to make computing in the home viable. . . . Standards are absolutely necessary for success in the home computer marketplace.'

With regard to video entertainment over a telecoms channel, one writer identified the key issue:

Although a rented videotape must be collected and returned, the cost, at about $0.50 an hour of usage, compares favourably with local telephone service at about $2 per hour.

Could the progress of technology become so rapid as to provide 4.5 MHz of video bandwidth for $0.50 an hour, when 4 KHz of telephone bandwidth presently costs $2 per hour?

According to an August 1992 forecast, although the multimedia 'consumer/entertainment' sector shared 18 per cent of a $626 million market in 1991, the same sector is forecast to share 55 per cent of a $12.4 billion market by 1996 – an increase of over 6000 times.

Domestic 'needs' may be classified as follows

- Commercial in-home
  Database, financial, shopping, security, entertainment, work-at-home
- Public in-home
  Network infrastructure, electronic mail, news, local schedules and emergency information, home security network
- Government in-home
  Government information, emergency services, polling, automated billing, local government bulletin boards

Home shopping with pictures, text, and sound, is a multimedia method of viewing, ordering, and paying for goods without leaving home, usually implying some form of interactive viewing system.

The Japanese started the Hi-Ovis scheme in 1976 in which 71 of the participants in experiments over a fibreoptic network used the 'home shopping' service which ran for a year in the Tokyo area. Still-picture transmission of goods was used as a substitute for a sales catalogue. Subscribers, using a TV display, could select, order, and pay without leaving home. The service was 'well accepted', although 'ways of improving the quality of TV broadcasting are needed', said a report. The service was supplied free. The total cost of Hi-Ovis was 25 billion yen – about $150 million. It is not known how much of this cost could be attributed to the home shopping experiment.

One of the earliest attempts in the United States was implemented by Teleaction, a J.C. Penney company. Experiments in Chicago using 125,000 'test households' gave 'positive' results. Shoppers could browse or shop by product category and 'could get close-ups of certain features and a detailed voice-over description'. Special technical arrangements, no doubt necessary to provide adequate bandwidth/resolution, were made by using 'shared facilities'. They included a local frame grabber relaying pictures (presumably a succession of frames at a rate of about one per second per household) to up to 40 households connected to a cable-TV video channel on a cable network. Customers issued their commands on a separate narrow-band telecoms channel – the PSTN. They dialled a special phone number using a standard 'touch-tone' telephone as a key pad.

In 1985 Littlewoods and Great Universal Stores in the UK started teleshopping services and Comp-U-Card set up a networked service for Commodore microcomputer users to access a database of 22,000 items, order, and pay by credit card. Several pioneering examples using Prestel were described in the following year.

In 1987 ex-Acorn founder Chris Curry planned to give away 500,000 simplified Prestel-like machines for home shopping, shops on the system being charged a 5 per cent commission on goods ordered. In this case the system was said to be able to accept everyday language commands.

In 1988 a company called Trintex, jointly owned by IBM and Sears Roebuck (CBS, a co-founder, pulled out), started to test their 'Prodigy' home shopping system, in which customers use their own home computers. The system provided for the necessarily slow transmission of images (limited by the bandwidth of a telephone line) with, like the text information, attached advertisements necessary to generate the revenue.

It is still hoped that a system called Keyline will be launched in the UK. Development costs will be £500,000 and 500,000 terminals are to be distributed free. The membership fee will be £50 and over 17 companies are committed to the system. In phase one, terminals will be provided for thousands of customers as a test activity. The terminal, to be plugged in to a telephone socket, includes a 1200 bps full duplex modem. It is said that it has enough spare capacity for managing electronic mail or holding a personal diary or phone directory. Keyline has reached an agreement with Mercury for communications over its X25 packet-switched network and all calls will be charged at the local rate. It will be competing with a number of less ambitious home shopping services running on Prestel.

Little is said these days about the need for the realistic presentation in colour of the goods for sale with a resolution at least as good as current 625-line TV – a feature of the Hi-Ovis system. Prestel, of course, is unable to provide anything but the most simple graphics. Home shopping providers seem to have resigned themselves for the time being to the bandwidth-imposed limitations allowing lists, descriptions, easy payments to be made, etc. (but see Teleaction below), without pictures.

The representation of goods on a CRT screen raises questions about realism. 'In the catalog home shopping business, one of the most common reasons for returning merchandise is that color does not meet the buyer's expectations' (Anon. 1995a). From a printed colour catalogue a human sees reflected colour; in a multimedia system it is transmitted from a CRT. Not only that, objects printed in colour, or for that matter the objects themselves, look different depending upon the colour spectrum of the light source. Some interesting comments are made in the discussion in this article (Anon. 1995a) which forms its main substance. One participant considers that it is colour that sells an item, and it's taken for granted that CRT colour is realistic. However, as another participant observes, people have different expectations for colour, 'engrained in their heads', just as they have different expectations for a variety of other factors in newspapers, television, or at the cinema.

It is suggested that 'With digital media you could easily make a calibration routine part of the log-on procedure'. This remark demonstrates the gulf that exists between engineers and ordinary people. However, another participant asked: 'if people are unable to set the clocks on their Video Cassette Recorders how can they be expected to colour-calibrate their multimedia receivers?'

CD-ROM might become an attractive method of distributing high-quality 'catalogues'. Lists, ordering, payments, etc. would be provided via an inter-active online terminal, with CD pictures triggered automatically for TV presentation.

Some comprehensive information about teleshopping comes from Jonathan Reynolds (1990, 1990/91). Reynolds was supported by retailers, notably Tesco Ltd, to enable him to do some thorough research. 'In the United States, J.C. Penney closed its Teleaction service in April 1989 with the company announcing write-off costs of $20 million on top of the $106 million already invested,' says Reynolds. One interesting aspect of this system was an attempt to overcome the barrier, even on a relatively wideband cable system, of presenting satisfactory images.

The IBM/Sears Prodigy system, which started with 10,000 subscribers in 1988, is claimed now to have over a million. By 1990 $600 million had been invested in it including 1000 man-years of work. A subscription costs $9.95 a month; it uses a videotex system. Reynolds provides a list of Prodigy's problems headed: 'Technology rather than customer led?: Limitations of display technology: Appropriate equipment?: Is Prodigy 15 years too early?' He includes a discussion of its advantages, namely: 'Large capital investment . . . willingness to commit to long term payback . . . well thought out and executed'. He also says that 'the respectability and track record of the main players in Prodigy may mean that these players can achieve success where others have failed . . . brand strength has been a critical factor'. Prodigy was still losing money in 1993.

Under the heading 'Hard lesson in the UK', Reynolds lists a number of benefits/requirements for home shopping systems: 'Speed of home delivery: Quality of service: Up-to-dateness: Prompt handling of returns: Ease of use: Reliability: Customer cost.' He discusses several UK systems which have failed because of the unsatisfactory nature of one or more of these items.

Of the French Minitel 'Supers à domicile' service, Reynolds says that the suppliers, given the critical mass of home teleservice users required to understand the characteristics of the marketplace, have targeted a customer base consisting of people open to the use of technology. They belong to households with children, within socio-economic groups which would permit them effectively to buy additional leisure time through the use of the tele-shopping distribution channel. He supplies a table of users and their reasons for using Minitel. Home deliveries and speed are the prime reasons. Like Prodigy, Minitel, when properly costed, is also steadily losing money.

US home shopping networks achieved a turnover of more than $3.5 billion in 1989, but home shopping in the United States should not be used for forecasting progress in Europe because it occupies a very particular niche. People have a high propensity to consume through mail order. The home shopper is a very different animal from those traditionally thought of as target markets for teleshopping.

Reynolds says that many consumers see teleshopping as an inevitable development but are not ready to welcome it with open arms. Fundamental social changes arising out of the incremental adoption of teleshopping are unlikely to take place in the 1990s. He identifies four key opportunities in the UK over the longer term:

- The opportunity to make shopping for essential goods easier.
- The opportunity to improve the quality of the non-essential shopping trip by providing additional choice within the home.
- The opportunity to ease the transfer of time from essential to non-essential shopping activity.
- The opportunity to inform the buying decision better.

Games

Games or to give them their more impressive title 'Interactive home enter-tainment', embody all the current ingenuity that multimedia programmers can provide. The small consoles dedicated to games from companies like Nintendo and Sega, where each game comes in a small plug-in cartridge, are an attempt to procure ongoing sales for more cartridges.

However, games on CD-ROMs and CDs have gained ground by reason of the falling price of drives and increasing PC processing power able to provide full-motion video, high-resolution graphics, high-quality sound, and fast decompression. The speed of games requires that 486 machines (at least) must be used otherwise the action will be slow. However, the fastest PC or Mac available is not essential for all CD games. For example, Links Pro from Access Software at a remarkable low $70 (£37 from Trinity Systems in the UK) featuring golf on the Harbour Town links, is intrinsi-cally fast as it is written in assembly code. Links Pro works best on a Power Mac but will run quite well on other Macs. A user selects clubs, shot type, direction, etc. for a golfer depicted on any of the holes, and the figure of a golfer strikes the ball, which falls according to the settings (Figure 12.1).

In 1994 Virgin Games' The Seventh Guest was considered to be one of the best CD-ROM games of 1994. It includes MIDI composed music, sound

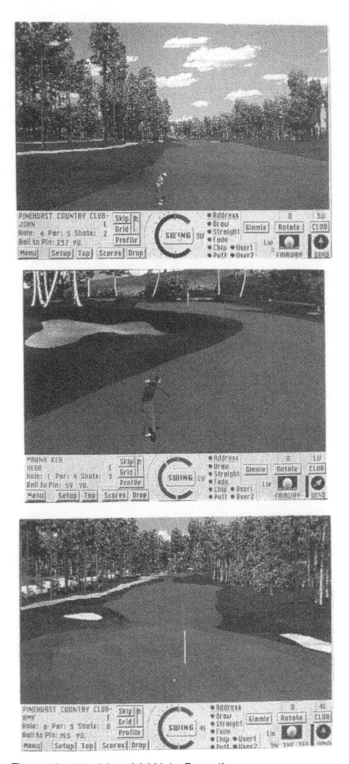

Figure 12.1 (a), (b) and (c) Links Pro golf

Source: Access Software

effects, morphing, and rendered 3D animation. All it requires to run it is clicks from a mouse. An improved version was produced for CD-I DV which removes the jerkiness from animated sequences.

Philips have introduced a number of games for CD-I such as Voyeur. It uses a new technique, also adopted in The Seventh Guest, where actors are superimposed on the background.

Under a Killing Moon from US Gold is supplied on 4 disks containing over 2 Gbytes of data. If run with a multimedia PC, this game of intrigue with good sound effects and speech is thought to be one of the best.

Chapter 13

Medical multimedia networks

One particular technique is not usually referred to as multimedia although it includes all the necessary ingredients for that label – CCD cameras, image capture and enhancement on workstations, associated text, voice, data compression, drawing tools, pattern matching, high-resolution displays, and high-speed networks. Everything is ready to be seized upon by the multimedia generalists as an example of an application which has taken hold to the extent that a complete issue of a journal has been devoted it.

Although singled out for special mention in the Ovum report mentioned below, the reason for its obscurity until recently is that it comes within the orbit of medicine, not information technology. I first came across it in a piece by Cowen (1989) about its use at Leeds University, and later, in full strength, as described by numerous authors in *Computerized Medical Imaging and Graphics* 15(3), 1991, pages 147–203. I am referring to Picture Archiving and Communication Systems or PACS. PACS systems embody new developments which are of interest to anyone involved in multimedia.

The objectives of PACS are to digitize, display, and if necessary enhance images captured by computed tomography, magnetic resonance, computed radiography, and other techniques, and bring order and accessibility via wideband networks to the files of film in which they are stored. PACS were called (uniquely to my knowledge) multimedia by Karmouch *et al.* (1991) in a French journal. This is a useful short review of PACS by some researchers from the Telecoms Research Institute of Ottawa. PACS include many interesting database, communications, and application activities. One aspect of multimedia which is steadily attracting more interest is how to deal with the immense amount of data required to represent high-quality pictures. This is a major issue in PACS systems. A computed radiography image contains $2000 \times 2000 \times 10$ bits = 40 Mbits of data. Wide bandwidths are needed for the networks which transport these data.

The Ultranet network with Sun Sparcservers type 490 connected to it is used to satisfy the general PACS yardstick of 4 Megabytes/32 Mbits per second (Stewart *et al.* 1991) data rates. The total data rate in the Ultranet hub required to manage five client-server exchanges of data is nearly 14 Megabytes/112 Megabits per second. At these speeds optical fibre with the FDDI Standard will be appropriate.

Since indexing images in a collection is a problem area, the piece by Taira *et al.* (1991) in the above journal about databases is of some interest. But there is no mention of any consequence about indexing or its problems in this or any of the articles in this journal.

The prototype of a new type of PACS system, described by Badaoui *et al.* (1993), is being used in France to handle 180,000 images. There are three parts to the system – the interface, a part which translates a user's query into a form understood by the system, and a dictionary containing the structure of the image data. In the French system a special relational database is used to retrieve images, associated descriptive data, and related documents such as reports. Other medical applications are mentioned in the Video-conferencing section in chapter 17.

New medical applications continue to be reported. Mezrich *et al.* (1995) describe a system for sending reports with images to referring physicians or consultant radiologists and for teaching purposes via the Internet:

- To demonstrate a mechanism for the distribution of patient reports with images;
- To provide a means for radiologists to exchange images for consultation and review;
- To provide teaching files of interesting cases to a wide audience;
- To provide universal access to a large database;
- To explore the use of interactive multimedia techniques including sound and cine to teach anatomy, pathology, and radiology to students at remote sites.

The data are managed on a server at a hospital in New Brunswick, N.J. and clients are distributed throughout the world. The server is a Mac Quadra 650 with a 1.5 Gbyte disk drive. Images from a GE imaging system are transferred as a $256 \times 256 \times 8$-bit array (about 65 Kbytes uncompressed) in Mac PICT format or in Graphics Interchange Format (GIF). JPEG 15:1 compression is used. Thumbnails 64×64 pixel are used as a form of index to the main images. Various kinds of client computers are used such as Mac IIxs, 486 PCs, and Sun Sparcstations. In late 1994 an average of 77 files were transmitted per day to 23 different countries in North America, Europe, and Australia. Indexes may be searched using words describing age, sex, examination reason, etc., but not patients' names. Delays in transmission are acceptable; the images, compressed by 10:1, occupy only about 6 Kbytes. The authors claim that the quality of the images when viewed remotely is similar to those viewed locally. It is surprising that original 256 $\times$ 265 images with 256 halftones are adequate for radiological detail.

A system being used between hospitals in Pittsburgh which employs diagnostic and monitoring techniques during brain surgery is described by Simon *et al.* (1995). It provides information for about 1600 cases every year. A neurotechnician operates a MedNet node during an operation or for diagnostic purposes and various tests are run which may be monitored with video images of the operation. An example is given showing electrical waveforms recorded during an operation in which a neurophysiologist observing the waveforms at a different hospital noted an abnormality when the operating surgeon clamped the right carotid artery. The surgeon was immediately informed and took the necessary remedial action. Multi-way communications are a part of the system.

The functional requirements of the system are as follows:

- Simultaneous acquisition and distribution of video, audio, neurophysiological, and autonomic data
- Real-time display and analysis of digital data acquired locally and remotely
- A reliable system for monitoring and collaboration
- Dependable convenient storage of all data

Digital information is carried on an Ethernet LAN with video conveyed on wideband cable. The network interconnects 44 operating rooms, 2 interventional neuroradiology rooms, 20 intensive care beds, 10 diagnostic laboratories, and several research labs. Each multimedia site, such as a workstation or a laboratory, receives a collection of data streams from different devices and measures are taken to ensure a given Quality of Service (QOS) – for example, stream synchronization.

Chapter 14

Museums and art applications

ORGANIZATIONS AND PUBLICATIONS

In sheer numbers of applications this field is at least as well known as any other because it is well organized and publicized. Much of the information provided in this section comes from the publications:

Archives and Museum Informatics   David Bearman
5501 Walnut St
Suite 203
Pittsburgh PA 15232-2311
USA

International Visual Arts Information   Jeremy Rees
   Network (IVAIN)   Isobel Pring
Suffolk College
Rope Walk
Ipswich
Suffolk 1P4 1LT
England

Museum Documentation Association
347 Cherry Hinton Rd
Cambridge
Cambs. CB1 4DH
England

Vasari Ltd   Dr James Hemsley
Clark House
Kings Rd
Fleet
Hants GU13 9AD
England

Journals and newsletters covering this field include:

Archives and Museum Informatics
5501 Walnut St
Suite 203
Pittsburgh PA 15232-2311
USA

Art Documentation
Art Libraries Society of America
c/o Rutgers University Art Library
New Brunswick
NJ 08903
USA

Chart Newsletter
Computers and the History of Art
43 Gordon Square
London WC1
England

MuseMedia
Sharon Kayne Chaplock
557 North 68th St
Milwaukee WI 53213-3954
USA

Museum Management &
  Curatorship
Butterworth Heinemann
Linacre House
Jordan Hill
Oxford OS2 8DP
England

Visual Resources
Fine Arts Library
Fogg Art Museum
Harvard University
Cambridge MA 02138
USA

The above list is a selection from a larger list published in *Archives and Museum Informatics*.

IVAIN publish a directory called Image Technology in Museums and Galleries (ITEM). Its major function is to provide short progress reports about projects in progress. The issues referred to here are 7 (1993) and 8 (1994).

The Museum Documentation Association publishes museum user lists of computer systems and software.

VASARI organizes an annual conference and exhibition at the National Gallery, London called the Electronic Imaging and Visual Arts conference (EVA). The 1993 and 1994 conference Proceedings and conference papers published in *Information Services and Use* are referred to here.

MUSEUM SYSTEMS

Multimedia systems are used in many museums and art galleries and pictures are the most important component in many of them. Lunin (1990) says: 'Increasingly museums and art departments are investigating the tremendous potential of videodisc and optical disc technology for projects such as collections management, research, fund raising, visitor interpretation and education, and exhibition design.'

According to Besser (1991):

Many museums, archives, and libraries have fine arts collections of either original objects or of surrogate images (such as slides) of original objects.

The items in these collections (be they original objects or surrogate images) are often either too large (wall sized), too small (slides), or too fragile both to attract textual explanatory material to them and to retrieve them easily when someone needs to examine them.

In an introductory piece to the proceedings of a recent conference Bearman (1991a) says:

Since the early 20th century museums have tried to be more than 'cabinets of curiosity' to be viewed passively. We may now witness the latest efforts to interact more assertively with visitors, but despite the introduction of new technology, they represent a continuity more than a radical departure.

Woolsey and Semper (1991) of Apple (San Francisco) point out that there are over 10,000 museums and visitor and science centres in the US which are visited by more than 50 million people every year.

Multimedia offers to people working in public space a set of new and exciting tools to augment their 3D displays and a way to extend the experience of visitors to greater depth and other environments. Through access to rich interactive kiosks in museums, for example, it is possible for visitors to move from a glancing experience to a deeper involvement with an underlying idea.

Although 'multimedia/hypermedia (M/H)' used to mean systems for providing on-screen presentations with text and line drawings, it now often means presentation systems with text, graphics, still or motion pictures, and sound. There is still a considerable gulf between the usefulness of M/H as claimed by the hardware/software hyper-authors responsible for pushing it onto the market, and its actual useful practical applications. This gulf is gradually narrowing and many museum and art applications are reported. Visser (1993) defines four different types of art/museum multimedia systems:

- Documentary, providing library/encyclopaedic information primarily for professional users
- General information covering a wide range of topics intended for the general public
- Supporting information system, for instance for use at exhibitions, etc., for providing limited information
- Point of information' stand-alone systems associated with a collection

Bearman reports on the failure of a number of museum projects due to lack of funds. The RAMA European Inter-Museum project was unable to pursue its telecommunications objectives. James Hemsley reviews 'Design and development of systems for museums and galleries' (Hemsley 1993b). He suggests that matters arising for a 'new paradigm' are as follows:

- Rising user power
- Increasing importance of 'content software' versus 'computer software'
- The switch from computing technology to two technologies – computing and video (multimedia) and then the inclusion of a third – telecommunications
- Increasing speed of technological change
- International collaborative efforts

In the United States, support seems very patchy. Scott Sayre (1993), in describing some activities at the Minneapolis Institute of Art in 'The evolution of interactive interpretive media', says that the Institute received $1 million from the General Mills Foundation for the development of interactive video programs.

Ruth Perlin (1993) from the National Gallery of Art, Washington, writes that their work was funded by the Annenberg Foundation 'including provision for giving 2,500 copies of the videodisc to educational institutions in every state'.

Philip Yenawine says in 'Multimedia and the politics of museum organisational change' (Yenawine, 1993) that

> we were unable to organise any forums for discussing specific issues involved for museums in multimedia publishing ... any attempt to get a large community of museum people to think beyond rather narrow and institution-bound issues, particularly considering policies with regard to reproduction rights and fees for 'venture' projects in multimedia, proved unproductive.

Yenawine is obviously disillusioned about the whole business, because he concludes: 'although we have given up all staff and our office because of the lack of funds, we still exist as an organisation ... etc.' These remarks have the same tone as comments made by David Bearman, editor of *Archives and Museum Informatics*, the co-publishers of the Proceedings containing Yenawine's contribution.

A number of advantages are claimed for multimedia in museums (Valls, 1994):

- Improved access to a collection with the minimum of risk
- Improved access to the content; visual as well as textual information available at the same time
- Greater ease in the research and planing for exhibitions
- Support for educational activities
- Interchange of information either by disk or telecoms link
- Saving of storage space
- Reduction in dependence upon verbal descriptions
- Active exhibition or working with the objects
- Reduction in cost of computer equipment needed for information maintenance

Valls also points out that there are a number of problems of several kinds – legal, technological, standardization, and resources.

Copyright presents some serious difficulties, particularly because the collecting societies have not formulated a policy for data in this form. The problem is taken seriously to the extent that difficulties in locating and negotiating with a number of object owners make some museum authorities avoid images in databases, thus lowering their completeness.

Some museums also think that the rapid rate of progress in image systems could quickly make image projects obsolete. Museums are making efforts to deal with incompatibility problems. The International Council on Museums has formed a task force within its Documentation Committee with a view to proposing an ISO Standard. The College of Art Association and the Getty Trust Art History Information Program have also sponsored a task force to work on Standards for descriptions and exchange of data.

IVAIN/ITEM

A further description of current multimedia systems in the arts in reference book form has been published by the International Visual Arts Information Network – IVAIN. Jeremy Rees (IVAIN, Ipswich, 1993) points out that although CEC funding is very welcome, the tackling of projects jointly by several institutions, encouraged by the CEC, adds to costs and complexity. Rees also says that funding under IMPACT is 'very modest'. He continues: 'one of the biggest problems facing any serious interactive multimedia project is one of distribution. As yet there is not a well developed means of point of sale access to such resources.' He asks whether people will be prepared to spend at least £100, sight unseen, on a CD-ROM or CD-I purchased at a bookshop or electrical shop.

A hundred and thirty-nine projects in 16 different countries are listed in IVAIN 1993, classified in various ways. Their titles include 'The Art Loss Register', 'Canal Builder', 'Journeys through London', 'Geology Information Programme', 'National Museum of Denmark Image Database', 'Uffizi Project', 'Interactive Multimedia Project for Diffusion of Energy Concepts' – to give a few examples of project diversity. 'Journeys through London', for instance, being prepared for CD-I using information from the Museum of London, will comprise journeys made from Roman times onwards, during which the 'traveller' may explore topography, architecture, society, and occupations.

Many of these 139 projects describe multimedia systems used within museums and art galleries but 40 of them have resulted or will result in published multimedia titles for wider use: 62.5 per cent of these are on videodisk, 12.5 per cent on CD-I, 7.5 per cent are on Macintoshes and the remainder on CD-ROM XA, CDTV, and PCs.

As Isobel Pring says in her Introduction to IVAIN 1993, this situation reflects multimedia's brief history, in which videodisk was for a time the only option. A videodisk will store about 54,000 NTSC analogue TV pictures providing an hour-long TV programme if used for that purpose. This emphasizes the only major disadvantage when changing to digital systems – the much greater bandwidth required for a digital picture system.

It appears as if other advantages of CD technology, advances in compression techniques, the rapid drop in price of players, and the versatility of systems such as photo-CD will result in these systems being adopted, presumably at the expense of videodisk.

Thirty-six new museum and art projects are listed in ITEM Issue 8 (Pring 1993–4) in the fields of visual arts and design, particularly modern and comtemporary art. Many more projects are listed later in this chapter.

EVA

At the 1992 EVA meeting, little was said about indexing problems in any of the papers, although I gave a short paper about the basic requirements.

A number of papers were delivered at the 1993 EVA conference (Hemsley 1993a). They covered descriptions of systems in use, existing and proposed telecommunications, and the acquisition, storage, display, and publication of images. Digital systems are used exclusively in those papers where a particular medium was mentioned. No new projects were described using videodisks.

I could find mention of indexing in only one other paper at the 1993 meeting – by Lewis and Draycott. They described the preparation of 56,000 pictures to be included in the Wellcome Institute's History of Medicine project. A 'cataloging' operation is included in the flowpath diagram provided, but that is the sum total of the comments about indexing.

Images are usually included in museum multimedia systems. Such systems are now becoming quite widely used in art galleries and museums. They may be interactive in order to encourage the participation of visitors who are otherwise passive observers. Multimedia used to be labelled 'a technique looking for an application' – a label which is no longer applicable in the arts field. Four of the projects described in the EVA papers are supported by CEC, ESPRIT, RACE, or IMPACT funding.

The variety of projects discussed illustrates the current range of electronic imaging activities. Three papers are about multimedia projects in museums. There are also three papers covering the subject of the intercommunication of imaging data. Other papers cover conservation, high-quality colour reproduction of pictures, historical applications, copyright, and indexing. The Apple Macintosh microcomputer is often used – it comes across as the dominant platform. Kodak photo-CD receives a mention as a very promising newcomer.

One of the first networked museum and art systems is at Delhi, India, and is described by Chaudhry and Roy (1990). The large inter-museum system described here, called the Access to Museum Archives (RAMA) telecoms system, is to be used for inter-museum access to databases. Planned PTT links will probably now be Internet links, as discussed below.

Delouis (1993) describes problems encountered when images are being sent between museums. The idea is to enable people studying the history of arts, fine arts generally, and museum objects to obtain the necessary information without having to consult archives in different museums. A few museum archives are already accessible – for example, the Beazley Archive in the Ashmolean Museum and in France the National Museums collections of paintings, which are partly accessible through Minitel. Presumably only data about images, not the images themselves, are available. A large number of plates, drawings, and prints are available for viewing on a 'high definition screen' at the Musée d'Orsay, running on a Vax computer for local viewing. Remote access to a collection at the Louvre from the Musée d'Orsay is being considered.

> Eventually in Europe, ATM networks might bring a single solution . . . compliance with property rights on images and other related rights such as copyrights are the most important aspect; these rights differ from one country to the other. Compliance with museum pricing policies is another essential point.

According to Van der Starre (1993) the early stage of the European Museum Network described by Delouis is confirmed, since 'it does not work as a network because of the lack of telecommunication facilities. . . . It is hoped that the EC will fund the second phase for building the system and the expansion into other countries.' However, in 1996 Cisneros *et al.* (1996) describe some ambitious arrangements for a similar purpose, supported under the EC RACE programme and by the Spanish government, to be set up on the Internet. This, of course, solves one major aspect of telecommunications because of the link exist. It introduces another because of the Internet's narrow effective point-to-point bandwidth.

The EVA 95 papers (*Information Services & Use* 1995) show that museums and galleries are thriving and are adopting electronic aids with enthusiasm; many museums are able to find the money to use state-of-the-art multimedia devices. Setting up a server on the World Wide Web has become commonplace, as Jonathan Bowen shows in the *IS&U* issue. He provides some statistics as evidence of the popularity of museum pages.

Iwainsky and Schulze describe 3D modelling techniques as a means of generating images of complete objects reconstructed from fragmentary data. Stanke and Paul pursue the idea further, describing sophisticated image-processing methods, including the reconstruction of the amplitude variations within the sound tracks of Edison cylinder negatives enabling the original sounds to be heard.

Special museum hardware and software

Apple's hypertext Hypercard system (see chapter 6) was an important contribution to Multimedia/Hypermedia image symbiosis; the facilities for controlling peripheral equipment on which pictures are stored makes Hypercard, or one of the several similar competitive products, a convenient and frequently used control method. Cards contain 'buttons' which, among other things, may be mouse-selected and 'clicked/pushed' to execute an external command or XCMD, routed through the appropriate 'driver' (software compatible with particular external peripherals such as a videodisk player, CD-ROM, etc.). Hypercard was developed primarily for the manipulation of cards containing text, with image-control as a bonus. The principle has been developed further for systems designed specifically to manage images and component parts of images.

In the Macromind Director multimedia software, the system is frame-based rather than card-based, with the means for controlling both external equipment and objects within one frame. The role of Director's 'XObjects' is to a frame similar to the role played by Hypercard's XCMDs to a card.

A publication from the Museum Documentation Association (Anon. 1993a) lists a large number of software and database software packages with the names and addresses of suppliers and a list of the two or three hundred museums, colleges, universities, trusts, and other organizations using them. MODES for cataloguing is the most widely used package by far, followed by MIS for inventory and Recorder for biological locality recording. DBase is easily the most widely used database.

From these data, it seems likely that in museums and similar organizations world-wide, perhaps 3000 are running computerized systems. Some hundreds of these are probably using or contemplating using images, with many more thinking about their introduction. Twenty-five different systems, running mainly in the UK but including others in five different countries, are described by Hoffos (1992).

1993 PCs are capable of a remarkable performance for special tasks with appropriate software. R.L. Miller (1993) describes the arrangements made to handle oceanographic images from the Advanced Very High Resolution Radiometers (AVHRR) aboard weather satellites. The PC's ability to display rapidly special types of high-resolution image indicates its potential for displaying high-quality pictures. Using a software package called Figment the time taken to calculate scale and offset for a display of 2048 × 1616 pixels was (in seconds) 159 for a 3240 concurrent multi-user multi-tasking mainframe, 21 for a Sun SPARC 1 workstation, 22 for a PC with 486 33 MHz processor, 59 for a PC with a 386 33 MHz processor, and 330 for a PC with a 286 10 MHz processor. The most suitable method of storing image data was found to be transportable 90 Mbyte Bernoulli cartridges. In some organisations very large collections require management. Sulger (1993) reports that at the New York Office of Mental Health there may be 100 million documents.

For files averaging up to 32 Kbytes in length, 16 2 Gbyte drives would be needed to store 1 million images. Removable optical storage will be needed.

A special package for museums has been introduced by Digital Collections Inc., of Berkeley, California. It receives high praise from Jones-Garmil (1994) and is described in chapter 6.

Steele *et al.* (1996) strongly recommend Kodak's photo-CD and discuss ways of using it. Recovering a high-quality image from disc now takes 2.5 minutes; last year it took 15 minutes. A photo-CD 24-bit colour 3072 × 2048 pixel image is comparable with a high-quality 35 mm film transparency. Capturing images of this quality using a Topaz scanner, Kodak Build-It software on a SunSparc station, and a Kodak CD Writer (total cost about £50,000) should provide a picture database of adequate and enduring quality whatever new hardware/software developments bring.

A system produced by Konica/Sony is expected in 1996, using Sony mini-disks. It will store 100 24-bit colour 3027 × 2048 pixel pictures. Presumably input image transfer costs and the required equipment will be much less that a comparable photo-CD outfit so Kodak can look out for some competition.

Examples of proposed or existing multimedia museum and gallery systems

A list of the examples discussed in this section is provided here:

The Berkeley prototype
The CMC (Delhi) Art Records prototype
Dallas Museum of Art Collections Information Center
European Museums Network
The proposed Globe Theatre system
The historic textile database at the University of Maryland
Micro Gallery, Washington, DC
Narcisse
National Archives of Canada
The National Gallery, London
National Railway Museum, York
Metropolitan Museum of Art, New York
History information stations at the Oakland museum
Réunion des Musées Nationaux, France
The Riverside Museum, Richmond, Virginia
San Francisco Museum of Modern Art
A working system at the Smithsonian Institution
The proposed Visual Thesaurus at Syracuse University
UK Museums and Galleries Consortium

The Berkeley prototype

Besser (1990) describes the Imagequery software implemented at the University of California at Berkeley. It will run on workstations, including SUNs, PS/2s with AIX, or MACs with AUXX. Besser talks about the often inadequate availability of rich information sources such as collections of photographs. His remarks about the problems of indexing objects in photographs are quoted in chapter 10.

UC Berkeley already run campus-wide online library services so it was proposed that Imagequery be made available as a kind of enhanced Online Public Catalogue (OPAC) over the existing network and workstations, allowing users 'to browse visually through the group of small surrogate images associated with an initial hit list'. Images would be taken from the Architectural Slide Library, the Department of Geography's Map Library, and the Lowie Museum's anthropology collection of photographs of their objects.

A form (spreadsheet) is first displayed, forcing the user to make the appropriate entries by selection options from pull-down menus. Thus the 'fields' menu for the architectural database offers the option 'place'. If 'Venice' is chosen, that word appears in the upper part of the spreadsheet. If the 'Authority list' is then chosen, classes of existing images are displayed for selection by the user, e.g. 'piazzas'. At this point a more complex Boolean logic query may be added or the 'do query' button pressed and a hit list displayed in the bottom part of the screen. For example, 'Venice ... San Marco' might be selected from the list. Upon selection of 'browse', thumbnail-size images are displayed on the right-hand side of the screen. The display area may be expanded to include the whole screen if necessary, allowing up to 30 thumbnails to be displayed together. Finally, any of these images may be replaced on command by a high-resolution colour enlargement.

The CMC (Delhi) Art Records prototype

Chaudhry and Roy (1990) describe a government of India scheme called the Arts Record Treasury System operated by CNC. A prototype art object imaging system is now in use at the Indian Centre for Cultural Relations. The objective of the scheme is to enhance an existing online Art Object Catalogue with images. The online catalogue is organized as an SQL/DS relational database running on an IBM 4361 in Bombay. It is accessed over the INDONET SNA network, which has nodes at a number of centres in India with a connection to CMC's London office via a gateway to an international packet-switch network. The catalogue covers a collection of Indian paintings, sketches, etchings, statues, sculptures, lithographs, etc., exhibited at various locations in India and abroad.

In common with image collections elsewhere,

a problem prevalent in the Indian scenario is the lack of uniformity in categorising various schools of thought, styles, etc., leading to an *ad hoc* classification scheme. Unlike books in the libraries the objects in a museum's collection are physically diverse and they have to be named before they can be added to the catalogue. A nomenclature for naming these objects has yet to evolve in India.

The image capture system consists of an Eikonix CCD type 850 camera for producing 4000×4000 pixel images in colour from standard size 22.5×15 cm photographs, a PC/AT microcomputer, and Philips optical disk storage. Compression is not used for fear of degrading the images. Each image is accompanied by a textual description of image attributes managed using Oracle RDBMS SQL software with interactive menu-control for user searching. Hits are picture identification numbers, each associated with an image displayable on a 500×500 pixel Mitsubishi colour monitor. Details of how the contents of pictures are described or the effectiveness of the *ad hoc* classification scheme are not provided.

Dallas Museum of Art Collections Information Center

A system has been established at the Dallas Museum of Art which includes eight networked digital imaging computer workstations. The workstations run JPEG compression and photo-CD software on 486DX 33MHz machines with CD-ROM drives and colour printers. Visitors can use the system to find information about 2000 artworks owned by the museum. Photographic collections stored in the Kodak photo-CD system may also be searched. Visitors use the system nearly 10,000 times each month. A Virtual Reality laboratory is planned including representations of a Mayan temple and a street in sixteenth-century Antwerp.

European Museums Network

One of the most informative EVA papers was by Friso Visser (1993), a member of the team formed from 8 museums – 3 in Germany, 1 in France, 1 in Spain, 1 in the Netherlands, 1 in Portugal, and 1 in Denmark, and 4 research or industrial organizations – 2 in Germany, 1 in Spain, and 1 in Portugal. The objective is to provide a multimedia visitor's program in English entitled 'Discoveries – traces of Europe's cultural integration'. It is to be a test for intercommunicating interactive multimedia to be made available to the public at each of the participating museums. The project, called the European Museums Network (EMN) project, ran from 1989 to 1992 with the support of the CEC through the RACE programme of application pilot projects.

The intercommunication aspect of the project could not proceed as planned since suitable telecoms were unavailable. It is interesting that in this and other related projects conceived in the late 1980s, unrealistic assumptions appear to have been made about the availability of European broadband telecommunications. Perhaps by sponsoring projects requiring the telecoms to be in place, the CEC felt that their optimistic forecasts would seem more plausible. Alas, they were not in place, but this did not stop other aspects of museum and arts systems from being tried out.

The European Museum Network's objectives were to provide the museums' administrators with the opportunity to get to grips with multimedia authoring and to try out the results on the public. To this end, data covering about 800 museum objects were input. The multimedia machine chosen was an Apple Mac IIfx with System 7.0 and Quicktime, and a Unix operating system. The machine includes a 24-bit video card, and viewing is done on 13" Trinitron monitors.

The information about the 800 objects is updated periodically by the museums, the main feature being digitized TIFF 1280 x 960 pixel 24-bit pictures. This is backed up by text, sound, and other images, with 30-second video clips and animation to be added later. Appropriate compression will be included when the video is added. The text includes basics, facts, explanations, titles and labels, copyright data, etc.

The system includes 'A short tour on . . . ' and facilities and button selection of functions. Navigation is assisted by the ongoing display of a 'personal keyword list' with thumbnail pictures as needed.

Visser states that

> the average manpower to describe one object to its full extent and store it digitally involved one full week of work. The average data referred to consists of the main image, some 15 pages of text, 15 additional images, and one or two fragments of sound.

Assuming the cost of labour and overheads to be a conservative £30,000 per annum, the weekly cost (48-week year) is £625. Describing the 800 objects therefore cost about £500,000. This does not include video or animation. The total cost of the EMN project was 10 million ECU (1 million ECU = £770,000). This multinational multimedia project would cost substantially more than a project undertaken by a single organization but it provides an idea of the authoring effort and finance needed to mount a comprehensive multimedia system in a museum.

The proposed Globe theatre system

To quote a recent feature article:

> The potential now exists to extend at least part of the public experience with all its drama and senses into the private world of the home. . . . A visitor-produced multimedia presentation which can be recorded at a public space site on to videotape can be taken home for viewing . . .

the development of the Globe theatre project will serve as a good set of concrete examples of what we are discussing here.

This idea will be used in the International Shakespeare Globe Centre, which includes the rebuilt Globe theatre. The original Globe, built in 1598, was closed by the Puritans in 1642 and demolished to make way for tenements in 1644. Sam Wanamaker decided to rebuild it; sadly he did not live to see its completion. A plaque on a brewery wall on the south bank of the Thames commemorates the original Globe. Rebuilding started in 1988.

A museum and research centre is being built on the site as well as the theatre. In October 1993 the building was held up by a shortage of suitable oak beams, but Wanamaker's dream is likely to be fulfilled with performances at the Globe in 1996. Some preliminary work on a multimedia system for use by visitors was done by IBM. Several modules were considered, including one to provide general information for visitors, a second to assist students, and a third to provide for several research options. An ambitious scheme described by Friedlander (1991) received Apple encouragement and is gradually being developed. Historical advice has been supplied by Andrew Gurr, Professor of English at Reading University. Part of the design provides for the production of animations using Macromind Director. Another part will enable Shakespearian plays to be made available as multimedia presentations. The plays could, for example, be 'edited' into various stage settings.

The historic textile database at the University of Maryland

The imaging system described by Anderson (1991) shows that image collections do not necessarily introduce difficult indexing problems. In this case the database consists of images of coverlets (decorative loom-woven bed-coverings) and carpets: 'Design motifs found in coverlet centerfields, borders, corner blocks, cartouches, and logos are coded on the back of the information sheet and then entered into the motif database. This makes it possible to search for specific design motifs.' Nothing more is said about the coding scheme except that 'untrained students would be hired to enter the data', so it must be relatively easy to update records and learn the basic tasks of entering, appending, and editing the data. Presumably an efficient coding scheme for all possible patterns has been devised and is easy to use.

The problems which arose in this case were not in the indexing area but in the imaging equipment. They sound predictable because 'the lack of funds forced many difficult compromises'. PicturePower software enables images to be imported from a video camera into a database running on a PS/2 via an image capture board, and integrated with text. Formats are compatible with DBASE III, chosen for the database. However, modifications were required because of the inconvenience of searching with this database.

Inadequate picture quality was improved by two methods. A standard camera was replaced by a professional camera and lens. System resolution was improved and colour was replaced by a 4-bit grey scale. It seems that 16 levels of grey were preferred to poor colour. The impression conveyed by Anderson is that the system does the job in spite of the cost constraints.

Micro Gallery, Washington, DC

Micro Gallery should be opening about the time this book is published. It is modelled on the system running at the National Gallery in London. The Washington Gallery will consist of seventeen interactive touch screen computers in a special room near the entrance. Animation and special graphics will be used to describe artistic purposes and techniques. Works of art permanently on view at the gallery will be described with artists' biographies, subject and atlas entries, dictionary terms, etc. The system is using Mac Power PCs with JPEG compression, Quicktime software, and Macro Media Director.

Narcisse

Christian Lahanier and Michel Aubert describe the 'network of art research computer image systems in Europe (Narcisse)' (Lahanier and Aubert 1993). This is a very ambitious project involving electronic storage and access to a large number of documents and paintings at cultural institutions in Europe.

The scanner being used will provide X-ray images of pictures of up to 8000×6000 resolution requiring 72 Mbytes of storage. A complete picture, requiring, say, 12 separate X-rays would require 864 Mbytes. 'Normal' resolution is 2000×3000 pixels. A monochrome photographic image is also generated, stored as 288 Mbytes. A prototype system comprising 300 paintings will require 5 optical disks, each with a capacity of 10 Gbytes.

A curious aspect of this system is that the images will be controlled by a multilingual text database in German, French, Italian, and Portuguese, although the article cited here is in English. A colour brochure in four languages, presumably the same four, has been published to attract more co-operation, and 2000 copies were distributed internationally. It seems odd that the English language is not featured in this project. However, the article includes one reference – the only one in the article – to an English publication, and an ancient one at that – *Leviathan* (1651) by Thomas Hobbes, a political philosopher. *Leviathan*, Hobbes' most famous publication, was critical of the power of the church and religious obedience.

National Archives of Canada

The ArchiVISTA system, a 'visual catalogue' of 20,000 cartoons and caricatures is described by Stone and Sylvain (1990). The requirement was 'to provide quick and easy visual access to the holdings of the National

Archives without having to handle original items, thus facilitating the long-term storage and conservation of the collection'. Images were captured at a rate of 150 per day on an Eikonix EC850 photo-digitizing camera and stored on a Laserdrive 5.25" 800 Mbyte digital WORM optical disk. Images were 1024 × 768 resolution with 8-bits grey scale per pixel. Some colour images were scanned with the same resolution at 32 bits per pixel, each occupying a 3 Mbyte file. Compression was not used.

A special arrangement for retrieval was devised by dividing each image into 4 NTSC video frames on videotape, transferred on to a 12" videodisk as one high-quality image. Retrieval is via a bilingual database by subject, artist, publication, place, date, or item number. Display time is 7 seconds per image using a minicomputer. The entire collection of 20,000 images is stored on two sides of a videodisk.

The National Gallery, London

The system running in the new Sainsbury wing at the National Gallery has been described by Rubinstein (1992). It took two and a half years to prepare. It is a visual image catalogue to the National Gallery's collection in five sections – a painting catalogue, artists' biographies, a historical atlas of western art, a types index, and a general reference index. It covers each of the 2200 paintings in the permanent collection.

Paintings may require eight pages of description covering the subject, technique, restoration, gallery details, etc. Thumbnail images abstracted by special software from the main images are provided for all the paintings. There are twelve 19" touch screen displays in the micro gallery, any of which may be used by a visitor without prior arrangement. Each screen is driven by a Macintosh II with its own 1.3 Gigabyte hard disk. The software was purpose-designed, and the display tubes provide a resolution of 82 dots per inch. The National Gallery already possessed 10" × 8" transparencies of almost the whole collection. They were scanned into the system by a Sharp JX-600 scanner in 24-bit colour. 8-bit colour is used on the displays.

The catalogue is said to include 21,000 articles with seven hours of sound, together with animations, music clips, and other items. Images may be displayed at 1024 × 768 pixels with 8-bit colour and the system contains 7000 photographs, charts, and graphics. Consideration is being given to a CD-ROM version.

The system's 12 monitors are open for use by the general public. Figure 14.1 shows one of them in use.

National Railway Museum, York

Work at the museum is well described by Ben Booth and Christine Heap in 'High resolution digital image storage at the National Railway Museum, York' (Booth and Heap 1993). In this project, images were scanned and

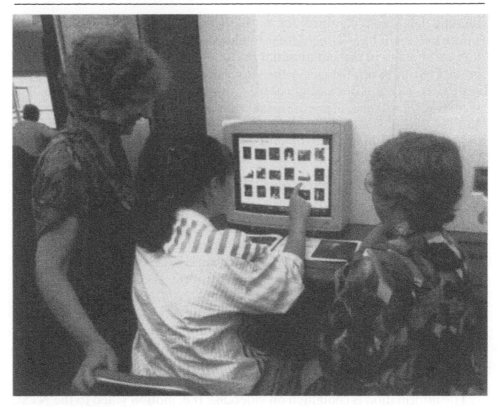

Figure 14.1 Multimedia at the National Gallery
Source: The National Gallery

stored at 2500×3500 pixels, expandable to 5000×7000 pixels in full colour. It seems that an important reason for adopting this very high resolution is that many of the negatives from the museum's photographic archive have deteriorated and the need for conservation is important. The imaging equipment and a modified workstation cost up to £70,000.

The museum (Heap 1993) is aiming to incorporate its collection of 75,000 photographs, eventually growing to over 1.25 million, on to WORM optical disks, each capable of storing 1 Gbyte of data. Each WORM will store 950 Mbytes, equivalent to about 1000 2500×3500 compressed monochrome images. The complete system was supplied by a company called Primagraphics. Pictures are managed at 2048×3072 pixels with an 8-bit grey scale, and are JPEG-compressed, normally at 13:1. They are indexed on a searchable 'image description sheet'.

Metropolitan Museum of Art, New York

At the Clearinghouse on Art Documentation and Computerization, based at the Thomas J. Watson Library, Metropolitan Museum of Art, New York, funding has been obtained for a 'Worldwide Networked Environment, where users will have direct access to files about the application of information technology to art and museum documentation issues'. The project will be tackled in several stages – the establishment of a network-compatible system, conversion of existing records, and standardization and access. The second stage will encourage the establishment of contributors to the scheme, and the access stage will investigate retrieval methods, with sophisticated indexing arrangements and direct access over the Internet.

History information stations at the Oakland museum

A number of 'history information stations' for the use of visitors have been installed at this museum. Each consists of a microcomputer, 19" monitor with touch screen, disk drive, videodisk player, and stereo amplifier and loudspeakers. The primary goal of the scheme is to 'provide, identify, and interpret, information about each of the 6000 artefacts on exhibition' (Cooper and Oker 1991). 'A clear favourite', say the authors, is the interactive map. The map includes 'landmark ikons to help visitors select the area in which they found the item in question'. A montage of display cases is shown, and the visitor selects the case and then the artefact. 'The map allows the visitor to filter out most of the gallery from the decision making process with one touch of the finger.'

The information is contained on videodisk (i.e. motion video to the NTSC Standard) with large-size text stored on the hard disk. The authors say that 'we chose to use a 286 class of computer because it has just enough speed to load full pages of text at an acceptable rate'. No doubt their choice today would be different.

Réunion des Musées Nationaux, France

In France the Réunion des Musées Nationaux is the state organization responsible for acquisitions, exhibitions, and events in art and culture. The objective in multimedia is to devise systems which appeal to the public and young people in particular, educators, and scientists. They are planning several major systems based on CD-ROMs, photo-CD, and CD-I. They include a guided tour and paintings of the Louvre, Versailles under Louis XIV, art collections for young people, historical themes centred on major figures including Leonardo da Vinci and Napoleon Bonaparte, major exhibitions, a porcelain catalogue of Musée Guimet and photographic archives of the Louvre, Orsay, and Versailles.

The Riverside Museum, Richmond, Virginia

Like the London Globe project, the Riverside Museum is appropriately situated. It is located on the site of the Tredegar ironworks and gun foundry on the James river at Richmond, the confederate capital. The works was the major industrial complex available to the South during the Civil War.[1]

The presentation uses Adobe Photoshop for image manipulation and enhancement, photo-CD for picture management, and Macromind Director for the touchscreen shows. The scheme was conceived by Frank Jewell, the museum's director, and executed by Pyramid Studios. It is a *tour de force* – one of the most ambitious multimedia and audio-visual schemes so far attempted.

There are four separate presentations at the museum:

- The historical section using LCD panels with an overlaid touchscreen. There are five screens running different historical stories driven by Mac Quadra 650 machines.
- The 'Sons of Vulcan' show (Figure 14.2) directed by Kevin Oldcorn from the UK and presented using nine slide projectors. This is a story about the industrial revolution in the South.
- The theatre containing a 6′ × 8′ central rear-projected screen driven by a laserdisk drive showing the general framework of the show accompanied by a set of large screen motors, one for every pair in the viewing audience, with stereo sound (Figure 14.3). The laserdisk delivers a program describing the social and cultural development of the city.
- A Light and Sound show projected on the front of the building using two 6Kw projectors, each containing a magazine of 85 images with scrolling control enabling 60′ × 80′ graphics to be presented as a continuous strip. At the same time 15 projectors are used to rear-project images on to the backs of the windows in the side of the building. Underground woofer loudspeakers are used to produce cannon fire and industrial effects. The show is accompanied by a four-channel soundtrack recorded by the Chamber Orchestra, also from the UK.

San Francisco Museum of Modern Art

The museum is developing a new system called 'Making sense of modern art'. Initially it will run on a publicly available kiosk. It will describe key works from the museum's collection of twentieth-century Western art. Animations and commentaries by artists, art historians, curators, and conservators will be used. It expects to publish a CD-ROM during 1996. The system's computer is a Mac Quadra or Power PC. The software includes JPEG compression, tools from Apple, and Macro Media Director.

A working system at the Smithsonian Institution

Part of the Smithsonian's 'Information Age' multimedia exhibition at the National Museum of American History on Constitution Avenue, Washington, is appropriately housed because this part of the Smithsonian contains such relics as Morse's original telegraph, examples of Bell's first

Figure 14.2 Scene from the Riverside 'Sons of Vulcan' show

Source: Valentine Riverside Museum

Figure 14.3 The Riverside theatre
Source: Valentine Riverside Museum

telephones, and the ENIAC computer. The system has been running since May 1990. Visitors may use interactive PCs linked by an IBM token-ring LAN. A number of the PCs embody touch-screen windows with choices provided by touching the image of a frame from a video clip.

Allison and Gwaltney (1991) say that

> the most popular program in the exhibition relates to code breaking. It runs on two stations. Visitors played it 314,564 times in the first year so it had approximately 471,846 viewings. With this program, visitors can encipher their name using a simulation of the German ENIGMA ciphering machine. They then decode it by remembering the machine rotor settings they used to encode it.

Finally they can see actual German messages that were intercepted and de-crypted during the Second World War. 'We believe that the subject attracts visitors and so does the fact that they can encode their own names. Making programs personally relevant to visitors clearly increases their popularity.'

The monitoring equipment, linked by an Ethernet LAN, handles the bar-coded guide used by visitors for logging-in to terminals, and is also used for checking operational status and collecting statistics about visitors' behaviour.

The proposed visual thesaurus at Syracuse University

The Globe project is one of a number of museum systems described in the Proceedings of the 1991 Pittsburgh conference. However, arguably the most interesting idea discussed in the Proceedings is the visual thesaurus.

Hogan *et al.* (1991) say:

> Many current information systems used to access images simply transfer the text-based methods of information storage and retrieval to computerized systems. Because the multiple aspect of visual access to images has long been neglected its development is still woefully inadequate. . . . The inter-relationships between text and graphics need to be thoroughly explored as do the creative possibilities in visual-based retrieval systems. . . . Visual thesauri and their applications to the museum community incorporate a complex mix of political, economic, and design issues.

Hogan *et al.* remind us that picture thesauri have been around since Joh Amos's *Visible World*, published in London in 1672. I remember being given a book called *The English Duden* many years ago. It was originally published in German. Every other page represented a scene showing many numbered objects. These pages were entitled 'The Car', 'The Farm', 'The Bank', 'The Railway Station', etc. The opposite pages contained the names of the numbered objects. This was the basic arrangement but there was also some kind of logical ordering of pages and the number of objects in each picture was very large. I don't remember whether there was any cross-referencing or duplication of objects in different scenes.

Hogan *et al.* say:

> It is relatively quick and easy to browse the page of a visual dictionary even though the book may have a large number of pages. . . . This type of browsing is difficult in a visual environment . . . rapid traversal of displays is difficult . . . what is lost to the user is the ease of determining the underlying structure which becomes quickly apparent with the use of a print dictionary,

and so on. However, there are some on-going attempts to extend this principle into computer-based system and Hogan *et al.* briefly discuss Besser's Imagequery, the NASA visual thesaurus, and the event display system used by physicists at CERN.

Advances in this area would, of course, be of great interest not just for museum collections but for all kinds of collections. Hogan *et al.* review research and then describe a prototype visual thesaurus being developed at Syracuse University. They make the point that 'visual images make it possible simultaneously to compare all the features of two patterns. Therefore information is matched in parallel . . . in contrast to features described verbally which are not all accessible at the same time and must be compared serially.' They also suggest that a computer can rotate images for pattern matching much faster than the brain can.

Unfortunately, pattern matching by rotate-and-try is only one of many actions needed for types of pattern matching with which the eye has no difficulty. An image which should match a query may be missed because of its angle, perspective, or other apparent difference which a computer is unable to retrieve although it may be an obvious match to the eye. Complex computing-intensive matching operations are currently receiving considerable attention, as in the system devised by Niblack *et al.* (1993) discussed on p. 276.

It is feasible to pose a question in the form required by a pattern-matching system, namely: 'Here is the kind of image I am seeking – which image in the collection most nearly matches it?' The user's simulation of a wanted image is the formulated query which he or she submits for matching. The machine signals the number of hits which may then be visually browsed by the user. Prompted by the resemblance, or lack of it, between his or her sketch and hit images, the user adjusts the sketch and the query is repeated.

UK Museums and Galleries Consortium

Consortium members include the National Museum of Science and Industry, the National Maritime Museum, National Museums and Galleries on Merseyside, and the Imperial War Museum. It also includes other museums in Leicestershire, Nottingham, Hull, and the Tate Gallery. The project is funded with half a million pounds and will be used to procure systems for imaging and public access at museums. The Imperial War Museum already has a system using laserdisks, videodisk player, and touch-screen access which provides public viewing of the museum's art collection, which includes paintings, sculptures, drawings, and posters. Each of about 800 items is accompanied by textual information. There is also an interactive explanatory programme about the museum and its collection.

Other multimedia museum systems

A system at the Bank of England has been described – a presentation seen by about 100,000 visitors a year, and at the British Golf Museum, St. Andrews – an elaborate system comprising eight laserdisk and three CD-I systems in an audio-visual theatre with many early video-clips.

At the Design Museum (London), an interactive computer-assisted design package which invites visitors to design a toothbrush is in operation. A comprehensive CD-ROM-based system covering museum objects and places of interest on the island is available at the Jersey Museum.

NOTES

1. Financial problems resulted in the closure of the Valentine Riverside Museum at the end of 1995. The Valentine Museum in Clay Street remains operational.

Chapter 15

Training and education

TRAINING

Multimedia training products which actively involve users in participatory tasks seem to rate much more highly than those which provide relatively low interactivity. An important requirement is tailorability – the ability to allow end-users to configure and change a multimedia package in order to meet a particular need.

Barker and King (1993) describe various facets of evaluation procedure and conclude that the quality of end-user interface design is paramount. The use of interactive multimedia in teaching has progressed far enough to prompt the European Commission to fund over 200 projects. Several organizations specialize in multimedia courses for training.

The Melrose company, London, provide a large, well-produced catalogue covering a huge range of subjects describing their many courses which are supplied on videotape cassettes or on CD-Is for interactive training.

The following headings have been taken from the 'Working with Aggression' course in the 'Communication & Presentation' section:

- Definition and personal experience of violence
- Body language indicators
- Verbal indicators
- Defusion techniques – to manage aggressive behaviour
- Preparation and ideas for reducing risk
- Levels of acceptable behaviour
- Causes of aggression
- Anger and its constructive use
- Assertive communication
- Body and verbal language from a multi-ethnic perspective

The range of subjects is divided into nearly seventy groups as diverse as Client Handling, Health, Marketing, Negotiating, Presentation, Computer Management, and Strategic Planning.

Xebec (Nailsworth, Glos, UK) offer similar training services. It has several generic courses on CD-ROM and offers a menu-based course for customization by a particular company. The company's CD-ROM Business Sense package runs on a 486 33 MHz MPC II machine with audio card and CD-ROM drive. The company also supplies business training packages covering Meetings, Team Leadership, Task Management, Cash Management, Budgeting, etc.

APPLICATIONS

National Council for Educational Technology, London

In 1995 ten projects were selected for support by the National Council for Educational Technology (NCET) in the UK. The objective is to 'promote the development of material for teachers to use with an open approach to integrated learning'. The subjects include lathe work, French, mapping, special needs, etc.:

AVP Computing	AVP Picturebase CD-ROMs in History and Art
Denford Machines	Design and technology manufacture using Mill CAM and Lathe Designer software
Longman Logotron	Supporting data in practical science using insight Data-Logging for Windows
New Media	Science curriculum materials and activities to support the chemistry set CD-ROM
Oak Solutions	Design and technology activities using Apollonius
Oak Solutions	Curriculum materials and activities to support CD Français
Shell Centre	Learning and investigative units using the COYPU software
SoftTeach Educational	Mapping skills and techniques using Local Studies mapping software
TAG Developments	Topic based courseware using Bodymapper, CD-ROM, and generic software
Widget Software	Special Needs language development using Choices and From Symbols to Sentences

Victoria & Albert Museum, London

The V&A has purchased four CD-I programs from Melrose for use in its new open learning centre to provide training for its staff of 800. The programs are entitled The Coach; Keeping Customers Cool; The Only Way, and The Team.

Training officers will evaluate the use of the new learning centre; all of its users must register and will be asked about their reasons. They will also be asked to provide feedback on the efficiency of the centre and how they put their training into effect in the workplace.

Deutsche Bundespost

The German postal organization built a system using Videologic graphic and multimedia products for interactive training claimed to have saved nearly £6 million in time and travelling costs. The system is arranged to provide flexible at-their-own-pace training for the Bundespost's nationwide workforce.

Ernst and Young

The company has developed a comprehensive system using Philips CD-I equipment and helped by the First Information Group in the preparation of a scheme called 'Figure it out – Finance for Non-Finance Managers'. Users are presented with a number of tasks in different business situations to improve their understanding, increase their competence, or test their financial knowledge. They can refer to a range of 'Factfiles' covering aspects such as financial statements, stock control, cash flow, forecasting, budgeting, etc., each providing definitions and explaining concepts.

McDonald's UK

McDonald's UK provides on-site interactive multimedia training for new employees and provides updates on new products for existing employees. The advantages are claimed to be the avoidance of having to send employees away for training.

EDUCATION AND TEACHING

Ignorance is like a delicate exotic fruit; touch it and the bloom is gone. The whole theory of modern education is radically unsound. Fortunately, in England, at any rate, education produces no effect whatsoever.

(Oscar Wilde)

Understanding learning

Plowman (1989) discusses the difficulties of system design in the face of uncertainty about how people learn: 'In spite of great steps forward in cognitive psychology, we have to admit that we still know very little in terms of how people learn' and 'Few programmes make any attempt to establish what the student already knows in the domain'.

The question is whether a better understanding of learning aided by multimedia systems will enable Oscar Wilde's assertion to be be firmly denied.

Theories of learning (Atkins 1993) embracing behaviourist and cognitive approaches suggest the following four design issues for multimedia teaching applications:

- Students are motivated to learn even when the 'gee-whizz' effect has worn off, and may prefer to learn from interactive courseware than from conventional teaching.
- Learning from interactive technology can be more efficient, but the benefit is lost if the interaction is complex.
- Students achieve a better mastery and remember more of what they have been taught from interactive courseware.
- The amount of structuring and control required is different for high-ability and low-ability learners.
- Some interactive techniques – for instance, the use of embedded practice questions – are highly effective for learning pre-specified factual content but may hinder the learning of more complex knowledge.

However, Atkins concludes, as did Plowman, that 'there is at present no coherent model of learning to support design'. Yildiz and Atkins (1993) review earlier media evaluation studies in which learners were assigned to a traditional control group or to a new media group in order to assess the relative gains in learning. They conclude that the 'evaluators stuck to an inadequate design' and that 'Many of the studies have shown no significant advantages of gains from use of the new technologies. The expectations of the media designers have not been realised in practice.'

After conducting tests (Blissett and Atkins 1993) on six mixed-sex groups, each of four pupils, it was concluded that 'To those who are designing the next generation of multimedia applications our findings suggest that effective design is problematic . . . there is little doubt that multimedia applications can be designed to be highly motivating and entertaining; making them also educational is more of a challenge.'

Wragg (1993), in discussing contributions at a conference, reports the remarks of van de Kuyl, who said that 'Multimedia has failed in any significant way to penetrate classrooms despite millions spent on kickstart projects. This is in stark contrast to industry where over 10,000 multimedia systems are delivering vocational training.'

To conclude this brief review of learning research, Plowman (1995) says: 'More than 90 per cent of UK schools have at least one CD-ROM player and the use of other technologies, such as CD-I, is accelerating.'

In spite of this massive investment of both public and commercial funds, little seems to be known about how children make sense of interactive multimedia. 'Some of the negative effects on comprehension caused by the highly fractured narrative can be diminished if the following guidelines are used to inform the design process:

- Narrative should be created specifically for interactive media. Keeping interaction simple will help to maintain the narrative dynamic.
- Narrative should be used so that tasks are integral with it. Tasks should be in short units which arise logically rather than as diversions from the narrative.
- The balance between media should receive consideration. Over-reliance on text should be avoided.
- A narrator can offer visual and auditory continuity.

Roger Schank is at the Institute for Learning Sciences at Northwestern University. He considers that teaching machines, as described in Skinner's widely read 1960 book, *Teaching Machines*, use out-of-date concepts. Skinner machines provided a series of questions and answers in which a student sees the correct answer if he gives an incorrect one, and then moves on to the next question. Schank thinks that flight simulators are a classic example of the 'learning by doing' approach and suggests some improvements. He is a well-known authority on Artificial Intelligence and has been considering educational goals since the mid-1980s. In Schank and Slade (1991) he concludes:

- Teach questions not answers. We want the students to learn how to think critically about new problems, not simply to memorize answers. In most real world situations there are no right answers.
- Teach from examples. Take advantage of the fact that people are well-suited to learning from experience. It is a natural form of cognition.
- Remove the stigma from failure. To learn from experience the student must first learn not to be afraid to fail. In this paradigm, failure is good in so far as the student can learn from his or her mistakes.

The use of multimedia teaching software has been described by Schank (1994). He believes that most multimedia programs fail because they 'merely add video and graphics to page-turning programs'. The student does not interact, the experience is passive, and the programs mimic television viewing. He describes two multimedia systems devised at the Institute for Learning Sciences. In one called 'Yello' the student is cast as an advertising agent and is required to present a proposal to a client in a scenario which includes several characters. In another system called 'Road Trip' the student takes simulated car trips round the United States.

Summarizing, Oscar Wilde would have been exaggerating if he had said 'multimedia produces no effect whatsoever'. Such a verdict would be premature; it seems that the jury is still out.

Demonstrations of faith

The designers of numerous multimedia teaching projects are not put off by the faltering progress just discussed. If they have any misgivings, the seductive attractions of new technology outweigh them.

Several computer-aided learning projects were put in hand in the United States in the 1960s and 1970s. The most ambitious were probably the Plato project covering accounting, biology, chemistry, English, and mathematics, and the Chicago City Schools project, which started in 1971 and where some of the Plato material was used and evaluated. In Plato, rented terminals were used, of which about 4000 were in the US and 40 in Europe. All were linked by telephone line to central computers. In a review of progress, Chambers and Sprecher (1980) thought that expectations had not been met although they expected advances with the arrival of microcomputer hardware. There was a surge of interest in microcomputer programs for computer-aided learning/instruction in the late 1970s, competing with recipe lists for the attention of users when microcomputers first arrived in homes and classrooms.

Eisenberg (1991) quotes from a 1990 paper in *Computers & Education* by Hawkridge who believes that the 'four basic rationales' for justifying computers in schools are:

- The social rationale
  Children should have an awareness of computers and be unafraid of them.
- The vocational rationale
  Computers are likely to be a part of future workplaces so children should be taught how to operate them.
- The pedagogic rationale
  Computers can teach.
- The catalytic rationale
  Computers can change schools for the better.

Note the curious way of expressing the 'pedagogic rationale' and the odd assumption that computers will somehow bring about unspecified 'improvements'. However, Hawkridge was considering the general benefits of computers in schools, which are not being considered here. We are considering only the effectiveness of multimedia in improving the processes of learning.

In the early 1990s the arrival of multimedia in the United States produced a mass of educational software – for example, a series based on the 'Peanuts' cartoons for teaching maths and geography. The National Geographic Kids Network successfully interconnected children in different countries. In the UK there is no doubt that the 1986 Domesday project drew the attention of schools to the possibilities of multimedia although the technology was then still in its infancy.

Domesday ran on an Acorn 8-bit computer with a 64K memory and a 160 × 256 16-colour display, which says something for the technical ingenuity of the software. Much of the data was collected by 14,000 schools throughout the country. Text with photographs about hundreds of small areas down to a size of 3 × 4 km and a variety of other information was stored on both sides of a 12" Laservision disk. The year 1986 was the 900th anniversary of William the First's survey of the country. The scheme was supported by the BBC and the University of Newcastle but it was badly priced and marketed. Expectations of selling 10,000 units at £1000 each were replaced by the reality of selling about 1000 at £3500; the system was subsequently taken over by a company and sold at a reduced price.

A sample of the titles for the CD-ROMs used in the 1992 UK National Council for Educational Technology (NCET) scheme follows:

Anglo-Saxons
Busy Towns
Creepy Crawlies
Frontier 2000
Just Grandma and Me
Hutchinson Encyclopaedia
Mammals Multimedia
Microsoft Art Gallery
Microsoft Dinosaurs
Microsoft Musical Instruments
New Kid on the Block
Photobase Landscapes
Picturebase: Victorian Britain
Planetary Taxi
Sherston Naught Stories
Silly Noisy House
Sitting in the Farm
Tortoise and the Hare
Usborne Exploring Nature
World of the Vikings
Worldbook Encylopaedia

The Council provided £700,000 for a CD-ROM trial in secondary schools using Acorns, the Apple LC475, or an RM 486 PC. In 1994 over 2000 primary schools took part in a NCET £4.5 million project where CD-ROMs and machines were supplied to support the National Curriculum.

Progress with multimedia learning systems is discussed by Pea (1991). Pea describes a system called Multimedia Works, which includes programs for composing, authoring and presentation, video clip editor, and search and editing tools. Pea claims various advantages for multimedia learning:

- Multimedia communication is similar to face-to-face communication.
- Multimedia is less restrictive than written text. Many people understand text better with broader media support.
- Multimedia can place abstract concepts in a specific concept. For example, refraction in physics might be depicted in a film of lens and light behaviour.
- Multimedia allows for individual differences in preferred sensory channels for learning.
- Multimedia lets you co-ordinate diverse external representations (with distinctive strengths) for different perspectives.

Multimedia Works supports two Mac II-based creation/presentation stations and six composition stations for classroom use. The limitations of the equipment used in respect of students' need to get to grip with real time effects are mentioned. Pea describes its use in boys' and girls' clubs and in middle schools. He concludes that 'we can easily make multimedia composition accessible to middle school students'. Unfortunately, nothing is said about total costs.

The development of multimedia technology and software to its present state and the fund of accumulated experience with learning/teaching material make it more likely that the huge investments made in educational systems will pay off.

> The enormous success of the early spreadsheet programs was not just brought about by their ability to total the rows and columns of known figures, but also because of the power they gave their users to pretend 'what if?' and perform calculations as to *what might be*. . . . What is likely to happen is that the computer as a tool for *imagining* will start to make a significant contribution to teaching and learning.
>
> (Whalley 1995a)

However, Whalley continues on a warning note: 'Educationalists have too easily fallen for each new technology as it has been presented as having the potential to revolutionise education, and none has been slicker than multimedia.'

Woolf and Hall (1995) suggest that the key factors in an active learning environment should be:

- Parameters of a database or simulation changeable by students
- System knowledge about the environment – for instance a model of the situation through mathematical formulas, scripts or semantic representation

- System reasoning about user actions and an immediate response.

They criticize commercial authoring tools for an absence of domain knowledge, inferences about students' knowledge, or strategies for responding to students' idiosyncrasies.

Although evidence to show the value of the payoff to be expected by an investment in multimedia learning systems is lacking, considerable funds have been provided for it in the US and in the UK. Government support for consortia has been forthcoming to produce something better.

Woolf and Hall conclude that multimedia learning environments, or 'Pedagogues', will 'At the very least enhance and improve the quality of learning', and in reference to networking, 'The global network will enable easy access to information.'

> Multimedia and artificial intelligence technology should play a central role in making this information more realistic and practical, providing knowledge and a variety of media forms. . . . The financial need for deployment is high considering the need for fast computers, CD-ROM drives, audio capability, and colour displays for every student seat. Fortunately the cost of these items keeps decreasing.

Woolf and Hall say that 'developing multimedia instructional systems involve extensive costs for multiple expertise such as contents experts, programmers, and instructional and graphics designers, and resources for planning, programming, observing student behaviour, debugging, and making the system bullet-proof'.

In the United States, the Department of Defense is funding a consortium with a range of expertise to build new instructional systems. The consortium consists of Apple, Houghton-Mifflin, PWS Publishing, and departments of the Massachusetts, Carnegie-Mellon, Stanford, and Colorado universities.

From September 1995 IT will be taught in the UK as part of the National Curriculum. The emphasis is on an understanding of IT rather than on its use as a teaching aid. An NCET booklet (Anon. 1995f) proposes a number of 'key stages' and 'activities', such as the stage 'Communicating and handling information' and the activity 'Illustration for a story'. The NCET chose ten projects in 1995 for support. The objective is to 'promote the development of material for teachers to use with an open approach to integrated learning'. The subjects include lathe work, French, mapping, and special needs.

A large act of faith – TLTP in the UK

The Teaching and Learning Technology (TLTP) programme is now running in the UK and the scale and comprehensiveness of the programme in higher education justify its special mention.

The screen shots in Figure 15.1–15.4 show details of one of the techniques – in this case at the University of Southampton. In Figure 15.1 screen dumps taken from a human morphology course are shown. A hyperlink has been used by clicking on 'carpal bones' in order to call up an illustration of the bones in the carpus or wrist.

Figure 15.2 is a 'self-assessment test' from the same course; a 'movie' showing wrist action is being shown in a small window. The program is designed to run on a PC so the small size of the window is accounted for by need to economize on hard disk space. Several such movies of any length would use it up at an alarming rate.

Figure 15.3 from an oceanography course in field study skills shows another hyperlink connection – from the word 'grab', to the picture of a 'Van Veen Grab' shown on the overlay. Figures 15.4–15.6 show screens where the student is invited to interact in order to move waveforms or to construct diagrams in an engineering course.

The computer department at Southampton University, authors of the course just discussed, have written a software package called Microcosm and have formed a company of the same name to market it. The software runs with Windows and Asymetrix Toolbox. Toolbox was first introduced in

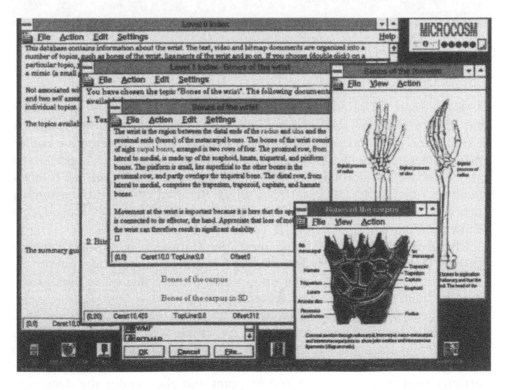

Figure 15.1 Human morphology course (1)

Source: University of Southampton

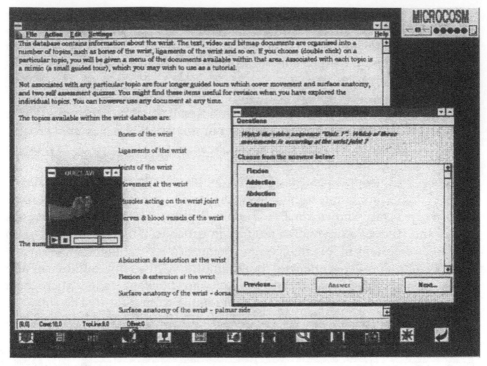

Figure 15.2 Human morphology course (2)

Source: University of Southampton

1990. Version 3.0 resembles other timeline-assembled authoring software capable of handling text, audio, video, etc. A further version, Toolbook CBT, is the one associated with Microcosm. It includes interactive course management and networking features. Toolbook also includes hyperlinking and database integration features which make up the Windows/Toolbox facilities required for Microcosm. A screen dump of clips and the assembly process, available for use with Microcosm course software when needed, is shown in Figure 15.7.

Microcosm demonstrates some interesting features of a multimedia application. There is now a very large fund of multimedia operating, authoring, and of other software available upon which the specifics of an application may be built. Microcosm takes advantage of it.

The general arrangement of the software is shown in Figure 15.8. Hyperlinks between two documents are created by observing a screen controlled by the application viewer layer at the top. This layer connects to storage via the link service layer shown at the bottom in a message-passing arrangement. Files are registered by point and click under the document control system and points to be hyperlink-connected are highlighted on both files by pointing and clicking in a dialogue box.

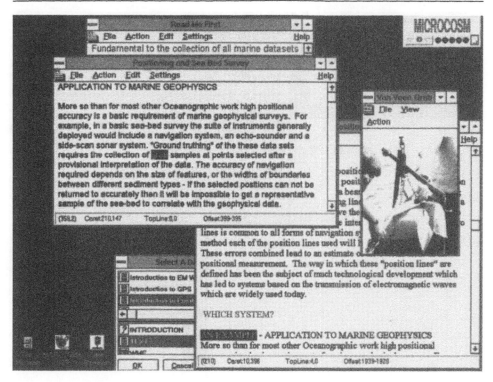

Figure 15.3 Oceanography course (1)

Source: University of Southampton

Data about the hyperlinked 'source anchor' and 'destination anchor' points are stored in link databases and the document files remain in their native language. There are different kinds of links, of which the 'generic link' is especially useful. When links are established between, say, two words in different documents, then all other occurrences of the word in the source file will also be linked to the word in the destination file.

Microcosm embodies several features associated more with information science than multimedia. For example, searching may be carried out by matching a query consisting of a word or several separate phrases to find documents containing matching items and the documents found are ranked in order of the frequency of matching terms.

The Windows clipboard is a useful feature whereby material from one or more documents may be moved on the clipboard, edited, and then merged into another document.

Jonathan Darby (1994), referring to the TLTP programme, thinks that 'There seems to be no real consensus as to what level of return is required to justify multimedia investment' and concludes that 'Without a change of attitude, multimedia will remain a tantalising possibility but not the core of academic learning that it could so easily become.' Darby is the head of the

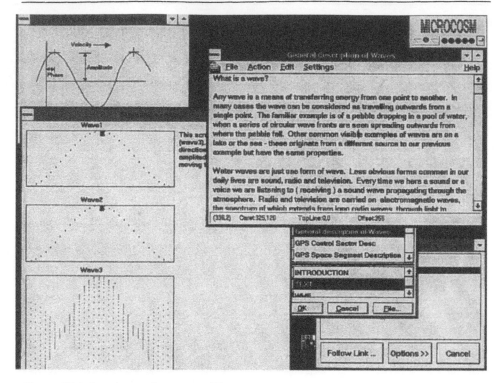

Figure 15.4 Oceanography course (2)

Source: University of Southampton

Computers in Teaching Initiative (CTI) unit at Oxford University, associated with the TLTP programme.

The TLTP four-year programme, financed mainly by the Universities Funding Council, is providing strong support for multimedia in education – £7.5 million spread over three years – with a further £2 million, provided in 1995 in support of on-going projects. The following are some of the participants:

- Mathematics Courseware Consortium
  6 universities led by the University of Birmingham
  Funding: £384,000 (first year).
  Objectives: help students in their first year; convince them of relevance of maths to application areas
- Teaching system for electronic design education
  8 universities and other organizations lead by UMIST
  Funding: £240,000 (first year)
  Objectives: develop material to support engineers and computer scientists in the design of circuits and systems
- Multimedia learning
  University of Southampton

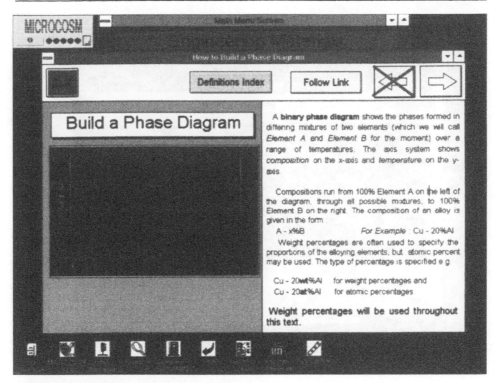

Figure 15.5 Engineering course (1)

Source: University of Southampton

Funding: £171,000 (first year)
Objectives: to shift university culture so that multimedia is used as an integral part of learning and teaching

- Biodiversity Consortium
  12 universities led by University of Leeds
  Funding: £291,336 (first year)
  Objectives: production of courseware at cellular, species, and ecosystem levels
- Earth Sciences Consortium
  25 universities led by the University of Manchester
  Funding: £118,000 (first year)
  Objectives: produce first-year courses in geology using Authorware Professional with 3D graphics

TLTP funding, provided by several bodies, is the largest amount of public funding ever committed to learning technology in UK higher education. The TLTP provides some information about its policy in its first newsletter (Price *et al.* 1994). The traditional idea to 'draw together the skills of the subject experts with the separate skills of the computer programmer' has been

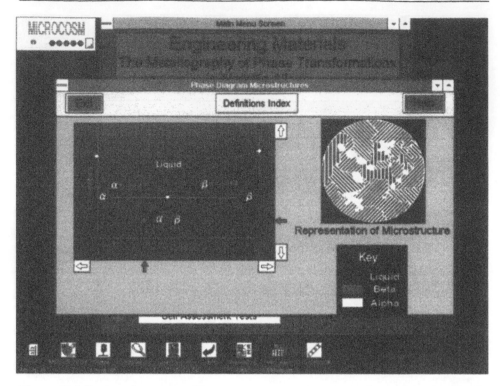

Figure 15.6 Engineering course (2)

Source: University of Southampton

replaced by separating the two skills 'through the encapsulation of all the advanced programming skills' in an authoring template. This idea, developed from the Asymetrix Toolbook system, is described in chapter 6.

In the second newsletter, John Wood produces a Really Good Proposal (Wood 1994) which falls short of a Really Excellent Proposal. Wood is talking about a multimedia mathematics course at Imperial College:

> Get some students who are hopeless at, say, complex number questions; expose them to interactive computer-based learning modules; check whether they are now better at complex number questions; then decide whether we've done it all quickly, cheaply, and cheerfully enough.

John Wood should do something more difficult but more interesting; he should divide his hopeless group into two, and ensure that each group is large enough to give the results some plausibility. One group should be exposed to computer-based learning, as he suggests, and the other taught conventionally. Resentment in the non-computer group could of course be a problem. At the end of a given period, which group has the better understanding of complex numbers? There would then be better evidence about whether or not the rather large investment in machines, software, etc. had been worthwhile. But perhaps such comparisons are unrealistic.

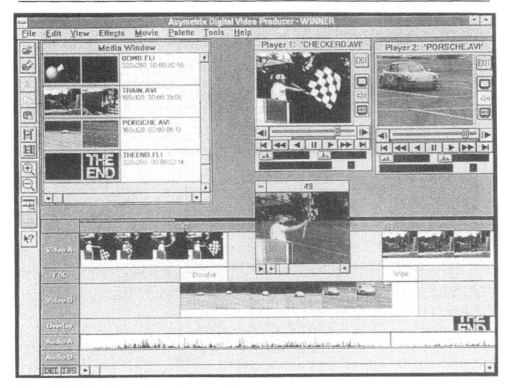

Figure 15.7 Toolbox multimedia assembly program

Source: Asymetrix

The market for multimedia educational systems and software has expanded enough to support an exhibition at the London Olympia. In a review of the 1994 exhibition, a number of items were singled out for special mention (Cole 1994). Cole points out that 'the four Cs – curriculum, conservatism, costs and control' have had their effect.

Many educational CD-ROMs are inexpensive. 'The Human Body', for ex-ample, from Anglia TV, costs £40 and is designed for 11- to 14-year old students. It includes pictures, text, and 50 video clips. Classroom worksheets may be printed out from it.

CD-I has relied on 'infotainment' disks from the US until now, but Philips has prepared disks specifically for the UK National Curriculum produced by Collins, Heinemann, and New Media. In the Horizon project, teachers and pupils created 80 of their own multimedia programmes – for example, 'A History of the Roman Soldier' for A-level students.

DISTANCE LEARNING

The Stanford University Instructional Television Network (SITN) was one of the first organizations to start a course-broadcasting service. It provided

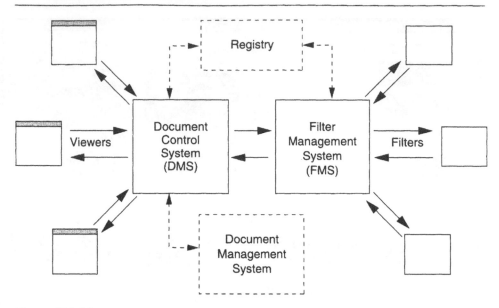

Figure 15.8 Microcosm processes

Source: AEC

engineering and computer courses as early as 1970. At present it broadcasts on four TV channels and supplies tapes to those out of range (Tobagi 1995). A multimedia education-on-demand system called the Stanford Multimedia Instructional Network (SMIN) is currently being set up in which video-recorded lectures will be compressed and stored on a server and transmitted to other servers over LANs or WANs for on-demand access. Information about the availability of on-demand courses will be stored on a separate database covering courses, lectures, server accessing data, and a list of servers subscribing to each course and to which of them video streams are distributed. The benefits claimed for the service are shown here:

- Distribution of digitized material in this way eliminates distance boundaries imposed by analogue broadcasts.
- The method of storage enables students to access the material at any time.
- Multiple users may simultaneously access the same material.
- The system provides for other methods of access – for example, retrieving material cross-referenced between courses.

The SMIN system provides interactivity by using satellite channels for data distribution to servers connected to a terrestrial network for two-way intercommunication to 'capture stations' containing the facilities shown here:

- Mpeg compression/decompression software
- Network interface for the server connection

- User software for initiating and terminating a capture operation
- Software for streaming data to the server

The TI IN satellite-broadcast education network is another service used all over the United States. It started as a service in Texas but has now been taken by over 6000 high school and thousands of other students (Anon. 1995e). Courses are provided in psychology, Latin, environmental science and other subjects. Course design is based on the Adobe Persuasion authoring system and students may telephone instructors for assistance.

However, according to the TI IN leaflet from Adobe, the system does not seem to embody the recommendations made by others discussed earlier. It uses a 'one touch' system enabling students to respond to multiple-choice questions. A telephone call to an instructor appears to be the justification for the statement that 'All 20 TI IN instructors broadcast interactive multimedia lessons'. The channel bandwidth of a satellite system permits direct inter-activity but each receiving station must possess the necessary equipment for beaming up signals to the source station via a satellite responder – a possible but expensive way of interacting.

The European Commission produced a booklet (Anon. 1994e) recommending a speeding up of progress towards an Information Society, and subsequently presented an 'Action Plan' (Anon. 1994g) to the Council and the European Parliament. In December 1994 the Commission set up an 'Information Society Project Office' in Brussels with access via a free telephone service and 'local' numbers (e.g. UK is 0800 962 114).

One of the new ideas is to identify 'initiatives . . . having a demonstration function which would help to promote their use'. 'Distance learning' is one of the ten launching applications. The idea is that once European telecommunications tariffs come right, 'industry will set up new service provider companies to supply distance learning services for vocational training'. The Commission would support 'quality Standards for programmes and courses'. The target is for pilot projects to be running in at least five countries by 1995, and that distance learning will be used by 10 per cent of Small and Medium Size Enterprises (SMEs) by 1996. The EC's track record in getting its recommendations off the ground is not good, but perhaps the new office in Brussels will be more successful.

Chapter 16

Multimedia databases

THE NEED FOR MULTIMEDIA DATABASES

Pictures are difficult to index. Perhaps that is why until quite recently very little work was done on that subject. Picture indexing was discussed in chapter 10. However, pictures are but one component of a multimedia database. Once multimedia databases become established and grow large, it will be realized that they are almost useless unless well indexed. It is not yet clear what difficulties have been met, how many large multimedia databases exist, or how great is the need for them.

Susan Mendelsohn (1994) quoted four factors which would determine whether 'the promise of multimedia would be realised'. They are 'ease of use (including the ability to customise), platform independence, affordability, and the development of authoring tools that will allow information workers to prepare multimedia reports, presentations, and so on in the context of normal day to day activities'. She then asked a number of librarians and information scientists whether they thought a multimedia database would be useful. The responses ranged from 'The only databases which I use in the course of my normal work are bibliographic and I can see no advantage in making them multimedia' (university librarian) to (in regard to the CD-ROMs already used) 'I would like to see all these products contain graphics, images, video, and voice. . . . Multimedia publishers will need to change the way they think about and realise multimedia versions of scientific publications and this generation of users must also change their ideas' (Information Service Centre Director).

Several of the applications described in this chapter include what amount to multimedia databases. You will note that in certain fields there is steady progress towards their use.

COMMERCIAL SOFTWARE FOR PICTURE DATABASES

Document Image Processing (DIP) for business documents is making rapid progress and systems for that field might be pressed into service for some kinds of multimedia collections. However, DIP systems are usually designed to manage a very large number of relatively small, not a relatively small number of large, records.

The Canofile 250 desktop electronic filing system, from Cannon (Crawley) is a typical example. It includes a scanner, magneto-optical disk drive, paper output delivery guide, display screen, and attached keyboard in one box. It will scan documents up to about 9" × 14" at 200 × 200 dots per inch (monochrome) at a claimed speed of 40 pages per minute. Images are stored on a removable disk of 256 megabytes per side. The systems costs about £9500, and an associated laser printer costs £1600. It will display retrieved pages on its LCD screen, which is about 5" × 10". Provision is made for simple indexing by words which are matched against query words for retrieval purposes.

A number of general-purpose microcomputer software packages for dealing with relatively small numbers of documents and/or pictures, usually including provision for rather basic indexing methods using words, are also available.

The difference between database prices, as between, say, Lotus Approach V2.1 (£99 from Lotus 01784 455445) and Microsoft Access (£280 from Microsoft 01734 2760001) lies mainly in the comprehensivity of 'help' screens, interfaces, editing facilities, etc.

One of the earliest picture database system was Picture Power from Pictureware – a software package for the IBM PC. It enabled a user to design an indexing form and to capture and edit a picture from a television camera. Picture Cardbox is a similar package including provision for indexing by words using a 'Term Manager' which enables a thesaurus to be constructed and operated; existing thesauri may be imported. Images may be displayed together with descriptive text and an image may be enlarged to fill a VGA display. A screen from this software is shown in Figure 16.1. It is claimed that a 300 megabyte hard disk will hold up to 15,000 images; an optical disk may be used if needed (Gray 1992). In the UK Picture Cardbox costs from £900.

Aldus Fetch 1.0 is a multi-user database for cataloguing images, animations, Quicktime movies, and sound files on Macintosh machines running Quicktime. It is suitable for various image packages including PICT, TIFF, Illustrator, Photoshop, Kodak photo-CD, Sound Edit, etc. Images may be imported from various sources. In a recent review of Fetch the author says:

> you can search for files by description or keywords rather than just file names, but generating this information can be quite a chore . . . with some

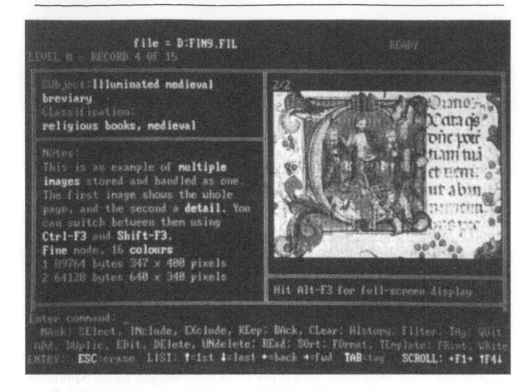

Figure 16.1 Picture Cardbox
Source: Picture Cardbox

procedural discipline all your files could have keywords and descriptions built into them, allowing Fetch to use all of its Apple searching capabilities.

Fetch costs $295.

The main feature on Kudo, an Image Browser from Imspace Systems (San Diego) is to scan forward or backwards through a thumbnail collection by pressing the 'riffle' button. Each thumbnail of 16K bytes per colour represents 'mixed-media' image files of unspecified quality. The browser 'is aware of the human eye's ability to perceive unrelated images at approximately 10 frames per second', says the blurb. The system will hold 32,000 or more images. Indexing is not mentioned.

Archis (commercial software) screen presentations consist of a picture and a photograph accompanied by various data in words including a caption describing the photograph. It is intended that workstations will be installed at major sites worldwide, so the system may be searched online before branches request particular photographs from the library.

As at September 1992 an Apple Macintosh system with scanner, optical disk, and Archis software could be purchased for less than £10,000. Archis enables users to input, store, retrieve, and output any type of document such as text, computer files, images (colour or black or white) slides, X-rays and digitized video, directly onto the desktop . . . users can search for information through a hierarchical structure or through the use of keywords.

The Kodak photo-CD system is described earlier, in chapter 11. Kodak have released software packages specifically designed for it. In the Kodak Shoebox software, arrangements are made to enable the user to provide a catalogue of thumbnail pictures, of which there will be about 100 derived from the full-resolution pictures stored on each photo-CD. The appearance of a screen produced by this software is shown in Figure 16.2. Thumbnails derived from other systems such as Apple Quicktime film strip ikons and pictures stored in TIFF and other formats may be imported into the same system.

A catalogue needs to be indexed in order to retrieve and display a wanted thumbnail. Indexing is provided by a user choosing a number of fields to cover some aspect of pictures in the collection – for example, colour(s) used, number of people in the picture, date, location, etc. However, no special measures are incorporated for effective retrieval by content.

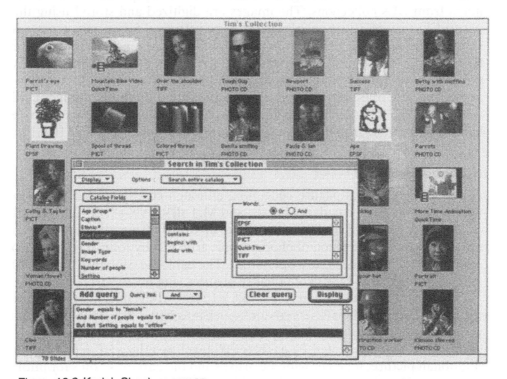

Figure 16.2 Kodak Shoebox screen
Source: Kodak

Kodak can also supply an image software package called PhotoEdge, which costs $135. It works on photo-CD, TIFF, and Macintosh PICT files. It will present a photo-CD thumbnail display, and enables any full-resolution image to be displayed in any one of five resolutions laid out in a chosen number of columns. It includes various tools, such as a tool for outlining an object within an image. The object may be lifted out and managed as a separate image.

IBM 'Tell Me' is a business system incorporating data from the Thomson Business Database. A screen from Tell Me running on a conventional PC is shown in Figure 16.3. It is designed for identifying types of businesses and their geographical location for planning a sales campaign.

Mathcad 5.0 (Figure 16.4) from Adept Scientific contains special facilities for equations using a range of stored symbols and for inserting graphics covering various functions in a choice of colours.

PICTURE DATABASES PROPOSED OR IN OPERATION

The British Library

The British Library's iBase image database contains data covering over 10,000 images of early photographs, sheet music, stamps, and many other items from BL's collections. The images are digitized and stored using the photo-CD system. iBase enables them to be retrieved for various purposes such as cataloguing, viewing for scholars, or accessing in galleries or museums. A number of thumbnails per screen may be browsed; twenty fields are used for indexing. iBase may be searched at several BL establishments and UK museums. To run it, a 486 PC with a 2 Mbyte graphics card is required capable of managing 16 million colours, together with a 1 Gbyte hard disk. Screens from the system are shown in Figures 16.5 and 16.6.

IBM John Wyeth collection

A good example of a picture collection, although created with equipment which is now rather dated, is Mintzer and McFall's (1991) IBM-devised art catalogue system, which will accommodate up to 10,000 pictures – it has been used to manage a collection of photographic artworks by John Wyeth. It also demonstrates the scale of such operations. The database contains $1024 \times 1024 \times 16$-bit colour (16.8 Mbit) high-quality pictures (Figure 16.7).

When 10,000 pictures are in place, $16.8 \times 10,000 = 168$ Gbits (21 Gbytes) of storage are used. When 32-bit colour comes into wider use, 10,000 pictures would occupy 336 Gbits (42 Gbytes). In an associated relational database, each picture is represented by a 200×200 pixel by 8-bit (320 Kbit) colour thumbnail picture, together with the artist's and the curator's notes for information, and for retrieval by word matching. A number of thumbnails may be displayed on a screen together.

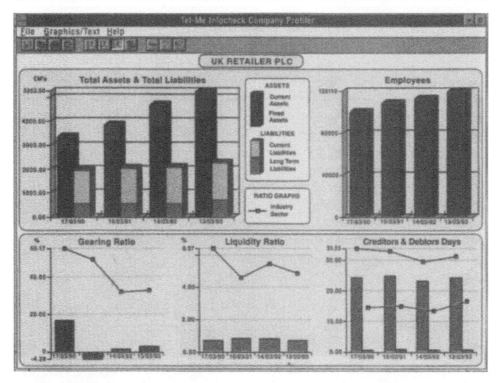

Figure 16.3 Screen from 'Tell Me'

Source: IBM

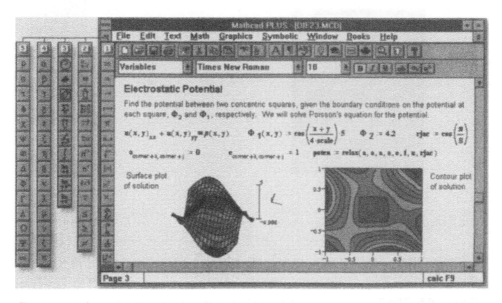

Figure 16.4 A screen from Mathcad

Source: Adept

Figure 16.5: The British Library's iBase system: selection and display
Figure 16.6: The British Library's iBase system: full-screen picture

Source: The British Library

Figure 16.7 A picture from the John Wyeth collection

Source: IBM

Browsing through a succession of rapidly presented blocks of thumbnails immediately brings to bear the most efficient selective system by far – the human eye/brain. Unlike a computer, a human can almost instantly ignore unwanted pictures. The number of thumbnails per screen depends on the amount of detail needed to identify a wanted picture, and on the screen size and resolution. As many as 25 to 30 can often be accommodated. If a human can discriminate between pictures in this manner, the need to provide an elaborate indexing scheme for discrimination purposes is reduced.

Hong Kong library

The slide collection in the Hong Kong Polytechnic Library (Yeung *et al.* 1992) is housed in 108 filing-cabinet drawers. There are 70,000 slides with sufficient storage space for 100,000. The slides cover paintings, sculptures, fashion, architecture, product design, aspects of Hong Kong, and other topics. The slides are catalogued according to the Anglo-American cataloguing rules (second edition) supplemented by US MARC formats for bibliographic and authoritive data. Slide titles may be searched on a computer keyword file.

British Petroleum

The photographic library at British Petroleum, Britannic House, London, has been described by Patel and Underhill (1992). It contains 300,000 photographs covering BP sites and activities. The library is currently entering the photographs on to optical disks capable of storing about 25,000 photographs. The equipment consists of Macintosh II work stations, archive server, and document server together with Panasonic WORM drives and Archis software.

Hulton Deutsch

Hulton Deutsch (Anon. 1993c) have recorded 2500 out of their collection of pictures of the 1930s on a CD-ROM. Searching is by associated keywords. The kind of indexing words chosen reflect action, background, location, mood, people, scene, and subject. Screenfuls of thumbnail hits are provided, any of which may be used to select a main image. Another disk called the People Disc is available containing 10,000 pictures of personalities and public figures. Further disks are planned.

University of Oslo Nansen collection

The University of Oslo Library (Aabo 1992) houses the Nansen collection of photographs, art work, drawings, and prints which have been scanned into Apple computer storage. The resolution of the system is up to 150 dots per inch. Provision is made for a 1 Gbyte hard disk to store the compressed pictures. The hardware includes a Macintosh IIfx machine operating on an Ethernet network. Apple's Quicktime software is being used. Searching is by words using Boolean logic.

Aviador

The Aviador (Anon. 1993b) is an interactive system linking a videodisk of over 40,000 architectural drawings from the Avery Library in the US to their online catalogue descriptions in the Research Libraries Group (RLG) on the RILN network. Searching is carried out by means of special software developed for use with Windows on a PC which includes an analogue videodisk-player. The database covers building projects, each of which requires a large number of drawings. A user who possesses the appropriate PC, videodisk drive, and the Aviador videodisk together with the Telecom software, may search RILN catalogue records for descriptions of drawings held on the disk, and immediately view them.

University of Kent

The University of Kent (Bovey 1993) holds about 80,000 original British newspaper cartoon drawings. They are accessible with Prism, a purpose-designed UNIX system implemented on Sun Sparc-stations using the

X-windows interface. Little is said about the indexing effort but judging by the amount of data shown in examples of retrieved records it must be considerable. Retrieved cartoons are displayed together with associated data.

One of the first large databases of this type being developed is being tackled in two stages – the first stage is a computer-based index to separately available pictures, and the second includes pictures with the index.

Beazley archive at the Ashmolean

Sir John Beazley's archive of Greek figure-decorated vases – Beazley spent much of his life collecting and researching – is held at the Ashmolean Museum, Oxford (Moffett 1992). A vase report is shown in Figure 16.8. The archive comprises 250,000 photographs and thousands of drawings indexed using the Ingres relational DBMS on the University's VAX cluster of computers. These data occupy (1992) 80 Mbytes of storage.

Each vase is indexed in several ways – by vase identity data, by attribution, by cataloguing history, by iconography, by references (published illustrations), by Text References, and by Terms based on the iconography. The system includes a report generator.

```
BEAZLEY ARCHIVE DATABASE
REPORT ON VASE 7043
--------------------------------------------------------------------
Technique : R                             Shape  : CUP B

  Signature : EUPHRONIOS EGRAPH [SEN] (EG)
  Provenance :

  Attributed to EUPHRONIOS Painter by SIGNATURE
  Attributed to 525-475 VY X
Decorated Area : A HYPNOS AND THANATOS WITH SARPEDON, AKAMAS
Decorated Area : B PYRRHIC, YOUTH PLAYING PIPES, YOUTH AND WOMAN
Decorated Area : I FLORAL COMPLEX, PALMETTES


Cataloguing history
--------------------

1 TEXH5            Texas, Hunt Collection
1 MALGLOAN7043     Malibu (Ca.), The J. Paul Getty Museum
1 NEWSXXXX7043     New York (N.Y.), Market - Sotheby's


Publication record
--------------------

 J. Paul Getty Museum Journal, 9 (1981) 24-26, FIGS.1-6 (I, A, B)
Wealth of the Ancient World, the Hunt Collections (Fort Worth,
1983), 54-57, NO.5, FRONTISPIECE (I, A, B, PARTS)
 Sotheby's, The Nelson Bunker Hunt Collection, New York,
19.6.1990 (New York, 1990), NO.6 (A, B, I, PARTS)
```

Figure 16.8 Beazley archive vase report

Source: Beazley archive

The archive has been available via the JANET UK University network, IPSS, and NSF-NETRELAY. The intention is now to supply 40-Kbyte thumbnail pictures of vases together with the retrieved data, estimated to consume 4 Gbytes of storage. The RAMA inter-museum network, mentioned earlier (p. 341), will be used. Experimental transmissions between the Ashmolean and the Musée d'Orsay have already taken place using the ISDN.

Elise

Elise – the Electronic Library Image Service for Europe – is sponsored as part of the CEC DG XIII programme by the IBM UK Scientific Centre, de Montfort University, Leicester, the Victoria & Albert Museum, and Bibliothèque Publique d'Information, Paris (Black 1993). The database will be accessed via the ISDN. The image archive will be composed of TIFF high-resolution images, normally unavailable online. Compressed images up to 1024×768 pixels will be available for users. It is intended to index the pictures using the AAT when appropriate. 'Images will be retrieved by their textual descriptions and so work is under way to investigate the difficulty of articulating in textual terms the search for a visual item.'

Relational database management systems were rejected, and three other packages 'are being evaluated further against a system specification and a choice will be made in the near future'. Unfortunately, this description tells us little about the way in which the system will be indexed. The ISDN will be used for communications.

CONCLUSIONS ABOUT WORKING SYSTEMS

Much of the available software appears to cater for the storage and retrieval of selected pictures to be incorporated in other material – for example, in multimedia presentations, desktop publishing, etc. The software examples provided here are a few of many packages available for multimedia work.

The examples given of operational collections represent a small fraction of the total in use. Almost all are indexed in some way using descriptive words keyed to each image, inserted by an indexer. Retrieval methods are usually similar, if not identical, to the methods which have been used for many years for text retrieval – text describing a picture is searched.

The fact that computer systems are used to manage such a variety of collections indicates a considerable general degree of interest in picture databases. The absence of critical comment about the various systems is very noticeable. Most are described with the 'I gotta picture system' enthusiasm by their originators or custodians – the enthusiasm which characterized the people saying 'I gotta text system' twenty years ago. Test results are not provided and the idea of 'failure analysis' is never discussed.

ORGANIZING A LARGE MULTIMEDIA DATABASE PROVIDING PICTURE RETRIEVAL

To generalize the database idea, suppose that there is a requirement for users to transmit a question to a database for picture retrieval and textual records, with the facility for supplying 'hit' pictures via a telecommunications network. A user may wish to change the question and repeat the operation if the first set of hits is unsatisfactory. Each complete operation needs to be quickly concluded – each picture should be received within a few seconds of posing a question.

Let it be assumed that the collection is large and consists of paintings, artworks, historic illustrated manuscripts, photographs, drawings, museum objects, images of items which are not normally accessible, and like items. These classes could reside in separate databases or could form a sectionalized single database. A large collection will require an index with a considerable power of discrimination, using a language which does not require a time-consuming indexing effort, or learning-to-use effort. It should be possible for the system to be amended or augmented and it also should be possible to scale it up to accommodate a still larger collection and more users. The effort and money expended in forming, indexing, operating, and maintaining a picture database depend on its planned size and diversity. Indexing, as explained earlier, which is often neglected, requires special attention.

Query-pictures will augment word queries as the techniques are refined for many kinds of questions; not all concepts can be better queried in this manner. Query-pictures will be introduced in due course to pose questions like 'What pictures are there showing ladies wearing medals?' or 'Are there any seventeenth-century pictures which include animal pets?'

The system should be able to handle 'information discovery' questions as well as 'information recovery' questions – that is, questions about data known to exist like 'Show me a selection of cartoons by Leonardo da Vinci'.

Design

The attributes and functions of a large diverse picture database could appropriately include:

- An updatable collection possibly divided into mutually exclusive sections, containing high-resolution full-colour images;
- The means for moving collections available in original, photographed, or other forms, into the system;
- The inclusion of 'thumbnail' (miniature representations of each picture) pictures which contain sufficient legible detail to represent parent pictures unambiguously;
- Queries by word terms or query-pictures;
- An indexing system;

- A mechanism for matching queries against contents and selecting hits;
- An optical multi-platter or a multiple magnetic disk store;
- A compression/decompression system;
- A staging mechanism to move data automatically from remote to local storage locations;
- A telecommunication network for receiving questions and transmitting hits;
- A community of users in different geographical locations with appropriate workstations.

Some design considerations follow for a system embodying these facilities and providing a service from a multimedia database.

Transmission costs and line bandwidth availability being what they are, it makes no sense to clog up the system when a number of users simultaneously want to pose questions, receive hits, modify the question, and receive some more hits, finally requesting the online delivery of one or more high-quality pictures.

Assuming that users have a CD-ROM player and a microcomputer or workstation, the initial selection procedures could be performed offline on the user's premises. For example, if the collection houses 20,000 images, 20,000 thumbnails must be indexed; they could be comfortably accommodated on one CD-ROM for in-house viewing. Provision could be made for word searching, just as it is in the inexpensive ready-made software previously described. Indeed, a software package might be selected from the widely available commercial packages for use in this system.

It is not known at present how good the indexing facilities must be if the user is already able to scan, say, twenty hits at a time before deciding on a wanted picture. Nor is it known whether software incorporating facilities for query-picture searching and matching could be easily integrated into the offline system. It seems likely that they could be. There is a wide choice of ready-made software for drawing, painting, clip-art selection, etc., which would provide the user with the means of posing query-pictures. Scanned images could be input for this purpose as well if necessary.

In any event, local offline thumbnail searches of this kind are feasible. The only traffic and operations left for the main online database are then to deliver requests for one or more high-quality pictures, perhaps when requested by a number corresponding to the number of the previously selected thumbnail. In this case no indexing or matching facilities are required on the database site. The system is simply concerned with retrieving a picture of the required number and dispatching it down the line.

If each picture contains $1000 \times 1200 \times 24 = 28.8$ Mbits, which is 3.6 Mbytes, reduced to 2.9 Mbits or 360 Kbytes when compressed by 10:1, then a 2.9 Mbit picture transmitted at 500 Kilobits per second will take 5.8 seconds to reach a user. The storage requirements for 20,000 compressed pictures will be $20,000 \times 0.36$ Mbytes = 7200 Mbytes or 7.2 Gbytes. If a CD-ROM contains 540 Mbytes, then fourteen such disks would be needed to house the entire collection. The database system must include the means of retrieving and dispatching pictures from these fourteen CD-ROM drives with their disks. A server containing a 80486 processor and EISA bus, connected to the drives by a SCSI interface would be satisfactory. It would be accompanied by a 486 microcomputer or a machine of greater power, as a monitoring work station, and as the device required to process image-query pictures if this method is used.

Such a combination would be capable of outputting data at a rate of up to 25 Mbits per second. The server must contain a card suitable for dispatching data down the chosen line – say, a Super JANET line. A SuperJANET plug-in telecoms interface card for a microcomputer does not yet exist, but it seems safe to assume that it soon will. A server such as the DEC Infoserver 150 or an Attica server would be suitable. The server would be capable of delivering data to a number of users simultaneously. It is assumed that those users would receive the data down SuperJANET, and that at each user site there would be a Hub with a LAN, or direct lines to each user's terminal. The server's delivery rate of 25 Mbits per second may be subdivided into the equivalent of separate channels (see under telecommunications section), each running at 500 Kbits per second. The system would be capable of handling requests to supply numbered pictures at that rate to each of 50 terminals.

Because imaging *per se* is 'fashionable', systems of all kinds and capabilities have been developed, usually disregarding the need for effective indexing and retrieval but employing methods of storing, transferring, communicating, and displaying pictures using a technology which increases in sophistication almost daily.

The idea of supplying blocks of hits as small thumbnails held in a store of moderate size for preliminary assessment, representing full-screen displays showing pictures from the whole collection, has much to commend it. The selected picture may be subsequently retrieved in its high-resolution full-colour format at a more leisurely pace.

Fifty terminals/users simultaneously accessing the system represents a large total population of users. For example, if fifty users at a time each have a two-hour session on the machine each week, and there are, say, 36 hours available per week, there could be 18 two-hour sessions providing a service for 900 users. All of the above numbers are theoretical, and would doubtless not be realized in practice, although they are probably of the right order.

A standard CD-ROM and drive delivers data at a rate of 170.2 Kbytes = 1.36 Mbits per second, comfortably exceeding the assumed rate of 500 Kbits per second. Faster 'Quadraspin' drives are now available rotating at 4 times the normal speed and capable of delivering data at 612 Kbytes = 4.9 Mbits per second. Such an arrangement would seem to be able to cope with a large user population with something in reserve if it was required to be scaled up at a later date.

To summarize, the system would consist of the following items:

14 CD-ROM drives
1 80486 microcomputer
1 Attica CD-ROM server
Software

An installation consisting of 14 CD-ROM drives, and a server with input interface cards, in two tower-type cases with 16 Mbytes of memory and a 125 Mbyte disk, 486 processor, EISA bus and cabling, together with a 486/EISA microcomputer for monitoring and auxiliary functions, but excluding an interface card to SuperJANET and also excluding installation and maintenance, would cost about £10,000 (Attica Cybernetics Ltd, approximate quotation). This company has had experience of supplying installations resembling the above, and the quoted figure should be correct to plus or minus 20 per cent. The server is capable of handling a maximum of 32 drives. It is claimed that it will support up to 100 simultaneous users. Users' access time to any CD would be about 14 milliseconds and only a simple inter-disk directory is assumed to be needed. Thus if a user specified picture no. 5282, the CD containing that picture would be selected.

No inter-disk directory at all would be needed if the collection was divided into as many sections as there are CDs, and users know in advance on which section their picture is contained, posing questions in the form of the CD-ROM number plus the record number.

The design for a system of this kind represents a set of compromises arranged according to circumstances. For example, the distribution or re-distribution of data across CD-ROMs might need to be organized in anticipation of demand patterns. For example, if all users simultaneously requested information stored on the same disk, there would considerable delays in delivery. Such problems could become low-probability events by arranging for multiple stored copies for most demanded data, the use of caching, and so on.

A number of companies would be capable of providing a suitable data-base system of the kind discussed here. They include Origin, Trimco, Epoch Systems, DEC, and IBM.

COMPOUND SYSTEMS: OLE, BLOBS, AND OPENDOC

Most existing database techniques, for instance the widely used relational database, were not designed to handle the complex objects that are encountered in multimedia, economic models, engineering systems, etc. An 'object' in this context is any chunk of information, be it text, images, motion video, charts, spreadsheets, etc., in displayable form, accompanied by 'native' data, not normally displayable, which enable the object to be processed or edited upon receipt of a message. The Binary Large Object (BLOB) – a description of an object of any kind in words, including images, occupying a field in a database and managed like any other record field – was introduced in an attempt to overcome this limitation. However, 'object-oriented' systems, as described below, seem to be more in line with users' requirements.

The idea that complex objects might be better managed by encapsulating appropriate processing methods with them, was used in an object-oriented program language called Simula-67, introduced in 1967. Since then various systems have been developed. Microsoft's OLE and Apple's OpenDoc, introduced during 1994, seem to be of most interest for multimedia.

An object may be 'linked' to a document where it will be displayed, with a reference to its native data, which are stored elsewhere; the document cannot be transferred to another computer. Alternatively, both the displayable and native data may be 'embedded' in a document, so that if the document is moved to another application or computer, it may be edited or processed at its new location. A linked object, updated by a message sent to its native data, will also be automatically updated in the linked document. In an object-oriented operating system, objects may be interchanged even when they reside in some remote part of a network.

Object Linking and Embedding (OLE) was introduced by Microsoft as a part of Windows 3.1. OLE 2.0 defines a document containing an object as a 'container'. Wayner (1994) provides an example of the usefulness of OLE 2.0:

> Suppose that the Container is a Microsoft Word 6.0 document and the inserted Object represents a range of cells in Excel 5.0 format. When you double-click on the spreadsheet object, Word's menus and frame controls magically become those of Excel. In effect, the word processor becomes a spreadsheet.

Apple's OpenDoc, in which Apple is associated with a number of others such as Sun, Xerox, Word Perfect, and IBM, is likely to be similar. Objects may be moved from one system to another. It is believed that translation software will be written enabling objects to be exchanged between OLE and OpenDoc. More details are provided by Gruman (1994).

Several 'multimedia database' software OLE packages at UK prices of between £100 and £300 were introduced in 1994. They require up to 6 Mbytes of RAM and run with Windows 3.1 on PCs, preferably at least 486s. They offer similar basic facilities for producing records by adding a field containing an object to another field, usually by presenting both fields on the screen with an appropriate menu-type interface to conduct the operation.

The difference between database prices, as between, say, Lotus Approach V2.1 (£99 from Lotus in the UK) and Microsoft Access (£280 from Microsoft) lies mainly in the comprehensiveness of 'help' screens, interfaces, editing facilities, etc.

STORAGE ARRANGEMENTS

If the database contains data which may be stored in more or less mutually exclusive sections, one section per disk, then a user's question may be routed directly to the appropriate disk. The retrieval speed will obviously then be faster than if the wanted picture is somewhere within a single large store.

The Kodak CD Jukebox system, for example, will provide rapid access to 30,000 thumbnail ('ikon') images, and slower access (5 seconds storage response time) to 60 Gbytes of storage on 2×50 CD jukeboxes containing associated high-resolution images. Sixty Gbytes amounts to 3333 $3000 \times 2000 \times 24$-bit (18 Mbyte uncompressed images), or 13,330 of the same images compressed by 4 times.

CD-ROM storage could well be a more convenient method of storage than large optical disks or jukeboxes. A considerable advantage of the CD-ROM is that a new disk may easily be produced for updating purposes. Moreover, individual CD-ROMs may be dispatched for use anywhere as needed. Parts or all of the Kodak photo-CD system could be pressed into service as part of the system to be described in the next section.

However, there is yet another option, which Kodak provide, and that is to store the pictures on CD-ROM at full resolution, with provision for calling them off at some lower resolution as 'thumbnails'. This has the advantage, assuming that telecom problems and costs can be overcome, of concentrating all activities at the database end and dispensing with the offline CD-ROM indexed-thumbnail arrangement operated at the user's premises.

For larger volumes of data, one idea is to store it hierarchically in order to position the data most likely to be needed closest to the user to minimize the time taken to retrieve and transmit them. A number of storage units are arranged so that archival least-used files are stored in the bottom row of stores, which are accessible relatively slowly (see Figure 16.9). Hierarchical Storage Management (HSM) software is available for managing such an arrangement where the available storage space appears to be infinite. The danger is that the system may be slowed up and the right choice of data migration rules may be difficult.

Files are moved upwards in stages to the local disk at the top, located in a user's workstation. All files are logically online. Staging is managed so that storage units never fill up. A user's activities are monitored and his or her most active files are moved into local storage.

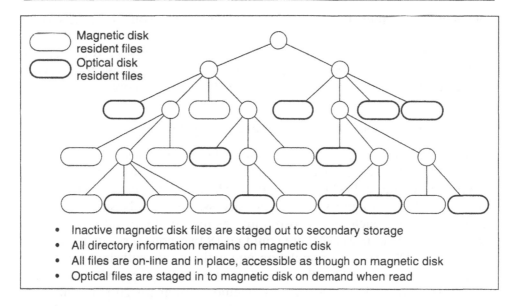

Magnetic disk
resident files

Optical disk
resident files

- Inactive magnetic disk files are staged out to secondary storage
- All directory information remains on magnetic disk
- All files are on-line and in place, accessible as though on magnetic disk
- Optical files are staged in to magnetic disk on demand when read

Figure 16.9 Hierarchical storage

Source: Epoch Systems

TELECOMMUNICATIONS

See also chapter 8.

The communications links between a picture database system and its users, assuming that users are geographically dispersed, could represent a severe bottleneck. Users must be able to participate in a question–answer fast-response session in order to home-in to, receive, and display wanted pictures using the remote system by trial and error. The response time depends mainly on retrieval from storage, telecoms transmission time, and the time it takes to present a high-resolution full-colour picture on a workstation. In order to consider the effect of the time taken in telecommunication transmission, the time to retrieve data from storage, etc., it will be assumed that a large diverse collection is to be accessed by people in different parts of the country. It will consist, as has already been assumed, of about 20,000 pictures, each occupying a picture file of 28.8 Mbits or 3.6 Mbytes. The total compressed size of 20,000 such files would be 7200 Mbytes or 7.2 Gbytes. If the user views the system as performing computations after a request is issued, then an average delay of 2 seconds is acceptable. Users tend to give up waiting for a response after about 20 seconds. A not unreasonable time to wait in the telecoms part of the system under discussion could be about 5 seconds. There will be other delays from the moment the user poses a question to the time he gets a picture retrieved from the system and displayed on his workstation, but if, say, the telecoms link can deliver the data at the rate of

500 Kbytes or 4 megabits/sec then a 3.6 Mbyte image would take 7.2 seconds in transit.

If a user is connected to a '30 × B' = 2.048 Megabits/sec total capacity ISDN system – the arrangement used, for instance, for connecting PABXs to the ISDN – then data speeds could be 500 Kbps or more.

User population and system peak handling capabilities

The maximum number of users who would be querying a system of this kind at any instant is a matter for conjecture. It would depend on the general usefulness of the collection, the way in which users connect to it, and the total population of users able to get access. As already suggested, if 50 terminals/users, each with a two-hour session, simultaneously access the system in a 36-hour week, there could be 18 two-hour sessions providing a service for 900 users – a population and activity rate sufficient for a fairly large system. In reality, the access pattern would probably resemble Bradford's law – i.e. 5 people (say) would account for 20 per cent of the total use, 10 for the next 17 per cent, 20 for the next 15 per cent, 40 for the next 12 per cent, etc.

The telecommunication delays would depend on the way the connecting links radiate outwards from the database centre to the users, and the ability of the retrieval mechanism to handle questions put by a number of users simultaneously. A set of local area networks, each with a few users, could be connected to a node via a Hub station. Users with heavy traffic could connect to the Hub with their own dedicated line.

Chapter 17

Videoconferencing and Virtual Reality

VIDEOCONFERENCING

> In the future, what we currently think of as separate applications such as work flow, conferencing, and text retrieval will become parts of a common service . . .

> Our goal is to make it possible for any two people on the face of the earth to communicate with each other visually over ordinary phone lines . . .

> Sales of desktop-based videoconferencing systems will soar from about 10,000 this year to nearly 800,000 in 1997.
> > (Quotations from articles in *Byte*, September 1993)

A number of qualifications are included in the *Byte* articles. In a piece entitled 'Video conquers the desktop', for instance:

> Video files could also spread problems for networks: frequent video-mail transfers could clog LANs. . . . Desktop videoconferencing systems typically compromise by offering smaller windows (as tiny as 80×96 pixels), grainier colour (8 bits per pixel instead of 24 bits), and lower frame rates (5 frames per second or less under certain conditions).

Marshall McLuhan, were he now alive, would certainly have been interested in videoconferencing; it represents a new form of technological determinism. I say new, but videoconferencing was being seriously considered at least twenty years ago – notably by AT&T with their Picturephone. The Picturephone was first demonstrated in Chicago in 1971 and cost a great deal to develop. According to Robert Lucky, Executive Director of Bell Labs (in his 1989 book *Silicon Dreams*) its expected success, like a disease, was based on contagion: 'when several of your friends got it, you were likely to get it too'. Lucky says it is still not understood why it failed. He thinks it was too intrusive: 'People did not want to comb their hair to answer the telephone . . . what is it worth to see the person you are talking to?' Lucky continues by quoting information transfer and problem-solving experiments conducted to try and quantify the effect of video; it was concluded that there was no advantage in having it, and 'there is an indefinable something about a real human being which is not conveyed by either the voice or the picture'.

Other suggestions about the failure of videoconferencing to take off in the late 1970s were made back in 1981: 'Teleconferencing was dominated by the belief that it was predestined to occur. Societal factors (e.g. energy shortages) and new technologies for holding electronic meetings, it was believed, were the only ingredients necessary for its emergence.' However, they were not. Videoconferencing did not emerge because readiness factors (energy shortages, new technologies, articulate promotional statements, public attitudes) did not develop into enabling forces (user-oriented systems, examples of success, enthusiastic advocates, believable justification).

Another sociological aspect is described by Short, Williams and Christie (1976). Commenting on the problems of the man at the other end during a face-to-face videoconferencing session, they said:

> We had arranged for coffee or tea to be served and he didn't have any. He sat there looking increasingly glum. The omission of social chat may have deleterious consequences. The busy executive may feel it advantageous to put in an appearance to chat with subordinates.

Substituting teleconferencing for travelling may save time and expense but there may be social losses: 'In the case of very large conferences it is not uncommon for a company to pay the expenses of its employees to travel and stay at a hotel to be wined and dined and generally mix business with pleasure.'

In the early 1980s, enthusiastic articles, usually including favourable comments about a rosy future for the Picturephone, were commonplace. Once again the forecasters were mistakenly making enthusiastic predictions about a new technology shortly to become a flop.

> National Data Corporation (NDC) predicts that the electronic meeting business will leap from $50M to about $220M by 1985.
>
> (*Telecommunications Policy*, 1981)

> TRW Inc has demonstrated big cost savings in presentations across America.
>
> (*Telecommunications Policy*, 1981)

> Video teleconference systems can be used effectively for a wide range of business meetings.
>
> (*Rev. Electrical Communication Labs*, 1981)

> There are many users and vendors who predict that teleconferencing will be as common in the office in 1990 as the typewriter is today.
>
> (*Data Communications*, 1982)

A conference at Wisconsin University was reviewed in *Telecommunications Policy*, December 1982. Ironically, enthusiasm at the opening of the Picturephone Meeting Service and the results reported about a major study by Satellite Business Systems (now defunct) were diminished by 'woefully inadequate audiovisual facilities ... antiquated rear-screen projection equipment which could not be focused automatically, etc.'

The same predictions for success, in some cases almost exactly the same, have been made for the 1990s; for some reason or other videoconferencing has been ten years in the wilderness. Someone must have cribbed the NDC 1981 forecast because the new version says: '$65.44M for 1990 and $296M for 1995' (*Financial Times*, 28 April 1992). But that's just for Europe. For the US it was '$894m for 1990 and [wait for it] $8.3 billion by 1995'!

Although the constraints on videoconferencing are steadily decreasing, 'acceptable' performance (the picture and sound quality which the industry thinks it can get away with) is still the criterion. Unless special machines are used which are interconnected by, and capable of working over a wideband channel, performance quality compared with TV is poor because of limited transmission bandwidth. Picture size and number of pixels are less, and frame repetition rate is reduced. Inter-frame motion compression is used but rapid movement is blurred. For the satisfactory reproduction of motion, frame repetition rates need to be 25 per second or above. If a station is transmitting frames at this rate and the receiving station is unable to process them, it simply drops frames and operates at its own specified rate.

Recent improvements have been brought about by a degree of agreement about the H.261 Standard (see chapter 9), advances in compression methods, chip-sets for PC boards, the arrival of 'Rollabout Units', falling prices, and wider availability of the ISDN. A Rollabout Unit may be used in any room – something of an advance because earlier machines suffered from 'howl-around feedback' or 'echo'. Special acoustically treated rooms were needed with careful placement of microphones and loudspeakers to prevent feedback, particularly in 'full duplex' connections. Echo feedback is now neutralized by subtracting an echo-replica signal from the signal itself. 'Full-duplex' means simultaneous two-way communication. 'To support video and voice over a single telephone line all signs point to the ISDN ... 27 times faster than the PSTN,' claims *Intel in its Solutions*, May/June 1993 publication.

I estimate that in practice the ISDN is only between 5 and 8 times faster. The *Intel* article says that Microsoft's Windows Telephony API interface 'will allow companies to develop products integrating the telephone and the PC'.

VIDEOCONFERENCING SYSTEMS

A number of illustrations of systems and systems in use are shown in Figure 17.1–17.5. Figure 17.1 shows the equipment fitted in a British Telecom experimental outfit called Mundi for exchanging pictures over a fibreoptic link – where the bandwidth would allow the minimum constraints on quality. Figure 17.2 shows a system containing a Picturetel Corporation PCS 1000 teleconferencing board; their very large screen unit is shown in Figure 17.3. The PCS1000 plug-in kit for PCs which sells for about £5000 in the UK is said to 'give users full colour full motion live video and high quality sound in a screen sharing collaborative computing environment'.

Figure 17.4 shows a screen using Loughborough Sound Images' MVP plug-in board, while 17.5 shows a session in progress in which the Indy computer described in chapter 5 is being used.

Today's range of videoconferencing facilities seem to vary between 'studio-level' equipment costing £30,000 or more, perhaps requiring a trained conference supervisor, hiring of equipped studios, using a VC7000 or similar machine, at £7500, or PCs in the price range $3000 to $5000 such as the Apple Quadra 840 AV at about $4500. The VC7000 will provide 360 × 288 pixel pictures at 25 frames per second, while the Apple includes facilities for marginally acceptable face-to-face teleconferencing (160 × 120 pixel window and 15 frames/second). There is some movement in the market. BT is said to have concluded a deal 'valued at around £400,000 as part of a call-off contract' with National Power for its VC7000 system which runs at 2 × 64K = 128 Kbps over dial-up ISDN.

At present, it seems that low price must be accompanied by low quality, which is not necessarily the same thing as 'low information capacity'. People accustomed to TV and cinema quality may sneer at low-priced video-conferencing quality which may yet be adequate to exchange the images of some kinds of documents. If you cannot see the small type, move it in closer and refocus on the required section.

However, that idea is over-simplistic and is complicated by 'whiteboard' considerations, where a whiteboard is an area on the screen for drawings, comments, or a prepared 'document' pasted on to it. Whiteboard data usually reside on the sending machine and are displayed on a remote receiving machine, having been prepared in advance at the sending end. The whiteboard is distinct from the area of the screen on which the image from a remote camera is displayed. This, and other inadequacies, and the conflict between machines complying with the CCITT Standard for compression and Intel's Indeo compression specification, are covered in chapter 9.

Improved facilities are likely to be added when the CCITT T123 working group recommends additional standards, including the provision of an interactively shared workspace. Commercial multi-point videoconferencing packages were unavailable as at December 1994, although AT&T is expected to make a system available in 1996 interlinking over twenty different

Figure 17.1 BT Mundi experimental fibreoptic system
Source: BT

machines. LANs and ATM protocol networks have the necessary bandwidth to interlink stations without unacceptable delays, enabling higher quality pictures to be exchanged.

However, there are as yet no Standards for networked videoconferencing. Garland and Rowell (1994) compare the performance of several hardware and/or software systems ranging in price from $500 to $6000, but requiring channels of appropriate bandwidth for the realization of their performance. For example, InVision's Desktop V 3.0 software, tested on a 10 Mbps Ethernet LAN and running on a 486 machine with Windows, provided a 160 × 120 pixel picture (see chapter 9), and ran at 2.9 frames per second during *Byte*'s 'VC bench high-motion' test. It does not support the CCITT Standard. The software price is $595.

Figure 17.2 The Picturetel PCS 100 system
Source: Liveworks

Descriptions of desktop machines, testing, and using via the ISDN are discussed in Anon. (1996b). The author considers that Focus PC 'is the best of the bunch' at £2800 in the UK. Some other products 'either did not work or were plagued with technical difficulties'. The conclusions are that 'desktop videoconferencing, while it has all the ingredients for being an attractive technology, has a long way to go before it can become a widely acceptable medium for sharing applications and data, using live audio and video'.

VIDEOCONFERENCING APPLICATIONS

A number of videoconferencing applications have been reported. One of the most ambitious is the Multimedia Integrated Conferencing for Europe (MICE) programme, a £5 million RACE-supported project. This is a large experiment to test interworking between European and US researchers using multimedia facilities. 'The MICE partners and the Internet community are providing multimedia services through applications that multicast directly to all sites in the conference' (Clayman *et al.* 1995).

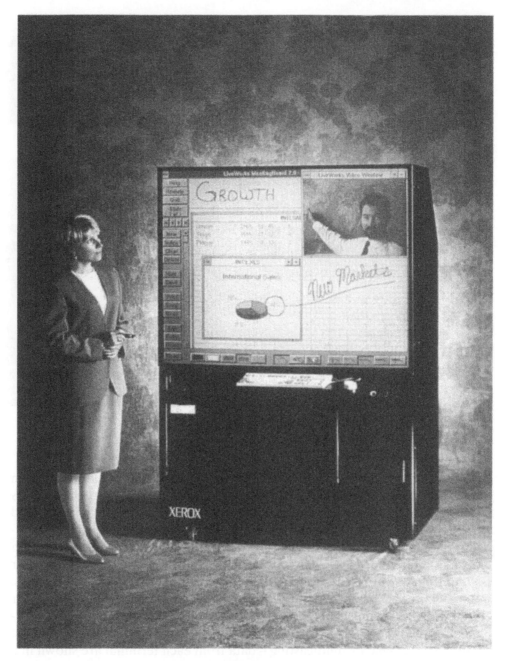

Figure 17.3 Picturetel large screen teleconferencing system
Source: Liveworks

Figure 17.4 Screen from Loughborough Sound Images' MVP system
Source: Loughborough Sound Images

At a 1993 meeting in Trondheim, Norway, for example, a demonstration was arranged between JENC (Trondheim), INRIA (France), RUS (Germany), University College London, Oslo University, Norway, and Lawrence Berkeley Laboratories, California. Most sites used Sun Sparc-Stations. The demonstration was artificial to the extent that the bandwidth of the interconnecting channels available for the participants was far wider than would be available to most people using videoconferencing links. Bandwidth ranged between 512 Kbps for the Nodunet link, 2 Mbps for London to Germany, and 34 Mbps within the UK. One part of the experiment provides for conferencing between a number of terminals on the Internet's M-bone by multicasting – data from each terminal are shown in a window on each participant's monitor. When terminals generate data in some other format, a Conference Management and Multiplexing Centre (CMMC) is interposed between those terminals and the Mbone. The CMMC modifies the format as necessary.

Videoconferencing has been used between Bellcore at Redbank USA, and high school students temporarily situated at the Smithsonian

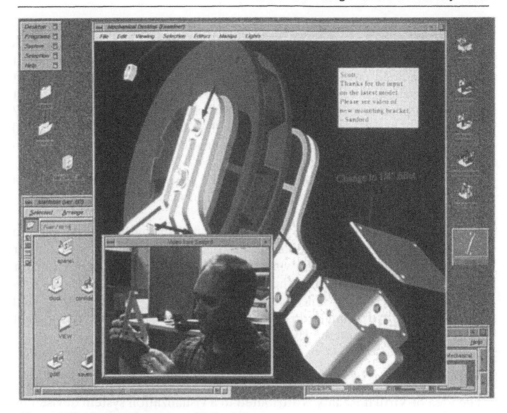

Figure 17.5 Videoconferencing with the Indy
Source: Silicon Graphics

Institution, Washington. Bellcore decided that clearly displayed facial expressions made interpretation easier so large screens were used. Plans are in hand to interlink 270 affiliated organizations using similar equipment, with the New York World Trade Center.

Whitehead (1994) reports a successful medical application of video-conferencing for consultation and training at remote locations. Only when systems became available working at 30 frames per second (NTSC Standard) over a 1.5 Mbps channel did videoconferencing become adequate for diagnostic quality images. Earlier systems lacked the necessary repro-duction quality. Systems in use now embody PCs which can also handle data from various medical appliances. Tests carried for dermatology were adequate for a remote physician to see different cell levels of the skin. Tissue samples could be examined at different sites by using a video camera attached to a pathology microscope. The Cleveland Clinic Foundation, now using the system on three different sites, is planning to set up links with affiliated hospitals and with hospitals in the Middle East.

The Bermed system at the German Heart Institute, Rudolf Virchow University Hospital, Berlin, has been described by Kleinholz and Ohly

(1994). Five hospitals and nine practitioners outside the hospitals are connected to the teleconferencing network via ISDN primary rate 2 Mbps links. At meetings between radiologists and orthopaedists a radiologist presents findings, physicians discuss cases, orthopaedists consult an expert radiologist about results of examinations from hospitals and learn about new developments in radiology. Sparc10 machines are used and 512×512 12-bit JPEG-compressed images are displayed on the screen in 5 to 10 seconds. This is considered to be good enough for short conferences but too slow for multi-image meetings.

The outstanding problems are considered to be inadequate security, a need for workspace management, and lack of synchronization. (Synchronization is covered in a section in chapter 8.)

Christie's have experimented with videoconferencing links between two of their London branches. Valuations can then be made on items sent in for auctioning to one branch by a valuer at the other one. In Scotland a major project was being planned at the end of 1993 to interconnect 13 colleges with videoconferencing links for teaching purposes. The Highlands and Islands Enterprise committed £400,000 to the project, and were trying to get a £5 million grant from the EC.

VIRTUAL REALITY

The idea of Virtual Reality is attributed to a visualization system devised by Ivan Sutherland (1965) called Sketchpad. Sutherland's work at MIT and Harvard was the founding research on the subject. By 1970 he had moved to the University of Utah where he developed the first interactive head-mounted display system. One of the first major applications was to simulate images for the pilots of military aircraft at the Wright Patterson base in the United States in the late 1980s.

VR is a computer technique in which a user or users seem to be surrounded by an environment sometimes called cyberspace, with which they are able to interact. The major components of a VR system are usually a helmet containing two display screens and sensors to detect the roll, pitch, and yaw of the head, headphones, and a glove or gloves to detect movements of the hand and the fingers with tactile sensors and pressure pads to sense foot pressures. The various sensors are connected to a computer with appropriate software in such a way that the user appears to react with a computer-created environment. Tracking of the user must appear to be natural without any time lag between user movements and system response. The display must have sufficient resolution to cover the user's field of vision with a smooth continuity of scene. Realistic scenes must be displayed at an appropriate repetition rate. The software must be adequate to provide the necessary support for animation, modelling, and dynamic behaviour of objects. A 1992 application received a good deal of publicity when a car called the Racoon constructed at Renault was designed and developed using VR. The car was 'driven' under virtual conditions which are said to have speeded up the design process so that it was completed only 13 months after the project started.

In October 1993 the journal *IEEE Spectrum* considered that the time had come for a special report about VR. The editorial comment (Adam 1993) opened with: 'Although virtual reality has become a popular buzzword with "frivolous" connotations, its ability to immerse users in interactive three-dimensional worlds of is of great significance for many scientific and industrial endeavours ... smell is being examined.' (Earlier movies known as 'the smellies' seem to have been a failure but they are bound to come.)

The complex structures of any desired shape, size, or complexity which are needed to represent VR environments such as a room, a landscape, or any object in a VR environment may be built up with sets of interconnected polygons. Comments about the required polygon construction rate have been made by G.W. Jones of ARPA:

> Many users are now content with 10,000 polygons per frame, but new users require one million per frame, repeating at 20-30 Hertz. . . . Users must be able to interact with a large complex geometry on the order of thirty million objects . . . dynamic access to more than 200 Gbytes of memory must be used.

The *IEEE Spectrum* editorial describes applications in tractor design, car engineering, military systems, health and medicine, research and education, and general amusements and entertainment. Collaboration between Paramount Pictures and Spectrum Holobyte is likely to produce a game in which users will be able to interact with characters aboard the *Starship Enterprise.*

An article by Steven Young in the *Daily Telegraph* of 24 November 1993 describes the training program for the repair of the Hubble orbiting telescope using VR. The system is also described in detail by Hancock (1993). A visual prototype was used to identify potential collision problems before designing the mechanisms needed to effect repairs. 'Viewers can position themselves anywhere around, and even inside, the Hubble Space Telescope, and zoom in for a close-up look at the Costar's arms deploying past the Wide Field Planetary Camera.'

Ralph Schroeder (1993) concentrates on applications in education and entertainment. In 1991, VR was used for educational purposes at the Human Interface Technology laboratory in Seattle, and in 1992 VR became a part of the standard curriculum at West Denton High School, Newcastle, UK.

Kaltenborn and Rienhoff (1993) review VR in medicine, providing 161 references. They cover applications in disability equipment, surgery, visualization of molecular structures, and psychiatry. At the Greenleaf

Medical Systems in the United States, data about wrist and hand movements are collected using a data glove for analysis purposes.

Alan Poulter distinguishes between a Virtual Library and a Virtual Reality Library. His Virtual Reality Library could be created using a software package called REND 386 for a 386 or 486 PC with a fast video card. It is available from the University of Waterloo, Ontario, Canada. The software enables a user to walk through each floor of a library and browse the contents of books by author and title. A representation of a 'volume', classified under an appropriate heading, may be found and its location marked, but there is no text display of the contents. Presumably the next step would be text records for volumes, retrievable from a very large database.

'Virtual Library' is also the label for a more nebulous concept reflecting the notion of the 'electronic book' and the possibility of providing information over a telecommunication network. Newby (1993) discusses the Virtual Library ideas put forward in the literature. They include access to multimedia databases and message systems, resource sharing, hypertext systems, etc. It appears that the word 'virtual' is sometimes used to add to the title of a system to increase its appeal, rather than to denote the arrival of a new concept.

Improvements in the mechanics of Virtual Reality continue. Recently a 640×480 pixel resolution screen the size of a 35 mm slide was announced. It consists of active matrix display using circuits deposited on glass.

A Frost & Sullivan forecast estimates that the VR market will be worth over 1 billion dollars by 1997, compared with $130 million in 1993, mainly because improvements in hardware and software will make it more acceptable.

Further applications of VR have been announced in 1994–95. Volvo use a VR system to illustrate safety features of its cars. The 'driver' dons VR equipment and test drives a Volvo 850, being able to see in any direction out of the interior of the car. An accident at 25 mph is simulated and the functions of safety features which enable the driver to survive are realistically shown.

IBM and a company called Virtuality have launched a complete system called Elysium, capable of providing an immersive presentation, selling for less than $50,000. Expectations are that it will be used to present a design for a building, kitchen, etc., providing a much more realistic idea of the item than using drawings, and enabling on-the-spot changes to be made by a client. A more futuristic idea is to use the system to simulate a networked 'virtually real office environment' to replace travelling to a meeting.

In the UK a VR research project is being funded by the DTI, the Engineering and Physical Sciences Research Council, and industry to produce systems for group work, with 'blockies' (virtual users) moving about in work spaces (Check 1994). The University of Surrey is developing systems to allow virtual people to enter hazardous environments with remote control by servo-mechanisms so that they move exactly as the controller is moving.

A medical application has been used at the Kaiser-Permante Medical Group in California to help acrophobics to overcome their fear of heights. Patients feel that they are entering a virtual environment simulating real situations – a therapy claimed to have a high success rate.

Medical applications in general have been reviewed by Satava (1994). He lists four areas for VR applications: assistance before and after medical and surgical procedures; medical education and training; medical database visualization; rehabilitation medicine. As an example he cites a VR model of a tumour visualized from the inside, constructed from three-dimensional scans. The tumour may be irradiated without damaging healthy tissue. As another example Satava refers to the training of surgeons by providing virtual organs on which virtual surgical procedures may be performed. He reminds the reader that the graphics available are still at the cartoon level but believes that as processing power is increased, realism will increase with it.

Chapter 18

Multimedia: prospects and growth

Gale (1990) foresaw 18 multimedia applications, 22 'market segments', and 14 'end-user platforms' by 1994. These precise estimates are blunted by an appropriate degree of segment broadness – for instance, 'documentation' is an application, 'consumer' is a market segment, and 'computerised entertainment/information systems' is an end-user platform.

The major markets in 1994 (in current millions of dollars) would be Consumer 4337, Heavy manufacturing 2211, Other 2103, Government 2055, Motion pictures 1239, Education and libraries 850, Computer and information Services 450, and Retail trades 352. Total $13.6 billion. Major manufacturers now consider it worthwhile to market 'multimedia systems'. These are really powerful microcomputers with extensions, integrated to be more easily managed than a micro plus some add-ons. This idea occurred to Commodore/Amiga back in August 1990 when they launched their 'CDTV' in the UK at around £700. Unfortunately it was a market failure.

Wilson (1991), at a time when applications were starting to emerge, divides the market into education, training, simulation, internal and external business communications, retail product information, museums, and domestic (home). Wilson says, after stressing the importance of the £2000 barrier, that 'Education is a growing issue' and in the UK the combination of performance with low cost is all-important.

Current activities by IBM, Apple, and others indicate that multimedia is now regarded as serious business and optimistic growth forecasts tell them what they want to hear. The business market for multimedia software and systems in the US and Europe will grow from £500 million in 1991 to £9 billion in 1997, according to yet another forecast. In 1991 there were only two significant uses for multimedia in business – interactive computer-based training systems and point-of-information/point-of-sale kiosks. But by 1994 a survey – based on detailed case studies of 25 systems suppliers, software developers, and users – reckons that there will be four main products operating system extensions that support multimedia, multimedia enhancements to spreadsheets and wp packages; business presentation packages, and information access packages that include publications, databases, and tools. By 1997 the survey adds two new categories which will extend the market still further – multimedia-enhanced electronic mail packages and groupware, including videoconferencing facilities. An organization called First Cities intends to create a significant marketplace for networked multimedia information and entertainment products and services by accelerating developments of a national infrastructure for entertainment, distance learning, health care, and electronic commerce.

According to Craig Fields, MCC chair and CEO, 'Our ultimate goal is the Telecomms Equipment, Cable TV, Broadcasters, Information Providers, and User Equipment.'

The information provided by the survey includes opinions about barriers to growth, a list of business and consumer applications and their expected time of arrival, degree of preparedness, organization vulnerability, and co-operation expectations. The biggest barrier to growth is considered to be 'end-user price unaffordable or uncompetitive'. The major 'market driver' will be the 'development of applications'. The first consumer application to reach critical mass will be 'games' (3 years), and the first for business, also in 3 years' time, will be 'business and financial news'. 'The most vulnerable companies' will be those in the 'video hire' business, with 'traditional print' not far behind. The survey finds that companies in print are 'less interested, less prepared, and less aware ... the most aggressive and enthusiastic are the cable companies'. The respondents in this survey are remarkably optimistic: '58% of them believe that the US domestic mass market will have access to network-based interactive multimedia by 1998–2000' – in other words the information superhighway will have arrived by then. While the conventional wisdom has it that the 'industry' will be entertainment-led, 54 per cent said that information products and services, led by education, will be at least as important, mainly because of people's desire to learn and keep on learning.

What can be concluded from this extraordinary collection of forecasts? The beauty of multimedia forecasting is that 'multimedia' is an elastic term. If you wish to include the best part of the computer and communications business in your definition, your forecast can be as optimistic as you like. You are still on safe ground because there no agreement about the extent of its borders. Unfortunately, the wider they are drawn, the less valuable the forecast. A broad-border forecast is not helpful if you wish to hear about the prospects for CD-Is or Corporate Presentation Software.

In the commercial world there have been several alliances between media and communications companies and publishers and entertainment organizations. The hardware people see the benefit of owning a complementary company to supply the 'software'. The early battles between VHS and Sony's Betamax recording systems might have gone Sony's way if Sony had been able to supply a volume of VHS consumer tapes. Sony soon pursued this principle. They purchased CBS records back in 1987 for $2 billion. In 1989 Sony bid $3.4 billion for Columbia Pictures, whose library of 2400 films included *Lawrence of Arabia* and over 20,000 TV shows. In 1989 Matsushita agreed a $100 million deal with 20th Century Fox.

This trend has continued. In 1995 MCI Communications and the News Corporation, chaired by Rupert Murdoch, agreed a $2.4 billion deal, their first project to be an electronic newspaper. News Corporation is the owner of 100 titles including *The Times*. MCI owns Internet MCI, which provides services such as electronic shopping, while the News Corporation runs Delphi Internet Services.

Some remarks made by John Priestley (1995) in his comments about the information superhighway seem equally appropriate when applied to multimedia generally. 'We have never been very good at predicting the future use of technology, even when we have had some success in predicting technology changes themselves,' he says.

> We may, by now, have shrewd ideas about some of the new tools that will be available to us, but we should be very wary indeed about assuming we know how they will make their impact. We know that we will have much more powerful and cheaper computing . . . we know too that we can bank on having a lot more communications capacity – and that an unstoppable combination of technological progress and political liberalisation will ensure lower prices, [but] we really should have learned by now that the availability of technologies is only one surprisingly small factor in a range of influences that determine social and behavioural change.

While the above remarks need to be taken into account, being aware of changes and reacting to them is a matter of equal importance. When should leaders of an organization consider and understand the possibilities of multimedia? David Kaye's remarks (Kaye 1994) include some pertinent advice to business leaders.

> Leaders in revolutionary times tend to have uncertain careers. Some fail because they are too slow to embrace revolution's possibilities and promises. Some fail because they cannot manage expectations. And some succeed either through a mixture of luck, energy and ability, or because they know how to make the many facets of inertia and change work together to their advantage, having the position, resources and commitment to make this happen. The drive for a leader to initiate the right IT-based change at the right time and to commit to its success comes either from competitors, or from a combination of personality or corporate culture, or from vision, or from all three combined.

References

Abbreviations
ICONCLASS Iconographic Classification System
IEEE   Institute of Electrical and Electronic Engineers
RARE   Réseaux Associés pour la Recherche Européenne
SPIE   Society of Photo-Optical Instrumentation Engineers

Aabo, S. (1992) 'A picture database; conservation needs and electronic access to the Fridtjof Nansen picture archive', *IFLA Journal* 18(3), 243–251.

Abernethy, T.W. and Munday, A.C. (1995) 'Intelligent networks, standards and services', *BT Technology Journal* 13(2), 9–20.

Adam, John A. (1993) 'Virtual reality is for real', *IEEE Spectrum* 30(10), 22–29.

Adie, Chris (1994) 'Network access to multimedia information', RARE Technical Report 8, Edinburgh University Computing Service.

Ajluni, Cheryl (1995) 'Security techniques ensure privacy', *Electronic Design* 43(8), 83–99.

Aleksander, Igor (1982) 'Modern pattern recognition and the classification of works of art', *Art Libraries Journal* 7(2), 61–66.

Allison, David K. and Gwaltney, Tom (1991) 'How people use electronic interactiveness', in D. Bearman (ed.) *Hypermedia and Interactivity in Museums*, Archives and Museum Informatics, Pittsburgh, pp. 62–73.

Alsberg, Peter A. (1975) 'Space and time savings through large database compression and dynamic restructuring', *Proceedings of the IEEE* 63(8), 1114–1122.

Ameil, Cécil (1995) *European information highways – which standards?*, European Parliament Economic Series W-18, European Parliament, Luxembourg.

Anagnostelis, Betsy (1995) 'Filtering for quality', *Inform*, December 1995, 3.

Anderson, Clarita S. (1991) 'A user's applications of imaging techniques: the University of Maryland's Historic Textile database', *Journal of American Society for Information Science* 42(8), 597–599.

Anon. (1977) *Whitford Report. Copyright and designs law*, HMSO Cmnd 6732.

Anon. (1981) UK Green Paper on copyright (for parliamentary discussion).

Anon. (1988) 'Symbolic projections', report of the ICONCLASS workshop, *Visual Resources* 5, 205–258.

Anon. (1992a) *The CD-I design handbook*, compiled by Philips and published by Addison-Wesley, Wokingham and Reading, MA.

Anon. (1992b) *The producer's handbook of multimedia authoring for CD-I*, Philips Interactive Multimedia Systems, Los Angeles.

Anon. (1992c) *Computerization project for the Archivo General de Indias*, Ministerio de Cultura, Madrid.

Anon. (1993a) 'Who's using what software for documentation where?' Report, The Museum Documentation Association, 347 Cherry Hinton Rd, Cambridge CB1 4DH, UK.

Anon. (1993b) 'The Avery video disc index of architectural drawings on RLIN', RLIN Information Center, 1200 Villa Street, Mountain View, CA 94041–1100, USA.

Anon. (1993c) 'Decades – the 1930s', Hulton Deutsch, 21–31 Woodfield Road, London W9 2BA.

Anon. (1993d) 'Main events and developments on the electronic information services market', Annual Report 1992 from CEC DG XIII/E, CEC Brussels.

Anon. (1994a) 'Esprit II project 5469: CITED (Copyright in Transmitted Electronic Documents'), Report available from the British Library, Boston Spa, UK.

Anon. (1994b) *Optical Fibre Networks*, Third report of the Trade and Industry Committee, HMSO, London.

Anon. (1994c) 'Preparing for the multimedia revolution', Touche Ross and the *Financial Times*, London.

Anon. (1994d) 'Information Superhighways. Opportunities for public sector applications in the UK', Report from the Government Centre for Information Systems (CCTA), Millbank, London.

Anon. (1994e) 'Europe and the global information society: recommendations to the European Council', Report from the EC Office, rue de la Loi, Brussels.

Anon. (1994f) 'The Internet and the European information industry', EC DGXIII Report, IMO (Information Market Observatory) working paper 94/3, Luxembourg.

Anon. (1994g) 'Europe's way to the information society: an action plan', The EC to the Council and European Parliament, rue de la Loi, Brussels, COM (94) Final.

Anon. (1995a) 'Color management and interactive home shopping: the imaging issues', *Advanced Imaging* 10(1), 22–29.

Anon. (1995b) 'Service actualités, nouvelles technologies, et épistel', European Parliament, Réunion du G7, DG de l'Information.

Anon. (1995c) 'Government Information Service. Access to information', CCTA, Norwich NR7 OHS, UK.

Anon. (1995d) Catalogue of 3000 colour photographs, Tony Stone Images, Bayham St, London.

Anon. (1995e) 'TI IN Educational Network', Adobe Systems, Mountain View, CA.

Anon. (1995f) 'Approaches to IT capability. Key stages 1& 2', National Council for Educational Technology, Science Park, Coventry, UK.

Anon. (1995g) 'Special Report. HDTV and the new digital television', *IEEE Spectrum* 32(4) 34–45.

Anon. (1995h) 'Uncle Sam logs off', *Byte* 20(7), 70.

Anon. (1995i) 'Beyond the telephone, the television and the PC', Consultative document, OFTEL, 50 Ludgate Hill, London EC4M 7JJ.

Anon. (1995j) 'Network Europe and the information society', Federal Trust, 158 Buckingham Palace Road, London SW1W 9TR.

Anon. (1995k) 'Banking and checking on the Net', *IEEE Multimedia* 2(4), 7.

Anon. (1996a) *Java Essentials: The Internet Springs to Life*, Sun Microsystem Computers Ltd, Bagshot, Surrey.

Anon. (1996b) 'Lab tests: videoconferencing', *PC User*, 23 January, 83–96.

Apiki, Steve (1991) 'Lossless data compression', *Byte* 16(3), 309–314, 386–387.

Aravind, R., Duttweiler, D.L. *et al.* (1993) 'Image and video coding standards', *AT&T Technology Journal* 67–89.

Atkins, M.J. (1993) 'Evaluating interactive technologies for learning', *Journal of Curriculum Studies* 25(4), 333–342.

Arlsberg, Peter A. (1975) 'Space and time saving through large database compression and dynamic restructuring', *Proceedings of the IEEE* 63(8), 1114–1122.

Arrott, Mathew and Latta, Sara (1992) 'Perspectives on visualisation', *IEEE Spectrum* 29(9), 61–65.

Badaoui, S., Chameroy V. and Aubrey, F. (1993) 'A database manager of biomedical images', *Medical Information* 18(1), 23–33.

Barberi, F., Bernstein, R. *et al.* (1991) 'Displaying morphological and lithological maps: a numerically intensive computing and visualization application', *IBM Journal of Research and Development* 135 (1/2), 78–86.

Barker, Philip and King, Terry (1993) 'Evaluating interactive multimedia courseware – a methodology', *Computers in Education* 21(4), 307–319.

Barnsley, M.F. and Demko, S. (1985) 'Iterated function systems and the global construction of fractals', *Proceedings of the Royal Society* A 399, 243–275.

Barten, Peter G.J. (1989) 'The effects of picture size and definition on perceived image quality', *Proceedings of SID* 30(2), 67–71.

Bearman, D. (1991a) 'Model agreement for owners of images licensing to multimedia producers', *Archives and Museum Informatics* 5(2), 9–10.

—— (1991b) 'Interactivity and hypermedia in museums', in D. Bearman (ed.) *Hypermedia and Interactivity in Museums*, Archives and Museum Informatics, Pittsburgh, pp. 1–16.

—— (1994) 'Guidelines for protecting intellectual property', *Archives and Museum Informatics* 8(2), 183–184.

Beaumont, J.M. (1991) 'Image data compression using fractal techniques', *BT Technology Journal* 9(4), 93–109.

Bell, Trude E., Adam, J.A. and Lowe, S.J. (1996) 'Communications', *IEEE Spectrum* 33(1), 30–41.

Besser, Howard (1990) 'Visual access to visual images: the UC Berkeley image database project', *Library Trends* 38(4), 787–798.

—— (1991) 'Imaging: fine arts', *Journal of the American Society for Information Science* 42(8) 589–596.

—— (1993) 'Visualisation of historic urban data', in Diane Lees (ed.) *Museums and Interactive Multimedia*, Museum Documentation Association, Cherry Hinton Road, Cambridge, UK.

Black, Kirsten (1993) 'ELISE – an online image retrieval system', *Aslib Information*, July/August, 293–295.

Black, Uyless (1995) *TCP/IP and related protocols*, 2nd edn, McGraw Hill, London and New York.

Blair, Nancy (1992) 'Device independent desktop colour: Kodak's new management tool', *Advanced Imaging* 7(4), 36–38.

Blakeman, Karen (1993) 'Internet up-date', IT Link, 5–7, September (Aslib, London).

—— (1995) 'Tales from the terminal room', IT Link, 13–16, June (Aslib, London).

Blank, Christine (1995) 'The FSN challenge: large-scale interactive television', *Computer* 28(5), 9–13.

Blisset, Gillian and Atkins, M. (1993) 'Are they thinking? Are they learning? A study in the use of interactive video', *Computers in Education* 21(1/2), 31–39.

Blum, Christofer, Hofmann, G.R. and Kronker, D. (1991) 'Requirements for the first international imaging standard', *IEEE Computergraphics and Applications*, March, 61–70.

Blunden, Brian (1994) 'Introduction and EP business review', in Brian Blunden and Margot Blunden (eds) *The Electronic Publishing Business and its Market*, IEPRC/Pira International, Leatherhead, Surrey KT22 7RU, pp. 1–45.

Bodson, Dennis and Schaphorst, R.A. (1983) 'Error sensitivity of CCITT standard facsimile coding', *IEEE Transactions on Communications*, COM-31(1), 69–81.

Bolt, R.A. (1977) 'Spatial Data Management System (SDMS)', Report, Massachusetts Institute of Technology no. 77 (Architecture Machine Group), MIT, Cambridge, MA.

Booth, Ben and Heap, Christine (1993) 'High resolution digital image storage at the National Railway Museum, York', in Diane Lees (ed.) *Museums and Interactive Multimedia*, Museum Documentation Association, Cherry Hinton Road, Cambridge.

Bordogna, G., Carrara, P., *et al.* (1990) 'Pictorial indexing for an integrated pictorial and textual IR environment', *Journal of Information Science* 16(3), 165–173.

Bornman, Hester and Von Solms, S.H. (1993) 'Hypermedia, multimedia and hypertext: definitions and overview', *The Electronic Library* 11(4/5), 259–268.

Bove, Tony and Rhodes, Cheryl (1990) *Que's Macintosh multimedia handbook*, Que Corporation, Carmel, Indiana.

Bovey, J.D. (1993) 'A graphical retrieval system', *Journal of Information Science* 19(3), 179–188.

Breward, Alastair (1993) 'The commercial exploitation of multimedia opportunities: a legal view', in David I. Raitt and Ben Jeapes (eds) *Online Information 93*, Learned Information, Oxford and New Jersey.

Brolio, John, Draper, Bruce A, *et al.* (1989) 'ISR: a database for symbolic processing in computer vision', *Computer* 22(12), 22–30.

Bryan, M. (1993) 'Standards for text and hypermedia processing', *Information Services and Use* 13(2), 93–102.

Burger, Jeff (1993) *The desktop multimedia bible*, Addison-Wesley Reading, MA, USA.

Bush, Vannevar (1945) 'As we may think', *The Atlantic Monthly*, July, 101–103.

Butterfield, Steve (1994) 'Process images fast with a real time OS', *Electronic Design* 42(8), 73–82.

Cappellini, Vito (1992) 'The Uffizi project', *Proceedings of the Conference on Electronic Imaging and the Visual Arts (EVA)*, Brameur, Aldershot (no pagination).

Carey, James W. (1981) 'McLuhan and Mumford: the roots of modern media analysis', *Journal of Communication* 31(3), 162–178.

Carr, Les, Davies, H. and Hall, W. (1993) 'Experimenting with HyTime architectural forms for hypertext exchange', *Information Services and Use* 13, 111–119.

Cavagioli, C. (1991) 'JPEG compression: spelling out the options', *Advanced Imaging*, 6(3), 44–48.

Cawkell, A.E. (1964) 'Cathode ray storage devices: TV by telephone line', *Electronic Engineering* 36(433), 142–149.

—— (1989) 'From Memex to Mediamaker', *The Electronic Library* 7(5), 278–286.

—— (1990a) 'Information theory is thriving', *Critique* 2(6), 1–12 (Aslib, London).

—— (1990b) 'Multimedia: hardware, software, costs, and applications', *Critique* 3(3), 1–12 (Aslib, London).

—— (1991a) 'Lethally innocuous visual display units', *Information Services and Use* 11, 33–42.

—— (1991b) 'Progress in documentation: electronic document delivery systems', *Journal of Documentation* 47(1), 41–73.

—— (1992a) 'Selected aspects of image processing and management: review and future prospects', *Journal of Information Science* 18, 179–192.

—— (1992b) Review of British Library R&D Department's image handling and multimedia programme, Report RDD/GC/901.

—— (1992c) 'Imaging systems and picture collection management: review', *Information Services and Use* 12, 301–332.

—— (1993a) 'Indexing collections of electronic images: a review', *British Library Research Review* no. 15.

—— (1993b) 'SuperJanet for information delivery', *IT Link* 3–4 (Aslib, London).

—— (1993c) 'Developments in indexing picture collections', in J. Hemsley (ed.) *Proceedings of the 1993 Electronic Imaging and Visual Arts Conference (EVA 93)*, Brameur & Vasari Enterprises, Aldershot, England, pp. 171–180.

—— (1994) 'Copyright and the First Amendment', *Journal of Information Science* 20(5), 368–369.

Chakravarthy, Anil S., Haase, K.B. and Weitzman, L.M. (1992) 'A uniform memory-based representation for visual languages', European Conference on Artificial Intelligence, Vienna, Austria.

Chambers, Jack A. and Sprecher, J.W. (1980) 'Computer assisted instruction: current trends and critical issues', *Communications of the ACM* 23(60), 332–342.

Chang, C.C. (1991) 'Retrieval of similar pictures on pictorial databases', *Pattern Recognition* 24(7), 675–680.

Chang, Shi-Kuo, Jungert, E. and Li, Y. (1990) 'The design of pictorial databases based upon the theory of symbolic projections', *Lecture notes on computer science*, Springer-Verlag, New York, pp. 303–323.

Chang, S.K. and Liu, S.-H. (1984) 'Picture indexing and abstraction techniques for pictorial databases', *IEEE Transactions on Pattern Analysis and Machine Intelligence* PAMI-6(4), 478–483.

Chang, S.K., Yan, C.W., Dimitrof, D. and Arnd, T. (1988) 'An intelligent image database system', *IEEE Transactions on Software Eng.* 14(5), 681–688.

Chaudhry, Anjali and Roy, Arup (1990) 'Art records treasury system: picture retrieval through image databases', *Proceedings of the 14th International Online Meeting*, Learned Information, Oxford and New Jersey, pp. 369–378.

Check, Martin (1994) 'Businesses waking up to virtual reality', *Computer* 27(12), 8–9.

Cherry, E.C. and Gouriet, G.G. (1953) 'Some possibilities for the compression of TV signals', *Proceedings of the IEEE* 100, part 3.

Cisneros, Guillermo, Bescos, J. and Martinez, J.M. (1996) 'Telemuseum services via Internet: present and future', *Information Services and Use* (forthcoming).

Clark R.S. (ed.) (1992) *Image Market '92. A strategic assessment of the international image and graphics management marketplace*, Frost & Sullivan, New York.

Clarkson, M.A. (1993) 'Hitting warp speed for LANs', *Byte* 18(3), 123–128.

Clayman, Stuart, Hestnes, Bjorn and Kirstein, Peter (1995) 'The interworking of Internet and ISDN networks for multimedia conferencing', *Information Services and Use* 15(2), 75–101.

Cleverdon, Cyril (1987) 'The Cranfield tests on index language devices', *Aslib Proceedings* 19(6), 173–194.

Cleverdon, C.W. and Lesk, M.E. (1966) *Factors determining the performance of indexing systems*, Aslib–Cranfield research project reports (2 vols). (Aslib, London).

Cole, George (1994) 'Multimedia goes to school', *Audiovisual*, March, 24–29.

Cole, Jonathan R. and Zuckerman, Harriett (1975) 'The emergence of a scientific specialty: the self-exemplifying case of the sociology of science', in Lewis Coser (ed.) *The idea of social structure: papers in honor of Robert K. Merton*, Harcourt Brace Jovanovich, New York.

Comerford, Richard (1995) 'Web sights', *IEEE Spectrum* 32(7), 71.

Cookson, Clive (1990) 'First auditions for the multimedia show', *Financial Times*, 11 October.

Cooper, Deborah and Oker, Jim (1991) 'History information stations at the Oakland Museum', in D. Bearman, (ed.) *Hypermedia and Interactivity in Museums*, Archives and Museum Informatics, Pittsburgh, pp. 90–113.

Cote, Raymond and Diehl, Stanford (1992) 'Monitors: beyond VGA', *Byte* 17(5), 208–234.

Cowan, A., Hartley, P. and Workman, A. (1989) 'Medical archiving: a picture of health', *Image Processing*, Autumn, 44–46.

Cronin, Blaise and Hert, C.A. (1995) 'Scholarly foraging and network discovery tools', *Journal of Documentation* 51(4), 388–403.

Cryan, Shelley (1994) 'Multimedia presentations', *Byte* 19(4), 189–195.

Cumani, A. Guidicci, A. and Grattoni, P. (1991) 'Image description of dynamic scenes', *Pattern Recognition* 24(7), 661–673.

Dackow, Tom (1995) Personal communication from Q Systems Research Corporation, 75, 6th Avenue, New York, NY 10012.

Dale, D.W. and Mitchell, D.J. (1993) 'Document management system – a strategic application for improved customer service', in Anon., *Proceedings of the Document Management Conference*, Meckler, London, pp. 441–455.

Daneels, Dirk, Van Campenhout, David *et al.* (1993) 'Interactive outlining: an improved approach using active contours', in W. Niblack (ed.) *Storage and retrieval for image and video databases*, Proceedings of the SPIE, vol. 1908, San José, CA, pp. 226–233.

Danziger, Pamela N. (1990) 'Picture databases: a practical approach to picture retrieval', *Database*, August, 13–17.

Darby, Jonathan (1994) 'Multimedia: so much promise, so little progress', in K. Beattie *et al.* (eds) *Interactive multimedia in university education. Designing for change and learning*, Elsevier, Amsterdam.

Dash, R.K. (1993) 'Image processing using quadtrees', *Dr. Dobb's Journal*, July, 44–49.

Davcev, Dancao, Cakmakov, D. and Cabukovski, V. (1992) 'Distributed multimedia information retrieval systems', *Computer Communications* 15(3), 177–184.

Davies, G.W.P. and Bianchessi, P. (1994) 'Human factors related to the use of visual display terminals in the European Parliament', *Information Services and Use* 14(1), 19–23.

de Benedetti, Carlo (1994) 'Superhighwayman', *Computer Weekly*, 13 October, p. 54.

Dejesus, Edmund X. (1996) 'How the Internet will replace broadcasting', *Byte* 21(2), 51–64.

Delouis, Dominique (1993) 'Telecommunications in museums', in J. Hemsley (ed.) *Proceedings of the 1993 Electronic Imaging and Visual Arts Conference (EVA 93)*, Brameur & Vasari Enterprises, Aldershot, UK, pp. 70–82.

Delp, H.R., Goertzel, G. *et al.* (1991) 'Color properties and color calibration for a high performance high fidelity color scanner', Report RC 17451 (no. 76941), IBM T.J. Watson Research Center, Yorktown Heights, NY.

de Sola Pool, Ithiel (1983) *Forecasting the telephone*, Ablex Publishing Company, Norwood, NJ, p. 76.

Dettmer, Roger (1996) 'Spinning the Web', *IEE Review*, January, 28–29.

Dickinson, Sven J., Pentland, A.P. and Rosenfeld, A. (1992) 'From volumes to views: an approach to 3-D object recognition', *CVGIP Image Understanding* 55(2), 130–154.

Diehl, Stanford (1991) 'The perfect pitch', *Byte* 16(13), 206–224.

Dijkstra, Joost (1994) 'A digital library in the mid-nineties, ahead or on schedule?', *Information Services and Use* 14, 267–277.

Dixit, Sudhir (1995) 'A look at the video dial-tone network', *IEEE Spectrum* 32(4), 64–65.

Doganata, Yurdaer N. and Tantawi, A.N. (1994) 'Making a cost effective video server', *Multimedia* 1, 22–30.

Doszkocs, T. (1984) 'Modern subject access in the online age' (untitled comments with W.R. Nugent), in P.A. Cochrane (ed.) *American Libraries* 15(6), 438–441, 443.

Doty, Philip and Bishop, A.P. (1994) 'The National Information Infrastructure and electronic publishing: a reflective essay', *Journal of the American Society for Information Science* 45(10), 785–799.

Dowe, J. (1993) 'Content-based retrieval in multimedia images', in W. Niblack, (ed.) *Storage and retrieval for image and video databases*, Proceedings of the SPIE, vol. 1908, San José, CA, pp. 164–167.

Eakins, J.P. (1992) 'Pictorial information systems – prospects and problems', Paper presented at the British Computer Society (BCS) Information Retrieval Specialist Group Research Colloquium, Lancaster.

Egan, Bruce L. (1994) 'Building value through telecommunications', *Telecommunications Policy* 18(8), 573–587.

Eisenberg, Michael B. (1991) 'Information technology and services in schools', in Martha E. Williams (ed.) *Annual Review of Information Science and Technology*, vol. 26, Learned Information, Medford, NJ, pp. 243–285.

Elliott, John (1995) 'Untangling the Web', *MacWorld*, July, 135–136.

Enser, P.G.B. (1991) 'An indexing-free approach to the retrieval of still images', in T. McEnery (ed.) *Proceedings British Computer Society (BCS) 13th Information Retrieval Colloquium*, BCS, London.

—— (1993) 'Query analysis in a visual information retrieval context', *Journal of Document and Text Management* 1(1), 25–52.

Enser, P.G.B. and McGregor C.G. (1992) 'Analysis of visual information retrieval queries', personal communications, August.

Equitz, W. (1993) 'Using texture for query by image content in QBIC', Research report, IBM Almaden Research Center, San José, CA.

Evans, Adrian (1991) 'BBC TELCLASS: basics of concept classification', Report, BBC Film & Videotape Library, Brentford, UK.

Fairman, Roger (1991) 'Networking CD-ROMs: theory and practical experience', *Aslib Information* 19(9), 356–362.

Farrell, Edward J. (1991) 'Preface to a visualisation issue of the journal', *IBM Journal of Research and Development* 135 (1/2), 3.

Feldman, T. (1991) 'Multimedia in the 1990's', BNB Research Fund Report 54, British Library.

Fink, E. (1980) 'Subject access to photographic reproductions of American paintings at the national collection of fine arts', in J. Raben *et al.* (eds) *Proceedings of the International Federation for Information Processing*, North Holland.

Flohr, Udo (1995) 'Hyper-G organises the Web', *Byte* 20(11), 59–64.

Foster, David (1992) 'Visualisation 2: IBM power', *Parallelogram*, 25, September.

Francis, Richard, Grigg, C. *et al.* (1992a) *Very spaghetti: the potential of interactive multimedia in art galleries*, Arts Council, London.

—— (1992b) *Very spaghetti: background notes for a report on interactive multimedia in art galleries*, Arts Council, London.

Freeman, David T. (1987) 'The false start of the electrical journal: a look at human factors and automation', *Proceedings of the ASIS Annual Meeting*, Learned Information, New Jersey, pp. 79–82.

Frenkel, Karen A. (1990) 'The politics of standards and the EC', *Communications of the ACM* 33(7), 41–51.

Friedlander, L. (1991) 'Electrifying Shakespeare: modern day technology in a renaissance museum', in D. Bearman (ed.) *Hypermedia and Interactivity in Museums*, Archives and Museum Informatics, Pittsburgh.

—— (1993) 'Making the punishment fit the crime', in Diane Lees (ed.) *Museums and Interactive Multimedia*, Museum Documentation Association, Cherry Hinton Road, Cambridge.

Fromont, J. (1993) 'State of the art regarding the various standards for contents related to text, still images, sound and video', *Information Services and Use* 13(2), 155–158.

Fromont, J., Creff, H. and Marie, X. (1993) 'The AVI initiative: functional requirements analysis and proposed framework for standardisation', *Information Services and Use* 13(2), 159–170.

Fuhrt, Borko (1994) 'Multimedia systems: an overview', *Multimedia* 1(1), 47–59.

Fuhrt, Borko, Kalra, D. *et al.* (1995) 'Design issues for interactive television systems', *Computer* 28(5), 25–39.

Galbraith, Ian (1993) 'The practicalities of document conversion', in Anon. *Proceedings of the Document Management Conference*, Meckler, London, pp. 85–94.

Gale, John C. (1990) 'Multimedia – how we get from here to there', in *Proceedings of the 14th Online Information Meeting*, Learned Information, Oxford and New Jersey.

Garland, Eric and Rowell, Dave (1994) 'Face to face collaboration', *Byte* 19(11), 233–242.

Gates, Rick (1993) 'The culture of net navigation', *The Electronic Library* 11(4/5), 335–345.

Gemmell, D. James, Vin, H.M., *et al.* (1995) 'Multimedia storage servers: a tutorial', *Computer* 28(5), 40–49.

Ghani, Din (1995) 'Charging and paying for information on open networks', *Aslib Proceedings* 47(6), 145–152.

Ghassemzadeh, A. and Regan, T. (1994) 'An environment for formal specification and implementation of interaction policies for distributed multimedia applications', *BT Technology Journal* 12(3), 64–71.

Ginsburg, Jane C. (1995) 'Putting cars on the "information superhighway": authors, exploiters, and copyright in cyberspace', *Columbia Law Review* 95, 1466–1499.

Gonzalez, R.C. and Wintz, V. (1987) *Digital image processing* 2nd edn, Addison-Wesley, Reading, MA, USA.

Goodrum, Charles and Dalrymple, Helen (1985) 'The electronic book of the very near future', *Wilson Library Bulletin*, May, 587–590.

Gordon, Catherine (1990) 'An introduction to ICONCLASS', in D.A. Roberts (ed.) *Proceedings of the 2nd Conference of the Museum Documentation Association*, 233–244.

Gore, Al (1994a) 'Why the world needs the information revolution now', *Business and Technology Magazine*, October, p. 13.

—— (1994b) 'Innovation delayed is innovation denied', *Computer* 27(12), 45–48.

Gould, C.R. (1973) 'Visual aids – how to make them positively legible', *IEEE Transactions on Professional Education* PC-16(2), 35–38.

Govindaraju, Venu and Srihari, R. (1990) 'Automatic face identification from news photo databases', *Advanced Imaging* 5(11), 22–26.

Grashoff, Tudor (1993) 'The pros and cons of producing your own CD-ROM', in David I. Raitt and Ben Jeapes (eds) *Online Information 93*, Learned Information, Oxford and New Jersey.

Gray, L. (1992) 'Information retrieval software: recent developments in the Cardbox family', *Aslib Information* 20(4), 164–165.

Gruman, Galen (1994) 'No missing link: OpenDoc and OLE: applications, but not as we know them', *MacWorld*, November, 89–96.

Guittet, Christian (1993) 'Turning an online database into a multimedia guide', in David I. Raitt and Ben Jeapes (eds) *Online Information 93*, Learned Information, Oxford and New Jersey.

Haddon, J.F. and Boyce, J.F. (1989) 'Simultaneous image segmentation and edge detection', *IEE Conference Publication* 307.

Hale, Diana and Grant, S. (1992) 'A multimedia database for heritage information systems', *Proceedings of the Conference on Electronic Imaging and the Visual Arts (EVA)*, Brameur, Aldershot, UK (no pagination).

Hales, Keith and Jeffcoate, Judy (1990) 'Document Image Processing: the commercial impact', Report, Ovum Ltd, 7 Rathbone St, London.

Halfhill, Tom R. (1994) 'The tools for new TV', *Byte* 19(3), 62–63.

Hancock, Dennis (1993) 'Prototyping the Hubble fix', *IEEE Spectrum* 30(10), 34–39.

Haskell, Barry G. and Steele, R. (1981) 'Audio and video bit rate reduction', *Proceedings of the IEEE* 69(2), 252–262.

Haywood, Trevor (1995) *Info-rich info-poor*, Bowker Saur, East Grinstead.

Heap, C. (1993) 'Photo negative database at the UK's National Railway Museum', *Advanced Imaging* 8(2), 36–39.

Helms, R.M. (1990) 'Introduction to image technology', *IBM Systems Journal* 29(3), 313–332.

Helmsley, James (ed.) (1993a) *Proceedings of the Conference on Electronic Imaging and the Visual Arts (EVA)*, Brameur & Vasari Enterprises, Aldershot, UK.

—— (1993b) 'Design and development of systems for museums and galleries', in Diane Lees (ed.) *Museums and Interactive Multimedia*, Museum Documentation Association, Cherry Hinton Road, Cambridge.

Hine, Graham (1992) 'The international art and antique loss register', *Proceedings of the Conference on Electronic Imaging and the Visual Arts (EVA)*, Brameur, Aldershot, UK (no pagination).

Hines, E.L. and Hutchinson, R.A. (1989) 'Application of multi-layer perceptrons to facial feature location', *IEE Conference Publication* 307, pp. 39–43.

Hirata, K. and Kato, T. (1993) 'Rough sketch-based image information retrieval', *NEC Research and Development* 34(2), 263–273.

Hirumi, Atsusi, Savenye, W. and Brockenbrough, A. (1994) 'Designing interactive videodisc-based museum exhibits: a case study', *Educational Technology Research and Development* 42(1), 47–55.

Hoekema, James (1990) 'Multimedia design for consumers: the case of Treasures of the Smithsonian', *Interactive Multimedia* 1(1), 7–22.

Hoffos, Signe (1992) 'Multimedia and the interactive display', Library and Research Report 87, The British Library Publications Unit, Boston Spa, West Yorks, UK.

Hogan, Matthew, Jorgensen, C. and Jorgensen, P. (1991) 'The visual thesaurus in a hypermedia environment: a preliminary explanation of conceptual issues and applications', in D. Bearman (ed.) *Hypermedia and Interactivity in Museums*, Archives and Museum Informatics, Pittsburgh, p. 202–221.

Hollis, Richard (1993) 'CD-ROM versus online: the UK perspective', *The Electronic Library* 11(4/5), 307–309.

Holt, Bonnie and Hartwick, L. (1994) 'Quick, who painted fish? Searching a picture database with the QBIC project at UC Davis', *Information Services and Use*, 14, 79–90.

Horowitz, Michael L. (1991a) 'An introduction to object-oriented databases and database systems', Report CMU-ITC-91-103, Information Technology Center, Carnegie Mellon University.

—— (1991b) 'The Alexandria Project', Project proposal, Information Technology Center, Carnegie Mellon University.

Huffman, David A. (1952) 'A method for the construction of minimum redundancy codes', *Proceedings of the Institute of Radio Engineers* 40, 1098–1101.

Information Services and Use (1995) special issue, 15(4) on 'Electronic imaging and the visual arts' (12 papers).

Jacobson, R.E. (1993) 'Approaches to total quality for the assessment of imaging systems', *Information Services and Use*, 13, 235–246.

Jacobson, Thomas L. (1994) 'The electronic publishing revolution is not global', *Journal of the American Society for Information Science* 45(10), 745–752.

Jagadeesh, J.M. and Ali, M. (1993) 'Framegrabber velociraptor', *Computer* 26(8), 86–88.

Jain, Anil K. (1981) 'Image data compression: a review', *Proceedings of the IEEE* 69(30), 349–389.

Jain, Ramesh (1995) 'World-wide maze', *IEEE Multimedia* 2(2), 3.

Jennings, Laura (1983) 'Why books will survive', *The Futurist* 17(2), 5–11.

Johnson, Andrew (1996) 'IBM to use Java to improve network connectivity', *PC User*, 23 January, 9.

Jones-Garmil, Kathy (1994) 'Embark', *Archives and Museum Informatics* 8(3), 255–260.

Kaltenborn, K.F. and Rienhoff, R. (1993) 'Virtual reality in medicine', *Methods of Information in Medicine* 32, 407–417.

Karmouch, A., Goldberg M. and Georgamas, N.D. (1991) 'Design considerations for a multimedia medical communications system', *L'Onde Electrique* 71(4), 7–12.

Kass, Michael, Witkin, Andrew and Terzopoulos, D. (1988) 'Snakes: active contours', *International Journal of Computer Vision*, 1, 321–331.

Katsuyama, T., Kamata, H., Okuyama, S. *et al.* (1993) 'Multimedia paper services, human interfaces and multimedia communication workstation for broadband ISDN environments', *IEICE Transactions on Communication* E-76-B(3), March, pp. 220–228.

Kaufman, Arie E. (1994) 'Visualisation', *Computer* 27(7), 18–19.

Kay, Alan and Goldberg, Adele (1977) 'Personal dynamic media', *Computer* 10(3), 31–41.

Kaye, David (1994) 'Managing the information revolution', *Futures* 26(4), 416–429.

Keating, Lawrence R., Reinke, C.A. and Goodman, J.A. (1993) 'Electronic journal subscriptions', *Library Acquisitions, Practice, and Theory* 17, 455–463.

Keefe, Jeanne (1990) 'The image as a document: descriptive programs at Rensslaer', *Library Trends* 38(4), 659–681.

Keen, E.M. and Armstrong, C.J. (1980) 'Visual processing in information retrieval searching', Report published by the Department of Information Studies, College of Librarianship, Aberystwyth, Wales.

Kitamoto, A., Zhou, C. and Takagi, M. (1993) 'Similarity retrieval of NOAA satellite imagery by graph matching', in W. Niblack (ed.) *Storage and retrieval for image and video database*, Proceedings of the SPIE, vol. 1908, San José, CA, pp. 60–73.

Kleinholz, Lutz and Ohly, Martin (1994) 'Supporting cooperative medicine: the Bermde project', *Multimedia* 1(4), 44–53.

Krol, Ed (1994) *The whole Internet user's guide and catalog*, 2nd edn, O'Reilly/Thomson, London.

Lahanier, Christian and Aubert, Michel (1993) 'Network of art research computer image systems in Europe (Narcisse)', in Diane Lees (ed.) *Museums and interactive multimedia*, Museum Documentation Association, Cherry Hinton Road, Cambridge.

Large, David (1995) 'Creating a network for interactivity', *IEEE Spectrum* 32(4), 58–63.

Larish, John (1995) 'The surprising digital side to the new Kodak advanced photo system', *Advanced Imaging* 10(11), 65–66.

Lee, J.H. and Liu, H.T. (1989) 'Digital image coding with high compression ratio', in Anon. *IEE Conference Publication* no. 307, IEE, London, pp. 595–598.

Lee, J.H. and Philpot, W.D. (1991) 'Spectral texture pattern matching: a classifier for digital imagery', *IEEE Transactions of Geoscience and Remote Sensing* 29(4), 545–554.

Lee, Newton S. (1991) 'Hypermedia authoring and annotation in InfoStation', *The Electronic Library* 9(6), 337–341.

Lee, Paul, Jeffcoate, J. and Mathews, J. (1995) 'Interactive television: the market opportunity (Update 3)', Report from Ovum, Mortimer St, London.

Lees, Diane (ed.) (1993) *Museums and interactive multimedia*, Museum Documentation Association, Cherry Hinton Road, Cambridge.

Le Gall, D. (1991) 'MPEG: a video compression standard for multimedia applications', *Communications of the ACM* 34(4), 46–58.

Lelewer, Debra A. and Hirschberg, D.S. (1987) 'Data compression', *ACM Computing Surveys* 19(3), 262–296.

Lennon, Anthony (1994) 'Hands-on testing: 46 powerful portables', *Byte*, 19(3), 156–181.

Leonard, Milt (1991) 'IC executes still-picture compression algorithms', *Electronic Design*, 39, May, 49–53.

Lester, Dan (1995) 'Yahoo – profile of a Web database', *Database*, December, 46–50.

Leung, C.H.C. (1990) 'Architecture of an image database system', *Information Services and Use* 10, 391–397.

Lewis, Ted (1995) 'The Nethead gang', *Computer* 28(12), 8–10.

Lindstrom, Bob (1994) 'Opening night for Premiere 3.0', *Byte* 19(1), 179–182.

Little, T.D.C. and Ghafoor, A. (1991) 'Synchronization protocols for broadband integrated services', *IEEE Journal on Selected Areas of Telecommunications* 9(9), 1368–1382.

Little, T.D.C. and Venkatesh, D. (1994) 'Prospects for interactive video-on-demand', *Multimedia* 1(4), 14–24.

Llewellyn, Richard (1991) 'Image storage and retrieval: a tool for museum collection management', in D. Bearman (ed.) *Archives and Museum Informatics*, Technical Report no. 14, Proceedings of the Conference on Hypermedia and Interactivity in Museums, Pittsburgh.

Lockwood, Russ (1994) 'Video acceleration in the fast lane', *Byte* 19(4), 28.

Loeb, S. (1992) 'Delivering interactive multimedia documents over networks', *IEEE Communications Magazine* 30(5), 52–59.

Looms, Lavin (1995) 'News of the Internet', *Infohighway*, 9–10, 31 May.

Looms, Peter O. (1991) 'Economic and design issues of large-scale multimedia databases', in D. Bearman (ed.) *Archives and Museum Informatics*, Technical Report no. 14, Proceedings of the Conference on Hypermedia and Interactivity in Museums, Pittsburgh.

Loveria, Greg (1993) 'Making the MPC upgrade', *Byte* 18(6), 176–192.

Low, Adrian (1991) *Introductory computer vision and image processing*, McGraw-Hill (Europe), Maidenhead, UK.

Lucky, Robert W. (1989) *Silicon dreams: information, man, and machine*, St. Martin's Press, New York.

Lunin, Lois (1990) 'An overview of electronic image information', *Optical Information Systems*, May–June, 114–130.

McClelland, Deke (1994) 'Photoshop's plug-in filters', *Macworld*, 99–104, November.

McLarnon, Z. and Muxie, J.P. (1994) 'Synchronisation problems faced by the multimedia producer now', *Advanced Imaging* 9(1), 62–64.

McLuhan, Marshall (1962) *The Gutenberg galaxy: the making of typographical man*, University of Toronto Press, Toronto.

McMahon, Ken (1994) 'Go on the record', *Personal Computer Magazine*, 151–167, June.

McMurdo, George (1995) 'How the Internet was indexed', *Journal of Information Science* 21(6), 479–489.

McMurdo, George and Simpson, Evelyn (1994) 'The White House files', *Journal of Information Science* 20(5), 305–313.

Makins, M. (ed.) (1991) *Collins English dictionary*, 3rd edn, HarperCollins, Glasgow, UK.

Maney, Kevin (1995) *Megamedia shakeout*, John Wiley & Sons, London.

Mansell, Robin (1994) 'Strategic issues in telecommunications', *Telecommunications Policy* 18(8), 588–600.

Marcus, Aaron and Van Dam, A. (1991) 'User-interface developments in the 90s', *Computer* 24(9), 49–66.

Marshall, I.W. and Bagley, M. (1995) 'The information services supermarket – an information network prototype', *BT Technology Journal* 13(2), 132–142.

Martin, James and Cowan, Mary (1994) 'Copyrights and wrongs', *MacWorld*, May, 99–106.

Martyn, John, Vickers, Peter and Feeney, Mary (eds) (1990) 'Publishing, new products, distribution and marketing', *Information UK 2000*, Bowker-Saur, London & New York, chapter 8, p. 161.

Maurer, H. and Williams, M.R. (1991) 'Hypermedia systems and other computer support as infrastructure for museums', *Journal of Microcomputer Applications* 14, 117–137.

Mendelsohn, Susan (1994) 'Would you like the databases you regularly use to be multimedia?', *Information World Review*, 36, November.

Menella, D. and Muller, A. (1990) 'Data capture of compound documents: solutions to the problems', in *Proceedings of the 14th International Online Meeting*, Learned Information, Oxford and New Jersey.

Mezrich, Reuben S., De Marco, J.K. *et al.* (1995) 'Radiology on the information superhighway', *Radiology* 195(1), 73–81.

Miles, I. (1993) 'Social implications', in D.E.N. Davies *et al.* (eds) *Communications after AD 2000*, Chapman & Hall, London, chapter 6.

Miller, Philip H. (1993) 'New technology old problem: determining the First Amendment status of electronic information services', *Fordham Law Review* 61, 1147–1201.

Miller, R.L. (1993) 'High resolution image processing on low-cost microcomputers', *International Journal of Remote Sensing* 14(4), 655–667.

Mintzer, Fred and McFall, John D. (1991) 'Organization of a system for managing the text and images which describe a collection', *Proceedings of the SPIE*, San José, (SPIE, Washington), 1460, 38–49.

Moffett, Jonathan (1992) 'The Beazley Archive: making a humanities database accessible to the world', *Bulletin of the John Rylands University Library of Manchester* 74(3), 39–52.

Mohageg, Michael F. (1992) 'The influence of hypertext linking structures on the efficiency of information retrieval', *Human Factors* 34(3), 351–367.

Moir, Michael B. (1992) 'The use of optical disc technology to improve access to historical photographs', *Archives and Museum Informatics* 6(1), 5–15.

Mooers, Calvin N. (1960) 'Mooers law – or why some retrieval systems are used and others are not', Editorial, *American Documentation* 5(2).

Moog, Robert A. (1986) 'Digital music synthesisers', *Byte* 11(6), 155–168.

Moroney, John and Mathews, J. (1995) *Applications for the superhighway*, Ovum Ltd, 1 Mortimer St, London W1N 7RH.

Muller, Nathan (1996) 'Dial 1-800-Internet', *Byte* 21(2), 83–88.

Mumford, Anne M. (1996) 'Networking multimedia – a supporter's nightmare', *Information Services and Use* 16(1), 43–50.

Mumford, Lewis (1963) *Technics and civilization*, Harcourt Brace & World, New York.

Murray, John (1995) 'Anarchy and chaos on the net', *Computer* 28(5), 87.

Mussman, Hans G. and Preuss, D. (1977) 'Comparison of redundancy reducing codes for facsimile transmission of documents', *IEEE Transactions on Communications* COM-25(11), 1425–1433.

Myers, Ware (1995) 'Compcon 95: technologies for the information superhighway', *Computer* 28(5), 101–103.

Nagy, G. (1985) 'Image databases', *Image and Vision Computing* 3(3), 111–117.

Nagy, George and Shirali, Nagesh (1991) 'Automated segmentation of printed pages for browsing', *Advanced Imaging* 6(3), 49–53.

Nahrstedt, Klara and Steimetz, R. (1995) 'Resource management in networked multimedia systems', *Computer* 28(5), 52–63.

Nance, Barry (1994) 'Four peer operating systems', *Byte* 19(12), 169–176.

Nelson, Theodor H. (1974) *Dream machines*, published privately; 1987 Microsoft Press, New York.

—— (1981) *Literary machines* published privately; 1987 Microsoft Press, New York.

Ness, Richard (1995) 'Set-top boxes: few standards but a rosy outlook', *Electronic Design* 43(9), 101–110.

Netravelli, Arun and Lippman, A. (1995) 'Digital television: a perspective', *Proceedings of the IEEE* 83(6), 834–842.

Neville, Peter (1989) 'The Mac shows its true colours', *MacNews*, 2 October, 12–15.

Newby, Gregory B. (1993) 'Virtual Reality', in Martha E. Williams (ed.) *Annual Review of Information Science and Technology*, vol. 28, Learned Information, London and New Jersey, pp. 187–229.

Niblack, W., Barber, R. *et al.* (1993) 'The QBIC project: querying images by content using color, texture, and shape', IBM Research Report RJ 9203 (81511), Almaden Research Center, San José, CA. NOTE: A similar paper by the same authors was subsequently published in W. Niblack (ed.) *Storage and retrieval for image and video database*, Proceedings of the SPIE, vol. 1908, San José, CA, pp. 173–187.

Nightingale, Charles (1991) 'Image processing in visual telecommunications – a light-hearted critique', in Don Pearson (ed.) *Image processing*, McGraw-Hill, Maidenhead, UK.

Nora, Simon and Minc, Alain (1978) 'L'informatisation de la société', Report to the President of France, La documentation française.

Nordgren, Layne (1994) 'Making sense of the new MPC Level 2 hardware choices', *CD-ROM Professional*, 35–42, January.

Nugent, W.R. (1984) 'Modern subject access in the online age' (untitled comments with T. Doszkocs), in P.A. Cochrane (ed.) *American Libraries* 15(6), 438–441, 443.

Nyquist, H. (1924) 'Certain factors affecting telegraph speed', *Bell System Technical Journal* 3, 324.

Oakley, J., Davis, D. and Shann, R. (1993) 'Manchester visual query language', in W. Niblack (ed.) *Storage and retrieval for image and video databases*, Proceedings of the SPIE, vol. 1908, San José, CA, pp. 104–114.

Obraczka, Katia, Danzig, Peter B. and Li, S.-H. (1993) 'Internet resource discovery services', *Computer* 26(9), 8–22.

O'Connor, Brian C. (1991) 'Selecting key frames of moving image documents: a digital environment for analysis and navigation', *Microcomputers for Information Management* 8(2), 119–133.

O'Docherty, M.H., Daskalakis, C.N. *et al.* (1991) 'The design and implementation of a multimedia information system with automatic content retrieval', *Information Services and Use* 11, 345–385.

Ohlgren, T.H. (1980) 'Subject access to iconographic databases. Theory and practice', in J. Raben *et al.* (eds) *Proceedings of the International Federation for Information Processing conference on databases in the humanities and social sciences*, August 1979, Dartmouth College, North Holland.

Olney, Lee D. (1995) 'Library networks and electronic publishing', *Information Services and Use* 15(1), 39–47.

O'Mara, William (1992) 'LCD dividends', *Physics World*, 36–41, June.

Oppenheim, Charles (1994) 'Lislex: legal issues of concern to the library and information sector', *Journal of Information Science* 20(2), 137.

O'Reilly, James (1994) 'Recordable CD, CD-ROM: cost-effective, secure, network storage?', *IMC Journal*, 26–28, November/December.

Ozsoyoglu, G. and Wang, H. (1993) 'Example-based graphical based query languages', *Computer* 26(5), 25–37.

Papadimitriou, Christos H., Ramanathan, S. and Rangan, P.V. (1994) 'Information caching for delivery of personalized programs on home entertainment channels', in Anon. *Proceedings of the International Conference on Multimedia Computing and Systems*, Boston, MA, May, IEEE Computer Society Press, pp. 214–223.

Parker, Elisabeth Betz (1985) 'The Library of Congress non-print optical disk pilot program', *Information Technology and Libraries*, 289–299, December.

Patel, P. and Underhill, C. (1992) 'Preview at B.P.: finding the right image', *Aslib Information*, 20, 333–335.

Pea, Roy D. (1991) 'Learning through multimedia', *IEEE Computer Graphics and Applications* 11(4), 58–66.

Pearson, Don (ed.) (1991) *Image processing*, McGraw-Hill, Maidenhead, UK.

Perlin, Ruth (1993) 'Education and access', in Diane Lees (ed.) *Museums and interactive multimedia*, Museum Documentation Association, Cherry Hinton Road, Cambridge.

Perry, Tekla S. (1995) 'Consumer electronics', *IEEE Spectrum* 32(1), 40–43.

Petersen, Toni (1990) 'Developing a thesaurus for art and architecture', *Library Trends* 38(4), 644–658.

—— (1994) 'Art and Architecture Thesaurus', *Archives and Museums Informatics* 8(2), 91–92.

Peterson, Gwen (1991) 'When image meets text; partners at last', *Advanced Imaging* 6(4), 76–79.

Petterson, Rune (1984) 'Laservision videodisc player and personal computer interaction', *Videodisc/Videotex* 4(1), 33–36.

Pichford, David (1995) 'World's largest High St', *Communications News*, 18, April.

Picone, Joseph W. (1993) 'Signal modeling techniques for speech recognition', *Proceedings of the IEEE* 81(9) 1215–1247.

Plowman, Lydia (1989) 'Learning from learning theories: an overview for designers of interactive video', *Interactive Learning International* 5, 165–174.

—— (1995) 'Narrative, linearity, and interactivity: making sense of interactive multimedia', *British Journal of Educational Technology* (forthcoming).

Popham, M.G. (1993) 'Use of SGML and HyTime in UK universities', *Information Services and Use* 13, 103–109.

Poulter, Alan (1994) 'Building a browsable virtual reality library', *Aslib Proceedings* 46(6), 151–155.

Pratt, W.K. (1991) *Digital image processing*, 2nd edn, John Wiley, New York.

Press, Larry (1992) 'Dynabook revisited – portable computers past, present, and future', *Communications of the ACM* 35(3), 25–32.

Preston, J.M. (ed.) (1988) *Compact Disk Interactive – a designer's overview*, 2nd edn, Deventer Kluwer, Antwerp.

Price, Mike (1990) 'The big squeeze', *PC User*, 25 April, 66–72.

Price, Simon, Hobbs, P. and Probert, J. (1994) 'Achieving efficiency gains through an authoring template', in *TLTP Newsletter* 1, 5–9, July 1994, Teaching & Learning Technology Programme, Northavon House, Bristol, UK.

Priestley, John (1995) 'Using the Information Superhighway', *Information Services and Use* 15(1) 25–29.

Pring, I. (1993) 'Video standards and the end user', *Information Services and Use* 13(2), 93–102.

Pring, Isobel (ed.) (1993–4) *Image Technology in European Museums and Art Galleries Database ('ITEM')*, Issue 5, April 1993; Issue 6, November 1993; Issue 8 November 1994. IVAIN, Suffolk College, Ipswich, UK.

Raittinen, Harri and Kaski, Kimmo (1995) 'Critical review of fractal image compression', *International Journal of Modern Physics* C, 6(1), 47–66.

Ramanathan, S., Vin, H.M. and Rangan, P.V. (1994) 'Architectures for personalised multimedia', *Multimedia* 1(1), 37–46.

Ramanathan, S. and Rangan, P.V. (1994) 'Towards personalized multimedia dial-up services', *Computer Networks and ISDN Systems* 26, 1305–1322.

Ramsden, Anne, Wu, Z. and Zhao, D. (1993) 'Selection criteria for document image processing system for the ELINOR electronic library project', *Program* 27(4), 371–387.

Rash, W. (1992) 'Multimedia moves beyond the hype: products finally arrive that solve real business problems', *Byte* 17(2), 85–87.

Rees, Jeremy (1993) 'Pages Interactive multimedia: the Brancusi project', in J. Hemsley (ed.) *Proceedings of the 1993 Electronic Imaging and Visual Arts Conference (EVA 93)*, Brameur & Vasari Enterprises, Aldershot, UK.

Reeves, A.H. (1965) 'Past, present, and future of PCM', *IEEE Spectrum* 2(5) 58–62.

Reguly, Eric (1996) 'Cable lays out the cash but fails to home on success', *The Times*, 6 February, 29.

Reguly, Eric and Tieman, R. (1996) 'Hollick deal heralds era of new media conglomerates', *The Times*, 9 February, 25.

Reinhardt, Andy (1994) 'The network with smarts', *Byte* 19(10), 51–64.

Repo, Aatto J. (1989) 'The value of information: approaches in economics, accounting and management science', *Journal of the American Society for Information Science* 40(2), 68–85.

Reynolds, Jonathan (1990) 'Teleservices in the US: two steps forward, one step back', *International Journal of Retail and Distribution Management* 18(2), 26–32.

—— (1990/1991) 'Is there a market for teleshopping?' *Marketing Review* 5(2), 39–51.

Reynolds, L. (1979) 'Progress in documentation: legibility studies – their relevance to present day documentation efforts', *Journal of Documentation* 35(4), 307–340.

Rickman, R. and Stonham, T.J. (1991) 'Coding images for database retrieval using neural networks', 3rd NERVES Neural Network Workshop, Grenoble.

Riezenman, Michael J. (1995) 'Government and Internet: little regulation needed except to aid education', *The Institute (IEEE Spectrum* supplement) 19(4), 1–2.

Roe, David B. and Wilpon, J.G. (1993) 'Whither speech recognition: the next 25 years', *IEEE Communications Magazine*, November, 54–62.

Rorvig, M.E. (1992) 'A method for automatically abstracting visual documents', *Journal of the American Society for Information Science* 44(1), 40–56.

Ross, Angela (1993) 'Making your own CD-ROMs – advances in CD technology', in David I. Raitt and Ben Jeapes (eds) *Online Information 93*, Learned Information, Oxford and New Jersey.

Roth, G.T. and Sullow, Claus (1993) 'The multimedia forum', in David I. Raitt and Ben Jeapes (eds) *Online Information 93*, Learned Information, Oxford and New Jersey.

Rowley, J.E. (1994) 'The 1991 census on CD-ROM: challenges for libraries', *Aslib Proceedings* 46(1), 25–27.

Rubinstein, Ben (1992) 'The micro gallery and the National Gallery', Private communication from Cognitive Applications Ltd, 4 Sillwood Terrace, Brighton BN1 2LR.

Russ, John C. (1995) *The image processing handbook*, 2nd edn, CRC Press, Boca Raton, FL.

Ryman, A. (1990) 'Personal systems image application architecture: lessons learned from the ImagEdit program', *IBM Systems Journal* 29(3), 408–420.

Saiedian, H. and Awad, M. (1993) 'Managing synchronisation and time factors in multimedia presentation', *Information and Software Technology* 35(11/12), 653–657.

Salton, Gerard (ed.) (1971) *The SMART retrieval system*, Prentice-Hall, Englewood Cliffs, NJ.

Samadani, R. and Han, C. (1993) 'Computer assisted extraction of boundaries and images', in W. Niblack (ed.) *Storage and retrieval for image and video databases*, Proceedings of the SPIE, vol. 1908, San José, CA, pp. 219–226.

Samadani, R., Han, C. and Katragadda, L.K. (1993) 'Content-based events selection from satellite images of the Aurora', in W. Niblack (ed.) *Storage and retrieval for image and video databases*, Proceedings of the SPIE, vol. 1908, San José, CA, pp. 50–59.

Sandbank, C.P. (ed.) (1990) *Digital television*, John Wiley, Chichester and New York.

Satava, Richard M. (1994) 'Emerging medical applications of virtual reality: a surgeon's perspective', *Artifical Intelligence in Medicine* 6, 281–288.

Sayre, Scott (1993) 'The evolution of interactive interpretive media', in Diane Lees (ed.) *Museums and interactive multimedia*, Museum Documentation Association, Cherry Hinton Road, Cambridge.

Schank, Roger C. (1994) 'Active learning through multimedia', *Multimedia* 1(1), 69–78.

Schank, Roger C. and Slade, S.B. (1991) 'The future of artificial intelligence: learning from experience', *Applied Artificial Intelligence* 5, 97–107.

Scheller, Angela (1993) 'The Open Document Architecture (ODA) and its HyperODA extensions', *Information Services and Use* 13, 121–130.

Scherr, Sol (1979) *Electronic displays*, Wiley Interscience, New York and Chichester.

Schifreen, Robert (1990) 'Ballade', *Personal Computer World*, August, 96–200.

Schmitt, Marilyn (1992) 'Art historians and the computer: the context for electronic imaging', *Proceedings of the Conference on Electronic Imaging and the Visual Arts (EVA)*, Brameur, Aldershot, UK (no pagination).

Schneider, Uwe and Strack, R. (1992) 'APART: system for the acquisition, processing, archiving, and retrieval of digital images in an open, distributed imaging environment', *SPIE Image Processing Interchange*, 1659, 288–298, International Society of Optical Engineers, Bellingham, WA.

Schorr, Joseph (1993) 'Presentation promotion', *MacWorld*, November, 43–47.

Schreiber, William G. (1995) 'Advanced television systems for terrestrial broadcasting: some problems and some proposed solutions', *Proceedings of the IEEE* 83(6), 958–981.

Schroeder, Ralph (1993) 'Virtual reality in the real world', *Futures*, 25, 963–973.

Schwartz, Michael F. (1993) 'Internet resource discovery at the University of Colorado', *Computer* 26(9), 25–35.

Searjeant, Graham (1996) 'BT head rejects network concept', *The Times*, 9 February.

Seloff, Gary (1990) 'Automated access to the NASA-JSC image archives. Retrieving information with interactive videodiscs', *Library Trends* 38(4), 682–696.

Servan-Schreiber, Jean-Jacques (1969) *The American challenge*, Pelican Books, Harmondsworth (English translation of *Le défi américain*).

Sevonius, Elaine and Witthus, Rutherford (1981) 'Information science as a profession', in Martha E. Williams (ed.) *The Annual Review of Information Science and Technology*, vol. 16, Knowledge Industries Publications, New York, pp. 291–316.

Sezan, M. Ibrahim and Tekalp, A.M. (1990) 'Survey of recent developments in digital image restoration', *Optical Engineering* 29(5), 393–404.

Shandle, Jack (1991) 'Multimedia computing hits a sour note', *Electronics*, June, 48–53.

—— (1993) 'Digital audio delivers non-stop innovations', *Electronic Design* 41, 53–66.

Shann, R., Davis, D. *et al.* (1993) 'Detection and characterisation of Carboniferous Foraminifera for content-based retrieval from an image database', in W. Niblack (ed.) *Storage and retrieval for image and video databases*, Proceedings of the SPIE, vol. 1908, San José, CA, pp. 188–197.

Shannon, Claude E. (1948) 'A mathematical theory of communication', *Bell System Technical Journal* 27(3), 379–423 and 27(4), 623–656.

Sharp, Oliver and Bacon, D.F. (1994) 'Measure for measure', *Byte* 19(10), 65–72.

Shetler, Tim (1990) 'Birth of the Blob', *Byte*, 15(2), 221–226.

Short, John, Williams, Ederyn and Christie, Bruce (1976) 'The decision to telecommunicate', *The social psychology of telecomunications*, John Wiley, New York, chapter 9.

Simon, Robert, Krieger, K. *et al.* (1995) 'Multimedia MedNet', *Computer* 28(5), 65–73.

Simpson, Evelyn, Duncan, Stephen and McMurdo, George (1994) 'Networking CD-ROMs: technical overview and the view from Manchester Business School', *Journal of Information Science* 20(1), 46–54.

Singleton, Andrew (1995) 'Cash on the wirehead', *Byte* 20(6), 71–78.

Smarte, Gene (1992) 'Active-colour notebooks arrive', *Byte* 17(5), 42.

Smith, John (1994) *Accessing the Internet – a guide for the UK and Ireland*, International Thomson Publishing, London.

Smith, Merril W. and Purcell, P.A. (1992) 'Developments in image technology for arts information', *Proceedings of the Conference for Electronic Imaging and the Visual Arts (EVA)*, Brameur, Aldershot, UK (no pagination).

Smura, Edwin J. (1983) 'Record structures for advanced information systems', *Computer* 16(3), 41–50.

—— (1986) 'Advanced information system structures', in A.E. Cawkell (ed.) *Handbook of Information Technology and Office Systems*, Elsevier, Amsterdam, pp. 779–801.

Snider, James H. (1995) 'The information superhighway as environmental menace', *The Futurist*, 29, 16–27.

Snow, Maryly (1991) 'The AAT browser at the University of California, Berkeley', in Toni Petersen (ed.) *AAT Bulletin* 19, AAT, Williamstown, MA.

Soares, L.F.G., Casanova, M.A. and Colcher, S. (1993) 'An architecture for hypermedia systems using MHEG standard objects interchange', *Information Services and Use* 13(2), 131–139.

Sowizral, Henry A. (1985) 'Expert systems', in M.E. Williams (ed.) *Annual review of information science and technology*, Knowledge Industry Publications, White Plains, vol. 20, chapter 7, pp. 179–199.

Sperling, George (1980) 'Bandwidth requirements for video transmission of American Sign Language and finger spelling', *Science* 210(4771), 797–799.

Steele, Michael, Murdoch, John and Arnott, Michael (1996) 'The emergence of Photo CD as a preferred method for image capture and storage', *Information Services and Use* 16(1), 7–13.

Stern, Barrie T. and Campbell, Robert (1988) 'ADONIS: the story so far', in Charles Oppenheim (ed.) *CD-ROM: fundamentals to applications*, Butterworths, London, chapter 8.

Stevenson, Iain and Howard-Healy, Marian (1993) 'ATM: market strategies', Report, Ovum Ltd, 7 Rathbone St, London.

Stewart, B.K., Honeyman, J.C. and Dwyer, S.J. (1991) 'Picture archiving and communication system (PACS) networking: three implementation strategies', *Computerized Medical Imaging and Graphics* 15(3), 161–169.

Stone, Gerald and Sylvain, Philip (1990) 'ArchVISTA: a new horizon in providing access to visual records of the National Archives of Canada', *Library Trends* 38(4), 737–750.

Stoneman, Geoffrey (1993) 'Worldwide trends in CD-ROM publishing', *The Electronic Library* 11(4/5), 299–302.

Strack, Rudiger and Neumann, L. (1992) 'Object orientated image database for an open imaging environment', *Proceedings of the Conference on Electronic Imaging and the Visual Arts (EVA)*, Brameur, Aldershot, UK (no pagination).

Sulger, Art (1993) 'Indexing image databases', *Dr Dobb's Journal*, August, 60–106.

Sutherland, Ivan (1965) 'The ultimate display', *Proceedings of the International Federation of Information Processing Congress*, 506–508.

Swain, M.J. (1993) 'Interactive indexing into image databases', in W. Niblack (ed.) *Storage and retrieval for image and video databases*, Proceedings of the SPIE, vol. 1908, San José, CA, pp. 95–103.

Syed, A. and Williamson, C.L. (1993) 'An experiment evaluation for video coding algorithms for ATM-based networks', in D. Phillips and P. Desrochers (eds) *Multimedia communications*, IOS Press, Amsterdam, pp. 247–256.

Taira, R.K., Stewart, B.K. and Sinha, U. (1991) 'PACS database architecture and design', *Computerized Medical Imaging and Graphics* 15(3), 171–176.

Thomasson, Kim (ed.) (1994) *Multimedia in the UK*, Keynote Market Review, Field House, Hampton, Middx, UK.

Thompson, Tom (1995) 'One box, two computers', *Byte* 20(4), 165–166.

Thompson, Tom and Smith, B. (1993) 'Apple, SGI, blaze video trail', *Byte* 18(10), 81–90.

Tobagi, Fouad A. (1995) 'Distance learning with digital video', *Multimedia* 2(1), 90–93.

Toda, I. (1993) 'The Japanese scene', in D.E.N. Davies *et al.* (eds) *Communications after AD 2000*, Chapman & Hall, London, chapter 4.

Tomek, J. and Maurer, H. (1991) 'Hypermedia – introduction and survey', *Journal of Microcomputer Applications* 14, 63–103.

Tonge, G.J. (1989) 'Current trends in image processing for broadcast television', in Anon. *IEE Conference Publication* 307, 257–263.

Toth, A., Bellisio, J. and Yasuda, H. (1993) 'Guest editorial: high definition television and digital video communications', *IEEE Journal on Selected Areas in Communications* 11(1), 1–5.

Truesdell, Dan (1992) 'Content based retrieval: imaging in multimedia', *Advanced Imaging* 7(5), 26, 28, 80.

Turtur, A., Prampolini, F. *et al.* (1991) 'IDB: an image database system', *IBM Journal of Research and Development*. 35(1/2), 88–96.

Udell, Jon (1994) 'Exploring Chicago', *Byte*, 19(11), 132–146.

—— (1995) 'Web search', *Byte* 20(9), 223–226.

Valls, Carina H. (1994) 'Multimedia museums. An overview of its developments', *Program* 28(3), 263–274.

Van der Starre, J.H.V. (1993) 'Visual Arts Network for the exchange of cultural knowledge (Van Eyck project)', in J. Hemsley (ed.) *Proceedings of the 1993 Electronic Imaging and Visual Arts Conference (EVA 93)*, Brameur & Vasari Enterprises, Aldershot, UK, pp. 84–92.

Van de Sompel, H. (1994) 'The electronic reference library at the University of Ghent', *Managing Information*, June, 44–46 (Aslib, London).

Vaughan-Nichols, Steven J. (1994) 'The Web means business', *Byte* 19(11), 26–27.

—— (1995) 'Free rides are disappearing', *Byte* 20(4), 26.

Vaxiviviere, Pascal and Thombre, K. (1992) 'Celesstin: CAD conversion of mechanical drawings', *Computer* 25(7), 46–54.

Virgo, Philip (1990) 'Putting true costs into the frame', *Daily Telegraph*, 12 November.

Visser, Friso E.H. (1993) 'The European museums network: an interactive multimedia application for the museum visitor', in J. Hemsley (ed.) *Proceedings of the 1993 Electronic Imaging and Visual Arts Conference (EVA 93)*, Brameur and Vasari Enterprises, Aldershot, UK, pp. 204–217.

Wadell, Pam (1993) 'The potential for electronic journals in UK academia', in Anon. *Libraries and and IT: working papers of the HEFC's Library Review*, UKOLN, Bath, pp. 240–271.

Wakimoto, K., Shima, M. *et al.* (1993) 'Content-based retrieval applied to drawing image databases', in W. Niblack (ed.) *Storage and retrieval for image and video databases*, Proceedings of the SPIE, vol. 1908, San José, CA, pp. 74–84.

Wall, Raymond A. (1993) *Copyright made easier*, Aslib, London.
—— (1994) 'Copyright and the First Amendment', *Journal of Information Science* 20(5), 369–370.
Waltrich, Joseph B. (1993) 'Digital video compression – an overview', *Journal of Lightwave Technology* 11(1), 70–75.
Wanning, Tyne (1991) 'Image databases for museum staff, visitors, and the outside world', in D. Bearman (ed.) *Hypermedia and Interactivity in Museums*, Archives & Museum Informatics, Pittsburgh, pp. 57–61.
Ward, David (1994) 'Number crunching production', *Audiovisual* June, 20–24.
Wayner, Peter (1994) 'Objects on the march', *Byte* 19(1), 139–150.
Weber, Jack (1993) 'Visualisation: seeing is believing', *Byte* 18(4), 121–128.
Weems, Charles C. (1991) 'Architectural requirements of image understanding with respect to parallel processing', *Proceedings of the IEEE* 79(4), 537–547.
Weyer, S.A. and Borning, A.H. (1985) 'A prototype electronic encyclopaedia', *ACM Transactions Office Information Systems* 3(1), 63–88.
Whalley, Peter (1995) 'An alternative rhetoric for hypertext', in C. McKnight *et al.* (eds) *Hypertext: a psychological perspective*, Ellis Morwood, Chichester.
—— (1996) 'Imaging with multimedia', *British Journal of Education* (forthcoming).
White, Andrew (1993) 'Copyright law, information services and the challenges of multimedia', in David I. Raitt and Ben Jeapes (eds) *Online Information 93*, Learned Information, Oxford and New Jersey.
White, Ian (1994) 'Graphics: top of the charts', *Audio Visual* 269, 22–27.
Whitehead, Rebecca (1994) 'Diagnostic imaging across distance: special conferencing needs tested', *Advanced Imaging*, 9, 50–53.
Wiley, Richard E. (1996) '1995: a regulatory review', *Telecommunications* 30(1), 17–18, 59.
Willis, P. and Dufour, I.G. (1995) 'Towards knowledge-based networks', *BT Technology Journal* 13(2), 87–93.
Wilson, Patrick (1990) 'Copyright, derivative rights and the First Amendment', *Library Trends* 39(1, 2), 92–110.
Wilson, Roger (1991) 'The market for multimedia', Report from Dragonflair Ltd, PO Box 5, Church Stretton, Shropshire SY6 6ZZ, UK.
Wood, John (1994) 'But what really works?', *TLTP Newsletter* 2, 3, Teaching and Learning Technology Programme, Northavon House, Bristol, UK.
Woolf, Beverly P. and Hall, Wendy (1995) 'Multimedia pedagogues', *Computer* 20(5), 74–80.
Woolsey, K. and Semper, R. (1991) 'Multimedia in public space', in D. Bearman (ed.) *Hypermedia and Interactivity in Museums*, Archives & Museums Informatics, Pittsburg, pp. 46–52.
Worthington, Shari L.S. (1994) 'Imaging on the Internet: scientific/industrial resources', *Advanced Imaging* 9(2), 17–25.
Wragg, E.C. (1993) 'Multimedia in education: bane or boon?', *Journal of Educational Television* 19(2), 73–79.
Wray, Stuart, Glauert, Tim and Hopper, Andy (1994) 'Networked multimedia: the Medusa environment', *Multimedia* 1(4), 54–63.
Wu, Zimin, Ramsden, Anne and Zhao, D. (1995) 'The user perspective of the ELINOR electronic library', *Aslib Proceedings* 47(1), 13–22.
Yager, Tom (1993) 'Photoshop now does windows', *Byte* 18(4), 49–50.
Yavatkar, Raj and Manoj, L. (1994) 'End-to-end approach to large scale multimedia dissemination', *Computer Communications* 17(3), 205–217.
Yeaton, Susan (1995) 'Powerful presentation for windows', *Byte* 20(1), 183–188.

Yeh, C.L. (1989) 'A lossless progressive transmission technique for image browsing', in Anon. *IEE Conference Publication* 307, 599–603.

Yenawine, Philip (1993) 'Multimedia and the politics of museum organisational change', in Diane Lees (ed.) *Museums and Interactive Multimedia*, Museum Documentation Association, Cherry Hinton Road, Cambridge.

Yeung, T., Burton, B. and Wong, N. (1992) 'Management and visual resources in Hong Kong Polytechnic Library: the case of the slide collection', *Aslib Proceedings* 44(11/12), 386–392.

Yildiz, Rauf and Atkins, M. (1993) 'Evaluating multimedia applications', *Computers in Education* 21(1/2), 133–139.

Zeng, Kencheng, Yang, C.-H., Wei, D.-Y. and Rao, T.T.N. (1991) 'Pseudorandom bit generators in stream-cipher cryptography', *Computer* 24(2), 8–17.

Glossary and acronyms

AAT Art and Architecture Thesaurus.

Accelerator A device fitted in microcomputers in order to speed up the process of moving data onto the display screen.

ACROBAT Postscript-based portable and revisable printing software introduced by Adobe Inc. It is able to reproduce graphics and images and supports SGML and may displace ODA.

A/D Analogue/Digital.

Adaptive Differential Pulse Code Modulation A method of encoding audio signals from changes between amplitude levels. It is used in CD-I systems.

ADPCM See Adaptive Differential Pulse Code Modulation.

ADSL Asymmetric Digital Subscriber Loop. A method of communicating over the PSTN, which has a nominal signalling limit of about 140 Kbps, at much faster rates.

ADSP Advanced Digital Systems Processing.

AIFF Audio Interchange File Format.

Aliasing The introduction of information, particularly in respect of visual displays, which was not present in the original data. For example, a jagged appearance noticeable on curves or diagonals displayed on a CRT screen, indicating inadequate resolution. The cause may be the use of data originally inadequately sampled. 'Anti-aliasing' can be provided by passing signals through a low pass filter to smooth fast transitions.

ALOHA An early type of Local Area Network (LAN) developed at the University of Hawaii in 1972.

ALU Arithmetic and Logic Unit.

AMLCD Active Matrix Liquid Crystal Diode. LCDs controlled by the switching action of thin film transistors bonded to the screen.

Analogue Digital (A/D) Convertor An electronic circuit used to convert a smoothly varying waveform (as, for example, a television picture waveform) into digital values.

Angstrom unit A unit of length. 1 Au = 10^{-10} metres.

ANSI American National Standards Institute.

Applet A special HTML tag used in Java browsers to carry application data.

ARPANET Advanced Research Projects Agency Network. A US government network which was subsequently incorporated into the Internet.

Ascender The upper part of the characters 'bdfh'.

ASCII American Standard Code for Information Interchange. A widely used code for numbers, letters, and other symbols.

ASIC Application Specific Integrated Circuit.

Aspect ratio The ratio of the horizontal to the vertical dimensions of a data field displayed on a CRT screen.

ATM Asynchronous Transfer Mode. A transmission technique which embodies the advantages of circuit switching and packet switching. However, the inter-packet time interval is usually only a few microseconds compared with milliseconds for packet switching. It may be used at data rates between 10 megabits to hundreds of megabits per second. ATM is the only technology which supports real-time voice and video and so is obviously of importance for multimedia transmission.

Atto- Prefix meaning 10^{-18}.

Authoring The operation of producing a multimedia presentation from concept to media product.

AVI

1 Audio Video Interleave. A Windows file format.

2 Audio-visual Interactive.

Backbone The 'main line' of a network which may have offshoots or other networks connected to it.

Barrel shifter Graphic software capable of manipulating pixel arrays *en bloc*, performing extremely fast shift operations in a single cycle; it can shift as many bits to new locations as it has bits. For example, a 32-bit barrel shifter can shift a 32-bit word by up to 32-bit locations in a single cycle. It also enables a field of pixels to be rotated.

Bernouilli disk A removable disk normally supplied in an external box, enabling disks to be removed to secure storage.

Bi-level A term used to describe a display in which pixels are either on or off – that is, the system is able to reproduce only either 'black' or 'white' pixels.

BIOS Basic Input/Output System. Software designed for IBM PCs and stored in ROM for controlling input/output functions and screen data.

B-ISDN Broadband Integrated Services Digital Network.

BitBlit A term used to describe the transfer of a block of bits in digital single processing systems.

Bit-map A method of organizing a CRT display where (in a black-and-white display) each pixel in a particular position on the screen is controlled by a 0 or 1 bit in an associated memory. In grey scale or colour displays there are as many memories ('bit planes') as there are bits to define the value of a screen pixel. Thus there would be one bit in each of 8 memories in order to represent the value of an 8-bit pixel.

Bitnet Because It's Time NETwork (United States).

Bit planes Memories which store the component digits of a pixel in order to speed up changes in a CRT display. For instance, a 4-bit code could control a pixel to display any one out of 16 grey levels on a CRT. Four digits delivered simultaneously from four bit planes in parallel can be delivered four times faster than serial delivery from a single store.

BLOB Binary Large Object. A description of an object which may be of any type, including an image, occupying a field in a database particularly in relational database management systems. BLOBs are indexed with words. For retrieval and storage purposes they are managed like any other record although they may be very large.

Boot To start up a computer with a program in permanent storage, automatically initiated when the computer is switched on. The program usually checks machine functions and loads up the operating system.

BT British Telecom.

BTLZ A method of compression used in V42 bis Standard for data compression. It is based on the storage of high-frequency codes which are substituted for longer words.

Buffer A temporary store to accommodate the difference in the data handling rate of two devices.

Bypassing A method, widely used in the United States, for bypassing the local loop telephone connection with some other form of connection – for instance, by wireless.

C A computer language particularly known for its use in UNIX systems.

C++ A development of 'C' which includes facilities for dealing with objects.

Cache A small auxiliary computer semiconductor memory arranged to store frequently used data, instead of the data being stored on disk and therefore taking much longer to retrieve.

CAD Computer Aided Design.

Cairo An operating system planned by Microsoft embodying object-oriented architecture.

Camcorder A television camera, microphone, and recording tape integrated into one portable unit.

Candela (Cd) The SI unit of luminous intensity equivalent to the luminous intensity of a black body normal to the surface at specified conditions of temperature and pressure.

CAV Constant Angular Velocity – the mode of rotation of disks such as gramophone (phonograph) records, floppy disks and hard disks. The driving motor runs at a constant speed, so that a given length of outer track is available for the same length of time as a shorter length of inner track.

CCD See charge coupled device.

CCIR Consultative Commission for International Radio Communication.

CCITT Consultative Committee for International Telegraphs and Telephones.

CD Compact disk.

CD-DA Compact Disk Digital Audio.

CD-I Compact Disk Interactive.

CD-R Compact Disk Writable. A CD created without the need for certain intermediate processes normally used to prepare it. CD-R is used for creating Kodak photo-CDs.

CD-ROM Compact Disk Read Only Memory.

CD-ROM XA Compact Disk Read Only Memory Extended Architecture. Its major feature is the interleaving of ADPCM audio data with graphical data.

CD-RTOS Compact Disk Real Time Operating System as used for CD-I.

CD-TV Compact Disk – Television.

CD-V Compact Disk Video.

Cel animation A method of animation in which motion is conveyed by adjustments to individual elements in successive frames.

CELP Codebook Excited Linear Predictive coding.

CEO Chief Executive Officer.

CIF Common Intermediate Format.

CGA See Colour Graphics Adaptor.

CGM Computer Graphics Metafile.

Charge coupled device A semiconductor element in which data are stored as an electrical charge which may be transferred to an adjacent, similar element by a control pulse. In a CCD image sensor, a charge is generated when light is focused upon it. Sensors may be arranged in the form of a strip of CCD elements associated with an electronic transport system.

After a given light exposure time, the charges are shifted by the transport system along to an output terminal where they represent a bit-by-bit serial representation of the light reflected from a strip of the image.

Chicago An alternative name for Windows 95.

Chorus A variation of the Unix Operating System based on a nucleus, claimed to provide a number of advantages.

Chroma Synonym for saturation.

Chrominance The difference between a colour and a specified reference colour of equal brightness, representing the hue and saturation values of that colour.

Chrominance signal A signal representing the colour of a given point in an image.

Circuit switching A transmission system where users are interconnected by a channel – for example, a telephone line – via conventional switches which make the user–line–user connections. It is a physical path set up for the duration of the call for the sole benefit of its only users.

CISC Complex Instruction Set Computer.

Client-server An arrangement consisting of a client computer able to search data stored on a file-server computer where both are connected to a network. The server computer on the network acts as a communal resource dedicated to the storage and retrieval of data simultaneously for a number of clients. A client/server architecture is claimed to be more efficient than a conventional general purpose computer where data storage and retrieval are but one of many of its functions. A dedicated server may be a fast microcomputer with large memory capacity. A non-dedicated file-server is a lower cost alternative where a workstation acts as a server as well as functioning as a user's workstation.

If the file-server PC is sufficiently powerful, a number of users can access it at the same time with some degradation of performance. For example, in throughput tests of a Storage Dimensions Filemaster II machine, the speed degradation when there were four users instead of one was 41 per cent. The Filemaster II contains a 33 MHz processor and 4 Mbytes of memory with cache and two 150 Mbyte disks.

Clip A file describing a multimedia presentation object. A video clip consists of a sequence of TV-like frames which run for a known period – say, 20 seconds. Usually it will be retrievable via a small ikon representing its subject matter. An audio clip, usually described in words, may be selected from a list, and may be represented as a waveform on the screen.

Clip art Files of useful drawings, logos, etc., which can be bought as a software package from which any object may be lifted into a user's design. For example, when a diagram of a computer network is drawn, a clip-art representation of a microcomputer can be lifted out of the package and inserted in as many places as necessary on the diagram.

CLUT See Colour Lookup Table.

CLV Constant Linear Velocity – a mode of rotation used for CDs. The motor speed is varied so that when the head is over an outer track the disk rotates more slowly, but considerably faster when the head is over an inner track. As a result each track can be filled with the maximum possible amount of data.

CMIP Common Management Information Protocol.

CMOS Complementary Metal Oxide Silicon.

CMS Colour Management System.

CMYK The colours Cyan, Magenta, Yellow and Key (black), combinations of which produce sensations of colour by the selective absorption of white light.

CODEC COder/DECoder.

Colour Graphics Adaptor (CGA) A printed circuit board installed in early IBM or IBM-compatible PCs. It provides for 320×200 pixels in 4 colours.

Colour Lookup Table A table containing a limited number of locations, say, 256 8-bit locations, each controlling a set of RGB values which select a far larger number of different colours, say $256 \times 256 \times 256$ (24-bit) alternatives. The table of 8-bit locations provides a far larger number of choices than would be possible by using the 8-bit number for directly selecting different colours. The numbers in the table may be changed to, say, $134 \times 223 \times 120$. The system provides for 2^8 colours displayed at one time out of any 2^{24} colours.

Colour temperature The colour of nominally white light, more accurately defined as the temperature of the source generating it. Thus a low-intensity source such as a candle produces a yellowish light at a temperature of 1800 degrees Kelvin, while clear sunlight represents a temperature of 25,000 degrees Kelvin.

Composite video The combined use of luminance and chrominance to represent colour.

Computer graphics metafile A method of encoding graphic elements so that graphics can be more easily exchanged between programs.

Convolution The combining of two sets of pixel intensity levels into a single value. The combination is effected by overlaying a set of pixels in an image with a set of pixels in a mask and executing the convolution with an algorithm.

Copeland A new name for a new version of Apple's Quicktime software, otherwise known as Quicktime 8.0.

CPU Central Processing Unit.

CRT Cathode Ray Tube.

CSMA/CD Carrier Sense Multiple Access/Collision Detection. A method used for LAN transmissions. If data elements collide, stations retransmit after a random delay period.

Cyberspace A computer-controlled space – for example, the space within which Internet activities take place.

D/A Digital to Analogue Convertor. See DAC.

DAC Digital Analogue Convertor. An electronic circuit used, for example, to convert digitized intensity levels into smoothly varying analogue waveforms suitable for varying the intensity of a cathode ray tube beam.

Three such convertors are used for colour CRTs to convert the three digitized signals representing red, green, and blue into analogue intensity levels for the three beams of the tube. Speed problems have almost disappeared in recent years – 8-bit D/A convertors are available to be clocked at up to 450 MHz.

Daisy chaining The stringing together of peripheral devices such as disk units, scanners, etc., to reduce the number of connections to a computer port controlled by SCSI software.

Daytona Alternative name for Windows NT.

DCE Data Circuit terminating Equipment.

DCT Discrete Cosine Transform. The processing operation performed on pixel blocks of an image, typically 8×8, in which the cosine terms of a Fourier transformation are retained and coded, the result being codes containing runs of consecutive zeros. This presents the opportunity for run length coding to achieve compression in such schemes as the JPEG scheme.

DDC Digital Dynamic Convergence.

Debug The elimination of faults in computer software or hardware.

DECT Digital European Cordless Telecommunications.

Default The state of computer hardware or software after various setting up adjustments have been made to organize the system for normal use.

DES Data Encryption Standard. A United States Standard for encrypting data.

Desktop publishing The preparation of material ready for printing, or of the printed material itself, using inexpensive equipment and DTP software. DTP became possible in the period 1984 to 1986 with the advent of the Apple Macintosh microcomputer, and the Hewlett Packard laserjet printer using Japanese Canon laser technology.

DHCP   Dynamic Host Configuration Protocol.

Dichroic filter   A piece of glass coated with a metallic film which allows the passage of light with a particular colour.

Digital Video Interactive   A system developed by General Electric/RCA, subsequently further developed by Intel, to enable video data to run for one hour on a Digital Video Interactive (DVI) disk – the same size as a CD-ROM disk.

DIP   Dual Inline Package. A collection of very small switches provided on some computer hardware for setting up purposes.

Dithering   A method of halftone printing with a laser printer by subdividing a bit-mapped area into small blocks of pixels – say, 4 × 4 blocks – and filling them with from 0 to 16 pixels in some prearranged pattern corresponding to the average brightness detected in corresponding areas of the original image. See also Halftone.

DMA   Direct Memory Access.

DMT   Discrete MultiTone. A method of signalling using the frequency spectrum within a channel divided into a number of bands with the signalling rate optimized within each band.

DOS   Disk Operating System. An operating system, then known as MS-DOS adopted by IBM for their personal computer.

Double click   The act of pressing a mouse button twice in rapid succession.

Download   Transferring a file from a computer, usually a remote computer via a telecoms link and a modem, to your own computer.

Drag   To move an object by observing a computer display, pointing the mouse at an object, and using software which enables the object to be dragged into a new position.

Driver   A file containing data which enable a computer to communicate with and control a peripheral device.

DSP   Digital Signal Processor.

DTE   Data Terminal Equipment.

DTI   Department of Trade and Industry (UK).

DTP   See Desktop publishing.

DVD   Digital Video CD. A system using a compact disk for storing a feature film using compressed video data.

DVI   See Digital Video Interactive.

DYUV   Delta luminance colour difference. A method of colour data compression in which brightness differences (Y) and colour differences (UV) between pixels are stored instead of storing colour values.

EARM   European Academic and Research Network.

EBONE   European BackBONE.

EGA   Enhanced Graphic Adaptor. An improved method of display introduced by IBM. EGA is normally 640 × 480 pixels with 16 colours.

EIA   Electronic Industries Association.

EISA Bus   Extended Industry Standard Architecture Bus capable of transporting data in 33 Mbyte bursts, and having 4 8-bit paths.

ELISE   Electronic Library Image Service for Europe.

E-mail   Electronic mail.

Embedded   An integral, rather than a separate, part.

EPROM   Erasable Programmable Read Only Memory.

Ethernet A network using a method of inter-station communication by data packets called Carrier Sense Multiple Access with Collision Detection (CSMA/CD). The maximum normal data rate is up to 10 Mbps.

ETSI European Telecommunication Standard Institute.

Fatpipe A telecommunications link between JANET and the NSFNET.

FCC Federal Communications Commission.

FDDI Fibre Distributed Data Interface

Femto- Prefix meaning 10^{-15}.

FFT Fast Fourier Transform.

Fibreoptic transmission Fibreoptic communication is achieved by modulating a light source such as a Light Emitting Diode (LED), or for greater energy a laser, with digital electrical signals. The modulated light is propagated along a thin glass fibre and detected at the other end by a photodiode which generates electrical signals when light falls on it. Laser-generated single-frequency data can travel very long distances with little attenuation.

Field An image scanned from top to bottom. In interlaced systems alternate frames contain odd and even scanned lines so two successive fields are required to complete a frame.

FIFO First In First Out.

File A collection of data listed under a file name. The data may be a computer program, a description of a series of video frames, a melody, or any set of data representing any kind of information.

File server See client-server.

Firewall A barrier to prevent unauthorized access to a file.

FIRP Federal International Requirements Panel.

Flash memory A semiconductor memory which does not require an applied voltage to store data and may be partially or completely reprogrammed within the host machine.

Flat file A database file laid out and retrieved in a simple address book manner (as opposed to the more sophisticated files used in a relational database).

Font (or fount) Font is a complete set of type in one style and size. (Sometimes used interchangeably with typeface).

Fourier Analysis Determining the harmonic components which make up a complex waveform. Such waveforms are composed of a series of sinusoidal waveforms with frequencies in the series f 2f 3f 4f . . . etc.

Fractal A property of many objects where small portions resemble larger portions, as in ferns, snowflakes, coastlines, etc. Codes may be devised to eliminate redundant information, so images may be scaled up or scaled down, thereby providing very high compression ratios.

Frame The complete representation of an image produced by scanning it. Two successive fields containing odd and even scanning lines form a complete interlaced frame.

Frame grabber A device for capturing a video frame and storing it on a computer. To capture colour, a frame grabber converts the YUV to RGB values by sampling the colour sub-carrier. The best conversion is obtained by 4:4:4 sampling – i.e. four samples of each component. 4:1:1, for example, would provide poor colour.

FTAM File Transfer Access and Management.

FTP File Transfer Protocol.

Fuzzy logic A method of representing smoothly variable functions in digital form. Fuzzy logic has an application in image matching where a match is deemed to occur when a query-picture approximately matches a picture in a database. Fuzzy logic enables a matching decision to be made even if the matching is inexact.

GaAs A chemical embodying a crystal lattice used in fast semiconductors within which electrons move much faster than they do in silicon devices.

Gamma correction A correction factor applied to a cathode ray tube monitor to provide linearity between intensity level and phosphor brilliance.

GATT General Agreement on Tariffs and Trade.

Genlock The process of synchronizing two sources so that, for instance, the timing of a computer is in sync with a video source in order that a video picture may have computer-generated text laid on it, the whole forming a stationary picture with overlaid text.

GIF Graphics Interchange Format.

GKS Standard The Graphics Kernel System Standard, now an ISO Standard, which defines the 'primitive' elements from which an image may be constructed – lines, arcs, polygons, etc. The elements may be described by a Standard code called CGM (Computer Graphics Metafile).

GNS Global Network Service (British Telecom).

GOSIP Government Open Systems Interconnection Profile.

Gouraud shading A means of altering individual pixels to produce smooth changes in appearance.

Graphics Interchange Format (GIF) A hardware-independent protocol devised by Compuserve Inc., for the interchange of graphics data. It is defined in blocks and sub-blocks.

Graphics Signal Processor (GSP) A GSP consists of two separate processors – the Graphics Processor, which receives CPU commands from a special instruction set, and the Display Processor. Both have access to a special form of buffer memory – a display Video Random Access Memory (VRAM).

A GSP, given the appropriate command, can execute complex operations on large blocks of pixels and can address (typically) 128 Mbits of memory – adequate to hold high-resolution representations of pages to be displayed or printed in colour.

Graphics User Interface (GUI) The part of a computer which gives rise to the 'look and feel' of the machine – namely the screen and the method of controlling it. The GUI was invented by Xerox and adopted by Apple with its WIMP arrangements – windows, ikons, mouse, and pop-up menu. For the first time a computer could be controlled by pointing and selecting instead of typing exactly correct code commands.

Green Book Volumes containing specifications for CD-I disks and players, Sony and Philips being the principal contributors.

Grey scale See Halftone.

GSP See Graphics Signal Processor.

GUI See Graphics User Interface.

Halftone An illustration broken up into dots for printed reproduction. The dots are created by photographing the illustration through a fine screen. For representing, say, 256 shades in a digital tonal scale form, each value in the scale would be represented by an 8-bit number.

Hashing The generation of storage addresses for data, derived from random numbers.

HDTV High Definition Television. HDTV has applications in high-quality text and image display for information systems, as well as for entertainment TV. It impacts semiconductors, display devices, and general consumer electronics and provides improved viewing approaching that of a cinema theatre. The number of lines is increased so that more detail becomes visible and the screen is made considerably wider.

A variation called Extended Definition Television (EDTV) – an improved but compatible version of the existing NTSC system – is a contender for adoption in the US.

High Sierra A software format for CD-ROMs agreed by major manufacturers which formed the basis of the ISO 9660 Standard.

Histogram A graphical representation of a set of values provided by adjacent rectangles, the length of each rectangle being proportional to a particular value.

HSI Hue Saturation Intensity. See HSV.

HSV An alternative to RGB as a way of specifying a colour. It is obtained by combining hue, saturation, and value (brightness) – properties which are more amenable for describing a colour in a way which relates to human perception.

HTML HyperText Markup Language. A simplified version of SGML used on the Internet for tagging parts of a document.

HTTP HyperText Transfer Protocol. A procedure for message control on the WWW (Internet).

Hue A colour named from its subjective appearance and determined by the frequency of its radiated energy.

Huffman Code A code in which the shortest code group is allocated to the symbol with the highest probability of occurrence, and the longest to the symbol with the lowest probability of occurrence. Thus in the English language, the letter 'e' will be allocated the shortest code, and a letter such as 'q' the longest.

Hypercard An Apple software product launched in 1987. A form of database using a card-like display with the means of jumping from one card to another and for controlling external peripheral units.

Hyperlink A method of inter-connecting data in a hypermedia system. Prompts are shown on a displayed collection of data enabling related data to be retrieved. Thus in a multimedia encyclopaedia, an outlined word such as 'cricket' might be a hyperlinking point. When moused and clicked the word is replaced with a movie of part of a cricket match.

Hypermedia A generic term for systems which enable non-linear access to information in one or more media.

Hypertext A word coined by Ted Nelson in 1981 describing software which breaks up text into non-linear inter-connected chunks enabling access from different perspectives.

Hytime Hypermedia Time-Based Structuring Language. An ANSI/ISO standard (ISO 10744) specifying how hypermedia document components may be represented using the Standard General Markup Language (SGML). It covers document structures, association of objects in documents with hyperlinks, and related matters.

Ikon

1 A pictorial representation of an object, for example a folder.

2 (Or Thumbnail) The miniature representation of a complete picture.

Illustrator Proprietary name of software originated by Adobe Inc., who also designed Postcript and which is used in conjunction with it. It provides for enhanced typographic and artistic effects.

IMA Interactive Multimedia Association.

Integrated Services Digital Network (ISDN) A telecommunications network arranged between PTTs overlaying the conventional telephone network and providing a user with either two 64-Kbps channels, one normally used for digitized voice, or with 32 64-Kbps channels to be normally used for connecting a PBX. Extra narrow-band channels are included for control purposes.

Interface

1 The boundary between computer, and peripheral devices or functions. The word

may be used to include details ranging from plug and socket pin connections to quite complex control software.

2 The boundary between the device presenting information and the human observing it.

Interlaced line system An arrangement used in television systems for reducing flicker by generating and displaying alternate fields with odd and even lines. Thus a '25 frame interlaced system' consists of 50 fields where successive fields contain odd and even scanning lines. A complete frame is made up of two successive fields.

Internet A network formed by the amalgamation of several separate American networks with connections to overseas computers and networks.

IP Internet Protocol.

IPng An improved method of addressing to be used in the TCP/IP protocol.

IPSS International Packet Switched Service.

IRE levels Standardized levels used in video cameras, originally agreed by the Institute of Radio Engineers. In NTSC video signals, 140 IRE corresponds to 1 volt peak-to-peak.

ISA Bus Industry Standard Architecture Bus. A bus for transporting data at 8 MHz with 2 8-bit paths.

ISDN See Integrated Services Digital Network.

ISO International Standards Organization.

IT Information Technology.

ITU International Telecommunications Union. The CCITT is one of its most well-known sections.

JANET Joint Academic NETwork.

JNT Joint Network Team.

Joint Photographic Experts Group (JPEG) The name of the committee which wrote a compression Standard, also used to refer to the compression Standard for still images which the committee devised. It covers the compression of colour pictures up to 24-bit and grey-scale (halftone) pictures.

The compression method is based on Discrete Cosine Transformation followed by Run Length Coding, together with the development of special JPEG chips to implement an algorithm and obtain image compression/decompression.

JPEG See Joint Photographic Experts Group.

LAN Local Area Network.

Laser Light Amplification by Stimulated Emission of Radiation. A laser consists of a cavity (the Fabry-Perot cavity) with partially reflecting mirrors at either end. In a semiconductor laser a layer of semiconducting material inserted into a p-n sandwich forms the waveguide cavity. Radiation occurs and the dimensions of the cavity reinforce radiation at a particular wavelength by resonant reflections between the mirrors.

The extraordinary benefits of a laser light beam for communication, industrial, or control purpose is that the light is radiated at a virtually single-frequency, very short, wavelength with the power concentrated into an extremely narrow beam. The beam may be easily controlled from its electrical source and optically by using collimating optics followed by directing mirrors.

LCD Liquid Crystal Display.

LCLV Liquid Crystal Light Valve.

LED Light Emitting Diode.

Linpack A benchmark, specified in Mflops, for expressing the floating point processing performance of a CPU.

Luminosity, luminance Synonyms for brightness.

MAN Metropolitan Area Network.

Matte A visual effect produced by storing images on separately controllable planes. For example, parts of a front plane may be made transparent to reveal parts of the back plane.

Mbps Megabits per second, sometimes used to mean Megabytes per second without a note to distinguish the difference.

Mbyte Megabyte; 1 million bytes.

Mflops Millions of Floating Point Operations Per Second.

MHEG See Multimedia and Hypermedia Information Coding Experts Group.

MIDI Musical Instrument Device Interface.

MIME Multipurpose Internet Mail Extension. A Standard for multimedia e-mail, defining data types and methods of encoding.

Mips Millions of Instructions Per Second.

MIT Massachusetts Institute of Technology.

Modem MOdulator DEModulator. A device for changing computer data into a form suitable for data transmission and vice versa.

Modulation transfer function An objective method of measuring and expressing the resolution of a display in terms of the response to a sinewave.

Moire fringe pattern A patterned effect formed by the intersection of sets of lines at particular angles, or by dots of different pitches.

Morphing Smoothly changing the appearance of one image into another with the aid of special software.

Mosaic An information retrieval and browser package designed for scientific information available on the Internet, developed at the National Supercomputing Centre at the University of Illinois.

Mouse A small device held against a flat surface by the hand. When moved, a corresponding movement of the cursor on a screen display is produced.

MPC See Multimedia Personal Computer.

MPEG Motion Picture Expert Group, also used to refer to a compression Standard for moving images devised by the group.

MSCDEX MS-DOS CD-ROM EXtension. An MS-DOS extension enabling a CD-ROM disk to be accessed like a hard disk, overcoming the inability of DOS to recognize a disk capacity exceeding 32 Mbytes.

MTBF Mean Time Between Failures.

MTC Midi Time Code.

Multimedia A computer-controlled system embodying at least two of the following media: text, images, pictures, sound, video, motion video, or graphics.

Multimedia and Hypermedia Information Coding Experts Group (MHEG) A group considering methods of standardizing object and interlinking data in multimedia disk-based publications, and perhaps ultimately in home entertainment systems. The proposed Standard will deal with Input Objects (e.g. menus), Output Objects (e.g. graphics), Composite Objects embodying both, and Hyperobjects – linked input and output objects.

Multimedia Personal Computer (MPC) A personal computer which includes a CD-ROM drive, an audio adaptor, Microsoft Windows with Multimedia Extensions and speakers or headphones. This is the MPC Marketing Council's definition so other collections of equipment embodying similar facilities may qualify for a similar definition.

Multiscan monitor A monitor capable of altering its scanning rate to accommodate a higher resolution display.

Munsell Colour System A method devised by Albert Munsell for allocating three attributes to a colour – hue (e.g. red, blue, green), brightness, and chroma or saturation. Saturation describes the amount of white in a colour; a pale colour has low saturation, but a vivid colour, high saturation.

Nanometre 10^{-9} metres or one thousand millionth of a metre.

NCET National Council for Educational Technology (UK).

NETBIOS Network Basic Input/Output System. A PC telecom protocol/interface for connecting IBM PCs, PS/2s, and compatibles to each other via a LAN.

NICAM Near Instantaneous Companded Audio Multiplexing. An improved method for reproducing television sound.

NII National Information Infrastructure.

NLM Network Loadable Module. A file used to drive CD-ROMs in certain networking systems.

NNI Network Node Interface.

Node

1 A connection point on a network.

2 A document or collection of data on the Internet.

NPL National Physical Laboratory.

NREN National Research and Education Network.

NSF National Science Foundation.

NSFNET National Science Foundation NETwork (United States).

NTSC National Television System Committee. US television specification for 525 lines with two 30-frame interlaced fields, repeated at 60 frames per second. During transmission, colour data are contained in a narrow segment of the frequency band occupied by the complete signal.

OCLC Ohio Computer Library Center.

ODA Open Document Architecture. A Standard undergoing modifications to cover multimedia. In spite of that it may not become widely used because of the probable popularity of ACROBAT.

OFTEL Office of Telecommunication, the UK regulatory authority.

OLE Object Linking and Embedding. Software which manages objects – units of code and data – capable of communicating by means of messages.

OPAC Online Public Access Catalogue.

OpenDoc An Apple software package compatible with OLE and with similar objectives.

OS/2 Operating System 2, a 32-bit operating system, introduced by IBM in 1987, for use on computers containing a 80386 or later processor.

OSI Open Systems Interconnection.

PABX Private Automatic Branch Exchange.

Packet switching A transmission network system where messages are split up into short packets which may be sent in 'time slots' within a data stream containing packets from other users. Each packet contains a destination address, so packets may be re-formed into a complete message when they reach the addressee.

If a gap occurs in data transmission between users – for example, during a telephone conversation – it is immediately occupied by as many packets from other users as there are time slots during that gap, so the data occupancy of the network is considerably higher than in a circuit-switched network. PS is usually used in networks with multiple connections between nodes. If one route fails, another becomes instantly available.

PACS Picture Archiving and Communication System. A method of formatting, transmitting, and storing medical images, such as radiographic images.

PAD Packet Assembly–Disassembly.

PAL See Phase Alternate Line.

Pantone A colour-matching system embodying a large number of standard colours, each referred to by its own number.

PCM See Pulse Code Modulation.

PCMCIA Personal Computer Memory Card Interface Association. A PCMCIA card is about the size of a credit card and carries a set of pins that plug into a definitive PCMIA socket.

PDF Portable Document Format.

Peer-to-peer Interconnection and communication between similar computers.

Pel Synonym for pixel.

Phase alternate line European specification for a television system formed from two fields of interlaced lines of video and synchronizing data to provide a frame containing 625 lines which is displayed 50 times per second. Colour data is contained in a narrow segment of the frequency band occupied by the complete TV signal. This specification is used in many countries outside North America. One of the two chrominance signals is reversed in phase for each alternate scanning line.

PHIGS Programmers Hierarchical Graphics System.

Phong shading An improved version of Gouraud shading capable of providing more accurate shadows.

Photo-CD A system introduced by the Kodak Company to enable CD images to be reproduced from domestic 35 mm film.

Photodiode A type of photosensor used in image scanners in a similar manner to a CCD element. A photodiode is a semiconductor device in which the reverse current varies according to the incident light.

Photoelectric scanning The original form of image scanning in which light reflected from the image is picked up by a photoelectric cell.

Photon A packet of electromagnetic light energy.

Photonics The study and operation of information technology systems using photons instead of electrons.

Photosensor A device which converts light energy into electrical energy.

Photo YCC A system for providing consistent colour used on Kodak photo-CDs.

Pico- Prefix meaning 10^{-12}.

Picon A symbol representing an object such as a section of audio, a video clip, used in Mediamaker software. Pointing and clicking on picon to drag it onto a timeline will cause the object which it represents to be moved to that position.

PIK See Programmers Image Standard.

Pipelining A technique to speed up a computer by overlapping operations which would otherwise occur in separate clock cycles.

Pixel Picture element; the small visible component of a displayed image. In the CRT of a digital computer system, data bits converted to analogue voltages are supplied to beam modulating electrode(s) in order to present a pixel on the screen. The pixel may be specified in 1 bit for black and white, or multi-bit to present a halftone or colour pixel.

PKA Public Key Algorithm. A component of a Standard method of data encryption.

Plasma panel A panel divided into small glass cells containing a gas which glows when a voltage is applied. Plasma panels are a potential replacement for the cathode ray tube, being thin, flat, and strong, but they are still relatively expensive.

Platform Generic term for the controlling computer in a system.

Plesiosynchronous A method of introducing pseudo-synchronism in STM systems by adding bits ('bit stuffing').

POAT Plain Old Analogue TV.

POP Point Of Access Point (to the Internet).

Postscript A programming language devised by Adobe Systems which controls the beam of a laser printer to print almost any kind of symbol or illustration. Computer-created dot structures are converted into vectors (quantities having magnitude and direction).

Thus a rectangle would be formed by specifying the co-ordinates of its corners, the thickness of a connecting line, and using the instruction 'move to'. These data become commands saved in a Postscript file. The benefits are economies in data, versatility, and resolution limited only by the printer in use.

POTS Plain Old Telephone Service.

Pre-caching Loading data from relatively slow to fast storage to enable faster data access and transfer times to be made.

Programmers Hierarchical Graphics System (PHIGS) An extension of GKS for describing 3D graphics by means of data arranged in a tree structure.

Programmers Image Standard (PIK) Under consideration by ANSI as an image specification for use in medical, machine vision, satellite imaging, and other areas.

PSS Packet Switched Service. See also Packet Switching.

PSTN Public Switched Telephone Network.

PTT Post, Telegraph, and Telephone. A 'PTT' is an acronym (originally for French words) for the national telecommunications authorities in Europe.

Pulse code modulation A method of digitizing analogue signals.

QBIC Query By Image Content. IBM software for inputting data about the shape, texture, and colour of objects within an image, in order to match them with the contents of an image database in an attempt to retrieve 'image hits'. Descriptive word searches may also be used.

QHY Quantization High resolution Y signal.

QOS Quality Of Service.

Quantization A division of a continuously variable signal into discrete levels so that each level may be transmitted as a digital code.

Quicktime An Apple 'Movie' file format for images, animation, or compressed 24-bit motion video.

Raster The pattern of scanning lines on a CRT screen produced by a spot which traces out a line and then rapidly flies back to trace another adjacent line beneath the first, and so on until the whole screen is traced.

Ray-tracing A semi-automatic process provided with certain kinds of imaging software which calculate the effect of imaginary rays of light on surfaces and then alter pixel values to improve realism and to provide a photographic quality.

Red Book Volumes containing specifications for CD-DA disks and players, with Sony and Philips as the principal contributors.

Refresh A single frame presented on a cathode ray tube rapidly decays. To provide an enduring image a succession of frames is rapidly displayed so that the eye perceives an apparently stationary image.

Rendering A method of improving the realistic appearance of an image by adding light, shade, and shadows to appropriate surfaces using a ray-tracing technique.

Resampling Changing the shape or resolution of an image by discarding or adding pixels by interpolation.

Resolution The capability of an electronic display to reproduce data of a given minimum size so that their detail may be seen.

Resource Interchange File Format (RIFF) An IBM/Microsoft multimedia file architecture for data exchange. It defines 'chunks' of data and covers playback, recording, and exchange.

RGB The values fed into the Red, Green, and Blue guns of a cathode ray tube to provide the right colour by combination in a triad phosphor dot.

RIFF See Resource Interchange File Format.

RISC Reduced Instruction Set Computer.

RLIM Research Libraries Information Network.

ROM Read Only Memory.

RS170 A US Standard laying down the format of NTSC television.

RS232 An EIA Standard first introduced in 1962 defining the electrical and mechanical characteristics of the interface between data terminal and data communication equipment.

RSA A method of enciphering messages based on factorizing large prime numbers, named after its inventors, Rivest, Shamir, and Adelman.

Run length coding An opportunity arises for compressing the data in a message when there are long strings of identical symbols. For example, in images a large area of black could be transmitted by a short code indicating that the following n pixels are 'black', instead of transmitting an individual data group for each black pixel.

Saturation The amount of white light in a colour contributing to the vividness of the hue. High saturation means a small amount of white.

Screen (printing) The photograph ('bromide') of a continuous tone illustration, used by printers to make a printing plate, is taken through a piece of glass with closely spaced lines ruled on it. This 'screen' produces lines of variable width corresponding to grey levels on the photograph which take up ink on the plate and produce a halftone reproduction. The screen is usually rotated through an angle – often 45 degrees – to avoid interference effects associated with vertical or horizontal lines in the original.

SCSI Small Computer System Interface. 'Scuzzy' is a fast interface for rapidly exchanging data between peripherals and a computer. A number of external disks or other peripheral devices may be 'daisychained' into one SCSI interface with a total cable length of up to 25 ft.

SDH Synchronous Digital Hierarchy. Data transmission rates based on multiples of 155.52 Mbps which will gradually replace STM.

SECAM Sequential Couleur à Mémoire. A 625-line 25-frames per second TV system where colour data are provided on alternate lines.

Server See client-server.

SGML Standard Generalised Markup Language.

Shadow mask tube Cathode ray tube for colour containing three electron guns converging on holes through which they are projected onto a phosphor screen containing closely spaced triad phosphor dots.

SIMD Single Instruction Multiple Data. A reference to the ability of recent processors to move data faster compared with earlier processors which had to execute several instructions to move a relatively small amount of data.

SIMM Single In-line Memory Module. A method of mounting RAM memory chips.

Skinning Applying a surface to cover a wire frame defining the shape of an object during the process of forming computer models.

SLIP Serial Line Internet Protocol.

SMDS See Switched Multimegabit Data Service.

SME Small and Medium size Enterprises.

SMPTE Society of Motion Picture and Television Engineers.

SMPTE time code A code used to identify a frame in a video sequence. The code was originated by the SMPTE and consists of a series of two-digit numbers representing hours, minutes, seconds, and number of frames. Any individual frame can be thereby identified.

SNMP Simple Network Management Protocol.

Soliton A wave which can travel enormous distances. The phenomenon seems to have been discovered in canals. There is a critical speed at which the displacement wave caused by a barge assumes a circular motion, rolls along the canal's bottom, and returns to the underside of the vessel, where it is travelling in the same direction of the vessel.

The important modern equivalent is the discovery of a light wave travelling along a single mode fibre for enormous distances. The effect is due to an interaction between dispersion and the fibre's non-linear properties. In 1991 it was discovered that a soliton can be amplified to make it travel almost limitless distances.

Sonet Synchronous Optical Network. Sonet will use the STH method of data transmission.

SPEC A suite of benchmarks which have become fairly widely used for technical and scientific programs and commercial and business applications.

Spreadsheet A software-controlled set of cells displayed in columns and rows to contain data. Data in any cell may be automatically altered by entering data into another cell according to the rules controlling the spreadsheet's operations. For example, if the bottom figure in a column represents the total of all the figures in that column, the column will be automatically correctly retotalled if a figure in it is altered.

Sprite A shape, usually small, which may be programmed to move to any position on a screen.

SQL Structured Query Language. A language used in relational databases.

SRAM Static Random Access Memory.

SSL Secure Sockets Layer. A method of encrypting data used in the software of certain suppliers of Web Internet software.

STDM Synchronised Time Division Multiplex.

STM Synchronous Transfer Mode. A method of data transmission based on bit rate multiples requiring bit-stuffing to make them plesiosynchronous or pseudo-synchronous. To be gradually replaced by SDH.

Sui generis Unique of its kind.

SuperJANET A high-speed network to interconnect a number of establishments in the United Kingdom, mainly universities, with a data rate of up to about 600 Mbits per second. SuperJANET will use the Asynchronous Transfer Mode (ATM) method of packet switching, which is able to carry data in bursts or continuously equally well.

Super Video Graphics Adaptor (SVGA) A control system for a display where the pixel format is as specified by the manufacturer at some level exceeding the VGA's 640 x 480 pixels, for example, 1024 × 768 pixels.

SVGA See Super Video Graphics Adaptor.

S-VHS The format introduced by JVC using the same size cassettes as are used in VHS, but providing better resolution.

S-Video A format for videotape providing improved colour reproduction.

Switched Multimegabit Data Service A service designed to supply bandwidth on demand to any user within a group of users.

System 7.0 Operating system used on recent Apple computers.

Tagged Image File Format (TIFF) A machine-independent Standard proposed by Aldus with the support of other companies for the interchange of digital image data between imaging devices such as scanners, cameras, word processors, etc. It includes provision for compression of the kind standardized for Group 3 facsimile machines.

A TIFF image file consists of a header, tag directory, and tags. Tags include such items as resolution, length, width, colour specification, compression used, etc.

Taligent An object-oriented operating system being designed by an American company of the same name. It may be adopted by IBM and Apple.

TCP/IP Transport Control Protocol/Internet Protocol. A protocol developed for

Internet which, because of the widespread use of it in that network, is becoming adopted in other systems.

Terahertz (THz) 10^{12} Hertz; a million million Hertz.

Threshold   The level at which the transition of black to white or white to black is set in a bilevel pixel system.

Thumbnail   A low-resolution small-size representation of a higher resolution image usually, but not always, contained in the same system. A rapid successive display of sets of thumbnails enables a user to home in to a wanted picture rapidly.

TIFF   See Tagged Image File Format.

Transform coding   The conversion of data to a different form – as used, for example, when compressing an image by processing blocks of pixels to reduce redundancy. The new JPEG Standard specifies transform coding. It works on the principle that a pattern of all-black or all-white pixels contain very little new information and may be rapidly processed. There is little redundancy in the rapid changes of detail in a chequerboard pattern, which must therefore be processed more slowly.

Transputer   A type of semiconductor invented by the INMOS company embodying communication links enabling a number of transputers to intercommunicate for parallel computing purposes.

Trichromatic coefficients   The relative intensities of the primary colours required to combine to produce a specific colour.

Trinitron colour cathode ray tube   A tube resembling a shadow mask tube except that the holes in the mask are vertical slots and the triad phosphor dots on the screen are in the form of stripes.

TRIPS   Trade Related Intellectual Property System.

TTL   Transistor–transistor logic. A logic circuit composed of directly inter-connected transistors designed rapidly to switch a high capacitance load.

Tweening   A method of creating frames in between the key frames which mark the beginning and end of a motion sequence in an animation.

Typeface   The size of a font or the print made from it (often used interchangeably with font).

UCLA   University of California at Los Angeles.

Ultimedia   A name adopted by IBM for its range of multimedia products.

Unix   A multi-task multi-user operating system developed at AT&T. It is claimed to be outstanding for software development and portability – that is, for transfer to other machines with different architectures. Others consider that it is difficult to work with.

URL   Universal Resource Locator. A scheme for naming any object on the Internet.

VAN   Value Added Network.

VBNS   Very high speed Backbone Network Service, a service being considered by NSF for use on the Internet.

VCR   See Video Cassette Recorder.

VDU   Visual Display Unit.

Vector   Many types of image may be broken down into component structures called vectors – lines, arcs, polygons, etc., described in terms of co-ordinates and dimensions. Such a representation is far more compact than a bit-map, and requires much less storage. Its advantages were recognized by Xerox and later Apple who used it in Lisa and in Macintosh's Quickdraw software.

   Vector software, particularly that designed for CAD/CAM use, provides fast action and storage economies. A form of vector representation has been adopted for the Postscript language.

Vertical blanking interval   The time interval between frames in a television signal.

VESA Bus Video Electronic Standards Association Bus. A fast bus introduced to handle video data.

VFW Windows For Workgroups.

VGA See Video Graphics Adaptor.

VHS Video Home System.

Video Cassette Recorder (VCR) A tape recorder which records and plays back video and audio signals.

Video Dialtone A method of combining telephoned requests and video data delivery via a cable network.

Video Graphics Adaptor (VGA) Graphic control system introduced by IBM to control a CRT display. Its specification became the *de facto* standard for a CRT resolution of 640 x 480 pixels and 16 colours.

Videophone An 'audiovisual' (sound plus vision) communication system where subscribers can see and talk to each other.

Virtual Reality Virtual Reality is a computer-generated environment within which the human user appears to reside and with which he or she interacts.

A typical system consists of computer and software, visor embodying head tracking device and LCD stereo colour display, joystick control, and feedback exoskeletal glove. The system provides the necessary real-time graphics, sound for instructions and effects, motion and tracking data, and a connection point to a LAN, enabling users to 'meet' each other.

Vision robotics Systems which attempt to model visual images. Information is contained in a TV-like representation of an image fed into the machine via its camera-eye. A set of stored rules will have been worked out in order to display an image reconstructed from information received by the 'eye'. At the present state of development the rules enable it to 'know' something about very simple schemes – for instance, the interior of a living room.

The machine examines edges contained in the electrical image – it might test for vertical edges consisting of a sequence of more than n elements followed by an abrupt change of contrast. When found, the sequence might be labelled 'wall boundary'. The machine might then explore long, not necessarily continuous, edges which join the wall boundary in order to construct the outline of the complete wall.

Its 'recognition' of an object may prompt further actions according to the machine's capabilities.

Visualization A technique used to change abstract or complex data into graphical, often three-dimensional, form. The significance of very large amounts of numerical data, difficult to assimilate, then becomes easier to understand.

VOD Video on Demand.

Voxel Volume pixel. A pixel positioned in a 3D display according to defined X, Y, Z co-ordinates. The 3D effect is produced by the Z data, which provide positional information about the location of a pixel on one of many 'slices' through the object.

VPN Virtual Private Network. A network providing a service similar to a private network but at a lower cost by companies such as Sprint. It features pay-as-you-use bandwidth on demand.

VRAM Video Random Access Memory.

WAIS Wide Area Information Service. The client-server system on the Internet enabling a client to search databases anywhere on the network using the operating system installed in their computer.

WAN Wide Area Network.

WFW Windows For Workgroups.

WIMP interface A program interface that uses windows (W), ikons (I), a mouse

(M), and pull-down menus (P). Windows and the Macintosh interface are both WIMPs.

Windows An operating system developed by Microsoft designed to bring a graphics user interface resembling that used on Macintosh machines into the DOS PC operating system.

Windows NT A version of Windows embodying a microkernel to enable it to support programs written for a number of different processors.

Windows 95 An improved version of Windows also known as 'Chicago'.

Winmark A speed benchmark used, for example, for assessing accelerators.

WINS Windows Internet Naming Service.

WORM Write Once Read Many. An optical disk where information may be written and stored once only.

WP Word Processing.

WWW World Wide Web.

WYSIWYG What You See (on the screen) Is What You Get (on the printer).

XCMD command A Hypercard command used to execute a resource. The resource may exist on an associated peripheral.

XGA Extended Graphics Array.

X-SERIES The CCITT Standards for data transmission over digital data networks. See separate entries.

X25 CCITT recommendation for the interface between asynchronous Data Terminal Equipment (DTE) and the point of entry to a packet-switched network (Data Circuit Terminating equipment (DCE)). Although an X25 link can handle hundreds of simultaneous connections, it can also be used for a single connection from a modem or PC with a Pad interface board.

The protocol is used in packet-switched networks implemented in the lower three layers of the ISO seven-layer model. An X25 packet consists of a flag, header, an area for data, a frame check, and a terminating flag. The protocol, known as the Link Access Procedure Balanced Protocol (LAP-B), controls data errors, and data flow rate.

The market for data networks was one of the first to be liberalized in Europe, and there were 16 operators of Managed Data Network Services (MDNS) with European revenues of more than ECU 3 million in 1992. X25 services are still dominant, according to a recent survey from Ovum. Telephone companies have an 80 per cent share of the X25 market which is worth ECU 2.3 billion, and which will grow to ECU 7.3 billion by 1996.

X50 A CCITT recommendation for the format of streams of 64 Kbps subscriber data in a multiplexed interconnection between synchronous data networks.

X75 CCITT recommendation for call control procedures and data transfer on international circuits between packet-switched data networks.

X86 Industry jargon for any processor in the Intel series ending with the digits 86.

X400 A series of CCITT recommendations for message-handling protocols to be used in computer-based message systems. They are particularly applicable to electronic mail systems, and are likely to become widely used.

Electronic mail started to be used in the 1980s, but subscribers to one service could not talk to subscribers of another. It was like the early days of the telephone when unconnected telephone exchanges were dotted about, each with their own subscribers.

The X400 recommendation appeared in the CCITT 1984 Red Book and was the first OSI Standard to be ratified. It provides the great potential benefit of 'universal electronic mail'. X400 resides in the OSI applications layer – the layer at the top which is of prime interest because that is the OSI 'telematics services' level

– the one closest to the user. Unfortunately, X400 does not include anything about how users should be addressed – a rather important requirement.

X400 1984 version adopted a rather convoluted procedure to identify name and position functions designated 'user agent', 'message transfer agent' and so on. The technology moved on and the CCITT didn't get the system quite right so people adapted it to their needs, with the result that Bloggs' e-mail X400 was different from Moggs' e-mail X400, and they could not intercommunicate.

The CCITT people put their heads together and came out with an added 'major feature' in 1988, primarily dealing with PC network functions – the most popular application. It is not clear whether '1984 X400' services are completely compatible with '1988 X400' services.

A message system, like a telephone system, needs a directory of subscribers in countries where there are systems, and it needs to be accessible in those countries. Agreement was awaited on another Standard – X500 – covering online directories.

Effective directory services are still awaited. For instance, both MCI Mail and Compuserve in the US conform to X400, but if you are running with one you cannot look up a number on the other. Another e-mail problem is that while e-mail providers will carry out a conformity test before allowing you to connect to their system (e.g. BT), that test is not necessarily the same one as is run by, say, MCI Mail, so a BT EM subscriber may not be able to connect to an MCI Mail subscriber. There does not seem to be any arrangement for international single billing either.
X500 A CCITT/ISO Standard for an address specification and global directory. One of the major intentions of the Standard is that it should be used in conjunction with X400.
Y signal A signal transmitted in a television system to represent average brightness.
YUV The luminance (Y) and chrominance (UV) components of a colour TV signal.
Zoom A means of providing an apparent progressive enlargement of a selected area of a screen or window.
Z39.50 An American National Standard containing information retrieval service definitions and a protocol specification for library applications.

Index

Printed and bound by CPI Group (UK) Ltd, Croydon, CR0 4YY

01/11/2024

01782599-0015